THE
MODERN
WORLD

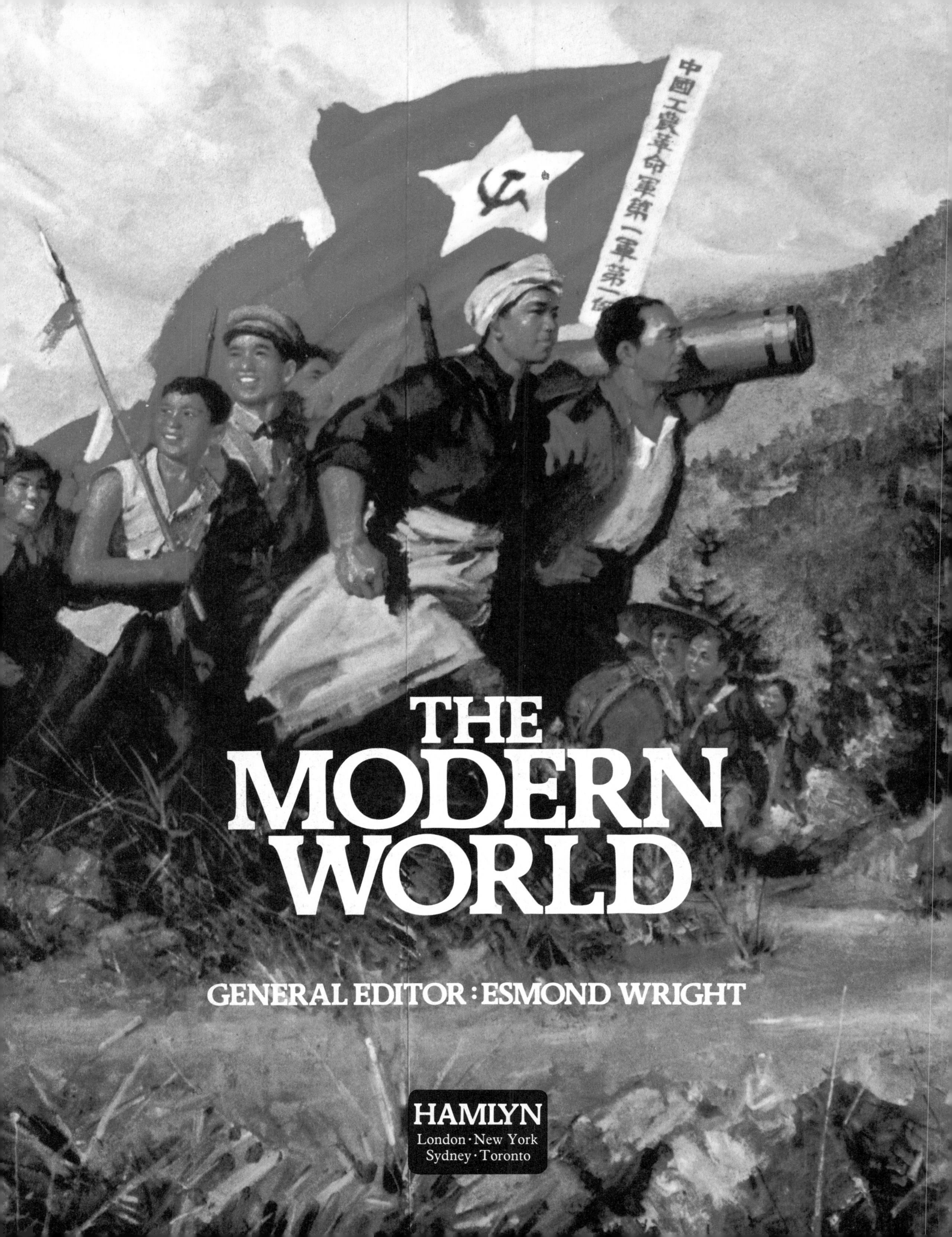

THE MODERN WORLD

GENERAL EDITOR : ESMOND WRIGHT

HAMLYN
London · New York
Sydney · Toronto

List of contributors
David Thomson
Christopher Andrew
Asa Briggs
James Henderson
David Gillard
George Shepperson
John Burnett
C. Duncan Rice
Esmond Wright
William H. McNeil

Published by
The Hamlyn Publishing Group Limited
London · New York · Sydney · Toronto
Astronaut House, Hounslow Road, Feltham,
Middlesex, England

Original text
© The Hamlyn Publishing Group Limited 1969
Revised and updated 1979
This edition
© The Hamlyn Publishing Group Limited 1979
Second Impression 1982

ISBN 0 600 39434 4
Printed in Yugoslavia

Part I
EUROPE AND
NORTH AMERICA IN
THE NINETEENTH
CENTURY
Page 9
Introduction

Chapter 1
The New Europe
Page 12

Industrial Europe
The transport revolution
The conquering bourgeoisie
The Disinherited
Reformers and utopians
The triumph of science
The romantic age
England after Waterloo
Middle class reform
The new poor law
The beginning of the Victorian Age
The Chartist challenge
The triumph of free trade
The British Empire
Britain's achievement

Chapter 2
The Springtime of Nations
Page 30

Germany and Poland
The birth of modern Belgium
The crisis of 1848
The Eastern Question
The awakening of Greece
The Egypt of Mehemet Ali
The dispute over the Holy Places
The 'sick man of Europe'
The Crimean War

Chapter 3
Russia: the Years of Conflict
Page 45

The Decembrists
Autocracy and orthodox
The new Russia
The intelligentsia
The consequences of the Crimean War
The abolition of serfdom
The Polish insurrection
The economic development of Russia

Part II
THE BALANCE OF POWER
Page 89

Introduction

Chapter 4
France from the Restoration to Napoleon III
Page 53

The restoration of the Bourbons
Charles X
The glorious days of 1830
The July Monarchy
Guizot's ministry
The revolution of 1848
The National Workshops
The return of Louis Bonaparte
The aristocratic empire
The Orsini Affair
The liberal empire

Chapter 5
The United States 1800–1865
Page 66

Thomas Jefferson
The Louisiana Purchase
Maritime problems
The War of 1812
The 'new nationalism'
Westward expansion
The South and slavery
The Jackson era
The American economy and the panic of 1837
Foreign policy and the American Indians
The Monroe doctrine
Manifest Destiny
War with Mexico
The growth of sectionalism
The compromise of 1850
The Republican party
The Dred Scott decision
Secession
The Civil War
The cost of the war

Chapter 6
Cavour and Bismarck
Page 92

Italian unification
Victor Emmanuel and Cavour
Giuseppe Garibaldi
The kingdom of Italy
Rome and Venice
Germany
Schleswig-Holstein
The French response
Sedan
The Peace of Frankfurt
The balance sheet

Chapter 7
The Modernization of Europe
Page 109

The physical sciences
Biology and medicine
The new science
The applications of science
A shrinking world
The world economy
The rise of the proletariat
Syndicalism
International socialism
Clerical liberalism
Pius IX
The expansion of Europe

Chapter 8
The New Imperialism
Page 123

Europe, Africa and Asia
The motives for imperialism
The British on the Nile
The Boer War
The French in North Africa
West Africa
The scramble for Africa
China and South-east Asia

Part III
DEMOCRACY AND THE NEW IMPERIALISM
Page 133

Introduction

Chapter 9
The Growth of Democracy in Britain and France
Page 136

Palmerston and Britain's world role
Gladstonian liberalism
Trade unionism
The Labour Party
The problem of poverty
Lords and suffragettes
The Irish question
Threats to the British Empire
The German challenge
The balance-sheet of industrialism
The fall of the Second Empire in France
Republic or monarchy?
The Dreyfus Affair
Anti-clericalism
Industrial development
The revival of French socialism
The problems of empire
France and the German threat

Chapter 10
Russia: Prelude to Revolution
Page 155

Russian expansion
Industrialization in the 1890s
Lenin and Russian Marxism
Empire in the Far East
The Revolution of 1905
Stolypin and the peasant problem

Part IV
THE FIRST WORLD WAR: CAUSES AND CONSEQUENCES
Page 207

Introduction

Chapter 11
Asia in the Nineteenth Century
Page 164

The challenge of the west
The Taiping revolt
The 'Arrow' War
The transformation of Japan
Asia's lesser lands
The South Seas
Japan defeats China
The powers close in on China
The Boxer uprising
The battle for east Asia
Japan's triumph
Sun Yat-sen

Chapter 12
The United States: Industrialization and Imperialism
Page 178

Reconstruction
Emigration
Railroads
The triumph of capitalism
The Populist Party
Progressivism
Imperialism in Latin America
Dollar Diplomacy
The Republican split
Wilson's dilemma

Chapter 13
Nations in Turmoil
Page 188

The *Kulturkampf*
The socialist threat
Restrained imperialism
William II and Germany's world role
The Habsburg Empire after 1848
The Compromise of 1867
The Yugoslav problem
Vienna
Revolution and repression in Spain
The Carlist Wars
Republican interlude
Spain's vanishing empire
Portugal
Italian Unification – the disappointed hopes
Crispi and Italian imperialism
Giolitti
The new Balkan states
The Young Turks

Chapter 14
The Approach of War
Page 210

The alliance system
German *Weltpolitik*
The Entente Cordiale
Tension in the Balkans
The naval arms-race
The Balkan wars
The Sarajevo crisis
The approach to war

Chapter 15
The First World War
Page 220

The Western Front
Verdun
The Somme offensive
The war at sea
America intervenes
Revolution in Russia
The Bolsheviks seize power
Victory in the West
The last German offensive

Chapter 16
Post-War Europe
Page 234

The reshaping of eastern Europe
The Civil War in Russia
The birth of the Weimar Republic
Fascism in Italy

Chapter 17
Europe and the Outside World
Page 245

The British Commonwealth of Nations
The Irish Free State
Imperial superiority
European rule in Africa
The Indian subcontinent
The Middle East

Part V
THE WORLD SINCE 1939
Page 287

Introduction

Chapter 18
Prosperity and Depression
Page 255

The European empires
The League of Nations
Latin America

Chapter 19
China and Japan
Page 260

The emergence of Japan
The Chinese warlords
Japan's bid for Asian mastery
The Manchurian incident
The rise of the Mao Tse-Tung
The Long March

Chapter 20
The Decline of Democracy in Europe
Page 269

The collapse of German democracy
Nazi Germany
Gleichschaltung
Stalin's Russia
The transformation of the Russian economy
The cult of personality
The retreat from democracy
Appeasement

Chapter 21
The Second World War
Page 290

Blitzkreig
The eastern front
Turning points in the struggle
Churchill and Roosevelt
Götterdämmerung
How the war was won
Resistance
The concentration camps
The Warsaw ghetto
Unconditional surrender
The aftermath
Russia and America

Chapter 22
The Headlines of History 1945–65
Page 313

Great Britain
Churchill resigns
The United States
The beginning of the Cold War
A wave of nationalism
Africa
The Middle East
The Caribbean and Latin America

Chapter 23
The Headlines of History 1965–78
Page 338

Europe
The Far East
Africa
The Indian continent
The Middle East
Latin and North America

Chapter 24
Behind the Headlines
Page 352

World economy
World welfare
Race relations
Peacekeeping
Science and technology
Education, art and belief

Part I

EUROPE AND NORTH AMERICA IN THE NINETEENTH CENTURY

Introduction

When in 1815 Louis XVIII returned for a second time to the throne of the Bourbons it seemed that an ugly and violent chapter in European history was at last closed. Although the French had again revealed their political instability by the enthusiasm they had shown for Napoleon Bonaparte when he escaped from Elba in March 1815, he was now safely incarcerated on St Helena deep in the South Atlantic and could not escape again; and the very moderation of the peace terms on which the British foreign secretary, Lord Castlereagh, insisted seemed to promise an opportunity for good sense to prevail after the twenty years of conflict. These hopes were reinforced by the conciliatory mood of Louis XVIII. He was declared king 'by the grace of God', and he graciously presented a royal charter to his grateful people. But he was wise enough to include in it the concession of those civil rights and rights to property which had been the permanent result of the Revolution and which had been won the hard way. The hope was for constitutional government on British lines.

Yet the form was clear: the watchword of the Congress of Vienna was 'legitimacy', even if the case for the restoration of the legitimate rulers and their descendants was that it was in the people's best interests. 'The principle of legitimacy', wrote Talleyrand to Louis XVIII, 'must be held sacred in the interest of the people themselves, because legitimate governments can alone be strong and durable, whereas illegitimate governments, relying upon force only, fall to pieces the moment that support fails them, and then the people are delivered over to a succession of revolutions of which no one can foresee the end.'

And so, for a variety of reasons, the Concert of Europe was born. The French foreign minister, Talleyrand, wanted to restore the pre-revolutionary map of Europe and get the best possible terms for France, Metternich dreaded a new wave of revolution lest it further weaken the diverse and chequered Habsburg Empire. Hardenberg of Prussia shared his fears. Alexander I of Russia, alternating between moods of repression and liberalism, sought a union with his fellow rulers 'as members of a single Christian nation' and opposed whatever might thwart

it. And Castlereagh's objective was primarily to re-create a power balance in a Europe torn and destroyed by a generation of war so that his island empire could absorb her widely scattered conquests to which there could now be no European challenge. Along with 'legitimacy' went the 'compensations'. And by them Britain did well indeed. She dominated the key strategic points – and the coaling stations for the coming age of steam – on all the oceans. For two generations she was the political and industrial pacesetter for the world.

It is easy now in retrospect to see how false were some of these assumptions and how short-lived the post-1815 stability. Yet the Holy Alliance and the conferences of the post-1815 years saw for the first time a genuine attempt to manufacture by diplomacy a European concert of power. It was for a purpose: the suppression at source of the first signs of unrest. Revolutions were put down by force, at speed and by foreign intervention: 1819 in Germany, in 1821 in Italy, in 1823 in Spain, in 1830 in Italy, in 1831 in Poland and in many countries in 1848–9. In 1830, in 1848 and in 1870 the barricades were raised in Paris; and throughout the period unrest and violence were endemic in Russia. There was no peace. When Metternich fled in 1848, there was still his replica, Schwartzenberg, to reign in his place. But, except in 1827 in Greek waters and in 1854 in the Crimea, there was no war in Europe either. The diplomats relied on the exhaustion of Europe, on the passiveness of a heavily rural society and on military force. And from their experiences they could hardly have acted otherwise. They ignored however the social and economic forces, the fact that the movement of armies carried with it the movement also of ideas, the growth of population, the development of railways, telegraph and postal services, the appearance in each country of a middle class that was the product of city life, commerce and schools, that would now break

the aristocratic pattern permanently and begin to grope towards an Internationale of trade. Metternich was intelligent, shrewd, every inch a realist, utterly devoid of Alexander's mysticism. He recognized, and was right to do so, the fragile character of human society. His ideal was limited but in its way noble. He laboured hard to maintain the equilibrium of Europe; as he wrote in 1824, Europe 'has acquired for me the quality of one's own country'. He was remarkably successful. He held the fort until 1848. But he ignored the three new creative and disruptive elements that were to make the years between the fall of Napoleon I and the rise of Bismarck so exciting; the industrial revolution and the forces of nationalism and socialism.

The industrial revolution was of course very uneven in its impact. Europe as a whole was still rural: serfdom was abolished in France in 1789 and in Prussia in 1807. But the effects of the abolition were varied. If small peasant farms became characteristic of western Europe, in the lands east of the Elbe a large, landless, agricultural labouring class was produced. And in Russia in 1815 there were still 16,000,000 serfs on the Crown lands alone. Serfdom brought acute problems to the Tsars, who had great difficulty in finding any solutions.

It was to this overwhelmingly rural world that the industiral revolution came. It came first in Britain and spread to western Europe: it was British capital and companies which applied steam to transportation on land and sea in France as well as Britain, so that a spider-like spread of railway lines appeared on the map of Europe between 1830 and 1870; coal and factory production boomed because of the use of steam engines. Ghent and Brussels, Liège and Lille, Namur and the Ruhr, Manchester and Glasgow became industrial centres of textiles, metallurgy, coal and steel.

The results were evident in the population boom – there was a fivefold increase in the British population between 1814 and 1914, and London grew from 875,000 to 2,000,000 in the years from 1800 to 1850 and to 5,000,000 by 1900; Cologne and Paris doubled in population in the same period; in 1800 there were 22 towns in Europe with more than a population of 100,000; by 1850 there were 47. There was also a series of cholera and typhus epidemics which led to a campaign for a public health service. Interest grew in wider and larger markets (hence the emphasis on the Empire of Britain and on the Union of the German States), state education and scientific invention and the development of joint stock companies. Napoleon was in nothing quite so farsighted as in his commercial code, which was adopted throughout most of western Europe; he was far more modern-minded than Metternich or Castlereagh.

Industrially, Britain was half a century ahead of Europe. She produced 10,000,000 tons of coal in 1800, 56,000,000 tons a year by 1850. This process did not occur in France until the years of the Second Empire: coal and iron production trebled between 1850 and 1870. And by 1871, aided by victory, Germany was, by rapid scientific training, outdistancing France. By 1871, though few appreciated this, British dominance was over. Between 1850 and 1910 iron production trebled in Britain, rose sixfold in France, but twenty-sixfold in Germany.

The same forces were at work in agriculture, with improvement in farming techniques, the abandonment of the fallow land system, the use of fertilizers, the specialization of crops and the cross-breeding of cattle.

And behind all these developments was money, not least in London, Paris and Amsterdam. Krupp was typical of one aspect of the industrial growth. What in 1826 was a near-bankrupt household business had become by 1870 a vast, private, paternalist empire of steel and bronze and guns, with pension schemes, hotels and stores – and no trade unions. The five Rothschild brothers from the Frankfurt ghetto managed the banking houses of Frankfurt, Vienna, London, Paris and Naples. When the transfer of funds over such distances was dangerous they could act as one, speedily and with confidence and trust. They invested shrewdly, especially in railways and shipping. They became barons of the Austrian Empire and assisted Disraeli over Suez, but they never overcame either envy of their skill or prejudice against their race. Yet, as their careers showed, it was possible to climb up the greasy pole, whatever your origins, your accent or your race. It was easier in Britain than in Europe. Or rather it was not easy at all: but it could be done.

Metternich's vision of Europe had a certain nobility – seen at least in the light of the problems of today. But it foundered, as did the fortunes of the Habsburg house he served, not only on indifference to economics but on ignorance of the emotional force of nationalism. So did the cause of aristocracy. The early nineteenth century was held together in its internationalism by the existence of a class whose manners were stylized, whose language was French and whose loyalties were less to territory and nation than to a sovereign. The chancellor of the German Empire in 1894, Hohenlohe, had a brother who was an official of the Emperor Joseph of Austria, another on service in Prussia and yet another at the Papal Court in Rome. Their loyalties were personal. The coming of the bourgeoisie meant the emergence of nationalism. Honour now became national, and nations began to take offence, to meet challenges that had been seen until then as purely personal. And the nationalism itself passed from the romantic and cultural force that it was to Chateaubriand and Mazzini to a hard, scientific, military force – a product of Darwin. The test of national honour by 1870 was conflict, and the national concept was in the process

brutalized, coarsened and devalued. Nationalist symbols and legendary grew, not least in Britain and the United States. But of its emotional power there could be no question. Loyalty was no longer to king or lord, class or creed, but to the republic one and indivisible. It became synonymous with notions of the rights of men and the career open to talent. It would be defended not by a professional class of warriors but by all its citizens. And it was for export. Belgium won its independence in 1830; Italy as a nation became more than a 'geographical expression'; each component part of the Austrian Empire struggled for self-determination; poets and historians kept alive the sparks of independence in Prague and Budapest, Belgrade and Athens. Greece won its independence and the map of the Balkans became a jigsaw of ever-changing boundaries. Every little language felt that it had to have a country all its own. Nationalism was a force that later both Bismarck and Hitler could exploit. And beyond nationalism was imperialism and the notion of the raj. By 1870, with the Suez Canal cut and a quick road open to India, an imperial age was about to be born. But the major force that emerged in these years was, in Europe at least, Socialism itself. Before long class would compete with nation for loyalty and allegiance, and some of the most difficult tensions and problems of our time would come to birth.

Three thousand miles away, on the other side of the Atlantic, a not dissimilar sequence of events had taken place. The United States had spent the first two thirds of the nineteenth century establishing its own nationhood, defining its own particular national characteristics that distinguished it from the European nations who had originally peopled it. Having established, in the Monroe Doctrine in 1823, its claim to its own sphere of influence, it could safely ignore events in Europe, its attention taken up with pushing its settlements ever further to the west.

The second main geopolitical problem inherent in the very establishment of the United States had also resolved itself by the last third of the century. This was the conflict, most importantly but not exclusively over slavery, between the rapidly industrializing and heavily populated North and the agricultural, more sparsely inhabited South. The Civil War had been bloody and bitter, but once the armies had withdrawn from the field the nation reunited remarkably quickly, social attitudes and an element of nostalgia perhaps excepted.

Now, the United States slowly took up its position as a world power whose rapidly growing economic and political strength could no longer be ignored by the major European nations. These may have reached the peak of their power only as late as the years between 1870 and 1914; but, not far behind, though scarcely noticed, lay the United States, which rapidly came to supplant them.

Above, London warehouses as depicted by the French painter Gustave Doré (1833–83): at the start of the nineteenth century the economies of western Europe and the United States were primarily agricultural. By the end they were primarily industrial, industrialization bringing with it the unplanned growth of big cities and of an urban proletariat.

Opposite, Tsar Alexander I, Francis I of Austria and Frederick William II of Prussia concluding the Holy Alliance, 26 September 1815. Though the document espoused Christian principles, it joined the three most powerful autocracies of central and eastern Europe in an alliance armed at self-preservation.

On page 8, Liberty Guiding the People *by Eugène Delacroix (1798–1863): this painting, executed in 1831 in the aftermath of political revolution in France, might be said to symbolize one of the nineteenth century's main aspirations, a popular yearning for national liberty. Though these hopes had by and large been fulfilled in western Europe by three quarters of the way through the century, central and eastern Europe, not to mention Europe's overseas territories, had to wait until the twentieth century. Musée du Louvre, Paris.*

Chapter 1

The New Europe

A man born in 1815 might reasonably have expected to live until 1870. Had he done so, he would have witnessed more changes – political, economic, industrial and social – than in any comparable period in history. While the Europe of 1870 was recognizably modern, that of 1815 was still in many respects medieval. After more than twenty years of revolution, war and destruction the old order was restored by the victors of Waterloo, and the deep cracks which had seemed to be breaking up the structure of European society in 1789 were temporarily pasted over. Except in France, the lot of the peasant had scarcely changed, and the land which still formed the basis of the European economy continued to be tilled in the same laborious way that it had been for centuries past. But the apparent continuity with the past was only superficial, and from about 1830 onwards scientific progress and social change accelerated spectacularly. Developments in industry, commerce and trade brought vast new wealth to western Europe but at the same time created a rootless working class and an intellectual protest that was ultimately to shatter the old order so carefully reconstructed in 1815. The lasting revolution was to be an economic, not a political one, its home in England, not in France.

At the beginning of the nineteenth century Europe remained essentially agricultural, and as in all agricultural societies life was directly affected by the state of the harvest. The absence of any permanent crop surpluses seriously hampered economic development: seasonal and annual crises, traceable to weather conditions, inadequate commercial organization and transport systems were followed at the end of the wars by a long period of falling prices which afforded no encouragement to change of any kind. With a few exceptions, agricultural techniques remained backward and unchanging. Great aristocratic landowners, uninterested in the processes of farming, were content to draw rents from their tenants and to value their estates in terms of the social status and political power that they conferred. Small farmers, though they might have the will to experiment and make changes, could rarely command the capital necessary to do so.

Throughout most of Europe, cultivation was still by the primitive methods of the Middle Ages. For lack of fertilizers land had to be kept fallow one year in every three, and much still lay in uncultivated waste: seed was sown 'broadcast' by hand, reaping was by scythe and threshing by flail. Crop yields were low, and undernourished animals, left to fend for themselves on rough pastures and commons, prevented any progress in scientific stock-breeding. The absence of developed communications and means of storing food compelled each country – and, often, each district – to be as self-supporting as possible, and it was only in a few luxury foods such as spices, sugar, coffee and tea that there was any important foreign trade.

Yet the first half of the nineteenth century was to see impressive agricultural progress, spurred on by growing populations and increasing demands for food. Change had begun in England in the previous century, where 'improving' landlords had enclosed scattered holdings into compact farms, had introduced new rotational systems based on the use of root crops and had greatly increased the size and weight of animals by selective breeding. Such practices became more widespread during the Napoleonic Wars and enabled England not only to survive the French blockade but to feed a population that grew threefold, from 6,000,000 to 18,000,000, during the century 1750–1850.

By the 1840s steam-ploughs and steam-threshers were coming to replace the labour of man, manure and artificial fertilizers (discovered by the German chemist Liebig) were enriching the soil and increasing yields, while the drainage of heavy clay lands, made possible by the mass production of non-porous pipes, was bringing ever more land under the plough. Altogether these changes meant a fundamental break with the past and a new concept of landownership for profit rather than pleasure.

Outside England there were two main types of agriculture in Europe. In France, the Low Countries, Switzerland and Northern Italy the suppression of feudal servitude had emancipated the peasants but had resulted in a pattern of small and medium-sized farms which were economically unable to take advantages of the new and costly agricultural techniques.

Elsewhere in Europe, vast manorial estates remained typical. In Southern Italy the landowning aristocracy practised absenteeism, leaving the management of their estates to stewards who let them out to tenant-farmers, often at exorbitant rents. Spanish lords also leased out their lands but were restricted by the *Mesta*, the powerful association of sheep farmers who monopolized vast areas of pasturage and were opposed to the development of arable farming.

In Prussia and eastern Europe the Napoleonic reforms were also abandoned soon after Waterloo, and peasants who had acquired land were now often compelled to restore part of it. On some Prussian estates, however, there was evidence of agricultural improvement on the English model, in contrast with the medieval conditions that still prevailed in Russia. Here, the land was owned entirely by the Crown and nobility; landowners kept back part for their own use and let the rest to serfs in small plots in return for payments and obligations of many kinds. Although Russia was the largest exporter of wheat in Europe, it was at the expense of a population that permanently lived close to starvation level. This contrast between eastern and western Europe, based on the different systems of land-ownership, resulted in glaring economic divisions which were to survive until recent times.

Industrial Europe

The new Europe – the Europe of machines and factories, railways and steam-engines – was hardly evident in 1815. Only in England, where industrialization had been growing at an increasing pace since about the middle of the eighteenth century, were the changes clearly visible. Here, a small population had

responded to a great overseas demand by mechanization, first of the spinning and weaving of textiles, next of the manufacture of iron and steel, and then of the actual means of power. Whether the British people had any peculiar inventive skill over other nations is doubtful: it is more likely that the industrial revolution began there because of a particular combination of circumstances – economic, social and political – that could not be found elsewhere at the time. But the fact was the discoveries of Hargreaves (the spinning jenny) and Arkwright (an early spinning machine driven by water power), of Watt (the steam engine), Cort (a process for purifying iron) and a score of others were not only turning England into the wealthiest and most powerful nation in the world but were ultimately to start a revolution throughout Europe, the consequences of which are still not fully worked out.

Britain, admittedly, had certain natural elements which favoured her early industrialization – coal and iron in great quantity and easily accessible, an old-established cloth industry which supplied a basis of organizational knowledge and experience, a vast colonial market for her goods, a developed banking system and a political structure that encouraged freedom and individual initiative. Before 1830, industrialization in France made only slow headway, delayed by poor communications and banking institutions and by the continuation of protectionist policies that only hampered progress. Here, the pace of change quickened noticeably after the accession of Louis Philippe: the iron industry developed rapidly under iron masters like Schneider at Creusot and Wendel in Lorraine, the number of steam engines in use doubled within six years, while the number of power-looms in Alsace and Normandy increased sevenfold between 1830 and 1848.

In Germany, the 'take-off' into industrialization was even slower. In 1830 the Ruhr was still a predominantly agricultural region, and Krupp, the great armament manufacturer of the future, employed only

nine workers: such industrial centres as existed were situated close to the ironfields of Saxony, the Saar, Upper Silesia and Bohemia. Only towards 1840 did the more intensive exploitation of coal fields and steam power indicate the real beginnings of technological advance. In Belgium, too, money from the aristocracy was by now beginning to stimulate the heavy industries in the valleys of the Meuse and Sambre.

Elsewhere in Europe there was, as yet, little sign of industrial progress. Some Italian cities were famous, as they had been for centuries past, for high quality workmanship in silk, leather and precious metals, but these were small-scale craft industries carried on in much the same way as they had been since medieval times. Here, as in Germany and other European states, the development of trade was seriously hampered by political divisions and the survival of local monopolies controlled by guilds and city corporations.

In spite of such impediments, it is likely that total European industrial output doubled between 1815 and 1848. Yet the progress of early capitalism was uneven, marked by booms and slumps which implied an inadequate adaptation to the market forces of supply and demand. Most countries attempted to protect their economies by complicated systems of tariffs and import restrictions which only served to keep down the total level of international trade. Such ideas were increasingly coming under attack from economists like Ricardo, Say and Mill who, deriving their theories from Adam Smith's *The Wealth of Nations* (1776), argued that wealth would be greatly increased if each country concentrated on producing what it was best fitted for by nature (whether food or manufactures) and then exchanged freely with all other nations. In the absence of artificial controls, production would always adjust itself to demand through the agency of the price mechanism.

Free trade found its first expression in England, where a gradual process of tariff or Customs duty reduction was begun in the

1820s by Huskisson and continued by Peel in the 1840s. Its most spectacular success came in 1846 with the repeal of the Corn Laws and the removal of the protection from wheat imports which farmers had long enjoyed: England would hereafter buy her food in the cheapest markets of the world and live by her manufactures.

The transport revolution

Industrialization required a fast and efficient system of communications for the movement of men, materials and goods. During the latter half of the eighteenth century, England had already made important developments in mobility by the construction of canals for the movement of heavy goods and the improvement of road surfaces for the transport of passengers. On the turnpike roads of Brindley, Telford and Macadam stagecoaches could carry twenty passengers at speeds of up to fifteen miles an hour.

The decisive change came with the steam locomotive, first successfully developed by George Stephenson in 1814. Originally, it was seen merely as a means of speeding up the transport of coal from mines, and the first railways, such as the Stockton to Darlington in England and the Saint-Etienne to Andrezième in France, were intended solely for industrial purposes.

But by 1830 Stephenson had produced a locomotive which could travel at thirty miles an hour, and the use of steel rails, automatic brakes and improved coaches made people aware of the railway's great potential for passenger transport. A 'railway mania' in England resulted in the formation of hundreds of private companies, some of them economically unsound but many paying

handsome dividends to shareholders. By 1850 almost all the principal towns had been linked by some 6,000 miles of rail, the average cost of which had been £56,000 per mile.

In other countries, development was retarded by distrust and the opposition of vested interests. Hostility came from landowners, coaching establishments and innkeepers – above all, sufficient capital was not forthcoming from investors, who preferred to put their money into land or safe government securities. Despite campaigns led by the banker Péreire and the economist Chevalier, the French network really only began after 1837, the first line, Paris to Saint-Germain, being sponsored by Baron Rothschild. Although it was an immediate success, there were still only 2,000 miles of French railways in 1848.

Railway construction followed in Belgium, Germany, Italy and in many countries throughout the world, often directed by British engineers and carried out by British workmen. In Germany the railway had a particular importance in the development of the *Zollverein* – the customs union by which Prussia was gradually forging a nation out of a collection of independent states: in 1850 Germany had some 3,500 miles of track and a great continental line from Aachen to Hanover and Berlin.

The economic and social effects of railways was revolutionary. Journeys were shortened from days to hours; the cost of moving goods was halved and the market for them vastly expanded; perishable foods in particular received a new mobility and could now be transported into the rapidly growing urban centres in good condition. Railways broke down the isolation of centuries and compelled people whose horizons had previously been bounded by the village

to think in terms of the nation: although they were a socially binding force it is probably true to say that they were a nationally divisive one.

But it is not in dispute that steam locomotion – whether by land or by the new steamships that were now crossing the Atlantic in seventeen days instead of forty – was one of the most powerful forces shaping modern civilization. Where the rail was laid, telegraph systems were constructed alongside, news and letters could be carried cheaply and swiftly, and national daily papers became possible. The new mobility that was thus given to the movement of ideas was at least as important as that conferred on people and goods.

The conquering bourgeoisie

Rich and poor there had always been, but industrialization tended to exaggerate the differences between plenty and want, to make the extremes more conspicuous, more exposed to public envy and concern. In countries which had not yet felt the impact of industrial change, the traditional two-tier system of aristocratic landowners and landless peasants persisted – in Southern Italy and in parts of Prussia and Russia, where social and political influence was still exclusively in the hands of a tiny territorial aristocracy.

However, in the industrially developing parts of Europe a third, middle class was rapidly rising to power and wealth, a class distinguished by its manipulation of capital rather than by ownership of land. These were the bankers and merchants of the new professions that complex financial undertakings and business relationships called into existence. At the extremities they merged imperceptibly into the classes above and below them; there was no single middle class, rather an infinite series of gradations. What characterized them, and distinguished them sharply from their social inferiors, was the ownership of capital or means of production on which they could employ others to work or the possession of special professional skills usually derived from some form of advanced education.

At the summit of the middle classes, barely distinguishable in wealth from the landed aristocracy, was the financial elite – a relatively few great families whose business lay in the use (to some the abuse) of money. These were the banking and financial houses, which dealt in money-lending on a grand scale, government credit, the discounting of bills of exchange and speculation in mining and the precious metals.

A general shortage of currency (still based on gold and silver) at a time of expanding trade, as well as the inadequate development of banking facilities, favoured such activities and their concentration into a few hands. Banking houses like the Barings in England, the Hopes in Amsterdam and the Rothschilds, with a family network extending through five European capitals, rivalled the wealth and influence of dukes and princes. The Jewish origins of some prevented their complete social acceptance, yet others were ennobled, became leading patrons of the arts and were famous for their lavish entertaining and hospitality.

Below the merchant princes were the upper middle-classes – the owners of textile factories and iron-works, the leading members of the professions and public administration, the army officers and diplomatic officials. Socially they were of mixed origins. Government service and army were still recruited mainly from the younger sons of nobility who, because of the rule of primogeniture, would not succeed to their fathers' estates: patronage assured them of remunerative sinecures, the actual work of which was done by poorly paid clerks. But in the ranks of the industrialists were found members of the nouveau riche, men of often humble origins who had carved their way to fortune by hard work, thrift and an unusual degree of intelligence or good fortune.

These various elements had in common the enjoyment of a degree of affluence which enabled them to educate and provide for their children and provided them with fine houses in the fashionable quarters and suburbs of the towns, armies of domestic servants who relieved their wives of all the household duties. Above all, they shared a

thirst for political power, a dislike of the aristocracy and a distrust of the working classes, a belief in free trade and free enterprise as the keys to economic success both for themselves and for the nation.

In the more advanced countries of western Europe they were already making a bid for power and, beginning to break the domination of the landed gentry. In England the middle classes were enfranchised by the Reform Act of 1832 and through the newly formed Conservative Party of Robert Peel won a remarkable success with the abolition of the Corn Laws in 1846: similarly the accession in 1830 of Louis Philippe, 'the bourgeois king', was the beginning of a period of increased power and influence for the French middle classes.

There were no overnight revolutions. Aristocratic power remained deeply entrenched, and even in England it was not until 1880 that middle-class members constituted a majority in the House of Commons: the important thing was that a shift in economic power was gradually bringing about a major political change and was causing a mounting attack on the aristocracy, its power and privileges.

The disinherited

In his famous work *Das Kapital*, first published in 1867, Karl Marx stated his belief that industrialization inevitably tended to divide society into two opposing groups of employers and employees, those who possessed capital and those who did not, and that the issue between them could be resolved only by revolution. To many observers in the first half of the nineteenth century his gloomy prediction seemed fully justified.

Above, Punch *cartoon of 1843 entitled* Capital and Labour, *a surprisingly acid comment on the structure of society.*

Opposite right, contemporary print depicting the three locomotives that took part in trials held in 1829 by the Liverpool & Manchester Railway: Stephenson's Rocket *won hands down. The Liverpool & Manchester, opened in 1830, was the world's first modern railway, that is, the first to operate on its own account regular passenger services hauled entirely by steam locomotives.*

Opposite left, power-loom for weaving carpets on show at the Great Exhibition, 1851: the industrial revolution had started in Britain, and in 1851 she was still the world's leading industrial power, though she would not remain so for long.

Even in the wealthy western countries of Europe, agricultural labourers, who still constituted the majority of the population in 1815, lived in destitution and semi-starvation, existing on a diet of bread, cheese and vegetables, with meat a rare luxury. Meagre wages were supplemented by the earnings of wives and children as soon as they were old enough to work at field-labour or domestic occupations like spinning and weaving.

In England the land enclosure movement had created a class of landless labourers entirely dependent on the wages paid by farmers. Elsewhere in Europe, small peasant farms had remained, but under such difficult conditions that the tenants had a constant struggle to escape from the extortions of landlords and moneylenders. Riots and risings were common occurrences in Russia, southern Germany and Ireland and were not unknown even in the 'peaceful' English countryside.

All over Europe there was a steady migration into the towns. Whether men felt dispossessed from the land or attracted by the greater opportunities of town life is difficult to say, and it is still impossible to draw up an accurate balance sheet of the gains and losses which such a transition involved. In factories and mines wages twice and three times as high as those of the agricultural labourer could be earned. On the other hand, workers had to submit to the impersonal discipline of the mill, to accept a working day of fourteen or fifteen hours, often in overheated and insanitary conditions, and to live in crowded slums shut out from the familiar peace and beauty of nature.

The employment of children from the age of five of six upwards in such conditions was a new a special evil which ultimately excited public concern and control, but the inhuman conditions under which thousands of men and women had to work – the tyranny and brutality of petty masters and overseers, the disease and early death that factory life often brought about, the drunkenness, immorality and prostitution that were all too common in the industrial town – seemed to pass almost unnoticed.

In England, Belgium and France the spontaneous reaction of workers to such conditions was often to break the machines that appeared to be depriving them of their livelihood. These 'Luddite' risings, like the sporadic strikes which were a common feature of early industrial society, were suppressed with great severity – none more so than that of the Lyons silk-weavers, which resulted in a thousand deaths. In the absence of effective trade unions such actions were doomed to failure. The only form of workers' associations which had any success in the period were the peaceful friendly societies formed by skilled craftsmen to insure themselves and their families against sickness and unemployment.

But almost from the beginning the growth of industrialization produced its critics. By the 1820s and 1830s the heightened contrast between wealth and poverty was leading some to question the very foundations of the new society and to propose, in the name either of Christian charity or social justice, fundamental reforms and new political systems.

Reformers and utopians

One of the most significant protests to develop from within the Church itself was the Liberal Catholic movement which began in France in 1829 under the leadership of the clerics Lamennais and Lacordaire with the support of the young peer, the Count of Montalembert. Totally opposed to the *ancien régime* and the control of the Church by the state, they urged through their journal *L'Avenir* freedom of conscience, of the press and education, the sovereignty of the people, universal suffrage and freedom of association. Considered dangerous to authority, the movement was condemned by the French government and by the pope in an encyclical of 1832. Nevertheless, the ideas survived and found expression in the work of a young student, Frederick Ozanam, who founded the Society of St Vincent de Paul for mutual aid and charity.

From outside the established order, and aiming at the overthrow of the capitalist

system as a whole, came a stream of socialist writings. Most of the early work was utopian and unrealistic, the product of the imagination of philosophers and intellectuals who were remote from practical politics, although their ideas contributed importantly to the later foundations of socialism.

One of the earliest was the Count of Saint-Simon (1760–1825), a ruined nobleman who became a violent critic of a social order based on competition and the exploitation of the most numerous class by a tiny minority of privileged owners. His conclusion was that it would be necessary to suppress this class, whose possessions and capital would thus revert to the state, the only legitimate owner. Society could then be reorganized and new classes constructed on the basis of ability, not wealth.

In place of the power of Crown and Church there would be the power of the creative sections of the population – intellectuals, bankers, industrialists, workers – all inspired by a common faith in service and progress.

Saint-Simon's influence was greater after his death than during his own lifetime. Two of his disciples, Enfantin and Bazard, tried to establish a small community in accordance with the principles of the master 'to each according to his ability, each man's ability to be judged by what he achieves', but, like many similar ventures, the project failed because of internal disputes and a law-suit brought by the state. Saint-Simon's significance lay in his challenge to a system which, to nearly all men, had seemed God-given and eternal and in the influence of his philosophy on his contemporaries and successors.

Among these was the English socialist, Robert Owen (1771–1858), who conceived a society in which all power would belong to the working classes, organized into co-operative societies which would both own and control the instruments of production. The son of a draper, Owen had a successful career as an employer in the cotton industry and then as manager of the largest cotton mills in Scotland, at New Lanark. It was during his time there as one of the few enlightened employers of the period that he developed his basic socialist principles: man is not good or evil by nature but largely as a result of the environment in which he grows up; and second, that the machine is not something to be feared and destroyed but to be encouraged for its power to lighten human labour and create vast new sources of wealth. However, to ensure that this wealth was fairly distributed among those who created it, Owen believed that the machine (including all the instruments of production) would need to be publicly owned and controlled and taken out of the hands of private capitalists. These shattering views were published in his *New Moral View of Society* as early as 1813.

Although he had important effects on the development of management, education and cooperation, as a practical socialist Owen was no more successful than Saint-Simon's disciples. A socialist community in the United States, inappropriately named 'New Harmony', collapsed after a few years, and Owen's Grand National Consolidated Trade Union (1834), which was to have taken over British industry after a general strike, was defeated by the combined action of government and employers.

Similar ideas were developed by another French socialist, Fourier. The state was to disappear and give place to self-governing socialist communities, each of about 2,000 people, which would be free associations in which all could devote themselves to the occupations of their choice. In this way, each would find personal fulfilment and happiness. Again, in the theory of Louis Blanc (1811–82), all private industries would be incorporated into social workshops, where workers would choose their employers and share the profits. Proudhon (1809–65) attacked the existence of private property ('property is theft'), the institutions of law and the state, even the sovereignty of the people ('universal suffrage is a lottery'). In his philosophy there was to be no system of government at all: he was the apostle of anarchy.

The very diversity of these views indicates that socialism was not, and could not be at this time, a political party with a well-defined programme. Its main theorists had been intellectuals and philosophers, often of aristocratic or middle-class background, remote from the hopes and aspirations of ordinary men. However, towards the end of the period socialism began to pass from the scholar's study to the mines and factories, as reformers began to organize the working classes for more effective political action.

In Paris in 1836 the Federation of Just Men was founded by a group of emigré German revolutionaries, of whom a tailor, Weitling, was the leading figure. In 1847, at the Federation's annual congress in London, the name 'Communist League' was adopted. It was on this occasion that Karl Marx and Frederich Engels drew up the *Communist Manifesto* (published 1848), which was to prove the most influential political document of modern times.

The triumph of science

But to many contemporaries it was not so much the development of new political ideas or the artistic achievements of the Romantic Movement that characterized the age as the spectacular advances in scientific knowledge and application. The origins of the scientific revolution lay much further back in the seventeenth century, when men had first begun to observe, measure, analyse and deduce laws from the natural world around them, but at this time science was still part of philosophy, the intellectual pursuit of gentlemen-scholars for its own intrinsic interest.

By the nineteenth century scientific knowledge had come to provide the very basis of industrial and technological progress, the life-blood of the new age, no longer the pastime of gifted amateurs but the activity of professional scientists and researchers.

The new science rested fundamentally on basic mathematical theory, which was greatly advanced by a group of scholars from many countries. One of the characteristics of the new knowledge was that it did not observe national boundaries but was developed by men of many countries, often working closely with each other by the exchange of ideas through meetings and publications. Thus Gauss, a professor at Göttingen University, did pioneer work in applying mathematical theory to electricity and magnetism; the Frenchman Monge largely established descriptive geometry, while Laplace demonstrated the stability of the solar system. The Norwegian Abel worked on mathematical astronomy and le Verrier, on the basis of pure calculation, discovered the existence of the planet Neptune which was only observed several years later by telescope.

Similar fundamental research was being pursued in physics which had developed little since its laws had been first established by Newton. Now, Biot and Arago made the first accurate measurements of the density of the air. Gay-Lussac discovered the laws of expansion of gas and Carnot defined the laws of thermodynamics (the science of the relations between heat and mechanical work) on which the Englishman James Joule later based his work.

Although these discoveries were the necessary basis for many new applications, their immediate contribution to human life and work sometimes seemed remote. Not so with the development of electricity, which, from early in the century, began to be used for a variety of purposes. In 1800 the Italians Volta and Galvani constructed the first electric battery: within a few years discoveries by the Dane Oersted, the Frenchman Ampère, the Englishman Faraday and the German Ohm had defined the laws of electromagnetism, established the idea of induction and expounded the mathematics of electrical currents. By the 1840s the electric telegraph, invented by Morse and Steinheil, was in use in England, France and in some other countries.

Discoveries in one branch of science frequently led to developments in others. Electrolysis was used to isolate new chemical substances such as potassium, magnesium, sodium, chromium and aluminium, many of which were to have highly important industrial uses. Similarly, the discoveries in organic chemistry by Chevreul and Liebig led to the development of artificial fertilizers and to much new knowledge about the chemistry of food. Already at the beginning of the nineteenth century Dalton and Avogadro were outlining the first modern theories of atomic structure.

Opposite top, the Count of Saint-Simon, one of the first French socialists: he found little support for his plans for the reorganization of society during his lifetime, though later his ideas gained in influence.

Opposite bottom, portrait by Gustave Courbet of Louis Blanc: his theories briefly took real form during the 1848 revolution in Paris, when the National Workshops were established. After their failure, he fled to Great Britain, only returning to France in 1871. Musée du Louvre, Paris.

Bottom, contemporary cartoon of Ned Ludd, the legendary leader of the Luddites, disguised as a woman.

Below, André Ampère (1775–1836): the pioneering work of this French scientist and mathematician in electromagnetism is recalled today in the word amp, used to measure the strength of an electric current.

Biologists, meanwhile, were investigating the nature of the cell, the fundamental element in the tissues, which was discovered in 1830. Advances in medicine and, in particular, the discovery of anesthetics were beginning to make treatment and surgery safer and more practicable, though until after the middle of the century hospitals continued to be places in which patients often died of diseases other than those with which they entered.

More fundamental research still was being undertaken into the nature of the earth itself. Detailed study of rocks enabled geologists to reconstruct the principal stages in the evolution of the earth's crust, while the examination of fossils by Cuvier laid the foundations of the science of paleontology. From here it was a short step to the posing of questions about the origins of man. Some of Cuvier's pupils remained convinced of the unchanged nature of species since their original creation, yet, to others, the discoveries of fossil remains, some of them closely similar to *homo sapiens*, seemed to argue some kind of evolutionary process from which modern man had developed. Why had some prehistoric animals disappeared from the earth while others had survived in changed, though recognizable form? Lamarck and Saint-Hilaire suggested a theory of evolution of species under the impact of changes in heredity and environment upon which Charles Darwin was later to build. Such views were, of course, irreconcilable with the teachings of the Christian church about the special creation of man and opened a long controversy between science and religion.

But the spirit of scientific enquiry was not confined to the exploration of matter. To many people in the early nineteenth century science was all-important and all-embracing, a tool that could unlock all doors and expose all secrets. Scientific method could be applied to history, to the civilizations of the past as readily as it could to physics or chemistry. It was in this spirit that Champollion deciphered the meaning of hieroglyphics and thus founded the study of Egyptology, while excavations in Greece and Mesopotamia began the modern study of archaeology. It was this profound belief in the power of science that gave to the age so much of its confidence, its sense of purpose and of the inevitability of progress.

The romantic age

Running parallel with the scientific movement of the day, in some ways complementary but in others contradictory to it, was the romantic movement. Its origins lay in the violent upheavals of revolutionary France and the Napoleonic era, which gave rise to changes in the ways of life, attitudes, tastes and feelings of a whole generation.

Napoleon had ultimately been defeated by the traditional monarchies and aristocracies of Europe, and romanticism found its first expression in writers wishing to affirm their anti-revolutionary faith. Romanticism was a philosophy of protest against prevailing circumstances, changing as the circumstances changed. Thus, the early writings of the exiled Chateaubriand showed a fiercely conservative outlook, and both the young Alfred de Vigny and Victor Hugo proclaimed themselves fervent monarchists. It was natural that among subject peoples conquered by the sword of France writers and poets should make themselves the champions of national feeling. They were anxious to assert their difference and individuality, to demonstrate their own distinct culture, language and literature. To oppressed peoples, history is a lifeline and a bulwark against the destruction of a nation's individuality.

But after 1815, the re-establishment of conservative monarchies throughout Europe and the absolutist policies of the Holy Alliance no longer satisfied romantic spirits eager for personal liberty and freedom. Some, like Victor Hugo, returned to the liberal camp and the literature of protest. Others retreated from the real world into a world of nature that had never been, endowed with sublime beauty, solitude and melancholy. The Germany of Goethe and Schiller was the principal home of literary romanticism, but England was also brilliantly represented by the poets Coleridge, Byron, Shelley and Keats and the historical works of Sir Walter Scott. Young people in many countries were fired with enthusiasm for the supposedly Celtic poems of the ancient bard Ossian – in fact, written by a Scotsman, James Macpherson, about 1760 – and Lamartine could write, 'Ossian was the Homer of my early years.' Romantics, no less than modern artists, were not uncommonly subject to self-deception.

In many European countries, however, romantics constituted an uninfluential minority desperately seeking to express their views against strongly entrenched, classical schools of literature. In France particularly they had to struggle to get their works published or produced on the stage, as did Lermontov against the forces of reaction in Russia. In such countries, where absolutist regimes had been re-established after the overthrow of Napoleon, romantics tended to be regarded as near revolutionaries, troublemakers, purveyors of anti-government literature, opponents of order, authority and religion. Some, it is true, were no more than wayward, angry young men; a few were wicked or depraved. But the death of Byron at Missolonghi, fighting for the independence of Greece against the despotic Turk, and the premature end of Lermontov, killed in a duel, symbolized the generous ideals, the courage and selflessness of the romantic spirit at its best. Such ideals were to find different, more positive outlets in the revolutions of 1830 and 1848.

England after Waterloo

In 1815 England came triumphantly to the end of a war in which she had been involved almost continuously for twenty-two years. In a real sense it was her victory. Although at the end, at Waterloo, the English armies had done little more than hold the line until the arrival of Blücher and the Prussians, England had been at the centre of the coalitions which ultimately defeated Napoleon and had provided the money and the war materials on which the armies were raised. Above all she had kept the seaways open and free from French domination. But victory had not been gained lightly. The long war left a crippling debt, an economy that had been subject to violent fluctuations and a working population which had been denied many freedoms in order that the enslaved of Europe should be freed. In some respects, the postwar difficulties and hardships were more acute than the wartime ones had been.

The England of 1815 remained, socially and politically at least, essentially the England of the eighteenth century. Despite the Industrial Revolution, which was rapidly changing the basis of Britain's economic wealth from land to industry and trade, all real power still remained in the hands of a territorial aristocracy numbering no more than a few thousand families. They represented the view – once arguable but by now irrelevant – that those who owned the land of Britain should control its destinies and public affairs. Since the 'Glorious Revolution' of 1688 Britain's system of government had been a parliamentary monarchy, with effective control of national policies in the hands of the two Houses of Parliament rather than the crown. The power of the monarchy had since been reduced further by the insanity of George III and the emergence of powerful parliamentary leaders like Chatham and Pitt. The peers of the realm had hereditary seats in the House of Lords where, together with the lords spiritual, they formed a solid bulwark not only against revolution but against reform. Although most legislation was now initiated in the lower chamber, the lords could always reject, delay or amend it out of recognition. In local affairs they also wielded immense influence through their appointment to the magistracy and county administration: their control of local justice and the administration of poor relief could be relied on to ensure a docile, even servile, rural population.

In theory the House of Commons, with members elected by the counties and boroughs of the four kingdoms, was a more representative body. But here, too, the right to vote and the right to election of a member rested on a property qualification which enfranchised a mere 150,000 out of a population of more than 15,000,000. Once flourishing centres such as the ancient port of Aldeburgh in Suffolk still sent more than

one representative to the Commons even though they were now reduced to small villages or hamlets (in Aldeburgh's case through coastal erosion sinking the city beneath the sea). In many 'pocket' and 'rotten' boroughs electors were sufficiently few for their votes to be bought or commanded, and it was common practice for wealthy young men seeking a political career to buy a parliamentary seat at a price of £5,000 to £6,000. Of 658 seats in the Commons only about fifty were actually fought by rival candidates.

By no stretch of imagination, then, could Britain's parliamentary system in 1815 be described as democratic. The privileged members of both Houses divided themselves between the two great parties, Whigs and Tories, the differences between which were by now all but lost in history. Originally, Tories had stood for the rights of the Crown and the Anglican Church, Whigs for parliamentary government, freedom of conscience and moderate reform. But both parties consisted of landowners equally devoted to the maintenance of the existing class structure and equally remote from the new centres of power that were beginning to reshape English society.

England in 1815 presented a strange contrast of the old and the new. In the countryside, where more than two-thirds of the population still lived, there was much that was traditional and unchanging: ways of life, methods of agriculture, food, dress and habits were still almost medieval, especially in the remoter parts of the West and North. But, by contrast, in the Midlands, Lancashire and Yorkshire industrialization had

made rapid progress during the wars, spurred on by the demand for guns and munitions, ships, clothing and army supplies of all kinds. Vast new centres of population sprang up as rural dwellers were attracted by the opportunities and earnings of industry. Within the first half of the century Birmingham trebled in size, Manchester quadrupled, Bradford increased no less than eightfold. This rapid and unplanned growth of cities created immense problems – of accommodation, sanitation, local government and recreation – whose solution lay far in the future. More immediately, it showed up the inadequacies and inequalities of a parliamentary system which gave two seats to a 'rotten borough' of a score of voters but denied representation to a great new city like Manchester.

But in one respect, at least, England had an advantage over other European countries. Here there was no impassable gulf between the aristocracy of birth and the aristocracy of wealth: the two met and mingled, their sons were educated together in the public schools, their families not infrequently intermarried. Robert Peel, the son of a successful Lancashire cotton manufacturer, could become an MP at twenty-one and, ultimately, prime minister; Richard Arkwright, the wandering barber who invented (some said stole) the idea of a water-powered spinning frame, could be knighted and created lord-lieutenant of the county of Nottinghamshire, an office usually reserved for a territorial lord. Industrialization offered to some glittering prizes of wealth and social mobility unknown to previous ages. To others, perhaps a majority

Above, The Election at Eatanswill, *a satire on the bribery and corruption common in elections before the 1832 Reform Act.*

Above left, portrait by Thomas Phillips of Lord Byron (1788–1824): both his writings and his fervent belief in political liberty (he helped Italian revolutionaries and joined the Greeks fighting for independence from Turkey) made him an inspiration to many European writers and poets, and his name is still commemorated in Greece today. National Portrait Gallery, London.

of the population, it offered misery heightened by the evidence of wealth about them.

At the end of the war England entered upon a long depression which brought to many even greater hardship than the war had done. Industries lay depressed with the sudden cessation of wartime demand, agriculture no longer enjoyed the protection that Napoleon's blockade had brought and began to contract, while European countries, impoverished after years of conquest and exploitation, could not afford to resume their former level of trade. It was, in fact, twenty years after 1815 before British exports recovered to their previous level. Added to the existing problems of unemployment and low wages were some half a million demobilized soldiers and sailors, suddenly thrown on to a labour market that could not absorb them. The years from 1815 to 1820 were among the darkest in English history when many feared, with some cause, a repetition of the events which had torn France apart in 1789.

Radicalism – an extreme form of politics which advocated fundamental reform of the constitutional and financial system – grew to brief importance under such popular leaders as Cobbett and Hunt. In their hatred of industrialization they preached a naive 'back-to-the-land' philosophy which seemed attractive to populations of former peasants exposed to the insecurities of town life. Significantly, the cause of the 'Peterloo Massacre' in Manchester in 1819, when a defenceless crowd was charged by squadrons of cavalry, was a speech by Hunt, not on the problem of wages or unemployment, but on the subject of land reform.

Most labour movements in the first half of the century had this strong agrarian background. A majority of the new town dwellers were peasants by origin, unaccustomed to

the regularity of factory work and the overcrowded life in slums and tenements. They tuned instinctively to solutions that offered simpler, better understood relationships in which men seemed to be something more than mere instruments of production. Working people gave their support to Radicalism, not because they understood or even cared very much about abstract democratic principles but because it represented a protest against the unacceptable conditions of life. To its few middle- and upper-class supporters it was much more – a progressive, democratic demand for a government responsible to the popular will and an administrative system based on efficiency rather than privilege.

To such suggestions the governments of the day responded with severe repression. The Tory party remained in office from the end of the war until 1830, first under Lord Liverpool, later under the wartime hero, the Duke of Wellington. Their belief was that the British constitution was perfect and that any attempt to disturb it must be put down firmly. Trade Unions were illegal until 1824 and even after that striking was still a criminal offence, public meetings and meeting-places required to be licensed and newspapers were subject to a crippling stamp duty of five pence a copy. Together with such measures went a crude system which paid a meagre dole to labourers whose earnings were inadequate to support their families (the Speenhamland System of poor relief) and which had the effect of impoverishing whole areas of the country.

In 1820 the mad George III was succeeded by his son, the former prince regent, who had been notorious as a beau and a rake. For many years now he had deserted his wife, Caroline of Brunswick, in favour of a succession of mistresses. Caroline had finally left England in 1814 to live abroad, and

George, the regent, had appointed a commission to investigate her conduct. Its report appeared in 1819, full of supposedly scandalous revelations about the intimate life of the Princess Caroline. She, however, refused to be divorced and published an open letter defending her own conduct and attacking that of George. In June 1820 she set sail for England to be crowned alongside her husband.

On her progress to London, and in the capital, Caroline was received by enthusiastic crowds who saw her as a wronged and innocent victim of a degenerate king. Divorce proceedings opened at Westminster in July, and the private lives of the British monarchy were exposed to the tales of lackeys and ladies-in-waiting. Public regard for the Crown had not been at a lower ebb since the Civil War of the seventeenth century, and there were many who predicted a republican future for the country which had developed the concept of constitutional monarchy. The court was unable to reach a decision, but ultimately Caroline was induced to yield by the payment of a handsome pension: one of the most ugly chapters in the English monarchy closed with an unseemly bribe.

The postwar depression and public disorder of the period between 1815 and 1820 had shown up the inadequacies – indeed, irrelevancies – of both political parties to the changing needs of the time. But after 1824 Tory policies began to receive a new direction at the hands of a group of enlightened young politicians – Canning at the Foreign Office, Peel at the Home Office and Huskisson at the Board of Trade – who appreciated the necessity of reshaping policies in the light of Britain's changing economic conditions and world role.

Middle-class reform

'Enlightened Toryism', which Sir Robert Peel was later to develop into the new Conservative Party, gave the government a fresh lease of life. Its appeal was particularly to the rising class of merchants and industrialists, who were favoured by reductions in the tariff system and by modifications to the Corn Laws. Under the Corn Law of 1815, passed in response to pressure by the landed interest, the import of foreign wheat was totally prohibited when the English price was less than eighty shillings a quarter. Whether it had very much effect on the price of wheat is debatable, but it certainly acted to the disadvantage of exporters who wished to sell to countries like Germany, Hungary and Russia who had little else but wheat to offer in exchange. The Corn Laws therefore constituted a serious hindrance to the expansion of world trade, from which Britain, as the greatest exporting nation, suffered particularly. By various acts in the later 1820s a sliding scale was substituted for the total prohibition, so that duties on imported

Gent. *No Gent.* *& Re gent !!*

wheat remained high when the English price was low and vice versa. These measures at least opened the way for the ultimate repeal of the Corn Laws in 1846.

Other reforms by the enlightened Tories were of benefit to the population as a whole. Peel, as home secretary, began to modernize the penal system by abolishing the death sentence on several hundreds of petty offences. At the same time, his establishment of the Metropolitan Police made the detection and punishment of crime more effective. In 1828 the Test Acts, which had debarred Nonconformists from the holding of public office as MPs, magistrates, etc., were repealed and, more significant still, Catholic emancipation was passed in the next year. This issue was forced by the 'election' of the Irish Catholic leader, Daniel O'Connell, for County Clare, and rather than face what might have been a civil war in Ireland the prime minister, Wellington, acceded to the demands of Catholics to be treated as equal citizens. After more than two centuries of persecution religious toleration was finally established in Britain.

Catholic emancipation did not solve the problem of Ireland. Tenants of English landlords, forced to pay tithes to the English Church and subjected by the Act of Union of 1800 to English political domination, the Irish now asserted their claims to absolute independence.

O'Connell and his Young Ireland party renewed their agitation. Monster demonstrations were organized, particularly between 1843 and 1847, and there was even an abortive attempt at revolution in 1848. But Ireland was crushed by poverty and exhausted by famine. In 1846 the potato crop on which the majority of the population depended was hit by blight, and thousands starved to death. Between 1841 and 1851 a million Irish – many of them the most intelligent and resourceful part of the population – emigrated to England and America. For the time being political issues were merged in national calamity.

Meanwhile, in England, agitation for parliamentary reform had been growing with an uneasy alliance between Whigs, Philosophical Radicals and some sections of the working classes. In 1830 the hated George IV died and was succeeded by William IV, of no great intelligence though more amenable. Revolutions in France and Belgium had some influence in England: in 1830–1 there was a large-scale rising of agricultural labourers throughout the eastern and southern counties demanding higher wages, fairer rents and an improved system of poor relief. Events were converging towards a major political change.

In the general election of 1830 the Whigs were returned to power under Lord Grey. Their first act was to introduce a measure for parliamentary reform, which passed into law in 1832 only after numerous amendments and an initial rejection in the House of Lords. Although always known as the 'Great Reform Bill' its provisions were modest enough and far less than the Radicals had hoped. It abolished the separate representation of small towns with less than 2,000 inhabitants and left towns with 2,000 to 4,000 with only one member; 143 seats were then available for distribution among the great new cities and among those counties which were not adequately represented.

Manchester and Birmingham for the first time received their own members of parliament, but even after 1832 an ancient borough of 2,010 inhabitants could still return its own representative. The other main provision of the Act was the extension of the franchise to householders in the towns rated at £10 a year and to £50 a year tenant farmers in the country – essentially the urban and rural middle classes: the electorate was thus increased to 600,000 voters. The Act did not enfranchise the working classes nor make voting secret. Parliamentary participation was still to rest on the possession of property as an indication of worth and responsibility. The Reform Act in no way converted English government into a democracy, though it was the first and in some ways the most decisive step in that process.

Above, meeting of the Birmingham Political Union in 1832: Political Unions – Birmingham's was one of the first and most important – were formed to press for parliamentary reform; the demands of some radical members for economic and social reform remained unfulfilled.

Above left, Cruikshank cartoon dating from 1816 satirizing the rakish life led by the Prince Regent.

Opposite, cartoon by George Cruikshank (1792–1878) of the Manchester Heroes of the Peterloo Massacre in 1819: economic depression after the Napoleonic wars led to a series of popular protests throughout the country, of which the meeting that led to the 'massacre' was one of the largest. In the 1820s the economy revived, and the threat of revolution, so feared by the established order, vanished.

The new poor law

The next task of the Whig government after the reform of parliament was reform of the poor law. A system which paid a dole to all and sundry, which encouraged the idle and discouraged the diligent and which acted as a deterrent to labour mobility was totally unacceptable to the 'practical' principles which inspired middle-class Whigs. In 1832 a Royal Commission, headed by the great classical economist Nassau Senior and the lawyer Edwin Chadwick, was appointed to investigate the existing provisions for the poor and to make recommendations for their reform.

Senior accepted the pessimistic view of the Reverend Thomas Malthus that population would inevitably outstrip the resources necessary to feed it unless kept down by 'natural checks'. Poverty was inherent in society, but pauperism could be eradicated by suitably stringent forms of relief. Under the Poor Law Amendment Act of 1834 the payment of doles, at least to those fit to work, was to cease: in future, the only form of relief would be in workhouses where conditions would deliberately be made 'less eligible' (i.e. more unpleasant) than those of the poorest paid free workers. Here, husbands and wives would be separated, fed on the sparsest diet and made to labour at the most uncongenial tasks. Behind the outward cruelty, however, there lay the hope that these measures would force up the level of wages, make labour more mobile and, not least, bring down the cost of poor relief. In this last respect the act was a marked success. As Carlyle commented cynically, 'If paupers are made miserable, paupers must needs decline in multitude. It is a secret known to all rat catchers.'

In a broad sense, the Amendment Act was in tune with the general philosophy of the Whigs of removing antiquated restrictions and bringing about greater freedom. The Municipal Corporations Act of 1835 reconstituted the local government of boroughs, establishing elected councils in all towns above the size of 25,000 inhabitants. More important, an Act of 1833 abolished slavery in the British Empire, so completing the work begun by Wilberforce who had earlier succeeded in stopping the slave trade in 1807. In the same year, 1833, the great East India Company was deprived of its monopoly of trading with the East and the gateway was thus opened for a remarkable expansion of British trade in India, China and Japan. All these measures were, in effect, advancing the cause of Free Trade, which became the guiding philosophy – almost the religion – of the Liberal Party later in the century.

The beginning of the Victorian Age

William IV died in 1837, to more or less universal indifference. England remained a monarchy, but for more than a century the

English people had had no feeling for their kings except amusement or contempt. A young girl of eighteen was now to regain the affection and respect that kings had forfeited.

For nearly two-thirds of a century (1837–1901) Victoria was to unite the people and the monarchy in an intimate, almost mysterious, relationship. Although she came to learn her position as a constitutional monarch very well and did not, after the first few years, attempt to intervene in party political issues, she was often able to represent the views and interests of the people to the government and hence to play an important part in the shaping of policy. In her simple, naive way she exercised a moral, moderating influence on politics, restraining the hot-headed, encouraging the timid and the humane, steadfastly opposing repression either at home or abroad.

Victoria had been an extremely unlikely

successor to the throne of England. The problem had presented itself during the lifetime of George III, when the royal family comprised seven princes, two of whom succeeded as George IV and William IV. But none of them had any children – at least, any legitimate children capable of succeeding to the throne. The Duke of Kent, who was deep in debt, agreed 'in the interests of the kingdom' to contract a 'reasonable' marriage. He left his mistress to marry a German princess, Victoria of Leiningen, a member of the distinguished Saxe-Coburg family. Of this union Victoria was born in May 1819.

The future queen was brought up strictly, seriously, even humbly for a person of her rank. At eighteen, she was intellectually unprepared for her role, though imbued with devotion to her task and a deep desire to raise the status of the monarchy from the ignominy of previous reigns. Political intrigue developed early around the young

queen whom every politician thought to influence, but Victoria acted mainly on the counsel of Lord Melbourne, the Whig prime minister after 1834, who offered wise and palatable advice on English constitutional practice. Victoria's marriage to her cousin, Prince Albert of Saxe-Coburg, also added strength, intelligence and moral purpose to the new monarchy.

In some important respects, the long reign of Victoria instituted a new kind of monarchy, one of the many adaptations that nineteenth-century England was obliged to make. Monarchy in the past had been associated with rural England, with the territorial aristocracy and the 'gentlemanly' pursuits of farming, sport and leisure. Such a role would have been impossible for the queen anyway, but, particularly through her husband, she chose to identify herself much more with urban and industrial interests, with the new sources of activity and wealth that were transforming England into a middle-class society. The royal court was still as magnificent as ever, there were still rural retreats in Scotland and the Isle of Wight (no longer Brighton), but the energy and moral purpose, the devotion to work and good causes of the royal couple were new characteristics of the monarchy, closely in tune with the principles of bourgeois life. The queen's unsophisticated taste in literature, music and interior decoration was mirrored in thousands of suburban homes,

Above, the reformed House of Commons meeting in 1835: ironically, in view of the vehement opposition to reform, the first parliament elected was, according to the diarist Greville, 'very much like every other parliament', and the south and the landowners maintained their dominant position. National Portrait Gallery, London.

Left, an early photograph, taken by Roger Fenton in 1854, of Queen Victoria (1819–1901) and Prince Albert (1819–61): the royal couple, who were married in 1840, were devoted to each other. Prince Albert had a difficult role which he fulfilled well, promoting especially industrial and social reform (the Great Exhibition of 1851 was his idea) and the arts.

Opposite top, painting by Benjamin Haydon of a meeting held by the Birmingham Political Union, 16 May 1832. Birmingham Museum and Art Gallery.

Opposite bottom, Bridewell prison, London, in 1808. Social reform, particularly of the system of poor relief and of the prison system, took a high priority among nineteenth-century radicals. Many debtors found themselves imprisoned in Bridewell and thus unable to pay off their debts.

and the extensive yet virtuous domestic life of the monarchy served to set a seal on the Victorian preoccupation with family, hearth and home.

The reshaping of the monarchy to essentially middle-class standards and ideals was only one of many adaptations that English institutions had to make in response to economic and social changes. By the 1870s complete free trade had been established except for a few duties kept for revenue purposes only. Recruitment to the expanded Civil Service had been established on competitive principles in place of privilege. The powers of local authorities had been enlarged to include responsibility for public health and, in part at least, for housing. More important still, in 1870 the state reluctantly accepted a duty towards popular education by instituting a system of public elementary schools. Although the composition of parliament was still unrepresentative of the changes taking place outside it, even here the beginnings of a modern party system were discernible, with stronger party discipline and greater concentration of authority in the hands of the cabinet. This development became marked only later during the great ministries of Gladstone and Disraeli.

The middle classes had made substantial gains in the early years of the queen's reign. But Victorian prosperity rested on a wide substructure of poverty in the working classes, for whom it must often have seemed that England had nothing to offer except unending toil, a slum dwelling and a pauper's grave. After the Reform Act of 1832 the alliance between the radicals and the middle classes collapsed; the workers were still unenfranchised and unrepresented and felt betrayed by those whom they had supported. Now there seemed no one to take their cause.

The saddest plight of all was that of the factory children, forced to work at the age of six or seven from five in the morning until seven or eight at night. Many were too exhausted to eat, some were maimed and even killed by the machines they tended. Industrialization in its early stages required cheap, amenable labour, and women and children could often perform the routine tasks it demanded with little or no training.

Direct political action by the working classes had, for the time being, been tried and had failed. Some improvements were to come, however, from philanthropists and humanitarians concerned for the sufferings of the poor and especially for the welfare of children. Lord Shaftesbury was particularly successful in compelling the investigation of conditions in factories and coal mines, which formed the necessary basis for the legislative control of employment which began in the Factory Act of 1833.

Robert Owen had already demonstrated at the New Lanark Mills, contrary to all popular belief, that humane factory management could reduce hours of work, pay higher wages and still make handsome profits. As an enlightened capitalist employer Owen was an outstanding success, as a socialist philosopher and educational theorist brilliant and inspiring, as a practical political leader an utter failure. His schemes for co-operative production and, more ambitious still, for the great Grand National Consolidated Trade Union (1833–4) intended to 'nationalize' British industry and run it socialistically, collapsed under the united attack of government and employers. The enduring memorial to Robert Owen, symbolic alike of his inspiration and failure, is the case of the Tolpuddle Martyrs (1834), sentenced to seven years transportation for having dared to form a trade union.

The Chartist challenge

The failure of Owen's schemes for a socialist millennium was to revive the agitation for direct political representation. The lawsuits which had struck at the trades unions, the harshness of the new Poor Law and the limited success of the Factory Act of 1833 all served to indicate to the worker that legislative policy would continue to be made regardless of his interests so long as he continued to be excluded from parliament.

In 1836 the London Working Men's Association was formed to campaign for parliamentary representation. It was, in itself, a moderate movement of working-class intelligentsia, deriving much of its programme from late eighteenth-century radicalism, but it quickly became caught up in much more violent agitations in the Midlands and North, particularly against the new workhouse 'bastilles'. In 1837 'The People's Charter' was formulated – a demand for six democratic reforms the most important of which were manhood suffrage, secret voting and the payment of members of parliament.

Chartism was the major working class movement of the first half of the century, dominating the stage from 1837 until 1848. Although outwardly a political movement, seeking to persuade parliament of the justness of its demands by the presentation of monster petitions, its root cause were economic and social discontent, and its main support came in the two major periods of depression and unemployment, 1839–42 and 1847–8. As one of its leaders, Joseph Stephens, put it, 'Chartism was a bread and cheese question, a knife and fork question.' It's appeal, especially after 'physical force' leaders like Feargus O'Connor took over command from those who advocated only moral persuasion, was to the hungry and destitute, the unemployed and the underemployed, the sweated workers and the casualties of industrialization.

Petitions presented in 1839 and 1842 were unheeded by parliament. The last, of 1848, which purported to contain six million signatures, was examined and found to include less than two million, many pages in the same hand and including such unlikely supporters as the Duke of Wellington and Mr Punch. The charter was laughed out of existence in an atmosphere of near hysterical relief.

Chartism failed for many reasons – because its aims were over-ambitious, because it was badly led, lacked funds and influence, and, not least, because it was firmly opposed by the ruling classes who alone might have championed it in parliament. Nevertheless, it has rightly been regarded as the first mass movement of an identifiable working class, and its very existence helped to draw attention to what Disraeli called 'The Condition of England Question'. Gradually a social conscience was aroused on specific evils, which found expression in legislation regulating the hours and conditions in factories and mines, the removal of street refuse, the conduct of common lodging houses and the adulteration of food and drugs.

In general, however, the mood of the mid-century was one of unbounded optimism and confidence in Britain's progress. After the depression of 1848 England seemed to move on to a new plateau of prosperity which began to bring gains, not only to the employing class, but to all sections of the community. The 'Golden Age', if it had not already dawned, was imminent.

The triumph of free trade

Britain's economic success in the middle of the century was in no small part a result of her adoption of a policy of Free Trade. It fell, ironically, to the lot of Peel, the leader of the Conservative Party from 1841 to 1846, to initiate the process of abandoning the Corn Laws in 1846. By so doing he acted against the wishes of the landed gentry which had helped to vote him into office and left his party split and in the wilderness.

Peel had become gradually convinced of the necessity for a free trade in corn, partly as a social reform which could cheapen the cost of bread to the working classes, partly as an economic measure which would enable Britain to sell more manufactured goods to countries which could only pay in food and raw materials. These and other arguments had been forcibly put by the Anti-Corn Law League under its founder, Richard Cobden, a Manchester industrialist of humble origins who had made a fortune in the cotton trade. The success of the League was in direct contrast to the failure of Chartism. It was efficiently organized and well led; it had the support of the middle classes and of many MPs, it used methods of propaganda such as the distribution of millions of pamphlets through the new penny post to ensure that its message was heard throughout the land. The campaign was a masterpiece of persuasion, essentially modern in its use of the mass media and its deliberate enlistment of influential support.

It seems that Peel had been convinced of the necessity for total removal of the Corn Laws by 1842 or 1843 and that thereafter he was only awaiting the right occasion. This came in 1846, with the Irish Famine, when thousands more would have died if the free import of wheat had not been allowed. Repeal was carried through parliament by a minority of the government (the 'Peelites')

Above, meeting of the Anti-Corn Law League at Manchester, 1841: this highly effective middle-class pressure group, whose aims were to abolish the duty on imported corn and extend Free Trade, achieved total success within seven years, a telling contrast with Chartism, whose aims were too extreme to gain any parliamentary support.

Above left, the National Convention of the Chartist movement, held in London in February 1839: the Convention – the first major gathering of the movement – revealed divisions between radicals and moderates that were never solved; these, combined with irresolute leadership and lack of contact with the nascent trade union movement, meant that the Chartists never became a force for effective political change. Most of their demands for parliamentary and electoral reform were enacted, however, within the next three quarters of a century.

Opposite, interior of a mid-nineteenth century doll's house, a perfect reproduction of the comfortable and solid though somewhat unimaginative style set by the royal family and followed by many of the more prosperous of their subjects. Bethnal Green Museum, London.

Text on the illustration:
BRITISH PROSPERITY. BASED ON FREE TRADE.

RIGHTEOUS EFFORTS OF MEN LEAGUED AGAINST TYRANTS, WHO WITHHOLD FOOD FROM THE LABOURER

GOD WILL PROSPER THE RIGHTEOUS

W. MARRIOTT MANUFACTURER OF THE CORN LAW REPEAL HAT

WE EXCHANGE OUR SUPERABUNDANT CROPS FOR BRITISH MANUFACTURES. ST ANDREWS ROAD, NEW KENT ROAD

NATIONAL ANTI-CORN-LAW LEAGUE FORMED IN LONDON

THE PEOPLE'S PRAYER, 1815 TO 1843
MARCH 27, 1839
"Give us this Day our Daily Bread"
ANSWERED IN 1844.
"We thank thee, O lord for what thou hast so bountifully provided"
FREE TRADE HAT.
W. MARRIOTT, 33 ST ANDREWS ROAD. NEW KENT ROAD. LONDON.

with the support of the Whigs and against the bitter opposition of the landowning Tories. It opened the way for the establishment of complete freedom of trade in the next decade.

By sponsoring repeal of the Corn Laws Peel split his party and committed political suicide. The young Disraeli made his reputation at this moment by denouncing his leader as a betrayer and putting himself at the head of the protectionist Tories. Gradually he welded a new Conservative party out of the ruins, dedicated to social reform at home and expansion of the empire abroad. 'Peelites' ultimately amalgamated with some of the Whigs to form the new Liberal party, of which Gladstone, the natural heir and successor of Peel, was to become the leader. Liberalism stood, above all, for Free Trade and free enterprise, for democratic reform and for a policy of peace abroad. These two great leaders were to dominate British politics until almost the end of the century.

The British Empire

With the War of American Independence (1776–83) the first British Empire had come to an end. But during the nineteenth century a second British Empire was constructed partly by acquisition, partly by conquest, partly by treaty, which was greater than the first – greater, indeed, than the world had ever seen – and which was at once her pride and the envy of other nations. Much of it had come by conquest at the expense of France and her allies, Spain and Holland, during the Revolutionary and Napoleonic Wars – huge areas in India and Canada, Ceylon and the Cape of Good Hope, many of the West Indian islands and strategic possessions in the Mediterranean like Gibraltar, Malta and the Ionian Isles. But there was little deliberate plan about the development of the empire – it has even been said that it was born 'in a fit of absence of mind'. A large empire, and the ability to maintain it and the sea routes between it, was a symbol of the power and status of the mother country. Some territories supplied useful products and raw materials, some provided substantial outlets for British manufactures, but in general the second British Empire came into being not so much from economic or military reasons but rather because of a rather ill-defined pride of possession often combined with genuine religious and humanitarian impulses.

The special pride of the Victorian Empire was India. By the end of the Napoleonic War Britain was firmly established in the territories of the Ganges and of the Deccan in the south but did not yet hold the whole sub-continent. The struggle against the Mahratta chiefs (1817), the conquest of the territories round the Indus and the war against the savage Sikhs of the Punjab occupied the first half of the nineteenth century. Then followed the task of governing and administering these vast dominions, a task accomplished on the whole with efficiency and honesty by the Indian Army and the Indian Civil Service, which was reconstituted on modern lines even before the reforms in home administration. For many functions the East India Company continued to act as the agent of the British government until 1858.

Protection of sea routes also assumed a major importance in the far-flung British Empire. St Helena, the Cape of Good Hope, Mauritius, Aden (acquired 1839), Ceylon and Singapore (1819) all became impregnable bastions and barriers to the colonial ambitions of other European powers.

Elsewhere, where outright conquest failed or seemed too costly, Britain contented herself with establishing a protective belt around her dominions. After the failure of the conquest of Afghanistan in 1842, the British army confined itself to fortifying the mountain passes of the Northwest Frontier. To the north of India the Himalayas provided a natural barrier capable of repelling any invader, while to the northeast Burma was at least partly occupied after two campaigns in 1826 and 1852.

India also served as a base for the domination of the Far East. The old East India Company had always claimed the monopoly of trade with all lands east of the Cape of Good Hope, though its success had been virtually confined to the mainland of India. Now, the search for ever wider markets was to open up the formerly closed countries of the Far East which had for centuries sought to insulate themselves against the influence of the West. The Opium War of 1840–2 forced China to open five ports to British trade, including the great cities of Canton and Shanghai, and to cede the island of Hong Kong, a trading centre and strategic port in the Pacific. In 1857 trade was opened with Siam, in 1858 with Japan.

In India and the Far East the motives of imperialism were economic and military, sometimes religious and philanthropic. It was never intended that British people should settle permanently in tropical and subtropical latitudes, where they were exposed to a harsh climate, endemic diseases and sudden, even violent, death. Countries which were so inhospitable, poor and already over populated offered little attraction to the English emigrant.

On the other hand, the mother country herself seemed to offer few prospects of health and happiness to many of those who laboured in the early days of industrialization, and there were parts of the empire – South Africa, Australia, New Zealand and Canada – where the climate was acceptable, where farmland could be had cheaply or even free, and where a man of energy and purpose could be master of his own destiny. There was a steady and continuous stream of emigrants from Britain, amounting, during the course of the century, to no less than twenty million people. Britain's human export, many of them men and women of above average intelligence and initiative, was perhaps her most important and enduring gift to the world.

To many, the Cape of Good Hope, acquired from Holland in 1815, seemed to offer the most attractive prospects. The original Dutch settlers, the Boers, were gradually pushed further back into the interior as more settlers arrived from Britain. Isolated and unprotected, they were unable to oppose the abolition of slavery in 1833, though this threatened to deprive them of the black labour force on which their agricultural economy depended.

In 1833 the Great Trek took the Boers from one side of the River Vaal to the other, into Natal. When this was annexed by Britain in 1844, the Boers trekked again, and Britain now recognized as independent the Republics of Transvaal and The Orange Free State. For the time being the issue seemed to be resolved – the diamond mines had not yet been discovered.

At the other end of the world Australia, remote and open, seemed less attractive to settlers and until the middle of the century was used primarily as a convict settlement. But the success of many ex-prisoners as sheep farmers, the availability of free land and the discovery of gold in 1851 soon began to exert a magnetic effect on emigrants. Rich lands also awaited the settler in New Zealand, where the warlike Maoris were defeated and pushed back into the hills. In Canada, especially in the state of Quebec, the situation was different. Here, English colonists encountered an existing white population of French descent, hostile to British domination and acutely aware of their distinct origins and culture. Little by little the French were swamped by continued migration, though they continued jealously to preserve their own customs and ways of life.

The spread of the 'white empire' posed new problems for the home government. The 'black' colonies, it was argued, constituted an 'empire in trust': they required the benefits of English law and firm government, of Christianity, educational and philanthropic provision generally and of military protection from more ruthless exploiters. In return for such benefits, England had a right to expect loyalty, trade concessions and treaty rights. But the lesson of history was well understood – that the attempt to impose such conditions on emigrated Britons had lost us the American colonies, the most highly prized pearl of the first British Empire.

It required little imagination to see that the new 'white' colonies must be treated differently and, in particular, be given a substantial measure of control over their own affairs. The new policy was initiated in 1847,

when Canada was granted a large degree of autonomy, her own parliament and a responsible minister, while Britain remained primarily responsible for foreign policy and defence. The process of self-government was thus begun which finally culminated in the Statute of Westminster of 1931.

The American colonies had been lost by England's attempt to control their trade and economic development. Now, Britain gradually abandoned her old colonial system by which the colonies had been obliged to trade only with the mother country. In 1825 Canada was permitted to trade with foreign countries, and in 1849 the repeal of Navigation Acts brought free trade to all the colonies. By this time, the 'white empire' was firmly linked to Britain not by political bonds but by common language and civilization and by unquestioned loyalty to the Crown. Queen Victoria's adoption of the title 'Empress of India' was symbolic of the

Above, British troops taking Cape Town in 1806: the colony, founded by Dutch settlers in 1652, was taken and lost several times before finally settling in British hands in 1815. The conflict between settlers of Dutch and British origin persisted throughout the century, flared up in the Boer War (1899–1902) and still exists today.

Top, view of Government House, Calcutta, executed by J. B. Fraser, c. 1825: British rule in India, at least until the last decades of the nineteenth century, was generally dedicated and enlightened and certainly avoided the exploitation, of both people and resources, that characterized European dominion elsewhere.

Opposite, the Corn Law Repeal Hat, manufactured by one W. Marriott, a South London hatter and supporter of Free Trade.

new role of the monarchy and of the strange power which a small island had to control the destinies of two hundred and forty million people throughout the world.

Britain's achievement

To other European countries in the first half of the nineteenth century Britain's success seemed remarkable and phenomenal. When thousands of foreign visitors attended the Great Exhibition in Hyde Park in 1851 they were impressed, even overwhelmed, by the industrial products and mechanical ingenuity of the British, as by the colonial pavilions displaying the resources of her far-flung empire. Designed, in the Prince Consort's words, 'to illustrate the point of industrial development at which the whole of mankind has now arrived', it in fact demonstrated for all to see the immense wealth of Britain and the great lead which she enjoyed over all other nations.

Yet it is important to remember that this position had been only recently acquired and, in the perspective of history, was comparatively short-lived. In 1800 France had been the 'great power', the conqueror of Europe, master of a vast empire, home of a

philosophy that seemed destined to swamp the world. By 1870 Britain's position was already coming to be challenged by newly industrialized nations, Germany and the United States, who seemed to possess in a marked degree the characteristics of industry and initiative of which Britain had thought herself the sole repository. Observers at the International Exhibition at Paris in 1867 were now struck not so much by the British contribution as by the remarkable progress of other countries.

Britain's tenure of unchallenged world leadership was, then, comparatively brief. She achieved it partly through the natural talents of her people and the abundant natural resources of her land, partly through the absence of any substantial rival. France after 1815 was defeated and exhausted, her economy virtually prostrate after a quarter of a century geared to war needs. Germany and Italy did not yet exist as nation-states and would not do so until the processes of unification had been completed in 1870, while the United States of America, 'united' in name, were not so in any real sense, as the Civil War of the 1860s was to demonstrate. None of these countries could yet command the political stability which seemed to be a

necessary condition of economic growth.

It would be a gross over-simplification to say that Britain in the nineteenth century chose to have an industrial rather than a political revolution. The evolution of democratic institutions went on alongside economic and social changes, often impelled by those very changes. On the continent political change frequently occurred which was not rooted in the economic fabric of society but was much more the product of philosophical ideas and intellectual ferment. Neither Robert Owen nor the Chartists ever brought Britain close to revolution, though Britain was the home of the first industrial proletariat and, in the Marxist logic, should have been the first to experience an open class war. The fact was that industrialization enriched as many – perhaps more – than it impoverished and in the course of time raised standards of living infinitely higher than they could ever have been under a rural economy. New wealth created new classes and new political parties which responed in a practical way to the pressures for change. In Europe such evolutionary change was often impossible, and there was no alternative to a sudden and violent overthrow of an existing regime.

GREAT BRITAIN IN THE EARLY NINETEENTH CENTURY

Date	Great Britain	British colonies	Scientific progress
1815	Corn law (1815)		
	Widespread distress and economic depression Peterloo Massacre (1819)	Revolt against British rule in Ceylon suppressed (1817)	
		Singapore founded (1819)	First steamship crosses the Atlantic (1819)
1820	Death of George III; accession of George IV (1820) Cato Street Conspiracy (1820) Canning foreign minister (1822)	Gold Coast becomes a crown colony (1821) Britain acquires Malacca (1824)	Stephenson builds first iron railway bridge (1823) Stockton-Darlington railway opens (1825)
1825	Duke of Wellington prime minister (1828) Sliding scale of duties on imported corn (1828)		Niepce makes photograph on a metal plate (1827)
	Catholic Emancipation Act (1829) Death of George IV; accession of William IV (1830)		G. S. Ohm defines electrical current, potential and resistance
1830	Whig government under Earl Grey (1830) Reform Act (1832)	Revolt in Jamaica (1831)	Construction of first US railway (1832)
	Abolition of slavery in British colonies (1833) Robert Owen's Grand National Consolidated Trades Union (1834) Tolpuddle Martyrs (1834)	Falkland Islands become a crown colony (1833) St Helena a crown colony (1834)	Faraday's laws on electrolysis (1834) Samuel Colt patents his revolver (1835)

Date	Great Britain	British colonies	Scientific progress
1835	Death of William IV; accession of Queen Victoria (1837) Chartist petition rejected by Parliament (1839)	Great Trek in South Africa; Orange Free State republic founded (1836) Rebellion in Canada (1837) Boers defeat Zulus at Blood River (1838) Act of Union in Canada (1840)	Samuel Morse develops telegraph (1837) Daguerre discovers daguerrotype process (1838)
1840	Robert Peel prime minister (1841) Chartists riots in Lancashire; second Chartist petition to Parliament rejected (1842) Bank Charter Act (1844)	New Zealand becomes a separate colony; Maori insurrection (1841) South Australia a crown colony (1841) Natal becomes a British colony (1843)	First use of general anaesthetic in an operation (1842) First screw-steamer crosses the Atlantic (1843)
1845	Repeal of the Corn Laws (1846) Failure of Chartist Movement (1848) Famine in Ireland	Responsible government in Canada (1846) Establishment of Orange River Sovereignty (1848) Annexation of Punjab (1849)	Sewing-machine invented (1846) Aneroid barometer designed (1847) Steam threshing machine invented (1850)
1850			

Above, Derby Day: *William Frith's (1819–1909) painting, completed in 1858, captures the exuberance and prosperity of mid-Victorian Britain when her industrial and imperial might was unrivalled. Tate Gallery, London.*

Opposite, interior view of the Great Exhibition of 1851.

Chapter 2

The Springtime of Nations

The political history of Europe between 1815 and 1870 is largely the history of the undoing of the attempt by the victorious allies to reconstruct the old order throughout the lands once conquered by France. In this sense, the results of the French Revolution were enduring. In the face of strong liberal and nationalistic movements, it proved impossible to turn the clock back to repressive government, and the peoples of Europe – whether in Germany, Austria, Italy, Greece or in France itself – constantly erupted into open revolt against governments which denied them the principle of democratic participation. The real 'challenge of the nineteenth century' was, then, the challenge of revolution – the necessity of reconciling the legitimate liberty of the individual with the ordered government of the state.

The peace treaties of 1815 had been designed not only to reorganize and make safe the frontiers of Europe, to punish France and reward her opponents, but also to conserve the firm position of tradition, order and religion against any possible return of revolution. It had been envisaged that there would be regular meetings of the four great powers – England, Prussia, Austria and Russia – to maintain these principles against any attempt at disturbance. But from about 1820 onwards, what has been called 'the Metternich System' had to defend itself constantly against a mounting and double attack from liberalism and nationalism. These concepts were in theory distinct, though in practice frequently unified.

Liberalism was largely the heritage of the ideas spread by the French conquests (civil and political liberty and equality, the sovereignty of the people and the right to democratic government). It had the support of many of the middle classes, who were hostile to rule by the minority and to the continuing powers and privileges of aristocracy and they found ready allies for their cause among the growing body of industrial workers in the cities.

Nationalist feelings owed less to the French Revolution itself, more to the spirit of patriotism which the Napoleonic conquests had awoken in many peoples not previously remarkable for their national loyalty. It was also the case that the peace

treaties of 1815 had divided populations with little consideration for such feelings, so that, for example, the Rhineland was given to Prussia and many Italians found themselves part of the Austrian dominions. Also, the policy of the allies of maintaining tiny principalities throughout Europe – inspired partly by a fear of powerful states – took no account of this growing sense of nationhood and desire for unity among peoples who shared a common language and culture.

The first congress planned by the allies was held at Aix-la-Chapelle in 1818 and was concerned exclusively with French affairs. It was decided that occupation troops could

now be evacuated and that France under the re-established Bourbon monarchy of Louis XVIII was sufficiently stable to join the Quadruple Alliance. But in Germany revolutionary agitation had already begun, led by a student body, the *Burschenschaft*, who in the course of a demonstration had burnt reactionary literature and other symbols of militarism. The rulers of three German states – Bavaria, Baden and Wurtemburg – were sufficiently alarmed to grant democratic constitutions to their peoples. Shortly afterwards, the assassination by a student of the journalist Kotzebue, a Russian agent who had been leading a campaign

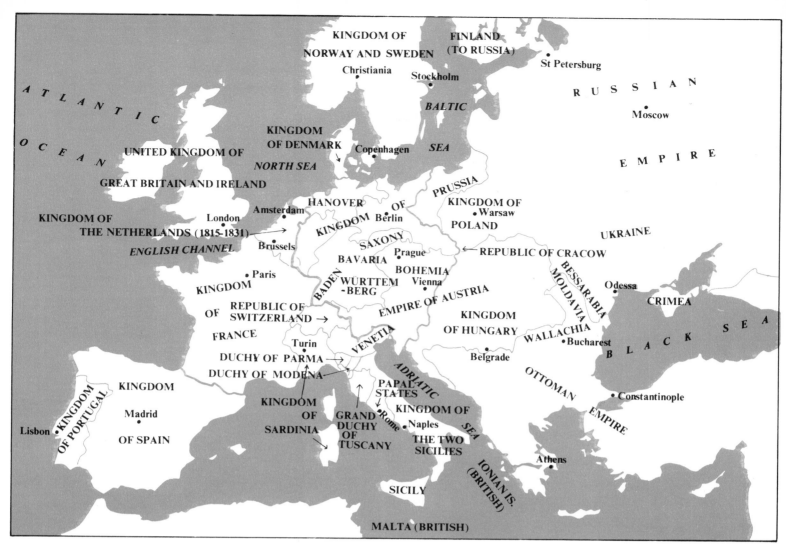

KINGDOM OF
NORWAY AND SWEDEN
FINLAND
(TO RUSSIA)

St Petersburg

RUSSIAN

Christiania
Stockholm

Moscow

ATLANTIC

BALTIC

EMPIRE

OCEAN

KINGDOM
OF DENMARK

SEA

Copenhagen

UNITED KINGDOM OF

NORTH SEA

GREAT BRITAIN AND IRELAND

PRUSSIA

HANOVER

KINGDOM OF

KINGDOM OF
THE NETHERLANDS (1815-1831)

Amsterdam

Berlin
London

KINGDOM OF
Warsaw

UKRAINE

POLAND

ENGLISH CHANNEL

Brussels

SAXONY

Prague

REPUBLIC OF CRACOW

Paris

BAVARIA

BOHEMIA

BESSARABIA

MOLDAVIA

Odessa

KINGDOM

WÜRTTEM
-BERG

Vienna

CRIMEA

BADEN

OF

REPUBLIC OF
SWITZERLAND →

EMPIRE OF AUSTRIA

KINGDOM
OF HUNGARY

WALLACHIA

Bucharest

BLACK SEA

FRANCE

Turin

VENETIA

Belgrade

DUCHY OF PARMA →

OTTOMAN

DUCHY OF MODENA

ADRIATIC

PAPAL
STATES

KINGDOM

KINGDOM
OF
SARDINIA

GRAND
DUCHY
OF
TUSCANY

Rome

Naples

SEA

EMPIRE

Constantinople

KINGDOM OF

Madrid

THE TWO
SICILIES

OF SPAIN

IONIAN IS.
(BRITISH)

Athens

KINGDOM OF PORTUGAL

Lisbon

SICILY

MALTA (BRITISH)

against liberal and nationalistic ideas, determined Metternich, the chancellor of Austria, to act. At Vienna in 1820 the German princes outlawed the *Burschenschaft*, imposed press censorship and brought the universities under strict control, though Metternich was unable to persuade the South German rulers to withdraw the recently granted constitutions.

In Spain, the restoration of the despotic King Ferdinand VII had brought to power a party which represented the deepest reaction. The country was now plunged into one of the unhappiest episodes in her unhappy history.

During Spain's struggle for independence against the French it had been shown that the local parliaments or *cortes*, where liberals were usually dominant, could produce enlightened and effective policies, but after the restoration of Ferdinand the *cortes* were ignored, thousands of liberal patriots were branded as French sympathizers, a strict censorship was imposed and despotic rule and corruption triumphed everywhere. The only resort left to liberals was to form secret societies against the government and to engage in plots, which always failed.

In 1820 in Cadiz, however, a much more serious situation arose. An army of 20,000 men had been assembled to be sent to South America to suppress revolution in the Spanish colonies there. Colonel Riego led many of the troops in revolt, demanding a liberal constitution. Successful in Andalusia, insurrection spread quickly to the provinces of Galicia and Catalonia, and the king was forced to adopt the constitution and to dismiss his unpopular ministers.

The apparent victory of the Spanish liberals now spread revolutionary ideas across the Mediterranean to Italy. Italy in 1815 was, in Metternich's famous phrase, merely 'a geographical expression'. She was a collection of independent states – Piedmont-Sardinia in the north, Parma, Modena, Tuscany and the Papal States in the centre and the kingdom of the Two Sicilies in the south. Austria possessed the kingdom of Lombardy-Venetia and wielded great influence in the affairs of many of the states. Everywhere there was censorship and police suppression of any attempt at liberal agitation. As in Spain, middle-class liberals had formed secret societies, known locally as the *Carbonari*, because their members met in the woods like charcoal burners.

Yet, at the news of the Spanish insurrection, army officers in Naples called out their troops in revolt in July 1820, and their leader, General Pepe, forced Ferdinand I of Naples to accept a democratic constitution

Above, Europe after the Congress of Vienna, 1815, called to settle European affairs after Napoleon's defeat: among the territorial changes were the establishment of the German Confederation, the union of Poland with Russia, the union of Norway and Sweden and the unification of the United Provinces and the Austrian Netherlands (Belgium) as the Netherlands.

Opposite top, contemporary illustration of the murder of August von Kotzebue (1761–1819), 23 March 1819, by Karl Ludwig Sand, a student at the University of Jena: Kotzebue had attacked the Burschenschaft, *quarrelled with Goethe and published anti-Romantic works.*

Opposite bottom, one of Goya's (1746–1828) etchings for his Disasters of War *series, done between 1810 and 1820, a foretaste of the bitter hostility and violence that was to surround Spanish politics in the nineteenth and twentieth centuries.*

similar to that granted in Spain. To many it seemed that this pattern of events marked the beginning of the end of autocracy.

Metternich's fear was that revolution would now spread through the whole of Italy. In 1820 the emperors of Austria and Russia, the king of Prussia and French and English representatives met at the Congress of Troppau in Silesia. Metternich converted the tsar to the idea of armed intervention against liberal movements, despite opposition from Castlereagh (the English foreign secretary) and the French delegate, who saw it as a move to increase Austrian influence in Italy.

At the Congress of Laibach, in January 1821, armed intervention was agreed on. Austrian troops dispersed the forces of General Pepe and entered Naples: the constitution was abolished and liberal leaders executed. But meanwhile revolutionary ferment had spread to students and army officers in Lombardy, with the object of freeing their state from Austrian domination. The king, Victor Emmanuel I, who had been restored by the allied powers in 1814, was hated by the liberals because of his reactionary policies and now abdicated in favour of his brother Charles Felix (1821). He lost little time in calling in the Austrians, who easily defeated the liberal forces at Novara.

The tide was also turning towards reaction in Spain. The liberal reformers who had secured the constitution from Ferdinand VII had no experience of government and did not succeed in maintaining order or in putting reforms into practice. Plots and risings occurred ceaselessly, giving Ferdinand the opportunity to call in outside help. The so-called 'Holy Alliance' of Russia, Austria, Prussia and France, formed in theory to conduct the affairs of Europe in accordance with Christian principles but in fact as an instrument for maintaining the status quo,

was more than willing to respond. The Congress of Verona (September 1822) was thus called to deal with the Spanish question.

Canning, who had succeeded Castlereagh as the British foreign secretary, declared himself strongly opposed to intervention in the internal affairs of Spain or her rebellious South American colonies. In officially recognising their independence Britain was, he announced, 'calling in the New World to redress the balance of the Old'. His message was lost on the other European powers. France was especially anxious to suppress revolution so close to her borders, as well as to demonstrate the military might of the restored Bourbon monarchy. Approval was given by the congress (Britain having withdrawn) to her intervention, and in April 1823 a French army of 100,000 entered Spain and quickly defeated the rebels at Cadiz and elsewhere. The repression which followed throughout the next ten years was more ferocious even than that in Italy, the liberal leader Riego and his comrades being mercilessly hunted down, shot and massacred. Until 1828 French troops continued to garrison fortresses throughout Spain in order to buttress the repressive policies of the Spanish minister of justice, Francisco de Calomarde.

For a few years in the 1820s the forces of reaction in Europe seemed triumphant: Italy and Spain lay prostrate under the heel of foreign autocratic domination. But in 1830 the Paris Revolution and the replacement on the French throne of the Bourbons by the 'bourgeois king' Louis Philippe caused reverberations throughout Europe which seemed to echo the storming of the Bastille by the Paris mob forty years earlier. Exiled *Carboneria* in Paris not unnaturally looked for French assistance in a new attempt to rid Italy of the hated Austrians. Secret revolutionary societies were again active in Lombardy, the Papal States and throughout central Italy.

Revolution in fact broke out in Modena in February 1831, quickly spreading to Parma, Bologna and the Romagna. In March an unlawful assembly at Bologna proclaimed the union and independence of the rebel provinces. Again, however, Metternich was master of the situation. He persuaded Louis Philippe that two of the Bonaparte princes were in the movement and that it therefore constituted a danger to the security of France. Austrian armies suppressed the rebels in Parma and Modena. In Bologna the rebels were either dispersed or arrested. Louis Philippe himself sent an expeditionary force to occupy Ancona.

By now the *Carbonari* had been thoroughly discredited by their repeated failures and their apparent inability to organize effectively. The spirit of revolt in Italy was kept alive, however, by writers and propagandists, many of them in exile. By far the most influential was a young Genoese, Guiseppe Mazzini, who founded a movement in Paris in 1832 known as 'Young Italy'. Its aim was a democratic republic, free of foreign domination: its slogan 'Unity and Republic, God and People, Thought and Action'. Mazzini's romantic personality attracted many followers, but his vague idealism was hardly what the situation demanded. More realistic policies were advocated by the Abbé Gioberti, who proposed a federation of the Italian states under the papacy by the historian Balbo, who gave to Piedmont the role of unifying Italy, and by Count Cavour, premier of Sardinia, who foresaw the necessity of defeating Austria militarily before independence could be achieved. All these ideas and aspirations were eventually to fuse in the *Risorgimento*.

Germany and Poland

In 1815 Germany, like Italy, was a mere 'geographical expression'. It consisted of thirty-nine independent states, some powerful like Prussia and Bavaria, others no more than tiny principalities, though equally proud of their separate identities. As yet there was little thought of national unity, though, as elsewhere in Europe, democratic thought had gained ground during the Napoleonic period.

The events of 1830 led to renewed demands for liberal reform in several states, and the rulers of Saxony, Bavaria, Brunswick and Hesse-Cassel were made sufficiently uneasy to grant constitutions to their peoples. The *Burschenschaft* was also re-formed in universities throughout Germany. As always, Metternich was alarmed at these stirrings of independent thought and, supported by Prussia, was able to get rigorous measures adopted by the Diet of Frankfurt (July 1832) including press censorship and the banning of unauthorized clubs and meetings. The writings of Heinrich Heine, Georg

Büchner and others were banned as subversive, and pressure was put on France to expel the large number of political refugees who had gathered there.

In fact, the idea of German unity was making progress in quite a different way. Prussia took the first step by founding the *Zollverein* or customs union, allowing the free passage of goods between states instead of the heavy tolls formerly charged. As a free trade measure it was a spectacular success, greatly increasing the level of commerce and economic activity generally: one state after another joined, until by 1834 nearly all had done so. More than this, however, the *Zollverein* facilitated the movement of people and ideas in Germany, undermined local prejudices and demonstrated the growing leadership of Prussia in German affairs.

Liberalism had an even harder struggle in Poland. This unhappy country had often been the subject of dispute and division among the powers, most recently in 1815 when the Duchy of Warsaw had been created a separate state and made part of the dominions of Russia. In theory it was endowed with its own parliament voting laws

and taxes, as well as its own army, though this was under the command of the Tsar Alexander's own brother, the brutal and authoritarian Grand Duke Constantine. The tsar's promise of a liberal, constitutional regime showed no sign of fulfilment.

In the other parts of Poland – Galatia, which had been ceded to Austria, and Posnan, which had been given to Prussia – there existed assemblies which were only partially representative of the people. Polish patriots, many officers and intellectuals had long been meeting together in secret societies, awaiting the moment to rise in support of unification and independence. At the news of the revolution in France in 1830, Constantine foolishly ordered the mobilization of the Polish army, and rumour quickly had it that he intended to use Polish troops to suppress the French liberals. The Poles in Warsaw rebelled, the Diet proclaiming the independence of the country and the deposition of the tsar in January 1831.

In spite of sympathy from France, none of the powers intervened to help the Poles, and the rebellion was soon crushed by the Russian army. There followed a more than usually severe repression, with mass hangings and deportations. Universities were closed, lands were confiscated and Russian was made the official language of the country. Thousands of Polish émigrés fled to France where they continued to hold up the torch of freedom.

The birth of modern Belgium

Only one of the many revolutions of 1830 was, in fact, successful – that of Belgium. In 1815 this little state had been given to the Netherlands – before that she had been, in turn, ruled by Spain, Austria and France. Although the union of industrial Belgium with agricultural Holland had been an economic success, there was almost nothing

in common between the two countries. Belgians spoke French (or Flemish), not Dutch; they were Catholics, not Protestants; they were in outlook liberal, not authoritarian. Moreover, the constitution was heavily weighted against them, with the Dutch William of Orange as king, only one Belgian minister out of a cabinet of seven, and fewer than 300 officers out of an army of 2,000.

In 1830 an alliance of Catholics and liberals rose in revolution, set up a provisional government and proclaimed the independence of Belgium. Everything now depended on the attitude of the great powers, particularly that of Britain whose traditional policy it was that the Low Countries should not be under the control of a strong and possibly hostile country. For this reason Britain opposed the offer of the Belgian crown to the Duke of Nemours, son of Louis Philippe of France. At the conference of London (December 1830) the powers formally recognized the independence and – significantly for the future – the neutrality of Belgium. The crown was accepted by a German prince, Leopold of Saxe-Coburg-Gotha, who became King Leopold I. Holland, who had still not accepted the situation, attacked the new country the next year, but England and France quickly came to her aid and forced the Dutch to withdraw. Holland officially recognized the existence of Belgium in 1839.

The crisis of 1848

The historian De Tocqueville wrote in 1848, 'Here begins again the French Revolution – this is exactly the same.' In fact, the events of 1848–9, though more widespread, violent and spectacular, were much more akin to those of 1821 or 1830 than to the localized events of 1789. As before, there was the same mixture of liberal and nationalist

aspirations, but a third element was now significant for the first time in the social conflict bred by industrialization. By 1848 many European cities had sizeable working classes which had been almost non-existent at the time of the French Revolution – populations of factory workers condemned to be the slaves of machines, confined to miserable lives in tenements and slums, who were beginning to demand a voice in their own destiny. Significantly, in Paris in 1848 the workers actually rose against the liberal middle classes, so opening a new chapter in the history of revolution which was to end in the accession to power of Napoleon III, the nephew of the former emperor. In the events of the mid-century, social and economic issues were fundamentally more important than the purely political.

More immediately, the events of 1848 had their origin in the Irish potato disease of 1845–6. This spread to the continent, causing an acute shortage of wheat which doubled prices in 1846–7 and resulted in food riots in France, Germany, Belgium and Italy. Commercial crises developed, as the banks used up stocks of gold to pay for wheat and could advance no more credit: there were numerous bankruptcies and a general lack of commercial confidence which resulted in heavy unemployment. While prices rose eighty to a hundred percent, wages were cut by an average of twenty percent.

The events of 1848 are confused and complicated; political demands are inextricably mingled with the social discontent, and there is an interaction or chain process which seems to sweep the infection across Europe, invading first one country, then the next. Revolution occurred first in Italy in January 1848, then in France in February, next in Vienna in March. By June the tide was running at its height, by the end of the summer it was already on the ebb.

In Italy the immediate cause of revolution was a combination of the economic crisis and the election of a liberal pope, Pius IX, from whom a lead in liberal reforms was expected. By the end of 1847 the whole peninsular was in ferment, and independent risings shortly broke out in widely separated states – in Sicily, demanding her independence from the kingdom of Naples, and in Lombardy in the north, where a boycott of Austrian tobacco sparked off bitter street fighting in Milan. Rulers were sufficiently alarmed to give way to demands for democratic constitutions in Naples, Tuscany and in Piedmont, where Charles Albert invited the revolutionary, Balbo, to join the government. In the Papal States Pius IX accepted laymen as cabinet ministers, and he too proposed a new constitution.

The most serious fighting was in Milan, where the revolution took the form of a truly national struggle against the Austrians. After five days of bitter street warfare (18–22 March) Austrian troops were forced to evacuate Milan, while in Venice, the other Austrian possession in northern Italy, the garrison was forced to capitulate by the patriots, led by Daniele Manin and Niccolo Tommaseo. The dukes of Parma and Modena, puppets of Austria, were also replaced by provisional governments.

With independent revolutions occurring throughout the peninsula, it seemed that the time had come for some state to take the leadership in the movement for unity and independence. The state of Piedmont in the northwest was ruled by Charles Albert and he and Count Cavour, who was then his chief minister, believed that it was Piedmont's destiny to lead an Italian crusade which would rid the country of the foreigner and unite the states under the Piedmontese dynasty. Piedmont entered the war on 24 March without any alliance from an outside prince or, indeed, the other provisional governments of Italy. For a time it seemed that Charles Albert's calculation was justified. Volunteers flocked in from Rome, Tuscany and Naples, and Manin collaborated by organising the defence of Venice.

At first there were early successes against the Austrians at Goito and Peschiera. Soon, however, the alliance began to falter. There were suspicions that Piedmont had territorial ambitions on other states and that her part in the movement was not entirely unselfish: Pius IX decided to withdraw the papal forces on the ground that the pope could not engage in war against Austria, the protector of the Catholic faith. Two more members of the alliance, Naples and Tuscany, quickly followed suit. Piedmont and Venice now remained alone against the might of Austria.

In Austria-Hungary, the ancient empire of the Habsburgs, the problems were complex. In the capital, Vienna, the revolution was primarily one of students and middle-class liberals in opposition to the absolutist régime of Metternich, the chancellor. Elsewhere nationalism was the main impulse and democracy only a secondary issue. The empire in fact covered a vast territory, inhabited by peoples of widely different beliefs, language and culture, and the motives of their protest were often obscure.

While Austria herself was largely German in language and customs, Hungary was mainly Slav. In theory a separate kingdom, she shared the common rule of the Habsburgs and was in most respects subservient to Austria. For many years there had been a movement for national independence in Hungary, led by some of the great landowners in what was still primarily a peasant country. There was also a body of liberal rebels led by men like Louis Kossuth and Ferenc Deák working for democratic reform and the development of a modern economic system. The fact that even Kossuth was less liberal in his attitude towards the Romanian and Croat minorities within Hungary was something that Metternich was subsequently able to exploit.

Bohemia was also a centre of national feeling in the empire – though she had not

Above, the revolution in Vienna, 13 March 1848, the day of Metternich's dismissal: the fall of three powerful rulers – Ferdinand II of Naples, Louis-Philippe of France and Metternich – within two months indicated the collapse of the old order and briefly brought about a revolutionary situation throughout Europe. Almost everywhere, though, the idealistic hopes of the revolutionaries were disappointed.

Left, Klemens von Metternich (1773–1859), Austrian foreign minister 1809–48 and chancellor 1821–48: one of the central figures of European diplomacy for over a generation, Metternich succeeded in maintaining a conservative autocracy throughout Europe against all nationalist and liberal influences until finally the wave of revolutions in 1848 swept him from office.

Opposite, representatives of the founding states of the Zollverein: the Zollverein was the first milestone along the path to a German state, and by 1834 seventeen states were members. Austria's refusal to join left the way open for Prussia to take a dominant position.

existed as an independent state since the seventeenth century and had since undergone a long process of Germanization. The Czechs had experienced a national reawakening led by poets and historians like Jan Kollár and František Palacký, and already by 1845 the Diet of Prague was showing opposition to the rule of Vienna.

In many parts of the empire, therefore, nationalists were waiting for the signal to rise. The day after the Paris revolution, on 12 February 1848, the students of Vienna began attacking the government forces, and after a few days of bitter fighting Metternich was forced to flee to safety hidden in a laundry van.

The Emperor Ferdinand granted freedom of the press and of assembly and promised a constitution. When published, it was thought insufficiently liberal, and a general insurrection then took place in May, at which Ferdinand now agreed to government by a constitutional assembly elected by universal suffrage. Vienna was firmly under the control of the students and the National Guard, formed by the middle classes to defend the revolution.

Elsewhere in the empire the revolution also seemed to be successful. In Hungary, led by Kossuth, independence was gradually being won, as the country gained the right to have its own army and financial system. In Prague a provisional government had been formed under the historian Palacký and a pan-Slav congress had met with a view to uniting the scattered Slavs of the empire into one state.

In Germany, too, there had been outbreaks of students, workers and peasants from February onwards, in the Rhineland in the north as well as in several southern states. Some rulers granted free speech and the right of constitutional assembly, abolished feudalism and the status of serfdom. The old King Louis of Bavaria abdicated in favour of his son Maximilian, while in Berlin a bloody riot in March forced King Frederick William IV of Prussia to withdraw his forces and promise a universally elected government. Tendencies towards national unity were also becoming noticeable. At Frankfurt an assembly of 600 delegates drawn from all parts of Germany agreed on the election of a constitutional parliament to prepare the way for a new, unified government for the whole country. This hopeful experiment in fact never had much likelihood of success. The parliament consisted mainly of notables and intellectuals, the commercial and business interests holding aloof. It soon showed itself to be a powerless debating chamber, quite impotent as an instrument of government.

Nevertheless, the very extent of the revolutions throughout Germany, Austria and Italy served to indicate the imminent break-up of the old Habsburg Empire. That it was able to survive the crisis was in no way due to the monarchy but to the loyalty of the professional army in the face of disaster.

In spite of the Viennese rising, Field Marshal Radetzky, the Austrian commander, decided to send his army first against the Italians. The Piedmontese army was attacked and defeated at Custozza (July 1848), Milan was occupied and Piedmont forced to accept an armistice. Already, two of the objectives of the *Risorgimento* had failed – to unify the Italian states under the head of the House of Savoy (Piedmont) and to involve the papacy in the national struggle. But there still remained Mazzini's ideal of a republic which would sweep away all incompetent monarchies.

Mazzinians were strongest in Rome itself, where many refugees had fled from other

states, and in November 1848 Count Rossi, Pius IX's anti-democratic minister, was stabbed. The Pope left the city in the hands of Mazzinians, who established a republic there in February 1849. Both Florence and Venice, under Daniele Manin, also proclaimed republican constitutions. New hope dawned of an Italy freed from both foreign oppressors and tyrannical rulers. Mazzini himself was triumphantly welcomed in Rome in March, and his lieutenant, Giuseppe Garibaldi, organized the army there.

This growth of republican feeling alarmed Charles Albert of Piedmont, who saw his chances of leading the Italian movement slipping away. Breaking the armistice, he re-entered the war but was utterly defeated by the Austrians at Novara and abdicated in favour of his son, Victor Emmanuel. Austria now invaded the smaller states of Parma, Modena and Tuscany and restored the dukes there. At the same time, Ferdinand of Naples regained control of Sicily.

In Rome, the success of the republicans now began to alarm foreign powers, in particular, France. The Catholic party there wished to support the Pope, while national interests were in favour of a military success which would limit the power of Austria in the peninsula. An expeditionary force of 7,000 men which arrived at Civitavecchia was beaten back by Garibaldi's amateur army, but with the help of reinforcements the French army entered Rome in July 1849, and Mazzini was forced to flee. Resistance continued only in Venice but, worn down by famine and disease, she too capitulated in August. The heroism and sacrifice of the Italian patriots had seemed to be in vain. Only in one state – Piedmont – did there remain a ray of hope. Though militarily defeated the new king, Victor Emmanuel, refused to abandon his constitutional regime. Advised by his minister, Cavour, he reflected on the lessons of 1848–49 and planned for the future.

What Radetzky had done in Italy, Marshal Windischgraetz was to do in Austria. He was a man of the sternest principle, once having declared that 'Blood is the only remedy for all the ills of the century – communism, radicalism, impiety and atheism.' Prague was bombarded, besieged and forced to submit to a military dictatorship in June 1848. The imperial cause was helped by the disunity of the rebel states, and particularly by the enmity between the Croats and the Hungarians. Hungary, under Louis Kossuth, had now come to the point of open rebellion against Austria, and the emperor cunningly gave command of the opposing army to the Croat 'Governor' Jellachich. At the news of the war against Hungary, the Viennese liberals again rose in revolt, hanged the Minister of War and forced Ferdinand to flee the capital.

In October Windischgraetz laid siege to Vienna, while the Croat army prevented aid coming from Hungary. Eventually the city fell and the democratic leaders were shot and their supporters arrested in great numbers. The emperor, now somewhat discredited by his weak handling of the situation, was, however, persuaded to abdicate in favour of his nephew, the Archduke Francis Joseph in December 1848.

From September 1848 Kossuth had headed the revolutionary government of Hungary and led the army of resistance against Austria. There was, however, an obvious limit to the capability of largely untrained volunteers against what was probably the best army in Europe, and despite all their efforts the Hungarians could not prevent Austrian and Croatian troops from entering the country in February 1849. By the spring, however, Kossuth had almost miraculously driven the enemy forces from the country and proclaimed the independence of Hungary and deposition of the hated Habsburgs in April 1849.

The emperor now entered into negotiations with the tsar, Nicholas I, for assistance. Nicholas was only too ready to help Austria in return for a free hand in the East against Turkey and immediately put an army of 130,000 men at the disposal of his ally. This meant virtual annihilation for the rebels. Kossuth resigned and sought refuge in Turkey. The last Hungarians capitulated at Vilagos in August 1849, and bitter reprisals followed against the patriots and all who had aided them. For the time being Francis Joseph had patched up his tottering empire: he was to live long enough to witness its virtual collapse.

At Frankfurt, the constituent parliament from all parts of Germany continued to debate the formation of a unified empire in place of the thirty-nine independent states. After endless discussions the hereditary crown of the new empire was offered to King Frederick William IV of Prussia, in spite of the protests of Austria and of the south German states who disliked the idea of a Protestant sovereign. There was, in fact, little choice in the matter. Prussia was incomparably the strongest of the German states, had re-established firm government in her own country and had demonstrated her ability to lead through the idea of the *Zollverein*. The only other possible contender was Bavaria, who had considerable influence over the Catholic states but was less powerful economically and militarily. But although Frederick William would have dearly liked an imperial crown, he was unwilling to accept one 'from the public streets, like that of Louis Philippe, a crown of rubbish made of clay and mud'. His chief minister, Bismarck, a firm believer in the divine right of kings, supported his decision.

Frederick William's rejection proved to be the death-blow for the Frankfurt Parliament. The Prussian deputies withdrew, and there was now no hope of effective leadership. But in numerous other German states – the Palatinate, Baden-Baden and Saxony – there were risings in the summer of 1849, and, significantly, these were much more working-class movements for social and economic reform than middle-class demands for nationalism or liberalism. The young Karl Marx, who was publishing the *Rhine Gazette* in Cologne at this time, learned much about the dynamics of the class struggle from a situation in which the middle classes increasingly allied themselves with the nobility in fear of the prospect of proletarian revolution.

But although Frederick William had refused the offer of an imperial crown from the people, he had not renounced the ambition of German leadership on his own terms. He now negotiated with the kings of Saxony and Hanover a scheme for unity to which twenty-eight of the German states were ready to agree: a congress at Erfurt was planned to settle the final arrangements. He had, however, to face the jealousy and distrust of outside powers. Austria, who

had now crushed her Hungarian revolt, strongly opposed this growth in the power of Prussia, as did the tsar. Saxony and Hanover were persuaded to withdraw from negotiations, and Prussia continued her plan with only the northern states.

Austria had decided that Prussia must be humiliated and that her own leadership of German affairs should be unchallenged. Schwarzenberg, the new chancellor of Austria, devoutly believed that there could be no Reich (German commonwealth) without Austria and sought an occasion to break up the league of princes which Prussia was sponsoring. The opportunity arose over Hesse-Cassel, where the tyrannical duke had recently been deposed: Prussia supported his subjects, Austria demanded his restoration. For a while the rival armies of Prussia and Austria faced each other poised for war, but two days later at Olmutz Prussia gave way and accepted all the Austrian demands including the dissolution of the proposed union.

By 1850 there seemed little left of 'the year of revolutions'. Austria had apparently re-established firm government in her empire and prestige among the German states. Democratic and nationalist movements had equally failed to take root, and the sufferings of the peoples of Europe seemed to be in vain. The enduring results were a liberal constitution in Piedmont and the abolition of feudalism in Austria and Germany. Moreover, two men had emerged from the crisis who were to become central figures on the European stage during the next twenty years. These were Cavour in Piedmont and Bismarck in Prussia. Under their leadership, the course of German and Italian unification was to take a new and decisive turn. But for the immediate future, the attention of Europe was drawn to the East, where similar nationalist aspirations were beginning to open great cracks in the once powerful Turkish Empire.

Opposite, Field Marshal Joseph Radetzky (1766–1858): commander in-chief in Lombardy from 1831, he was forced to leave Milan in 1848 but reoccupied the city a few months later. He was governor-general of Lombardy and Venetia until the year before his death.

Below left, Charles of Albert, king of Piedmont, enters Pavia, 29 March 1848.

Below, Louis Kossuth (1802–94), leader of the Hungarian revolution and for a short time governor of the independent Hungarian state declared in 1849: in exile in Great Britain and the United States during the 1850s he attracted a considerable following as a freedom-fighter, but after twice staging unsuccessful risings against Austria in the 1860s he spent the rest of his life in quiet retirement in Italy.

ÉLJEN KOSSUTH LAJOS.

The Eastern Question

At the beginning of the nineteenth century the Turkish Empire, despite an already long history of decadence, still remained a vast conglomeration of states placed at the crossroads of three continents, Europe, Africa and Asia. Her territories covered the great peninsula of the Balkans and extended eastwards into Asia Minor and westwards along the North African coast as far as Algeria. Yet it was not so much the strength as the weakness of the Turkish Empire that produced the Eastern Question of the nineteenth century. Her declining power and supposed imminent collapse roused the territorial ambitions of both Russia and Austria. Britain was also concerned since she had no wish to see a strong power in this area which might endanger her trading routes to India and the Far East.

But the European powers were also interested in the affairs of the Orient on religious grounds. The Turkish Empire, officially Muslim in faith, contained substantial minorities of Christians within its borders who were regarded as *raia* (no more than cattle). They were subject to many special disabilities, taxes and dues which made them very much the most profitable subjects of the empire. Only if converted to Islam could they become full citizens, but the Turks, who wanted to keep the Christians weak and vulnerable, did not encourage such additions to Allah. In general, the Christians maintained their beliefs as members of the Greek Orthodox Church, of which Russia regarded herself as the protector.

For many years groups of rebels – half-patriots, half-brigands – had sought independence of the Turkish yoke. Here, too, the French Revolution had spread ideas of democracy and independence, and in the disturbed conditions of war bands of Serbian *haidouks* and Greek *palikares*, forerunners of modern freedom-fighters, had begun to attack the hated Turkish army. Ever since 1804 the Serbs had been rebelling under their leader Kara George and had suffered terrible reprisals. In 1815 revolution broke out again, led by Miloš Obrenovich, but this time the sultan acted with more prudence, fearing the possibility of Russian intervention on the side of the Serbs. Obrenovich was granted the title 'Chief of the Serbs' and made a pasha, responsible for the government of the province. The Turkish Empire had unwittingly taken the first step towards its own dissolution.

The awakening of Greece

'Come, children of the Hellenes, the hour of glory has arrived. . . . Macedonians, rise up like wild beasts: spill the blood of all tyrants.' This song, based on the 'Marseillaise', appeared in 1797 at the beginning of the movement for Greek independence. In fact, the Greeks were among the most favoured subjects of the Ottoman Empire, allowed to practise their religion under their own Patriarch, holding four of the great offices of state, and largely monopolizing Mediterranean trade with their great merchant fleet. It was this measure of freedom and power that gave the Greeks their desire for more, that magnified their sense of injustice and reminded them of their former glories.

Significantly, the movement for independence sprang from the wealthy merchant communities spread around the Mediterranean shores and islands, traders who could command between them 600 ships manned by 17,000 sailors. In the great Turkish city of Constantinople Greeks dominated the *Phanar* (the business quarter) and furnished numerous of the sultan's administrators. In Odessa on the Black Sea Greeks had formed a secret society, the *Hetairie*, to prepare for revolution. Throughout the ports and the islands a secret network was gradually built up, linking the Greek communities together in a dream of freedom.

For the rich Phanariots of Constantinople and the Anatolian Greeks who dreamt of 'The Great Idea', time stood still after 1453. The great social, economic and intellectual upheavals of the West bypassed them. The Renaissance, the Reformation and the Industrial Revolution never touched them.

Towards the end of the eighteenth century some Greeks were pitchforked from the past into the hardy ideals of contemporary Europe. The writings of eighteenth-century French liberals and revolutionaries were translated for (if imperfectly understood by) the merchant circles of Smyrna and the Greek *Frontisteria* of Dimitsana and Trebizond. Their effect was devastating.

In 1821 Alexander Ypsilanti, a general of Greek origin who was in Russian service, was appointed military leader of the movement. The time seemed propitious, as the sultan was occupied with a revolt of the Pasha of Janina, who was trying to establish his own dynasty in Albania. Ypsilanti called on the Greeks to rise in March 1821 and the Archbishop of Patras launched an appeal for independence. The campaign was, in fact, ill-led and failed to receive the expected outside support from Russia; the rising in Walachia was easily crushed by the formidable Turkish janissaries (soldiers, originally forming the sultans's guard). But at sea, on the islands and in the Morea, bitter guerrilla fighting continued which the Turks could not suppress.

By the beginning of 1822 the whole of the Morea was in Greek hands, and deputies of the rebellious districts, meeting at Epidaurus, proclaimed the independence of the Greek nation. A National Assembly, presided over by Alexander Mavrokordatos, voted the first Hellenic Constitution in

euphoric recollection of the democracy of classical times. In savage revenge for their defeats, the Turks seized the island of Khios, where they perpetrated horrible cruelties on a defenceless people – 23,000 inhabitants were killed and 47,000 carried off into slavery. Two daring Greek sailors, Canaris and Miaoulis, set fire to the Turkish fleet in the roads at Khios and incurred the lasting gratitude of their people.

The situation was now transformed by the intervention of Egypt's powerful army and navy on the side of the sultan. The brilliant but unscrupulous Mehemet Ali, an Albanian Muslim who had been tax gatherer, tobacco merchant and commander of the Albanian contingent in the Ottoman army, had recently expelled the Turks from Egypt and set himself up as pasha there. He now offered his efficient army and navy to the sultan for the suppression of the Greeks in exchange for Crete and the provinces of Syria and Palestine.

Egyptian armies quickly overran the Morea while her fleets dominated the Aegean. European opinion was appalled to discover that hundreds of Greeks were being sold as slaves in the markets of Cairo, but the mutual rivalry between the powers and the belief that 'legitimate' governments must be maintained at all costs prevented any joint action. Austria and Britain remained highly suspicious of Russian ambitions in the Balkans, and, equally. Tsar

Below, the Balkans and the Near East in the nineteenth century: at the root of the 'Eastern Question' was the problem of the future status of the European territories controlled by the decaying Ottoman Empire. Disputes over these territories were largely responsible for the Crimean War, 1853–56 (the main battlefields of which are shown in the inset), which checked Russia's influence in southeast Europe.

Below left, Marshal Radetzky on the battlefield of Novara, where he defeated the Piedmontese for the second time in less than a year. Heeresgeschichtliches Museum, Vienna.

Opposite, Austrian troops under Marshal Radetzky leaving Milan after the March 1848 uprising: the Piedmontese immediately declared war on Austria but were twice defeated, and within eighteen months the status quo *had been restored throughout Italy, all hopes of unification squashed. Museo del Risorgimento, Milan.*

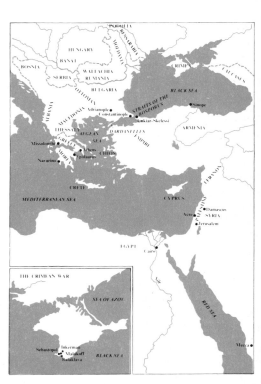

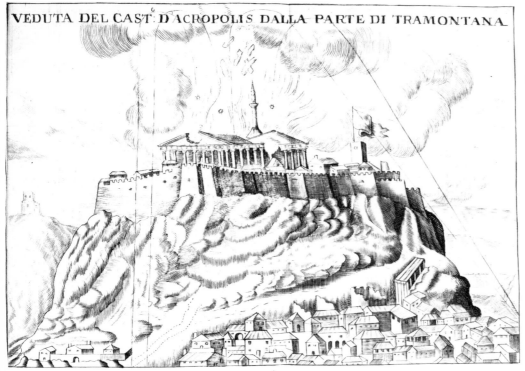

VEDUTA DEL CAST: D'ACROPOLIS DALLA PARTE DI TRAMONTANA

Bavarian prince, who became King of Greece as Otto I.

The issue of Greek independence, in itself relatively insignificant, was of profound importance for the future of Europe. It demonstrated on the one hand the chronic weakness of Turkey, 'the sick man of Europe', on the other the might and ambition of Russia for influence in the Balkans. It marked, too, the virtual end of the autocratic government of Europe by congress and Holy Alliance, as it did the increasing participation of Britain in the affairs of the Near East and in support of liberal movements generally.

The Egypt of Mehemet Ali

Mehemet Ali was by birth an Albanian, whose family had settled in Macedonia. He was working as a successful tobacco merchant when conscripted for military service in Egypt against the Napoleonic armies, where he showed great courage and daring. Having reached high office in the army, he had himself declared Pasha of Cairo by popular consent after the departure of the French. Now he gradually gained control over all the sources of power and wealth – the land, the army, commerce and trade. Ali was the classic example of the unscrupulous adventurer, clever, treacherous, always awake to the main chance and his own advantage.

After establishing himself in Egypt he turned to a policy of expansion, seizing the holy cities of Mecca and Medina, conquering the Sudan and founding the city of Khartoum. The Egyptian army, manned mainly by Albanians, was made the most modern and efficient fighting force in the Near East, and it was typical of his Machiavellian way of conducting affairs that his method of expelling his Mameluke mercenaries was first to invite them to a banquet and then to have them killed.

The more positive aspect of his policies lay in modernizing the antiquated institutions of Egypt. Agricultural techniques were improved, cotton spinning and sugar refining industries established, harbours equipped and a modern merchant fleet founded. Foreigners were encouraged to bring Western knowledge to Egypt, and young Egyptians of promise were sent to study in London and Paris.

Above all, Mehemet Ali wished to legitimize his rule, to make lawful the independence that he already possessed in fact. By 1830 he was sixty-one (Mehemet Ali, Napoleon and Wellington were all, by a strange chance, born in the same year) and needed to make his title hereditary so that it could pass to his son, Ibrahim. He also demanded Syria from Sultan Mahmud as the price of his military assistance against Greece and as compensation for the loss of his fleet at Navarino. When Turkey refused, Ibrahim invaded Syria in 1832, seizing Acre and Damascus and overrunning the Taurus.

Alexander had no wish to offend two such powerful nations.

Metternich commented at the Congress of Laibach in 1821, 'Over there, on the other side of our eastern frontiers, three or four hundred thousand people hanged, butchered, impaled . . . all that hardly matters.' Not all accepted his counsel of despair. From all over Europe democrats and patriots flocked to the cause of Greek independence, inspired more by the vision of what had once been Greece than by the realities of the savage conflict. The French Colonel Fabvier offered his sword to the rebels, the great poet Byron joined Mavrokordatos at Missolonghi, only to die of fever two months later (1824).

Village by village, the Egyptian armies extinguished the flame of Greek independence. Missolonghi fell heroically in 1826, the last defenders setting fire to the powder-kegs and blowing themselves up with their attackers: a year later Athens was forced to surrender. There remained in Greek hands only a few islands where the rebellion had begun six years before.

Unlike the issue of Italian independence, Greek independence ultimately succeeded because the European powers came to her aid. The invitation to intervene was made by George Canning, the British foreign secretary, who viewed Greece as the original home of European civilization. France accepted out of sympathy, Russia because she also wished to win independence for her fellow Slavs in Serbia. Austria and Prussia were not interested in supporting a rebellion against a lawful authority, even if it were an authority as unworthy as that of the Turk.

In the Treaty of London (July 1827) Britain, France and Russia agreed to mount a 'peaceful' naval blockade on Turkey which would force her, if negotiation failed, to recognize the rights of self-government of her Greek subjects. As the Turkish and Egyptian fleets, under the command of Ibrahim, son of Mehemet Ali, were at anchor in the roads of Navarino, the allied fleet drew near to make a show of strength. On 20 October 1827 what was intended as a naval manoeuvre erupted into war. A chance shot fired at the French flagship was taken to be a hostile act, and within a few hours of bitter fighting the Turkish and Egyptian fleets were destroyed. The Triple Alliance was now inevitably drawn into war by the outraged sultan, and the politicians at home were forced to uphold the actions of their commanders in the field. The Greeks owed their freedom to the mistake of a Turkish sailor.

Charles X sent a strong French force to the Morea. Russian troops attacked in the Caucasus and on the Danube, while a British fleet was sent to Alexandria. By 1829 Russia had entered Adrianople, and the sultan was forced to sue for peace. The mixed motives of the allied intervention were demonstrated clearly enough in the peace settlement. By the Treaty of Adrianople (1829) Russia acquired strongholds in the Caucasus and Armenia, two ports on the Black Sea and the right for her merchant ships to pass freely through the Straits of Bosporus and trade with the Turkish Empire. The sultan also recognized the independence of Serbia and of the Romanian provinces of Moldavia and Walachia. The recognition of Greek independence came almost as an afterthought, and only partially, for the new state was not to include Thessaly or Crete and excluded many Greek-speaking peoples. In 1832 the crown of the little state was offered to a

Ibrahim's army decisively defeated the Turks, commanded by the Grand Vizer Pasha Rashid, at Konieh. Again, the sultan had to look for outside aid and in desperation turned to the Russians who had so recently been his enemies: 'A drowning man clutches at a serpent', Mahmud is reported to have said. Again, the European powers became alarmed at the likely increase of Russian influence in the Balkans, and Britain, France and Austria all put pressure on the sultan to make concessions to Mehemet Ali and end the conflict; in the Treaty of Koutaieh (1833) Turkey agreed to cede Syria to the rebel. However, the sultan also signed the secret Treaty of Unkiar-Skelessi with the tsar by which Russia guaranteed the safety of Turkish territory in return for the closure of the Dardanelles to all foreign ships. Under this agreement the Black Sea would be virtually a Russian lake, denied to the trade of the world, and Russia would have established a practical protectorate over the Turkish Empire.

When the terms became known Britain felt her interests particularly threatened, and Palmerston, the Foreign Secretary, promised British aid for the reorganization of the sultan's armed forces: in return, he negotiated a trade agreement by which Turkey lowered her tariffs to a nominal amount. British forces were also permitted to occupy Aden, key to the Red Sea, to prevent further expansion of Mehemet Ali's power.

Under the aggressive leadership of Palmerston, the British Foreign Office was now anxious to extend still further British influence in the Turkish Empire as a counterbalance to that of Russia. For his part, the sultan had never accepted the independence of Syria except under duress, and in 1839, encouraged by Britain, he sent a strong army against Ibrahim. It was crushingly defeated at the Battle of Nezib, while shortly afterwards the Admiral of the Turkish fleet treacherously handed it over to the Egyptians.

Mahmud did not live to witness these tragedies. At the point of collapse, as it seemed, his empire passed into the hands of a seventeen-year-old boy, Abdul Medjid.

The new sultan had, at least, a sensible awareness of his country's failings and a genuine desire to reform. He began his reign by launching the *Tanzimat*, a programme of reform and modernization which was to include a properly organized system of taxation and regular military recruitment: its good effect was, however, to some extent nullified by the apathy and reaction of the old guard.

It was Britain who now intervened to save Turkey from Mehemet Ali. Russia, Austria and Prussia were all in favour of a mediated settlement of the Eastern Question, France alone now supporting Ali. By the Treaty of London (1840) a ten-day ultimatum was delivered to him, under which he was to receive Egypt as a hereditary

title and Palestine for life but was to give up his other conquests and his fleet to the sultan. This the pasha refused, supported by Louis Philippe and his minister Thiers. A leading French newspaper at the time declared, 'France should remember that, although alone in her position, she could resist the rest of Europe.' In the event, however, France was quite unprepared to take on a war against the three strongest powers of Europe. Palmerston, in a typical display of what has come to be known as 'gunboat diplomacy', sent a fleet and small expeditionary force to Syria, which was sufficient to persuade Mehemet Ali to submit. At the Conference of London (1841) Egyptian independence was ratified by the powers, subject to the payment of an annual tribute to the sultan and a limitation on the size of the Egyptian army. Although his greater ambitions had failed, Mehemet Ali's original dream of establishing an Egyptian dynasty had been realized.

At the same time, the powers came to an agreement over the Black Sea in the Straits Convention by which the Bosporus and the Dardenelles were to be closed to the warships of all nations. This agreement, cancelling the terms of Unkiar-Skelessi, was a triumph for Lord Palmerston, as was the Treaty of London as a whole. He had now prevented the future growth of the Egyptian army, halted the expansion of French influence in the Turkish Empire, and stopped Russia from converting the Black Sea into a private lake from which her warships could dominate the Eastern Mediterranean. In 1841, it seemed, the Eastern Question had been answered.

The dispute over the Holy Places

Under its new sultan the Ottoman Empire made some progress towards constitutional reform and the westernization of her archaic

Above, Mehemet Ali (1769–1849), Viceroy of Egypt from 1805: adventurous and ambitious (he founded the dynasty that ruled Egypt until 1952), he was the first major nationalist leader outside Europe, drawing on European culture and technology while attempting to assert an independent national identity.

Top, the Battle of Navarino, fought on 20 October 1827 in the Bay of Navarino in the southwest Peloponnese.

Opposite, the Turks attack the Acropolis, Athens, during the Greek War of Independence: Greek national aspirations slowly revived during the eighteenth century, revolt broke out in 1821 and the Greeks became the first subjects of the Ottoman Empire to attain full nationhood.

inevitably involved in the dispute, since Russia regarded herself as the protector of the Greek Orthodox faith and Roman Catholics tended to look to France as theirs. During the Revolutionary and Napoleonic Wars France had been in no position to honour that role, but by 1850 there were good political reasons for the new government of Louis Napoleon to do so.

At the end of 1850 Louis Napoleon's government, anxious to win support from the French Catholics, made official protests about the custody of the Holy Places. Ali Pasha, the Turkish foreign minister, attempted to avoid offence to either side by establishing a mixed commission to try to reach agreement. As this did not satisfy anyone, it was very soon replaced by an all-Muslim commission. This eventually suggested a compromise by which Catholic monks were to hold the key of the main door of the church of Bethlehem but not the right to hold divine service there and a complicated arrangement by which the Christian sects were to follow each other in a kind of rota in the Sanctuary of the Holy Virgin. Such a solution was, of course, only likely to produce further quarrels in the future.

The 'Sick Man of Europe'

In a situation in which the host country, Turkey, was unquestionably weak – some thought on the point of death – the policies and postures of the European powers were all-important. For her part, Russia had ambitions to expand southwards into the Balkans and control of the Black Sea; equally, Britain regarded this as a threat to her Eastern and Oriental interests. It was also significant that British public opinion, especially that part of it represented by the jingoistic policies of Palmerston, was strongly anti-Russian and regarded Nicholas I as evil, despotic and treacherous.

Nicholas believed, however, that he might reach an agreement with Britain, and it was in this hope that he declared to the British Ambassador, 'We have on our hands a sick man . . . let us reach an agreement to divide his inheritance.' He suggested that Britain should take Egypt to safeguard her route to India and that Russia should receive Moldavia and Walachia, Bulgaria and Constantinople, which would be made a free port. The moment for such a surgical operation seemed to the tsar opportune. France was on the point of re-establishing the empire after the coup d'etat of December 1851, which gave Napoleon III dictatorial powers, and Austria was still feeling indebted to Russia for her help against Hungary in 1849.

Prince Menschikoff, the tsar's aide-de-camp, was sent to Constantinople with a demand for immediate satisfaction in Jerusalem and a treaty which would grant Russia a virtual protectorate over the

institutions. Revolts in the Lebanon and in Bosnia were dealt with firmly but with clemency, and the vigorous application of the measures of the *Tanzimat* was beginning to bring progress to a country which had seemed rotten with decay.

A new and explosive crisis was, however, soon to develop. For centuries there had been dispute between the Greek Orthodox and the Roman Catholic churches as to which monks should have guardianship of the Holy Places in Jerusalem, Nazareth and Bethlehem. Historically, the Catholic monks had had custody, but in the seventeenth

century Orthodox monks had succeeded in ousting their rivals. On several subsequent occasions there had been open fighting between Greek pilgrims and Catholic monks, even in the Church of the Holy Sepulchre in Jerusalem.

In a sense, the problem of the Holy Places was a trivial ecclesiastical dispute which need never have grown to critical proportions. Turkey recognized that the great sanctuaries of the Christian world should be under Christian care, and to her it was a matter of indifference which sect was given that privilege. But political issues were

20,000,000 Orthodox subjects of the sultan. Before replying, Abdul Medjid consulted the British ambassador to Turkey, Lord Stratford de Redcliffe, who was held in special respect as a known friend of Turkey and implacable enemy of Russia. In the event, Redcliffe advised acceptance of the tsar's demands, and throughout the negotiations, contrary to what was once thought, urged moderation on the sultan. Nevertheless, Medjid rejected Russia's demands, probably on the calculated risk that, whatever the British ambassador was bound to advise officially, the British government could be relied on as an ally if necessary.

Britain and France continued to look for ways towards a negotiated peace, but in 1853 Russia occupied the principalities of Moldavia and Walachia and Turkey gave an ultimatum for her withdrawal within one month. The first shots were exchanged between Russia and Turkey in October 1853, and a month later the Turkish fleet in the Black Sea was destroyed off Sinope. Russia's refusal to compromise had, it seemed, made war inevitable, and public opinion in Britain and France moved strongly in favour of early intervention on the side of the friendless Turk. In 1854 the two countries concluded a treaty of alliance with Turkey by which they agreed to defend Ottoman territory and not to seek any advantage for themselves. War with Russia was officially declared in March.

The Crimean War

By the time that plans had been made and armies assembled Russia had already been driven out of Moldavia and Walachia by Turkey unaided. The war was therefore conceived as principally a naval exercise, the point of attack being the great Russian naval base of Sebastopol in the Black Sea. A combined force of about 50,000 men was landed in September 1854 after the allies had won the Battle of the Alma and encamped near Balaklava. Meanwhile Sebastopol had been heavily fortified and resisted a long siege through the cold of the Russian winter. The necessity for the war – if 'necessity' it had ever been – had now largely disappeared with the evacuation of the principalities. Why the particular target of Sebastopol was selected was never very clear, nor what strategic advantages would follow from its capture. It is likely that all that was in mind was some blow inflicted on Russian pride.

The Russians made two attempts to break through the allied lines – at Balaklava, where the Light Brigade was wiped out by the Russian guns, and at Inkerman, but cholera and frostbite took a far greater toll of the invaders than the enemy. The Crimean campaign soon became a public scandal for the gross inefficiency of its conduct, the mistakes of its military leaders and the neglect to ensure appropriate clothing, supplies and medical services for the troops.

France had to recruit another 140,000 men for the campaign, while Piedmont supplied an expeditionary force of 15,000 so that she might take a place alongside the powers in any future disposition of European affairs.

A new general attack was launched in the summer of 1855, and in September a French division under General Mac-Mahon at last succeeded in taking the fort of Malakoff and breaching the defences of Sebastopol. The city surrendered shortly afterwards, and the new tsar, Alexander II, was prepared to sue for peace. Though Palmerston, who had now become British prime minister, was in favour of a vigorous continuation of the war to some more dramatic victory, he was

Above, the Charge of the Light Brigade at the Battle of Balaklava, 25 October 1854: the Charge (the Brigade lost a third of its men dead or wounded) served only to highlight the inefficiency of the military command. The resulting criticisms led to radical reforms of the army.

Top, the British lines at Sebastopol. The Crimean War was the first recorded by photography and the first reported by war correspondents.

Opposite, Delacroix's painting Greece Expiring at Missolonghi, *painted in the aftermath of the Greek defeat there: the Greek struggle for independence caught the imagination of writers and artists throughout Europe. Musée des Beaux-Arts, Bordeaux.*

persuaded by Napoleon III that honour had now been fully satisfied and that a lasting peace in the Balkans could be made. 'The Empire is Peace' Napoleon had said on his accession. France had already lost 100,000 men in the Crimea, 85,000 of them killed by disease.

The peace treaty, signed in March 1856, decreed that the Black Sea was to be neutral (neither Turkey nor Russia being allowed to maintain a war fleet there), that Moldavia and Walachia were to be independent (Moldavia being enlarged by the addition of part of Bessarabia from Russia), that there should be free navigation of the Danube and that Russia was to resign her protectorate over the Orthodox Church in Turkey. In return, the sultan promised to confirm the privileges of his Christian subjects.

The treaty thus secured for the allies all the aims for which they had professed to enter the war. For the time being, Russia was humiliated and crippled; France, for the first time since 1815, was restored to the rank of a great power; little Piedmont, represented by the brilliantly able Count Cavour at the conference table, was able to air publicly the wrongs of Italy at the hands of Austria. The empire of the Turk had been once more propped up, and the 'sick man's' illness halted, if not cured. Finally, the Treaty marked a considerable expansion of French influence in Turkey, evidenced by the establishment of a French lycée there and a considerable export of French capital.

In fact, the Peace of Paris solved none of the long-term problems of the Balkans. By 1870 Russia had renounced the Black Sea clauses of the treaty, and the powers had acquiesced in her faithless act; Moldavia and Walachia formed the independent kingdom of Romania in 1866, so confirming the break-up of the Ottoman Empire which had been begun by Greece. Above all, Turkey remained weak and impotent, a prey to internal crises and to foreign ambitions which were to carry within them the seeds of the First World War.

Chapter 3

Russia: the Years of Conflict

nations which would preserve the peace of Europe in accordance with Christian principles. We have already seen how this well-intentioned scheme became an instrument for the suppression of all reformist movements, a mere buttress for the maintenance of despotism and privilege. In Russia itself the tsar's policy was now no less illiberal: students were forbidden to study abroad, foreign teachers dismissed, and all the apparatus of a police state was erected in an attempt to prevent any criticism of the government or its policies.

The period between 1815 and 1870 also witnessed revolutionary changes in the eastern world no less far-reaching than those in the west. Russia, convulsed by her defeat in the Crimean War, passed from autocracy to a more liberal regime under Alexander II, who freed the serfs and established a process of modernization and westernization. When the forces he had unleashed seemed to be passing out of control, reaction returned and his reign ended in repression and terrorism. But despite her internal difficulties Russia continued to pursue an expansionist foreign policy.

Russian history in this period is to a considerable extent the history of the tsars and the tsarinas who ruled the country with autocratic power: 'the people' seem shadowy, unsubstantial figures, moved here and there, like pawns, at the whim of rulers and nobles. Under Peter the Great and Catherine II Russia had been brought into western political life, though no concessions had been made to those democratic ideas which had exploded in France in 1789. On Catherine's death her son, Paul I, a mentally unbalanced tyrant, ruled for only five years until his assassination in 1801. With the accession of Alexander I hopes for reform revived. In particular, the tsar's minister, Speranski, was a great admirer of Napoleon and wished to introduce a representative system into Russia as a first step towards a constitutional monarchy.

But any progress towards liberalization was soon dashed by the French invasion of Russia in 1812. Napoleon and all that he stood for was now the arch-enemy, and the Russian nation suddenly became united in a determined effort to repel the invader and resist the spread of subversive ideas. Speranski was sent into exile and his enemies promoted to high office. One in particular, Arakcheyev, an extreme opponent of any change, was largely instrumental in turning Alexander's views from liberalism to autocracy. Under the influence too of the extremely pious and visionary Julie de Krüdener, the tsar became increasingly aloof from political life and inclined towards a well-meaning but vague form of mysticism.

It was in this spirit that, after the final victory of the allies in 1815, Alexander conceived the Holy Alliance – a union of

The Decembrists

In an unexpected and unintended way, however, the ideas of the French Revolution were to have profound effects in Russia. Russian armies had fought Napoleon in Europe and had been stationed in France after his defeat. Soldiers of all ranks returned to the homeland full of liberal ideas, convinced that Russian government and institutions were backward and corrupt. The effects of European culture and attitudes were most marked on the young officer class who, despite the aristocratic origins of many, seemed suddenly to have developed a social conscience and humanitarian instincts.

Freemasonry, made illegal during the reign of Catherine II, was now revived and became a focus for liberal thought and discussion. Secret revolutionary societies multiplied throughout the country, including some of the highest nobility like Prince Paul Trubetskoi among their members. But such societies were mainly debating arenas for intellectuals, hardly action groups. Some advocated the establishment of constitutional monarchy, some a republic, others, like the United Slavs, a union of Slav peoples beyond the confines of Russia. Among the more extreme of the revolutionaries, however, some positive plans were being formulated. Men like Ryleiev and Colonel Pestel, son of a former chief of police, were among the strongest advocates of a republic, prepared even to assassinate the tsar and the royal family as the principal obstacles to their plans.

The death of Alexander I in 1825 posed a problem of succession, since the tsar left no direct heir. He chose to grant the crown to his second brother, Nicholas, but this was disputed by his elder brother, the Grand Duke Constantine. Ultimately, Constantine was persuaded to renounce his rights to the throne, but the whole occasion had provided an opportunity for the revolutionaries to take advantage of the uncertainty. On the morning of 14 December 1825, many officers who were members of the secret societies raised a body of troops in the belief that Constantine, who was being held prisoner in Warsaw, would not agree to a renunciation. The rebels formed up in Senate Square, St Petersburg, where the new tsar

Opposite top, contemporary photograph of French trenches and, on the horizon, the fort of Malakoff.

Opposite bottom, the signatories of the Congress of Paris, 1856, convened to settle the Eastern Question at the end of the Crimean War.

Autocracy and orthodoxy

For the thirty years of his reign Nicholas remained an implacable enemy of liberalism and the principal buttress of conservative ideas. He had come to the throne 'at the cost of the blood of my subjects', as he wrote to his brother Constantine, drawing from this experience a profound fear of any concession that might seem to encourage revolution. At the same time, he was acutely conscious of the responsibilities of his office, was hard-working and devotedly attached to the army and its iron discipline. These were hardly endearing qualities, and the new tsar's regime quickly became a byword in the West for severity and inhumanity. De Tocqueville described it as 'the cornerstone of despotism in the world' and the Marquis de Custine in 1839 wrote that 'the Russian government has substituted the discipline of the camp for the order of the city: a state of siege has been made the usual state of society.'

Nor did the church escape the strict control of the government. A colonel of the Hussars was appointed to the holy synod (ecclesiastical assembly) and was given powers greater even than those of the patriarch, the nominal head of the Orthodox Church. The watchwords of the regime – 'orthodoxy, autocracy, nationality' – were officially proclaimed by Count Uvarov, the minister of education.

The enforcement of such precepts required a ruthless and efficient police state, which effectively muzzled press and public opinion, banned secret societies, trade unions and all expressions of opposition to the state. An ardent nationalism and pride in Russia was to be impressed on the young, and it was in keeping with this that foreign travel was made almost impossible and French tutors and governesses – supposed sources of dis-affection – placed under strict supervision.

There were, however, some more positive aspects of the Russian dictatorship. Speranski was recalled to complete the massive codification of Russian law and in 1830 the Complete Collection of the Laws of the Russian Empire was issued, which brought together some thirty thousand promulgated over the centuries.

Nicholas was also anxious to reorganize the cumbrous administration of the empire and planned new central and local institutions which would bring greater efficiency into the archaic structure of Russian government. The only practical outcome of these plans was, however, the creation of a new government department – the tsar's 'personal chancery' – which was responsible among other things for the police régime. Nicholas saw public order as the necessary condition of social progress. Once efficient government was established throughout his vast dominions, freedom and civil liberties could follow, the serfs could be emancipated from bondage and the subject peoples of the empire given control of their own affairs. Any hopes of such a gradual relaxation of

Nicholas was to come to take his oath, but they were dealt with swiftly and efficiently. Artillery opened fire on the barricades, the rebels dispersed and arrests followed. The same pattern was repeated in the south, at Kiev, where loyal troops again suppressed the insurrectionaries. A trial of prisoners was carried out with apparent meticulous justice: 121 of the accused were brought before the High Court, where they defended themselves with great courage. Pestel declared at his trial, 'My greatest fault is to have tried to reap the harvest before I had sown the seed.' He and another were hanged, the rest of the conspirators being deported to Siberia.

Pestel's words were an apt comment on the failure of the Decembrists' rising as a whole. They had planned insufficiently, had counted on greater support from the people and had not imagined that so many of the troops would remain loyal to the tsar. But in one vital respect the rising of 1825 was significant. For the first time in Russian history members of the aristocracy had been allied with workers against the interests of their own class and had been involved, not merely in a squabble over the succession, but in a fundamental attempt to change the nature of the state. The Decembrists left both a legacy and an inspiration to the revolutionaries of the future.

Above, painting, dating from the 1830s, of the December uprising in St Petersburg, December 1825: the uprising, a military conspiracy that had originally planned to assassinate the tsar in May 1826, misfired, initially because of his death in November the previous year and then because of the collapse of the plotters' morale.

Left, contemporary print of the Russian royal family: flanking the heir to the throne, the Grand Duke Alexander (who as Alexander II ruled 1855–81), are the Emperor Nicholas I (ruled 1825–55) and the Empress Alexandra. Nicholas' regime was socially and intellectually repressive; though Alexander was more liberal – the serfs were emancipated, elected provincial assemblies were established – he too mercilessly put down a Polish revolt and severely repressed all signs of revolutionary activity at home.

Opposite, Tsar Alexander I of Russia (1777–1825, ruled 1801–25): a liberal at the beginning of his reign, he became increasingly pietistic and reactionary, founding the Holy Alliance in the hope of resisting revolution in Europe. Royal Society of Medicine, London.

policy were shattered by the revolution in France in 1830 and its repercussions in Russia, where the military garrisons in Novgorod rose in a revolt reminiscent of that of the Decembrists five years earlier. Although easily suppressed, the renewed threat of revolution brought to an end any move towards a more liberal policy.

In fact, Nicholas saw his greatest danger in the subject peoples who had been annexed to the empire after 1815 – the Finns and Swedes of Finland, Germans, Estonians and Latvians in the Baltic provinces, the Poles, Lithuanians and Jews of Poland, the Georgians of Transcaucasia – none of whom had any sense of loyalty to the Russian crown and might be expected to seize any opportunity to shake off alien control. At the end of 1830, after revolutions in France, Belgium and Italy, the Poles rose in revolt, and the Grand Duke Constantine, military governor of Warsaw, was forced to flee. Polish officers and landowners fought bravely for a year against the might of Russia, inflicting and receiving heavy losses, but by September 1831 Warsaw had been subjugated and the rebels captured or dispersed. Thousands were exiled to Siberia and the last vestiges of Polish freedom were suppressed: for all practical purposes Poland disappeared, to be absorbed into the tsarist empire.

The new Russia

But not even Russia could remain unaffected by the changes that were transforming western Europe. During Nicholas's reign Russia underwent the first stages of an industrial revolution, much of it necessarily initiated by the state in the absence of a sufficiently large and wealthy middle class. The tsar himself drew on a map with a ruler the route of the railway line from St Petersburg to Moscow, work on which began

after 1838, though no line yet connected Russia with the West. Much road development also took place, enabling the freer movement of goods and people. At the tsar's accession in 1825 Russia had 5,000 factories employing 200,000 workers: within ten years there were already 10,000 factories with 500,000 employees and economic growth was to continue apace. In her vast domains Russia had most of the raw materials necessary for industrialization, while her large population provided at once a ready labour force and a potentially huge market. Already she was able to replace previously imported products like textiles with her own manufactures.

But, as elsewhere, industrialization brought about social change and social problems. The growth of industry and trade offered opportunities for middle class manufacturers, merchants and professional people generally. Equally, it created a new urban working class alongside the serfs of rural Russia. Nicholas's deliberate policy was to encourage this new middle class and to ally it firmly to the monarchy. A class of 'notable citizens' was created with special privileges, who were to hold important positions in the civil service, commerce and the professions. But despite this development, significant for the future, Russia remained essentially a two-class society, with all real power monopolized in the hands of some 120,000 landed nobles. Russia was still a land of farms and villages and, with few exceptions, the towns were no more than overgrown market centres for the surrounding countryside, with wooden houses, unpaved streets and a total lack of sanitary provision. In 1838 there were 11,000,000 serfs, subject to laws which made them virtually the slaves of their lords, compared with the mere 80,000 free peasants, the numbers of whom grew only very slowly. Most

lords continued to regard their serfs as chattels to be bought and sold, exchanged or pledged at the bank as security for a loan, brutally punished or imprisoned if they dared to offend. A police report of 1827 stated, 'the peasants await their liberation as the Jews await their Messiah.'

The tsars faced an impossible choice of policy – to modernize the institutions of Russia and so liberate forces which might overthrow their regime or to try to maintain their autocracy in spite of the mounting pressure for change.

In particular, the promise of public education, made necessary by the increasing industrialization of Russia as well as being desirable on social and moral grounds, tended to whet the appetite for economic and political changes which the tsars were totally unwilling to concede. Nicholas's policy of limited and hesitant liberalism was to prove quite inadequate to resolve the country's problems.

The intelligentsia

Leadership in the movement for the reorganization of Russia now increasingly passed to the intelligentsia of students and teachers. As educational opportunities widened some young men from the lower classes began to find their way into university, and it was largely from such students, inspired by German romantic philosophy, that the revolutionary lead now came. Contempt for riches and conventions, hatred of tyranny and a somewhat mystical yearning for progress were its main characteristics, though it was sometimes also mixed with a strong sense of patriotism, the belief that the Russians were a chosen people and should go their own way independently of western influences. Whatever their ideological differences, the intelligentsia were, however, all agreed on one thing – that, as Herzen expressed it – 'the Slav race will take the initiative in the Renaissance of humanity.'

These attitudes were clearly reflected in the cultural developments of the new Russia. Already the poet Alexander Pushkin (1799–1837) had begun to free Russian literature from classical and French influences, showing that English and German writers were models more akin to Russian traditions: another, Lermontov, wrote the epic *Heroes of our Time* in a style closely similar to that of Byron. During the reign of Alexander I Pushkin wrote a number of what were soon to become classic works – *The Prisoner of the Caucasus*, *Eugene Onegin* and *Boris Godunov*. But it was the work of a new writer, Gogol, that marked a decisive turning point by using literature to take up a moral standpoint. 'The writer', he said, 'should make judgments in the service of humanity', and, especially in his *Dead Souls*, he daringly attacked the shortcomings of Russian society and administration. The same period also saw the emergence of Ivan Turgenev, whose masterpiece was *Fathers and Children*.

The work which caused the greatest sensation was, however, Nicholas Turgenev's *Russia and the Russians*, published in France in 1847 where the author had fled after the December Revolution. The book was a bitter denunciation of the evils of serfdom and the vices of the tsarist regime. Such works had a limited, and necessarily secret, circulation among the Russian intelligentsia. With a strict press censorship and police supervision they ran a terrible risk, and in 1849 all the members of one political and literary club – the Petrachevists – were arrested and the leaders sentenced to death. As they stood on the scaffold awaiting execution, the tsar's pardon was proclaimed. The event left a lasting impression on one of the condemned men, Feodor Dostoyevsky, who in *The Idiot* described the mounting panic on the scaffold and the cruelty of the delayed reprieve: the nature of their offence had been officially described as a 'conspiracy of ideas'. For this, Dostoyevsky was deported to a prison camp in Siberia where he wrote his *The House of the Dead*.

The Russian intellectuals of the 1840s were not revolutionaries thirsting for direct action against a corrupt state so much as artists and idealists who used the political scene as the dramatic background for their canvas. But the intellectual ferment they created, and the public criticism that they levelled at the tsarist regime, was to take on a deeper significance in the next decade when the power and authority of Nicholas I was to suffer its first great defeat.

The consequences of the Crimean War

'War', wrote Karl Marx, 'is the forcing-house of democracy.' In victorious Britain, the ineptitude of the conduct of the Crimean campaign brought reforms to the army and

the civil service based on promotion by competition and ability in place of wealth and privilege. In defeated Russia, the consequences were even more far reaching. The Treaty of Paris, signed in 1856, marked, for the time being at least, the end of Russian ambitions of territorial expansion and the reversal of the steady growth of influence in Western affairs which had been built up for long centuries past. For thirty years Nicholas had been the greatest champion of counter-revolution in Europe, the arch-enemy of any change towards more liberal policies in the conduct of affairs. Dying at the beginning of 1855, he did not live to see the complete collapse of his system.

The Russian autocratic regime had been able to command the loyalty and submission of its subjects so long as it was militarily successful. Once defeated in the field, the faith in Russian supremacy which had silenced the voices of the critics was broken. The Crimea came as a shattering and traumatic experience to the armies which still

Above, illustration from an 1890s edition of Fyodor Dostoevsky's (1821–81) The House of the Dead.

Top, Mikhail Lermontov (1814–41): A Hero of Our Times, described by the author 'a portrait composed of the vices of all our generation', is a work of social and political criticism, whose hero, Petchorin, wastes his life aimlessly, scornful of the court, yet remains cut off from the ordinary people by his European education.

Top left, view of Moscow in the early nineteenth century.

Opposite, Russian and Polish cavalry clashing during the Polish uprising in 1830: Nicholas I easily but severely repressed the revolt, absorbing the nation into his empire. Only in 1918 did an independent Poland come into being, for the first time since the eighteenth century, and that state too has once again suffered Russian imperialism. Muzeum Wojska Polskiego, Warsaw.

rested on their laurels of 1812. To be beaten was bad enough, but to be beaten on her own soil by the two great liberal powers, France and Britain, assisted by the despised Turk, was catastrophic. The Crimean War was widely interpreted as a failure for autocracy, a success for liberalism. Russia experienced an agonized period of guilt and self-analysis, during which an outpouring of literature passed secretly from hand to hand, criticizing all those who had been involved in the conduct of the war but chiefly the Tsar himself. 'Awake, oh Russia', proclaimed one of the pamphlets; 'Awake from your long sleep of apathy and ignorance. Arise, prepare yourself, and demand before the despot's throne that he render account for the disaster that has befallen the nation.'

The abolition of serfdom

Nicholas had once said, 'My successor will do what he pleases: I myself cannot change.' In many respects it was the epitaph of the old regime. His son, Alexander II, came to the imperial throne at the age of thirty-seven, intelligent, tolerant, well-prepared for the role he was to play. In the manifesto in which he announced to the Russian people the end of the Crimean War, Alexander stated that internal reform was necessary. A government which protected itself by silencing public opinion, a people of whom the majority were still bound by serfdom – such things were incompatible with a modern state and largely explained the defeat of the armies in the field.

The key to reform was, however, to be gradualness. Little by little a greater degree of freedom was given to the press, the universities and to public opinion in general. There was much discussion of the need for modernization of Russian institutions along Western lines, for the development of railways, banks and industrial companies and for the improvement of education and agriculture. Pressure for change was kept up by Russian exiles, of whom the revolutionary leader and writer, Alexander Herzen was among the most outspoken in his journal *Kolokol* (*The Bell*).

Shortly after his accession the new tsar announced that he intended to emancipate the serfs, though not immediately. In fact, the problem was an exceedingly delicate one and was examined in great detail by a Secret Committee for the Amelioration of the Situation of the Peasants, which was set up in 1857. Were the serfs to be freed with or without possession of their lands, and if granted land rights were they to have free possession or some kind of tenure? If, on the other hand, emancipation were not to carry land with it, would it not merely weaken the position of the peasants and possibly create a vast and dangerous rural proletariat?

Influenced by liberal advisers, Alexander II chose to grant freedom and land. Provincial land committees were established to investigate the problems locally and to report directly to the tsar, who presided over the Central Committee. Alexander also toured the provinces personally, appealing for a spirit of generosity and conciliation among the great noble landowners. On 19 February 1861, the sixth anniversary of his accession, the tsar signed the manifesto announcing the greatest reform in Russian history.

By this bold measure, 47,000,000 peasants were granted personal liberty – 21,000,000 the serfs of lords, 20,000,000 of the Crown, and the rest a mixed body of servants and workers. The actual terms of the emancipation were, however, complex and not as generous as many had hoped. The peasants were granted freehold possession of their houses and the ground immediately surrounding; the farmland on which their livelihood depended was assigned to the collective ownership of the *mir* or village council, which then granted to the peasants the use of specific parts. A clear indication of the fact that the land was not his own was that the *mir* was charged with making a periodic redivision of the property; even the *mir* was not the owner in the fullest sense since it was still subject to certain seignorial rights reserved by the lords. In fact, the reform satisfied no one. The lord, deprived of his forced labour, now had to hire workers or hand over all his estates to the *mir*. Equally, the peasant believed that the land he tilled should have become his and felt cheated by any survival of the lord's authority.

But in one respect at least, the institution of the *mirs* was an outstanding success. They introduced to the Russian people the idea of local self-government, free from the control of the former lords. They administered, judged and kept order on the democratic principle of equality in a society which had formerly been sharply divided into those who had rights and those who had none. The village *mirs* were grouped together into larger units, the *volosts* (cantons), above which again were elected municipal corporations. Thus, the Russian peasants were given a complete system of local self-government, which ensured that, for the first time, the voices of the poorest and meanest of the tsar's subjects could be heard. In 1864 the same principle was extended to the major units of provincial administration, the districts and the provinces, which were given the right to elect councils (*zemstvos*) by universal suffrage and charged with responsibility for roads, schools, hospitals and provisions against famine. In these important regional assemblies the nobility were more strongly represented, yet nevertheless this new system of local government proved to be one of the main instruments that brought the nobility and the peasantry into contact and alliance with each other in the pursuance of common interests. The building of thousands of schools and the modernization of agricultural techniques were two of their more important achievements. The growing number of towns also received a measure of self-government when the merchant corporations and craft guilds were allowed to elect representatives to the municipal council (*duma*). It seems, however, that Alexander was conscious of the possible dangers of allowing too much power to these democratic bodies. *Zemstvos* and *dumas* were never permitted to take joint action: the tsar was to remain the sole link between the two.

Another major reform, undertaken between 1862 and 1865, was the reorganization of the system of justice. The courts were increased in number and modelled on Western lines: juries were established, secret trials, torture and corporal punishment abolished. The most important principle was that the judiciary was to be separated from the executive arm of government and so freed from royal control. As in the British constitution, the judges were to be independent and able to arrive at their decisions without fear or favour.

In the early years of Alexander's reign a new spirit of freedom and conciliation seemed to be moving through Russia. The country which had once sought to suppress public opinion now seemed anxious to stimulate criticism and change. Press censorship was eased, control of the universities was relaxed, and many scholarships were granted in order to spread higher education among those formerly excluded on the grounds of cost. To many it seemed that a new Russia, freer and greater than the old, was about to be born.

The chief beneficiaries from these more enlightened policies were the intelligentsia and students, but far from drawing them into alliance with the tsar the new taste of freedom served only to alienate them from his regime. In recognition of the growing danger, Alexander went back on some of his earlier reforms after 1861, for example by forbidding the universities to admit women or any student who could not subscribe to the orthodox religion. As the country began to take steps towards a more modern, industrialized society, the social problems of the towns and their inhabitants increasingly forced themselves on the public's attention and the intellectuals turned for guidance and inspiration to the writings of the French socialists and to Hegel, Marx and Engels.

Increasingly, the younger and more educated classes came to see revolution as the only means of creating a new world in which there would be no distinctions of rank or wealth, no nobles or serfs but a classless society in which each man would be free to give of his talents to the common good. This idealism was compounded of many elements – liberalism, socialism, and not least a devout religious faith which still inspired many young Russians as it had their fathers for generations before. Dostoyevsky in *The Possessed* described the atmosphere of mysticism which hung around the revolutionary intelligentsia. The organization necessarily had to be secret, for despite his liberal sympathies the tsar could never have tolerated a body the whole object of which was aimed at the foundations of his power.

In 1861 Nikolai Chernyshevsky, a publicist and critic, founded the most influential of these secret societies, 'Young Russia', which had the support of most of the intelligentsia and was in close contact with Russian emigres abroad and with political prisoners exiled to Siberia. In the next year, Chernyshevsky was himself arrested and deported to the prison camps, but others were soon willing to follow the lead he had given, and in 1863 the society 'Land and Liberty' took up the struggle. In a climate of opinion that now regarded any public criticism of the régime almost as treason, it was impossible that these dissentient elements could form a constitutional opposition party as they might have done in western Europe: their only recourse was direct action and terrorist activities against the state.

The hopes of the young Russian revolutionaries were raised by the growth of national feeling in Poland. Since the revolution of 1831 this poor country had suffered under the harsh yoke of Nicholas I, who had tried to stamp out all vestiges of independence. But under the more liberal régime of Alexander II Polish hopes for political independence and for the recovery of the lost Lithuanian provinces revived. Increasingly 'Young Russia' saw the expression of its own hopes in the struggle of the oppressed Polish people.

The Polish insurrection

To the Polish people, the blunders and prevarications of the Russian government seemed a mockery. A strong nationalist spirit had persisted there ever since the abortive rising of 1831, strengthened by a fervent Catholic faith which further separated the Poles from the Russian Orthodox Church. The seeming impossiblity of any kind of peaceful negotiation with their Russian masters led, in the absence of any organized Polish army, to the outbreak of guerrilla warfare in 1863. Within a short time fighting had spread to the whole country, and the Russian army was taking bitter reprisals against the civilian population, ostensibly for harbouring the rebels. Once again, the sympathy of the European powers was not translated into action. Abandoned to their fate, the Poles now lost all remnants of independence, and Russia was allowed officially to absorb the state into her dominions. By 1866 resistance had been crushed: Russian was made the official language, and the former kingdom was carved up into ten regions forming part of the vast tsarist empire.

In effect, the Polish insurrection hindered rather than helped the liberal cause in Russia. Although some of the young revolutionaries hailed it as a bold blow for

freedom, the more general reaction in Russia was to condemn the Poles as ungrateful rebels and to rally public support solidly behind the government in its policy of 'pacification'. Liberal opinions, once tolerated and even encouraged, now came to be condemned as unpatriotic. The turning point in attitudes occurred in 1866 when a young student, Karakozov, unsuccessfully attempted to assassinate the tsar. The government was able to take advantage of the public alarm to put down all supposedly subversive movements. The members of the secret societies were tracked down and hundreds deported. The liberal experiment in Russia was at an end.

The 1860s therefore form a decisive decade in Russian affairs. A definite break had occurred between liberal opinion and government policy: there could be no accommodation between the two, no steady progress towards a liberal constitution. From the time of Karakozov war was declared on the tsar and all his policies, and terrorism became the order of the day. In 1881, fifteen years after the first attempt on his life, Alexander II died at the hands of an assassin.

Above, Russian peasants greeting Alexander II in front of the Winter Palace in St Petersburg, 19 February 1861, the day of their emancipation.

Top, public reading of the statutes emancipating the serfs on an estate near Moscow: though emancipation was in many respects the beginning of the end for the old autocratic regime, making further reforms almost inevitable, many peasants were worse off than before and were still tied by debt to their village.

Date	France	Russia	Other European countries	Date	France	Russia	Other European countries
1815	Restoration of Bourbons; Louis XVIII	Holy Alliance (1815)	Battle of Waterloo	1845	Affair of the Spanish marriages	Occupation of Danubian provinces	Revolutions in several countries (1848)
	The Ultra-Royalists come to power	Nicholas I tsar (1825)	Holy Roman Empire becomes German Confederation under Austria		Revolution in Paris (1848)	Start of Crimean War (1854)	Campaigns of Garibaldi in Italy
	Chambre introuvable	December uprising (1825)			Election of Louis-Napoleon Bonaparte as president	Alexander II tsar (1855)	Crimean War (1854)
			Uprising in Greece (1822)			Liberation of the serfs in the royal domain (1858)	
	Assassination of the Duke of Berry (1820)	Capture of Erivan (1827)	Independence of Serbia		Military expedition to Rome (1849)		
	Expedition to Spain (1823)				Coup d'état of 2 December (1851)		
	Accession of Charles X (1824)				Establishment of the Second Empire (1852)		
	The Liberals are elected				Assassination attempt by Orsini (1858)		War between Austria and Sardina (1859)
	Capture of Algiers and Oran				Franco-Sardinian alliance		
1830	July Revolution in Paris	The Polish revolt (1830)	Independence of Belgium (1830)	1860	Acquisition of Nice and Savoy	Emancipation of the serfs (1861)	Bismarck comes to power in Prussia
	Louis Philippe becomes king	Russians take Vassorie (1831)			Intervention in Mexico	Creation of the *zemstvos* (1864)	Sadowa—Prussia defeats Austria (1866)
	Treaty with Abdul el-Kader (1834)	Treaty of Unkair-Skelessi (1833)	Victoria Queen of England (1837)		Liberal concessions (1867)	Attempted assassination of Alexander (1866)	Opening of the Suez Canal (1869)
	Capture of Smala from Abdul el-Kader (1843)	Straits Convention (1841)			Ollivier ministry		
	French Moroccan War (1844)				War against Prussia	Municipal reform	
					Sedan		
				1870	Fall of the Empire		

To some extent, the return of ruthless repression at home was compensated by a successful policy of expansion which helped to buttress the prestige of the tsarist regime. By the late sixties middle-class liberals had been alienated by the policy of stern despotism, and the more extreme revolutionaries had turned to the new philosophy of nihilism, a creed which challenged every aspect of the old order while having nothing positive to offer in its place. Against this mounting opposition, the government of the tsar had two popular causes to offer – the unification of the peoples of the empire and the conquest of central Asia.

In the Caucasus, the primitive mountain people, Muslim in faith and owing allegiance to the Imam Schamyh, had resisted Russian advance for twenty years; they were finally defeated in 1859. Between 1865 and 1868 Turkestan, to the east, was overrun after the capture of Tashkent and Samarkand. Further east still, the crumbling Chinese empire was forced to cede the maritime province in which Russia founded Vladivostock, the 'key to the East', in 1860. For many people, Russian despotism again seemed to be justified by its military success, though externally her expansion was watched with growing concern by Britain and, before long, by the new and ambitious power of Japan. Conquest alleviated but did not cure the ills of Russia.

The economic development of Russia

Terror and autocracy might also have been compensated by the material progress of the Russian people, by economic and industrial developments and by a rising standard of living which could have brought prosperity comparable with that enjoyed by some western European countries. Russia was vast and populous, rich in material resources largely unexploited, and with a people noted for their hard work, imagination and inventiveness. Precise statistics on the Russian economy in the 1860s are not available, but it is likely that at this time some ninety percent of the people lived in villages, only ten percent in towns. Russia was predominantly agricultural, with rather more than half her 260 million acres now in the hands of peasants. But the average size of holdings was only eight to nine acres per household, and many were too small to support a large family. The land was still divided up into tiny strips, often widely scattered, as it had been in Europe in the Middle Ages, one-third of it allowed to lie fallow and unproductive each year.

The consequence of this was that modern methods of farming – the use of agricultural machinery, rotational systems and fertilizers – were almost unknown on most Russian farms. Even scythes, one of the simplest of all agricultural tools – had to be imported, and the primitive ploughs in use did little more than scratch the surface of the land. Despite the great fertility of her 'black earth' Russian wheat yields were only half those of Austria and France and one-third those of England.

Whether or not Alexander II's reforms produced any measurable change in the standard of life of the Russian peasant is doubtful. Just before the First World War the *Encyclopaedia Britannica* (eleventh edition 1910–11) commented:

The present condition of the peasants – according to official documents – appears to be as follows. In the twelve central governments they grow, on average, sufficient ryebread for only 200 days in the year – often for only 180 and 100 days. The peasantry are impoverished, and in many parts live on the verge of starvation for the greater part of the year.

Although technically emancipated, the serfs were free only in name. They bore the brunt of Russian taxation, both direct and indirect, and were also taxed by the *zemstvos* on which they had only indirect representation. For the most part they lived in huts of wood and mud with earthen floors and usually with no water supplies or sanitation: the single room was shared with pigs and poultry, and infectious diseases took a tremendous toll of human life. Even at the beginning of the twentieth century the Russian deathrate was the highest in Europe – thirty per thousand per year compared with sixteen per thousand in Britain – and one child in every three died during its first year. In 1914 only twenty-one percent of the whole population could read and write, and the figure would have been smaller still in the 1860s. Count Witte, the prime minister in 1905–6, commented:

The peasants are free from the slaveowners. But they are now slaves to arbitrary power, legal disabilities and to ignorance. The peasants have ceased to be private property. . . . That is all that remains of the reform of 19th February, 1861.

There was little more evidence of progress in the Russian towns than in the countryside. Although St Petersburg and Moscow were centres of culture and fashion for a few thousand nobles and rich bourgeois, the great majority of town dwellers lived in conditions no better than their country brothers. They were crowded into insanitary shacks and tenements and forced to labour at sweated trades, hardly yet affected by mechanization, for a mere pittance. Rich material resources of coal and metals had scarcely begun to be exploited, and as late as 1914 only about one-thenth of the country had been geologically surveyed. Coal production was only one-twenty-seventh and iron-ore production only one-twelfth that of the United States of America. This state of industrial backwardness was to some extent actively encouraged by the crown and nobility, who feared the growth of a powerful urban proletariat as a possible source of change – even of revolution. Ultimately, as the events of 1917 were to demonstrate, their fears were amply justified.

Chapter 4

France from the Restoration to Napoleon III

The French Revolution bequeathed to its birthplace a heritage of problems – political, social and economic – which successive governments strove vainly to solve. To reconcile liberty with order, to give effect to the democratic principles for which Frenchmen had fought while re-establishing the necessary authority of the state taxed the energies and imaginations of statesmen and politicians for more than half a century, and to achieve this while at the same time providing the conditions of economic growth and military power ultimately proved an impossibility. Monarchy, republic and empire all fell victims to the same enemies from within, and in this sense the eventual consequence of the French Revolution was the humiliating defeat of French arms on the battlefield of Sedan.

The restoration of the Bourbons

The last Bourbon king had fallen victim to the guillotine. Now, in 1815, Louis XVIII was restored to the throne, brought back 'in the baggage of the allies' after more than twenty years of exile. The new king was intelligent enough to know that the *ancien régime* could never be re-established, that the middle classes were prepared to accept a monarchy only if the essential freedoms of the Revolution were confirmed. Thus at the outset of his reign, Louis XVIII was brought face-to-face with a fundamental philosophical problem which demanded immediate and practical solution.

Although intelligent, cultured and refined, Louis XVIII was ill-equipped to provide such an answer. His long exile had taught him to be patient and amenable and to accept the position of a constitutional monarch which was the condition of his restoration; on the other hand, he had no intention of playing only a nominal part in affairs of state. Unfortunately, his closest associates, led by his brother the Count of Artois, were more royalist than he himself and were not prepared to make concessions to the principles of 1789.

Under the new constitution of 1815 the king was the head of state and the executive power: he had the right to choose his own ministers, who were not responsible to the

parliament. The latter was to consist of two houses – an Upper Chamber nominated by the king and a Chamber of Deputies chosen by an electorate limited to men over the age of thirty who paid at least 300 francs a year in taxes. There were less than 100,000 voters in all, and the working classes were totally excluded from political power. Moreover, even the 'democratic' Chamber of Deputies could only discuss legislation and vote taxes: since they had no executive power there was no means of enforcing their decisions unless the king also agreed.

Yet, despite its very limited nature, the constitution was regarded as revolutionary by many of the nobility and clergy, who dreamed of a restoration of real power to the ancient pillars of the state. They had influential leaders like the Count of Artois, the Count of Villèle and the writer Chateaubriand, as well as their own organ in the *Gazette de France*.

Ranged against them were those who benefited from the new constitution – essentially the middle classes and professionals who had been brought into political competence, supported by a few enlightened nobles. These 'Constitutionalists' were led by the historian François Guizot and expressed their views in the *Courrier Français*. To their left stood a more extreme group, led by Benjamin Constant and the veteran Marquis de Lafayette, who had no faith in the constitution and were uneasy at the excessive influence of emigrés and clergy in the new government. These 'Independents' drew most of their support from the lower middle classes: their objective was a more democratic constitution in which the elected chamber would have real power.

One of the king's promises on his restoration had been an amnesty for all those Frenchmen who had supported Napoleon at the time of the Hundred Days, but in the country as a whole anti-republican feeling was running high. In several cities known Bonapartists were assassinated by mobs, and in the first post-war election the Ultra-Royalist party surprisingly won a majority in the Chamber of Deputies. Louis, who had not dared to hope for such support, described it as 'The Unknown Chamber'.

The king was now urged – probably not wholly against his will – into a policy of repressive conservatism. Talleyrand, the moderate prime minister, was replaced by the royalist Richelieu. Eighteen high-ranking officers who had fought with Napoleon at the end – including the once-popular hero Marshall Ney – were condemned and shot, while a general purge of the courts, the universities and local government removed some 9,000 from public office. Finally, the Bonaparte family, and all those who had had any part in the execution of Louis XVI, were banished from France.

But if the royalists wished to restore the *ancien régime*, the king knew that to do so would lose him his crown. Making an astute appraisal of the political feeling of the

Above, Louis XVIII (ruled 1814–24): Louis' reign was a time of reconciliation for France, brought about as much by an improving economic situation as by the king's moderate, efficient and honest government.

while secret presses continued to pour out broadsheets and songs denouncing the government and the Jesuits. In the universities student demonstrations against control by the Church were often violent, especially when popular professors like Guizot and Victor Cousin were suspended from their duties.

Among some of the more extreme revolutionaries the belief grew that Villèle's regime could only be ended by armed insurrection. Republicans like Lafayette and Cousin formed secret *charbonneries* with cells of twenty members directed by a high command. Badly organized and idealistic, they were no more successful than their Italian counterparts and had little support from the public at large. The ease with which their local risings were put down indicated that the government had the situation well in hand and that they constituted no real threat to the authority of the Ultras. But in September 1824 the old king died and was succeeded by his brother, Charles X, who in a few months was to destroy what little credit the French Crown had left.

Charles X

Where Louis had been shrewd, moderate and easy-going, Charles was unintelligent, stern and autocratic. At sixty-seven he was the epitome of the *ancien régime*, proud, haughty and unbending, a staunch adherent of the Church and an implacable enemy of paganism and reform. 'I had rather chop wood', he had once said, 'than reign after the fashion of the King of England', and his coronation ceremony was symbolically performed at Reims with the full pageantry of medieval rites. One of his first acts was to increase the penalties for sacrilege, and it rapidly became clear that Charles intended to put the clock back to 1789. His abolition of the National Guard, who had demonstrated in favour of constitutional reform, and his granting of compensation to the emigre nobles were especially unpopular. In the Chamber, Constitutionalists and Liberals allied together in a powerful opposition headed by Guizot and in the next elections won a majority of 250 seats against the government's 200. Villèle had no alternative but to give his resignation to the king in January 1828.

Charles was now faced with an unmanageable Chamber and a seemingly impossible situation. To gain time, he first appointed a Constitutionalist, Martignac, who completely failed to win the support of the deputies. Increasingly, the feeling grew that the king was planning a coup d'état to overthrow the constitution and restore the *ancien régime*. This view seemed to be confirmed the following year when he dismissed Martignac and appointed Prince Polignac, one of the original emigres and a man who had refused to swear allegiance to the Charter of 1815: one of his stranger

country, Louis dismissed the chamber in September 1816 and held another election in which the Royalists lost many seats and the Constitutionalists gained a small majority. For the next four years France was to experiment with more liberal policies.

The old king now had an opportunity to show his wisdom and shrewdness in steering a middle course between the two extremes of reaction and reform. Though he never became a popular figure – the memories of France's departed glories and the bitter pangs of Waterloo were too strong for that – he succeeded ably in maintaining peace and prosperity while paying off the country's war indemnity and liberating her soil from foreign armies. Under the new prime minister, Décazes, the electoral law was altered in order to reduce the influence of the great landowners over their tenant voters, military conscription was replaced by a volunteer army of a quarter of a million and, again to reduce aristocratic power, officers were selected by competitive examination and promoted by seniority and merit. Finally, in 1819, press censorship was abolished, and in future cases concerning publications were to be tried by jury in the assize courts, no longer by special tribunals appointed by the government.

One of the unforeseen results of this general relaxation of control was a large increase in the circulation of liberal newspapers, and in the 1819 elections the Independents gained considerable ground. Décazes, alarmed at the strength of the forces he had unleashed, brought his programme of reforms to an end, dismissed several of his most liberal ministers and increasingly allied himself with the Right. Groups of extreme anti-clericals had formed themselves into secret societies on the model of the Italian *Carbonari*, and in 1820, when there were revolutionary outbreaks in Pied-

mont, Naples, Spain and Portugal, there were disturbances in France culminating in the murder of the king's nephew, the Duke of Berry, by a Bonapartist fanatic. Under pressure from his own family and the country, Louis dismissed his friend Décazes. The Ultra-Royalists quickly seized power in the council, appointing one of their own number, the Count of Villèle, as president.

There now followed the undoing of much of Décazes' patient reconstruction. Villèle, the puny little member for Toulouse, was a shrewd administrator who understood clearly enough the realities of political power. In order to halt the progress of the liberals he abolished the new electoral law and, moreover, introduced double voting rights for that quarter of the electors who paid the most taxes: political competence was to rest upon economic foundations, not on abstract principles of justice and equality. As a result, the liberals lost heavily in the elections of 1820, and Villèle completed their defeat by reimposing censorship of the press and the hearing of cases by special tribunals: in this way the publication of most opposition journals was stopped.

Villèle's policies relied in part on a renewed energy and spirit in the Roman Catholic Church, which through a determined onslaught on the schools and universities was attempting to reconquer areas of French life which had lapsed into paganism during the Revolution and subsequent war. Villèle strongly supported the *Congrégation*, an association dominated by the Jesuits, and placed the universities under the supervision of the bishops.

But despite the attacks on them, the opposition continued a vocal criticism of the government and its policies. The fifteen members of the left in the Chamber of Deputies included some outstanding orators like Benjamin Constant and General Foy,

delusions was that he received direct guidance from the Virgin Mary.

The glorious days of 1830

The political crisis of 1829 had resulted in
important regroupings of the parties, the
Republicans growing in strength and, more
important, a new party led by the Duke of
Orléans emerging in the forefront of affairs.
This was a party of moderate Royalists,
anxious to safeguard the interests of the
middle classes and having the support of
influential men like Talleyrand and Adolphe
Thiers. Their ideal was a constitutional
monarchy like that of England, where power
was shared between the sovereign and the
houses of parliament.

Faced with growing opposition in the
Chamber of Deputies, Polignac now dismissed parliament and prepared for an open
conflict. On 25 July 1830, royal ordinances
were issued which limited the freedom of the
press, dissolved the Chambers and altered
the electoral law. Although the king had
authority under Article 14 of the Charter to
do this, it was clearly a provocative gesture,
especially as the new electoral law limited
the franchise to those who paid land tax or
property tax and so deliberately excluded
many professional and businessmen who
were known liberal supporters.

It was the journalists who reacted first,
on 26 July, by issuing a declaration that they
would continue to publish newspapers without the required permission.

Next day, workers from the poorer
quarters of Paris erected barricades in the
streets, but the final spark to the revolution
was given on the 28th, when the government
announced that the hated General Marmont, who had betrayed Napoleon in 1814,
had been given command of the royal
armies. There followed three days of disorder and fighting, when thousands of
Parisians of all classes marched through the
streets with tricolour flags at their head.
Students of the Polytechnic had previously
seized several army barracks and distributed
arms to the population. Those royal regiments which had not gone over to the rebels
were quickly overcome, and after the capture of the Louvre and the Tuileries Marmont, defeated, evacuated the capital.

The revolution of 1830 was over before
most French people realized what was
happening. The events had happened entirely in Paris, so that the royalist strongholds in the provinces were unable to
move until it was too late. But in some ways
the strangest part of the revolution was its
outcome. Its leaders had been mainly
Republicans or Bonapartists, anxious to
establish in France either a presidential
constitution or a second empire under one
of the children of Napoleon. In fact, the
result was neither of these but a bourgeois
monarchy under Louis Philippe, the head
of the House of Orléans, who as a young
man had fought in the revolutionary armies
and had subsequently known sorrow and
poverty. The Orléanists, essentially the
party of the middle classes and professionals,
were able to turn events to their advantage
partly because they were better organized
than their political opponents, partly because a constitutional monarch who would
accept the Chamber and honour the tricolor

represented a middle way which the majority of French people could support. It was therefore relatively easy to persuade the two Chambers, on 30 July, to send a deputation to Louis Philippe offering him the crown, in much the same way that William of Orange had been invited to take the English throne in 1688. The Parisian mob, at first somewhat hostile, were won over when Louis Philippe appeared on the balcony of the Hôtel de Ville, draped in a tricolour flag, and warmly embracing Lafayette, 'the grand old man of the revolution', who had announced his adherence to the Orléanists.

Meanwhile, Charles X made a last bid to rescue the situation for the Bourbon dynasty, abdicating in favour of his young grandson the Duke of Bordeaux and suggesting that Louis Philippe should act as Regent until he came of age. This Louis refused, and after further threatened attacks by the Paris mob Charles escaped to England. The throne of France was officially offered to Louis Philippe by the two Chambers on 9 August.

The July Monarchy

There could hardly have been a greater contrast between the new king and his Bourbon predecessors. To outward appearances he was the personification of the petty bourgeois – a shabbily dressed man who loved to stroll through the streets of Paris with his umbrella under his arm, a devoted father of five sons and three daughters, a man of simple tastes and no pretensions. Behind this very ordinary exterior there also lay much courage and resolution, a sound business sense and a determination to raise the authority of France from the low levels to which Charles X had reduced it.

Louis Philippe accepted a constitution considerably more democratic than that of 1815. By a series of amendments, the

king no longer had the power to promulgate ordinances having the force of law, press censorship and double voting were abolished, and in future the choice of prime minister was to lie with the two Chambers. Thus parliamentary supremacy over the legislative function was clearly and absolutely established. By additional clauses, the National Guard was permitted to choose its own officers, the hereditary peerage was abolished and the Chamber of Peers opened to the middle classes, and the property qualification for the vote in the Chamber of Deputies was lowered from those paying taxes of 300 francs a year to those paying 200 francs thus doubling to 200,000 citizens.

The new king's policy was clearly to try to steer a middle course between the two extremist groups, the Republicans and the

Bonapartists. Like all compromises, it satisfied few people. The Republicans regrouped under the leadership of such men as Carrel, the lawyer Garnier-Pagès and the chemist Raspail and through the now free press launched a campaign for universal suffrage. Again secret societies sprang up to prepare the ground for the next general election. Even within the Orléanist party, differences of opinion appeared between the more conservative leaders like Casimir Périer and Guizot, who believed that reform had now gone far enough, and liberals like Laffitte and Lafayette, who wished to continue reform towards an even more democratic constitution. Louis Philippe had to choose between the two: he chose the liberals under the leadership of Laffitte, 'the king of bankers and the banker of kings'.

One of Laffitte's immediate problems was the trial of Charles X's former ministers. Justice seemed to require that they should be punished for the injuries they had inflicted on the French people: the more extreme elements demanded their execution, the upper house contented itself with sentencing them to life imprisonment. Widespread demonstrations had accompanied the trial, and early in 1831 there was a wave of violent anti-clericalism when Roman Catholic priests were insulted and attacked. In an attempt to win popularity, Laffitte lowered the taxes on alcoholic drinks, which only had the result of producing a budget deficit of forty million francs.

Louis realized that the situation demanded a firmer hand. Dismissing Laffitte, he appointed Casimir Périer, another banker but an authoritarian of more conservative views, determined to suppress public disorder. Within a few months the budget was again balanced and the new minister could turn his attention to a serious situation which had appeared in Lyons, the centre of the great French silk industry. In November 1831 the weavers, wretchedly paid and housed in miserable slums had taken up arms against their employers, and had occupied the town after two days of bloody fighting against the police and the army. Whatever the rights or wrongs of the situation, Louis Philippe's government could not allow such a threat to public law and order to continue, and General Soult was ordered to march on the city.

The army regained possession of the city on 5 December, the silk workers then being disarmed and treated as rebels: if anything, their conditions subsequently grew even worse. It was thus clearly demonstrated, early in the new reign, that the rights of the property-owning middle classes were to be regarded as paramount and that the Revolution of 1830 had served merely to confirm the power of the bourgeoisie, leaving the workers as excluded from political participation as they had been under the Bourbons.

The stirrings of the Lyons proletariat had hardly been suppressed when a new threat to the monarchy appeared. In 1832 the Duchess of Berry, widow of the murdered Duke and mother of Prince Henry, the heir of Charles X, landed in the Vendée, western France, in an attempt to rally support for her son's cause. In the event, she drew few followers and was arrested shortly afterwards in Nantes. At least the episode demonstrated that royalist opposition to Louis Philippe was no longer a serious threat.

More disturbing was the growth of the Republican movement. In June 1832 there was a serious rising of Republicans against the government, when over 800 died in bloody street fighting. Two years later another insurrection, inspired by the Society for the Rights of Man, resulted in the deaths of a further 300 rebels in Lyons. Such risings could be put down with relative ease because the army remained loyal and because the National Guard, essentially a middle class body, could always be relied on for support, but they demonstrated an inherent weakness in Louis Philippe's regime that it was not firmly based on the respect and affection of all classes of Frenchmen.

In 1835 an attempt on Louis' life served as the pretext for laws directly aimed at the Republicans. One imposed severe penalties for attacks on the monarch, including the caricatures of Louis Philippe by Honoré Daumier and other artists which had been circulating; the other officially outlawed Republicanism and laid down special rules for the trial of political offences.

Within about four years, therefore, Louis Philippe's government, now under the leadership of conservatives like Guizot and Thiers, had brought the liberal experiment to an end, though at least that had established firm government. For the time being, the Republican menace was halted, both in the Chamber of Deputies and in the country at large, and for a few years France was to enjoy a period of calm during which economic expansion and a growth in prosperity seemed to justify the political conservatism of the July Monarchy.

Guizot's ministry

For some years after 1835 Louis Philippe virtually ruled France himself. Technically, a series of puppet ministers presided in the Chamber, and the middle classes, enjoying a period of unusual economic growth and prosperity, were for a while content to allow him to hold the reins of power. In the elections of 1839, however, the prime minister Molé, was defeated, and after some months of hesitation Louis gave the leadership to Guizot, a distinguished academic historian who was a staunch royalist and conservative. To Guizot the constitution of 1830 was perfect: the art of the politician was to make it work, to give the monarch a position of real influence in government while allying the representatives of middle class wealth and culture solidly behind the throne.

But the first task of any government, Guizot believed, was to maintain order. He inherited a confused situation in which Republican and dissident elements, secret societies and subversive literature constituted a serious threat to public order and to France's economic development, and in the very year of his taking office 700 rebels belonging to one of the secret societies known as 'The Seasons' occupied the law courts and police headquarters in Paris. Precisely what they intended to do is not clear, though it seems that they hoped to overthrow the constitution and establish a republic. Guizot's new government dealt with them easily and effectively, surrounding the rebels and arresting the leaders Barbès and Blanqui, yet the episode demonstrated the continued and growing attraction which the idea of a republic had for many Frenchmen.

The other strong current of opposition opinion was Bonapartism. As the years went by, the tyranny and oppression of the empire was forgotten, only its glorious victories before which the powers of Europe had trembled were remembered. Historians,

Above, portrait by Hippolyte Delaroche of François Guizot (1787–1874): his refusal to extend the franchise and to make any concessions to radical thinking led to his overthrow in 1848.

Top, army and silk weavers facing each other on the Place des Bernardines, Lyons, 22 November 1831: the revolt was bloodily crushed, as was a further rising sixteen months later.

Opposite top right, the Parisian crowd attacks the Louvre, 29 July 1830.

Opposite top left, four of the leaders of the 1830 Revolution: from left to right Jacques Laffitte, Casimir Périer, the Marquis de Lafayette and Marshal Gerard.

Opposite bottom, Louis Philippe (1773–1850, ruled 1830–48), the 'citizen king', portrait by Franz Winterhalter. Château de Versailles.

poets and pamphleteers, combined to venerate the Little Emperor, to reinterpret his defeat during 'The Hundred Days' and to record his reminiscences and conversations from his exile in St Helena. It was symbolical of this process of rehabilitation that in 1840 his ashes were brought back from St Helena to be given honourable burial at Les Invalides in Paris, the funeral carriage being followed though, by an immense crowd. As yet, it was too soon for the Bonapartists to overthrow the strong government of Louis Philippe.

The head of the Napoleonic house was Louis Bonaparte, nephew of the great Napoleon and son of Napoleon's brother who had once held the throne of Holland. He was a strange, studious young man, convinced of his imperial destiny and unabashed by the utter failure so far of his attempts to seize power in France. Already in 1834 he had unsuccessfully tried to win over the garrison of Strasbourg. Now in 1840, when he landed at Boulogne, the French army, instead of rallying to his cause,

merely captured and imprisoned him in the fortress of Ham. Yet, in retrospect, the origins of the Second Empire are discernible plainly enough in the events of 1840.

For the next six years Guizot's conservative ministry continued to resist all political change. Industry and agriculture prospered, and in 1842 plans were drawn up for the construction of a huge railway network converging on Paris. The philosophy of 'grow rich, pay taxes, and you too will enjoy the vote, gradually brought a few more Frenchmen into democratic competence, and in the elections of 1846 the government was overwhelmingly returned to power. In all outward appearances at least 'the bourgeois king' was more secure than at any time since his accession.

The revolution of 1848

The beginning of the trouble was an economic crisis, caused by a failure in the wheat and potato harvests in the autumn of 1846. As prices soared, bands of starving

people began looting the bakeries, spreading terror throughout the countryside, while in the towns factories closed and the number of unemployed multiplied alarmingly. At the same time, the disclosure of a series of government scandals gave the opposition their opportunity to demand changes in the electoral system and the lowering of the property qualifications for the franchise to 100 francs. Unwisely, but predictably, Guizot refused all pressure for change. The opposition leaders now decided to put the issues before the public, organizing mass meetings at which they exposed the government's failures to large and enthusiastic audiences of workers. Republicans like the journalist Louis Blanc and the author Alphonse de Lamartine quickly came to the forefront, campaigning for universal suffrage and the improvement of economic conditions.

'The wind of revolution is blowing', wrote de Tocqueville. The storm burst on 22 February 1848, when Guizot refused permission for a public banquet to be given

Above, the proclamation of the Second Republic at the Hôtel de Ville, painting by J.-J. Champin. Musée Carnavalet, Paris.

Left, members of the Provisional Government, formed on 24 February 1848, an uneasy mixture of republicans, such as Lamartine and Ledru-Rollin, and socialists, such as Albert and Louis Blanc: after the shattering socialist defeat in the April elections and the bloody suppression of the June uprising, power returned to the propertied classes, and in December Louis Napoleon Bonaparte was elected president. Four years later he became hereditary emperor.

Opposite top, Napoleon Bonaparte's funeral cortege in the Champs Elysées, 15 December 1840. Bonapartism remained weak throughout Louis Philippe's reign, though it revived rapidly after 1848.

Opposite bottom right, Louis-Philippe's throne being burnt by the Parisian crowd, 25 February 1848.

Opposite bottom left, cartoon by Honoré Daumier (1808–79), the celebrated painter and caricaturist, of Louis Philippe fleeing to England; the king travelled as plain 'Mr Smith'.

by the Republicans. A protest demonstration turned into a riot when a frightened army patrol fired a chance volley into the crowd. By the 23rd the National Guard had joined the rebels and Louis Philippe's dismissal of Guizot came too late to retrieve the situation. As in 1830, arms were seized from the barracks and barricades erected in the streets, but, as in 1789, it was the 'Marseillaise' that was on everyone's lips. After some skirmishes with the remaining royal troops the crowd marched to the Tuileries were Louis abdicated and shortly afterwards fled to England.

The speed and easy success of the revolution startled even the Republicans. Their problem now was to make sure that the victory was not wrested from them. To do this meant excluding the deputies from any share in the success. The crowd took possession of the Chamber, Lamartine reading out the names of the new government to the Parisians who crowded into the benches and galleries. The Republic was then officially proclaimed from the Hôtel de Ville.

Louis Philippe's government had given France for eighteen years an unaccustomed measure of peace and prosperity, but ultimately it failed because it was not broadly based on the popular will. By devoting itself to the avarice of the middle classes it had alienated that growing body of workers on whom the wealth of France depended, and they, in anger and despair, had ended the life of a monarchy which had either treated them with contempt or ignored their very existence. Now these same workers were flushed with success, but unorganized, inarticulate, an easy prey to the demagogue who could promise all.

At the same time as Lamartine was proclaiming the new Republic, another group had strong supporters in the crowd. These were the Socialists, followers of Louis Blanc and Albert, who had derived their ideas from earlier French philosophers like Saint-Simon, Fourier and Proudhon and were now advocating fundamental economic, not merely political, changes. At the meeting at the Hôtel de Ville they had tried to substitute

The first general election to be held under conditions approaching manhood suffrage was, therefore, a shattering defeat for socialism. It illustrated, perhaps, the victory of common sense and practicality which has rescued France from more than one crisis, for it was clear enough that a country on the brink of economic disaster was hardly the place for utopian experiments. The government had urgently to find money, yet with the future so uncertain the policy of raising loans by the issue of government bonds was a miserable failure. Appeals to French patriotism were in vain, yet to increase the level of taxation was equally unthinkable. There remained the possibility of reducing government spending.

For this reason, if for no other, Louis Blanc's idea of cooperative production was doomed. He and other Socialists had advocated the setting-up of National Workshops, where workers would both own and control the processes of production and would divide the profits among themselves. Initially, the state would provide the capital to buy premises, machines and materials, but thereafter workers would be free to run their own affairs independently of their former capitalist masters. Part of the profits would be set aside to purchase more workshops, so that ultimately the whole of the nation's economy would be socialist.

Obviously, such ideas held great attraction for the poor and unemployed of the French cities, but equally clearly they faced immense problems of finance and organization. It was, to say the least, unlikely that the middle classes who had sunk their fortunes in industry would voluntarily renounce their ownership, and the new minister of public works, who himself opposed the whole idea, was easily able to wreck any chance of success that the National Workshops might have had. Although work of a kind was certainly provided for the unemployed, he made no attempt to select men for tasks according to their skill and no attempt to create work which could show a profit. Men were directed into planting trees or digging trenches which they then filled in again. Workers soon became disheartened, abandoned their support of the Socialists and spent their time either in idleness or fruitless political agitation. The National Workshops had skilfully been turned into objects of public ridicule and scorn.

Meanwhile, reaction was setting in in the government. All real power was concentrated in an Executive Committee of five members which, although it contained Republicans like Lamartine and Arago, had no Socialist representative. In May an armed demonstration resulted in the arrest of the Socialist leaders Barbès, Blanqui and Albert and the closure of the revolutionary clubs, while one of the first acts of the newly-elected Assembly was to order the closure of the National Workshops. Workers were

the red flag of socialism for the tricolour of the republicans, but Lamartine had rushed forward and in a famous speech had condemned their emblem as the flag of blood and hatred. He was not, however, able to prevent the inclusion of the socialist leaders in the new government.

The Republicans knew clearly enough that the immediate cause of the revolution had been the economic crisis and the miserable poverty of many of the working classes, but even if they had wanted to exclude the proletariat from power there was no way of doing so. Universal suffrage which had been proclaimed and would now enfranchise nine million pople instead of a quarter of a million. Freedom of the press and of public assembly resulted in the appearance of hundreds of revolutionary newspapers and political clubs. For the first time, it seemed, a new working-class consciousness had emerged, in which they were no longer content to accept the leadership of middle-class liberals but wanted a complete reconstruction of society on their own terms. To outside observers like Marx and Engels, publishing their Communist Manifesto at this time, it seemed that the hour of the proletarian revolution had struck.

In the uneasy situation the new government played for time, appointing a special commission to enquire into working conditions in industry, which resulted in a substantial reduction of hours. But there were growing signs of a rift between the middle classes and the socialists over the timing of the general election, the one urging delay, the other pressing for immediate action. Popular discontent was further heightened by increases in taxation made necessary by

the government's critical financial position.

In fact, the postponement of the elections favoured the Socialists rather than the Republicans. Lamartine and his followers believed that people instinctively recognized the truth when it was presented to them and that propaganda was therefore wasted on intelligent and discriminating human beings. More realistically, the Socialists knew that many of the French working classes were poor and illiterate and believed that they were entitled to a period of instruction to remedy the effects of their political inexperience. Demonstrations and mass meetings were therefore organized throughout France, sometimes attended by as many as 100,000 to listen to renowned speakers like Louis Blanc. On some of these occasions public order was only kept by the National Guard, and a growing rift became apparent between the two groups who had so recently been allied to bring about the revolution.

On 23 April for the first time millions of Frenchmen went to the polls. The results were as the Socialists had feared. France was still a predominantly rural country, and the strength of socialism was almost entirely among the exploited working classes of the towns. The peasant was traditional and conservative in outlook, a staunch supporter of property and order and suspicious of the Parisian trouble-makers. The newly-elected Assembly was moderate and middle class, hardly dissimilar from that of Louis Philippe's closing years. Of 900 Deputies only 100 were Socialists, fewer than the 130 Royalists of the extreme right: the rest were moderate Republicans, pledged to suppress disorder and to restore financial stability to France.

given the choice of two unattractive alternatives – military service in Algeria or work draining the mosquito-infested swamps of Sologne in central France. For the middle classes, it seemed a good way of removing a disorderly mob from Paris, but the men of the National Workshops who had once dreamed of being their own masters had no intention of accepting either. Once more the barricades went up in the streets of Paris, but this time Republican was against Socialist.

For a while it seemed that the government forces were taking little action. In fact, General Cavaignac first cut off the infected areas of the city like the Latin Quarter and then made organized attacks; only after several days of very bitter fighting did these become successful. Middle-class opinion had been outraged by accounts of the brutality of the rebels, such as the fatal injury of the Archbishop of Paris who had tried to intervene in the dispute, and the Assembly now wreaked terrible vengeance; 10,000 Socialists were executed, a further 15,000 imprisoned. In future the Socialist working class and the Republican middle class, who had once fought together behind the barricades, were divided by the blood spilt in June 1848. The inevitability of the class war, which Karl Marx had predicted, seemed to be amply justified by the turn of French events.

The return of Louis Bonaparte

With public order re-established so dearly, the first task of the Assembly was to prepare a constitution. That this was to be a Republican one was never in doubt, but beyond this there were almost as many opinions as deputies. Ultimately, a constitution resembling in some respects that of the United States of America was agreed, its main principle being to establish a president with executive power sufficient to guarantee public order. He was to be chosen by universal suffrage for a period of four years – long enough, it was hoped, to make his mark but not to establish a dynasty. As the legislative arm there would be a single National Assembly, also elected by universal suffrage, though the precise relationship between the Assembly and the president was not clearly defined. The principle of 'the right to work' was specifically not mentioned: it was replaced by 'the freedom to work'.

The presidential elections took place in December. A number of candidates entered the lists – Lamartine, the revered writer and Republican, Cavaignac, the general who had saved Paris from the mob, two Socialist leaders and, finally, Louis Bonaparte, returned from England where he had quietly been waiting for the call. He was elected at the head of the poll by a majority of more than four million votes.

By a series of unlikely chances – the early death of Napoleon's own son, then that of his elder brother, killed during *Carbonari* violence in Italy – Louis had become the heir to the Bonapartist succession and legend. Although possessing few of his uncle's qualities, he had lived a life of some daring and adventure in Switzerland and Italy, had twice before made a bid for French power and had escaped from his final imprisonment in the fortress of Ham to England in 1846. Here he waited until the events of February 1848 brought him rushing back to France. At forty he was still hesitant and timid, a poor orator who fumbled his speech as a newly-elected deputy, but he had the name of Napoleon which still passed in every Frenchman's memory for discipline, power and military renown.

There could be no mistaking the relief with which the French electors turned to a candidate who had the advantage not only of the name but of having been apart from the vacillations and shabbiness of French politics in recent years. Here, it was thought, was a president who would be above politics, who could be loved at home and respected abroad. Louis was elected overwhelmingly, polling 5,400,000 votes compared with 1,400,000 for Cavaignac: the rest were far behind, at the very bottom the poet Lamartine with a mere 20,000.

Elections for the Legislative Assembly were held a year later – in May 1849. The result was a major defeat for the moderate Republicans and a victory for the Conservatives, but also significant was a substantial gain for the extreme Republicans led by Ledru-Rollin. The strange situation was already occurring that out of a republican revolution had emerged a president who was a prince and an Assembly elected by universal suffrage which was solidly conservative and which, indeed, contained many royalists. One of the first acts of the new government was to send a French expeditionary force to Rome, not to support the republic of Mazzini, but to overthrow it. Ledru-Rollin and others who had attempted an insurrection against the campaign were sent into exile.

It soon became clear that the Republic and its president were no democrats or tolerators of free thought. The spread of socialism, it was believed, had originated with teachers of 'advanced' ideas in schools and colleges, and in order to prevent such people from practising the Falloux Law of 1850 was passed, limiting the right to teach to those who held a university degree. An even greater restriction followed in May 1850, when the parliamentary franchise was made conditional on having lived in the constituency for three years and having never had any crown conviction, even for the most trivial offence. This removed the franchise from 3,000,000 of the former 9,000,000 voters: in particular, it hit at Socialists and extreme Republicans, many of whom had been technically guilty of political offences and were precisely the people who never

Above, Louis Blanc (1811–82): Blanc had long opposed competitive industry and favoured co-operative workshops and had set out his ideas in L'Organisation du travail *(1840). Though the provisional government did establish a form of National Workshops, they were little more than a means of providing unemployment relief and certainly did not realize Blanc's own aims. Even these failed and after the June days he fled to England.*

Opposite, the Archbishop of Paris faces a firing-squad during the June days. The June days were a virtually spontaneous outburst of almost leaderless popular fury, partly stimulated by the closure of the National Workshops. The uprising lasted two days, was brutally put down and left the republicans and socialists bitterly divided.

stayed long in the same place. The Assembly had very effectively removed political power from their opponents without incurring the unpopularity of restricting the franchise by a property qualification.

Louis Napoleon was sufficiently astute to let it be known that he personally disapproved of the measure and thus could continue to stand as the representative of freedom and equality. It seems likely that he was already preparing the ground for his coup d'état, the seizure of power by which he could again make Bonapartism a reality. In retrospect, there is an inevitability about the course of events.

The elected president found himself in a chamber in which he had no personal following and from which he could expect no support; he was by temperament a liberal and a nationalist, yet he was forced to acquiesce in conservative policies at home, even to support the pope against the Republicans in Italy. The constitution stipulated that the president should hold office for four years and was not eligible for re-election. The nephew of Napoleon, who had risked all to return to France, was unlikely to accept such transitory power.

The president now carefully prepared the ground. First, the military governor of Paris was dismissed on a pretext and replaced by one of his own supporters. The Africa Corps, on whose loyalty he could depend, were also quartered in the capital. He next undertook a series of tours throughout the provinces, rallying support at mass meetings in which his supporters had been carefully planted to lead the cry of '*Vive l'Empereur*'. Finally, he began a campaign to alter Article 45 of the constitution to allow the president to serve for a further term of office of four years. In doing so, Louis Bonaparte probably calculated on the Assembly's rejection; if so, his prediction was justified. His amendment to the constitution was finally rejected in July 1851.

From this time, an open conflict had really become inevitable, but the president still chose his time carefully. The selected date was to be 2 December, the anniversary of his uncle's coronation as Emperor of France and of his great military victory of Austerlitz. On the evening of the 1st, he gave a splendid reception at the Elysée Palace, where he was seen to be unusually charming and courteous. At one point, however, he slipped away to give instructions to an inner circle of conspirators – his half-brother Morny, Maupas the Prefect of Police, and Saint-Armand the military commander. During the night the plan was put into effect – occupation of the Assembly, arrest of all the principal leaders who might have organized resistance, including Thiers and Cavaignac, and military occupation of strategic points in Paris. An announcement was made dissolving the Chamber of Deputies and re-introducing universal suffrage.

When Paris awoke the next morning, the takeover was already accomplished. A few deputies tried to resist, objecting that the president had broken his oath, had violated the constitution and was therefore deposed. Few took any notice, and those like Victor Hugo who tried to urge the people to take up arms against a tyrant found no support. Parisians had suffered and died at the barricades only three years before and had gained nothing from their middle class allies. Louis Napoleon was seen as a democratic deliverer who would restore the Rights of Man and again make France respected throughout the courts of Europe.

The coup d'état succeeded brilliantly in a city overcome by lethargy and bored by the succession of civil disorders. One of the few instances of courage occurred when the deputy Baudin was urging the workers to help him to build a barricade, and one of them called out: 'Do you think we are going to get ourselves killed to protect your twenty-five francs a day?' (The official salary of a deputy). Baudin replied: 'Stay there, my friend, and you will see someone killed for twenty-five francs a day.' Shortly afterwards he was killed at the barricade. On 4 December there was shooting on the boulevards, which terrorized Parisians, and armed risings in the provinces which were put down with terrible severity. In all, some

1,200 innocent citizens were killed in the coup, 10,000 more deported, and sixty deputies, including Victor Hugo, expelled from France. Louis Napoleon's seizure of power was thus achieved by fraud, duress and murder, yet it also had the overwhelming backing of the French people. On 21 December a national plebiscite was held, and by 7,350,000 votes to a mere 650,000 France expressed her approval of the prince-president's acts.

A new constitution became immediately necessary and was quickly drawn up. The President of the Republic was to hold office for ten years. Under him was to be a Council of State, a silent body whose debates were never made public but which had the crucial role of proposing legislation to the Legislative Assembly. There was also to be a Senate of dignitaries and notables. The new constitution thus approached that of a monarchy, giving considerably greater power and security to the president than would be usual under a republic.

Clearly, Louis' position was now firmly established, but would the European powers accept a Bonapartist on what had, for all practical purposes, become the 'throne' of France?

Louis Napoleon, elated with success, had already observed to the Sardinian Prime Minister, 'Now I can do what I want, I shall do something for Italy', and it was the fear that a revived Bonapartism in Europe might reawaken nationalist feelings among subject Italians, Poles, Hungarians and Slavs that most alarmed the rulers of Austria and Russia. Even in Britain, where there was admiration for the president's liberal and democratic ideas, there was also concern that a Bonaparte was again in command in France, placed there by the force of arms and known to be looking for military glory. His frequently asserted claim that 'the Empire is Peace' seemed genuine enough, however. Britain recognized the new president, Russia and Austria remained suspicious but had no way of intervening.

Precisely a year after the seizure of power, on 2 December 1852, a hereditary

Empire replaced the Republic which had had nothing republican about it except its name. In a strange calm a new empire was born and a new figure stepped onto the European stage. Still not acceptable socially, the new emperor was not permitted to marry into any of the legitimate royal families of Europe but in January 1853 took as wife a beautiful young Spanish countess, Eugénie of Montijo.

The aristocratic empire

For the first few years of his reign the emperor ruled personally and with a strong hand. Normal political life practically ceased: the opposition was either cowed or exiled, and the few who, like Victor Hugo, dared to raise their voice against 'the Little Napoleon' made no headway.

The press was effectively muzzled, and any criticism of the emperor quickly resulted in suppression. Even elections, which had been the great national preoccupation of recent years, ceased to be of much interest when only loyal candidates were able to stand. The local prefects kept a complete control over the conduct of election campaigns, to such good effect that when opposition candidates tried to present themselves they found it impossible to hire halls for meetings or to find printers who would publish their literature. Prefects openly canvassed for the 'official' candidates, factory owners warned their workers to 'vote properly'. Political passion had, for the time being, been suffocated.

In some respects the France of the early empire seemed to turn back to the attitudes and values of Louis Philippe. If political life was sterile and unrewarding, at least in the new stability of domestic conditions one might make money and enjoy oneself. It was an era of heavy investment and great banking development, the government leading the way by financing enormous public works, road and railway building programmes. Paris itself was to be reconstructed, the Prefect of the Seine, Baron

Haussmann, being commissioned to prepare plans to build the most magnificent capital in Europe, a city to dazzle the foreigners who had scorned the elected emperor.

Great new boulevards were cut through the heart of Paris, at once giving a plan and symmetry to the capital which it had never had before and, in the process, destroying many of the slums which had disfigured it. The wide roads with their tarmac surfaces were beautiful and impressive: at the same time, they made army manoeuvres easier and deprived Parisians of the paving-stones which rebellious mobs had been accustomed to fling from behind the barricades. Haussmann's remodelling of Paris therefore had many motives – economic, social, aesthetic and military. Not least important, it provided employment for those evicted from the National Workshops and gave immense opportunities to investors, speculators and businessmen of many kinds.

Paris in the 1850s was a city of feverish activity and frivolous gaiety, admirably

Above, the fashionable Boulevard des Italiens. Musée Carnavalet, Paris.

Top, contemporary print depicting Felice Orsini's attempt to assassinate Napoleon III and the Empress, 14 January 1858: after the assassination – Orsini had been disgusted at Napoleon's failure to assist Italian unification, which the Emperor had supported as a young man – Napoleon's interest in Italian affairs revived.

Top left, Victor Hugo (1802–84): a Napoleonist until 1848, Hugo was elected to the National Assembly in 1848 and again in 1849 but fled the country after the 1851 coup.

Opposite right, the Emperor Napoleon III and Eugénie in their wedding costume.

Opposite left, deputies being arrested during Louis Napoleon's coup d'état, 2 December 1851: popular in the provinces, Napoleon met scarcely any resistance in Paris, still smarting from the violence of the previous few years.

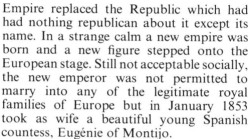

reflected in the popular light operas of Offenbach, *The Tales of Hoffmann* and *La Belle Hélène*. The reputation of Paris as a city of easy virtue, if not positive wickedness, dates especially from this period, when the emperor of the French could devote time to playing Blind Man's Buff or, less innocently, to his mistresses.

For many of the working class, too, times were good, with regular employment, booming trade and rising wages. For that growing section who now had some margin of income over necessary expenditure there were new pleasures, new recreations, great new stores like 'Bon Marché' where customers could find all that they needed at moderate prices under one roof or could simply come to stare.

The countryside also shared in the prosperity of the capital. Roads and railways brought a new mobility to people and goods, enabling farm produce to be sold profitably in the growing towns and bringing the benefits of civilization to formerly remote areas. Agriculture was still the mainstay of the French economy, some two-thirds of the whole population still living on the land and cultivating their small peasant farms. For them, the political events of the last few years had been remote, almost irrelevant, but now they could take pride in a revived empire and share in the benefits of a programme of national development. Even the sandy wastes of the Landes area in western France came to be planted with fir trees to provide pit props for the expanding coalmines, while in the Alps the daring project was begun of driving a tunnel through the heart of Mont Cenis.

But for the Second Empire to become a complete reality it needed to spread its wings beyond the confines of France and establish a colonial hegemony. It was in pursuance of such an object and in the face of ridicule and scepticism by Britain, that in 1859 work was begun on cutting the Suez Canal in Egypt. A sea route to India and the East could bring back the Mediterranean into importance in world trade, could revive the great ports of southern France and begin to move back the balance of maritime power from the British-dominated Atlantic. With these great purposes in view the foreign policy of the empire was bent towards extending French influence throughout the Mediterranean world – intervention in Italian affairs, the pacification of Algeria and the defence of the Holy Places in Palestine which involved her in a victorious war against Russia. With the signing of the Treaty of Paris in 1856, France had successfully reasserted her place in the conduct of European affairs.

The Orsini affair

For the first few years the reign of the new emperor was undisturbed by the political crises which had come to be regarded as almost the normal condition of French life. The opposition party made some small gains in the elections of 1857, though insufficient to constitute any real threat to the security of the government which was bringing an unaccustomed measure of order and prosperity to the country. In 1858, however, a more serious event occurred. As a young *Carbonari* before his accession to power, Louis Napoleon had vowed that he would help the Italians to liberate their country from the Austrians: now, as emporer, he was more prudent and cautious, seeming to betray his Italian friends. One of the most extreme of the Italian nationalists, Orsini, was driven to make an attempt on the emperor's life, his bombs killing or wounding over a hundred people. Napoleon himself escaped injury.

The 'Orsini Affair' was, however, influential in shaping French attitudes. At home, the attempt provided the government with good grounds for tightening security by permitting the prefects to deport any suspect by simple adminstrative order. Over 300 Frenchmen were so exiled on evidence which would scarcely have satisfied a court of law. France quietly acquiesced in a policy which some regarded as a move towards autocracy, even dictatorship, on the part of an all-powerful emperor.

The liberal empire

Unaccountably, however, Napoleon suddenly retracted his policy and proceeded to introduce a series of liberal reforms. In fact, it seems likely that it was the growing opposition from Catholic and the industrialists, who had formerly supported the regime, that forced the change. Increasingly, Napoleon had to seek an alliance with the political left as the right deserted him.

The Catholics he had offended by insufficiently backing the temporal power of the Pope in Italy. Industrialists were claiming that the Free Trade Treaty signed with Britain in 1860, which allowed the passage of goods without duty between the two countries, would ruin the French economy. Napoleon, ahead of his people, had become a confirmed free trader, impressed by the success of the policy in England, but most French industrialists believed that their continued prosperity depended on maintaining the protection afforded by the tariff system which their goods enjoyed in the home market. Now the two disparate groups made common cause in resentment against the dictatorial aspects of the regime which they had once been only too ready to support.

The Catholics were the first to launch an open attack against the emperor in the columns of the influential Catholic newspaper *L'Univers*. The government responded by suppressing the religious society of St Vincent de Paul. But the chief power of the Church lay in its control over the schools, and the Minister of Education now decided to attack this. His real desire – to establish a system of state elementary schools throughout the land – proved impracticable, but he did set up the lycèes (secondary schools) for girls in direct competition with the convents and himself planned a course of ethics and morals to replace instruction in religion. The great struggle between church and state – a central issue in European politics since the Middle Ages – had been reopened.

The emperor therefore had to fall back on his old enemies, the liberal Republicans, and in order to gain their support concessions were required. An amnesty was granted for many political offenders, freedom of speech was allowed to deputies and the right of publication of parliamentary debates. In the general election of 1863 the opposition polled two million votes, and Thiers, the liberal, was returned to office. The new policy also made a greater appeal to the working classes, and trade unions were granted the legal right to strike in 1864. Two years previously, permission had been granted for a delegation of working men to go to London to meet English workers: out of this meeting was born in 1864 the International Working Men's Association which, under the influence of Karl Marx, was to become a powerful force in international socialism.

Once again, the pattern of events which had shaped French history ever since the revolution of 1789 reasserted itself. Autocracy could survive so long as the people were content: when opposition appeared, concessions had to be made which only served to demonstrate how little freedom the people really had and it whetted the appetite for more.

In other ways, too, the strength of the regime was ebbing. The strong men of 1848, including the emperor himself, were now older and feebler than they had been twenty years before. Foreign affairs had not gone with the flair and success that an empire seemed to demand, and, in particular, France had been obliged to watch with growing concern the rise to power of Prussia and her overwhelming defeat of Austria on the battlefields of Sadowa in 1866. The policy of concession in no way abated the mounting opposition to the regime, which became increasingly dangerous as Republicans and Socialists sank their former differences and became reconciled in a common opposition to the policies of the Empire. The failing power of the government was amply demonstrated in the elections of 1867 when, despite all efforts to gain support, its majority was drastically reduced and the combined opposition of Catholics, Republicans and Socialists polled more than 3,000,000 votes. Further concessions to the freedom of the press and of assembly followed in a desperate attempt to curry favour.

For the last two years of his reign the emperor was the subject of ridicule, even public dislike. One of the consequences of the now free press was an outpouring of satirical comment on Napoleon and his government, most brilliantly handled by the journalist Rochefort in *La Lanterne*. By 1869, when in fresh general elections the opposition polled almost half the total votes, the situation had become extremely dangerous; either the Empire must make some drastic bid for popularity or must quickly fall.

At this critical point in French affairs, help suddenly came from an unexpected quarter. One of the Republican opposition to be elected was Emile Ollivier, at first a bitter critic of the emperor who later came to support him. By 1869 he found himself prime minister. His responsibility, as he saw it, was to the Assembly rather than to the emperor, and here he gradually built up a powerful group of moderate liberals which became known as 'the Third Party'.

By 1870 it seemed that a parliamentary Empire modelled on the lines of the British political system might at last become a reality. A new constitution was framed on liberal principles, submitted to a national plebiscite, and accepted, to the immense relief of the emperor, by nearly 6,000,000 votes. The Republican-Socialist opposition was crushed, and the Empire seemed even more secure, and rooted in popular support than it had been in 1852. 'On whichever side we look,' declared the new prime minister,

'there is an absence of troublesome questions; at no moment has the maintenance of peace in Europe been better secured.' Precisely one month later a war broke out which was to sweep away Ollivier, Louis Napoleon and the Empire and to result in the appearance of a powerful, united Germany on the stage of Europe.

Above, Émile Ollivier (1825–1913), the liberal deputy chosen in January 1870 to head a parliamentary government under Napoleon: he was dismissed seven months later in the wake of Prussian victories in the Franco-Prussian War.

Opposite, rebuilding the rue de Rivoli in Paris, 1859: as Prefect of the Seine département from 1853, Georges Haussmann (1809–91) was responsible for rebuilding Paris; he installed a sewerage system and the water supply, built a new opera house and created the Bois de Boulogne.

Chapter 5

The United States, 1800–1865

When the United States achieved independence from England in 1783 she was beset with numerous problems. Most important was the need to establish a form of government which would effectively unite the thirteen colonies scattered along the eastern edge of the North American continent. Vital also was the need to pursue a foreign policy which would prevent the European powers from taking advantage of American weakness to win control of large areas of the new country.

A massive step towards achieving national unity had been taken when the new constitution had been put into effect in 1789, but even yet the United States was vulnerable to foreign powers. Although her economic prosperity was increasing rapidly, the United States had extremely weak military forces, and many of her citizens were opposed to any increase in military power. The outbreak of the wars of the French Revolution gave the United States the opportunity to take advantage of European divisions but also posed the danger that the extensive American maritime commerce would involve her directly in the wars.

In the 1790s the United States first had a crisis in her relations with Great Britain which almost led to war and then from 1798 to 1800 engaged in an undeclared war at sea against the French. Fortunately for Thomas Jefferson, who was elected president in 1800, he took office in March 1801 at a time when American foreign relations had improved strikingly as a result of a temporary cessation of the European wars.

Thomas Jefferson

When Jefferson assumed the presidency in 1801 he had long been a towering figure on the American scene. If he had never been president, his name would still have lived as the author of the Declaration of Independence. His career as governor of Virginia had not been successful, but as a legislator in that state his achievements were massive. They included the Virginia statute for religious freedom, the codification of the law (including reforms in the laws of inheritance) and a passionate espousal of the expansion of educational opportunity.

As secretary of state in President Washington's first administration, Jefferson had become leader of a group who were to form the Democratic-Republican party. It was as leader of this party that Jefferson came into office in 1801. The Federalists, who under the inspiration of Alexander Hamilton had held office in the 1790s, had accomplished the major task of welding a nation from disparate states, but it was Jefferson and his Democratic-Republicans who were prepared to show the faith in popular government that had been expressed in the American Revolution.

Although Jefferson was obliged in practice to modify some of the ideas he had expressed in his public writings and letters, the influence of his philosophy of government was to be felt throughout the nineteenth and into the twentieth century. Jefferson expressed a belief in democratic majority rule, tempered by a respect for the rights of the minority. He also believed in the subordination of military to civil authority, in strict economy in government and in an educated electorate. He felt that a healthy nation was based on a strong group of active, educated yeoman farmers. He distrusted cities and urban mobs and hoped that the United States would be governed by a natural elite, an elite that would be given the opportunity to rise to the top through education and which would be elected and supported by an educated electorate.

Jefferson disliked slavery but as a slave-owning Virginian was unsure whether the negro was equal in body and mind to the white man. But for his time and place,

Jefferson demonstrated a remarkable belief in man's capacity to govern himself. When it is remembered that he was also an active scientist, architect and inventor it is clear that few nations have ever been blessed with a man of his calibre to guide their early years.

The Democratic-Republican victory in 1800 inaugurated a period of rule which lasted until the break-up of the party in the late 1820s. The years from 1801 to 1825 were those of the 'Virginia Dynasty'. All three presidents in these years were from Virginia: Jefferson until 1809, James Madison for two terms until 1817, and James Monroe from 1817 to 1825. The Federalists never held control of the national government again after 1801. This failure was not only because of the greater faith of the Democratic-Republicans in the democratic process but also because the best ideas of the Federalists were adopted by the Democratic-Republican party.

As president, Jefferson soon discovered that he could not in practice grant the individual states the freedom he had argued for in theory and that his advocacy of strict construction of the constitution had been far more practicable for a party in opposition than for a party in power. He did not make any basic changes in conducting the executive branch of the government.

Jefferson's first term was a triumph. The pause in the European war from 1801 to 1803 meant that American ships could sail the seas unmolested, and the increased trade produced increased revenue from the customs. Jefferson's secretary of the treasury, Albert Gallatin, was thus able to eliminate

the excise taxes long opposed by the Democratic-Republicans, balance the budget and even reduce the national debt. He was aided in this by the cuts in the military forces which accorded well with the general Jeffersonian philosophy of government as well as finance.

Not all went as well as Jefferson hoped. He was obliged to fight a short and exotic naval war against Tripoli to protect American shipping in the Mediterranean, and at home he was ultimately rebuffed in an attack on the Federalists entrenched in the federal judiciary. But the setbacks were overshadowed by the triumph of the Louisiana Purchase, a triumph which owed as much to luck as to judgement.

The Louisiana Purchase

The American settlers who since the Revolution had been advancing across the Appalachians into the Mississippi Valley depended for their economic well-being on an export trade down the Ohio and Mississippi river systems to the Gulf of Mexico. This was the only practical way to find a market for bulk produce, but the trade was made difficult by the presence of the Spanish. They owned the territory west of the Mississippi, New Orleans and a strip of land eastwards along the Gulf through the southern parts of modern Mississippi and Alabama and the whole of modern Florida. From 1795 the United States had the right to ship goods through New Orleans and deposit them in that port before export, but this working relationship was threatened after 1800.

In 1800 Spain ceded the Louisiana Territory to France in exchange for warships and for territory in Italy. This Louisiana Territory was a vast area west of the Mississippi River, stretching north and northwest to the Canadian border and the Rockies. France had dreams of re-establishing her New World empire, and Louisiana would be the source of supplies for the sugar-rich West Indies. This French dream was to collapse within a few years. Since the 1790s the island of Santo Domingo had been in revolt. The slaves, believing that they too should share in liberty, equality and fraternity, had risen against their masters, and in the years after 1800, led by the great leader Toussaint L'Ouverture, they resisted French efforts to restore control. A whole French army was wiped out by yellow fever, and by 1803 Napoleon was ready to cut his losses and withdraw from the complicated New World situation.

Although France did not take over Louisiana from the Spanish in 1800, rumours of the change in ownership reached the United States in 1801, and by 1802 Jefferson knew that instead of impotent Spain the France of Napoleon was about to control the outlets of the United States on the Gulf. This fear was increased in the autumn of 1802 by the news that the right of deposit at New Orleans had been suspended. Although this action had been taken by Spain, it was naturally assumed that France was responsible. The Westerners now cried for war and the capture of New Orleans. To avoid military action Jefferson decided to attempt to buy access to the Gulf. In 1803 James Monroe was sent to join American

Above, New York street scene in the early nineteenth century. New York Historical Society.

Opposite, the Capitol building, Washington, in about 1800: Washington was designated the nation's administrative capital in 1790 not least because its geographical position meant it could be claimed by neither north nor south. The government moved there in 1800, but construction work proceeded very slowly. The Capitol was extended in 1851 when chambers for the Senate and House of Representatives were added.

minister Robert Livingston in France with instructions to buy at least New Orleans and if possible the Floridas. Nothing was said about the vast area of the Louisiana Territory, although Jefferson showed a definite interest in the region at this time by sending Lewis and Clark to explore all the way west to the Pacific.

In France Napoleon had decided to sell the whole of Louisiana. Napoleon in 1803 did not want to send another army to Santo Domingo. It was clear that the war with England would soon be renewed (England declared war in May), Napoleon needed money for a European campaign, and he could not defend New Orleans against the British fleet. Although the American envoys had been empowered to spend no more than $10,000,000 for New Orleans and the Floridas, they agreed to pay $15,000,000 for New Orleans and the whole Louisiana Territory, with no mention of the Floridas. When Jefferson heard the news he had qualms regarding the constitutionality of the transaction, but his cabinet persuaded him not to ask for a constitutional amendment. The territory of the United States had been nearly doubled and the foundation laid for expansion westwards to the pacific.

Maritime problems

United States foreign policy in the years from 1805 to 1812 was dominated by the dangers presented to American ships and seamen by European maritime warfare. Jefferson's triumphant first term was succeeded by a second term of major disappointments, and James Madison, who had done so much to frame the American government, had to serve as president in a time of foreign crisis which ill suited him. These were decisive years in the experiment of American independence, for once the United States had weathered this crisis it

was not until the American Civil War that the United States was again in such danger.

The basic problem confronting the United States in these years was her desire to trade at a time when Europe was engaged in general war. By her 1807 Orders in Council Great Britain declared that United States ships could trade with the possessions of Napoleon if they first came to England to be licensed. By his Berlin and Milan Decrees of 1806 and 1807 Napoleon declared Great Britain in a state of blockade and announced that neutral ships which obeyed British regulations would be liable to seizure. In theory, American ships were liable to be seized whatever they did. In practice, both sides were anxious for some trade and connived at a variety of evasions. Their safety depended however, on the whims of Great Britain and France.

Although Napoleon inflicted some damage on American commerce, the British were for the most part in command of the seas, and the weight of their restrictions was felt much more heavily, particularly as Great Britain was the old enemy of the Revolution. Moreover, the British particularly infuriated American opinion by their practice of impressment. Many British deserters found service in American merchantmen, and the British claimed the right to stop these ships and seize any British deserters found on board. British captains, if they lacked hands to man their ships, also frequently removed American seamen. Several thousand Americans were impressed, and this practice was viewed as a particular outrage by American citizens who had fought a revolution to establish their freedom from Great Britain.

In the years after 1803, as the war between Great Britain and France became more intense, difficulties at sea increased, and in June 1807 a crisis which seemed likely to lead to war developed between the United States and Great Britain. In stopping an

American frigate, the *Chesapeake*, to search for British deserters, the British *Leopard* fired into her, killing American seamen. Many Americans demanded war, but Jefferson took steps to avoid it. His motivation was mixed. As a practical man he knew that the United States possessed extremely weak military forces, indeed he had reduced their effectiveness during his administration and had no desire to risk the gains of independence in a risky war against Great Britain. As an idealist, Jefferson had long maintained that the United States should demonstrate to the decadent powers of Europe that countries could attain their ends without war. His solution to the dilemma in 1807 was to adopt the idea, used by the American colonies before the Revolution, of economic coercion as an alternative to war.

In December 1807, at Jefferson's request, Congress passed an embargo, which confined all American ships to port and prohibited all exports. Earlier Congress had passed a non-importation law against selected imports. Jefferson hoped that British industry would starve for lack of American cotton and that British manufacturers, who depended so heavily on the American market, would force their government to remove their restrictions on American commerce to obtain a renewal of American trade.

Jefferson's experiment in economic coercion failed because in 1808 Great Britain was not prepared to make concessions which might aid France, even though these would also ease the plight of the manufacturing districts. Moreover, Jefferson was unfortunate in that Napoleon's invasion of the Iberian peninsula threw open the Spanish and Portuguese colonies in Latin America to British goods and helped to offset the losses in trade to North America which resulted from the embargo.

Shortly before he left office in March 1809 Jefferson repealed the embargo, and in the next three years the United States floundered. The main measure of economic coercion had failed. The alternative was war, but with the country divided, and with inadequate military forces, it seemed likely that war would only add to America's problems. Also France's hostility made it unclear whether the United States should fight one, both or neither of the great European belligerents.

Uncertain of how to proceed, the United States first followed the embargo with a weaker method of economic coercion (the Non-Intercourse Act against Great Britain and France) and then in 1810 threw open her trade, promising, however, a friendly neutrality to that power which would remove its restrictions on American commerce. Napoleon took advantage of this offer (although in reality still seizing American shipping), and early in 1811 the United States resumed non-intercourse against Great Britain.

The War of 1812

Having failed to acheive her ends by peaceful means, the United States at last began to move towards war. This policy reversal was made easier because since 1807 the British in Canada, fearing an American invasion, had supplied and organized the Indians on the frontiers of the United States. This gave another grievance to Americans, who became convinced that Great Britain would not respect American ships and seamen unless compelled to do so by an American invasion of Canada.

From 1810 an enthusiastic group of young men in Congress – the War Hawks – began to press for war to save national honour and to force Great Britain to respect American maritime rights. Their leader was young Henry Clay of Kentucky. This move for war met determined resistance from the Federalists, who wanted to continue trading and who believed with good reason that American commerce would suffer still more if war was declared. They also feared Napoleonic ambitions more than they disliked their old colonial enemy, Great Britain.

Eventually, however, in June 1812 the Democratic-Republicans, led by young men from the West and the South, obtained enough votes for war. Ironically, two days before the United States declared war, the British government had intimated in London that the Orders in Council would be withdrawn; this news was not known in the United States for several weeks.

The Federalist opposition continued into the war itself. Many in New England would give no support to the war effort, and many even supplied the British in Canada. In December 1814 in the Hartford Convention the New Englanders discussed the possibility of extreme action, possibly even secession. Eventually, however, they settled for a list of proposed constitutional amendments designed to restrict the power of the South.

American strategy in the war was to invade and conquer Canada and to use this as a pawn to force maritime concessions from Great Britain. Many thought, wrongly, that the conquest of Canada would be accomplished with little difficulty. Even those who argued for war were prepared to admit that the United States had little hope at sea. The tiny American navy was overshadowed by the great British naval power. Forgotten even in America was the fighting quality of individual American ships and the numerous merchantmen that could be fitted out as privateers to raid British commerce.

In the first year of the war the British public was shocked, and that in the United States surprised, by American victories over British frigates in single-ship engagements – the *Constitution* over the *Guerrière*, the *United States* over the *Macedonian* and the *Constitution* over the *Java*. These were great morale boosters for the American people, but by the summer of 1813 British ships were placing a tight blockade around the American coast and for the rest of the war effectively controlled American trade. American privateers still escaped, however, and until the end of the war seized British merchantmen.

Above, illustration from the diary of an expedition member of Lewis and Clark holding a council with the Indians.

Top, the US frigate Constitution *engaging the* Java *off the coast of Brazil, December 1812: after her masts and rigging had been shot away, the* Java *surrendered. This was one of several engagements in which the young American navy performed brilliantly against the far more experienced British. US Naval Academy, Annapolis, Maryland.*

Opposite left and right, William Clark (1770–1838) and Meriwether Lewis (1774–1809), who were sent by Jefferson to explore the territories acquired by the Louisiana Purchase: their expedition, which took eighteen months, reached the Pacific and blazed a trail in the northwest that settlers were soon to follow.

The invasion of Canada failed disastrously. All the efforts of 1812 and 1813 produced only slight inroads into British territory. By the close of 1813 the United States faced a tight blockade around her coasts and the prospect of heavy reinforcements for the British military forces. As the power of Napoleon collapsed in the spring of 1814 the British had ships and troops ready for transfer to America. In 1814 it was no longer a question of the United States conquering Canada in order to force a change in British maritime policies; the United States was now in danger of defeat and dismemberment. That she managed to avoid this fate was, like the Louisiana Purchase, the result of chance just as much as of good management.

In August it appeared all was lost for the United States. After landing in Chesapeake Bay a British force routed the Americans at Bladensburg, marched into Washington D.C., and burned the public buildings. With its trade shattered, the country was bankrupt and unable any longer to meet the interest on the national debt. In the New England states some people were talking of secession, and veteran British armies were preparing to invade in the north and south.

The sudden change in affairs was so remarkable that it seemed to the Americans that their nation was blessed by divine providence. In September the British left Washington and tested the defences of Baltimore. It held firm. The British commanding general, Robert Ross, was killed in a skirmish, and although the British navy bombarded Fort McHenry it resisted attack and inspired the writing of the song that eventually became the American national anthem. The British army decided not to attack and withdrew to the fleet.

In this same month of September 1814

ten thousand British troops marched south along Lake Champlain. It seemed that nothing could stop them, but at the naval battle of Plattsburg Bay on Lake Champlain the American fleet totally defeated the British. The British army, fearing that its line of communications could now be severed, halted the invasion and then withdrew to Canada.

The repulse of the British was decisive because in Ghent British and American commissioners were discussing the terms of peace. The British had been delaying, hoping and expecting that news of major victories would force the Americans to grant large territorial concessions in any peace treaty. When the news of the British withdrawals arrived in Europe, it helped to persuade the government to make peace. On 24 December 1814, the Treaty of Ghent was signed. There were no major changes in the treaty; it merely brought the war to an end. The main reason for fighting had disappeared with the end of the war in Europe.

Although the war was over, one major and important battle was still to be fought. There was no way for the British to stop the army that was already assembled to attack New Orleans. The British failed to advance swiftly when first landing near the city in December, and by the time they finally attacked on 8 January it was against entrenched American positions and troops well commanded by Major-General Andrew Jackson. As the British advanced across the flat ground they were shattered by the American fire. When they withdrew their total casualties amounted to over 2,000; the Americans had suffered little more than seventy. The British commander, Wellington's brother-in-law Edward Pakenham, had been killed.

The 'new nationalism'

The year 1815 was a turning point in American as well as in European history. The miraculous survival in 1814 and the news of the remarkable victory at New Orleans sent a surge of enthusiasm through the American people. The founding fathers had been convinced that in creating a new republican nation they were setting an example for the rest of the world, that they were showing the world that a nation could be safe, prosperous and democratic. Now, after 1815, as American prosperity increased, a belief in the ultimate greatness of the United States became very strong among the American people. A surge of nationalism swept through the country, and although eventually the national spirit faced a major clash with growing sectionalism in the South the years after 1815 saw an enhancement of national power.

The Democratic-Republicans now showed themselves willing to use the power of the federal government in a manner which they had attacked when earlier proposed by the Federalists. In 1816 they conceded that the developing American industry needed protection by placing a moderate tariff on imports, and they also completely reversed Jefferson's earlier stand when they agreed to charter the Second Bank of the United States. Some Democratic-Republicans, particularly those from the West, also argued that the federal government should spend money on internal improvements to improve the nation's communication system. Congress was almost evenly split on this proposal, and Presidents Madison, Monroe and Jackson all vetoed internal improvement bills on the grounds that they believed such expenditures unconstitutional.

As the Democratic-Republicans espoused an increasing number of policies that had once been Federalist, they gradually became the completely dominant party. James Monroe became president in 1817 after an easy victory and three years later in 1820 won re-election with only one electoral vote cast against him.

The enhancement of federal power that took place in these years was aided considerably by the attitudes and decisions of John Marshall of Virginia, who was Chief Justice of the Supreme Court from 1801 until 1835. Marshall consistently interpreted the American Constitution and the relationship between the central government and the states in such a manner as to enhance federal power. Although he was roundly criticized, particularly in the southern states, his work endured and was a most important ingredient in creating a powerful central government.

The power of the federal government was developing rapidly in the first three decades of the nineteenth century, but the problems that confronted it were also increasing with remarkable speed. Indeed, the question was

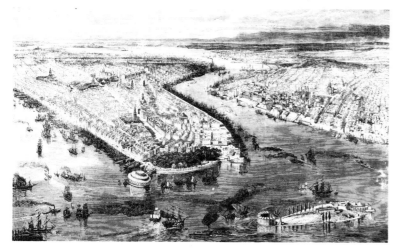

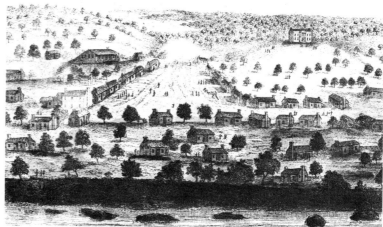

arising whether the powers of the central government could increase rapidly enough to cope with the problems presented on the one hand by a nation that was constantly expanding in size and on the other by an area of the nation – the South – that was becoming particularly sensitive to its own particular problems. The westward advance of American pioneers, while helping to create a nation that spanned the continent, also complicated the organization of an efficient national government and accentuated the already serious difficulties with the South.

Westward expansion

In the years from the beginning of the seventeenth century to the Revolution the American people had pushed inland only as far as the Appalachian mountain barrier. In the years immediately before the Revolution they were just crossing into the modern states of Kentucky and Tennessee. Although

it had taken 150 years to move 200 miles inland, within 100 years after the Revolution a network of states and territories extended across the whole 3,000 miles of the American continent.

From its inception the American government had decided not to establish a colonial regime beyond the Appalachians but rather to create new states which would enter the Union on an equal basis with the older states. Under this arrangement the thirteen original states were soon outnumbered by the new admissions of the nineteenth century: five new states were created before 1815, another six by 1821, seven more between 1836 and 1850, and five more between 1858 and 1864.

This expansion was made possible by a remarkable increase in the American population. From nearly 4,000,000 in 1790 the population increased to over 9,600,000 by 1820, to over 17,000,000 by 1840, and to over 31,400,000 by 1860. The great natural increase was aided by the immigrants who poured into the United States during the

Above, Austin, Texas, in 1840: Texas was admitted to the Union in 1845; its rich farmlands soon attracted settlers from the east.

Above left, view of Manhattan from the south, 1855: New York was the destination of almost all immigrants to the USA, among whom Germans and Irish predominated during the first decades after independence.

Top, James Monroe (1758–1831, president 1817–25): he recognized the independence of the Spanish American republics and in 1823 laid down in the Monroe Doctrine that 'the American continents ... are henceforth not to be considered as subjects for future colonization by any European power.'

Top left, the Battle of New Orleans, 8 January 1815, at which American forces, commanded by Major-General Andrew Jackson, later to become president, defeated the British. The War of 1812 was the last occasion on which the United States had to defend itself on its own territory against foreign intervention.

Opposite, Oliver Perry capturing a British naval force on Lake Erie during the War of 1812.

71

nineteenth century, attracted by the prospect of land, economic prosperity and a degree of religious and political freedom unknown in much of Europe. As in colonial days great numbers of immigrants came from England, Scotland, Wales, northern Ireland and Germany, but during the first half of the nineteenth century they also entered in increasing numbers from Scandinavia and from southern Ireland.

In the years after 1815 the younger sons of farmers pushed west to find new lands and new opportunities. The new states they established pressed the federal government for expenditures on internal improvements and for more liberal land policies, and many in the east resented these new areas which were reducing the power of the older states, attracting eastern population, and asking for larger expenditures of federal tax money. This east-west division was complicated by an increasing rift between northern and southern areas of the Atlantic seaboard and by a different type of western expansion north and south of the Ohio River in the Mississippi Valley.

The South and slavery

Although indentured servants had been a more important labour force than slaves in early colonial days, slavery had become an integral part of the American scene by the time of the American Revolution. Of an American population of nearly 4,000,000 in 1790 some 700,000 were slaves. The great majority of these slaves were employed on the plantations of the southern states.

In 1808 Jefferson's administration abolished the foreign slave trade but did not interfere with slavery itself nor with internal trade in slaves. The desire of many in the South to retain a system of slavery was strengthened in the first decades of the nineteenth century by the opening up of the rich lands of the southwest and the expansion of the British cotton market. Those who had once thought that slavery was likely to be economically unprofitable on old, worn-out tobacco lands were hopeful of rich profits from the cotton lands of Mississippi and Alabama, and even the upper South could profit from this by selling slaves to the new areas.

Slavery had already been extended into Kentucky and Tennessee in the Revolutionary period, and after 1800 increasing numbers of slaves were taken into the lower southwest to what is now Mississippi and Alabama and after 1803 to Louisiana. This movement grew after 1815 and produced great problems of future political allegiance. There was no doubt that the southerners expanding south of the Ohio River would be able to take slaves with them, and even within the bounds of the modern state of Louisiana it was clear that slavery would be allowed to continue, but for the vast area of the Louisiana Purchase north of

Louisiana there was considerably more doubt. In the Northwest Ordinance of 1787 slavery had been prohibited between the Ohio and the Mississippi Rivers, and some in the north were beginning to question the desirability of the further expansion of a slave system.

The question involved far more than simply the continuation or restriction of the expansion of slavery. It had major political and economic implications. Those states who had large numbers of slaves were engaged for the most part in the production of extensive agricultural surpluses for sale overseas and in the north. The economy of the South was much less diverse than that of the northeastern and middle states. Accordingly, the Southerners wanted to avoid high tariffs and generally feared too great an addition of power to the central government, which if too powerful might threaten slavery itself and with it the whole social system of the South.

In view of this, the extension of slavery to newly created states became of great importance to the southern states, for they wanted to be quite sure that they could not be outvoted in Congress. In the House they were falling behind, because northern population was growing more rapidly than southern, but in the Senate, where there were two senators from each state regardless of size, they could hope to maintain a balance.

The first major crises on the question of the expansion of slavery arose in 1819 when Missouri applied for admission to the Union, and representative James Tallmadge of New York proposed an amendment which would provide for the gradual abolition of slavery in the new state. At this time there were thirteen slave and thirteen free states in the Union, and the issue of slave expansion was debated bitterly both in

Congress and in the country at large.

The compromise that was eventually worked out after extensive debate did not remove the causes of difficulty but merely delayed the clash. It was agreed that Missouri could enter the Union as a slave state, but that Maine, which had long wanted to separate from Massachusetts, would be admitted as a free state. In the future, the dividing line between slave and free states west of the Mississippi would be set at 36° 30′.

The quarrel over the admission of Missouri to the Union made it quite obvious that the old parties were falling apart and that sectional splits were posing a major threat to national unity. These tendencies became particularly clear in the presidential election of 1824. Although the Federalists could present no real opposition to the Democratic-Republicans, the latter party had four candidates in the race, representing different sections of the country: John Quincy Adams of Massachusetts, William H. Crawford of Georgia, Henry Clay of Kentucky and Andrew Jackson of Tennessee. Adams had made a brilliant reputation as secretary of state, Crawford was the natural successor to the Virginia dynasty, and Henry Clay was becoming increasingly prominent as a spokesman for a policy of economic nationalism; his 'American System' called for high tariffs, federal expenditure on internal improvements and a strong Bank of the United States.

Andrew Jackson was a new type in the race for the American presidency. A Tennessee settler, he had made his local reputation as a lawyer and politician but achieved national fame as an Indian fighter and a legendary reputation as the victor over the British at the Battle of New Orleans. As a plantation owner and leading Tennessee figure, he was never the man of the people that his backers proclaimed him to be, but he was able to win general national support.

Although Jackson gained the most electoral votes, no candidate had an absolute majority in the 1824 election, and so it was thrown into the House of Representatives. There Henry Clay gave his support to John Quincy Adams, who was second in electoral votes, and Adams gained the presidency. John Quincy Adams, son of the second president, was a man of many talents, but he had an unfortunate presidency. His opponents charged him with making a 'corrupt bargain' with Clay, and the Jacksonians immediately began to make preparations for the 1828 election. The Democratic-Republican party had fallen apart, and out of the supporters of Jackson arose the Democratic party of the 1830s.

In the 1828 election Jackson gained popular support because of his military reputation, but he also had influential backing from the new entrepreneurs of the west who were anxious to end eastern dominance and special Southern strength through the vice-presidential candidate John

C. Calhoun and the assumption that a Tennessee plantation owner would be sympathetic to the Southern point of view. Jackson won a resounding victory in 1828, and to the easterners long established in government positions in Washington his victory was looked upon as a disaster: a backwoodsman was to end the rule of eighteenth-century aristocrats. This feeling was increased at his inauguration when his supporters crowded noisily and tumultuously into the White House.

The Jackson era

Andrew Jackson showed himself more willing to enhance the powers of the presidency than any earlier president. He used his veto power more regularly and showed himself quite willing to contend with Congress, the federal judiciary and the individual states. Instead of placing full reliance for advice on his official cabinet, he formed an unofficial 'kitchen cabinet' out of his most ardent supporters; they gave him the support of men who were entirely dependent on him for their power. In general, Jackson showed himself far more willing than any previous president to reward his followers with the spoils of office, even to the extent of removing previous office holders to make room for them.

Jackson's first term proved a surprise to many who had supported him in 1828. The Maysville veto in 1830 disappointed those

who had hoped that he would be willing to overcome any constitutional qualms concerning the expenditure of federal funds on internal improvements. But his major difficulties with his former supporters came from the South. Although the South had shared in the nationalistic enthusiasm of the immediate post-1815 years, disillusionment set in during the 1820s. The struggle over the admission of Missouri, Marshall's Supreme Court decisions and in particular the tariff question produced an increasing development of Southern sectionalism and resistance to federal policies. South Carolina assumed the leadership in this movement not only because of the calibre of her politicians but also because of the decline in her prosperity owing to the competition of the new, rich cotton lands of Alabama and Mississippi.

In 1816 many Southern congressmen, including John C. Calhoun, overcame their deep-seated hostility to commercial restrictions and in the cause of national prosperity voted for a moderate protective tariff. In the 1820s, feeling that national policies threatened Southern prosperity and a way of life, Calhoun led the Southerners in intense opposition to high tariffs. The increase in 1824 was strongly opposed, and in 1828 the tariff forced through Congress over Southern opposition was christened 'the tariff of abominations'. Calhoun anonymously wrote *The South Carolina Exposition and Protest* in which he argued for the

Above, illustration by the British caricaturist George Cruikshank of the celebrations at the White House on President Andrew Jackson's inauguration day: Jackson (1767–1845, president 1829–37) brought a new style to the presidency, one more in line with life on the western frontier than in the old-established eastern states.

Opposite, illustration entitled 'Selling Females by the Pound' from a book on slavery published in 1834: the South had primarily a one-crop, labour-intensive economy, and its advocacy of slavery rested at least partly on economic grounds.

doctrine of nullification: individual states would have the right to reject those laws of the federal government which they thought unconstitutional.

It was soon apparent that the alliance that had elected Jackson could not hold together once he was in office. Calhoun men in the cabinet soon clashed with the followers of Secretary of State Martin Van Buren, the New York politician who had done so much to build support for Jackson in that state and region. Tension between Jackson and Calhoun increased rapidly as it became clear that Jackson had a concept of national power which accorded ill with Calhoun's hopes for the South.

Indicative of the tension in the administration was the social crisis over Secretary of War John H. Eaton's marriage to Peggy O'Neale, a young woman who had been seen with Eaton before her sailor husband had died. Mrs Calhoun led the group who snubbed this daughter of a Washington tavern-keeper. Jackson's own wife Rachel had been attacked during the 1828 campaign, shortly before she died, and Jackson took up the cause of the Eatons. With such stresses and strains, it was not surprising that in 1831 Jackson reorganized the cabinet and reformed it without the Calhoun men.

The full crisis came in 1832 when Congress again passed a tariff much higher than that desired by the South. In November a South Carolina convention declared the tariffs of 1828 and 1832 'null and void'. Calhoun resigned as vice-president, and Jackson faced the greatest threat to federal power the country had yet known. He rose to the occasion in a manner which belied his own southern origin. He asked Congress for a Force Bill and made it clear that if necessary he would invade South Carolina to enforce the law.

Open hostilities were avoided by the desire, both in Congress and in South Carolina, to avoid if at all possible an open clash and by the efforts at compromise led by Henry Clay. In the spring of 1833 both the Force Bill and a compromise tariff bill passed Congress. The compromise tariff, called for a gradual reduction in duties over the next nine years. Once again, as in the Missouri Compromise, the ultimate problems had been left unsettled. This was made particularly clear when South Carolina rescinded her nullification of the tariffs but nullified the Force Bill, an important symbolic gesture even though the bill had by now become unnecessary.

The other major issue that beset Jackson in the election year of 1832 was the rechartering of the Second Bank of the United States. Since Nicholas Biddle had become president of the bank in 1823, this institution had assumed a vital role in the nation's finance and general economy, acting as a restraining force on local banks and gaining great power through its function as the government bank of deposit. The bank had made a great many enemies who for various reasons desired to see its power reduced.

Many of the rising financiers and entrepreneurs in the west and other regions of the country resented the power of the old-establishing ruling clique. To oppose the bank they formed a strange alliance with two very different groups: farmers who resented the restraining influence of the bank and who as debtors would have been happy if the local banks had created an inflationary situation and another group (Jackson leaned to this argument) who put their faith in hard cash and felt that banks merely lived on the work of others.

During Jackson's first term Biddle became fearful for the future of the bank and increased his lobbying activities. Some of his actions, such as advancing loans to congressmen, were of a dubious nature. Biddle was also involved in the political complications of Jackson's first term.

As the Democratic Party came into being under Jackson its main opposition at first was the alliance of Henry Clay and John Quincy Adams, men who in the 1832 election ran as the National Republicans. They supported the 'American System' of Henry Clay, and in looking for an issue for the 1832 election they seized upon the bank. Clay persuaded Biddle to apply for a recharter of his bank in 1832, although the old charter did not have to be renewed until 1836. In this way the Clay group hoped to force Jackson to take action which would hurt him in the 1832 election.

For a time everything proceeded as planned. Congress passed a recharter bill, and Jackson vetoed it with a ringing attack in which he charged that the bank was a monopoly which allowed the rich to oppress the poor. The National Republicans were delighted. They believed that Jackson could be defeated on this issue. Henry Clay ran for president as a National Republican and Jackson as a Democrat. There was also a third party – the anti-Masons – who originating in western New York as a rural movement distrusting the foreign and the unusual, had been used by the politicians as an anti-Jackson movement in a number of northeastern states. For the first time national political conventions nominated the candidates, and it soon became clear that Jackson had an excellent sense of popular attitudes. He won an easy victory.

In his second term Jackson's weaknesses in economic policies became more apparent. Rather than waiting for the bank to expire naturally, he determined to attack it directly by ending its function as a government bank of deposit. He began to distribute federal funds to a variety of state banks – the 'pet banks' – and essentially destroyed the effectiveness of the United States Bank as a check on local banking.

The American economy and the panic of 1837

The American economy had taken tremendous strides since 1815. In spite of a setback in 1819, the constantly expanding population, the abundant natural resources and a government which gave internal peace and opportunity combined to bring a flourishing economy. American shipping was still to be seen all over the world, and the large export trade in tabacco was soon surpassed by the cotton trade as the rich cotton lands of the southwest opened up in the years after 1815.

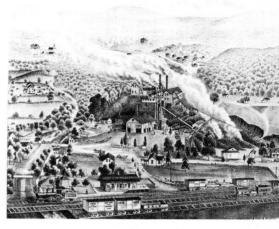

The real American industrial revolution was not to occur until after the Civil War, but already in the first decades of the century New England and the Middle States were laying a solid base for industrial expansion, particularly in textiles and the iron industries. Internally, communications had grown at a rapid rate. Before 1815 the country depended on river traffic and inefficient roads, but between 1816 and 1840 a whole network of canals (aided by the development of steamboats) boosted the economic expansion of the nation. The success of the Erie Canal (connecting the Hudson Valley and the Great Lakes), which was completed in 1825, inspired states to begin canals which could never hope to have the same trade and revenue potential. States borrowed money, confidently expecting to repay it by revenue earned from the finished canals. Many underestimated the costs of upkeep and were also placed in a difficult position by the steady growth of railroads in the 1830s. These were to expand with great rapidity in the following decades: by the end of the 1860s they spanned the continent.

In the late 1820s and in the early 30s the United States was in a boom period. Foreign commerce flourished, states feverishly built canals, railroads were beginning to be constructed, settlers poured west and land was being sold at an ever-increasing rate. As revenue flowed in from the tariff and land sales the nation had a strange new embarrassment: an excess of money. The national debt was rapidly being paid off (it was repaid by 1835), and yet even though facing a surplus the government had difficulty in reducing its revenue. The compromise tariff could not be tampered

with, and the price of public land could not be reduced without infuriating those easterners who already objected vehemently to the ease with which the eastern states were deprived of population.

In 1836 the government took steps to deal with the surplus. Henry Clay had long argued that his should be distributed to the states for them to use for internal improvements. This had been objected to on the grounds that it was unconstitutional, but in 1836 it was agreed that all funds over five million dollars in the Treasury on 1 January 1837 would be distributed to the states in four instalments. To avoid constitutional difficulties this would be a loan not a gift. The decision meant that federal funds on deposit all over the country would have to be transferred. In the summer of 1836 the Jackson administration also acted to curb the inflationary situation. Lands bought from the government would have to be paid for in gold and silver not banknotes.

By early 1837 there was a great pressure for specie (payment in coinage), and with the obvious signs of instability in the American economy foreign creditors began to press for payment of all outstanding obligations. The general pressure was too much to bear. Banks all over the United States suspended specie payments in the spring of 1837, and the financial panic that followed led to a prolonged depression whose effects were not thrown off until the 1840s. Then the economy again leaped forward.

The panic of 1837 inevitably delivered a blow to the fortunes of the Democratic Party, but fortunately for Jackson's supporters the election for president in 1836 took place in an atmosphere of continued

Above, view of the waterfront at Cincinnati, Ohio, in 1843, already an important manufacturing centre: the Ohio (on which Cincinatti stands) and Mississippi Rivers were important waterways, along which settlers travelled westwards and goods eastwards.

Top, iron works alongside the Erie Railroad in upstate New York: railroads played an enormous part in opening up the interior and in the growth of industry. The 1850s were the boom decade – more than 21,000 miles of line were built, bringing the total to over 30,000 – and by the 1860s a fully developed network was in existence in all the states east of the Mississippi.

Above left, View on the Erie Canal by J. W. Hill, 1830–32: opened in 1825, the Canal linked the Atlantic and the Hudson River with the Great Lakes, so opening up a new, fast route to the west. New York Public Library. Stokes Collection.

Opposite, The American Slave Market, 1852: for many southerners – though by no means all – slaves were a commodity to be bought and sold like any other. Chicago Historical Society, Illinois.

prosperity. Jackson had welded together an effective party while the opposition had difficulty in cementing a political alliance. By 1836 both anti-Masons and anti-Jackson southerners had joined with the National Republicans to form a new Whig party (named from its opposition to 'King Andrew I'), which was to exist into the early 1850s.

The basic weakness of the Whig party was its diversity and a lack of unified beliefs. The Southern plantation owners who joined the party because of their hatred of Jackson were also opponents of Clay's economic policies. In 1836 the Whigs ran several candidates, hoping to throw the election into the House of Representatives, but with the support of Jackson, and with a country not yet beset by economic difficulties, the Democrats won under their candidate, Martin Van Buren.

Van Buren had a most unfortunate presidency dominated by the economic distress of the country, and the Whigs were in an excellent position for the 1840 election. Their candidate was William Henry Harrison, a man in his late sixties, who had come to national fame as the victor over the Indians at Tippecanoe in 1811 and as a general in the war of 1812. Learning from the Jacksonian techniques, the Whigs ran Harrison as a western man of the people in the 'log cabin and hard cider' campaign. To gain southern support John Tyler of Virginia was given the vice-presidential nomination. The Whig candidates ran under the banner of 'Tippecanoe and Tyler Too.'

The panic was too great a liability for Van Buren to overcome, and the Whigs took office. Within a month Whig hopes were shattered by the death of the president and the succession to the presidency of John Tyler. It soon became all too apparent that while Tyler was anti-Jackson he was certainly no Clay Whig. The resulting clash caused a

bitter intra-party fight, which made the administration ineffective.

The Democrats had emerged from the 1830s as a reasonably coherent party. The Whigs, however, never really succeeded in obtaining unity and depended more on those who disliked the Democrats than on policies that could be supported by the whole party. They entered the election of 1844 with the legacy of an administration of intense internal fights and at a time when the Democrats were better sensing the mood of the electorate in regard to the rapidly developing problems in foreign relations.

Foreign policy and the American Indians

In the years after 1815 there was a dramatic change in the relationship between the United States and foreign nations. In the first thirty years of American independence the United States had been in constant danger and had devoted much of her energy to avoiding entanglement in the European wars. After 1815 there was no general war involving Great Britain, the European continent, and general maritime blockades for another hundred years. Not until the First World War were American ships again to be beset with the problems they had experienced after 1793.

After 1815 the United States, without major interference, was able to expand over much of the North American continent and to begin to extend her general influence through Latin America as well. Instead of being in danger herself, the United States posed a threat to those powers who held territory adjacent to her in North America. The basis of this expansion was the rapid increase in the American population and the determination of American citizens to seek a better life on new lands to the west.

To the inhabitants of the United States the presence of vast, rich, undeveloped lands acted as an irresistible lure. To many it was a vast 'empty' continent ready to be cultivated by those who had the energy to build a new life.

In reality, of course, not even the undeveloped lands within the actual bounds of the United States were empty; they were occupied by a variety of Indian tribes who had no desire to yield their lands to the American pioneers. Before 1815 the American government argued that American expansion would benefit the Indians, because as they yielded their land the Indians would be given the benefits of American civilization and would be assimilated within the American nation. After 1815, as it became clear that most Indians did not want to accept American civilization, an increasing number of Americans accepted the argument that the Indians were doomed, that they would be swept aside and would eventually disappear as obstacles in the path of progress.

When in the 1830s the Indians east of the Mississippi River were moved to lands west of the river it was still argued by some that this would help to save the Indians, but others were now more ready to accept the argument that the Indians were an inferior race, destined to be engulfed in the advancing stream of American civilization. Although the Indians fought fiercely to prevent the American advance, it was a futile fight. Not until after the Civil War was the American government again to think as seriously of the possibility of assimilation as they had before 1815.

Apart from sweeping aside an aboriginal population, the Americans had the problem of land in the possession of other nations in their rapid advance across the American continent. Though the land immediately

west of the Mississippi had been bought from France in a stroke of fortune in 1803, and other purchases proved possible later in the century, possession of much of what is now the United States had to depend upon diplomatic pressure and war.

The possessions of Spain in East and West Florida had been desired by some in the United States since the Louisiana Purchase in 1803. Jefferson attempted to buy West Florida and placed severe pressure on the Spanish government. In 1810 a revolution at Baton Rouge gave part of the area to the United States, and during the War of 1812 American troops occupied and kept possession of Mobile.

After John Quincy Adams became secretary of state under Monroe in 1817, he made determined efforts to secure the Florida region and resisted a cabinet attempt to censure Jackson when he led troops across the Spanish border in pursuit of the Indians. In 1819 the Spanish, realizing that they had no way of protecting the Florida region, yielded to American pressure and, under the Adams-Onis Treaty, sold it for $5,000,000. However, this money was not to leave the United States but was to be used to pay claims of American citizens against the Spanish for damage suffered to their property in the European wars. As part of the agreement the United States acknowledged Spanish ownership of Texas, and Spain ceded to the United States any claim she had to the land north of California on the Pacific coast.

The Monroe Doctrine

John Quincy Adams, more than any other American statesman during these years, envisaged a United States which would own much of the North American continent and would also extend her sphere of influence throughout Latin America. His chance to assert positively the hopes of the United States came both because of the situation on the distant northwest coast of North America ('the Oregon country') and because of the situation in Latin America.

In the early nineteenth century several powers had hopes of controlling the North American coast north of California. Spain's long-lasting claims were given up in the Adams-Onis Treaty of 1819, but the United States, Great Britain and Russia continued to have an interest in the region. Britain and the United States had claims based on exploration, while Russia, who had advanced into Alaska in the eighteenth century, was anxious to extend her control down the west coast of North America. In 1812 a Russian post was established north of San Francisco, but Russia's attempt to assert a claim to the region was resisted by Adams in the early 1820s.

The various regions of Latin America that had been in revolt from Spain since the Napoleonic wars were anxious to secure recognition from other powers. The United States sympathized with the aspirations of the area, both because of a supposed similarity with her own Revolution and because of the opening of new trade opportunities, but had delayed recognition in the years after 1815 because of her desire to obtain the Floridas from Spain. After that transaction was completed, however, the United States rapidly moved to recognition, even though there was some fear in the early 1820s that the Holy Alliance powers of Europe would come to the aid of Spain in recovering her Latin American colonies. In 1823 the United States also made a general assertion of the principles she was trying to uphold on the American continents by issuing the Monroe Doctrine.

The occasion for the issuance of the Monroe Doctrine was a British request that the Americans should join in a declaration in opposition to any European efforts to help Spain to restore her power in Latin America. John Quincy Adams turned down the British request but persuaded the American government to act unilaterally and assert the position of the United States. Accordingly, in his annual message of December 1823, President Monroe incorporated a statement summarizing the American position.

President Monroe declared that the United States would view as unfriendly acts any new colonization by the European powers on the American continent or any attempt to change the forms of government: as the United States did not wish to interfere in European affairs, European powers should not interfere in the western hemisphere. In 1823 the United States did not have the military power to enforce her desires, but as Great Britain, who controlled the Atlantic, did not want any major European interferences in the New World the general principles could be upheld.

The interests of the United States and Great Britain were not in accord, however, on the Pacific coast north of California. Russia had agreed to withdraw from this region in the mid-1820s, but Britain and the United States both maintained their claims and merely agreed that for the time being the area would be open to citizens of both countries.

While John Quincy Adams and the American government asserted the general principles upon which the United States was acting, American settlers continually advanced the bounds of actual settlement. From 1821, with Mexico now independent from Spain, Southerners and their slaves began to move in increasing numbers into Mexican Texas. For much of the period this movement received Mexican encouragement, although for a time Mexico tried to stop the immigration as she realized the dangers it posed to the region. By 1835 over 25,000 Americans had crossed into Texas. They attempted to gain greater independence while the Mexican leader Santa Anna pressed for centralization. The friction led to open warfare. The American government did not involve itself officially in Texas, though individual Americans gave aid.

Santa Anna advanced into Texas early in 1836 and in March helped to arouse Texas resistance when his army, after meeting great opposition, stormed the Alamo in San Antonio and killed all the defenders (under 200), including the famous frontiersmen Davy Crockett and Jim Bowie. The Mexicans continued their advance, but on 21 April 1836 at San Jacinto the aroused Texas, led by Sam Houston, completely defeated the Mexican army and captured Santa Anna. He was freed after promising to acknowledge Texan independence but later broke the promise.

Andrew Jackson would have liked to incorporate Texas into the Union – this was strongly desired by the Texans – but he did not wish to provoke war with Mexico and also had to contend with the resistance of northerners who did not want to see an addition to the power of the slave states. Accordingly, Jackson merely recognized Texan independence before he left office.

Manifest Destiny

By the 1840s the long-established American interest in expansion on the North American continent had erupted into a popular surge of enthusiasm usually described by the phrase 'Manifest Destiny'. Americans' confidence in their destiny and mission reached reached new heights; not only was the United States clearly intended to expand to the Pacific, it was also argued that this would help bring about a new age of democracy and republican government in the world. The American advance would expand the area of freedom, it was argued, and if Mexicans blocked the way they, like the Indians, would be overwhelmed.

In the election of 1844, when the Whigs were already in dire trouble because of their internal splits, the Democrats began to take advantage of the new national enthusiasm and helped to guide it. James K. Polk, the Democratic candidate, was prepared to take strong action to accomplish American aims, both on the Pacific coast and in the southwest. The slogan of 'Re-annexation of Texas and the reoccupation of Oregon' stirred American blood and helped to elect the Democrats.

The first practical result of the Democratic victory was that lame-duck President Tyler, before handing over to his successor, considered he now had a popular mandate to

annex Texas, and this was done by joint resolution of Congress in March 1845. A formal treaty for annexation was avoided as this would have needed a two-thirds majority in the Senate and would have met opposition from the northeasterners.

American pressure on the Pacific coast and on the southwest had been made possible by the activity of American traders and settlers in those regions. In the previous decades American traders had settled in the ports of Mexican California, and an overland trade had been built up from the central Mississippi Valley states to Mexican Santa Fe by way of the Santa Fe Trail. In the 1840s the trade interest was followed by that of the American pioneer farmers who travelled the Oregon trail across the Continent. They set out west from the vicinity of Independence, Missouri, trekking along the Platte into the Rockies and then over to Oregon, or perhaps by a southern cut-off to California.

In the early 1840s several thousand pioneers found their way across the continent to Oregon, following missionaries who had arrived there a decade earlier, enabling the American government to reopen the Oregon question with Great Britain. Although extravagant claims had been made to an area extending northwards as far as

the southern boundary of Alaska, actual control of the region was rather different. British fur trading interests had long held effective control over the region between the forty-ninth parallel and the Columbia River, and American settlers had moved only into the region south of that river.

President Polk exerted strong pressure on the British government, at first arguing that he wanted the boundary at 54° 40′. But, eventually, in the Oregon Treaty of June 1846 he accepted the line of the forty-ninth parallel as the boundary to the Pacific (Vancouver Island was given to the British). The boundary was not what Polk had originally demanded, but he actually won control of an area that the British had previously dominated. As other United States-Canadian boundary problems had been settled in the Webster-Ashburton Treaty of 1842, British-American relations from now on improved markedly.

War with Mexico

California and the southwest presented a more difficult problem for the American government, as Mexico had no desire to give up this section of her country. Since the 1820s the United States had been urging Mexico to sell portions of this region, but Mexican-United States relations became bitter after Texas obtained her independence. Mexico believed, with good reason, that the northern regions of her country were in imminent danger from the advancing American pioneers, and the United States complained of Mexican intransigence in refusing to negotiate and also of the Mexican failure to pay claims of American citizens for the loss of their property in the frequent Mexican revolutions.

When the United States annexed Texas in 1845, Mexico broke off diplomatic relations, and many Mexicans urged war against the United States. Polk was still anxious to secure what he wanted by negotiation and in November sent John Slidell to try to obtain Mexican recognition of the annexation of Texas. He was also to secure recognition of a Rio Grande boundary between Texas and Mexico and to try to buy New Mexico and California.

The Mexicans refused to negotiate with Slidell, and in the spring of 1846 tension between the two countries erupted into open conflict. American troops were ordered into the disputed territory immediately north of the Rio Grande, and Polk resolved to ask Congress for war. His task was made easier by the news that Mexican and United States troops had clashed north of the Rio Grande. On 13 May 1846, the American Congress declared war on Mexico.

The Mexican War was a complete victory for the United States. While American troops took possession of New Mexico and California, General Zachary Taylor invaded the provinces of Mexico south of the Rio Grande. His victory at the Battle of Buena Vista in February 1847 won control of the region for the United States. By that time New Mexico had been taken by an American force which marched overland from Fort Leavenworth, and California had already been conquered by a combination of internal revolt and American troops.

In March 1847 the American government took more direct steps to end the war. Polk, who was becoming increasingly concerned at General Taylor's growing popularity, had placed Winfield Scott in command of an army which was landed by sea at Vera Cruz. The Mexicans put up a stubborn and brave resistance, but in September the United States troops took Mexico City.

Polk had sent Nicholas P. Trist with Scott's army to conduct peace negotiations,

The growth of sectionalism

The years between 1820 and 1850 brought a marked deterioration in American national unity; in particular the South became a distinct section, dedicated not only to the preservation of slavery, but also to distinct economy and a whole way of life. The 1830s were decisive years in the creation of a solid South. Although there was opposition to slavery before 1830, it was the foundation of William Lloyd Garrison's newspaper *The Liberator* in 1831 that marked the real beginning of a radical abolitionist movement in the North.

In the following years hundreds of abolitionist societies were formed in the northern states. Their periodicals and other publications poured abuse upon the Southerners, depicted the worse cruelties of the slave system and demanded that the institution should come to an end. Although those involved were a small minority of the northern population, their arguments produced a strong reaction in the South. Instead of Southerners arguing that slavery was a necessary evil, as many had done in the years following the Revolution, they began to maintain that slavery was a positive good, that the negroes were an inferior race who were happier in their slave condition than if free, that their lot was better than that of the northern factory workers, and that slavery had been the basis of all great civilizations. They also showed fear that northern arguments would inspire slave insurrections: a rising led by Nat Turner in 1831 had resulted in the deaths of fifty-five white and had sent a shudder of fear throughout the South.

With tempers inflamed by the argument over slavery, the other basic issues separating North and South were contested far more vehemently. The acrimonious tariff struggle between President Jackson and South Carolina in the early 1830s was followed after 1836 by another argument over the admission of Texas. The North feared a major addition to slave power if that region were annexed to the United States.

Underlying the whole quarrel was the continued Southern desire to maintain enough votes in Congress to block any undesirable political, social or economic legislation. This was becoming more difficult as the population of the free states continued to grow more rapidly than that of the South, giving the South an increasingly weak position in the House of Representatives and making it all the more important for the Southern slave system to control new states and provide new Senate votes.

and, although Polk had ordered him to return, Trist signed the Treaty of Guadalupe Hidalgo in February 1848, and Polk decided to submit it to the Senate. The treaty gave California and New Mexico to the United States and acknowledged the Rio Grande as the boundary of Texas. The United States agreed to pay $15,000,000 for these areas as well as to assume $3,250,000 in debts owed by Mexico to Americans.

It was a crushing defeat for Mexico, made all the more galling because early in 1848 gold had been discovered in California. In 1849 thousands of Americans made their way to the goldfields overland, by the way of Panama, and around the Horn. This discovery was ultimately to lead to the expansion of the mining frontier over the whole region of the Rockies.

The American enthusiasm for Manifest Destiny was to continue into the 1850s, and there was talk of annexing Cuba, but the only addition of territory was by the Gadsden Purchase from Mexico in 1853, which gave to the United States a strip of land in the southwest suitable for a railroad route to the Pacific.

In 1783 the United States had been bounded by the Mississippi on the west, the Great Lakes on the north and Spanish territory to the south. Within seventy years the country had assumed her modern dimensions on the North American continent, with the exception of Alaska which was bought from Russia in 1867. Not only had these areas come under the sovereignty of the United States, her settlers were also rapidly advancing throughout the continent: by 1850 California was a state, Oregon a territory and Mormon settlers had established the nucleus of a future state by the Great Salt Lake. It now seemed that the only threat to the development of the United States into one of the greatest powers in the world was internal dissension, for now the threat of civil war was becoming ever greater.

The compromise of 1850

The war with Mexico produced an immediate crisis in the relations of North and South. Nationalistic enthusiasm had produced general support for the conflict at the beginning of the war, but northern Whigs soon expressed their opposition to a war of conquest and to any further extension of slavery. As early as 1846 representative David Wilmot of Pennsylvania had introduced into Congress the Wilmot Proviso, which stated that slavery should not be permitted in any of the territory obtained from Mexico.

While American armies conquered a huge addition to the territory of the United States, Congress argued about the Wilmot Proviso, which did not have enough votes to pass the Senate. Some were now contending that slavery should be allowed to expand into any area that wanted it, others maintained that the Missouri Compromise line of 36° 30′ should be extended to the Pacific. But what would happen to California, an area that was already asking for admission to the Union?

In the 1848 presidential election both candidates played down the basic issue, and military hero Zachary Taylor was able to win the second and last Whig presidential victory. His opponent Lewis Cass had become known as an advocate of the idea that the territories should decide for themselves whether or not they would have slavery, but he laid little stress on this in the election. Ominous for future unity was the third party – the Free Soil party – who ran ex-President Martin Van Buren on a platform against the future expansion of slavery. Taylor's victory had been based on both Northern and Southern votes, but it was now clear that it was becoming increasingly difficult for either main party to hold together such bipartisan support.

Taylor urged California to apply for admission to the Union and was willing to abide by the state's decision whether or not to be slave or free; in late 1849 California formed a free constitution and applied for admission. The South, fearing that all the land acquired from Mexico would be free, bitterly opposed the admission of California on these terms, and in 1850 Congress engaged in an impassioned debate on the future expansion of slavery. The eventual solution was devised by Henry Clay, now near the end of his long career, and was pushed through Congress after the death of President Taylor had brought Vice-President Millard Fillmore to the presidency.

The Compromise of 1850 consisted of a number of measures passed in the hope of giving some concessions to both North and South. Many on both sides voted for those measures they liked and were prepared to abstain when those measures they did not like were voted upon. By the compromise California was to enter the Union as a free state, New Mexico and Utah were to be organized as territories with no specification whether they were to be slave or free, the slave trade (but not slavery) was to be abolished in the District of Columbia, and a stricter Fugitive Slave Law was enacted. In addition, Texas was compensated for ceding her claims to part of New Mexico. The compromise pleased neither side. Southerners objected to restrictions on slavery anywhere in the West, and northern abolitionists protested against the harsh Fugitive Slave Law, and insisted that the future expansion of slavery should be prohibited.

The increasing emotional impact of the issue of slavery was well demonstrated by the phenomenal success of Harriet Beecher Stowe's novel *Uncle Tom's Cabin*, which was published in 1852. This melodramatic depiction of slave life moved millions of northern citizens as a book, in serial form and as a play. As the North became more stirred by the moral implications of slavery, and as the South became convinced that it was losing political power, it became impossible to maintain political compromises.

The Compromise of 1850 collapsed within four years. The election of 1852 was fought between a Democratic party still anxious to maintain the unity of its Northern and Southern wings and a Whig party that was finally falling apart. The undistinguished Franklin Pierce of New Hampshire won an easy victory over Whig Winfield Scott. Pierce had a tumultuous presidency, and once again the fiercest arguments came over the westward expansion of slavery.

Although American settlers had pushed all the way to California and Oregon in the 1840s, there had long been a reluctance to advance on to the Great Plains. With good reason it was feared that the lack of timber and an uncertain water supply would present problems unknown in the eastern half of the continent. Yet, as the more desirable areas were populated and pioneers still looked for land, the adventurous began to encroach upon the Plains, and in the 1853–4 session of Congress a bill was introduced for the organization of the area west of Iowa and Missouri as Nebraska Territory. Although settlers were moving into this region, the bill also stemmed from the ambitions of Senator Stephen A. Douglas of Illinois.

In the 1850s there was a new breed of politicians in Congress. After the deaths of Clay, Calhoun and Webster, in both North and South some politicians had less patience for compromise. Men such as Senator Charles Summer of Massachusetts poured scorn upon their enemies. Of the new group of prominent political leaders, Democratic Senator S. Douglas appeared the most anxious to achieve compromise and preserve national unity; in his case it was bitterly disputed whether it was patriotism or personal ambition that led him to take this course.

As chairman of the committee on territories, Douglas introduced the bill to organize Nebraska Territory. He was interested not only in the settlers in that region but also in a trans-continental railroad. Since the 1840s there had been talk of such a link, and in the 1850s it was a major political issue; there was great competition from those areas seeking to be the eastern terminal of

Opposite top, the US sloop Saratoga *engaging two Mexican steamers off Vera Cruz, 1860: for much of the nineteenth century, US foreign policy, though hostile to European interference, believed it to be the USA's 'manifest destiny' to spread over the entire continent; today Latin America is still held to be a sphere of influence of the USA.*

Opposite bottom, contemporary print depicting Nat Turner's revolt, 1831: occasional uprisings such as this did little to advance the emancipation of the slaves but rather confirmed many whites in their fear of the negro. Freedom did not come for thirty years and then for a mixture of reasons.

the railroad. Douglas was pressing for Chicago – he had a personal interest in the Illinois Central Railroad and in land speculation as well as a Senator's interest in his own state – but he realized that the area through which the line would pass needed a form of governmental organization if the railway was to be more attractive to Congress.

The question of Nebraska Territory sent Congress into turmoil. Nebraska would presumably enter as a free state, and to meet Southern objections it was agreed that the region would be divided into two territories: Kansas and Nebraska. Douglas also agreed that instead of the line of 36° 30′ dividing slave and free areas, as decided in the Missouri Compromise, 'popular sovereignty' would prevail in the territories. Douglas argued that, rather than Congress making the decision for an area, it would be more democratic for each area to decide for itself whether or not to have slavery. The advantage to Douglas was that this would also meet the wishes of the Southern section of his own party and help his presidential ambitions.

In spite of Northern objections, the Kansas – Nebraska Act was pushed through Congress, repealing the Missouri Compromise and allowing the territories to decide for themselves on the issue of slavery or freedom. From that time on there was little respite in the steady slide into Civil War.

There was no doubt that Nebraska would be a free area, but from 1854 until the Civil War the situation of 'bleeding Kansas' constantly aggravated relations between the North and South. Both Northerners and Southerners attempted to arrange the migration of pioneers who would vote Kansas slave or free, and the general turmoil was increased by the opportunists and criminals always attracted to the edge of the frontier. They speculated in land and ambushed and burned for personal rather than national motives.

The Republican party

The Kansas – Nebraska Act also helped to bring about the final disintegration of the Whigs and to create the new Republican party, a Northern party composed of ex-Whigs, Democrats who opposed Douglas and the Kansas – Nebraska Act and the old free-soilers, all uniting on opposition to the expansion of slavery. A third party, the Know-Nothings, appealed to prejudice, opposing Catholics and immigrants, and tapped the nativistic tradition in American politics, i.e. the tradition favouring those actually born in America. The Republicans spread quickly throughout the old northwest and New England, and the Whig party, which was a national party however disunited, was now replaced by a sectional party.

The bitterness of the Republicans was increased by the situation in Kansas. Soon two governments existed – one pro-slavery, one for freedom – and violent incidents multiplied. After a pro-slavery group had attacked the town of Lawrence, the unbalanced John Brown, with his sons and friends, murdered a group of Southern sympathizers. The breakdown of order even spread to Congress itself. In the Senate in 1856 Charles Sumner launched a vituperative personal attack on Senator Andrew P. Butler of South Carolina. Butler's nephew, Congressman Preston B. Brooks, heard about it, entered the Senate and beat Sumner on the head with his cane. Brooks was censured by the House but after resigning was swept back into Congress by his district in South Carolina.

In the 1856 election the Democrats nominated the mediocre James Buchanan while the Republicans, already strong enough to contest the presidency, nominated the national hero, soldier and explorer John C. Frémont. Ex-president Fillmore ran on the Know-Nothing ticket. Buchanan won, but it was ominous for the South that Frémont obtained 114 electoral votes to Buchanan's 174 and Fillmore's 8.

The Dred Scott decision

Buchanan's problems began immediately, for in March 1857 the Supreme Court, which had a majority of Southerners, declared in the Dred Scott case that the Missouri Compromise was unconstitutional. Slaves were property and the constitution protected individual rights of property. By this decision the Supreme Court made it clear that neither the federal nor the territorial government could constitutionally exclude slavery.

The Dred Scott decision brought impassioned arguments in the North, but it was also a crushing blow to Douglas, for the decision went further than his popular sovereignty in satisfying the Southerners; according to the Supreme Court an individual's ritht to own a slave was protected by the constitution, and even a democratic majority could not outlaw slavery in a territory. Douglas was placed in an even more difficult position when President Buchanan decided to ask Congress to admit Kansas to the Union under the provisions of the 'Lecompton Constitution'. This was a pro-slavery constitution supported by only part of the Kansas population and never voted on by all the people of the territory. Although this did not pass, it further divided the Democratic Party. The dilemma was revealed dramatically in Douglas's senatorial re-election campaign in Illinois in 1858. His opponent was Abraham Lincoln.

Lincoln was the son of a pioneer farmer, who, after his famous son's birth in Kentucky in 1809, moved on into Indiana and finally into Illinois. Lincoln became a lawyer

in the 1830s, although for the most part he was self-educated. He also became a Whig and served one term in Congress after his election in 1846. He was a competent state-level politician but was not at all well known as a national figure.

In the 1850s Lincoln began to take a strong stand against the further expansion of slavery, although he was not at this time an abolitionist. He soon became an important figure in the new Republican party and in 1858 ran for the Senate against Douglas in Illinois. The debates the two engaged in received major national attention, and although Douglas won Lincoln obliged him to choose publicly between popular sovereignty and the Dred Scott decision. At Freeport Lincoln forced him to answer whether or not the people of a territory could exclude slavery. Douglas answered that they could and in so doing alienated the Southern Democrats, who wanted Douglas to accept the Dred Scott decision.

The last years of Buchanan's administration brought a breakdown of responsible government. The division between Northern and Southern extremists was such that Congress had difficulty in conducting any of its business. Tension reached a high point when in the autumn of 1859 John Brown led a small group of followers into Virginia to attack the federal arsenal at Harper's Ferry. He wanted to arm the slaves and begin a revolt. After they had seized the arsenal the attackers were themselves besieged, Brown was captured, quickly tried and hanged. In life Brown was a fanatic; in death he became a martyr to the cause of freedom. His act was a fitting prelude to the climactic election of 1860.

When in the spring of 1860 the Democrats met in Charleston to nominate their candidate for president, the logical candidate, Douglas, could not obtain the votes for the nomination. Neither North nor South would compromise, and the Southern delegates walked out. The Democrats tried again in June at Baltimore, again failed to agree and eventually the Northern and Southern wings of the party nominated separate candidates: Douglas for the North, John C. Breckinridge of Kentucky for the South. As the Southerners had been unwilling to accept even the moderate Douglas, they now created an opportunity for the sectional Republicans. In May the Republicans nominated Abraham Lincoln for president, choosing him over the more extreme William H. Seward of New York. For the South the vital section of the Republican platform was that which opposed slavery in the territories.

A third party – the Constitutional Union party – attempted to hold the nation together with an appeal for national unity, but their candidate – John Bell of Tennessee – had no chance of success. Lincoln won the election with 1,866,000 popular votes; Douglas had 1,383,000, Breckinridge

848,000, and Bell 593,000. Although a minority president in terms of popular votes, Lincoln had an absolute majority of electoral votes.

Secession

The victory of Lincoln could not be accepted by the South. In half a century they had lost the dominant position in the nation. Between 1789 and 1825 Virginia had provided all the presidents but one, and Southerners had dominated public office, so much so that some in New England had thought of secession. In 1860 the North elected a president from a party which unalterably opposed the extension of slavery. With no possibility of expansion, the South would be outvoted in Congress, policies would be adopted against Southern wishes, soon perhaps the institution of slavery itself would be threatened, and the South would be faced with a massive economic loss and a general social readjustment. By withdrawing from the Union many in the South hoped to preserve intact their economic and social system.

The first Southern state to act was South Carolina. In December 1860 she seceded from the Union and by the beginning of February had been joined by Mississippi, Florida, Alabama, Georgia, Louisiana and Texas. At Montgomery, Alabama, in February 1861 the seven seceding states set up the Confederate States of America. President Buchanan vacillated, and although various compromise plans were suggested there seemed no way to reunite the Union save by a swift use of force.

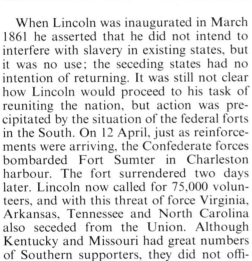

When Lincoln was inaugurated in March 1861 he asserted that he did not intend to interfere with slavery in existing states, but it was no use; the seceding states had no intention of returning. It was still not clear how Lincoln would proceed to his task of reuniting the nation, but action was precipitated by the situation of the federal forts in the South. On 12 April, just as reinforcements were arriving, the Confederate forces bombarded Fort Sumter in Charleston harbour. The fort surrendered two days later. Lincoln now called for 75,000 volunteers, and with this threat of force Virginia, Arkansas, Tennessee and North Carolina also seceded from the Union. Although Kentucky and Missouri had great numbers of Southern supporters, they did not officially leave the Union.

The Civil War

The discrepancy in force between the United States and the Confederacy was very great. The North had over four times the free population of the seceding states, by far the largest industrial development and the most extensive railroad system. She also had the naval power to blockade Southern ports. Southern hopes were based on the knowledge that a stalemate would benefit the South and that it was the North's task to wage a positive, offensive war. The South was also hopeful of foreign aid, particularly from Great Britain, the main consumer of Southern cotton. These hopes proved illusory. Although relations between Great Britain and the United States were strained at the beginning of the war, the strength of anti-slavery opinion in Great Britain was such that any suggestion of joining with the South met with great opposition.

At the beginning of the war the Confederacy gained a false confidence from the ease with which it resisted Northern armies. The politicians pressed the Northern army into action before it was ready, and this produced disastrous results on the main eastern front of the war: the stretch of country between Washington D.C. and the Confederate capital of Richmond, Virginia. At the first Battle of Bull Run in July 1861 the Northern armies were completely defeated. The elderly Winfield Scott was now removed from command, and George B. McClellan replaced him.

Until the spring of 1862 McClellan devoted his attention to the organization and training of the 'Army of the Potomac'. He then attempted to attack Richmond by having his main army of over 100,000 men landed by sea on the peninsula between the James and the York rivers while another force of over 40,000 advanced overland from Washington D.C. The campaign failed. In a running seven-day battle at the end of June Confederate General Robert E. Lee, aided by Stonewall Jackson, forced McClellan to retreat. Lee, who had served in the regular army before the war, had returned to his native Virginia to join her fight. He proved to be a masterly defensive general.

Throughout 1862 the Northern armies continued to suffer defeat on the Washington-Richmond front. In August Lee and Stonewall Jackson overcame the Northern armies at the second Battle of Bull Run, and Lee advanced into Maryland. In September he was obliged to withdraw after the bloody, indecisive Battle of Antietam in which total casualties amounted to over 20,000 men.

Even though Antietam was indecisive it enabled Lincoln to take a decisive step in the conduct of the war. The abolitionists had been urging the freeing of the slaves, and

Lincoln knew that he could also ensure British neutrality if he took the step of fighting for the end of slavery. He did not wish to appear to be freeing the slaves out of desperation, but after the partial victory of Antietam he issued the preliminary Emancipation Proclamation; the final proclamation was issued in January 1863. Yet, though the Confederacy was denied foreign intervention, it still seemed she could save herself, for 1862 ended in disaster for the North when General Ambrose E. Burnside threw his troops into suicidal attack against the Confederate positions at Fredericksburg and lost over 10,000 dead and wounded.

The first eighteen months of the war had seen the complete failure of the main Union effort to drive south from Washington

Left, President Lincoln with generals and staff of the Union army: though the North could call on far larger reserves of manpower than the South, the cream of the pre-war officer corps joined the Confederacy, and, at least in the first years of the war, the North suffered from unimaginative, over-cautious leadership.

Below left, men of the Richmond Grays, the 1st Virginia Regiment: the South waged war to defend a way of life in which it fervently believed and fought that war principally on its own territory. Such total commitment to the cause did much to raise morale in the early years of the war but could do nothing to prevent the military and economic inevitability of the final collapse.

Opposite top right, the guardhouse and guards of the 107th Colored Infantry at Fort Corcoran, Virginia.

Opposite centre right, the aftermath of battle, by Matthew Brady, one of the earliest war photographers: the war claimed 620,000 dead on both sides.

Opposite bottom, the 1st Connecticut Artillery encamped within sight of Washington DC. Chicago Historical Society, Illinois.

Opposite left, the battle between the Confederate Merrimac and the Union Monitor in Hampton Roads, Virginia, 9 March 1862, the first major engagement between ironclad vessels: Federal command of the seas ensured a naval blockade of the South, so depriving it of much needed supplies.

against the Confederate capital. There was extensive criticism of Lincoln and much disaffection in Northern areas. It was as well for the Union that other pressures on the South were weakening her resistance. Particularly effective was the blockade, which ruined Southern commerce. Also Northern naval forces eventually combined with land forces to split the Confederacy.

Union troops in the Mississippi valley were at first more successful than those in the east, and in April 1862 General Ulysses S. Grant won the Battle of Shiloh, with terrible losses, and forced the Confederate troops to retreat. In the same month a naval squadron under the command of David G. Farragut captured New Orleans and pushed up the Mississippi. In the next year

the Northern armies slowly fought their way south to join up with the naval forces on the Mississippi and split the Confederacy. On 4 July 1863, Grant took Vicksburg, and a few days later the North had succeeded in winning complete control of the Mississippi River.

The first days of July 1863 were the turning-point in the history of the Confederacy, for while Grant was preparing to take Vicksburg Lee was making a decisive move which he hoped would end the war. In May, Lee and Stonewall Jackson (who was killed) defeated Northern forces at Chancellorsville. Lee now decided to advance into Pennsylvania and by a decisive victory force the North to concede that the South could leave the Union.

From 1 to 3 July Lee met the Northern army of General George Meade at Gettysburg. The slaughter was immense, and on the third day Lee sent General George E. Pickett's men in wave after wave against the Union line. They could not break it, and Lee withdrew southwards. From July 1863 it became increasingly obvious that the South had lost the war, but unfortunately for future relations between the two sections the desperate struggle continued for nearly two more years. Lincoln could now quiet his critics, and in 1864 he won re-election over the Democratic candidate General George B. McClellan.

In 1864 and 1865 the federal armies plunged deep into the South to bring the Confederacy to its knees. The Northern armies in the Mississippi Valley were repulsed for a time at Chickamauga in September 1863, but in November after the Battle of Chattanooga the Southern forces retreated into Georgia. In 1864 the Northern armies moved to split the Confederacy again by driving into Georgia to Atlanta and then to the sea, while further north General

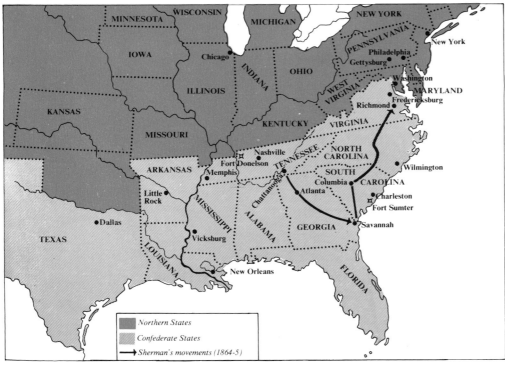

Grant, who had been transferred to command on the Washington-Richmond front, attempted to advance south towards Richmond.

There was intense fighting throughout the spring and summer of 1864. In May and June Grant fought a series of battles in the Wilderness and encircled Richmond, which was well defended by a series of trenches and fortifications. It was the following year before he could force Lee's army to withdraw from these positions.

General William T. Sherman and his

THE UNITED STATES AND LATIN AMERICA, 1800–1870

Date	United States	Mexico and Argentina	Rest of Latin America
1800	Presidency of Thomas Jefferson (1801–09) Louisiana Purchase (1803) Presidency of James Madison (1809–17)	British occupation of Buenos Aires (1806)	Unsuccessful revolt by Miranda in Venezuela (1806) Abortive attempt at independence in Ecuador (1809)
1810	War with Britain (1812–14) Presidency of James Monroe (1817–25) Spain cedes Florida to USA (1818)	Beginning of Mexican struggle for independence (1811–15) Argentina independent (1816)	Venezuelan independence proclaimed (1811) Spain reconquers Venezuela (1814) San Martin liberates Chile (1818) Greater Colombia founded (1819)
1820	Missouri Compromise (1820) Monroe doctrine (1823) Presidency of J. Q. Adams (1825–29) Presidency of Andrew Jackson (1829–37)	Mexico independent (1821) Mexico a federal republic (1824) War between Argentina and Brazil (1827–28)	Peru independent (1821) Final liberation of Venezuela (1821) Liberation of Ecuador (1822) Brazil independent (1822); Pedro I emperor (1822–31) Bolivia a sovereign state (1826) Uruguay a sovereign state (1828)
1830	Beginning of Abolitionist movement First Mormon Church (1831) Republic of Texas established (1836) Presidency of Martin van Buren (1837–41)	Santa Anna President of Mexico (1833–35) Rosas governor of Buenos Aires (1835) Santa Anna defeated by Texans at San Jacinto (1836)	Venezuela and Ecuador separate countries (1830) Pedro II Emperor of Brazil (1831–89); regency established Brazilian separatist movement in Rio Grande do Sul (1835–45) Flores assumes power in Ecuador (1839) Chile destroys Bolivian-Peruvian federation (1839)

Date	United States	Mexico and Argentina	Rest of Latin America
1840	Presidency of W. Harrison (1841) Presidency of J. Polk (1845–49) Britain gives up Oregon (1846) Conquest of California (1847) Gold rush in California	Rosas dictator of Argentina Argentina at war with Paraguay (1845) War between Mexico and United States (1846–48) Treaty of Guadalupe Hidalgo (1848)	Reign of Pedro II begins (1840) Carlos López president of Paraguay (1844) Overthrow of Flores (1845) Castilla president of Peru (1845)
1850	Clay compromise (1850) Foundation of Republican party (1854) Lincoln-Douglas debates (1858) John Brown's raid (1859)	Revolt of Urquiza in Argentina Urquiza defeats Rosas at Caseros (1852) Secession of Buenos Aires (1853) Dissolution of the Order of Jesuits in Mexico (1855) New Mexican constituion (1857) Civil war in Mexico—Juárez against Miramón (1858) Buenos Aires rejoins Argentinian federation (1859)	Abolition of slavery in Colombia (1851) and Venezuela (1854) Fall of Monagas regime in Venezuela (1859)
1860	Election of Lincoln Secession of eleven Southern states (1860–61) Formation of the Confederate States of America (1861) Lincoln proclaims the emancipation of the slaves (1863) Surrender of General Lee (1865) Assassination of Lincoln (1865) Military occupation of the South	Juárez President of Mexico (1861) Bartolemé Mitre President united Argentina (1862–68) Maximilian Emperor of Mexico (1864) Maximilian executed (1867) Juárez re-elected president of Mexico (1867)	Liberal regime in Chile (1861) Argentina, Brazil and Uruguay at war with Paraguay (1865–70)
1870			

armies from the Mississippi Valley had more dramatic success. Atlanta fell in September, and Sherman marched to the sea, taking Savannah in December. He was now able to turn north, and in the spring of 1865 the Confederacy collapsed. In April Lee was finally forced to retreat from Richmond; on 9 April at Appomattox he found there was no way of retreat and surrendered to Grant. Other small forces soon capitulated, and the war was over.

The cost of the war

The North had lost 359,000 dead, the Confederacy 258,000 dead. Much of the South had been devastated: plantations ruined, fortunes lost, railroad tracks torn up, cities destroyed. The Union had been preserved, and the slaves had been freed, but a monumental task of reconstruction and a deep legacy of bitterness and hatred remained. To climax the tragedy, on 14 April Lincoln was shot at Ford's theatre in Washington D.C. The nation faced the task of reconstruction without its great leader. Andrew Johnson of Tennessee became president.

Yet, even after this great war, the United States was ready to become one of the most powerful countries in the world. Although hundreds of thousands had been killed and maimed, Northern prosperity had suffered no severe injury. Industrial development, railroad construction and commerce were leaping forward. The South would remain a problem, but the vast unified United States spanning the North American continent would quickly press forward to new heights of prosperity and strength. A unified nation which offered a combination of political and religious freedom and economic opportunity attracted even more millions of immigrants from Europe in the years after the Civil War. To judge the advantages possessed by the United States, even after a bloody conflict, one had only to turn to South America to view the sad history of a fragmented continent which had obtained its independence from Europe but which had failed to obtain either the prosperity or the freedom of which some of the early revolutionaries had dreamed.

Opposite top, Yankee volunteers marching into the South: the north's assertion of its political and cultural way of life soured relations between the two parts of the Union for decades.

Opposite bottom right, a refugee family leaving the war zone, their belongings loaded on a cart: the armies of both North and South left a trail of destruction behind them, though none was exceeded by the devastation and looting of Sherman's army as it marched across Georgia in 1865.

Opposite bottom left, the United States during the Civil War, 1961–65: the final victory of the northern states preserved the Union, but at the cost of more than 600,000 dead.

Part II

THE BALANCE OF POWER

Introduction

The nineteenth century had no monopoly of nationalism and imperialism – they seem to be as old as the earliest, organized human societies. But it was in the nineteenth century that the search for power and glory, the essential element in nationalism and imperialism at any time, was intensified by forces largely unknown in previous ages. Historians may debate which of these forces was the most influential in the promotion of nationalism and imperialism, but there is little doubt about what, in the main, they were: challenging developments and discoveries in science and technology which placed into men's hands – particularly into white men's hands – powerful agents for both construction and destruction; profound changes in the economic and social systems of Europe and America; the tensions of democracy; severe threats to the traditional faiths; and the agonizing search for new ones.

By the second half of the nineteenth century, Europe and its white offspring overseas were well advanced in the process of transforming themselves into areas in which new nation-states, flush with the enthusiasms and pretensions of novelty, co-existed uneasily with the older countries. Impelled by the new and often ill-understood forces of the century, both the old and the new nation-states of Europe found that the customary means of preserving their freedom of action by balancing their power, the one against the other, were no longer adequate; and, in the process of discovering new ones, changed not only themselves but the world overseas – white, black, brown and yellow.

The relations of white men with the old civilizations of the East, particularly in the second half of the nineteenth century are especially significant. By this time, the wheel which Europe had set in motion in the thirteenth century with such ventures as Marco Polo's journeys across Asia was coming full circle. The awe of white men at the power and the wealth of the East was being replaced by the East's respect for the power and wealth of white men.

In this process, the United States of America, that part of the New World upon which Europeans had stumbled accidentally in the fifteenth century in their search for the lands and riches of the East, was to play an important part. Indeed, it could be argued that the arrival in Tokyo Bay of the American naval expedition under the command of the militantly-minded Commodore Matthew Perry in 1853 was as important an event in the relations of white men with the non-European world as Columbus' voyage to the Caribbean in 1492.

Even within Europe, the remarkable growth of American political, economic and technological strength had a disturbing effect. The powers and peoples of Europe rarely acted in any sphere (political, economic, social or ideological) without some consideration of the American position.

Even the literature and language of the imperialism of the late nineteenth century reflected this. When, for example, Hilaire Belloc, the Anglo-French writer, produced in 1898 his satirical poem, *The Modern Traveller*, on the advances of the British Empire in tropical Africa, the famous couplet which he assigned to an English adventurer facing a crowd of hostile Africans,

Whatever happens, we have got
The Maxim gun and they have not

would have been impossible had not the inventor of this weapon been one Hiram Maxim, a gentleman of American origins. Hiram's brother, Hudson, an expert on explosives, also gave his name to a means of destruction – maximite (a high-explosive bursting powder for use in torpedoes), which helped to change the fate of nations and empires in Europe and in Europe's spheres of influence elsewhere. And when Rudyard Kipling produced his celebrated poem on the responsibilities of imperialism, he was stimulated by the American victory in the Spanish-American War of 1898, which made them heirs to the remains of the Spanish Empire in the Pacific and the Caribbean. Addressing his poem to these new American imperialists, Kipling declared that they must also take up 'the white man's burden'. This hypnotic and deceptive expression, indeed, might never have been coined if Kipling had not kept the United States constantly in mind.

Yet the core of what the great English writer, John A. Hobson, called 'the new imperialism', of the late nineteenth and early twentieth centuries, remained European.

It was promoted, in particular, by the challenge to the conventional balance of power in Europe by the unification of the German and Italian nation-states in the 1870s. The new Germany precipitated the new imperialism. The overthrow of the French Second Empire by the leaders of German nationalism, the Prussians, at the Battle of Sedan on 1 September 1870 was an ignominious defeat for the nation which had produced Napoleon I.

His nephew, the French emperor Napoleon III, who had all of his uncle's pretensions but little of his power and ability, was taken prisoner. The French nation – especially its army, with its ambitious officer class – could seek consolation in the extension of its overseas empire. Not for nothing did the English imperialist, F. D. Lugard, himself an ambitious army officer actively engaged in extending British territory in tropical Africa, say in 1893 that the Franco-Prussian War was indisputably linked to the scramble for Africa by the powers of Europe. Strangely enough, it was the pretensions of Napoleon III and his Second Empire, before its debacle in 1870, which launched the term 'imperialism' into the popular speech of Europe. But, in the last thirty years of the nineteenth century, the term was to acquire a variety of meanings which owed little to the Second Empire.

Most of all, perhaps, under the influence of the socialists and Marxists, the term 'imperialism' came to signify economic rather than political pressures behind the overseas expansion of the white nations. Undoubtedly, there were very important economic pressures behind the new imperialism. But there were also powerful political forces at work – if, of course, it is ever possible or realistic to attempt to disentangle political and economic elements. The new nationalism, in all its complexity, was one of them. And, as the influential German philosopher, Friedrich Nietzsche, who died at the beginning of the twentieth century, pointed out, there was the basic human drive of the will to power, flowing into the new European expansionist channels.

There was also an element in the new imperialism which can be too easily overlooked: disgust at the achievements and values of Europe and a desire to escape to the so-called 'uncivilized' lands overseas. Arthur Rimbaud, the French poet who served in the army of the Paris Commune in 1871 but who deserted France in disgust at the Western world, to wander in Asia and Africa for the remaining sixteen years of his life, exemplifies this tendency. There was a *fin de siècle* pessimism about such men, which the Jewish-Hungarian writer, Max Nordau, discussed pungently in his *Degeneration* of 1895. Nordau was an ardent Zionist who believed that the Jews should accept the offer of land by the British in their new possession of East Africa. For Nordau's pains, an attempt was made on his life by a Jew who was opposed to the scheme to found a new Zion in East Africa. It was psychological and political problems of this sort which made the pattern of the new imperialism more complex.

To complicate this even further, there were the reactions to the new imperialism and nationalism of Europe in the overseas lands to which they penetrated. In 1896, for example, the Ethiopian emperor, Menelek II, defeated the Italians at Adowa, forcing them to sign a treaty recognizing the absolute independence of his country. Nine years later, a resurgent Japanese nationalism,

having learnt well the industrial and military techniques of the West since Commodore Perry's visit half a century before, defeated the Russians and stripped them of some of their empire. Within a decade, the imperial pretensions of two white nations had been defeated by two 'coloured' countries. The new imperialism of Europe continued to search 'wider still and wider': but it was now less sure of itself, since it was compelled to consider the threat of what the new, cheap, popular press called the 'black peril' and the 'yellow peril'. The age of European dominance, apparently at the peak of its power at the beginning of the new century, could already be seen drawing to a close.

Chapter 6

Cavour and Bismarck

While the Westerners were pressing into the Far East, the European balance of power was changing. In 1871, after its crushing victory in the Franco-Prussian War, a triumphant and united Germany declared the Second Reich. The year before the Italians had occupied Rome and completed the formation of modern Italy. Two countries which had been disunited since the Middle Ages now took their places as great powers. They had achieved this under the leadership of two great men. Cavour and Bismarck, at the expense of Habsburg Austria.

Both nationalist movements were supported by businessmen, who sought wider markets for the products of the rising industrial system. The flourishing new bourgeoisie were also champions of liberal institutions, which gave them the voice in government needed for their commercial interests. Yet unification came about in very different ways in Italy and Germany. In one country liberals and democrats allied behind the monarchy of Savoy. In the other the Prussian army united the nation by smashing the power of France. In Italy the new constitution was essentially democratic. In Germany liberalism made little headway against the ruling militarist caste.

Italian unification

In many ways, however, the movements for Italian and German unification were very similar. They went on side by side from 1850 to 1870. Neither resembled in any way the popular uprisings of 1848. What happened was that one of the states within each country became strong enough to dominate and finally unite all the rest. Both these states, Piedmont in Italy and Prussia in Germany, were opposed to the Austrians. Both their leaders, Cavour and Bismarck. made masterly use of a new form of 'power politics'.

However, unlike the Germans, the Italians did not gain unity by surrendering to their own army. The Piedmontese army played an important part in fighting the Austrians, but they were greatly helped by popular unrest, guerrilla warfare, and the work of amateur generals like Garibaldi. After the war was over, Garibaldi retired to his farm on Caprera.

Indeed the diffidence of the Garibaldians created marked difficulties. Romantic supporters of unity like his 'Redshirts' did little to organize an Italian state after 1870. This was left to the hardheaded statesmen of Piedmont. But at least unification here had a likeable spontaneity which saved it from the domination by the military which was the price of Bismarck's success.

Before 1848 the Italian patriot, Guiseppe Mazzini, had dreamt of a republic ruled from Rome, in which the power of the papacy and the individual princes would be broken and cast aside. The defeats of 1848 showed the weakness of his hopes. Republicanism, as he saw it, not only antagonized the Austrians but also horrified the Vatican and the rulers of the Italian states.

Mazzini's idealism was too extreme and impractical, and only a minority followed him. The alternative plan of the Abbé Vincenzo Gioberti, for an Italian confederation under the pope, was equally unworkable. Italy, especially northern Italy, was an Austrian sphere of influence. Even under the liberal Pius IX, the papacy could hardly afford to usurp the powers of the Habsburgs, its principal supporters.

As the 1850s opened, both the Mazzinians and Gioberti's 'neo-Guelphs' were discredited. Hopes turned to a third plan of liberation, that of accepting the leadership of the constitutional monarchy of Savoy, or Sardinia-Piedmont, which had already shown itself moderately liberal. Perhaps if Savoy renewed the attack on Austria, it could join with Lombardy and Venetia to form a kingdom of Northern Italy. Beyond this Italian patriots worked out very little. They thought vaguely of organizing some form of federation between the north, the Papal States and Naples in the south. At least this seemed to be a more realistic proposition than Mazzini's republican pipe dreams.

After 1848, Italy, like the rest of Europe, moved into a phase of reaction against liberalism and nationalism. Even the once-idealistic Ferdinand of Naples had become an arbitrary despot. His kingdom of the Two Sicilies remained the most backward in Europe, its peasants too miserable even for revolution. When Mazzini's followers arrived in Naples in 1857 to try to organize a revolt against Ferdinand, there was no support for them, and they were easily wiped out by the Bourbon troops.

In Rome, Pius IX had been restored but now lived in terror of all liberal experiments. The constitution he had granted in 1848 was not restored; he was protected by a French garrison; and power passed increasingly to his diehard conservative secretary of state, Cardinal Antonelli. The rulers of Parma, Modena and Tuscany had become Austrian puppets.

Like Austria-Hungary itself, Lombardy-Venetia, which was still ruled directly from Vienna, had become a police state. After the 1848 revolt alone Metternich's officials there sent 4,000 rebels to prison and 1,000 to the gallows. In London, Mazzini continued to

dream impracticable dreams. The Austrian police crushed his network of Italian revolutionary committees in 1852. Yet he tried to raise the standard of revolt in Milan the very next year. The authorities acted swiftly, and forty republicans died on the gibbet. In the northern Italian states at least, not even the most optimistic patriots could see any solution but the leadership of Savoy.

Victor Emmanuel and Cavour

In 1849, after the bloody Austrian victory over the Piedmontese at Novara, Victor Emmanuel II came to the throne of Savoy. The new king was a homely little man, with an incongruous set of bushy black whiskers. He enjoyed great popularity in his capital of Turin, where he was nicknamed *il re galantuomo* ('the cavalier king'). His good public image was probably linked with his enthusiasm for trimming the privileges of the clergy, who were much less revered in the north of Italy than in Naples for example. This in itself produced a long series of quarrels between Victor Emmanuel and Pius IX. The man who was to make him king of Italy, Camillo Benso, Count Cavour, became a member of the cabinet in 1850.

Cavour had been born in Turin forty years earlier. He was unusually cosmopolitan for an Italian aristocrat. His mother was Swiss, and he himself was educated in France. Afterwards he travelled in England to study its politics and agriculture, before returning to Piedmont to edit the constitutionalist newspaper, *Il Risorgimento*. He had also spent a short time as an officer with the Piedmontese engineers, before losing his commission because of his liberal views.

Once in the cabinet, his rise was meteoric. First appointed minister of agriculture, marine and commerce, he became secretary of the treasury within a few months. After a very short spell out of office, he replaced D'Azeglio as prime minister only twenty-five months after taking his first cabinet post. From 1852 until his death in 1861, aside from a few months in retirement on his estate, he ruled Piedmont.

When his first government was formed, Cavour was forty-two, rich and one of the most popular men in Italy. The people of Turin called him 'Daddy Camillo'. He quickly launched a programme of reform. Unpopular convents were suppressed to the profit of the government. The army was modernized by La Marmora. Above all, Cavour aimed at interesting foreign businessmen in Piedmont's survival and success. British investors sank money in his railway expansion. Communications with France were improved, particularly when work on the Mont Cenis Tunnel started, to bring the magnates in Paris closer to those of Turin.

These measures raised the flagging hopes of Italian nationalists, who deserted Mazzini to follow the Sicilian exile, La Farina, now a champion of unification under the Piedmontese. Cavour was pledged to oppose Austria, and it was only a matter of time until he provoked a crisis. All he lacked for the struggle was a strong ally.

Above, Count Camillo Cavour (1810–61), Prime Minister of Piedmont from 1852 to 1861 (except for a short break in 1859): one of the foremost architects of Italian unification, he worked ceaselessly for it, dying only a few weeks after the first Italian parliament had proclaimed the new king. Pinacoteca di Brera, Milan.

Top, Victor Emmanuel (1820–78), King of Savoy from 1849: he was proclaimed the first King of Italy in 1861, though the whole nation was finally united only in 1870, when the French occupation of Rome came to an end. Museo del Risorgimento, Milan.

Above left, the uprising in Naples; on 29 January 1848 Ferdinand II was compelled to grant a constitution.

Opposite, cartoon by Daumier entitled Le Reveil d'Italie *(Italy Awakes) depicting Italy as Gulliver being jerked awake by the Lilliputians: it needed forty years of political agitation and armed uprisings to achieve unification.*

He found such an ally in France. Napoleon III still had the vestiges of a liberal reputation as a result of his youthful involvement with the *Carbonari*, the romantic republicans of the years after the Napoleonic Wars. He was known to sympathize with the Italians. However, he was somewhat chary about unification, since this would inevitably lead to papal opposition. Even worse, it would offend groups of important Catholic voters in France.

Napoleon was no match for the brilliant diplomacy of Cavour. His master-stroke was to send a handful of crack Piedmontese troops to help the French and British in the Crimean War against Russia. La Marmora and his men gained much of what little credit was to be had from this disastrous campaign, and Cavour was invited to the peace talks in Paris in 1856. Napoleon, as usual clumsily anxious to appear as the champion of nationalism, denounced the oppression of northern Italy in front of the astonished Austrian delegates. Naturally they refused to discuss the subject, but Cavour had gained exactly what he wanted. He had drawn attention to his cause, Piedmont had appeared as a European power, and the other powers had been warned of the general importance of the Italian situation.

Piedmont now went from strength to strength. The whole nationalist movement was swinging over to constitutionalism. In Lombardy-Venetia, even the Mazzinian leader, Daniele Manin, the hero of the 1848 rising against the Austrians, gave support for unification under Victor Emmanuel shortly before his death in 1857. The flamboyant Garibaldi, who had been Mazzini's right hand man in 1848, offered his sword to Piedmont as its reputation for liberalism improved. Loyalty to Victor Emmanuel

grew stronger throughout the north Italian states, including the Austrian ones.

On the other hand, Mazzini lost support as fast as Cavour gained it. Indeed he sponsored the abortive rising of 1857 in Naples to prevent the loss of his republican followers to the monarchists of Turin. If the Bourbons had been defeated in the Two Sicilies, republicanism would have swept through the whole of Italy. After the miserable failure of this revolt, however, the Mazzinians, with their warm, romantic idealism, became a voice in the wilderness. Only success could succeed, and in the 1850s all the successes were Cavour's.

Cavour meanwhile continued trying to inveigle Napoleon into an alliance. '*Italia fara da se*' ('Italy will go it alone'), the slogan of 1848, had become outmoded, and Napoleon's help was essential for the attack on Austria. However, Cavour's hopes for an alliance were set back by the 'Orsini Plot'. One January evening in 1858, when Napoleon and the Empress Eugénie were on their way to the Paris Opera, they narrowly escaped assassination at the hands of an Italian refugee, Felice Orsini.

The concern of this most misunderstood of emperors for those injured by Orsini's bomb shows better aspects of his character than those stressed by critical historians. In the long run, Orsini's attempt actually helped the cause of unification. His appealing letters to the emperor, and his dignified call for help to Italy from his scaffold, increased French sympathy for the nationalists. After the first violent protests to Turin, Napoleon accepted his would-be murderer's advice to 'do something for Italy'. Cavour and he met secretly at the little resort of Plombières in July.

In fact neither Cavour nor Napoleon was interested in uniting Italy. Napoleon had no

wish to antagonize Pius IX, and Cavour shrank from having prosperous Piedmont saddled with the backward southern states. However, they agreed that after war with Austria, a kingdom of northern Italy should be formed, in exchange for which France was to gain Nice and Savoy. Princess Clotilde of Piedmont was to marry Napoleon's cousin. It was vaguely agreed that all Italy was to become a federation under the pope. Piedmont, however, was to go to war with Austria only on a pretext which would justify French intervention on her side. This conspiratorial bargain became the basis of a formal treaty in January 1859.

Cavour at once prepared to set Piedmont on a war footing. He floated new loans, had Garibaldi organize groups of guerrillas, and began to mass troops on the Lombard frontier. A much more difficult problem, however, was preventing Napoleon from changing his mind about the whole plan. As soon as the possibility of war became real, characteristically he began to talk vaguely in favour of an international conference on Italy. It had dawned on him that Paris bankers, and the conservative and clerical parties who supported him, were firmly opposed to French involvement.

Fortunately for Cavour, Napoleon's mind was made up for him by an Austrian blunder. In April Vienna delivered an ultimatum demanding Piedmontese disarmament. After it had been rejected, on the 26th, war was inevitable. Cavour's delight was expressed in his famous (and probably rehearsed) comment '*Alea iacta est*. [The die is cast.] We have made history – so now to dinner!' France dutifully entered the war against Austria.

When the French crossed the Alps and joined with the Piedmontese a month later, they were slightly outnumbered by an

Austrian army of 200,000 men. The first set battle of the war was at the small market town of Palestro, where the personal bravery of *il re galantuomo* was so striking that he was made an honorary corporal in Napoleon's zouaves. The Austrians fell back, and were defeated more decisively at Magenta. But although the allied monarchs rode into Milan in triumph, the Austrians under General Benedek simply fell back on the virtually impregnable fortresses of the Quadrilateral, which controlled the basin of the River Po.

They struck back at the French savagely on 24 June at Solferino, checking the advance of Mac-Mahon and the Piedmontese. Although this was one of the bloodiest battles of the century, and the tales of its slaughter prompted the foundation of the international Red Cross, it was in effect a draw. Control of northern Italy still lay in the balance.

The gentle Napoleon was horrified by the carnage he had witnesses. He was escorted vomiting from the battlefields of Magenta and Solferino. The imperial linen was even offered to augment first aid supplies. After Solferino, he took the first chance of making peace. In fact there were good reasons for the French to draw back. Mac-Mahon's shattered troops were unlikely to make much impression on the Quadrilateral. At home, anti-war feeling was growing – even the Empress Eugénie supported it. Prussia was moving forces up to the Rhine, to emphasize her leadership of the German states.

In Italy itself, the nationalists were doing rather better than Napoleon wished. In Tuscany, Cavour's agent, Ricasoli, deposed Grand Duke Leopold II in favour of a provisional government which offered the crown to Victor Emmanuel. Modena and Parma also fell to the rebels. Worst of all, the papal legate was forced to flee for his life from the Romagna. The rage of Napoleon's clerical supporters made it impossible for him to support Italian nationalism any further. In mid-July the French and Austrians signed the Peace of Villafranca. Napoleon and his army returned across the Alps hated by the Italian nationalists. They seemed to have deserted when the Austrians were on the verge of total defeat. Cavour's hopes for a kingdom of northern Italy had apparently come to nothing. He resigned and returned to his estates.

Cavour did not remain out of office for long. When he formed a new government early in 1860, however, French opinion, partly because of the stability of the provisional government in Tuscany, had changed. It was also clear that a restoration of the expelled rulers of the Italian states would be impossible. Secret negotiations between Cavour and Napoleon reopened, and it was agreed that Piedmont should expand into central Italy. Lombardy had already been given to her at Villafranca, and she was now to gain Parma, Modena and Tuscany. Savoy and Nice, however, were to go to France. Napoleon's condition was that these moves should be preceded by plebiscites to avoid the appearance of disregarding nationalist feelings. Naturally all the Italian population consulted declared overwhelmingly for union with Piedmont. In Savoy the ballot, whether rigged or otherwise, demanded annexation to France by 130,538 votes to 235, and the same decision was reached in Nice by 24,448 votes to 160.

Although the kingdom of Northern Italy was now declared it appeared that Napoleon had been well rewarded for his half-hearted pains. The remaining absolutist princes were appalled at the disregard for

the rights of their colleagues in the north and moved even further to the right. The papacy remained doggedly opposed to liberalism, perhaps partly because Napoleon had now moved over to attacking it. Soon after Villafranca he had sponsored a French pamphlet calling for the removal of the secular power of the Vatican.

In Naples, the Bourbon government was if anything even more wedded to its ancient traditions of reaction. Indeed northern and southern Italy might as well have been two separate countries. The north had become an industrial state characteristic of modern Europe. Its financiers and businessmen flourished and had a voice in the affairs of the state. But the kingdom of the Two Sicilies had changed little since the Middle Ages, its agriculture was still feudal, and it was quite without industry. Overseas trade and the modernizing contacts which went with it were also lacking.

Certainly, feudalism had been technically abolished in 1818, even on the island of Sicily itself. A small proportion of aristocratic land, and a number of church fiefs, had even been put on the market. But the peasantry, who lived by subsistence farming, had little money, and those who did buy holdings soon went bankrupt. The old feudal magnates at once moved in to buy land which had theoretically been confiscated from them.

In the end the system remained essentially unaltered, except that a few of the tiny Neapolitan middle class managed to buy land and began aping the ways of the aristocracy. Even in 1860, the miserable people of the Two Sicilies were dominated by a handful of backward-looking barons. Cavour would certainly have avoided liability for this archaic and poverty-stricken land if it had not been forced on him by the romantic nationalist Garibaldi.

Giuseppe Garibaldi

Garibaldi was fifty-four in 1860. In his teens he had been a sailor on the route to the Black Sea and the Levant. He left the sea out of enthusiasm for Mazzini's 'Young Italy' movement in the 1830s. After being condemned to death by Charles Albert, Victor Emmanuel's father, in the Piedmontese rising of 1834, he was pardoned and emigrated to South America. He fought for the insurgents of Rio Grande Province against the Braganza emperor, Dom Pedro I of Brazil. In the Uruguyan War of Independence against Argentina, which was eventually successful, he fought at the head of a battalion of Italian volunteers.

When the dramatic news of 1848 reached Uruguay, the Italian community in Montevideo collected money to send Garibaldi home, and he sailed for Europe with his young American wife, Anita Ribeiros. After fighting at first for his old enemy the House of Savoy, he went to the aid of the Mazzinian revolutionaries in Rome. When Pius IX was restored by Oudinot's French soldiers, he fled to New York, where he worked briefly as a candlemaker before going back to sea. His wife had died during the flight from Rome.

Garibaldi returned to Nice, the town where he had been born, in 1854. Like most Italian nationalists in these years, he came to see unification under Piedmont as being

the only realistic hope. He and his irregulars, the 'Hunters of the Alps', gave the war of 1859 a note of glamour which impressed all Europe. Next year he and his redshirted volunteers, the 'Thousand', prepared to sail for Sicily to assist a revolt against the Bourbon government. With little expectation that this would succeed, but glad to cause trouble in the south, Cavour helped to equip the expedition. However, its success was so dramatic that Piedmont became deeply involved in Naples and was eventually pushed into absorbing it.

Garibaldi landed at Marsala in May 1860. Although the peasants showed little enthusiasm and the landowners none, he had proclaimed Victor Emmanuel King of Italy and taken Palermo in a month. Unfortunately it was no easier for a liberal to improve the lot of the peasants than it had been for the Sicilian nobles. Their only interest was in land, and as the insurrection spread they rose savagely against their masters – just as the French peasants had done in 1789.

No concessions could stop civil war from spreading throughout Sicily. Not even Garibaldi had any brief for anarchy of this sort. The unfortunate aristocracy now saw the 'Thousand' as the only force which could save them, became nationalists overnight and flocked to the banner of Piedmont. Hundreds of bewildered peasants were shot or thrown into the dungeons of the Bourbons. Yet Garibaldi's advance continued through the island. Messina fell at the end of July, and the Redshirts prepared to cross the straits and threaten Naples itself.

Francis II, King of the Two Sicilies, wavered. He offered a new constitution to try to fob off the revolutionaries. However, he was probably not as frightened as Cavour, who had visions of an embarrassing Mazzinian revolution sweeping through the

south. He frantically ordered Garibaldi not to begin the advance on Naples. He dreaded a revolt in Rome which would bring foreign intervention.

Garibaldi's nationalism was much more uncompromising. With his romantic vision of ancient Italy reunified, diplomatic complications were meaningless. Nor did he see the difficulties of uniting north and south. Cavour did not want Naples, because his first concern was for Piedmont. Garibaldi did want it, since his first care was for Italy.

Garibaldi went ahead with his plans. He crossed the Straits of Messina, defeated the Austrians on the Volturno and sent Francis scuttling from his capital to Gaeta. Cavour now had to intervene. He soon gained the approval of Napoleon, who could easily be persuaded that anything was better than a republican Rome. Cavour's agents stirred

Above, Garibaldi's followers in action.

Top, Garibaldi's volunteers, the 'thousand', embarking for Sicily: they needed only three months to take the whole island. Museo del Risorgimento, Milan.

Top left, Giuseppe Garibaldi (1807–82): his romantic patriotic zeal did much to further Italian unification. Museo del Risorgimento, Milan.

Opposite top, the Neapolitan royal family attending a hunt: ruled by the house of Bourbon until 1860, when the city fell to Garibaldi, Naples was still an undeveloped feudal society, its economy and lifestyle quite remote from that of the industrializing north. Galleria d'Arte Moderna, Florence.

Opposite bottom, life in rural Sicily, as recorded by Chierici in his painting Gioie di una madre. Galleria d'Arte Moderna, Florence.

up rebellion in the papal states, and massed troops on its borders. On the pretext of defending liberal movements which the pope was attacking in Umbria, the Piedmontese then defeated the surprisingly stubborn papal army at Castelfidardo.

Meanwhile, Garibaldi had taken Naples. Cavour's army marched south to join him, carefully avoiding Rome itself. Although Garibaldi had at first said that he would hand Naples to Victor Emmanuel only if Rome was taken first, he handed over power to the Piedmontese army peacefully. After the inevitable plebiscites, which must have been meaningless in peasant areas at least, Naples, Sicily and the occupied areas of the Papal States were annexed by the kingdom of Northern Italy. The first parliament of all Italy met in Turin in February 1861. The following month it was announced that 'Victor Emmanuel II assumes for himself and his successors the title of King of Italy.'

The kingdom of Italy

The outlook for the new kingdom was not very bright. Though Cavour had taken his chances when they came, he had not wanted unification at this stage. He still had to pay the Piedmontese army and to complete his communications system. Pius IX remained steadfastly opposed to the new regime. Worst of all was the backwardness of the south. Cavour had never wanted it and knew that forging a new Italy from the disparate north and south would be as difficult as the tasks he had already accomplished. The Two Sicilies were far removed from the brave new world of the industrialized kingdom of Northern Italy.

Cavour died eleven weeks after his master had been proclaimed King of Italy. Even today, the slums of Naples show that the gigantic task he began has not been accomplished. In the 1880s and 1890s, hundreds of thousands of southern Italians flocked to the United States and Latin America in search of a better world. Joseph Conrad's novel *Nostromo* gives a fine picture of the life of such emigrant labourers.

At home, life in Naples and Sicily went from bad to worse. The romantic liberalism of Garibaldi's Redshirts had done very little for the southern peasantry. Although unification meant that the markets of northern businessmen expanded into the Two Sicilies, its economic needs were modest. Disgruntled merchants complained that the only things they could sell to the peasants were rosary beads. Southern life therefore had to be standardized to create a need for northern merchandise. The peasantry were ruthlessly taxed to pay the salaries of the officials who were to do this, yet gained few benefits from unification.

The first Italian governments, not surprisingly, were northern and shrank from spending money in an area with little business potential. As for the southern barons, their position was left all but untouched. They still controlled local government, and the new officials from Turin did little to help the peasants against their masters. In fact, the new government bought the loyalty of the magnates by guaranteeing their ownership of the land and their control over the peasants. Indeed they were net gainers from the revolution, since they had the assets to buy up land which Garibaldi in his sincerity had distributed among the peasants.

Although redistribution of land was begun again in 1861, with the compulsory breaking up of the greatest fiefs, the barons did what they had done after 1818 and quickly repossessed their land. The only difference was that they were now joined by a sprinkling of rich middle-class businessmen, many of them northern. They too found it easy to cheat the simple and usually illiterate peasantry, who found themselves perilously placed tenant farmers – exactly the position they had occupied since the tenth century. Not only this, but all classes in the south had to meet national taxes geared to the prosperity of Italy as a whole and unrelated to their small means.

The hope of industrializing the south under the new regime soon faded. What tiny amounts of capital were available were leeched off to the north, for no corresponding return. Little was spent on communications and irrigation in Naples and Sicily, where they were most needed. Perhaps worst of all, the self-confident north soon removed tariff barriers which were essential for the protection of infant industries in the south. Low-priced imports now came not only from Piedmont and Tuscany but from Britain and France. The modest family and craft concerns of Naples were destroyed.

Disillusionment with the government of united Italy partly explains the prevalence of banditry as a way of life in the mountain areas of the south. There is a great deal of glamour about our modern picture of the Sicilian bandit. But this does not hide the fact that he was often a man who had found that even with the utmost initiative it was not possible to make a living within the limits laid down by well-heeled officials from Turin. Although there was no leadership to mount a real organized resistance, the bandits were also encouraged by Bourbon agents trying to disrupt the government of the new nation. Indeed the latter was often goaded into clumsy measures of repression, which made the bandits public heroes and bred violent hatred of the north. Italy was not able to solve the problem of Naples in the nineteenth century.

Rome and Venice

After Cavour's death, his successors continued the policy of centralization in the north. But all their efforts could not hide the fact that Turin was not the natural capital of Italy. The country could only be fully united from the centre, from Rome, which was still occupied by a French garrison determined to defend Pius IX's rights. There was also the haunting fear that Garibaldi or some other extremist might do something rash to create a crisis over Rome or the *Italia irridenta* still under Austrian control.

After Garibaldi had been narrowly prevented from invading the Austrian Trentino, in the north, by the personal order of Victor Emmanuel, he gathered a group of alarmingly determined volunteers in Palermo and attacked Rome in August 1862. Although he was captured by the Italian army before he was able to attack the French, his expedition seriously compromised the new

Piedmontese government of Rattazzi at home and abroad. Successive governments fell, and after long negotiations with Napoleon a temporary Roman settlement was reached. The French agreed to a staged withdrawal of their troops, while the Italians were to symbolize their renunciation of Rome by moving their capital from Turin to Florence.

Although the deal over Rome horrified nationalists throughout the country – not least those of Turin – they were more encouraged by gains made in 1866 by the government of La Marmora, the hero of the war of 1859. Part of Bismarck's preparation for war against Austria had been to ensure that France would stay neutral by an agreement made at Biarritz. To guarantee trouble for the Austrians on their southern frontier, he also formed an alliance with the Italians. But although Bismarck crushed the Austrians easily, Victor Emmanuel's troops were heavily defeated at Custozza and the little Italian navy destroyed off Venice, at Lissa. The only successful actions in this disastrous war were the skirmishes led by the inevitable Garibaldi on the borders of Venetia. Nevertheless, at the Peace of Vienna a much-humbled Austria, with a very ill grace, disgorged Venetia. After the usual plebiscite, it became Italian.

But Italy had not yet been united, even by the end of 1866. Rome was still in the clutches of Pius IX, or Pio 'No, No!', as the London *Times* called him. In the northwest, Vienna still controlled Trieste and the Trentino. Naples and Sicily were still not fully subdued. During the war Palermo itself had revolted against the oppression of its overlords in the north.

The Roman problem seemed insoluble. The functions of church and state in the Holy See were bewilderingly interwoven.

Above, voting in Naples during the plebiscite held in October 1860 on annexation to the kingdom of Italy: the vote in favour was practically unanimous. Private Collection.

Opposite right, Garibaldi's triumphant entry into Naples, 7 September 1860: in political manoeuverings during the weeks after the fall of Naples, Garibaldi failed to retain power in the south and had to abandon his hopes of a march on Rome.

Opposite left, painting by Ignazio Alfani of one of Garibaldi's Redshirts departing for battle. Museo del Risorgimento, Florence.

While the Italian government were debating the niceties of this situation, Garibaldi again raised the standard of revolt in Rome itself, in September 1867. Garibaldi was captured and, as usual, sent back to Caprera. However, he escaped in time to fight against a French division which was landed at Cività Vecchia, forty miles north of Rome. They defeated and captured him at Mentana. Although European opinion turned very much against Napoleon's intervention, the French garrison remained in Rome.

Within Italy, the republicans were beginning to gain ground. Opinion was turning very much against a régime which would do nothing for Rome. It is even doubtful whether the kingdom of Italy would have survived if it had not been handed to Rome by the crisis of the Franco-Prussian War of 1870. The French garrison was withdrawn for other duties, and Napoleon was deposed. Victor Emmanuel could argue that he had no obligations to the new Third Republic.

The Italian army swept into Rome in September. Pio Nono made no consessions and considered himself a prisoner in the Vatican until his death in 1878. Indeed it was only with the Lateran Treaty of 1929 that Italian difficulties with the papacy were settled through the creation of the Vatican City State. Again, Trieste and the Trentino remained Austrian until 1918. But in 1870 Rome declared sweepingly for unification with the rest of Italy. The House of Sardinia-Piedmont now ruled over a united country from the capital of the Caesars.

Germany

German unification was to change the course of European history even more dramatically than the emergence of the kingdom of Italy. The Battle of Sedan, which had given the Italians the chance to seize Rome, upset the balance of power in the West. The traditional Europe had been dominated on land by France and Austria and at sea by Britain. It was replaced by a new state system, with the massive land power of united Germany precariously balanced against Britain and her continental allies. This balance survived until the disaster of 1914 and re-emerged under Hitler. After the Second World War, yet another system of international relations took its place, Soviet Russia replacing Germany as the main threat to the other countries of Europe.

After the failure of the 1848 revolutions, Germany, like Italy, remained as disunited as she had been since the Middle Ages. However, the number of independent states left had been reduced to thirty-eight, and all were members of an extremely weak confederation. Its nominal head was the Habsburg emperor of Austria, and all states sent members to a central though powerless diet or parliament in Frankfurt. Certainly German liberals had developed a sense of common nationality. But the individual princes,

from the emperor in Vienna downwards, were jealous of their privileges. All resented Austrian domination, but this did not mean that they would listen to any plans which would threaten the integrity of their little statelets.

As in Italy, the 1848 failure had disillusioned the intellectuals who had led it. They drifted away from republicanism towards the strongest power which had shown any liberal inclinations – Prussia. Even here, hopes of success were low. After 1848 Austrian pressure had brought all the German states, including Prussia, into line against liberalism. Frederick William I was now an old man. The Prussian government was controlled by mediocre and thoroughly conservative ministers. Although second only to Austria within Germany, Prussia was still a second-rate power.

Yet the groundwork of future Prussian greatness was being laid. More than any of the neighbouring states, Prussia had gained from the Zollverein or German Customs Union. Formed under Prussian domination, this had defeated all other attempts to create free trade areas within Germany by the end of 1833, after which most of the other states joined it. Key seaports like Hamburg, however, remained outside. More significantly, Austria remained aloof and was excluded even when the Zollverein was reorganized and strengthened in 1853. Prussian businessmen were given the opportunity of extending their interests throughout a wider area of Germany, and industrialization was speeded up. Another important effect of the union was that the

German railway system came to be centred on Berlin, a factor which was eventually to give Prussia considerable advantages in time of war.

During the decades before German unification, quite apart from the Zollverein, industrialization went on apace. The contry's vast mineral resources were tapped, and production was revolutionized by complexes like that of the great ironmaster Alfred Krupp. Britain was no longer the only country with an industrial landscape. Germany was not spared the ugliness of industrialization, the dirt of its sombre factories and the misery of its poorest workers.

However, German society adapted readily. The hard-working middle classes were quick to adopt new methods, quick to re-invest their profits, and quick to make their businesses large and modern enough to compete with any others in the world. Even the solid, old-fashioned *Junkers*, who had ruled the villages and countryside of Prussia since the Middle Ages, were affected. They began to invest the profits from their land in industry or look for easier profits underneath it. Trade was not looked down on by the north German aristocracy, in spite of the Prussian love of military display, and industrialization was all the easier for it.

Prussia's modernization was encouraged by its ruling house, the Hohenzollerns. William I came to the throne in 1861, at the age of sixty-four. Not an original man, the new king was a competent administrator and, like most of his family, devoted to the army. The Berlin government was heavily

weighted towards soldiers, and the equivalent of secretary of state was the military strategist von Moltke, the uncle of the general of the First World War. In 1862, however, the government faced serious opposition to its plans for extending conscription from two to four years. It fell in September. The Kaiser's new prime minister was Count Otto von Bismarck.

Although Bismarck became the greatest diplomatic genius of the century, he was the most human of statesmen. Apart from unifying Germany, he invented his own favourite drink, the black velvet, a mixture of champagne and stout. The most important man in Europe was also a man whose unreasonable greed for pickled herrings made his old age a hell of indigestion. He was born in 1815, into a good Brandenburg *junker* family. They had always been modest landowners, with generations of service in the Hohenzollern armies behind them. Bismarck's sophisticated mother was an exception for a Bismarck wife, and her experiments in Berlin salon life had very nearly ruined the family by the time her son Otto came of age.

He was a strange mixture of brilliance and eccentricity. One moment he would be a great hearty giant of a man, the next an obnoxious and moody bore. Athletic and startlingly clever when he chose to work hard, he was proud of being a *junker* and proud of being a Prussian. As a young man he was known as a madcap, a fearless horseman and a massive drinker, and yet he worked frantically to set his family's affairs in order and pay off his mother's debts.

There was not the slightest trace of the revolutionary about Bismarck. Like other landowners, his main interest was in preserving the position of his estates, his class and his country. He opposed emancipation of the Jews and saw the vicious Prussian game laws as a bastion of society. No doubt it was because of his conservatism that he became a member of the united Prussian Diet in 1847. In the same year he married his gentle Lutheran wife Johanna von Puttkamer.

Bismarck lost no time in earning a reputation as an arch-reactionary. He struggled for counter-revolution in 1848. Bismarck had little sense of German nationality. He always thought in terms of Prussia annexing the other German states rather than true unification. But he was not foolish about his patriotism. When Austria humiliated Prussia in the Olmütz agreement of 1854, he spoke very sensibly against the hotheads who wanted to march on Vienna forthwith. He shared the feeling that honour was worthless for its own sake with his master Frederick William and was rewarded well for his loyalty. He was Prussian delegate to the weak Frankfurt Diet throughout the 1850s and then became ambassador successively to St Petersburg and Paris.

Later Bismarck made full use of the experience these posts gave him. He realized that Austria was the real obstacle to Prussian supremacy in Germany. He also had an opportunity to work out the way in which Napoleon's dreaminess laid him open to being duped by talk of liberalism and nationalism. He himself was not troubled

Above, the Krupps works in the mid-nineteenth century.

Opposite, 1852 cartoon from Kladderadatsch *(the German satirical journal) showing Prussia trying to persuade recalcitrant non-members to join the* Zollverein.

▓	*Kingdom of Prussia in 1861*
░	*Acquired by Prussia in 1866*
╱	*Other members of the North German Confederation*
- - -	*Southern boundary of the North German Confederation*
	Countries expelled in 1866 from the German Confederation of 1815
⊥	*Alsace-Lorraine*
▬	*Frontier of the German Empire in 1871*

by platitudes of this sort. A real opportunist, his political life was never hampered by any set of ideals.

His first concern was his own career, his second the welfare of the Hohenzollerns and his third the greatness of Prussia. For the sake of all three objectives, he turned his powerful mind towards bringing Germany under the overlordship of Berlin. Unification for him had nothing to do with progress or change. He feared and hated both, though he would use their supporters when he could. Because of his flexibility, he was able to dupe those more idealistic than himself and seize all possible opportunities of increasing Prussian power.

Strangely enough, Bismarck hated force. He may have spoken about blood and iron, but he detested the clumsiness of actually using them. Yet he knew that his brilliant diplomacy would only be effective if backed by real military power, and he knew that this military power would eventually have to be used or the impregnable position he wanted for Prussia could not be gained without it.

His real genius appeared not in fighting wars against Denmark, Austria and France but in outmanoeuvring those who might have objected to such wars. His first task was to leave Austria without friends outside Germany. He won the regard of Russia by appearing as the only European statesman willing to help in the tsar's savage repression of the Polish revolt of 1863. After the Convention of Alvensleben, where Bismarck agreed not to give sanctuary to any refugees from Poland, he could rely on Russian friendship. France and Italy were the other two powers which might have been expected to object to Prussia's taking over German leadership from Austria. We have already seen how Napoleon was won over

at Biarritz and La Marmora persuaded to join in the war which led to the disasters of Custozza and Lissa.

Schleswig-Holstein

War with Austria eventually broke out over rival claims to the Danish duchies of Schleswig and Holstein. Both belonged to the Danish royal family but contained substantial German minorities anxious to join the German Confederation. When Christian IX was crowned in Copenhagen in 1864, he created a European crisis by announcing that he intended to incorporate Schleswig, Germans and all, into Denmark. Austria and Prussia together attacked the Danes on behalf of the German Confederation, and Christian was forced to give up both duchies. They were temporarily put under joint Austro-Prussian control.

Probably Bismarck had not thought out the implications of this situation. However, when he attempted to discredit Austria by questioning her administration of Schleswig, Vienna accepted the challenge. Francis Joseph had now promised Venetia to the Italians and thought they would not fight. The past record of the Habsburg army was good, and the southern German princes resented Prussian control of the *Zollverein* and suspected Bismarck's intrigues. It was Austria, not Prussia, which declared the war which would decide who was to lead Germany.

The Austrians had underestimated the brilliance of von Moltke and his army. Prussian discipline was splendid, and Austrian territory was invaded with bewildering speed. The power of the Habsburgs was smashed once and for all on 3 July 1866 outside the Bohemian town of Sadowa. The

news of the Austrian collapse galvanized Europe. Although Napoleon moved troops up to the Rhine, he could not act decisively on behalf of Austria when he had pledged himself so often to support liberalism and the rights of nationalities. Italy herself was crushed at Custozza, the British admired the Prussians and were unlikely to intervene in far-off Eastern Europe, while Russia had been bought off at Alvensleben. Bismarck was left to make peace in his own way.

In fact the Peace of Prague was most statesmanlike. Bismarck realized that a humiliated Austria would become an even more bitter enemy of future Prussian ambitions. The Habsburgs only lost their stake in the duchies and Venetia, both of which were commitments they could well do without. However, Prussia's gains within Germany were enormous. She absorbed Hanover, Schleswig, Holstein, Frankfurt, Nassau and Hesse. The weak confederation was swept away.

With Austrian power broken, Bismarck was also able to form a North German Confederation, under Frederick William's presidency, including all the states north of the River Main. As president, the King of Prussia was to appoint a chancellor – Bismarck – and to be advised by a council consisting of the rulers of the various states. A central parliament or Reichstag was to be elected by universal suffrage. Economically, this was a great advance over the *Zollverein*, since control of currency and trade was to rest with the central government. Other aspects of policy, like foreign policy and control of army and navy establishments, were centralized, although the sovereign states still dealt with internal affairs. Apart from the confederation, twenty-five million Germans were now ruled from Berlin.

The French response

Napoleon III, as he gazed across the Rhine and the Main to Berlin, was alarmed by what he saw. His efforts to construct a nationalist Europe had simply set the

Above, Field-Marshal Helmuth von Moltke (1800–91): he served in the Prussian Army for 66 years, becoming Chief of the General Staff in 1857, and was responsible for the successful campaigns against Denmark, Austria and France in 1864, 1866 and 1870 that led to unification.

Above left, the Battle of Custozza, Lombardy, 24 June 1866, at which Austrian forces, led by the Archduke Albrecht, defeated the Italians, allies of Prussia: Austria's victory brought her no benefits.

Left, Prussian troops advancing at the Battle of Sadowa, 3 July 1866, the chief battle of the Austrian-Prussian war: peace was signed three weeks later, and from now Prussia replaced Austria as the major central European power.

Below left, William I (1797–1888), King of Prussia from 1861 and Emperor of a united Germany from 1871, opening the Reichstag of the North German Confederation: the Confederation, formed in 1867, which Bismarck governed as Chancellor (the two assemblies had little power), was a union of virtually all Germany north of the River Mainz so designed to facilitate the membership later of the southern German states. Prussia was the dominant power.

Opposite right, Otto von Bismarck (1815–98), as portrayed in a photograph taken in 1863: Chief Minister of Prussia from 1862 and Imperial Chancellor from 1871 to 1890, he was a dominant figure in German unification and also in the establishment after 1870 of Germany as a world power.

Opposite left, Germany in the mid-nineteenth century.

Hohenzollerns in place of the Habsburgs as a threat to French security. His response was a written demand for territory to compensate France for Prussian gains. Bismarck (in private) contemptuously dismissed the note as an 'innkeeper's bill' and sat back to let the unhappy Napoleon make a fool of himself in the eyes of Europe. Although he at first did this with the simple intention of weakening French prestige as much as possible, he delightedly saw Napoleon's blunders push the south German states into alignment with Prussia.

First Napoleon asked successively for the Rhineland and part of Belgium but was assured their cession was politically impossible. Finally he lowered his sights to trying to buy Luxembourg from the King of Holland. The grand duke at once appealed to the North German Confederation, and Prussian detachments were moved in to support him. Bismarck took good care to make Napoleon's floundering public, and the German states became united in hostility to France. The most which was conceded was a guarantee of Luxembourg's neutrality and the withdrawal of Prussian troops.

In his old age Bismarck recorded that he avoided a war at this time because, although he had decided that a conflict with France would be essential to unification, he wished to give his military reforms time to make the Prussian army unbeatable. But it is not likely that he thought of war or even unification until 1870. By then Napoleon's extraordinary bungles had left all the German princes clamouring for Prussia to lead them to battle. Bismarck then seized the opportunity of destroying the French threat on the Rhine, annexing the border states for his master the King of Prussia and thus 'unifying Germany'.

To do him justice, Bismarck did ensure that the Prussian army became the most efficient fighting machine in Europe. Arms were poured into Berlin's new dependencies and the increasingly friendly states of southern Germany. The French were much worse off. Recruitment had dropped, while conscription did not affect the rich and faced serious public opposition. Plans for mobilization were antiquated and ineffective. It was probably because they knew this that the general staff put so much pressure on Napoleon to guarantee the Rhine frontier against Prussian expansion. Indeed they were frightened and second-rate men compared with Bismarck's purposeful generals. Occasional reforming officers like Marshal Niel, who tried to reorganize the weak National Guard while war minister, ran up against solid opposition in the purblind Corps Législatif.

The pressures on Napoleon to bluster against Prussia were increased by the unstable nature of French politics. The empire was under heavy attack from the republicans and in May 1870 granted a new constitution. Control of affairs had really passed out of Napoleon's hands. He is something of a

tragic figure in these last months of the régime, ill, muddled and scared. All his advisers misjudged the real power of Prussia. The Empress Eugénie, the new prime minister, Émile Ollivier, the foreign minister, the Duke of Gramont, all gave the wrong advice to a man who was incapable of making up his mind for himself. The Second Empire faced its last crisis without decisive leadership.

The French response to the 'Hohenzollern Candidacy' for the throne of Spain gave Bismarck the chance to fight a war on exactly the terms he wanted. After the 'Glorious Revolution' of 1868 sent the Bourbons into exile from Madrid, the liberals led by General Juan Prim y Prats began what the Spanish press called a 'lottery of kings'. The Kaiser's cousin Leopold von Hohenzollern announced he would become a candidate in June 1870. Gramont, for once with the support of all parties, announced belligerently that France would consider foreign control of the Spanish crown a threat to her security.

However, the Kaiser, who had always been opposed to harrying the French through Madrid, eventually persuaded Leopold to withdraw. Matters would have ended there if Napoleon's final stroke of folly had not given Bismarck the opportunity he wanted. The Kaiser was on holiday in the Rhineland resort of Ems when Benedetti, the French ambassador, brought him a demand from Paris that Prussia should humiliate herself by refusing to renew the candidacy. He replied politely that he approved of the withdrawal and had nothing to add to it.

Bismarck had never dreamt the French would play into his hands in this way. He at once published an edited version of Kaiser Wilhelm's telegram telling him of Benedetti's demands. The 'Ems telegram' brought the countries to the brink of war. Its text

gave the impression that the ambassador and the Kaiser had exchanged mutual insults in an interview which closed with Benedetti being refused a further audience.

Ollivier at once moved towards war, which he announced he could now wage lightheartedly (*d'un coeur léger*). France declared war against Prussia on 19 July. Not even the wildest optimist in Germany could have expected France to take on this responsibility. She had no allies while the Prussians had no enemies. Even Alexander II had been friendly with the Hohenzollerns since the Kaiser entertained him at Ems in May.

Sedan

The Franco-Prussian War surprised Europe not by being so short but by not being even shorter. Although Leboeuf, the French war minister, reassured doubters by claiming that his preparations were complete down to the last gaiter-button, more important aspects of planning had unfortunately been neglected. The first French troops at the front were outnumbered two to one. The famous French *chassepôt* was as good as the German rifles, but unfortunately Leboeuf had not ensured that all his men had one. The German artillery was immensely superior. Worst of all, the French General Staff had no member who could match the brilliance of von Moltke.

His first army pushed a French army led by Mac-Mahon, the hero of the war of 1859, out of Alsace. A second army under von Moltke's own leadership advanced towards the great fortress at Metz, routing five army corps under General Bazaine. They re-formed in Metz itself, and the Germans surrounded the city. Thanks to Bazaine's halfheartedness – or treachery – this French army of 173,000 remained out of action until the end of the war.

Left, the Battle of Sedan, 1–2 September 1870, at which Napoleon III surrendered with some 85,000 of his troops: after this there was no hope left for France.

Opposite, Prussian infantry storming a French village at the Battle of Metz, 18 August 1870.

Left, William I receives Napoleon III's letter of surrender on the field of Sedan.

Left, French and Prussian troops fighting for control of a railway line: the war, which left lasting bitterness between France and Germany, announced Germany's arrival, under Prussian leadership, as a major world power.

However, Mac-Mahon had redeployed round Châlons and might have presented the Prussians with a serious threat if the dithering Napoleon had not arrived at the front to direct the French defence. He ordered Mac-Mahon to try to relieve Metz, the very plan which was easiest for the Germans to counter. The rescuing forces were themselves surrounded by the Germans at Sedan, on the Meuse. After two attempts to break through the German ring, Napoleon offered to surrender on 2 September. The emperor became a German prisoner, and Moltke and the Kaiser marched unopposed towards Paris. Seventeen days later, they had placed the capital under siege. It appeared that the war had practically come to an end.

In fact France had not yet been defeated, although the fall of the empire had become inevitable. The Third Republic was proclaimed in Paris the day that news of the surrender at Sedan arrived. After tentative attempts to open negotiations with Bismarck, the provisional government's minister of the interior, Léon Gambetta, set about placing France on a footing of all-out national warfare.

On 7 October he himself left Paris by balloon, to sail across the German lines and rally support in the provinces. He and the Bonapartist d'Aurelle de Paladines formed a new army on the Loire and regained Orléans, while General Faidherbe checked the rather surprised Germans in the north.

Although Gambetta never managed to lift the siege of Paris, and Bazaine remained ineffectively cooped up in Metz, France's temporary recovery was startling. It could not last. The two sections of Gambetta's Loire army were defeated at Loigny and Le Mans, and the heroic Faidherbe at Saint-Quentin. In Paris itself, the Germans did not bother to waste men in a frontal attack, but simply sat down and waited for surrender. In the end the poorest Parisians genuinely faced starvation, while even the most fashionable restaurants were reduced to feeding their patrons on the inmates of the Tuileries Zoo. Paris could not have lasted much longer even if Bismarck had not ordered a bombardment which claimed 400 civilian casualties.

On 23 January 1871, Jules Favre, the Republican foreign minister, began to negotiate an armistice. When a new National Assembly was called, it declared overwhelmingly for peace and appointed the veteran statesman Adolphe Thiers as its plenipotentiary or 'Chief of the Executive Power' in negotiating with Germany. Meanwhile, Paris itself was on the verge of revolting to form the 'Commune'. In March radical rebels, some of them socialists, seized the city. Late in May Mac-Mahon, himself a thinly disguised royalist, reconquered it block by block against bitter resistance. Indeed the Third Republic's first task at home was the bloody suppression of the 'communards' in its own capital.

The Peace of Frankfurt

Since unification of Germany had suddenly become a practical possibility, Bismarck had to make peace on the terms which would make that unification as smooth as possible. Anxious to appear as the protector of the southern German states, he could easily argue from Napoleon's erratic behaviour that Germany's neighbour was violent, greedy and irresponsible. Germany thus had to gain a frontier which would make French attack impossible (or, alternatively, make a German attack on France easy). This was why Bismarck demanded that the peace of Germany should be guaranteed by giving her the area on the left bank of the Rhine round the fortresses of Strasbourg and Metz. He argued that in German hands these would be used defensively, as a guarantee of peace. He warned Prussian diplomatic officials, somewhat unconvincingly, that 'in twenty wars we have never been the aggressors against France, and we claim nothing from her but the security she has so often threatened.' The beauty of this standpoint was that its appeal to the south German states made the prospect of unification under Prussia a reality.

When the final peace settlement was signed at Frankfurt in May, Alsace-Lorraine

Left, William I, General von Moltke and Bismarck in the Prussian lines during the siege of Paris: Paris did not prove an easy target as the imperial armies had expected and withstood a siege from 19 September 1870 to 28 January 1871, its population facing starvation and, from early January, nightly bombardment.

Centre, William I, King of Prussia, is proclaimed Emperor of Germany in the Hall of Mirrors in the Palace of Versailles, 18 January 1871, the final scene in Prussia's long struggle to control a united Germany.

Bottom, Jules Favre, foreign minister of France, and Otto von Bismarck signing the Treaty of Frankfurt, 10 May 1871. Under the Treaty France ceded Alsace and most of Lorraine to Germany and agreed to pay an indemnity of five billion francs; the former provision provided a lasting grievance, the second was met within a few years.

Opposite, painting by Adolph von Menzel of William I, King of Prussia, leaving to join the army in the field, 31 July 1870: within six months he had been crowned emperor of a newly united Germany. Nationalgalerie, Staatliche Museen Preussischer Kulturbesitz, Berlin.

was ceded to Germany, and it was agreed that German troops were to remain in eastern France until an enormous indemnity of 5,000 million francs was paid. The disgrace of these losses was keenly felt in France. The Mayor of Strasbourg died of shock on hearing the news of the peace. Although the people of Alsace-Lorraine were given the option of taking French citizenship, relatively few did so. Far more became settlers in Napoleon's great colony, Algeria. Later the *colons* became the most French of French exiles. Although Alsace and Lorraine were duly absorbed into the Second Reich, Bismarck's mistake was not to see that this ultimate humiliation would produce a France unlikely to rest until it had reversed the Peace of Frankfurt. This was one reason why the Europe he constructed slid so easily into the First World War.

The new German Empire was not very liberal and not very nationalistic. Even in the Catholic south, German life was standardized on a Prussian model, not a true German one. Although a constitution was granted, power remained where it had always been in Prussia, with the small class of *junkers* under the Hohenzollerns, themselves the principal *junker* family. But Bismarck had taken his chances and made Prussia the greatest power on the continent. The German princes were united under the Hohenzollerns on Hohenzollern terms because of the enormous success of the Peace of Frankfurt. It was no accident that the Second Reich was proclaimed on 18 January 1871 in the *Galérie des Glaces* of the Palace of Versailles, at a point when it was clear that France would give all the concessions necessary to win over the German princes to Prussia.

Even so, the organization of the empire in the preceding months had perhaps been Bismarck's most difficult task. He himself

had probably wished to avoid a union with the decadent popish south when the war broke out, and although his own ideas changed during the autumn by no means all German rulers wished to bind themselves to Prussia. Several princelings, particularly the more powerful rulers of Baden, Würtemburg and Bavaria, proved stubborn about surrendering their privileges. Louis II of Bavaria was only won over by being allowed to retain control over his army, post office and railways. He also gained a secret pension of £20,000 per year (taken from the revenues of the exiled King of Hanover) and a promise that the Bavarian brewing industry would be protected by a reduced duty.

The greatest problem of all was to win over the Kaiser. He was unimpressed by the new-fangled idea of becoming Emperor of Germany. His interests were Prussian and not German, and unlike Bismarck he saw no reason for disguising Prussian greatness with the fiction of a nationalist empire. He distrusted popular power and was only converted when Bismarck managed to persuade Louis of Bavaria to write to him on behalf of the princes of Germany begging him to accept the crown. Even at the ceremony in the *Galérie des Glaces* he shook hands with all the dignitaries present except Bismarck. The chancellor had had him proclaimed as 'Emperor William' instead of 'Emperor of Germany', a subtle difference which avoided the implication of true kingly power over Germany.

The balance sheet

Ten years before, no one had dreamt that Piedmont would unite Italy or that Prussia would unite Germany. Neither Bismarck nor Cavour had been an exception. Their early aims had been limited but had expanded as the weaknesses or blunders of other powers gave them opportunities to increase their strength, which they faultlessly seized. The result was the emergence of the united countries German and Italian liberals wanted, although they were ruled respectively by soldiers and businessmen rather than by intellectuals.

For Europe as a whole, the result of the rise of Germany and Italy was revolutionary. Unfortunately Bismarck's successors failed to see that he had used force in 1870 as an adjunct to his diplomacy. Since they still possessed the world's finest fighting organization, they fell back on using it to gain whatever they wanted. This was the more dangerous since France also looked forward to the war of revenge which would give her back Alsace-Lorraine. The result was the war of 1914.

Although greatly different, both Germany and Italy gave new opportunities to industry and to the rising middle classes. The businesses which profited from the large new national markets mass-produced more and more new inventions. Many of their products

were later sold in the widening markets of Asia and Africa. Partly for this reason, partly because of the desire for prestige connected with very new nationhood, Germany eventually began the 'scramble for Africa'. Italy also came to play a part in annexing territory overseas. At the same time, the expansion of the working class at home produced new social theories which brought the industrial states to the verge of revolution.

Chapter 7

The Modernization of Europe

Europe changed dramatically in the later nineteenth century. Nationalism upset the traditional relations between its states, and imperialism eventually extended its rule throughout the world. Neither, however, had effects as far-reaching as developments in industrial and intellectual life. As industrialization speeded up, in old and new nations alike, business units increased in size. Europe moved into the age of trusts, cartels and monopoly capitalism. Its need for machinery also gave an immense stimulus to inventiveness. The scientific and technological revolutions had even more startling results than the industrial one.

By 1900, modern medicine, electrical power and even the petrol engine, were accepted as part of European daily life. But at the same time as scientists were meeting the needs of the business world, it was creating new forces which would challenge it. Industry required labour, and as its workers were gathered together in Europe's growing cities they began to consider new theories of society which rejected the capitalist system which employed them. Karl Marx is as much a figure of the nineteenth century as Count Cavour.

Sir Lewis Namier, one of the greatest historians of our century, has called 1848 the year of the revolution of the intellectuals. These intellectuals were defeated by monarchists throughout Europe. The result was profound disillusionment with the hope of changing the social and political structure from within. It now seemed more realistic to abandon piecemeal reform. There was an increase in the numbers of socialists, who planned to substitute the rule of the community for the rule of kings and capitalists alike.

The most advanced of them, Karl Marx, tried to apply the laws of science to his interpretation of society. His *Communist Manifesto* was actually issued during the 1848 revolutions and thereafter rapidly made converts. Marx's prophecy that proletarian revolution would erupt throughout the world still remains to be fulfilled, but his theories of class structure have deeply affected all the modern 'social sciences'. Some disillusioned intellectuals went even further than Marx and abandoned the study of society and its ills completely. Some even joined the ranks of the great scientists and inventors of the nineteenth century. Their discoveries made changes in the life of the West – and the world – which had never been dreamt of by the men of 1848.

The physical sciences

By the nineteenth century, most elements known to modern science had been discovered. The next task was to classify them. In 1869 this was done by the Russian researcher Dmitri Ivanovich Mendeleev. He was of Siberian birth, the fourteenth son of a schoolteacher, and rose to be professor of chemistry at the University of St Petersburg. It was already known that matter was composed of atoms grouped into molecules of different formations, in turn linked in varying ways. Mendeleev grouped the elements according to their atomic weights ranging from the lightest (hydrogen) to the heaviest (mercury). This classification provided the groundwork for modern chemistry and may have been the most important work by a nineteenth-century scientist.

Equally significant progress was soon made by physicists. The whole field of astrophysics had been opened by the research of two German scientists, Kirchhoff and Bunsen. In their research on the physical properties of light, they developed the technique of spectrum analysis, which in turn was applied to chemistry. This not only made it possible to locate elements like rubidium but also led to the discovery of helium in the matter composing the sun before it had been isolated on earth.

In 1850, another German, Rudolf Clausius, who became professor of chemistry at Berlin at the age of twenty-eight, demonstrated the connection between heat and energy. His findings were supported by William Thomson, Lord Kelvin, the foremost British scientist of the age. In 1861–2, another Scot, James Maxwell, professor of physics at Aberdeen and later London, postulated the electromagnetic nature of light. Twenty years later the existence of the electromagnetic waves of which he had written was experimentally proven, and the discovery was eventually applied to radio transmission. Modern organic chemistry had been founded by the research of the French scientist Jean Baptiste Dumas on the chemistry of the alcohols. The next step was to apply all these advances to industry.

Biology and medicine

The nineteenth century also saw advances in biology and medicine, as both were taken into the laboratory. The theories of Claude Bernard first suggested that the body represented a complete and interdependent mechanism, to which experimentation could be applied as successfully as in any other branch of science.

Above, Robert Bunsen (1811–99), who, in addition to his pioneering work with Gustav Kirchhoff on spectrum analysis, can claim credit for several inventions, among them a galvanic battery and the Bunsen burner.

Opposite, French cartoon of 1870 showing Bismarck's dominant position in Europe.

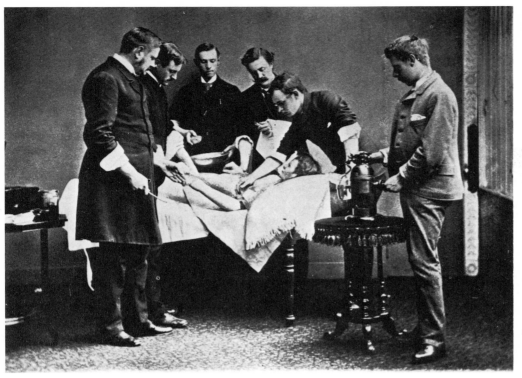

Louis Pasteur (1822–95) was perhaps the most influential of all. He used his training as a chemist and his skill with the microscope to solve practical problems for vintners, brewers and dairymen. Examining spoiled wine under the microscope, he found living organisms in addition to the yeasts which produced fermentation. He concluded that these 'bacteria' caused decay and also spread infection in animals and humans. He was able to develop the process of 'pasteurization', in which heating of liquids for a prolonged period destroyed the infection-carrying bacteria they contained. He also found that the risk of infection among domestic animals could be reduced by inoculating them with weak strains of bacteria.

It was a short step onwards from his discoveries to develop antibiotics to fight the micro-organisms which cause human diseases like tuberculosis. Joseph Lister, professor of surgery at Glasgow and later Edinburgh, applied these theories to surgery. At King's College, London, he was able to reduce fatalities during operations through the use of antiseptics. Pasteur's work had begun a medical revolution.

Against the background of these discoveries, Charles Darwin was working on the most controversial of all theories of biology – the theory of evolution. His *Origin of Species* was published in 1859, after long years of research he had begun in 1831 on a round-the-world voyage as naturalist on the survey ship HMS *Beagle*. Although he

worked from the classification of species carried out by the great eighteenth-century Swedish naturalist Carl Linnaeus, Darwin rejected his assumption that the species were immutable and had been created in their current form.

Darwin argued that life had begun at the lowest possible level and that only those species which had come to terms with their environment had survived. This constituted his law of survival of the fittest, which governed the selection process by which humanity had emerged as the highest form of existence. In turn, not all humans would survive. Influenced by the gloomy theories of Thomas Malthus, Darwin was obsessed by the thought that as population outstripped world resources only the fittest would manage to survive. But it was not a pleasant thought to be descended from an ape, or something worse. Darwin was ostracized. Churchmen throughout the world were horrified and wrote learned treatises to defend the biblical account of the seven-day creation.

They had little success in refuting Darwin's startling heresy. The revolution in scientific attitudes went on apace. However, the discoveries which would have made Darwin's case unassailable went unnoticed. The researches of Gregor Mendel, a monk from Moravia in Czechoslovakia, were only recognized in 1900. Mendel had spent the years between 1858 and 1866 studying generation after generation of garden pea plants. He discovered that their hereditary characteristics appeared at set intervals between generations.

From this he was able to evolve 'Mendel's Laws' on heredity. Not only plants but animals and humans transmitted their characteristics by heredity, these characteristics changing slowly to meet new conditions in the way Darwin had suggested. Thirty years later the Dutch scientist Hugo de Vries discovered Mendel's work and confirmed his findings. The science of genetics had been founded.

At the same time, Pavlov's dogs were making history. This Russian biologist found that once they were accustomed to having a bell rung immediately before feeding time, the dogs salivated on hearing the bell even when no food was forthcoming. This research produced the theory of 'conditioned reflexes', which was the first step towards the development of psychology as we know it.

Also towards the end of the century, Sigmund Freud and his English popularizer Havelock Ellis began to write on the psychology of sex and the importance of sexual motivation in human behaviour. Since it could be argued that psychological as well as physical characteristics were likely to be passed down from generation to generation, the stage was now prepared for the controversy that was to last a long time among the great scholars over the importance of environment versus heredity.

Left, caricature of Charles Darwin (1809–82) produced at the time of the publication of his Origin of Species in 1859: his theory of evolution through natural selection, which met enormous resistance for many decades, provoked a fundamental change in scientific method and thought.

Opposite top, an operation in progress during the mid-nineteenth century: the work of Louis Pasteur (1822–95) and Joseph Lister (1827–1912) had a revolutionary effect on surgery and laid the foundations for the development of bacteriology, thus making possible for the first time the defeat of diseases such as typhoid, diptheria and cholera.

Opposite bottom, Ivan Pavlov (1849–1936) with his colleagues and one of his dogs: his research on dogs produced theories of behaviour applicable in general to human beings.

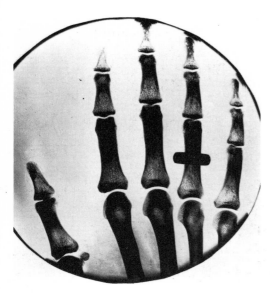

The new science

The most revolutionary findings of all, those of early atomic physics, were made in the last years of the century. In 1895, the German scientist Wilhelm Roentgen, who had studied under Clausius as a student, discovered X-rays. Three years later an even greater triumph came with Pierre and Marie Curie's isolation of the first known radioactive element, radium. The research of the Curies stimulated the work of Ernest Rutherford on the structure of the atom. This in turn looked forward to the time when the atom would be split and atomic energy harnessed, for better or worse.

The whole structure of science was changing. New subjects were being examined even in the most traditional of universities. 'Laws' of science which had been accepted for centuries now became the butt of scholarly ridicule. The data available was expanding with alarming rapidity, and scientific methods of study changed accordingly. Now, scientists would propose a hypothesis which they accepted as the best possible approximation to the truth. They expected future experiments to suggest a better hypothesis, when the first one would be discarded. And its value would not have been explaining an aspect of nature so much as in suggesting new areas of research. The German writer Max Weber even suggested that society should be studied through constructing hypothetical 'ideal types', against which its actual conditions could be measured. It is on his work and that of other scholars of his generation whom we would now call 'social scientists' that the new subject of sociology has been built.

The applications of science

The nineteenth century did not make its scientific discoveries for their own sake. Science was to be applied to technological advances, which could be used in the dominant industrial system of the West. But

in spite of the discovery of new metals and new sources of power, the late nineteenth century was still the age of steel and coal.

Steam was still the main source of energy used in industry and communications. It had improved immensely since the days of Watt and his kettle, because of the use of the compound engine, which increased efficiency by using steam that once heated was repeatedly recycled. Again, the invention of the Parsons' steam turbine made long distance ocean transport faster and more reliable. By the middle of the century, the great private steamship companies, plying from Liverpool, Southampton, Cherbourg and Le Havre to New York, were making enormous fortunes for their owners. By 1900 the ships used had become floating hotels, carrying their passengers in unparalleled luxury.

The steam turbine was also adapted to generating electricity in power stations. Electricity had not yet replaced steam as a source of industrial power, but the nineteenth century was the time of the inventions which made its harnessing possible. A clumsy electric motor had been invented in Belgium as early as 1869; twelve years later the brilliant German businessman, Werner

Siemens, had the first electric streetcar running in Berlin. More important for industry was the success of the French engineer Deprez in transmitting electrical power by means of high tension wires, the forerunners of the lines of pylons which march across the landscape.

Power could now be distributed cheaply from central generators to industries hundreds of miles away. Factories would soon be able to move away from the coal mines towards the markets they served. On the whole this meant that they were no longer confined to the most unattractive localities. Since the first experiments in harnessing hydro-electric power had also been made, the basic components of the system of electrical power on which modern industry depends had been invented by the end of the century.

Soon it would also be possible to use electricity outside the factory. No nineteenth-century invention now seems as indispensable as Edison's humble domestic electric lamp. In international communications, the first ocean cables had been laid as early as the 1850s. On the completion of the transatlantic cable – under the direction of the physicist Lord Kelvin – New York

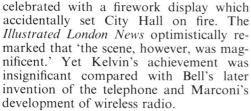

Above, Magnus Volk's Electric Overland and Submarine Railway, the first electric railway in Britain, it started operations along the Brighton seafront in 1883.

Left, the electric tramway at the Paris Electricity Exhibition, 1881: electricity soon became the prime source of power in industry but had only a marginal impact on transport, being chiefly used for urban streetcar networks, until electric locomotives began to be introduced on a large scale in the 1950s.

Below left, the opening of the Kaiser Wilhelm Canal (now known as the Kiel Canal), 21 June 1895: the canal was primarily built for strategic reasons, to give the German fleet rapid access from the Baltic to the North Sea, and reduced the journey by several hundred miles.

Opposite right, Pierre and Marie Curie (1859–1906 and 1867–1934), who in 1898 isolated radium: their discoveries, along with those of Röntgen, Antoine Becquerel (who discovered radioactivity) and Ernest Rutherford, completely altered the way in which scientists viewed the physical world.

Opposite left, an X-ray of a human hand taken in 1907: Wilhelm Röntgen's discovery of X-rays in 1895 marked an important advance for medical science.

celebrated with a firework display which accidentally set City Hall on fire. The *Illustrated London News* optimistically remarked that 'the scene, however, was magnificent.' Yet Kelvin's achievement was insignificant compared with Bell's later invention of the telephone and Marconi's development of wireless radio.

But the nineteenth century was not to feel the full impact of electricity. The same was true of early experiments with the internal combustion engine. It was first used in commercially available motor cars in 1885, when the German firms of Daimler and Maybach, and Benz, both offered models to the public. In the same year, Gottlieb Daimler even produced the first recognizable motorcycle. By the turn of the century, improved with the invention of the pneumatic tyre by Dunlop and Michelin, the motor car was known throughout Europe. The French manufactured it most enthusiastically,

largely through the firms of De Dion, Panhard and Peugeot.

But the motor car was still an aristocrat's toy in 1914. Even with the application of Rudolph Diesel's heavy engines to some areas of marine transport, little inroad was made into the supremacy of steam as a motive power. In the year the First World War began, ninety percent of all Europe's fuel for industry and transport came from coke and coal.

A shrinking world

As the output of industry increased, the long-distance transport which carried its wares improved to meet its demands. By 1914 the Kiel and Panama Canals had been added to Suez as the world's greatest artificial waterways. Steel-hulled, screw-driven ships had taken over the greatest share of

the world's ocean transport. Railway communications also improved, especially in the United States, where the Atlantic and Pacific coasts were linked in 1869. On 10 May, Union Pacific Locomotive No. 119 chugged up to Promontory Summit, Utah. It carried the company chairman, Dr Thomas C. Durant, to a ceremony at which he and Leland Stanford, President of the Central Pacific, tapped gold spikes into the final section of transcontinental track.

No European achievement in railway building equalled this. Nevertheless, the continental rail system expanded dramatically from about 1850 onwards. In many cases construction went on under the supervision of British engineers. The greatest plan of all was the completion of the Trans-Siberian Railway, which carried its first train in 1904. The mastermind behind it was the Russian minister of finance, Count Sergei Witte. The long journey from Moscow to Vladivostock, once one of several months, could now be made in favourable conditions in just under a fortnight. Trains in general became swifter. Lighter but more powerful engines and more comfortable coaches carried their passengers more cheaply and comfortably than ever before. The danger of accidents lessened as steel rails were substituted for faulty iron ones.

Competition between railway lines remained, with a resulting wastage of capital investment. But duels like the one between the North British and the Caledonian on the run from London to Scotland meant that schedules were pared and passengers were treated with unfailing consideration. The last years of the nineteenth century and the first of the twentieth were the heyday of the European railways.

Though few Europeans could afford to travel on the ocean liners or the great transcontinental railways, more modest advances affected the whole population. Even the poorest began to use the bicycle to release themselves from the monotony of town life. Again, the expensive Daimlers and Le Dions of 1900 were not far removed from the

Model T Ford and Baby Austins manufactured a generation later – or indeed from the Vauxhalls and Buicks of 1970. Soon the bicycle would be replaced by the mass-produced motor car.

It was only after 1900 that the lighter-than-air balloon gave way to the aeroplane. Even then, the dream of flying in machines heavier than air had fascinated inventors for so long that it was difficult to have any faith that it was possible for anyone to do so. The flight of the Wright brothers on the lonely shore at Kitty Hawk, North Carolina, attracted little attention, in their own country or elsewhere. At the end of 1903 Orville Wright's clumsy monoplane, built in his brother's own workshop, staggered through its first flight. Two years later the same machine stayed airborne for thirty-eight minutes. Yet the Brazilian aviator Santos-Dumont, when he made the first European flight in 1906, in a machine rather similar to a box kite, genuinely thought he was the first man to fly in a craft heavier than air. However, at least Santos-Dumont's achievement created some interest.

There was even greater popular enthusiasm when Blériot crossed the English Channel between Calais and Dover in his neat little monoplane in 1909. After this flying came to have an enormous glamour in the public eye, which made the Royal Flying Corps one of the most difficult services to enter during the 1914–18 war, though the military possibilities of aircraft were at first little understood. During the first part of the war they were considered one of the frills of the armed services.

On the other hand, it was well understood that the new invention would soon have commercial possibilities. Even the modest Wrights had been primarily businessmen. They flew in sober three-piece suits, starched collars and neat ties. The only article of city dress they left on the ground were their bowler hats. In the last few years before the war, other speculators began to build, improve and sell aircraft. Though the United States War Department had

originally scorned the Wright's toy, governments soon began to buy aeroplanes. Certainly early critics considered that the heavier-than-air machine, like the balloon, would be useless except for reconnaissance. They considered the problems of shooting or bombing from vehicles travelling at the breakneck speed of 60 mph to be insuperable. Nevertheless, this startling invention of the early years of the century was soon to revolutionize warfare. It would also have the greatest effect of all on international communications.

The world economy

As communications within and between the nations improved, it became possible for industry and agriculture to specialize. Produce could now be carried cheaply and quickly from one end of the world to the other. To take three examples, Ontario could concentrate on growing wheat, the Scottish border towns on producing woollens, the Ruhr on producing steel. Each area could provide the world with its speciality and avoid wasting time on producing the general necessities of life. These could readily be shipped from other regions in turn devoted to exporting other commodities. Another result of the improvement in communications was that it now became economical for both Europe and America to import raw materials from the

under-developed areas absorbed by 'new imperialism'. Specialization became the keynote of the world's economic life, as steam and steel reduced the area and widened the scope of the world market.

In the late nineteenth century, industry quickly adapted to the use and to the manufacture of the new inventions. Communications improved its sources of raw materials and expanded its markets, and factories in turn throve on creating the materials required for these communications. At the same time, advances in the processes of production increased industrial output. For instance, Europe's production of steel had increased and made cheaper ever since 1855, when Sir Henry Bessemer invented the converter which made steel by passing air through molten cast iron. A greater advance came with the Siemens-Martin process, using furnaces fired with superheated gas, which permitted the production of larger quantities of highly tempered steel.

Advances in mining made it possible to exploit mineral-bearing areas like Pennsylvania and South Africa. Huge new deposits of increasingly important metals like copper, tin and zinc were discovered in Russia, Canada, the USA and even West Africa. Lighter metals, which were to be of the first importance in twentieth-century industry and technology, were added to the traditional ones. Aluminium, for instance, had first been isolated in the laboratory in 1854 by two scientists working independently,

the Frenchman Sainte-Claire Deville and the German Friedrich Wöhler, professor of chemistry at Göttingen. The latter also isolated two other metals, beryllium and titanium, which were later put to use in making light alloys of steel.

In industrial terms, however, a more important discovery came in 1886 when the American Charles Hall evolved the method of producing aluminium economically by electrolysis. It had long been known that steel could be hardened through the addition of tungsten. Duralumin, a light and hard substitute for steel, was first produced in 1908 by combining aluminium, copper, manganese and magnesium. The basic metals used in modern technology were now available, and metal production bounded ahead. One hundred and fifty times as much steel was produced in 1913 as in 1850.

Industry also began producing articles which had previously been unknown and which sent Europeans all over the globe to find raw materials. For instance the infant automobile and aero industries were indirectly responsible for the devastation of the Belgian Congo. After the invention of the pneumatic tyre by Michelin and the introduction of vulcanization by Goodyear, world demand for rubber became insatiable. The one staple which the Congo could produce was crude rubber, and its unfortunate population was decimated by the refusal of European factors to accept tribute in anything else.

Above, the smoking chimneys of Stoke-on-Trent, the centre of England's china manufacturing, a scene that was repeated in every industrial centre in Europe and North America.

Opposite top right, the P & O Company's liner Himalaya in 1895: the opening of the Suez Canal in 1869 considerably reduced sailing time to India, the Far East and Australia.

Opposite top left, construction work in London on the world's first underground railway: the line, which ran between Paddington and Farringdon Street, was opened on 10 January 1863. Other major cities were slow to follow London's lead and waited until the early twentieth century to inaugurate a rapid transit system, though the first line of the elevated railway in New York started operating in 1867.

Opposite bottom, planting the first pole of the overland telegraph at Darwin, September 1870: the line ran 1800 miles to Adelaide, mostly across barren wilderness, and, once linked with a cable from Darwin to Java, put Australia in telegraphic communication with London.

With less disastrous results, the huge British textile industry searched for new sources of raw cotton once its main supplies were cut off by the American Civil War. India had always grown cotton in moderate amounts, and by the end of the century a substantial amount of Lancashire cotton was coming from Egypt, now effectively a British colony. Improvements in dyeing and patterning processes meant that more and more cotton prints could be produced to sell throughout the world. The British woollen industry had expanded in the early nineteenth century using the fleeces of Cheviot sheep which landlords had used to stock the Scottish Highlands after enclosing their estates and expelling their tenants during the Clearances. It now expanded even further to absorb the fine wool produced in Australia after the introduction of the Merino.

Widespread use of synthetic fibres would have to wait for the great chemical manufacturing complexes of our own century, but the textile industry was now far removed from the old era of craft production controlled by small businessmen. Textiles, like most other enterprises, were moving into an age of mass production when the great captains of industry effectively elbowed lesser men out of the economy. More and more men who would once have owned their own businesses sank to being employed by others.

The same was even true of farming itself, traditionally the preserve of men with little capital. The specialization made possible by improved communications was profitable, but in the first instance it was also costly. Australian sheep farming was only one area where the capital needed to begin farming was enormous. In other branches, new machinery and effective fertilization made yield higher, though this also meant that a larger unit had to be cultivated to give an economic return on capital invested. Once again the small man went to the wall.

The process was accelerated by the fact that competition could now be felt thousands of miles away from the places where crops were produced. Until subsidies and tariffs were introduced, for instance, it became uneconomical for European farmers to grow wheat, since North American imports could be sold so cheaply. The smaller producers were forced out of the market, while larger ones diversified the crops they grew or began to clamour for tariff protection. Even then, much European farming sank to being a form of glorified market gardening. The fruit farming of Britain and the Low Countries is a case in point. Even the French wine industry falls partly into this category, although it seemed likely to be wiped out by the scourge of phylloxera after 1868, until the European vine was saved by grafting it on to hardy Californian stocks. In agriculture in general, small farmers who failed had the choice of working for other farmers, moving into the towns or emigrating.

At all levels, units in the world economy grew larger. Free competition destroyed competition as the great industrial trusts swallowed one another up and became monopolies. Even if this did not happen, competition between huge concerns meant that the small businessman could not survive. By the end of the century companies had appeared in Europe which carried out every stage of the production of whatever article they made. In turn such companies raised capital for their enormous operations through borrowing from the bankers' trusts which dominated the new phase of 'finance capitalism'. The bankers' return for investing in any given company was to claim a number of its directorships. Great financial houses like Morgans, Barings and Rothschilds thus came to have a finger in most industrial pies and could effectively control the operations of the business world as a whole.

The only direction in which they could not control it was in its tendency to manufacture too much for its own good. Overproduction was the bane of the mature capitalist system of the nineteenth century. Each time the bulk of commodities on the market outran world demand, a slump resulted. The years 1877, 1893, 1907 and 1929, to mention the worst examples, saw disasters of this kind. Nothing could be done to curb the seesaw boom/bust pattern of business life until governments intervened to prevent overproduction. Meanwhile the industrial nations frantically searched for new markets to absorb their surpluses.

The slumps which caused industrialists so much worry had even worse effects on the masses of working men who had been gathered to work in the new factories. At each recession large numbers of them were left without jobs and the division between employers and employed appeared harsher. Industry was now controlled by a very few entrepreneurs. Small businessmen had become wage-earners, and farmers who had failed to withstand growing competition moved into the towns to join them. All became slaves of the factories, a solid 'proletariat' at odds with the captains of industry. In the *Communist Manifesto*, Marx argued that in this class capitalism had created its own ultimate enemy, the force which would overthrow it. For the present, however, the proletarian worked on at his monotonous task: 'He becomes an appendage of the machine, and it is only the most simple, most monotonous, and most easily acquired knack that is required of him.' Yet this humiliated workman, Marx thought, would be the revolutionary of the future. Eventually there would be a slump from which capitalism could not recover, since it would have no further markets to absorb its surpluses.

Later Lenin argues that the 'new imperialism' had postponed this final crisis by annexing territory which would become new fields for investment and salesmanship –

but after these had been used up, he maintained, the revolution would come. After prolonged slump, the proletariat, organized by alienated middle-class leaders, would turn on their masters and destroy the capitalist system.

Undoubtedly the speeding up of European expansion overseas was to some extent connected with the need to find wider and wider market areas. Yet the final crisis which Marx and Lenin prophesied has not come about. What they underestimated was the flexibility of the system they criticized. They could not look forward to the time when the liberal English economist John Maynard Keynes would advise governments to spend as much money as possible, even if this involved increasing public debts, to guarantee markets for their national industries. Nor could they imagine that the capitalists would ever change their nature to the extent where they would deliberately pay high wages so that their workmen could buy enough to prevent industry falling on hard times.

Marx would have been even more astounded if he could have been transported to the world of the 1960s. In his own time no one had thought of sophisticated advertising devices which make it possible to sell articles which rational enquiry proves to be useless. No one had thought of the even more sophisticated practice of selling articles which must be replaced regularly because they have been specifically designed to fall to bits as soon as decently possible. The capitalist system actually had a great deal more strength and adaptability than Marx had imagined. The structure of industry which emerged in the West in the late nineteenth century survives in our own day.

Until the appearance of Keynes' startling theories, however, European and American industry had its troubles. The saving grace was that many businessmen quickly developed an acrobatic knack of making money out of their own difficulties. When fears of overproduction, or perhaps hints of diminishing gold supply, led to alarm on the stock exchanges, nothing was simpler for those who had reserves of money than to buy shares at low prices and then to sit back to wait for conditions to improve. There was no capital gains tax in the 1890s. From making profits out of stock exchange fluctuations, it was a short step to engineering them. False rumours could start panic among speculators as well as true ones, and exactly the same profits could be made by buying cheap and selling dear. By these means and more honest ones, the numbers of extremely rich men increased.

There were more millionaires in America than anywhere else – from having twenty in 1840 the USA could count over four thousand in 1900. The size of individual fortunes increased too. John Jacob Astor, in the forties, had been worth a miserable seven and a half million. The great Scottish-

American steel magnate Andrew Carnegie, whose money founded several of the greatest British public libraries, including the Mitchell Library in Glasgow, died in 1919 leaving five hundred million. Exactly the same was happening in Europe. Marx was certainly right in arguing that the gulf between rich and poor had increased, although he was wrong in prophesying that it would go on increasing.

The rise of the industrialists also meant that the relation between farm and factory changed. Until the nineteenth century, perhaps even until the end of the nineteenth century, the richest men in Europe had been landowners. The increase in the size of business units, however, made it possible for men like Krupp in the German steel and armaments industry, Michelin in the French rubber industry or Morgan in American banking to amass fortunes undreamt of by earlier generations.

As for the legions of labourers required to man the factories, they were provided partly by draining off the population of the countryside. Farmers who did not survive the worsening conditions of competition in agriculture naturally sought a better livelihood in the growing industrial towns. It was only for very few that the hope of riches was ever fulfilled. The lure of the city meant that by the end of the century the characteristic European was coming to be a townsman rather than a peasant, though this development did not go ahead at a uniform speed. France, for instance, retains much of her rural character up to the present day. Only half her population were town-dwellers when the First World War began. Britain had reached this proportion as early as 1851. Even so, France was highly urbanized compared with the backward countries of Eastern Europe.

The new industrial complexes were also helped to find adequate labour by the population explosion of the latter part of the nineteenth century. Europe had a population of 293 million in 1870 and 490 million in 1914. This rise resulted not from change in the birth rate but from a startling increase in life expectancy. The death rate fell as hygiene improved and medical research concentrated on preventing disease rather than dealing with it once it had arrived.

Europe's growing towns created many difficulties for those responsible for governing them. Not the least was that the workers who lived in the towns began to combine in efforts to improve their condition, in ways which threatened the supremacy of their employers. A more immediate problem, however, was that of health. The more enlightened European governments and local authorities had to set about dealing with the risks created by filth and overcrowding in the massive cities of the new industrial world. The most important pioneer of the new science of urban administration was the British 'philosophic radical' Edwin

Chadwick. Pasteur's work afterwards made it clear that the removal of slums was extremely urgent.

By the end of the century it was agreed that towns should be planned to give their inhabitants at least reasonable amounts of light and space. It was recognized that the risk of infection meant that sewage and garbage disposal and the provision of uncontaminated water supplies were services which had to be provided for the public good, whether by central or local authorities. Some advanced towns set magnificent examples – Berlin almost doubled in population in the nineteenth century and yet had the most modern sanitary services in Europe. As the pattern of growth combined with more rigid health precautions was repeated in every city, so the old cycles of recurrent epidemics like typhoid and cholera gradually disappeared. At the same time, the role of the state in governing citizens' lives for their own good widened. European civil services swelled and on the whole became more efficient. Traditional groups of government employees were joined by a new and continually expanding class of trained local government officials.

Above, engraving of Parisian slums towards the end of the nineteenth century: measures to improve public health began to be put into effect during the second half of the nineteenth century, but slums such as these survived well into the twentieth century.

The rise of the proletariat

As the city populations swelled, the differences between those who owned businesses and those who worked in them sharpened. More significantly, as workmen were crowded together, they became aware that they had common interests and shared grievances against the captains of industry who controlled their lives. A true mass working class had now appeared. As a mass electorate, it was to revolutionize European politics after the First World War. In the late nineteenth century, sections of the workers set about expressing and organizing their opposition to the capitalist system. Strike action became more militant, and genuine socialist parties appeared throughout the West. The Socialists' First International, founded prematurely in 1868, had collapsed by the seventies. But the formation of the Second International in 1889, and the frequent congresses it held from that time onwards, signalized the organization of the proletariat as a force in world politics.

The international socialist movement, pledged to destroying capitalism, had itself been produced by the changing industrial order. This also involved a great expansion in the city-dwelling middle class. Its new members were men whose education was good, whose salaries were comfortable and whose posts depended on the prosperity of the great industrialists. But the fact that ownership was now concentrated in such few hands diminished their opportunities of rising up the scale.

The characteristic middle-class man of the nineties no longer owned his own small business but was employed in someone else's large one. He might also be a professional man disturbed at the low reward given to his specialized skills relative to industrial incomes or a humanitarian genuinely distressed at the misery he saw in the working population around him. Unlike the workers, none of these groups had the slightest intention of destroying the capitalist system. This would have been to take the bread out of their own mouths. But they did set out to try to mitigate its abuses. It was they who were most enthusiastic about improvements in the conditions of work in industry. Above all, they used their votes to bring pressure to bear on those richer and more powerful than themselves, entering into temporary alliances with workmen for this purpose.

This was the liberal impulse as it emerged in the later part of the century, giving rise to the organization of the great European liberal parties, the best example of which is the British one. All such parties, incidentally, were strongly patriotic and did much to sweep their countries into overseas expansion at the time of the 'new imperialism'. Socially, however, they were far more wedded to the existing system than even the most conservative trades unions and labour parties which were emerging throughout Europe at the same time.

The most effective bargaining counter which the workers possessed was their labour. They had everything to fight for. Working conditions were miserable, hours outrageously long, pay low and security or hope of advancement nonexistent. Although many dreamed of a new socialist order where these abuses could not exist, others joined the liberals in working for short-term improvements of their position. But where the liberals trusted in the political mechanism, the workers' hope was to force concessions through direct action. They therefore set about organizing strong labour unions to use the weapon of the strike most effectively. In doing so, they could be sure of some middle-class support. In the nineties, they were even encouraged by the Catholic Church, which cast aside its traditional conservatism in an enlightened attempt to win the poor away from the atheistic assumptions of socialism.

But the first problem of the trade unions was that not only their strikes but their existence were illegal in most European countries. Collective bargaining could also be defined as conspiracy in restraint of trade, and it was only gradually that the unions gained protection for their funds and had the rights of striking and picketing recognized.

Trade union history in each European country followed different lines according to the political structure and industrial sectors involved. In Britain, the Trades Union Congress, the first of its kind, initially met in Manchester in 1868. Its success in extorting legal recognition of its status and the right to strike from Gladstone and Disraeli inspired trade unionists throughout Europe. But the TUC remained a relatively conservative body dominated by skilled workmen.

When the 1875 recession threw thousands out of work, unskilled labourers also formed their own unions. The 'new unionism' was deeply influenced by socialist thought and developed political goals. At the Edinburgh Congress of 1896, British unionists called for a nationalization of mines and railways. Though this generation of leaders did not achieve anything so startling, their ties with the Parliamentary Labour Party, which worked in partial alliance with the liberals after its foundation in 1893, produced much of the legislation on working conditions which was fought for. The Liberal government further conciliated the Labour Party by providing for limited but compulsory National Insurance against sickness and industrial injury. By 1914, it seemed that the representation of the British working-class electorate through parliament had enabled them to lobby for advances in the conditions and security of their labour.

Although no other country had a union movement as successful as the British one, all show comparable developments during this period. In Germany, for instance, the union movement was well represented in the *Reichstag* through the Social Democrat Party. This had more seats than any other single party by 1912. Because of this success, both genuine revolutionary socialism and straight concentration on collective bargaining were underplayed in Germany. German unionism also had undertones of nationalism disturbing to socialists elsewhere. The Gotha Programme of 1875, for instance, stirred Marx to violent opposition because of its admission of the need for a 'people's army', presumably to fight nationalist wars. With the successes gained at the polls, there seemed no need for revolution or even forceful direct action in industry. Indeed the bulk of German unionists were opposed to the socialists.

When the German equivalent of the TUC first met in 1890, its general secretary, Karl Legien, even argued that the hope of organizing a general strike was a delusion. Its inevitable failure would destroy the patient advances made by previous generations of trade unionists. In 1906 the Social Democrat Party itself took exactly the same standpoint. If this was socialism, it was not the form envisaged in the *Communist Manifesto*. Indeed Marx, Engels and later Lenin, spent much of their time denouncing German 'revisionists'.

Syndicalism

France's trade unions or *syndicats* were much more radical than those of Germany. The recognition of trade unions by Jules Ferry's brilliant government of 1883 was followed in 1886 by the formation of the Fédération Nationale des Syndicats. This was strongly Marxist and suspicious of previous labour activity through the existing political machinery, though its leader Jules Guesde did not extend this ban to the Fédération itself. But early progress was slow. Ferry's law of 1884 forbade the formation of unions among state employees, who included the important railway workers. There was bitter and sometimes violent opposition to unions at all levels of French society. At the end of the century less than 600,000 French workers held union cards.

Much of this weakness was a result of disunity. The unions not only included men like Guesde but those interested in using them as workers' friendly societies, which could administer funds or relief during periods of unemployment or sickness. These were the aims of the Bourses de Travail set up in 1887 and federated five years later, though they could also be used as bases for much more radical anarchist or 'syndicalist' agitation. Although the Bourses joined in a new national organization, the Confédération Générale du Travail (CGT), in 1902, this division was to bedevil unity in the French movement for many years.

The more radical unionists also made the creation of any wide workers' front difficult because of their tactically wise refusal to accept any concessions from bourgeois or 'opportunist' politicians. They felt that any such acceptance could only weaken the genuine radical labour opposition. In fact French statesmen in general were still haunted by memories of the radical 'Commune' of 1871, and any concessions made were moderate. They were also badly received. When the socialist Alexandre Millerand became secretary of commerce in 1899, his sell-out to bourgeois politicians was seen in labour circles as direct treachery. Not even his creation of a new labour department, his extension of minimum wage and maximum hour legislation to all public employees and his institution of the eleven-hour day restored his good reputation.

The French labour movement, then, was more militant than those of Britain and Germany. In 1906, the CGT reaffirmed its faith in the general strike in the Charter of Amiens. By this time it had been deeply influenced by the 'syndicalism' of Georges Sorel, which involved use of the trade unions as training units to prepare for violent revolution. Indeed the movement had none of the encouragement to work through existing institutions given to the Social Democrats by their success in the *Reichstag* or to the British Labour Party by its success in extorting acceptable legislation from the Liberal Party.

In 1914, the CGT strongly opposed labour participation in the 'fratricidal' conflict. No other major European labour organization was far enough divorced from the nationalism of the middle classes to be able to do the same. French labour, on the other hand, was forced by the conservatism of the levels of society above it to reject contacts with the middle class completely. It was only in Italy and Spain, where the franchise was narrow enough to make hopes of constitutional reform faint, that other labour movements rejected all reform from above and followed France in a leaning towards syndicalism and anarchism. At the other end of the scale, the most backward unionism of all was that of Russia, which was legally recognized in 1906 but at once forced underground by tsarist police methods. In 1914, few could have foreseen that it would be in imperial Russia that the first socialist state would be founded.

International socialism

In nineteenth century socialist circles, Karl Marx now seems the most influential and purposeful figure. His assumptions about the structure of society influence most modern scholars, and the *Communist Manifesto* and his *Das Kapital* still provide much of the ideology of the underdeveloped nations which have gained their independence since that era. However, this should not obscure the fact that Marx was by no means unchallenged as the leader of socialists of his own generation. First, Marx was firmly in opposition to cooperation with bourgeois, clerical or aristocratic socialists, far less with liberals – 'the people, so often as it joined them, saw on their hindquarters the old feudal coats of arms, and deserted with loud and irreverent laughter' – thus the *Communist Manifesto*. Yet the feudal coats of arms were not enough to make all workers reject the gains they could make through such alliances. Much more serious opposition to Marxist socialism came from the anarchist wing of the labour movement. This became very clear when socialists tried to unite in launching the First and Second Internationals.

The First International, officially entitled the International Working Men's Association, was formed in London in 1868. It drew support from all parts of the labour movement, but in spite of the disunity this caused it made rapid gains and had about 800,000 members by the end of the decade. An increasing number of these members were Marxist socialists, who were gaining at the expense of the followers of Pierre Joseph Proudhon. Proudhon was the self-educated son of a French barrel-maker, who had become a printer by trade. He had won a large section of European labour over to a belief in attacking capitalism through workers' education and the formation of worker-owned cooperatives. The threat of the Proudhonites, however, was not as great as that of the anarchists.

The leader of the anarchist attack on the Marxists was Count Mikhail Alexandrovich Bakunin, the greatest of the Russian aristocratic revolutionaries. A complete nonconformist among nonconformists, one of his leaders in the Paris revolt of 1848 had exclaimed of him – 'What a man! The first day of the revolution he is a perfect treasure, but on the next day he ought to be shot.' It is

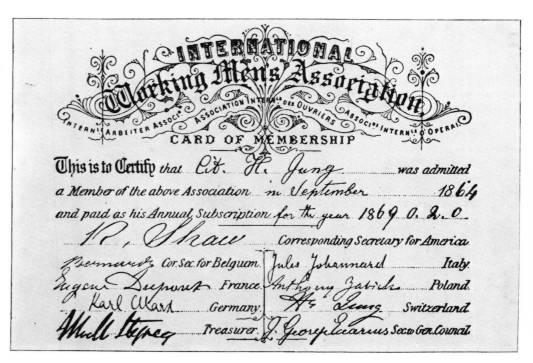

Above, Count Mikhail Bakunin (1814–76), Marx's chief opponent in the First International: Bakunin believed not in the dictatorship of the proletariat but in the destruction of all state organization and appealed not to the industrial proletariat but to the peasantry and workers of the less industrialized nations.

Top, membership card of the International Working Men's Association for the year 1869.

likely that Turgenev modelled the character of the dedicated revolutionary Insarov in *On the Eve* on his close friend Bakunin. After 1848, he spent eight years in jail in Saxony. The Saxons handed him over to the Russians, who in turn sent him to Siberia. Predictably, he escaped, via China, and sailed from Yokohama in Japan to the United States and thence to London.

His hopes of replacing all state agencies with self-governing workers' communes horrified Marxists, who thought in terms of rigidly centralized proletarian revolution. But his ideas appealed in countries where there was little hope of revolution as Marx understood it and less of constitutional gain. When Bakunin and his followers appeared at the 1869 Congress of the International, they received strong support from Swiss, Spanish and Italian delegates but were spurned by the French, Germans and British.

Bakunin clearly intended to cut the International loose from the 'German authoritarianism' of Marx, and he and his friend Nechaev worked hard to gain support. The confused network of even more confused secret societies they formed are bitterly satirised in Dostoevski's *The Possessed*. The anarchists were expelled from the International in 1872, but their opposition was so great that the organization fell apart. Although Marx cleverly moved the remnants of the International's headquarters to New York, it was dead by 1874.

Bakunin died in 1876 and Marx in 1883, but the European labour movement remained as disunited as ever. However, at least the trade unions made steady progress, and the earliest socialist parties were founded in the eighties. In 1889 delegates from all the European nations met in Paris to form the Second International. Among them were the Scottish socialist Keir Hardie and the German 'revisionist' Eduard Bernstein. Their programme was simple. They announced that they would work for universal suffrage and better working conditions and hold a one-day token strike on May Day of each year. What they did not do was provide any permanent organization or office, and this was only set up in Brussels in 1900.

The Second International had learned enough from past experience to try to exclude anarchists, although its inaugural meetings were frequently interrupted by the Italian Bakuninite Dr Merlino, who sneaked in, in various disguises and abused the organizers at most of the sessions. Anarchists or no, the International continued to waste effort in bitter disagreements. Even when it was formed in Paris, there were two rival conferences to celebrate the centenary of the revolution of 1789. The regular Marxist/trade unionist one eventually formed the International, while the other one was a meeting of 'possibilist' or opportunist socialists ready to work through existing parties. Yet all these elements had to be incorporated in the International if it were to remain a working force.

LE CONGRÈS SOCIALISTE

The new threat was not anarchism but 'revisionism'; the assumption that working-class prosperity and growing capitalist strength had now indefinitely postponed the revolution. The new role of the labour movement was thus to have wages raised and force concessions on suffrage and working conditions from liberal politicians.

Since the British were fully integrated into the International, because of the peculiar form of their socialism, the main spokesmen for the revisionists were the Germans. Their leaders Eduard Bernstein and August Bebel became the main opponents of the orthodox Marxists. Given German success in liberal politics, it was easy for them to illustrate their arguments from their own experience. Sure of their success through constitutional means, they even stuck to the damaging slogan, 'the general strike is general nonsense!' The Marxists were championed by the Frenchman Jules Guesde, now leader of the Parti Ouvrier Français (POF), so that the argument fell partly along nationalist lines. Each annual conference of the International ended in a violent exchange of insults connected with this division of policy.

However, the national socialist movements were in many cases divided internally as well. Even in Britain, where the working class vote apparently made revolution unnecessary, the Social Democratic Federation remained independent from the Labour Party and took a revolutionary position. The situation was far worse in France, where socialists had been debating Millerand's betrayal in joining the Waldeck-Rousseau cabinet in 1899. Guesde's attacks on the relatively mild Jaurès, with his belief in constitutional action, produced conflicts which reduced the movement's meetings to what Briand called 'annual scissions'.

In Russia, Lenin's chief opponent in the years before 1917 was the revisionist Karl Kautsky. Indeed Kautsky replaced Bernstein as the European leader of the revisionists. The International was still prostrated by this disagreement when its unity finally disappeared in debate over the question of whether socialist parties should support their governments in the First World War.

Hopes of organizing a European revolution against the masters of the industrial system had faded. Socialist goals had not been abandoned, but it was increasingly felt that these could be reached by peaceful methods. In the first decade of the century, socialist parties and trade unions had become genuine powers which could exert genuine pressure within the capitalist structure of society. The future lay not with violent revolutionaries but with Bernstein's revisionists, or so it seemed until the stress of war made the Bolshevik revolution of 1917 possible.

Meanwhile, revisionism was all the more attractive because it did not involve abandoning national loyalties. The 1912 Conference of the International rejected a French resolution that the weapon of the general strike should be used to prevent a capitalist war. This involved an admission that direct and violent action had been given up in favour of 'evolutionary socialism'. But it also made it clear that for a majority of European socialists loyalty to the small unit of the state came before loyalty to the wider unit of the working class. The long fragmented Second International finally collapsed under the additional strain of the 1914–18 war. It was hard to talk of class brotherhood when socialist politicians from Britain and Germany had voted for taxes to fight against one another.

Clerical liberalism

The difficulties of the Second International were not wholly its own fault. The increasingly liberal capitalist system had simply acted to give timely concessions which would dampen the ardour of a large section of the socialist rank and file. The working-class vote and the improvements in conditions of labour in the factories were reforms which blunted the revolutionary impulse. Yet they left the essential structure of European society unchanged. There was still a class of very rich men in control of industry and with real power over the lives of the great mass of those poorer than themselves.

Changes were being made so that the position of the upper-middle and even middle classes might be preserved from attacks from below. This is nowhere more evident than in the attitude of the churches towards reform. The Catholic Church in particular began to campaign for concessions to labour after the death of Pio Nono in 1878. No doubt there was sincere humanitarianism in the new radicalism which appeared among churchmen. But they also hoped that workmen could be kept close to Christianity by diverting their attention from the appeals of atheistic socialists.

Pius IX

Prior to this, however, the Catholic Church had passed through an extraordinary period of medieval reaction during the long pontificate of Pius IX. Although he had become pope as a relatively young man, it had only taken two years of exposure to the startling radicalism of the Italian nationalists to drive him into dogged opposition to all reform, political or theological. After his flight from Rome in 1848, he became one of the most important supporters of the old order in Italy and throughout Europe. His conservatism deeply affected his theology. In 1854, in the Bull *Ineffabilis Deus*, he took it upon himself to outline the doctrine of the Immaculate Conception. This meant reviving a mystical aspect of Catholicism which was naturally under attack in an increasingly scientific age.

Even more archaic was Pius' insistence on reaffirming the doctrine of papal infallibility, a standpoint also open to rational doubt. Finally, he succeeded in antagonizing nationalists throughout the Catholic world through his 'ultramontane' assumptions on the power of the papacy over the individual national churches. Until his death in 1878, he was involved in a bitter struggle with the 'Gallican' Catholics, who insisted that each bishop should be given a degree of independence within his diocese.

Vatican attitudes to reform in general during Pius' pontificate were summarized in his encyclical *Quanta Cura* and his *Syllabus of the Principal Errors of our Age* (1864). Nationalism, liberalism, socialism, doctrinal revision and above all the toleration of these errors were roundly condemned. European liberals were horrified, and their opposition in some cases merged with that of the Gallican faction, who denied papal infallibility in matters of dogma. These they considered should be settled only by councils of the church. It was in response to the conservatism of Pius IX that Bismarck launched his *Kulturkampf* ('struggle of civilizations') against the Vatican.

Catholicism was not alone in reacting so strongly against the rapid changes of the modern world by attempting to shut them out. If anything the Protestant churches found themselves under even more severe attack from the new scientific thinkers, particularly those who accepted Darwin. Later, some clerical theorists were to adapt to the post-Darwinian world by arguing that the Protestant Christian nations had survived as being the fittest and that their duty was to rule other races and religions – including the Catholics – who had been less blessed in the struggle for existence. A rationalization

for supporting the capitalist system was also provided by 'Social Darwinism', since it apparently proved that those who became richest were those who had been most able to adapt to the conditions of modern life and at the same time were the most scrupulous in applying religious ideals to their business life.

The first Protestant reaction to Darwin, however, was much more critical. His removal of God from the history of the world provoked ministers into a horrified rejection of his heresies. Their first instinct was to combat his ideas by falling back on fundamentalism and arguing that since the literal reading of the Bible contradicted the *Origin of Species* Darwin's conclusions were wrong if not actually sinful. The same kind of uncompromising opposition to a new intellectual movement appears in both Catholic and Protestant responses to the rise of socialism. At first it was regarded as an atheistic system which had to be attacked root and branch.

It was perhaps because of such a frontal attack was failing so conspicuously that the churches set about offering counter-attractions to socialism. If social reform could not be avoided, the most constructive plan was to carry it out freed from its atheistic connections and under the supervision of liberal churchmen. This was most obvious in the case of the Catholic Church, under Pius IX's brilliant successor, Leo XIII. Encouraged by this versatile and charming man, liberal Catholics who had been repressed by Pio Nono turned to destroying the appeal of socialism by improving the conditions of the working class in the Catholic nations of Europe. Working along with the rising liberal parties, they also organised extensive programmes of workers' education, which were intended to spread the belief that substantial reform could be achieved without abandoning religion.

Leo XIII himself set the new liberal Catholicism in perspective. His Bull *Immortale Dei* of 1885 allowed French Catholics to cooperate with the Third Republic, which had previously been disavowed by the Vatican. With more far-reaching effects, the Bull *Rerum Novarum* called for concessions to the new mass working class: 'The more that is done for the benefit of the working classes by the general laws of the country, the less need will there be for special means to relieve them.' The new pope even encouraged the Catholics of southern Germany to conciliate Bismarck in the hope of destroying the appeal of the *Kulturkampf*. It was only after Leo's death in 1903 and the election of Pius X, that Rome began to retreat from its position as a major force in international liberal politics. Pius X, like Pius IX, spent the rest of his life waging war against 'modernism', excommunicating large numbers of liberal Catholics to do so. Unlike Leo XIII, he was quite prepared to abandon the working classes to the socialists. Since his own theology was not far removed

Above, Pope Pius IX (1792–1878, elected Pope 1846): his reign saw the incorporation of all the papal lands into the new kingdom of Italy, only the Vatican City enclave remaining under the Church's control.

Opposite, magazine report of the 1900 Congress of the Second International, held at Paris: among the participants were, top left and top right, the German socialists Karl Liebknecht (1871–1919), who was murdered during the German Revolution, and August Bebel (1840–1913), leader of the Social Democrats in the Reichstag, bottom right, Jean Jaurès (1859–1914), founder of L'Humanité, who was assassinated a few days before the outbreak of the First World War, and, bottom left, Alexandre Millerand (1859–1943), at that time minister of commerce.

from that of the thirteenth-century scholar St Thomas Aquinas, it is not surprising that his Bull *Pascendi* condemned 'modernism' as 'the synthesis of all other heresies'.

The Protestant churches were not so unfortunate as to pass through such a period of reaction. In Britain middle-class nonconformists formed the backbone of the Liberal Party and by and large remained in it until its collapse after the First World War.

The expansion of Europe

Protestant and Catholic churches alike shared the strengthening missionary impulse which sent their most devoted clergymen to the corners of the earth. No doubt this filtered off many of the most enterprising young men in Europe's theological colleges and diverted their attention from more radical movements at home. But the missionaries of the late nineteenth century were also centrally important in the 'new imperialism'. In one sense this simply involved the annexation of the heathen part of the globe by the Christian part. Indeed all the rapid changes which have been described here reinforced the burst of European expansion overseas after 1884. The changing Church produced evangelical missionaries, the rising population provided emigrants. A strengthened industrial system, working through the new nation states, began to look overseas for new markets, sources of raw materials and opportunities for profitable investment. Medical improvements made life in the tropics tolerable, while Europe's new technology made light of primitive resistance. Better links by rail and sea provided the communications essential to expanding empires. The net result, over the space of a few years, was the extension of Western rule throughout the world. It may even be that the rivalries which the nations formed overseas were important causes of the Great War.

Even the critics of the new industrial order had a part to play in the history of the expansion of Europe. When the colonies of the 1900s became the emerging nations of the fifties, their ideology was largely drawn from European socialist thought. All in all, the late nineteenth century was the time when the world became recognizable as the one we live in today.

THE MARCH OF THE NINETEENTH CENTURY

Date	Politics in the West	Industry, labour and technology	Politics in the wider world	Date	Politics in the West	Industry, labour and technology	Politics in the wider world
1815			Raffles acquires Singapore (1819)	1868		First Trades Union Congress (1868)	Meiji Restoration in Japan (1868)
			British occupation of Rangoon (1824)			Suez Canal opened (1869)	
		Stockton & Darlington Railway (1825)				Mendeleev's classification of elements (1869)	
			British claim all Australia (1829)			First electric motor (1869)	
	Revolutions throughout Europe					American transcontinental railroad track completed (1869)	
1830		Darwin's voyage on the *Beagle* (1831)			Hohenzollern candidacy Franco-Prussian War, Battle of Sedan		Massacre of Catholics at Tientsin
		Opening of Lyons-Saint-Étienne line begins French railway construction (1831)		1870	Rome capital of a united Italy		
	English Reform Act (1832)	Faraday invents dynamo (1832)			Second Reich proclaimed (1871)	Anarchists expelled from International (1872)	Livingstone and Stanley meet at Ujiji (1871)
	Emancipation of slaves in British colonies (1833)	Robert Owen founds Grand National Consolidated Trades Union (1834)			Communards rule Paris (1871)	Gotha Programme for German labour (1875)	British buy Suez (1875)
	Formation of *Zollverein* (1834)		Great Trek (1836)				Queen Victoria becomes Empress of India (1876)
			Opium War breaks out (1839)		Leo XIII becomes pope (1878)		
1840	English Corn Law Repeal (1846)		Treaty of Nanking begins 'Era of Concessions' (1842)			Edison electric lamp (1879)	
	Pius IX becomes pope (1846)	Elias Howe invents sewing machine (1846)	California annexed by USA (1848)	1880			De Brazza extends explorations in the Congo
	Year of revolutions (1848)					Siemens electric tramcar in use (1881)	Boer revolt breaks out (1881)
	Victor Emmanuel takes Piedmontese crown (1849)		Livingstone's first journey (1849)				British bombard Alexandria and occupy Egypt (1882)
1850	Cavour takes office (1852)	Great Exhibition in London (1851)	Taiping Revolt begins (1851)			Death of Marx (1883)	Germans seize Togoland (1883)
	French Second Empire proclaimed (1852)				Berlin Conference on colonies (1884	Parsons steam turbines applied to shipping (1884)	Berlin Conference prepares for partition of Africa (1884)
	Outbreak of Crimean War (1853)		Commodore Perry arrives in Japan (1853)				Mahdists take Khartoum (1885)
	Garibaldi returns to Italy (1854)	Isolation of aluminium (1854)				American Federation of Labor founded (1886)	Gold discovered in Transvaal (1886)
	Paris Peace Conference (1856)	Bessemer Converter introduced (1856)	'Arrow' War (1856)				French Indo-China is organized (1887)
		Brunel's *Great Eastern* built (1858)	Indian Mutiny (1857) Peace of Tientsin ends		Negro slavery ended in Brazil (1888)	Second International (1889)	
	Orsini Plot (1858)	Atlantic Telegraph Cable laid (1858)	'Arrow' War (1858)	1890	British Parliamentary Labour Party founded (1893)	World slump (1893)	*Union Coloniale* formed in France (1893)
	Pact of Plombières (1858)		French take Saigon (1858)				Sino-Japanese War (1894)
	First Austro-Italian War (1859)	*Origin of Species* published (1859)				Confédération Générale du Travail founded (1895)	
1860	Garibaldi's Sicilian campaign	Siemens-Martin smelting processed perfected	Russia seizes Vladivostock			Marconi wireless telegraph invented (1895)	Jameson Raid increases Anglo-Boer tension (1896)
	Russian serf emancipation by Tsar Alexander II (1861)					Röentgen discovers X-rays (1895)	French annex Madagascar (1896)
	First Italian parliament (1861)					French annex Madagascar (1896)	Fashoda Incident (1898)
	American Civil War breaks out (1861)		Speke proves his and Burton's findings on source of Nile (1862)				USA gains Hawaii, the Philippines, Puerto Rico (1898)
	Cavour dies (1861)				Spanish American War (1898)		Outbreak of Boer War (1899)
	Bismarck takes office (1862)		Cambodia becomes a French protectorate (1863)	1900			Boxer Rebellion
	Polish revolt (1863)						Peace of Vereeniging ends Boer War (1902)
	American emancipation proclamation (1863)	Pius IX promulgates *Syllabus Errorum* (1864)			First Russian Revolution (1905)	Orville Wright's first flight (1903)	
	Prussia fights Denmark over Schleswig-Holstein (1864)	First International (1864)			First *Duma* (parliament) meets in Russia (1906)	Trans-Siberian Railroad completed (1904)	Russo-Japanese War (1904)
		Lister introduces antiseptics (1865)			Algeciras Conference strengthens Anglo-French ties (1906)	Charter of Amiens (1906)	
	Austro-Prussian War, Battle of Sadowa (1866)		Rholfe crosses the Sahara (1867)		Anglo-Russian Entente (1907)	Santos-Dumont makes first European flight (1906)	
	Roman Revolt (1867)				Second Moroccan crisis (1911)	Stock market recession (1907)	British and Russian zones in Tibet, Afghanistan, Persia settled (1907)
	North German Confederation formed (1867)				Sarajevo and First World War (1914)	Blériot crosses the Channel (1909)	French occupy Casablanca (1907)

Chapter 8

The New Imperialism

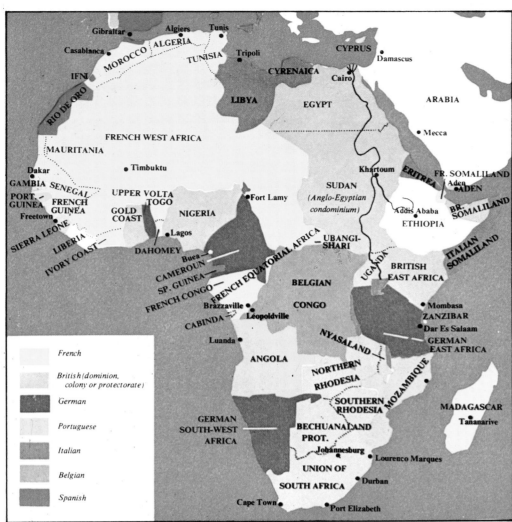

Above, the European 'scramble' for Africa in the second half of the nineteenth century: by 1912 only Ethiopia and Liberia were free from European domination or influence.

At the end of the nineteenth century, the overseas policies of the Western nations changed dramatically. Where they had once struggled to gain concessions and bases for trade, they now set about annexing swathes of territory in Africa and Asia. New anxieties were created with the rise of new nations. Bismarck's united Germany played a central part in the scramble for Africa. In 1898 the United States took its place as an international power by seizing Puerto Rico and the Philippines from Spain.

The old imperial powers, Britain and France, also annexed whatever territory they could. All the Western nations joined in a mad rush to seize unexploited land, often just to prevent other powers getting it. Patriotic enthusiasm supported all annexations, which were also linked to the advances in business and technology which made it essential to find foreign markets. Thus it was that in western Europe patriotism and industrialism combined to produce the 'new imperialism'.

Europe, Africa and Asia

Whatever was new about the new imperialism, there was also much about it that was old. Europe had been expanding ever since the Crusades or even earlier. The great Portuguese and Spanish colonists had first blazed the trail to Asia, Africa and the New World. The rise of the Dutch in the seventeenth century ruined both their empires, and the Dutch were pushed to the wall in their turn by other powers. We have already seen that the British and French were the dominant nations in China in the first part of the nineteenth century. They also had colonies in the West Indies and Africa, while the British ruled over Canada, India, Australia and New Zealand. Indeed the history of modern Europe may be seen as a constant struggle between the powers for an empire overseas.

After about 1880, however, the kind of empire which the powers wanted changed. New nations and new industries sought markets and territory overseas, and all Europe became involved in their ambitions. The pace of expansion quickened, its characteristics changed. Nations like Britain

and France, which had long been established in Africa, now had to widen their interests to protect themselves from interlopers and each other. In West Africa, for instance, the British had previously been content with owning a few coastal forts. By the end of the century they had annexed all of modern Nigeria and Ghana and had consolidated their settlements in Sierra Leone, and Gambia. Africa was soon dismembered. Asia was only saved from the same fate by a delicate balance between the interests of Japan, now a modern industrial state, and the individual Western powers. America absorbed the remnants of the Spanish Empire. The twentieth century dawned on a world in which little territory was not owned by Japan, the USA, the nations of Europe or, as in the case of Latin America, their offshoots.

Historians have found it difficult to explain this sudden burst of expansion. Clearly it is linked with the new needs of industrialism and with the rise of nationalism. After 1850, too, European population rose sharply, and emigration increased. In the middle of the century peasant emigrants, for instance the Irish displaced by the potato blight or the Scandinavians and southern Germans, flocked to the USA and Latin America. After about 1880 a new wave of emigrants left the poorer parts of southern

Italy and eastern Europe. Communications had improved and cheapened, and the attractions of the New World as described by shipping companies and American emigration agencies were great.

For others, however, the New World had less glamour. Many adventurous young men from the educated classes of the nations involved in the new imperialism set out as explorers and in the end became the administrators and engineers who opened up the Asian and African territories annexed by the West in the eighties and ninties. Rising scientific curiosity and the eagerness of such men to travel in unknown areas meant that this was also the period when the parts of the world which remained unexplored were first visited by Europeans. The drive towards exploration was all the stronger since so many Europeans were interested in bringing Christianity to black, brown and yellow heathens. It is difficult to imagine how the new imperialism would have arisen without the scientific and missionary impulses which encouraged exploration.

The greatest explorer of all, David Livingstone, well illustrates the complexity of motive of his generation of imperialists. Born in Scotland, he painstakingly scraped money together while working in a Lanarkshire cotton mill to begin his education and eventually to go to Glasgow University. By the time the London Missionary Society sent him to Africa he had a medical degree as well as strong interests in botany, zoology and astronomy. A committed abolitionist, he believed that opening Africa to Protestant missionaries would crush the slave trade. This continued in West Africa in spite of the efforts of the British West Africa Squadron to capture slavers and flourished more than ever through the East African depot in Zanzibar. He made three main journeys through unexplored Africa from 1849 onwards. On the first he crossed the continent, exploring the course of the Zambesi, and on the second he discovered Lake Nyasa.

The activities of explorers had become good press, and the whole of Europe and America followed the last journey, which he began in 1868. When he went missing, the *New York Tribune*, a paper which had fought against American slavery and was now the organ of the Republican Party, sent its ace reporter Henry Morton Stanley to look for Livingstone. The search took three years. In 1871, at Ujiji, on Lake Tanganyika, the reporter met a very sick and weary Livingstone with a handshake and the famous though superfluous question, 'Dr Livingstone, I presume?' Racked with fever and worn out by his labours, poor Livingstone was found dead by his bearers only two years later, in 1873.

Stanley himself continued the work of exploration, still sending his despatches back to the *Tribune* when he could do so. Travelling from Zanzibar in the east, he reached

the headwaters of the Congo and followed it down to the coast. Soon afterwards King Leopold of Belgium tried to expand his interests in the Congo, which together with the sudden intervention of Germany precipitated the 'scramble for Africa'.

Livingstone and Stanley were not the only great travellers of this period. In 1880 the French explorer de Brazza sailed up the Ogooué River from the coast of Gabon, cut across country to the Congo, and founded the post of Brazzaville, later the capital of the French Congo. Before Stanley, Livingstone and Brazza had showed the way into Central Africa, even more attention had been given to trying to discover the sources of the Nile. The riddle of this river had puzzled scholars for generations.

In 1858 the Royal Geographical Society of London sponsored the expedition of Burton and Speke, which discovered the Great Lakes – Tanganyika, Victoria, and Albert. Unfortunately the scholarly world could not believe that the controversy over

the source of the Nile had been settled, and Speke was denounced as a charlatan when he claimed that the river flowed out of a huge lake system in Central Africa. In 1862, however, he was able to prove his point by marching round Lake Victoria Nyanza, finding the outlet of the Nile and descending it as far as the first cataract. Since the successive expeditions of Mungo Park, Hugh Clapperton, and the Lander brothers had revealed the course of the Niger by 1830, European knowledge of Africa's main river systems was now complete.

In the late 1860s, the land routes across North Africa and the Sudan were also covered by two Germans, Gerhard Rholfe and Gustave Nachtigal. Rholfe trekked from Tripoli to Conakry in Guinéa in 1867. Nachtigal's achievement was to find a route from Libya to Lake Chad, turn eastwards to Khartoum and return home down the Nile. The names of such explorers became household words throughout Europe. More important, their work provided enough

knowledge of Africa to make penetration possible.

The interior of Asia received less attention from explorers than Africa. However, the imagination of Europeans was stimulated by travel accounts like that of the colourful medical missionary to China, Charles Gutzlaff. After 1870 even more attention was attracted by the voyages of the German traveller Richthofen. Another exploit was Garnier's exploration of south east Asia. He sailed up the Mekong, discovered the dramatically beautiful ruins of the Khmer palace at Ankgor Wat and penetrated into China's Yunnan province. The European public heard as much of the heroism of explorers in Asia as it did of those in Africa. The French poet Rimbaud reflected their enthusiasm when he wrote *Le Bateau ivre* ('The Tipsy Boat'). Indeed Rimbaud himself died while exploring part of Abyssinia. The publicity given to explorations no doubt helped to prepare European voters for later annexation of African and Asian territory.

The motives for imperialism

There were other factors behind the new imperialism as well as enthusiasm for the exploits of missionaries and explorers. Sometimes events proceeded almost by accident, with ambitious young men on the frontiers of European expansion annexing territory without orders from above. For instance the forward policy of the French in Indo-China was partly moulded by the enthusiasm of Gallieni. A similar case was the initiative of the British officer Frederick Lugard in seizing territory in Uganda.

However, it is unlikely that such men would have received the backing of their governments if deeper forces had not been at work. Sometimes these arose in the territory which was to be conquered and not in Europe. In West Africa, for instance,

traders had to appeal to their governments to move in when the local states on which they had previously relied for protection collapsed under the strain of generations of slave trading. The Boer War was also fought partly for internal reasons. Again, the Russian advance into Manchuria, where tsarist troops eventually clashed with the Japanese, was dictated partly by the need to find a frontier which was settled and stable on the other side. There were also direct economic motives for expansion. V. I. Lenin, the great leader of the Russian revolution, maintained that it arose because capitalism had to find new areas for investment to escape from the problem of overproduction at home.

Nevertheless, whatever economic interests were involved, the missionary factor in the new imperialism cannot be overestimated. No doubt some of the enthusiasm of the missionaries was linked with improvements in education which meant there were more young ministers than there were parishes for them to find jobs in. But the missionary movement was now given new scope among the tens of millions of heathens living in the vast new territories discovered by men like Livingstone and Garnier. The middle classes who had risen because of industrialization were fervently interested in missions, probably with complete sincerity.

The hope of spreading Christianity was linked with changing attitudes to race. It now appeared possible to fit the non-European races into the framework of *The Origin of Species*. If human history, like natural history, was governed by the survival of the fittest, the races of the West, with their advanced technology, had obviously survived most effectively. Clearly, therefore, their Christian duty was to extend their humane leadership throughout the world. This theory of the 'white man's burden' is best expressed in the poems of the great imperialist poet Rudyard Kipling and the popular novelist Rider Haggard. A

Above, the coffee harvest on the plantation at St Austin's Mission, Nairobi, 1902: imperial expansion was motivated by a complex mixture of national self-aggrandizement, commerce and evangelical zeal.

Above left, Gustav Nachtigal (1834–85), the pioneer German explorer: in addition to his Sahara expedition, he also annexed Togoland and Cameroun for Germany in 1884.

Opposite, illustration from a contemporary account of the Pierre de Brazza's (1852–1905) expedition to the Congo: here the explorer is shown treating with native chiefs.

STANLEY IN AFRICA.

IMPERIAL FEDERATION — MAP OF THE WORLD SHOWING THE EXTENT OF THE BRITISH EMPIRE IN 1886.

generation of British schoolboys grew up reading these works.

Yet Lenin's theory of a link between capitalism and imperialism is of some importance. As technology advanced, the naval strength of the powers increased, especially in the cases of Japan and Germany. Influenced by the great American theorist Alfred Thayer Mahan, they all considered it essential to have large navies to protect their overseas interests. These interests in turn expanded, as industrial Europe demanded more and more raw materials and produced more and more goods for which markets had to be found. Spokesmen like Joseph Chamberlain in Britain or Jules Ferry in France could argue that new territory had to be found overseas to stave off the recurrent slumps which plagued the European nations. There is no single cause which explains the new imperialism. But it may be closely linked to the rapid changes in European industry, technology and ideas described in the last chapter.

By no means all Western statesmen were in favour of the new imperialism. Bismarck tried to keep Germany out of involvement in Africa and Asia, though his successors reversed this policy. In France, Jules Ferry was ably opposed by nationalists determined to concentrate on revenge against Germany. As for Britain, it has recently been discovered that Lord Salisbury, who was prime minister during the years when Britain annexed most of her new territory, spent his spare time in the sixties writing anonymous anti-imperialist articles for the *Saturday Review*. 'Love of Empire', he concluded, 'is inevitably a love of war.' Joseph Chamberlain and his followers were usually at odds with liberal and conservative leaders alike.

Chamberlain's group were usually called the 'jingoists'. The name comes from a popular song written during the Russo-Turkish War of 1878:

We don't want to fight,
But by jingo, if we do,
We've got the men, we've got the ships,
We've got the money too.

Chamberlain himself was the son of a Manchester manufacturer, the grandfather of the later prime minister, Neville Chamberlain. Convinced of Britain's destiny as an imperial race, he was less disposed than other statesmen to lose sleep over international complications which might be caused by an aggressive policy outside Europe. He was not alone in his assumption that God was on the side of the empire and that other nations and above all other races were less favoured. The age of the new imperialism was brash, self-confident and in some ways devout. Chamberlain was its most typical mouthpiece. It was partly as a result of his cavalier attitude to foreign affairs that Britain became involved in the Boer War.

Although the new imperialism was certainly responsible for creating trouble with other powers, Britain's worst colonial troubles of the nineteenth century came in the old empire and not in new territory. As early as 1857 the precious possession of India had burst into revolt in the Indian Mutiny. Revolt swept across central India and the middle section of the Ganges, destroying everything European which stood in its way. Although they announced loyalty to the old Mogul emperor Bahadur Shah, the mutineers lacked organization or any real plan. Bengal and most of southern India remained loyal. At the end of the year, the relief of Lucknow by General Campbell made it possible to disperse the huge numbers of rebels.

Although relations between Britons and Indians had been poisoned for generations, Indian government was reorganized under the Indian Civil Service. India was still Britain's richest possession and the key-point in imperial strategy. It was defended against the French by the British annexation of Burma in 1886 and against the Russians by an agreement over Tibet and Afghanistan in 1907. India's communications were also guarded by a line of way-stations stretching from London to Bombay, Gibraltar, Malta, Cyprus, the Suez Canal, British Somaliland, Aden and Bahrein.

Again, the British controlled the approaches to the Indian Ocean from their foothold in South Africa, while the maintenance of stability in Egypt, as the Canal Zone, was simply essential to them. These were the interests which led them into taking control of Egypt and fighting the Boer War.

The British on the Nile

The building of the Suez Canal had been a French enterprise, directed by Viscount Ferdinand de Lesseps. Indeed Egypt became very much Frenchified in the 1860s. In 1875, however, the Khedive of Egypt, Ismael Pasha, faced bankruptcy as a result of his speculations in railway-building. Since the French had their own troubles at the time, Disraeli was left to bale him out of his difficulties by buying the khedive's personal shares in the Canal. Disraeli actually received the news that the shares were on sale while dining with Baron Lionel de Rothschild, a fellow-gourmet and another Jew who had broken into the circle of the European aristocracy. The four million required for the transaction were promptly raised from him. Britain became the principal shareholder in the Canal. Further complications arose when Ismael Pasha subsequently cancelled the interest on international Egyptian debts. The British

THE LION'S SHARE.

and French accordingly formed a consortium to make him manage his money more sensibly. Among other economies, they had 2,500 army officers put on half-pay. These men joined with the masses of peasants suspicious of Western influence and crushed by taxes from Alexandria. When the Europeans responded to their criticism by deposing Ismael Pasha and installing his son Tewfik Pasha, they forced the whole Egyptian Civil Service into alliance with the discontented elements.

A series of disturbances followed. The French did not intervene, although their North African interests were expanding with the consolidation of Algeria. The British shelled Alexandria on their own initiative and landed an expeditionary force to restore order and take over the government. They were left in control of the Canal and the Egyptian capital. To consolidate their position, always thinking in terms of protecting the route to India, they found themselves forced to expand further and further inland. Ismael Pasha had never managed to bring the Sudan fully under control or stamp out the slave trade there.

In 1882 conditions deteriorated completely when a holy war or *jihad* was begun by a Muslim prophet calling himself the *Mahdi* or 'chosen one'. 'Chinese' Gordon, who had helped to train the Manchu troops to fight the Taiping, had already advanced to Khartoum on the White Nile. The Mahdi's hordes took the city in 1885, killing all its defenders, including Gordon, a few days before a relief force arrived. The British could not leave the hinterland of Egypt under Mahdist control, although the Mahdi himself died a few months later. It was only in 1898, however, that the 'dervish' troops of his successor were defeated at Omdurman. Egyptian troops led by British advisers took control of the Sudan. Egypt and the Canal were now safe.

The Boer War

By a coincidence, the British general at Omdurman was Kitchener, later the hero of

the relief of Ladysmith in the Boer War. The more general connection between these two conflicts is close. Control of the Cape was as essential to the protection of India as the Canal itself. Cape Colony, which had been taken from the Dutch during the Napoleonic Wars, controlled the entrance to the Indian Ocean. Its change of ownership, however, did not remove the Dutch population. From 1835 to 1837, the Afrikaans-speaking farmers of the Cape set out on the 'Great Trek' northwards, led by Piet Retief and other heroes of Boer history, to escape British rule. On reaching the rich grasslands they wanted, against bloody opposition from the Zulu *impis*, they formed the little republics of Transvaal and the Orange Free State, which were recognized by Britain in 1852 and 1854. Bitterness between Britain and the old-fashioned Calvinist Afrikaners, was increased by Sir Bartle Frere's unsuccessful attempt to re-annexe the Transvaal in 1881, after the Zulu War.

The hatred of the Afrikaners for those who wished to upset their way of life was further increased by the gold strikes of 1886 in the Witwatersrand. Boer society was threatened by the arrival of modern-minded businessmen and engineers, the *Uitlanders* or foreigners. A much worse threat was the covetousness of the great British imperialist Cecil Rhodes. The head of De Beers Mining Corporation and prime minister of Cape Colony from 1890 to 1896, he dreamt of a line of British territory from Cape Town to Cairo. This would link the Suez route to India with the Cape one and would make the British Empire in India impregnable.

Since a strong Boer Transvaal stood in the way of this plan, Rhodes tried to force it into a British-dominated federation ruled from Cape Town. He then harried the Transvaal by annexing the territory around it. When its president, Paul Kruger, stood firm, he took the part of the dissident Uitlanders and then mounted the disastrous Jameson Raid on Johannesburg on their behalf. It failed dismally and enabled the kaiser to make capital out of British blunders by denouncing this attack on the 'infant republic'.

Chamberlain fully supported Rhodes' plans and in spite of Salisbury's doubts he went ahead to provoke the Boer War, Britain's greatest conflict since the American Revolution. This unnecessary war broke out in 1899, after Sir Alfred Milner, the British High Commissioner at the Cape, made impossible demands on behalf of the Uitlanders. The superb irregular cavalry of the Transvaal and the Free State gave an excellent account of itself. The first British reinforcements were outfought but recovered ground after Lord Roberts, or 'Bobs' as his men called him, took command. His most successful generals were Kitchener and Sir John French, the future hero of Ypres.

After bitter guerrilla warfare, Kruger signed the Peace of Vereeniging in 1902. Given the brutality of the war, the settlement was statesmanlike. The British actually gave £3,000,000 in reparations to make good the damage done by their scorched earth policy. In 1906 Campbell-Bannerman's liberal government gave self-government to the Transvaal and the Orange Free State. Four years later they united with Cape Colony and Natal to form the Union of South Africa, the federated unit of which Rhodes had dreamt. With Egypt, Burma

Above, Boers manning their trenches outside Mafeking during the siege of the city: despite the valour of the Boers, the outcome of the war was inevitable. The British could call on far greater manpower reserves than the Boers, and British command of the sea prevented any European nation helping the Boers.

Left, unloading provisions and matériel at Casablanca, 1906: in that year, although technically still independent, Morocco effectively came under French control.

Opposite top right, gold miners in the Transvaal, 1888: the discovery first of diamonds, then of gold, in southern Africa led to an influx of capitalist interest and, along with the threat posed by increasing European intervention elsewhere in Africa, strengthened British determination to maintain control.

Opposite top left, Scottish troops pose at the Sphinx for the camera after helping to defeat the nationalist uprising in 1882: British intervention was provoked by the need to guarantee passage through the Suez Canal, and Egypt remained under a loose form of British occupation until the mid-1950s.

Opposite bottom, Paul Kruger (1825–1904), President of the Transvaal from 1883: strongly anti-British, Kruger had gone on the Great Trek as a boy and took a leading part in the Boer revolt in 1881.

and South Africa under British control, the safety of India was guaranteed.

British interests in Africa were not confined to Egypt and South Africa. Spurred on by the activities of other powers, Britain joined in the 'scramble for Africa' after the Berlin Conference of 1884. Kenya, Uganda, Nigeria, the Gold Coast, Gambia and British Somaliland were all annexed during this period, not to mention swathes of territory like Bechuanaland, Zululand, Pondoland and Rhodesia itself, which were seized in the south under Rhodes' influence.

The French in North Africa

The Joseph Chamberlain of the Third Republic was Jules Ferry. He too carried his aggressive policies against strong opposition from both left and right. By the nineties, however, his ideas had been taken up by a pressure group in the Chamber led by the Algerian-born deputy Eugène Etienne. He cooperated with two bodies out of doors,

the *Comité d'Afrique Française* and after 1893 the *Union Coloniale*. Indeed it was only after 1890 that France made her main gains south of the Sahara.

France's first commitment in Africa, of course, was to Algeria. Although she had defeated 'Abd el Kadar by 1845, the first programme to dispossess the tribesmen of their land did not come until 1871, when the first *colons* from Alsace were settled. This produced a serious uprising. It only brought confiscations which were given to new bodies of settlers. Although Algeria technically became part of metropolitan France, its franchise was narrow, and rule still lay effectively with a governor appointed in Paris.

The impossibility of winning the loyalty of its tribesmen did not prevent the French from turning their attention to Tunisia, which became their protectorate in 1881, in spite of the ambitions of the newly united Italy there.

The last part of French North Africa to be annexed was Morocco. Constantly in a

state of disorder, its independence was a standing threat to the Algerian border. In 1903 Colonel Louis Lyautey was sent in to restore stability, and Morocco became a French sphere of influence after Casablanca was occupied in 1907. In spite of strong German suspicion of France, the powers recognized a French Moroccan protectorate in 1912. Lyautey's wise administration and the defeat of the fierce nomadic Tuaregs on the Algerian frontier ensured that North Africa was firmly under French control by 1914.

West Africa

Although other annexations were going on throughout the world, no area shows the rivalries of the imperialist powers better than West Africa. Although control of forts at Lagos, in the Gold Coast (Ghana) and Sierra Leone made the British strong in the area, the French had maintained trading stations on the Senegal since the great days of the slave trade in the eighteenth century. They also had interests in modern Guinea and the Ivory Coast, though they had not carried out any inland penetration.

It was Senegal which first became a real French colony. The greatest of the French colonialists, Louis Léon César Faidherbe, became governor there in 1853. In his first few years in office, he attacked the Senegalese traders who levied an exorbitant 'tribute' on all trade passing down the Senegal. He also checked the expansion of the Muslim leader Al Hajj 'Umar, whose strong state on the upper Niger was threatening to extend into the Senegal Valley. During tours of duty which went on until 1886, Faidherbe re-modelled Senegal. Its Islamic population became loyal citizens of the Republic, and the Senegalese riflemen came to be one of the crack units of the French Army.

Faidherbe, and other French leaders, began to dream of a French Empire which would stretch from Senegal across the Sudan to the Indian Ocean. This would also link up with the new territories in North Africa. On the other hand, it could not avoid clashing with the plans of Rhodes and the British to secure communications from Cairo to the Cape.

Equally difficult was the subjugation of West Africa itself. Al Hajj 'Umar was not

THE RHODES COLOSSUS
STRIDING FROM CAPE TOWN TO CAIRO.

the only Islamic leader who waged the *jihad* against the French. His son Ahmadu Bello, ruling a state of great sophistication which dominated the western Sudan, was only finally defeated in 1893. After this there was still resistance from Samori, the most likeable and least cultured of these Muslim princes, which went on until 1898. Indeed the European advance in West Africa was at least partly governed by the behavious of the strong Islamic states which stood in its way.

The scramble for Africa

The advance was also moulded by the relations of the powers with one another. King Leopold's interests in the Congo and the intervention of the Germans created fears that if territory were not seized soon, it would no longer be available. Between 1883 and 1885, the Germans annexed Togo, Kamerun, German East Africa (Tanzania) and German South West Africa. In 1885, the Congress of Berlin, called by Bismarck, in effect laid down the rules for the partition of Africa. Although it also gave the Belgian Congo recognition and access to the sea, this alarmed the French into seizing the French Congo to the north of Leopold's state. Sir George Goldie, a director of the Royal Niger Company, was alarmed by the German and French advance into seizing Nigeria, which had been brilliantly subdued by Lord Lugard by the end of the century. The French advanced into Guinea, the Ivory Coast, and eventually Dahomey. To keep them out of the Gold Coast, the British pushed their long-standing grievances with the kingdom of the Ashanti to a conclusion in 1896.

130

Meanwhile British concern over German interests in modern Tanzania produced a similar policy in East Africa. Salisbury had Kenya declared a British sphere of influence in 1886, and it became a protectorate in 1893. In 1890 Lugard had arrived in Kampala with his one maxim gun, and had taken the part of the Protestants or wa-ingleza (the English party) against the wa-franza (the French party), Catholics converted by Lavigerie's famous White Fathers. The Imperial British East Africa Company then opened up the territory, and it too became a protectorate in 1894. The last power to enter the scramble was another new one, Italy, which managed to satisfy its hunger for national greatness by seizing Eritrea, on the Red Sea, and part of Somaliland in 1889.

Unfortunately this first stage of the scramble did not solve the problem of conflict between British and French imperial ambitions, which cut directly across one another. In 1896 the French, long humiliated by Germany at home and determined to compensate by seizing the kind of empire they wanted abroad, sent Marchand from the Congo to forestall British Cape-Cairo ambitions by annexing the headwaters of the Nile. Marchand and his tiny force sailed up the Ubangui River on their little steamer, the *Faidherbe*. When it could go no further, they dismantled it and dragged it through the jungle, in the hope of being able to relaunch it on the Nile. After two years of travel, they reached the station of Fashoda, on the Nile. Four days later it was approached by Kitchener, with a greatly superior British force, fresh from the victory of Omdurman.

A full-scale conflict was only avoided by the courtesy and tact of these two soldiers, who agreed that until orders arrived the British flag should fly over the town and the French one over the fort. Even this did not prevent a major international crisis. Only the threat of war persuaded Delcassé, the French foreign minister, that Marchand's troops should be withdrawn. Once the crisis blew over, however, the main barrier to Anglo-French understanding had been removed. From now on the two nations gradually moved together to become allies in the First World War.

China and southeast Asia

While the European nations were dividing the spoils of Africa, they continued the expansion of the earlier part of the century in the Far East. To protect India against the French advance in Indo-China, the British annexed Burma in 1886. However, French penetration had been greatly slowed up by the disaster of 1871 and by Garnier's discovery that control of the Mekong would not give the expected access to China's markets.

Attention now turned to the Red River and the Gulf of Tonkin. Although Hanoi was taken in 1873, the state of Annam (north Vietnam) was surprisingly strong, and the ancient city could not be held. The only result of further attempts to take Hanoi was a disastrous reverse in 1883. This provoked Ferry and the French jingoists to a firmer policy. After bombarding Foochow, outside Canton, to discourage Chinese protests, the French finally annexed Annam. It was soon pacified, while neighbouring Laos became a protectorate a few years later. Although Siam remained independent, Britain and France had now divided all of mainland southeast Asia between them.

China itself was a little luckier. Although the Manchus were constantly humiliated during the era of concessions, they did at least remain in possession of the bulk of their land, if only because the mutual jealousies of the powers kept them cautious about annexation. Nevertheless, such scramble as there was in China was again triggered off by German action, when Admiral Tirpitz took the port of Kiaochow in 1897. Russia at once grabbed the precious warm-water harbour of Port Arthur, the French took Kwang-chow in the south and the British bullied the Chinese into granting a lease of Wei-hai-wei.

In 1898, the Americans also gained a foothold in the China Sea by conquering the Spanish Philippines. Anxious to gain further advantages in China, John Hay, the American Secretary of State, confirmed the delicate balance of Western interests by announcing (untruthfully) that the powers had agreed to his 'open door' policy. Any concession gained by one Western power was now to be open to all. In the next year, 1900, the powers actually cooperated in putting down the Boxer Rebellion. Fanatical anti-Western rebels besieged the Peking diplomatic community in the British legation. Eventually the siege was lifted by an international task force. This action confirmed first that the powers could not fully dismember China against each other's interests, second that the Manchus had become powerless and finally that America had become a world power.

Part III

DEMOCRACY AND THE NEW IMPERIALISM

Introduction

The closing years of the nineteenth century and the opening ones of the twentieth are from one angle best thought of as an epilogue, from another as a prologue. During the last decade of the nineteenth century contemporaries placed almosy equal emphasis on *fin-de-siècle* and on 'newness'. During the *belle époque* which ushered in the twentieth century there was an obvious contrast between surface glitter and structural disturbance. There were, indeed, many symptoms of violence before the greater violence of the First World War shattered the old world for ever.

In these years, ways of working, living, thinking and feeling were all transformed as a result of industrial development. The first great changes had taken place during the late eighteenth century with the exploitation of coal, iron and steam, but it was not until the 1840s, 50s and 60s that the railway, symbol of industrial progress, completed the British industrial revolution and intro-

duced industrial revolutions in other countries. Factories and furnaces were visible signs of a new dispensation. So, too, were industrial cities and regions. There were invisible signs also – new feelings about 'class', 'mobility' and the prospects for further technological and social advance. The transformation, moreover, was not confined geographically to a few countries where economic progress was most rapid: it affected countries which remained primarily agricultural, setting the terms of their relationship with the rest.

This great transformation is not easy to chart, for the history of industrialization is concerned not so much with events as with processes. There were spurts and lags and different chronologies of growth, disturbance and adaptation in different countries. By 1914 the processes were still incomplete. Many of the new techniques developed between 1870 and 1914 had not been fully exploited; many of the innovations had not left their impact on daily life. We can, nonetheless, trace back to the world before 1914 the origins of what we now take for granted – not only material comfort of a kind never before enjoyed but 'welfare states' in which governments intervene in the working of the market and large business organizations.

In the long run, industrialization meant greater wealth. Between 1870 and 1900, as many countries industrialized, world industrial production increased nearly four times. Between 1900 and 1914 the amount of world trade in manufacturing goods doubled. In consequence, there were marked improvements in standards of living along with the aspirations which went with them. Yet in the

short run, as industrialization proceeded, there were fluctuations in income and employment from year to year and wide disparities in every year in the distribution of wealth both within and between countries. These fluctuations and disparities were traced quantitively by men who developed the study of statistics, extending it to cover social as well as economic indices – birth and death rates, for example, or industrial accidents alongside figures relating to prices, wages and profits.

Between 1870 and 1914 there was rather less confidence in the rhetoric of industrial progress than there had been in mid-Victorian Britain, the pioneering industrial country. In Britain itself, where the early lead was beginning to be thought of as something of a handicap, businessmen were worried by foreign competition and by smaller profit margins: at the same time workers, skilled and unskilled, were becoming more organized, the latter for the first time in history. Critics of society as it was and as it was becoming complained not only of continuing poverty in the midst of plenty but of the wastes of early industrialization. In continental Europe, trade-union and political movements refused to accept the logic and authority of the profit-making industrial system. For every new opportunity which industrialization afforded there were parallel problems. The social costs of industrialization were difficult to measure, and those changes in the physical environment and in human relations which could not be measured quantitatively stimulated both intellectual argument and moral and political protest.

As many of the new techniques and innovations discovered before 1914 transformed the texture of daily life only during the 1920s and 1930s – electrical power, automobiles and wireless are obvious examples – so many of the criticisms of nineteenth- and early twentieth-century industrialization which were voiced before 1914 became effective in social and political terms only much later. There were time lags in experience and response, particularly in political response, as well as in the history of invention. In the meantime, the technology behind industrialization continued to change. Britain which at first was the 'workshop of the world' had established its lead on the basis of coal and iron – 'carboniferous capitalism'. Germany and the United States forged ahead in 'the age of steel'. 'The age of steel' is itself an inadequate label since there were striking developments in steel technology which now makes the early age of steel seem as distant as the age of iron.

There were differences also in organization and in scale. The British industrial revolution had depended on the free initiative of individuals: in later industrial revolutions the state counted for more. So, too, did science. Individualism itself proved inadequate to direct large-scale industry, and the development of industry depended increasingly on organizational efficiency. The industrial growth not only was uneven but the experience associated with industrialization varied as it progressed at different times in different countries. By 1914 Japan was the one Asian country to have undergone an 'industrial revolution', a distinctive experience which must be considered in relation to the developments in nearby China at that time and to the progress of the industrial revolutions which preceded and succeeded Japan's.

The experience of individual countries must always be studied within a bigger frame than that which they themselves provide. As a result of developments in transport and finance, an international economy came into existence between 1870 and 1914 within which Europe, with its growing population and its developing technology, played the dominant role in the world. By the First World War sixty percent of all manufactured goods were exported from three European countries, and although Britain was no longer the workshop of the world London still remained the centre of international economic transactions. Britain's share in world trade was declining, yet it was still the great trading country. It continued to provide both international economic services and a huge market, a free trade market for foreign goods. It served, in a phrase of J. M. Keynes, as 'the conductor of the orchestra'. As the world's largest creditor country, it never exploited its position to accumulate such large stocks of gold that it drained the resources of other countries within the gold standard system. Smaller countries could afford to let London lay down the rules. Free movements of capital, stable exchange rates and the 'legal order' of the gold standard were thought by many to be essential aspects of any international economic network, and though there were rumblings from below and complex pressures which pointed to fundamental disturbances in the future, the system held until 1914.

There was irony in the fact that the collapse of the system in 1914 and during the years of unanticipated attrition which followed would not have been so catastrophic had not industrialization affected warfare as much as the making of wealth. The skills which had been applied to the making of machines and of consumer goods had been capable of being applied also to the making of weapons of destruction. The scale of destruction between 1914 and 1918 – and the scope of the organization which was necessary to wage war successfully – depended on the record of technical and economic progress before war broke out. It is apparent, moreover, that before 1914 industrialization played a larger part in influencing the fortunes of states in their rivalry, often ancient rivalry, with each other, a rivalry grounded in fear and mistrust, than it did in remodelling their internal forms of government. In administration even more than in politics old ways persisted after industrialization had posed new issues and demanded new remedies.

Below, saluting the flag in a New York school in the 1890s; especially between the 1860s and 1920s, the USA really was a new world for millions escaping poverty and oppression in Europe.

Opposite, members of the international relief force sent to Peking in 1900 to quell the Boxer rising and maintain western influence pose for the camera outside a photographer's studio.

On page 132, French soldiers occupying a railway station during a strike of railway workers, 1910: the years before 1914 were marked by increasing trades union activity, as organized labour came to realize its strength.

Chapter 9

The Growth of Democracy in Britain and France

Britain was the pioneer of the new industrialism. Since the late sixteenth century England had been renowned as a rich and powerful trading nation. During the seventeenth and eighteenth centuries she had fought a series of wars and thereby acquired a great commercial and territorial empire overseas, which left her trading rivals in western Europe far behind. British manufacturers seized the opportunity to produce for an almost unlimited market abroad as well as for Britain's own rapidly growing population.

The lead was given by enterprising manufacturers of cotton goods. In the second half of the eighteenth century improvements in textile machinery raised output dramatically. New steam-driven machines and the men, women and children who worked them were concentrated in factories. Other British industries followed suit in the quest for profitable inventions and profitable ways of organizing labour. In the nineteenth century trade was freed. Raw materials for the factories and food for the growing number of town-dwellers could now be imported cheaply. Railways revolutionized Britain's communications, while her trading competitors were much slower to change. Until the latter part of the century she had no rival in supplying and fostering mankind's demand for manufactured goods. By 1850 Britain had become, in the familiar phrase, 'the workshop of the world'.

The social cost of pioneering such a change was high. The entrepreneurs who organized industrial change made their fortunes out of it, while the early generations of factory workers had less cause to be grateful. Although it is possible that many of them were marginally better fed, better clothed and better housed, they had to adjust themselves to an entirely new and alien way of life: to the harsh and monotonous grind of factory discipline, to grim and cheerless factory towns, to the ever-present fear of losing, through no fault of their own, a job which was essential if the still greater tyranny of the workhouse were to be avoided. For these pioneers it was a bleak age.

Living conditions were much more obviously man-made than in an agricultural society, and it seemed reasonable to demand that the makers and upholders of industrial society should better these conditions. From the late eighteenth century onwards discontented workers organized themselves to win enough power to back up their demands. They often came into violent conflict with authority. As agricultural workers were suffering from an equally man-made transformation of the countryside in the interests of large-scale farming, they too erupted at times in protest. Down to the 1840s it seemed at least possible that the price of pioneering industrialism could be social revolution.

Yet despite the mounting fears of the propertied classes this point was never reached. Britain was to remain one of the few states, like America and Japan, where the social tensions brought by industrialization did not lead to political breakdown.

Compared with their more self-conscious successors in the rest of the world, the British industrialized slowly and casually, and the problems of social change emerged correspondingly slowly. There was no swift and sudden build-up of tension such as was induced by tsarist Russia's hectic pace of industrialization at the end of the nineteenth century. As pioneers the British had no precedents to guide them, but their political system, like that of America and the Scandinavian countries, proved remarkably responsive to the new era. It was a flexible system, which allowed more freedom of action for those seeking change than was usual in most countries at any time. Political societies, trade unions and polemical literature could flourish just sufficiently to act as a safety valve. Enterprising families could share power with the ruling aristocracy after a generation or so's apprenticeship in accumulating the necessary wealth and land.

The ruling classes contained enough able, intelligent and enlightened men to edge parliament in the direction of timely concessions to the middle and working classes. Reforms made in the first half of the nineteenth century left many people dissatisfied, but they bred optimism about the political system's capacity for changing both itself and the conditions in which people lived. It was significant that many of the reforms were the work of Sir Robert Peel, son of a cotton magnate and the first prime minister from the new manufacturing class.

By the 1850s more people than ever before were experiencing the rewards of industrialization in the form of higher earnings and a greater variety of goods to buy with them. The rewards were still scanty, and dismal poverty remained the lot of millions, but industrial society was at last accepted as a means and not a bar to progress.

The British could look back on the previous 100 years as a remarkable success story. They had pioneered an industrial revolution and had made themselves the most prosperous nation in the world. They had made enough political and social changes to avoid the revolutions which engulfed most of Europe in 1848 and could claim to be the most stable state in the world. And they controlled such a vast territorial and commercial empire and had beaten off so many challenges from their greatest rivals, France and Russia, that they could claim to be the most powerful nation in the world.

Palmerston and Britain's world role

The rewards of industrialization were, therefore, not only material ones. It had strengthened immensely the economic power which underpinned Britain's world role. Emotional satisfaction in the greatness of Britain's power was freely available to millions of her people who had to be content with a meagre share of her new wealth.

The symbol of this greatness was Lord Palmerston, who between 1830 and 1865 was the most influential figure in the conduct of Britain's foreign policy. He is the only British foreign secretary whose name is still familiar the world over, epitomizing breezy, cocksure diplomacy. Palmerston had style, and his boisterous handling of international business matched his own rakish and full-blooded private life. He breathed a self-confidence which was very reassuring to a generation perplexed by the hazards and uncertainties of industrial society. International problems, at least, could be made to look simpler by applying superior naval and military force. Power remained the most popular criterion by which a country earned respect and admiration. Palmerston proved that Britain had more power at her disposal than any of her rivals.

He used that power with great skill in furthering what most of his fellow countrymen would have agreed were the nation's interests: the security of its empire, the development of its commerce and the spread of the British kind of constitutional government. He used British forces to ensure the triumph of constitutional government in Spain and Portugal in the 1830s. In 1839–42 and again in 1856–8 he used war to force the Chinese empire to trade according to 'Western' rules. He used both diplomacy and war to prevent Russia from gaining control over the Ottoman Empire, Persia and Afghanistan, an area crucial to the long-term defence of British India.

Admittedly, in these and other cases Palmerston provided only temporary solutions. Constitutionalism never prospered in Spain or Portugal. The consequences of rousing the Chinese giant so rudely and unceremoniously are still working themselves out. The climax of his Eastern policy, the defeat of Russia in the Crimea in 1854–6, merely diverted Russian imperialism to Central Asia well out of range of British sea power. But his dramatic and skilful improvisations abroad, though often criticized, contributed towards a national unity and pride badly strained by the developments at home.

Palmerston was a dangerous model for statesmen in other countries exhilarated by the power industrialization had placed in their hands. The most famous incident of his career was a trivial one. In 1850, he sent an ultimatum and a naval squadron to Greece to extract compensation for one Don Pacifico, whose property had been destroyed in a riot and who claimed to be a British citizen. His critics claimed this was outrageous bullying. Palmerston retorted that a British citizen anywhere should get the same protection once afforded to citizens of the Roman Empire. This was splendid rhetoric and is testimony of his effect on national morale. A *pax Britannica* was an illusion, however, for other powerful empires were soon to come into being as industrialism spread. They, too, would seek a world role of the kind which Palmerston had made so glamorous and successful.

Gladstonian liberalism

The 1860s and 70s were decades in which most European governments were experimenting with modernization with the centre of authority shifting away from absolute monarchy. The timing is explained by the common experience of revolution in 1848 and a great series of mid-century wars. Both exposed dangerous defects in the states involved and offered serious warnings to others.

Although her economy was the most advanced in the world, in other respects Britain was badly in need of modernization. The constitution, the civil service, the legal system, education, the army, even the navy no longer answered the needs of an industrial society with world-wide commitments. The third quarter of the nineteenth century was to bring radical reform of the country's main institutions.

The most burning issue was that of parliamentary reform. The first reform of parliament in 1832 had scarcely affected the predominance of the landed gentry in the House of Commons. But it was the thin end of the wedge. It whetted the appetites of those who wanted a really sweeping change in the way the British people were represented in parliament. By the 1850s there was wide agreement among political leaders that further reform was inevitable in such a rapidly changing society. There was equally wide disagreement as to what form it should take.

During this same period party politics were in a state of flux. Sir Robert Peel's Conservative Party had split in 1846 over his decision to repeal the Corn Laws, which for decades had protected British farmers from having to compete with cheap grain imports. Because of the potato famine in Ireland, Peel got rid of this last big barrier to free trade. During the next twenty years Peel's opponents in parliament built a new Conservative Party – a conservative

section of the party, under the growing influence of Benjamin Disraeli. In the same years a new Liberal Party was emerging as a complex alliance of great Whig landowners, supporters of Peel on the Corn Laws issue and radicals. Its leader was William Ewart Gladstone, who as chancellor of the exchequer introduced a remarkable series of budgets which cut tariffs and reduced government expenditure. British politics in the 1860s and 70s were dominated by the rivalry between Gladstone and Disraeli.

By the 1860s both parties were alarmed by the scale of popular agitation for parliamentary reform. The result was Disraeli's comparatively radical measure of 1867, the Second Reform Act, which gave the vote to all male householders in towns. This meant that most urban voters would in future be from the working classes.

Above, Punch *cartoon, captioned 'A Bad Example', of the two great political rivals of the 1860s and 1870s: on the left, William Ewart Gladstone (1807–98), four times Liberal prime minister, reformer and a fervent opponent of repression, and, on the right, Benjamin Disraeli (1804–81), twice Tory Prime Minister, an enthusiastic reformer at home and imperialist overseas.*

Disraeli's hopes that these new working-class voters could be rallied in support of the Conservatives proved premature, and a general election in the following year returned the Liberals to power. Between 1868 and 1874 Prime Minister Gladstone's government enacted a series of overdue reforms: voting in parliamentary elections was at last made secret; a start was made in providing elementary education for all; the law courts were reorganized on simpler lines for the more efficient administration of justice; recruitment to the civil service was open to anyone who could pass a competitive examination. The army, after its poor showing in the Crimean War was thoroughly reorganized: country regiments were established; flogging was abolished together with the practice of allowing officers to purchase their commissions. Thus many of Britain's institutions became more democratic and efficient.

The principle of democracy was relatively new to British politics. The idea that every citizen was entitled to the vote and that a government's authority should rest on the consent of the majority of the people had been pioneered in France and America. Though political democracy was not a by-product of industrialization, it was in industrial areas that the working classes could most effectively organize themselves to demand political rights. The direct involvement of the whole population in politics, therefore, tended to follow in the wake of industrialism.

After the Second Reform Act it was only a matter of time before full parliamentary democracy was obtained in Britain. The Franchise Act of 1884 and the Redistribution Act of 1885 were logical extensions of the principles recognized in 1867. The Franchise Act gave the vote to working men in rural areas, just as its predecessor had enfranchised the towns. The Redistribution Act remapped the constituencies so that each member of parliament would represent roughly the same number of people. Representation of the British people in parliament still fell somewhat short of universal male suffrage, and none of the nation's women won the vote until after the First World War, but Britain now had a mass electorate of some 5,000,000 voters.

Both the composition of parliament and the style of British politics changed with the coming of democracy. The composition of parliament changed slowly, however, and working-class candidates initially got little support from the predominantly working-class electorate. This was partly because of the aristocratic and middle-class politicians who so quickly saw the need for a new style of politics. Gladstone in 1879–80 and the Birmingham radical Joseph Chamberlain in 1885 sought out the new electorate by personally campaigning throughout the country in support of their programmes. They set a fashion which other political leaders were obliged to follow. After 1867, both Liberals

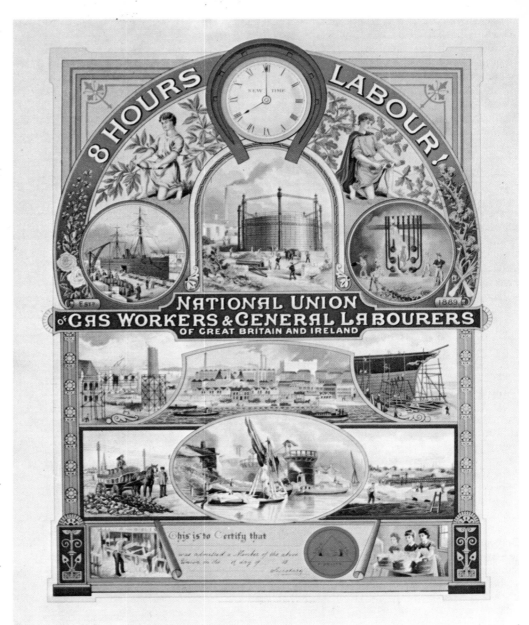

and Conservatives groped their way towards new ways of organizing their parties so as to mobilize as much support as possible on polling days. The modern party 'machine' was coming into existence.

Because of the larger electorate, the drift of public opinion was much less predictable than in the past. The popular press helped to organize public opinion and projected the views of its owners. The *Daily Mail*, one of the first of the dailies deliberately aimed at millions made literate by the Education Act of 1870, was founded by Alfred Harmsworth in 1896. It was selling nearly a million copies a day by the end of the century. Dramatic and simplified presentation of the more emotionally charged issues of international affairs made politics seem exciting and relevant to the electorate, even when its material interests were being neglected. As in the days of Palmerston nationalist sentiment had a unifying effect.

The ruling classes in Victorian Britain had brought off a remarkable feat of political engineering. Political stability in an age of social and economic revolution was rare. For a while the history of the nineteenth century seemed to confirm a widespread belief in the possibility of steady and peaceful progress; but as the century wore on, doubts about the future became more prominent and there was apprehension about the future shape of British government and society now that the balance of political power had shifted from the middle to the working classes. Phrases like 'a leap in the dark' and 'shooting Niagara', used about the Reform Bill of 1867 expressed the sense of uncertainty. Demands for social and economic equality seemed likely to follow the winning of political equality. How could it be accommodated without wrecking the whole Victorian scheme of things, which assumed that everyone would find his proper level in society by the use of talent and energy and that the interests of the whole community would regulate themselves in the long run? Reality did not justify these gloomy predictions of 1867, however, and the newly franchised classes proved far from revolutionary in their demands.

There was apprehension as to the future of the British Empire. It remained the envy of its rivals, who saw it as the secret of Britain's power and wealth, and expanded dramatically between 1882 and 1890 when Britain won the lion's share in the partition of Africa. The financial coup through which Disraeli increased her stake in the Suez Canal in 1875 was of tremendous importance to Britain because of the value of the canal in reaching India. The British were, nevertheless, aware of the empire's vulnerable foundations. The unity of the United Kingdom itself was threatened by Irish discontent; and further threats to the empire multiplied in the later nineteenth century as Russia, France, Germany and America made spectacular gains in Africa and Asia. The task of providing against such threats became increasingly onerous, expensive and uncertain success. Britain's survival as a world power seemed at stake.

There was also apprehension about the economy. Though much of the nation became more prosperous and the rate of industrialization accelerated, progress was less smooth in the last quarter of the nineteenth century. It fluctuated enough for businessmen in the 1870s and 80s to talk gloomily and prematurely of the 'Great Depression'. British agriculture suffered from the rising imports of cheap foreign grain from America and Russia. British manufacturers had to compete with rivals from America, Germany and other newly industrialized states. In the face of such competition British industry adapted itself with only partial success, and Britain ceased to be the workshop of the world. Her future role in the international economy was obscure.

Trade unionism

The rise of trade unionism, the formation of a Labour party and the growing acceptance of the idea that the state should make itself responsible for the welfare of its poorer citizens proved again how well the British social and political system could adjust itself to change.

British workers had pioneered trade unionism during the first half of the nineteenth century. It was a long, slow process of trial and error. There was never any shortage of men willing to experiment in how best to wring better wages and conditions of work from their employers, and their persistence in face of repeated failure was eventually rewarded. By the middle of the century a booming economy and a shortage of skilled labour created the right conditions for successful agitation. The experience of previous decades enabled union leaders to take advantage of them.

The Amalgamated Society of Engineers, established in 1851, set a new standard for the movement with its large membership, ample funds and nationwide organization. The economic benefits of trade unionism were made apparent to an ever-growing army of industrial workers.

But they had not yet won respectability. The courts denied their legality, and the law did not protect their funds from absconding treasurers. In the 1860s the principal union leaders entered politics and agitated for the extension of the vote to working men. Union support was given to sympathetic parliamentary candidates, while at the same time a growing number of trade unionists stood for parliament themselves. The unions' case was forcibly put to the Royal Commission on trade unions, which reported in favour of legalizing them.

In 1868, the Trade Union Congress first met to provide a national forum for discussing labour problems, and in 1871 it set up a parliamentary committee to lobby M.P.s. This political activity proved effective, and the legislation enacted by Gladstone's government in 1871 and by Disraeli's government in 1875 reflected the new climate of opinion by making the unions a recognized British institution with legal status.

Only a minority of mostly skilled and 'respectable' workers were yet represented by trade unions, and to many workers the unions had become too respectable. In the 1880s and 90s a 'new unionism' developed, with a new generation of union leaders like Ben Tillett and Tom Mann, who organized the great mass of unskilled workers. Their tactics were more aggressive, their political thinking often socialist. The great London dock strike of 1889 won the dockers the sixpence an hour they demanded, and the 'dockers tanner' marked the triumphant arrival of the 'new unionism'.

The Labour Party

The 'new unionism' swelled the ranks of the labour movement, but it also made trade unionism less acceptable to middle class opinion. This was at a time when trade unions generally found themselves under renewed fire. Employers' associations increasingly resisted their activities, encouraged by the success of their counterparts in America. The courts tended to decide against the unions in test cases; even the legality of picketing, essential to the success of strikes, was again in doubt. Trade unions were blamed for the decline in competitiveness of British industry because they raised costs and resisted innovation. The position they had won for themselves after so many decades of struggle no longer seemed secure.

By the end of the century the union leaders were conscious of their political weakness. Since the 1860s they had counted on being

Above, members of the Matchmakers Union, 1888.

Opposite, membership certificate of the National Union of Gas Workers & General Labourers.

able to persuade the Liberals and, more indirectly, the Conservatives to look after their interests in parliament. Since 1885 working-class men elected to parliament had sat with the Liberals as 'Lib-Labs'. A new political party to represent working class interests, however, had been regarded as impracticable and unnecessary. Now even the most moderate union leaders were not so sure.

The demand for a new party had sprung from the revival of British socialism after 1880. The most influential of the various socialist groups formed at this time were the Social Democratic Federation and the Fabian Society. The Social Democratic Federation, led by H. M. Hyndman, was a Marxist organization too addicted to the idea of violent revolution to have a wide appeal to British workers. The Fabian Society, whose most famous members were Bernard Shaw and Beatrice and Sidney Webb, rejected revolutionary Marxism and believed in 'permeating' the existing parties with socialist ideas. Though the SDF and the Fabian Society were both predominantly middle class in leadership, the socialism they propagated spread to a small but enthusiastic section of the working classes. To many of them an entirely new political party seemed the obvious way of realising social and economic equality.

In 1893 representatives of various socialist societies and labour clubs met in Bradford to found an Independent Labour Party. Its programme was broadly socialist, but its prime aim was to attract as much working class and especially trade union support as possible for a parliamentary party working for the general interests of labour. Its leading light was the Scottish miner, Keir Hardie, who in the previous year became the first working man to sit in parliament independently of the main parties.

Although the ILP had little success at the polls, its activities helped to swing trade union opinion. In 1889 the Trades Union Congress decided to investigate ways of establishing a distinct group in parliament. In 1900 the unions joined with the ILP, the SDF and the Fabians to set up a Labour Representation Committee. Its secretary was Ramsay MacDonald, later to become the first Labour prime minister.

Many union leaders still remained unconvinced, but what convinced them was the Taff Vale Case of 1901. In that same year the House of Lords upheld a claim by the Taff Vale Railway Company against the Union of Railway Servants for damage to railway property done by its members in a strike called by the union. The union was ordered to pay £23,000 in compensation, which caused much resentment among trade unionists who regarded the judgement as an overt attempt to suppress strikes. In the general election of 1906 the strong feelings aroused by the Taff Vale case helped to return twenty-nine MPs to constitute the new Labour Party.

The problem of poverty

Through trade unions and the Labour Party the more energetic of the new voters had organized themselves for industrial and political action. Gradually the older parties came to see the wisdom of anticipating some of Labour's demands and began to tackle the worst evils of poverty.

Nineteenth-century liberalism had believed that the state should interfere as little as possible in the lives of its citizens. The best goods and services would be produced, to the benefit of all, if everyone pursued his own interests and knew that if he did not help himself no one else would. Charity and legislation like the poor laws and the factory acts reflected the belief of the upper classes in the virtues of hard work.

By the end of the century, however, it had become clear that leaving the system to regulate itself meant too high a cost in human suffering. Investigators like Charles Booth in London and Seebohm Rowntree in York produced startling figures of the extent and depths of poverty in a country which was renowned for its creation of wealth. The realization that nearly a third of the people of London, the richest city in the world, lived in misery, squalor and hopelessness shocked public opinion. With socialism putting forward radical solutions to the victims of poverty, who could now vote, both Conservatives and Liberals had cause to reconsider the perils of letting the state interfere with the economy.

But traditional ideas died hard, and the Liberals and the Conservatives were cautious about social reform. Disraeli had in his younger days written eloquently of the 'two nations' into which the country was divided by the poverty line; but during his

second administration (1874–80) a relatively moderate programme of social legislation was attempted: a factory act for the further protection of women and children, a public health act and an act enabling local authorities to do away with slums.

But between 1885 and 1905, when Britain was governed almost continuously by the Conservatives, his successors, Lord Salisbury and Arthur Balfour, accomplished little except in the field of education. Elementary education became free in 1891, technical education was belatedly developed when its value to Britain's trading rivals was demonstrated and Balfour's Education Act of 1902 re-organized both elementary and secondary education on more efficient lines. In the long term no social reform could be more important than making education available to the whole of the nation's children, but the problem of ensuring their health and well-being deserved equal priority.

What was to become the 'welfare state' took shape after the Liberals came to power in 1906. Already, during the second half of the nineteenth century, enterprising municipal governments had made many of Britain's cities cleaner, healthier and pleasanter to live in through schemes for slum clearance, sanitation, transport services and the supply of water, gas and electricity. During their long spell as the minority party many Liberals had come to accept that the state should take direct responsibility for the welfare of its citizens. In the election campaign of 1906 (the first one for the Labour Party) they denounced the Conservatives for their incompetency in the Boer War and appealed to the country with a platform which called for the enactment of measures favourable to organized labour and a programme of social legislation. The Liberals won a considerable majority and thus began a new era for Great Britain, replacing the liberalism of Gladstone with the radicalism of men like David Lloyd George, who had a much deeper concern for the economic and social welfare of the masses.

Despite the opposition of the House of Lords, the Liberals succeeded in enacting the Workingmen's Compensation Bill and the Small Holdings Bill of 1907 which authorized the County Councils to acquire land suitable for small holdings and to sell or lease it to agricultural labourers or other persons desiring a small stake in the land. The most important legislative achievement of 1908 was the passing of the Old Age Pension Act, which provided for the payment of small pensions to people over the age of seventy whose yearly income did not exceed £31 10s. In the summer of that same year Lloyd George, who had been made chancellor of the exchequer, visited Germany and made a study of the German system of state insurance against sickness, accidents and old age. Deeply impressed by what he saw, he introduced his National Insurance Bill in 1911, which brought in a national insurance scheme to insure the working population against sickness and, to some extent, against unemployment. The British were at last doing what the old-fashioned paternalist government of the German Empire had done twenty years earlier.

Lords and suffragettes

The 'leap in the dark' towards democracy had been less hazardous than the old ruling classes had feared. Enough of the new mass electorate were as aware of the possibility of progress as the middle classes had been after 1832. Yet the slowness with which the two traditional political parties accepted the idea of actively promoting some redistribution of wealth put a strain on this belief in the years before 1914. Many trade unionists began to rely more on massive industrial action than on their representatives in the House of Commons, and a great wave of strikes hit the country in 1911–12. The railways and the docks were at times paralysed, and there were violent clashes with police and troops. But the strike movement died away, and syndicalism – the use of strikes to promote class struggle and political change – did not become the philosophy of the British labour movement.

The fundamental issue of this period was that of curbing the power of the House of Lords, which because of its hereditary character was not subject to popular control, was always dominated by the Conservative Party and hence obstructed a good deal of Liberal legislation. After 1906, although the Liberal government had won a massive majority for the first time since 1880, the Lords continued their wrecking tactics.

The long awaited clash between the Commons and the Lords came in 1909. The Liberal prime minister, Sir Henry Campbell-Bannerman, was forced to retire in 1908 and was succeeded by Herbert Asquith, who was in turn succeeded as chancellor of the exchequer by Lloyd George. Because of the cost of old-age pensions and other social legislation and the great increase in naval expenditures brought about by the competition with Germany, Lloyd George was immediately confronted with an enormous national deficit. In his 1909 budget he proposed to make use of the older forms of taxation such as the income tax, inheritance tax, luxury taxes on liquor and tobacco; but in addition he proposed to use the expedient of imposing a supertax on larger incomes. Another ingenious form of raising revenue was a tax on the sale of land, which was of course bitterly opposed by the landowners, many of whom were in the House of Lords. For six months this budget, the object of which was to wage war against poverty, was hotly debated in parliament. The Lords defied constitutional precedent by rejecting it after it had passed the Commons; but Lloyd George and his colleagues were not averse to a fight on this issue and managed to win the ensuing general election. Deferring to the popular mandate on the budget, the House of Lords finally passed it.

With the struggle over the budget out of the way, the Liberals turned to the central issue of curbing the power of the Lords. In April 1910 the Asquith government introduced the Parliament Bill, which abolished the right of the Lords to veto a money bill and established the procedure that any bill, other than a money bill, if passed in three successive sessions of the Commons was to become law, despite the veto of the Lords,

Above, suffragettes under arrest in Hyde Park, London: the 'votes for women' movement became increasingly militant between 1906 and 1914, though without making much impression on official attitudes. Female suffrage – granted to women over thirty in 1918 and to those over twenty-one ten years later – came about as a result rather of the crucial role on the home front played by women during the First World War.

Top, an old woman evicted from her south London home just before the First World War: by now old-age pensions and the national insurance scheme had laid the basis of the welfare state, but few municipalities recognized a duty to house their citizens.

Opposite, pupils at a London infants school in the late nineteenth century: only in the last decades of the nineteenth century was a national system of primary education established, and secondary education did not become compulsory until 1944.

provided two years had elapsed between the first reading of the bill and its final passage.

Only after another general election in 1910, which was in reality a referendum on the Parliament Bill, and a threat that the king would be asked to create enough Liberal peers to swamp their Conservative majority, did the Lords give way. An obvious anomaly in the British democratic system was removed and the House of Lords, like the Crown, became an appendage to the British system of government. The drama and high feeling of this major constitutional crisis were less important than the fact that it was peacefully and democratically resolved.

Another colourful constitutional issue of these years was the fight to win women the vote. As with most of the other emerging democracies, sex was more important than class in determining who should be excluded from the franchise. In 1903 Mrs Emmeline Pankhurst founded a movement which campaigned with ever increasing militancy to extend the vote to women. At first, her supporters confined themselves to heckling, but failure to get results turned the extremists to window-breaking, arson and other attacks on property. The campaign made female suffrage a more urgent political issue than it otherwise would have been, but the 1914 war intervened, and women's role in it proved their case more conclusively than suffragette militancy.

The Irish question

Grudging acceptance of social reform, hesitancy over women's suffrage and the reactionary stand of the House of Lords suggested that the ruling classes had difficulty in adapting themselves to democracy. Nevertheless, they did adapt themselves, and the impatient violence of the strikers and the suffragettes was a passing phase.

The real threat in the half century before 1914 was to the political unity of the United Kingdom and to Britain's ability to defend her overseas empire and the homeland from external attack. The first of these threats stemmed from failure to solve the Irish question.

Britain was a multi-national state in a century which was an age of nationalism. Though the Scots and the Welsh found close political union with the English profitable, the Irish did not, apart from the Protestant minority in the north of the predominantly Catholic island. Very few were bent on full independence, however, and the search for a form of union which would satisfy both the Irish and the rest of the British had been a major issue in British politics throughout the century.

The search failed. The turning-point was the great famine of 1845–9. Ireland had a rapidly expanding population which its primitive agriculture could not support. About half the Irish depended for their survival on the potatoes they grew. Crop failures were frequent and usually local, but in 1845 the whole country was affected by potato blight. It was in response to this crisis that Robert Peel repealed the Corn Laws and took more direct relief measures. In 1846 blight struck again, followed by a further failure in 1848. The result was famine, which Peel's successors handled disastrously, and in the wake of the famine came typhus and other diseases. Something like a million of Ireland's 8,000,000 people died from starvation or disease, and about the same number were forced to emigrate to America. The horror of these years bred deep and lasting bitterness. It would have taken an unusually imaginative statesman to bridge the gulf between the Irish and the rest of Britain.

Gladstone was such a statesman. Sooner than his fellow politicians he realized the scale of the problem and the danger of leaving it unsolved. From the time he first became prime minister in 1868 until he retired from public life in 1894 he made repeated efforts to reconcile the Irish to inclusion in the United Kingdom. He could have won over the Irish, but he failed to win over the English to the concessions he believed they had to make.

British complacency about Ireland was shaken, however, in the 1860s by the activities of a revolutionary nationalist organization, the Fenian Brotherhood. Public opinion accepted that something had to be done. Gladstone's early measures of reform combined with coercion won general support. In 1869 he disestablished the Anglican Irish Church, to which a resentful Catholic majority had hitherto been forced to pay tithes. His Land Act of 1870 tackled Ireland's basic problem by trying to prevent landlords from exploiting the poor tenant farmers who formed the majority of the population. Although it was an important first step towards solving the land problem, the Land Act was not enough and provided no security for fair rent, fixity of land tenure or for the free sale of land to Irish tenants.

In 1881 Gladstone put through another Land Act which recognized dual ownership of the land and created a land commission to mediate between landlord and tenant, thus contributing greatly to the solution of the agrarian problem.

By this time the Irish Nationalists in the House of Commons were demanding Home Rule for Ireland, and in 1875 Charles Stewart Parnell, who was soon to assume the leadership of the Nationalist Party, won a seat in the House of Commons. He also accepted the presidency of the Land League in Ireland, which had been organized to unite peasants and politicians against landlordism and which employed violent methods of reprisal against anyone who took over land from which a tenant had been evicted. One of their most effective methods of coercion was boycotting, named after a Captain Boycott, the despised English land agent of a large landowner in County Mayo.

By 1885 Gladstone, whose second Land Act of 1881 had proved inadequate, had become convinced that Home Rule was the only way to solve the Irish problem. His conversion split the Liberal Party, opponents of Home Rule allying themselves with the Conservatives as the Liberal Unionists. The most important of the Liberal Unionists was the great radical Joseph Chamberlain. It was clear that the majority of people in Britain were unsympathetic to Home Rule and apart from a brief spell (1892–5) the Liberals were out of office until 1906. The Irish Nationalist Party, too, which had been a dominant force in British politics in the 1880s, declined in influence after 1890 when Parnell was forced out of the leadership after being named as co-respondent in a divorce suit.

The Lords had frustrated two Home Rule bills introduced by Gladstone, though because of the restrictions of the Parliament Act of 1911 they could merely delay the third Home Rule Bill passed for a second time by the Commons in 1913. By this time, the prospect of Home Rule had precipitated a crisis in Ireland. The Protestants of Ulster, under the leadership of Sir Edward Carson, announced their determination to oppose Home Rule. This marked the beginning of the antipathy and religious hatred which still persists in Northern Ireland.

Asquith's Liberal government found itself faced by the threat of open rebellion on the part of Protestant Ulster. A force of Ulster Volunteers was formed, and in the south similar military organizations appeared to oppose it. Civil war seemed imminent in Ireland. The Conservative opposition in the House of Commons was strongly sympathetic to the Ulster cause. In March 1914 several officers of the British Army at Curragh, a large military base near Dublin, declared that they would resign their commissions rather than join in military measures against Ulster. The Home Rule Bill was due to be passed for the third time in May 1914, and Britain seemed on the verge of civil war. She was saved from such a disaster by involvement in another: on 4 August 1914 Britain entered the First World War. The Home Rule Bill was enacted as law in September, but to satisfy the Ulster Protestants a suspensory bill was passed by Westminster to delay the execution of Home Rule until the end of the war.

Threats to the British Empire

The cause of preserving the political unity of the British Isles was in the end lost. After a period of revolution and savage repression during the First World War, independence was conceded to all of Ireland except Ulster when a treaty was signed in 1921 setting up an Irish Free State. The war of 1914 did however stave off the other major threat of the preceding fifty years – the danger of attack on the British Empire and on the British Isles themselves.

A great expansion of the empire had been accomplished in the last fifteen years of the nineteenth century. A thrilling sense of global power gripped the British people as it did so many nations at this time. The British Empire was incomparably greater than any other and comprised some four hundred million people, about a quarter of the world's population.

Disillusion soon followed, however, when the empire's weaknesses became increasingly obvious. It was too vast and sprawling to be easily defended by a nation of 40,000,000, traditionally averse to conscription. It was safe as long as other powers were weak or inactive, but the renewed imperialistic interests of the European states and the United States put the empire at risk.

Britain's hasty acquisition of so much African territory was stimulated by fear that France, Germany and Italy would seize strategic areas of a continent which lay between Britain and her Asian possessions. The Fashoda crisis had ensured control of the Nile valley and hence Egypt and the Suez Canal. Even more important to communications with India however was the Cape of Good Hope. Between 1899 and 1902 Britain tried to crush a possible threat to her domination of South Africa in a war against the republics of Transvaal and the Orange Free State, which were inhabited by Boers of Dutch descent. A nerve-wracking and humiliatingly long struggle against a small nation of farmers ensued; and when victory came, imperialism had turned rather sour.

The Boer War occurred when fear about Russian expansion in Asia was at its height. Though backward Russia had more cause for alarm, as the Crimean War had shown, her defeat in the Crimea was followed by a burst of modernization and by a vast extension of her frontiers in Central Asia. In the 1890s Russia tried to industrialize rapidly and close the gap between her power and that of Britain and Germany. Russian advances in Asia seemed likely to give her predominance in China, and Britain, who had felt her hold on India uncertain as a result of the Indian Mutiny (1857), foresaw the balance of power in Asia shifting to Russia's advantage. Britain allied herself with Japan in 1902. Russian encroachments in Korea and Manchuria aroused the apprehensions of the Japanese, who precipitated war by attacking the Russian fleet at Port Arthur. In less than seven months Japan startled the world by defeating Russia and proving her strength as a new imperialistic power.

Imperialist fervour in Britain and anxiety about the empire's future combined to

Above, evicting a peasant from his holding: the poverty-stricken Irish peasantry's resentment of prosperous English absentee landlords was just one contributory factor in the unstoppable demand for Home Rule and the dissolution of the Union of England and Ireland.

Opposite, illustration from an 1857 edition of the Illustrated London News *of Irish emigrants leaving home: between 1841 and 1861 the population of Ireland fell from over 8 million to 5.8 million, the result of death from starvation or disease and of emigration, mostly to the USA.*

produce plans for strengthening it by closer political and economic links. Joseph Chamberlain, colonial secretary between 1895 and 1903, worked towards expansion in Africa and for imperial federation; but self-governing colonies like Canada and Australia were bent on greater independence, not tighter control. Chamberlain then tried in 1903 to foster unity by adopting the idea of a preferential trade agreement within the empire. This meant restriction of free trade with other countries, long regarded as one of the keys to Victorian prosperity. Chamberlain's resignation to campaign for tariff reform split the Conservative Party and paved the way for the Liberals' return to power in 1906. The empire remained vulnerable and beset by dangerous rivals.

The German challenge

Although much of the alarm about the future of the British Empire was premature it underlined the difficulties of holding together such scattered possessions. Without command of the sea, Britain herself would be open to blockade and invasion. The British had often before been jittery about the strength of their navy, but the great development of the German fleet at the beginning of the twentieth century offered the first real challenge to Britain's security since the time of Napoleon.

Industrialization in the second half of the nineteenth century had made Germany the richest and strongest state in Europe. By building a navy to match her army, Admiral von Tirpitz hoped to make Germany a world power. Britain's Admiral Fisher responded with a revolutionary battleship, HMS *Dreadnought*, which was launched in 1906 and made all existing battleships obsolete. Other navies followed suit, while the British strove to consolidate their lead.

This was a triumph for British technology, but the cost of the naval arms race was high, and finding the money to pay for such Dreadnoughts as well as social security had been the reason for Lloyd George's controversial budget of 1909. The Germans were simultaneously experiencing political conflict over the taxes needed to finance their armaments drive. Industrialization had made war vastly more expensive.

Though Germany never succeeded in outbuilding Britain in warships, it was believed in government circles that Germany was a major threat to the British Isles. Britain cleared up outstanding overseas disputes with France in 1904 and with Russia in 1907 in an attempt to reduce her international commitments, and she was to cooperate more and more with these two powers, who had already allied themselves against Germany. Gradually Britain was drawn into plans for participation in a European war which was generally thought to be in the offing; hitherto she had intervened in continental politics only occasionally and without lasting commitment. Talks with the French over the use of the small professional army, which the Liberal war minister R. B. Haldane had so effectively reformed after 1906, signalized the British government's growing acceptance of positive action to check Germany. Whatever the justification, it came to mean involvement in the 1914 war with its appalling cost and human sacrifice.

The balance-sheet of industrialism

Industrialism had made Britain the giant of nineteenth-century states, but she could not sustain the role once industrialism had spread. British industry only partially managed to meet the challenge of new and enterprising foreign competitors. There was

a decline in the growth of British industrial production at the very time when newcomers like Germany and America were setting a particularly gruelling pace. Even if the British economy had responded satisfactorily, the boost which industrialization gave to the power of rival states still would have strained Britain's capacity to defend her empire. The global character of the empire gave her more rivals than anyone else, and coping with the problems of defence in an age of industrial giants drew Britain into two world wars in the first half of the twentieth century. The cost of victory in both eventually convinced her that the task was beyond her strength.

On the other hand, the British surmounted the difficulties presented to all societies experiencing industrial change, and in the area of social legislation they outdid all except the Scandinavian states. The stresses of social and economic revolution and international crisis did not prove too much for what were on the face of it obsolete and inappropriate institutions. The monarchy, the aristocracy and parliament adapted themselves sufficiently and survived. Power was exercised in a restrained and civilized fashion which had no parallel among the other industrial giants. The demand for political change was expressed in an equally restrained and civilized way. This was an even more remarkable achievement than pioneering the industrial revolution, though its impact on the course of world history has, of course, been negligible in comparison.

The fall of the second Empire in France

France moved much more slowly than Britain towards urban industrial society. In about 1870 when a majority of the British lived in towns, less than a third of Frenchmen did. But, together with the Belgians,

the French were the first to adopt British methods of production, and in the nineteenth century they experienced the social tensions which usually accompany economic change. Although France was less industrialized than Britain, the strain of social tensions was greater because the French were deeply and bitterly divided as to the merits of the different kinds of monarchy and republic they had experimented with since 1789. There was a greater temptation than in Britain to remedy discontent by changing the political system rather than by individual reforms. Between 1815 and 1870 there were two monarchies, two republics and an empire. Thus, while France's economic development was comparatively unspectacular, it gave rise to political instability and violent change.

Napoleon III, whose regime was the outcome of revolution in 1848, tried to accelerate industrial progress by establishing a railway network and encouraging freer trade, which helped to make France a considerable industrial state, far behind Britain but ahead of the rest of Europe. Although change bred discontent, Napoleon used plebiscites to show that the majority of Frenchmen accepted his régime. He might have withstood the turbulence of French politics better than his predecessors but for his dangerous meddling in foreign affairs.

A series of diplomatic defeats was followed in 1870 by war with Prussia. The Prussian army was in general better equipped and organized than the French and very much better led. Napoleon's armies were quickly overwhelmed near the frontier, and the Prussians marched on Paris. His regime was too shallowly rooted to withstand military defeat, especially as he had made the mistake of personally commanding the army and being captured by the Prussians at Sedan. On 4 September 1870 revolution broke out in Paris and a republic was proclaimed.

In the revolutionary wars at the end of the eighteenth century the First Republic had saved France from the invader. The Third Republic was expected to perform the same miracle and for a brief moment seemed to be doing this. The most colourful personality in the provisional republican government was a young lawyer, Léon Gambetta. When the Prussians beseiged Paris at the end of September 1870, he escaped by balloon to organize resistance in the provinces. The large and enthusiastic volunteer forces which he mobilized disconcerted the Prussians, prolonged the war and restored French self-respect, even though the Prussian grip on France was never seriously shaken. After an agonizing four months under siege, the Government of National Defence signed an armistice for three weeks, ignoring the protests of Gambetta. Paris surrendered. The rapidly elected National Assembly agreed to negotiations with Bismarck at Versailles, which were to involve making peace with Germany at the cost of losing Alsace-Lorraine.

Although the new republic had failed to save France from the invader, it did save the country from social revolution – a prospect feared more than defeat by most Frenchmen. The elections of February 1871 produced a highly conservative National Assembly, the majority of whom favoured a return to some form of monarchy. Adolphe Thiers, a veteran politician, who had warned Napoleon III against war with Prussia, became head of state and was entrusted with negotiating peace. Most of the country wanted peace, even on humiliating terms. Paris did not and was seething with discontent. It had borne the brunt of the war, and its staunchly republican citizens resented the arrangements for peace made by the monarchist assembly. When the National

Assembly while still sitting at Bordeaux tried to deprive the National Guard of its pay and its weapons as part of the return to peace, Paris rose in revolt.

The Prussian occupying forces now witnessed a second siege of Paris conducted by troops of the French government. The professional revolutionaries, who haunted the political underground of Paris, took control of the insurrection. They represented various brands of republicanism and socialism, but they were united in their hatred of the wealthy bourgeoisie, the Catholic Church and the remnants of the old aristocracy. They dominated the emergency municipal government, elected on 26 March 1871, and called themselves the Commune, after a similar body in the French Revolution. Although the revolutionaries were in a minority, the government and its supporters saw the Commune as a threat to property and the social order. As defenders of both they attacked the Commune with savage determination, and after bitter street fighting and the slaughter of some 20,000 Communards the Commune was overthrown.

The main troops of the insurrection had been the industrial workers who had been saved from starvation by their service in the National Guard during the Prussian siege of Paris. Little had been done by any regime to alleviate their harsh working conditions, and it was not surprising that they looked to the revolutionaries for salvation. Their earlier protest in 1848 had also been brutally crushed. This second blood-bath in a generation intensified class hatred and provided European socialism with a legend of great emotional force. Thiers' triumph was in the long run to undermine the social stability it was meant to secure.

Its most dangerous opponents destroyed, the government could concentrate on recovering from defeat by the Germans.

The peace treaty was harsh. France had to pay an indemnity of five thousand million francs, to accept the presence of German troops until it was paid and to surrender the provinces of Alsace and Lorraine with their one and a half million inhabitants and rich resources. In addition, France had to adjust herself to a period of weakness and isolation. Prussia's victory in 1870 had enabled her to form a German Empire out of the confederation of Northern German States who had fought side by side with the South German states against France. Germany was in the middle of an industrial revolution which was quickly to consolidate her position as the strongest power in Europe. France's prospects of revenge and the recovery of Alsace-Lorraine seemed remote.

Nevertheless, French revival was swift. Thiers was a reassuring figure to the conservative-minded majority of Frenchmen, and he reinforced their confidence in him by avoiding innovation and experiment. This made it far easier for Thiers to raise the large public loans needed to pay off the indemnity, and as a result the French had the satisfaction of seeing the evacuation of German troops from her soil by 1873. France's renewed financial strength allowed her to begin rebuilding and modernizing her army by the mid-1870s. Although France was a long way from winning security and revenging the loss of Alsace-Lorraine, the Third Republic got off to a good start in the eyes of its citizens and of Europe.

Republic or monarchy?

It was by no means clear, however, that the Republic would survive. After the defeat of the Commune, a monarchy seemed likely to emerge. Thiers' career as a minister had been in the service of King Louis-Philippe, who

had been overthrown in 1848, and the National Assembly elected in February 1871 was predominantly monarchist.

Those who favoured a return to constitutional monarchy were divided as to who should be king. Some supported the Orleanist dynasty in the person of Louis-Philippe's grandson; others supported the old Bourbon dynasty and the grandson of its last king, Charles X, whom Louis-Philippe had supplanted in 1830. The Bourbon candidate would not accept the tricolour as the flag of France because of its revolutionary origins. His supporters knew that this attitude would make him unacceptable to the overwhelming majority of Frenchmen, but they would not switch their allegiance to an Orleanist while a Bourbon candidate was available. This deadlock was to destroy the prospects of monarchy in France.

Time was on the Republican side, and by-elections showed that the monarchist majority of 1871 was a fluke. Thiers himself quickly realized that a republic would divide the French less than any other regime provided it was conservative and not radical in its policies. The monarchists were of course incensed and insisted that Thiers be replaced as president by Marshal Mac-Mahon, who was to prevent any irrevocable decision about France's future form of government until the monarchists had agreed on who should be king. They left it too late. France could not go on indefinitely without an agreed constitution. In 1875 constitutional laws were finally agreed by the Assembly, but they were couched so as to avoid calling the regime a republic. Then a deputy named Wallon introduced the word in an amendment, which, because of quarrels in the monarchist ranks, got through by a majority of one. The Republic was no longer provisional – it was formally in being.

The first parliamentary elections under the new constitution took place early in 1876. The royalists secured a slight majority in the senate and the Republicans secured a majority in the Chamber of Deputies. A constitutional crisis now gave the Republic a chance to establish itself. Marshal Mac-Mahon dismissed the new Republican ministry, appointed a royalist prime minister, and held fresh elections in 1877 with the government using all the means of pressure at its disposal to secure a monarchist majority. They failed, Thiers and Gambetta joining forces in a successful campaign for the Republic. Mac-Mahon accepted the verdict of the electorate and resigned. Support for any kind of monarchy faded, and the Third Republic survived until 1940.

One reason why the Republic won such wide support was that during the decade 1879–89 the moderate republicans controlled the Chamber of Deputies and the good sense of its leaders compared favourably with the behaviour of the squabbling monarchists. Republicanism had freed itself from its revolutionary associations and represented the interests of the propertied classes in a country where landowning peasants predominated. Its conservatism and respectability made it popular.

The only drastic change contemplated concerned Republicanism's old enemy, the Catholic Church. Anti-clericalism was one of the strongest emotions uniting Republicans. One of their ablest leaders, Jules Ferry, was determined to end the Church's control of education. The nation's children were to grow up as loyal citizens of the Republic; they must not be taught by a church traditionally favourable to monarchy. The education laws of 1880–1 went a long way towards ensuring this. But this was the extent of the radicalism of the moderate Republicans.

In contrast with the governments in Britain and Germany, the Third Republic gave low priority to social reform. Although the slow pace of industrialization in France made it seem less urgent, she could not isolate herself from the effects of rapid change elsewhere. The world slump in the 1870s eventually affected France, and massive exports of cheap grain from America hit hard at her agricultural economy. By the 1880s, there was a good deal of discontent about the Republican regime which had failed to cushion people against the effects of world competition.

Disenchantment with the Republic was expressed through support for the colourful General Boulanger, who was made minister of war in 1886. The enemies of the Republic pictured him as a new Bonaparte leading a revitalized France to revenge against Germany. In 1887 the respectability of the Republic was shaken when the president had to resign after charges of corruption were brought against his son-in-law. Supported by various right-wing groups like the League of Patriots, Boulanger became a candidate for election to the Chamber of Deputies wherever by-elections occurred, the last being a constituency in Paris in January 1889. Paris crowds, discontented with the Republic, urged him to seize power, but his hesitation allowed the Republicans time to close ranks. Boulanger fled the country and committed suicide two years later.

Although Boulanger had proved a paper tiger, the remarkable support he had so easily won was a grim warning to the Republicans. The old royalist threat of Bourbon and Orléans was fading fast. The Napoleonic tradition was very much alive.

It was some of Boulanger's supporters who unearthed the Panama scandal. Ferdinand de Lesseps, who had won fame a generation earlier by building the Suez Canal, had been trying since 1881 to build a Panama canal linking the Atlantic and Pacific Oceans. The scheme proved a costly failure, and in 1889 his Panama Canal Company went bankrupt. In its final efforts to stave off bankruptcy, the company had tried to raise money by methods which needed parliamentary approval. In 1892 it was revealed that many deputies, including some ministers, had

been bribed to vote for the company's proposals. Two Jewish financiers had arranged the bribery.

The scandal severely damaged the Republic's reputation and gave further substance to the allegations of corruption made by its opponents on the Right. The way in which the scandal was used, moreover, confirmed that a new 'right' was emerging in France. Its leaders were strongly nationalist and anti-semitic; it charged the Republic with allowing Jewish and other alien influences to corrupt the nation and its traditions.

The Dreyfus Affair

The battle between the new French Right and the forces of Republicanism was joined over a miscarriage of justice in the French army. The army did not directly play at politics and saw itself as the loyal instrument of whatever government the democratic process threw up. But its upper ranks were dominated by men who would have preferred a royalist and clerical form of government. Republicans, therefore, viewed the

Above, General Georges Boulanger (1837–91), appointed war minister in 1886, leaving Paris in 1887 for a provincial command: he did, amid popular protests, indeed return, as the slogans fixed to the locomotive proclaimed he would, and almost staged a coup d'état *in 1889, drawing back, to the disappointment of his supporters, at the last moment.*

Opposite, the statue of Napoleon Bonaparte in the Place Vendôme, Paris, overthrown by Communards: the Commune's most constructive achievement was the myth of a genuinely socialist society it left behind it, reinforced by the viciousness with which it was repressed; in reality it had neither the time nor the ideological strength to establish anything remotely like an ideal society.

army with the same suspicion and dislike as they did the Catholic Church. Their suspicion and dislike were raised to fever pitch by the Dreyfus Affair.

In 1894 Captain Alfred Dreyfus was convicted of spying for Germany and condemned to life imprisonment on Devil's Island, the notoriously harsh penal settlement off the coast of South America. At first, the case seemed uncontroversial except for the stimulus it gave to anti-semitism. Dreyfus was the first Jew who had succeeded in becoming a staff officer. His apparent treachery seemed to justify the more usual practice of excluding Jews and fed the flames of the campaign against French Jewry currently being waged by the journalist Edouard Drumont.

In 1896 Colonel Picquart, the newly appointed head of counter-espionage, discovered that Dreyfus was innocent and that the real spy was another officer called Esterhazy. The army now made the fatal mistake of trying to suppress Picquart's evidence. Through Picquart the story reached political circles, and a small but influential group began to campaign on behalf of Dreyfus. The army hastily court-martialled and acquitted Esterhazy and posted Picquart abroad. The reputation of the army was held to be more important than the fate of Dreyfus.

In their anxiety to avoid a scandal the army authorities had made things worse. Public opinion was initially anti-Dreyfus, and the government had no desire for a row with the army; but a brilliant press and parliamentary campaign by the Radical politician Georges Clemenceau, the novelist Zola and others eventually forced a re-examination of the case in 1898. The minister of war discovered that documents to put Dreyfus's guilt beyond doubt had been manufactured by an intelligence officer, Colonel Henry, who was arrested and committed suicide. The establishment of Dreyfus's innocence seemed only a matter of time.

But much more than the fate of Dreyfus was now at stake. So little solid evidence had been available to the public during the controversy that it was possible to believe whatever one's prejudices seemed most likely. To most monarchists, Catholics, nationalists and anti-semites, it was obvious that a corrupt group of Republicans was trying to help a Jewish traitor to escape his just deserts. To the more radical and anti-clerical Republicans, as well as to the socialists and others on the far Left, it was equally obvious that the reactionary forces in the Church and the army had condemned an innocent man as part of their campaign to undermine the Republic. The debate about Dreyfus became an occasion for releasing pent-up political emotions. Settling the guilt or innocence of Dreyfus would also mark a propaganda triumph for either Right or Left.

The Right could hardly win. They had the disadvantage of having backed the wrong horse in the Dreyfus case itself. Although the army condemned Dreyfus again at a re-trial in 1899, he was quickly 'pardoned' and freed; his formal rehabilitation was eventually arranged in 1906. Moreover, most Frenchmen continued to back the Republic, which meant not so much the Dreyfusards who so passionately defended it as the more conservative Republicans who had governed France moderately and unspectacularly for the past thirty years. The Republican governments during the years of controversy had initially trusted the army's version and gradually moved over to a more sceptical attitude. This was probably in tune with the great majority of French voters. The Right, therefore, lacked mass support. They were divided, too, as to what they wanted in place of the Republic.

The Republicans, on the other hand, again showed their ability to unite when the regime was in danger, as during the height of the crisis when the nationalist writer Déroulède attempted a futile coup. A strong Republican ministry emerged which took effective counter-measures. The Republic had lasted longer than any other regime since the French Revolution in 1789. The frequent changes of government and the mediocrity of so many of its politicians made it look deceptively weak and unstable. The Dreyfus Affair showed that the Republic had formidable enemies but it also showed that the Republic could prove more than a match for them.

Anti-clericalism

The coalition of the moderate and radical republicans in the Chamber of Deputies which Premier Waldeck-Rousseau had formed in 1899 survived the Dreyfus crisis. In this coalition known as the 'Bloc' the radicals had the edge over the moderate opportunists or progressists, who had enjoyed predominance during the 1880s and had tried to reconcile hostile elements to the Republic. The passions revealed by the Dreyfus Affair made the task seem too difficult, and the radicals, who believed in 'Republicanizing' France, were now given their head. The minister of war was given control of army promotion to ensure that loyal Republicans got preference. Above all, there was a return to the anti-clericalism of the early years of the Republic.

Many Catholics in France had long desired to end the ancient feud with the Republic, but they were in a minority. Even when Pope Leo XIII lent his support to the idea of reconciliation in the early 1890s, the response from most Catholic bishops in France was cold. Hatred of Republicanism and all it had stood for since the French Revolution was too deeply rooted. The vision of France united by liberal Catholism and moderate Republicanism quickly faded, but after the Dreyfus Affair the Republic and the Church seemed set on a collision course.

Between 1899 and 1905 a new offensive against the Church's power was launched, and most of the rich and influential religious orders were dissolved and their schools closed. The death of Pope Leo XIII in 1903 made reconciliation even more remote, because his successor, Pius X, was uncompromising and tactless and offended even sympathetic Republicans. Relations between the Vatican and Paris deteriorated to such an extent that diplomatic relations were broken off.

In 1905 the French government took the final step of scrapping Napoleon's Concordat with the Pope, which had been the basis of church-state relations since 1801. State and Church were now completely separated, and the Church lost its official status and its revenue from the state. When the Pope refused to accept the Separation Law the Church's property was confiscated.

Thus the Church lost its ability to intervene in politics, as it had done in the Dreyfus Affair, and a further step had been taken towards consolidating the Republic. The Church's loss of wealth was not altogether detrimental to spiritual life, and its influence was still exerted in less provocative fashion. Both sides benefited from the lowering of tension which separation brought.

Industrial development

With so much time and energy devoted to anti-clericalism, the ruling Republican parties had little time to spare for social reform. Even the radicals, who talked of it, did little when they had the chance. Electoral backing for the Republic might have been fatally undermined if it had decided to tax the peasant majority for the sake of the proletarian few. Income tax, for example, was not introduced until the First World War.

French industry continued to expand, but not enough to make the industrial population a majority, nor enough to put France on a par with Germany, Britain or America. France suffered from certain disadvantages, having fewer natural resources, like coal and iron, than her rivals and a slower rate of population growth. There was no urge to overcome these disadvantages, since the French economy as it stood supplied the needs of too many Frenchmen. France could not only feed herself but was the third

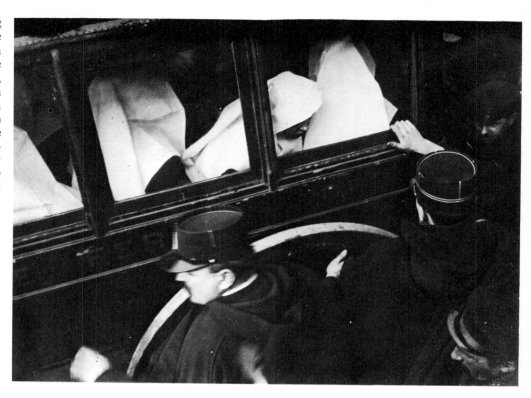

largest grain exporter in the world. Her reputation for manufacturing luxury goods like furniture, silks, jewellery, cosmetics and fashionable clothes was unsurpassed. The traditional preference for a family business of a size the family could directly manage continued to appeal to most industrialists. Sacrificing the good life in the quest for ever greater profit would have been alien to another French tradition. The sort of attitude which helped to build the giant firms of Germany and America was rare in France; and for peacetime government to urge the development of large corporations in the interests of national strength, as had happened in tsarist Russia, was alien to the political thinking of the Republic.

Hence there was a growing number of industrial workers destined for a long time to remain a minority of the electorate. In contrast with British and even German workers they saw little prospect of improving their conditions by conventional political methods. While the British and German labour movements became increasingly absorbed into the existing political system in the years before 1914, French workers became more revolutionary in their approach to politics. France had too little industrial development for her security in Europe but too much for domestic peace.

The revival of French socialism

The defeat of the Commune in 1871 had shattered the French socialist movement and destroyed thousands of its most militant supporters. Within a few years it had begun to revive, and in 1880 an amnesty for the Communards who had been sent into exile stimulated interest.

Above, nuns leaving their convent after the passing of the Separation Law, 1905: anti-clericalism had been a continuing theme of French politics since the Revolution of 1789; now that separation had been achieved it lost much of its potency.

Opposite, contemporary drawing of the crucifixion of Captain Alfred Dreyfus (1859–1935): General Mercier, the Minister of War, who willingly accepted the fabricated evidence against Dreyfus, is offering him a sponge soaked in vinegar. The Dreyfus affair split the country into two bitterly hostile camps and brought into the open the extensive anti-semitic feelings latent in France, as elsewhere in Europe.

As in the earlier period of French socialism the movement was deeply divided as to doctrine. The principal difference among the Socialist leaders, as in the rest of Europe, was between the Marxists and the 'reformists'. The Marxists, led by Jules Guesde, saw their task as preparing the workers for their role in the revolution which would overthrow capitalism. The reformists wanted pressure through conventional political channels to win immediate reform of working conditions and a gradual transfer of power to the working classes.

Socialists of all kinds did well at the polls in 1893 after the Panama scandal had shaken the Republic. The forty-nine socialists elected included Guesde and the two ablest of the reformists, Jean Jaurès and Alexandre Millerand. In 1899 Millerand became minister of commerce in the Waldeck-Rousseau government formed to ward off the challenge to the Republic during the Dreyfus case. Despite his success in carrying reformist principles into practice by securing a minimum wage and reduced working hours for public employees, his acceptance of office in a bourgeois government scandalized a large section of the movement.

Socialists overcame their differences sufficiently in 1905 to form a united socialist party. Guesde's influence was strong, and cooperation with the radicals in government was ruled out. But the old divisions were never far below the surface, and on the eve of the 1914 war French socialism lost its most attractive and powerful leader when Jaurès was assassinated. The parliamentary socialists had made themselves a force in French politics, but their hopes of real power remained slight.

The record of the organized socialist parties was not such as to impress workers in search of rapid and fundamental change. France's underprivileged citizens had a long tradition of revolutionary violence to secure quick results. The bloodshed of 1848 and 1871 had deepened class hatreds and engendered the distrust of bourgeois political leaders, which included most of the parliamentary socialists. They were sceptical of winning socialism by parliamentary methods and they did not want to wait for the distant revolution promised by the Marxists. The gulf between the trade unions and the socialist parties, in sharp contrast with developments in Britain and Germany, further weakened French socialism.

When trade unions, or *syndicats*, were legalized in 1884, they saw themselves less as organisations to improve working conditions than as agents of revolutionary change. Syndicalism, as their programme came to be called, relied on a general strike to paralyse capitalist society and enable workers to seize power. The *syndicats* would then be the units of the future socialist society based on producer-cooperatives. The syndicalist doctrine was formerly adopted in 1892. It was re-affirmed more explicitly in the Amiens Charter of 1906, after syndicalists meeting

in a trade union congress at Amiens had defeated those who wanted cooperation with the parliamentary socialists.

Between 1906 and 1909 the syndicalist creed was put into practice with a wave of strikes culminating in an abortive general strike. Trade unionists were a small proportion of the French population – half a million at the turn of the century rising to a million by 1909 in a country of 39,000,000 – but concentrated in the major towns they could cause a good deal of disruption. Prime Minister Clemenceau's government acted ruthlessly against the strikers, and there was a lot of violence. When further strikes broke out in 1910, Clemenceau's successor, Aristide Briand, who in his early days had advocated syndicalism, mobilized the railwaymen who had paralysed communications and forced them to do their jobs in uniform. Syndicalism was spectacular in action, but it failed.

Doctrinal disputes among the socialist politicians and violence among the trade unionists were only to be expected in a country which industrialized slowly and whose politicians felt no urge to anticipate trouble by social reform. The prospect of a socialist majority seemed so remote that any programme of action could be shown wanting by its opponents, thus producing endless

debate in the chamber. A feeling of impotence among politically conscious workers in France was bound to be strong and often explosive. Also for a time the anarchists felt driven to violence, which in the 1890s took the form of bomb outrages and political assassination. The pattern was repeated in many other countries of Europe as part of the price of slow industrialization unaccompanied by adequate social reform.

The problems of empire

Under the Third Republic France built the second largest colonial empire in the world – Indo-China, Madagascar and vast areas of northwest Africa, including Tunis and Morocco, were conquered or made protectorates. The acquisition of an empire became an important way of compensating the French people for the humiliation of the 1870 defeat. Frustrated soldiers and other men of action could find fame and fortune by carving out an empire. The emphasis on North Africa was natural for a state doubtful of its security and anxious about its Mediterranean flank.

In theory the French favoured the assimilation of their colonial subjects, by which they would gradually come to share the

Above, contemporary illustration of a march through the mining villages of northern France during the April 1906 miners' strike.

Opposite top, strikers on their way to a meeting in central Paris, 1909: though the left was in power after 1905, the division between parliamentary and industrial socialism was never overcome.

Opposite bottom, Jean Jaurès, the French socialist leader, speaking at a demonstration against the three years' law, a proposal to increase the period of conscription from two to three years, May 1913 (the law was passed in July): on 31 July 1914 Jaurès was assassinated on his return from an unsuccessful attempt to maintain international socialist unity by persuading German socialists to strike rather than mobilize.

benefits of French citizenship and absorb the values of French civilization. One of France's most distinguished colonial administrators, Lyautey, summed up the ideal by declaring that France was a nation of 100,000,000 inhabitants. As the empire became more vast, the idea of an immense nation ceased to be a practical possibility, and the concept of assimilating a native elite to cooperate with the French in the work of government tended to take its place.

In any case, for most Frenchmen the empire was of secondary importance to affairs in Europe. Dreams of revenge or fears of another German invasion were always in the last resort more important than imperialist expansion overseas. Both the ministries of Jules Ferry were brought down because he was alleged to have diverted France's energies overseas – in 1881 by taking Tunis and in 1885 by conquering Indo-China. In 1882 the French government declined to join Britain in an expedition to Egypt, which marked the beginning of Britain's long predominance over the Nile valley and the Suez Canal. The Fashoda crisis of 1898 showed that the French were to regret their decision – their withdrawal from the possibility of war showed that the reasoning behind the decision of 1882 still held good. Despite its vast imperial gains, the Republic had discarded the Napoleonic tradition of foreign adventure on a grand scale, and the new French Empire was won with little risk of conflict with other powers.

France and the German threat

The 'German question' haunted the Third Republic throughout its history. The phrase had its origins in the German invasion of 1870 which was to be repeated in 1940 and destroy the Republic. France's dilemma after 1871 was that no French government could think of abandoning Alsace-Lorraine for ever, yet Germany's military superiority and her astounding industrial and commercial development were so great as to make avoidance of war a prime necessity.

Neither security against a further invasion nor revenge for the last one could be obtained without allies, and for the first twenty years of its existence the Third Republic was isolated. The German chancellor, Bismarck, was determined to keep France in isolation and had negotiated alliances with Austria-Hungary, Russia and Italy. The only other major European power was Britain, whom the French regarded as an enemy second only to Germany.

France's chance of breaking out of isolation came in 1890 when Bismarck fell from power and his successors tried to reduce and simplify Germany's obligations. They incautiously dropped the Russian alliance, leaving Russia isolated and threatened by the same two states whose power menaced France – Germany and Britain. An alliance between France and Russia was an obvious

SAISON RUSSE 1909 OPERA ET BALLET

Left, poster by Léon Bakst advertising the 1909 season of Diaghilev's Russian Ballet.

Opposite, Tsar Alexander III of Russia (1845–94) and Sadi Carnot (1837–94, President of France 1887–94) shake hands to symbolize the Franco-Russian defensive alliance signed in January 1894.

move, because Germany would hesitate to face a war on two fronts.

What stood in the way was the tsar's hatred of republics and the fact that Paris was a centre for Russian revolutionaries in exile. He was gratified, however, by the arrest in Paris in May 1890 of a large group of these revolutionaries, which signalized a change in French government policy. Moreover, since 1888 Russia, desperately in need of foreign capital, had been floating loans very successfully in Paris with the active encouragement of the French government. The makings of an *entente cordiale* were present.

A dramatic colonial agreement in 1890 between Britain and Germany convinced both Paris and St Petersburg, wrongly as it happened, that their two main enemies were on the point of making an alliance. In July 1891 a French naval squadron visited Kronstadt, Russia's Baltic fortress. During the festivities Tsar Alexander III gave startling proof of Russia's new policy by standing bareheaded while a Russian band played the 'Marseillaise', the battle hymn of the French Revolution. Negotiations followed, and in January 1894 a defensive

alliance was signed. The ecstatic welcome given to the Russian fleet when it visited Toulon in October 1893 was a measure of the French relief at emerging from isolation. A further diplomatic success for the Republic came when Britain not only settled her differences with France and Russia but was drawn into ever closer cooperation with Germany in the years before 1914.

In all the Republic had enjoyed remarkable political success. It had beaten off its enemies at home and had built a coalition against Germany which enabled France to survive invasion in 1914 and win back Alsace-Lorraine at the end of the war.

The Republic did a great service by surviving so long, and within its political framework most of the French nation enjoyed a steadily growing prosperity. Nevertheless, it failed to solve two fundamental problems. Like all the other European states France could find no answer to the problem of surviving in a world torn by imperialist rivalry except by fragile alliances of the kind likely to provoke war. Moreover, France could not afford even a successful war like that of 1914–18, which exhausted her and made her all the less able to withstand the renewed

German challenge in the 1930s. The Third Republic also failed to unite the nation, and a dangerously substantial minority wanted a change in the whole system. Hostility from the Right persisted under the powerful influence of Charles Maurras, whose nationalist paper, *Action Française*, first appeared in 1899. The ruthlessness with which the Republican parties dealt with strikers embittered still further the socialist Left, whose numbers were bound to increase as industrialization proceeded.

Consequently, the Republic always had an air of the provisional about it despite its long life. In terms of both French history and the history of the world, the Republic is most likely to be remembered for the extraordinary array of painters who worked in France during these years. The exhibition by Impressionist painters in 1874 signalized a revolution in art, and by 1914 Paris had seen a succession of revolutionary developments in painting. Monet, Toulouse-Lautrec, Degas, Renoir, Cézanne, Van Gogh, Gauguin, Matisse, Picasso and many other great painters contributed to this astonishing artistic ferment. France's writers at this time were almost equally fertile in creating new literary forms, such as the symbolist poetry of Rimbaud and Mallarmé and the naturalistic fiction of Zola and Maupassant. It was in Paris that Diaghilev's Russian ballet and Stŕavinsky's music made their revolutionary impact. Paris was more than ever the cultural capital of Europe. The bold experiments of its creative artists were in strange contrast to the cautious and conventional acts of its statesmen; but both were responses to the same bewildering new world of industrial civilization.

Chapter 10

Russia: Prelude to Revolution

While the British and the French were pioneering industrialization and political democracy, Russia remained the most backward of all the major European states. She was ruled by an autocratic emperor, and about ninety percent of her inhabitants were peasants, who were either serfs and the private property of a small class of landed gentry or state peasants controlled by the government. They eked out a miserable existence by primitive agricultural methods and were at the mercy of the landlord who owned them. There were few towns, and in 1851 only about eight percent of Russia's 67,000,000 people lived in them. Although industry did develop in Russia in the first half of the nineteenth century, it was a slow growth and the gap between Russia and western Europe was widening all the time.

Just how wide the gap had become was brought home to Russia's rulers by the Crimean War. The war is remembered in Britain for the inefficiency with which it was fought and organized by the British army commanders: the futility of the charge of the Light Brigade, the scandalous provision for the wounded and the work of Florence Nightingale are the best known episodes. For Russia it was one of the greatest humiliations of her history. Since the time of Peter the Great, Russia had been renowned above all for her formidable army, and between 1815 and 1854 she was thought to be invulnerable. When the tsar's armies failed to dislodge the comparatively small and poorly led armies of Britain and France from Russia's soil, the shock was tremendous.

It was clear to the new tsar, Alexander II, who came to the throne during the war, that Russia's failure was a result of her economic backwardness. Like Peter the Great, who in the wake of defeat had introduced western European civilization into Russia, Alexander II proceeded to do the same. He freed the serfs from bondage in the hope of revitalizing Russian agriculture; he gave Russia an enlightened legal system; he created new organs of local government, the *zemstvos*, with elected members; he made the army more efficient and humane; he reformed Russia's finances. By instituting these changes he hoped to bring about conditions favourable to business enterprise and industry, which had given Britain and France a decisive edge over Russia in economic and military strength.

Alexander II wanted economic change without political change, however, and did not propose to give up any of his power to elected parliaments. He wanted to make the old autocracy work better so that Russia could regain her position as a great European power. Between 1855 and 1917 the tsars strove to catch up with their European rivals in military and economic strength, while at the same time trying to preserve autocratic government.

After such a long period of stagnation, Alexander's reforms stimulated a demand for much more sweeping changes; but Alexander's determination to preserve autocracy led to the growth of a revolutionary movement which was to undermine and finally supplant the tsar in 1917.

The middle class in Russia was small and insignificant, in striking contrast with most western European countries. Resistance to tsardom was led by discontented and conscience-stricken members of the intelligentsia – students, authors, teachers, doctors and so on – most of whom were of noble birth. One of them, Alexander Herzen, waged a propaganda war against the tsarist regime from exile. He initially greeted Alexander II as the 'Tsar-Liberator' but was quickly disillusioned and gradually inspired a younger and more radical generation than his own to seek change through revolution.

Student revolutionary societies were formed in the early 1860s. As they were suppressed, others emerged more militant and better organized, aiming not merely at overthrowing autocratic government but at establishing peasant socialism. Village communes in Russia ran their own affairs on roughly democratic lines, and Herzen had hoped the commune would be the unit of a peculiarly Russian kind of socialism, which would make it unnecessary for her to go through an industrial revolution, whose results in western Europe had horrified him. The movement aimed at this was known as 'Populism'.

Populists were at odds as to how best to bring about their revolution. In the 1870s thousands of young people went off to the countryside to bridge the gulf between the educated classes and the peasantry and to incite the peasants to revolt. The movement was a dismal failure which simply demonstrated that the gulf between the peasants and the educated Russians was too wide to be bridged so easily. Though hopes of a great mass uprising faded, hopes of overthrowing tsardom were kept alive. In 1876 a revolutionary society called 'Land and Liberty' was formed to organize a systematic campaign of propaganda in town and country. Its more impatient members saw a short-cut to success in terrorism.

The Land and Liberty movement was encouraged by the case of Vera Zasulich, who in 1878 had shot and wounded the

the repressive system of Nicholas I was restored. In the face of rising discontent among the educated classes Alexander II had, on the morning of his assassination, finally given his approval to a scheme for introducing some elected representatives into the work of central government. This might have been the first tentative move towards a breach in autocratic government and might someday have led to a constitution. It was quietly buried. Opposition to the government could still be expressed only through revolution, and it was only a matter of time before a new and wiser generation of revolutionaries was to emerge.

Russian expansion

While the regime was fighting off revolutionaries within Russia, it was experiencing mixed fortunes in its struggle to revive Russian power abroad. Between 1864 and 1884 Russian troops conquered a vast region of Central Asia, partly controlled by the principalities of Khiva, Bokhara and Khokand and otherwise occupied by nomadic tribes. These conquests brought Russia's frontiers in line with those of Persia and Afghanistan, beyond whose borders lay the British Empire. The battle for influence over these two unstable buffer states was now more urgently waged than ever. British nervousness increased, but there was no chance of a new Crimean War to warn the Russians off because Turkey was now anti-British and would not let British warships and troops through the Dardanelles into the Black Sea. British sea power was helpless to check Russia, as became clear in 1885 when the two nations came to the brink of war.

military governor of St Petersburg because he had ordered the flogging of a political prisoner. Her acquittal by the jury in defiance of the evidence showed the state of public opinion.

In 1879 'Land and Liberty' split over the question of terrorism, the terrorists forming a new society, called 'The People's Will', which believed that the assassination of the tsar would bring down the regime. This small group of men and women, hunted by the police, made numerous attempts to kill Alexander II and finally succeeded in March 1881, when bombs thrown during a street procession fatally wounded him.

The assassination did not bring down the regime, however, and Alexander III, who succeeded his father, ruthlessly repressed the revolutionary movement. Populism was crushed for a decade. Many of Alexander's reforms were watered down, and much of

Although British fear for her Indian empire was an agreeable form of revenge for Russia's Crimean defeat, she was still very vulnerable in regions less remote than Central Asia, as she realized during two great crises in the Balkans from 1875 to 1876 and again from 1885 to 1887. Both times Russia had tried to use rebellion against the Turks to bring Bulgaria under her influence, because Bulgaria was an excellent base for striking at the straits of the Bosporus and the Dardanelles, which, especially since the Crimean War, Russia had regarded as the key to her back door. To maintain her position in the Near East Britain was able to organize enough opposition among the powers to make Russia climb down. In 1878 Russia was particularly incensed at having to abandon a valuable peace treaty, which had cost her a year's bitter fighting. From these two crises Russia learned that she was still not strong enough to contemplate a European war.

In 1890, she lost her only remaining ally when the German emperor, William II, decided not to renew the treaty with Russia which had been negotiated by his former chancellor, Bismarck. Alexander III had little alternative but to ally himself with

France, although such an alliance might increase the risk of Russia having to fight Germany, now the strongest power in Europe. The conquest of vast regions of Central Asia made a spectacular triumph, but the diplomatic buffetings Russia received in Europe reminded her rulers that she lagged far behind the advanced industrial powers.

Industrialization in the 1890s

Russia's backwardness was underlined again in humiliating fashion when famine struck in 1891. The inability of the authorities to deal with the situation and organize food supplies made Russia the target of sneering remarks abroad, especially in Germany. Alexander III's pride was badly hurt by these comments and other evidence of Russia's low international standing. He was impressed by the arguments of Sergei Witte that only rapid industrialization would enable Russia to become a world power in keeping with her vast population and resources.

Witte came from a family of German origin which had long been in the service of the Russian state. He had worked his way up to an important post in the administration of Russia's railways, which were belatedly transforming the country's notoriously bad communications. He came to the notice of Alexander III and went to St Petersburg as minister of communications. In 1892 he became minister of finance, a post whose responsibilities were so wide as to make him virtual overlord of the whole Russian economy. He held the job until 1903 and presided over a massive drive by the Russian government to industrialize the country and thus acquire the immense power which industrialization had conferred on rival states like Britain and Germany.

Witte believed the task was an urgent one because of the intense competition for empire and influence among industrialized nations in the late nineteenth century. Russia had to equip herself to join the imperialist race to carve up the world or become a prey to the imperialists like Turkey or China. Russia could not wait for private enterprise to do the job, so the state must take the lead. Russia had too little capital, so foreign loans were sought. As mentioned earlier, great quantities of Russian government bonds were absorbed by the French market for the construction of the Trans-Siberian Railway and the equipment of the army. This investing was one of the factors which encouraged the alliance between France and Russia in 1894. In 1897, to stop the fluctuations in the value of the currency, Witte made gold the standard of Russia's monetary system and thereby created a further inducement for capitalists to invest in Russian enterprises.

Something like an industrial revolution was launched in Russia in the 1890s. Great

new industrial regions sprang up in the Ukraine with its coal and iron ore and in the Caucasus with its petroleum. Older industrial regions like Moscow and St Petersburg witnessed great expansion and modernization. Coming late in the day, Russian industrialization was able to take advantage of the latest machinery and techniques.

Although Russia achieved a quite extraordinary rate of economic growth in these years and was on the way to becoming a major industrial power, she was still essentially a peasant society. In 1900, there were only about 3,000,000 industrial workers out of a population of 133,000,000; these workers were concentrated in a few parts of the country, including politically important areas around St Petersburg and Moscow. If industrialization brought more discontent than prosperity, as it usually did in its early stages, these 3,000,000 workers could be a grave danger to the tsarist regime.

Lenin and Russian Marxism

Trouble for tsardom as a result of industrialization had been prophesied by George Plekhanov ten years before Witte began his work. Plekhanov had been one of the 'Land and Liberty' revolutionaries who refused to believe that terrorism would bring down the regime. After the assassination of Alexander II had proved him right, he had abandoned

Above, factory workers in 1888: because of its late start, Russian industry missed out the small units that had characterized the early industrial revolution in western Europe and went immediately into large-scale production.

Above left, the Nadezhdinsky iron and steel works, 1898: rapid industrialization in the last years of the nineteenth century could do little to alter the agricultural base of the economy.

Top, the Trans-Siberian Railway at the point where it crosses the River Volga: construction of the railway, nearly 6,000 miles long, started in the early 1880s and was completed in 1904. The line would, it was hoped, strengthen the Russian military strength in the Pacific, help internal migration and attract trade.

Opposite top, the assassination of Tsar Alexander II (1818–81, tsar from 1855), 13 March 1881 at St Petersburg: Alexander had been responsible for a programme of domestic reform including improvements in the legal system, education and local administration and, most important, the emancipation of the serfs in 1861; his heir, Alexander III, made no attempt to continue his father's policies.

Opposite bottom, the ringleaders of the assassination are executed, 3 April 1886.

Opposite centre, Gregory Guerchouny, one of the organizers of the assassination of Alexander II and a member of People's Freedom, which had already made at least seven unsuccessful attempts on the Tsar's life.

Populism, with its belief in a peculiarly Russian brand of socialism, in favour of Marxism. From exile in Switzerland, he argued that Russia would pass through the same stage of capitalism as the West and that the Russian revolution would be the work of the proletariat not the peasantry. Revolutionaries must await the coming of industrialization and prepare the workers for their future role.

In 1883 Plekhanov formed in Geneva the group called 'Liberation of Labour', the forerunner of the party which was to rule Russia after tsardom collapsed. As Plekhanov had predicted, its propagandist literature attracted a growing number of workers. When Russia's main cities became swollen by masses of harshly exploited and resentful factory workers, revolutionaries turned to them as the source of the explosion which would destroy tsardom.

The most remarkable of Plekhanov's disciples was Vladimir Ulyanov, one of whose underground pseudonyms was Lenin. Lenin had been born in 1870 at Simbirsk, on the Volga, the son of a local school inspector. His elder brother, Alexander, was hanged in 1887 for his part in a students' plot to assassinate the tsar. Lenin qualified as a lawyer in 1891 and at about the same time was converted to Marxism. He quickly became an important writer and organizer in the revolutionary movement in St Petersburg and, later, in exile.

Although a Marxist party, the Social Democrats, was founded in Russia in 1898, it was not until 1903 that representatives of all the various Russian Marxist groups met in Brussels and later in London to plan the new party's future. A split developed over whether the party should be restricted to dedicated professional revolutionaries or open to all active sympathizers, Lenin favouring restricted membership. His supporters were in the majority during the latter part of the congress because of a walkout by another group, and they took the name of 'Bolsheviki' (members of the majority). His opponents, led by Martov, incautiously accepted the name Mensheviks (members of the minority). The two factions in the Social Democratic Party continued to quarrel over most issues until 1912, when Lenin formed his Bolsheviks into a separate party.

Plekhanov and most other Russian Marxists were prepared to wait until capitalism produced the same conditions in Russia as existed in the more advanced industrial states. Lenin believed that the Russian revolutionary movement should adapt itself to Russia and that the small and backward proletariat should be guided by an elite of professional revolutionaries drawn from Russia's intelligentsia. After the Revolution of 1905, Lenin came to see the peasants as a valuable ally. The Russian masses in town and country alike could be a powerful force for revolution if properly harnessed. Lenin's blending of Populist and Marxist thought proved to be a successful formula

for the Bolsheviks' seizure of power in 1917.

Even though the Bolsheviks eventually succeeded the tsars as the rulers of Russia, their chances of achieving this succession in the early years of the twentieth century looked no better than those of their rivals, the Mensheviks, the Socialist Revolutionaries and the liberals. The Socialist Revolutionaries were in the old Populist tradition but they accepted that industrialization could not be reversed and were anxious only to keep it in its place. The peasants were to play the key role in the coming revolution and in the new society that revolution would bring. Russian liberals, who aimed at a constitutional government on western European lines, had had valuable administrative experience in the *zemstvos* set up by Alexander II. They too began to organize themselves for political action at a national level.

At the turn of the century Russia's first political parties were taking shape. It was at a time when a world economic crisis was shaking Russia and halting the remarkable growth of the nineties. The peasants had been taxed to the limit, and peasant revolts became common for the first time since the emancipation of the serfs by Alexander II. The threat of these revolts together with a wave of strikes signalized a new stage in the tsar's battle for survival. Liberals, Socialist Revolutionaries and Social Democrats all sensed the approach of a great national crisis.

Empire in the Far East

During the period of growing political agitation, industrial strife and peasant revolt, Russia got involved in a war with Japan. Alexander III had confined his wars to central Asia, but his son, Nicholas II, who succeeded him in 1894, was less cautious and allowed himself to be drawn into two disastrous wars, the second, from 1914 to 1917, marking the end of the monarchy in Russia. The war fought in 1904–5 provided a dress rehearsal. In each case Nicholas seems to have gambled on victory restoring his popularity – in each case defeat meant revolution.

Like the unrest at home, the war with Japan resulted partly from Witte's industrialization programme. Russian expansion in the Far East was itself nothing new, since Russians had reached the Pacific in the seventeenth century and Siberia had gradually been colonized. Alaska, too, was part of Russia until its sale to America in 1867. Between 1847 and 1860 Russia extended her frontiers at China's expense, a gain which was to be a source of conflict between the two powers a century later. In the 1890s Russia became more ambitious. Witte believed that Russia could capture the vast Chinese market for her manufactured goods, which would further stimulate industry. Between 1891 and 1903, when the Trans-Siberian Railway was being built, China

began to turn to Russia for financial and political aid and in return was forced to allow Russia substantial economic concessions and military bases in Manchuria. Witte's scheme was working well. China looked like becoming a victim of Russian economic imperialism.

By disregarding Japanese interests in the Far East, however, Nicholas II and his ministers overplayed Russia's hand. When Japan went to war in 1904 to counter Russian expansion, there was an outburst of patriotism in Russia very reassuring to her harassed rulers. The shortsighted government failed to take advantage of the public mood to win over moderate opinion by a few timely concessions, relying instead on false hopes of victory.

The Revolution of 1905

The year 1904 brought political ferment at home and humiliating defeat by the Japanese on land and sea. The regime could still have averted the danger of revolution by conceding even limited participation in the work of government to an elected assembly. But Nicholas II believed it his sacred duty to pass on his autocratic power to his heirs. The unyielding attitude of tsardom was dramatically expressed in the events of 'Bloody Sunday'.

One Sunday in January 1905 a peaceful demonstration took place in St Petersburg when Father Gapon, an Orthodox priest, led a deputation of unarmed workers to petition the tsar at his Winter Palace. Gapon had organized a workers' union in St Petersburg with government aid in an attempt to keep labour relations under control. The petition to be delivered on 22 January had

Above, troops firing on demonstrators outside the Winter Palace, St Petersburg, on Bloody Sunday, 22 January 1905: though disturbances including a general strike and mutiny in the armed forces continued throughout the year the tsarist regime came through by and large unscathed, though a constitution was granted and a parliamentary assembly, the Duma, established.

Opposite, Japanese painting of a Russian warship exploded by a mine during the Russo-Japanese War, 1904–05.

resulted from strikes and general discontent among workers in the capital and contained a demand for the redress of grievances and for the convocation of a national parliament to be elected by the people. The march had not been forbidden by the authorities, but when the workers reached the Winter Palace they were fired on by troops and hundreds were killed or wounded.

Bloody Sunday destroyed popular faith in the tsar. Belief in the tsar as the father of his people was strong among millions of Russians who had traditionally attributed their sufferings to the gentry and to the tsar's advisers rather than to the tsar himself. Many of the workers who marched to the Winter Palace carried religious icons and pictures of the tsar.

Since Russia was an autocracy, the whole moral authority of the government rested on trust in one man, the tsar. In the months that followed Bloody Sunday it became clear that the government's authority throughout the country was collapsing. Strikes spread to all the industrial centres of Russia and involved white-collar workers as well as workmen in factories. In St Petersburg and elsewhere workers set up soviets (councils) to organize public services and act in general as alternative centres of authority. Peasant unrest affected many provinces, and for the first time the peasants began to organize themselves and transformed their *mirs* into petty republics. Then began the process under socialist leaders of organizing the republics into the giant federation called the Peasant's Union. Local government leaders and the professional classes added their vigorous support to these activities. Political protest was publicly voiced as never before in Russia.

Disaffection spread to the army and navy, the most spectacular demonstration being the mutiny of the battleship *Potemkin* at Odessa in June 1905, where street fighting raged for several days. The *Potemkin* crew,

however, failed to win the support of the entire Black Sea fleet; mutiny, immortalized in Sergei Eisenstein's film, ended in anti-climax with the crew sailing off to internment in Romania. It was, nevertheless, an alarm signal to the government. In August 1905 when the war ended with victory for the Japanese, the fate of the tsar's regime depended on troops who had been demoralized by defeat.

Nicholas had attempted after Bloody Sunday to restore his authority with gestures of conciliation. He agreed to the establishment of an elected assembly, but one which would have no real power and would exclude members likely to be hostile to the government. This gesture was rejected by even the most moderate opponents of the regime. In October, when the St Petersburg Soviet was formed, a railway strike was followed by a general strike which paralysed the cities of the empire. Practically the whole of Russia was in revolt.

At this point Nicholas II consulted Count Witte, who had been dismissed in 1903 after criticism of his industrialization policy but had been recalled in 1905 to negotiate the best possible terms in the peace talks with Japan. Witte saw only two alternatives open to the tsar: military dictatorship or the granting of a constitution. Though Nicholas preferred military rule, his most trusted generals regarded this as too risky; and therefore he accepted Witte's advice to grant a constitution.

Witte then drafted a manifesto, which announced the end of centuries of autocratic rule. Russia was to be a constitutional monarchy, whose parliament, the Duma, could veto legislation and supervise the activities of the tsar's ministers. Civil liberties, like freedom of speech and assembly, were to be guaranteed. The October Manifesto marked the failure of the tsarist bid to weld the new forms of economic power to the old autocracy.

The manifesto split the revolutionaries. The majority were prepared to accept it, but the Soviets were determined to secure a democratic republic. The Soviets grew in size and authority and appeared an admirable instrument of revolution to Social Democrat leaders like Leon Trotsky and Lenin, who had returned from exile. Strikes, mutinies and disorders in town and countryside continued to break out during the remainder of the year. Right-wing organizations added to the chaos by terrorizing non-Russian nationalities, especially Jews, who had long been victims of tsarist persecution and were understandably prominent in the ranks of the revolutionaries.

As the weeks went by it became clear that the revolutionaries were losing control over their supporters. The crisis had dragged on too long and the workers had borne the brunt of a struggle which no one seemed to know how to bring to a satisfactory climax. Calls to strike met with less response. Although the loyalty of many army units remained doubtful, the government felt safe enough to arrest the leaders of the St Petersburg Soviet. A summons to insurrection was answered in Moscow, where savage fighting ensued during December 1905, but this was a final despairing effort. Punitive expeditions against the centres of peasant revolt continued, but the Revolution of 1905 was over.

The constitution promised by the October Manifesto was set out in the Fundamental Laws of May 1906. The tsar kept most of his old power over the armed forces and foreign policy. He could rule by decree when the Duma was not sitting; and ministers were responsible to him, not to the Duma. Legislation had to be approved not only by the Duma but also by the tsar and an extremely unrepresentative upper chamber, half of which was chosen by the tsar himself. The Duma did not even have full control over the budget, the right most prized by any parliamentary assembly. The promised

guarantees of civil liberty were hedged around with exceptions. The constitution violated the whole spirit of the October Manifesto. The tsar and his advisers believed they they had won and that there was no need to keep faith with revolutionaries.

How fully the authorities had regained control of the country was shown when the new Duma made its first challenge. Elections for the Duma took place in March and April 1906. The old tsarist belief had prevailed that the peasants were loyal when not being led astray by agitators; therefore the government had framed an electoral law reasonably representative of an overwhelmingly peasant society. This proved to be a complete miscalculation of the state of peasant feeling, and the free elections produced an overwhelmingly radical Duma. The leftwing of the Liberal Party – the newly formed Constitutional Democratic Party, usually known as the Kadets – was the most successful of the rash of political parties which had sprung up and which took their seats when the Duma was first assembled in May in the Taurida Palace in St Petersburg. The Social Democrats and Socialist Revolutionaries had boycotted the elections because they refused to sit as deputies in a Duma created by the tsar. During the first few months of the Duma there were chaotic parliamentary manoeuvrings and clashes between the government's ministers and the Kadets and their colleagues in the Labour parties. Nicholas, disappointed in the character of the Duma, dissolved it, whereupon the Kadets called on the people to refuse to pay their taxes until the restoration of the Duma. There was no response to this appeal. After the upheaval of the previous year most Russians found voting for their first parliament a sufficiently revolutionary experience.

Eventually the government allowed new elections, thinking that they now had more influence over the voters. The second Duma

which met in March 1907 was even more radical than the first however and was dissolved by the government in June. By altering the electoral law, the government the third Duma in 1907 and in the fourth five years later.

Stolypin and the peasant problem

Even before the 1905 revolution it had been widely recognized that something would have to be done to improve the lot of the peasants. They had been freed from serfdom in 1861, but they had generally got a raw deal over the distribution of land, and they had had to pay a high price for it by instalments. The population was increasing so fast that there was, in any case, too little land to go round.

From 1906 to 1911 the Tsar Nicholas' principal minister was Peter Stolypin. Stolypin's career as a provincial governor had won him a reputation for pitiless suppression of peasant uprisings, but at the same time it had given him a deep appreciation of the peasant problems and a determination to solve them. Stolypin believed that the regime would be safe from revolution only if it could win the loyalty of the peasantry, who constituted the great majority of the Russian people.

In common with others who had studied the peasant question, Stolypin saw the village commune as the chief obstacle to a healthy agriculture and a contented peasantry. When the serfs had been emancipated by Alexander II, it was decided that the land allocated to them in each village was to be owned not by individual peasants but by the commune. The self-governing commune distributed the land periodically in strips to ensure that each household had its fair share. Stolypin had observed that communal ownership of the land offered no

incentive to the enterprising peasant to improve strips of land he might only hold temporarily. Moreover, the commune regulated its affairs by majority decisions, and the enterprising were not likely to be in a majority in a generally illiterate and hidebound society.

Stolypin believed that if peasants were allowed to own a piece of land and pass it on to their heirs they would have a stake in society. Like the French peasants they would then be inclined to be conservative because of their property interests. Between 1906 and 1911 Stolypin put through laws which allowed the head of a peasant family to withdraw from the commune with his own land, not in strips but a solid field, which thereafter would be his property to sell or pass on to his sons. During the period of Stolypin's premiership, something like two or three million individual farms were created in this way. Other measures intended to secure more arable land and raise

agricultural production were also put into effect; a credit system for buying land was established and the colonization of Siberia begun.

Stolypin's ambition to create a nation of conservatively-minded peasant proprietors loyal to the tsar would have taken a very long time to fulfil. What he called his 'wager on the strong' set in motion a revolution in agriculture just as Witte had precipitated an industrial revolution.

In 1911 Stolypin was assassinated while attending a gala performance in the opera house at Kiev. His strong and constructive government in the aftermath of the 1905 revolution had given the regime a misleading appearance of stability. The economy recovered, and industrialization proceeded at a slower but very impressive pace. Agrarian reform was at last under way. The revolutionary movement was in disarray, and tsardom seemed to have won its struggle for survival.

In fact, it had won no more than a breathing space. It had survived because enough of the army had remained loyal and because its opponents had been doubtful as to how to use the revolutionary crisis to win political power. In the next crisis things would be different. Even an impotent Duma would serve as an alternative centre of authority more convincing than the palace. The revolutionaries knew that they had a new weapon in the workers' soviets, which they could use to advantage in a crisis. Though the question of who should rule Russia remained undecided, there was wide agreement that it should not be the tsar.

Nicholas' unsuitability as a ruler was recognized even by the supporters of an absolute monarchy. The influence of Gregori Rasputin at the tsar's court was one of the major factors which contributed to this feeling. Rasputin was a Siberian peasant, who posed as a mystic monk with strange healing powers. A number of such religious quacks haunted the imperial court at the invitation of the Empress Alexandra, who hoped they might be more successful than doctors in healing her haemophiliac son. Rasputin earned her unshakable devotion by being able to halt Alexei's bleeding, apparently by hypnotism. Unfortunately, Rasputin was given to vices and orgies which scandalized St Petersburg. There were wild rumours about his relations with the empress and a feeling of alarm about his influence on decisions of state. From 1912 onwards he was attacked by members of the Duma and eventually by people who had supported the dynasty throughout its troubles.

The tsar was unlikely to survive the next great crisis, and with Nicholas II at the helm such a crisis was only too probable. He was a poor judge of men and events, disliked his ablest advisers, Witte and Stolypin, dismissing Witte as soon as the revolutionary threat had subsided and threatening Stolypin with dismissal. After 1911 Nicholas governed under the influence of his even less judicious wife and of ministers congenial to them. His chances were slight of being able to steer Russia successfully through a period of rapid social and economic change and mounting international tension.

The Lena goldfields massacre of 1912 began a new period of strife at home. Police killed hundreds of workers protesting against intolerable conditions while the government ostentatiously approved the police action. A wave of industrial unrest followed when Mensheviks and Bolsheviks seized their opportunity to revive the cause of revolution. How near Russia was to a new crisis on the scale of 1905 is open to dispute, but the symptoms were ominous. Moreover, the tsar was facing a crucial challenge to his traditional role as defender of the Slav nations as Austria-Hungary, supported by Germany, prepared to destroy the power of Serbia, Russia's Balkan ally. Another diplomatic humiliation at a time of domestic tension could be fatal for the regime. When the moment of decision came in July 1914, the tsar took up the challenge. The result was a war of unprecedented disaster.

Above, patriotic postcard issued in 1916 of Tsar Nicholas II, who became supreme commander of the Russian armies in September 1915.

Above left, Nicholas II (1868–1918, tsar 1894–1917) with the Tsarina Alexandra and his family: a weak and autocratic man, he could find no glimmer of sympathy or understanding for his subjects' desire for change.

Below left, the Duma in session: the four Dumas between 1905 and 1916 managed to achieve some reforms but are perhaps more remarkable for being the only democratically elected assembles ever in Russia.

Opposite top right, a Russian village in the 1890s: the peasantry was numerically such a dominant sector of society that both the revolutionaries and the tsarist regime attempted to engage their support, the latter by limited reforms after 1905. In the event neither succeeded.

Opposite bottom right, Gregori Rasputin (1871–1916) with some of his court followers: his sinister influence on the royal family was yet one more factor that helped to discredit it.

Opposite left, Peter Stolypin (1862–1911), prime minister from 1906 until 1911: cautious reform was the hallmark of his administration, accompanied by social reaction, including the introduction of a property qualification for the franchise and the encouragement of anti-semitism.

163

Chapter 11

Asia in the nineteenth century

At the time of the Crimean War, which resulted in the momentous revolutions of Russian political and economic institutions, China and Japan were also forced to adjust themselves to the fact of western military superiority. China's response was slow and ineffective, while Japan responded with a revolution from above, but a revolution carried through more systematically and successfully than in Russia. These differing responses shaped the history of Asia during the nineteenth and twentieth centuries.

In the mid-nineteenth century about half the world's population lived in Asia. They were mostly peasants, and Asia's industrial activity was confined to hand-made quality goods. Half Asia's population had come under European and American rule by the end of the nineteenth century. They bought the cheap manufactured goods produced by European and American factories, and they were exposed in time to democratic and nationalist ideas which bore fruit in the independence movements of the twentieth century. Little native industrialization developed, however, even in India, where British rule revolutionized communications by a vast railway network. Even though the British provided a background of law and order, the traditional way of Indian life offered no stimulus to private enterprise. Moreover, the European rulers had no interest in promoting competition for their home industries and looked on colonial territories as profitable markets and a great source of raw materials for their own factories.

For Asia the most important effect of the industrial revolutions was the strengthening of the nations which had already built empires in Asia and those which were ambitious to do so. The British, the French and the Russians extended their empires, and the Americans and the Germans entered the imperialist fray in the later years of the century. The older imperialists in Asia – the Spaniards, the Portuguese and the Dutch – were less active, but they were not in the forefront of industrialization. The aggressive imperialism of the others had alarming implications for the few remaining independent Asian states. Persia, Afghanistan and Siam were the weakest, but they maintained a precarious existence as buffer states

– the first two between the British and Russian empires, Siam between British India and French Indo-China. It was China and Japan whose position was most changed by the spectacular increase in power of the alien empires which surrounded them.

The Chinese Empire had towered over the rest of Asia for centuries. It was a huge and powerful centralized state on which had been based one of the world's greatest civilizations. Medieval Europe had borrowed extensively from Chinese science and technology, which was then the most advanced in the world. Europe's own scientific revolution of the sixteenth and seventeenth centuries had enabled her eventually to outstrip China, but it was not until the nineteenth century that China had cause to be disturbed by the results. Until then, the Chinese emperors had seen themselves as the centre of the world order. They treated the small squabbling western European states which had built commercial empires in Asia with the disdainful tolerance that a quiet giant might display towards noisy pygmies. Serenely confident of their cultural superiority and invulnerable strength, the Chinese refused to negotiate with European governments on equal terms. The most they would concede was limited trading privileges on the coast or at the border.

Japan had been strongly influenced by Chinese civilization but, politically speaking, was a very different sort of state. Its emperor was a figurehead, and real power lay with a warrior aristocracy headed by a shogun, or generalissimo. While China disdained the 'barbarian' world of Europe, Japan was afraid of it. The activity of European traders and missionaries during the

sixteenth century had proved unsettling to Japanese society. From the seventeenth century onwards Japan's ruling class forbade contacts with the outside world, except China and Holland, the latter having been more discreet in its use of the trading connection than other Europeans.

The challenge of the west

Between 1833 and 1860 Great Britain forced China to abandon her traditional attitude to the outside world and to accept a code of international behaviour convenient to European and American trading interests.

The demand for Chinese tea, porcelain and silks was high, and British merchants had secured the largest share of this lucrative trade. China was largely self-sufficient, and the Chinese government had never regarded foreign trade as important to the empire. Foreign merchants were restricted to the ports of Canton and Macao and forced to operate under highly unfavourable

conditions. The merchants put up with these in view of the vast profits to be made, but at the same time they pressed the British government to negotiate with the Chinese for improved trading conditions. British representatives who travelled to Peking in 1793 and 1816 were rebuffed by the emperor, who saw no need to make concessions to a state which had nothing to offer her in return.

The situation changed when foreign traders found there was an almost inexhaustible demand for opium in China. By the 1830s over half of British exports to China consisted of opium. Importing opium at Canton was banned, but by providing local mandarins with lavish 'presents' it was possible to smuggle the drug past the officials whose job was to exclude it. Their salaries were small, the profits of the trade vast. In effect, British merchants soon found that they could sell as much opium in China as they could carry there.

The effects on the Chinese population were disastrous. Early missionaries record that even the crews of coasting junks took it in relays to go into a drugged stupor. Apart from the cost of the trade, it was clearly ruining the health of the people. In 1839 the Tao Kuang emperor decided to appoint a high commissioner to deal with the situation at Canton. The man he chose was a capable official, Lin Tse-hsü, the Viceroy of Hunan. Much to the surprise of British merchants, he forced them to hand over all the opium in their possession and afterwards had a million *chin* (about 4,000,000 pounds) of it destroyed in lime pits dug on the banks of the Pearl River.

This energetic action soon brought war. Commissioner Lin continued to blockade Canton forcibly against the opium smugglers, and in the summer of 1840 a strong British naval force, some of it steam-powered, appeared off Canton. After sealing up the port, it took the nearby city of Tinghai, thus reducing the imperial defences to confusion. Officials had expected nothing less than the enormous strength of the Royal Navy. After some negotiation, it went on to bombard Canton.

The emperor had little to set against the greatest sea power in the world. Although resistance went on until 1842, the outcome was never in doubt, except in the minds of Chinese officials. Lin's mistake would have been even more disastrous if it had not been for China's enormous size. Although the prohibition of opium in Britain itself did not prevent Queen Victoria's government from protecting those who smuggled it into China, the cost of genuine conquest and annexation would have been prohibitive. After British troops advanced up the Yangtse River to Nanking, the Tao Kuang emperor sued for peace, and the Opium War ended with the Treaty of Nanking of 1842.

This was the first of the 'unequal treaties' between China and the West, and it gave British merchants all the concessions they wanted. This was not purely protection for their sordid opium smuggling but genuine trading equality, without the humiliating assumption of Chinese superiority. The Co-Hong was abolished, and British merchants given free trade rights in five ports, most importantly Shanghai and Canton. Hongkong was ceded to Britain, and an indemnity of £5,000,000 paid. The kowtow, with its implication of paying tribute, was no longer to be demanded.

Similar treaty rights were granted to the Americans and French immediately afterwards. The Opium War made it clear that the Chinese could no longer hope to stave off the power of the West. It may even be seen as the most important turning-point in 2,000 years of Chinese history.

Above, the ceremonial signing of the Treaty of Nanking, 1842, which gave Britain a dominant position in trade with China.

Opposite top, Gillray cartoon satirizing Lord Macartney's (1737–1806) embassy to China, 1793, to ask for free trade and diplomatic representation: the Chinese received Macartney as the representative of a submissive state, their assumption of the superiority of their own culture paralleling that of western imperialists only a few decades later.

Opposite bottom, Chinese sketch of a British sailor during the Opium War 1839–42: as a result of the war, the Chinese were forced to grant trading concessions to western merchants, the first dent in their deliberate refusal to recognize western military and commercial power.

The Taiping revolt

Few Chinese realized the significance of what had happened, and modern Chinese historians call the time which followed 'the twenty precious years when China stood still'. But Manchu power had declined drastically. In their difficulties the many enemies of this foreign dynasty banded together against them. The most formidable threat they had to face was that of the Taiping, which has been seen as the first modern nationalist movement in China. It also had many of the characteristics of a traditional peasant revolt. In either case, it kept the imperial troops at bay for thirteen long and bloody years, from 1851 to 1864.

The prophet of the Taiping was Hung Hsiu-ch'üan, a Cantonese student who had failed to pass civil service examinations. Embittered by his failure and neurotically ambitious, he was nevertheless an inspiring leader with an ability to put forward an appealing and coherent programme of reform. A smattering of mission Christianity appears to have been enough to convince this highly unstable character that he had been divinely chosen as the redeemer of China.

When he began to agitate among the discontented Hakka or immigrant population in southern China, his claim, probably sincere, was that he was the younger brother

of Christ. Yet he was much more than a simple revivalist. His message included demands for a series of radical social reforms, including improvement in the inferior status of women and equal distribution of land and all other property – which naturally appealed to a peasant population frequently on the verge of starvation. There was also to be a return to simplicity in religion, with opium, alcohol, tobacco and prostitution forbidden. Even the long pigtail worn in Manchu China was to be replaced by short hairstyles.

In 1851 Hung was proclaimed leader of the *T'ai-p'ing t'ien-kuo*, or 'Heavenly Kingdom of Absolute Peace'. He had launched the greatest peasant revolt in modern history, which aimed incidentally at removing the European influence which the decadent Manchu had encouraged. The Taiping took Nanking in 1853, while Shanghai fell to other rebellious sects. The Manchu were powerless.

Only the Westerners could save the dynasty. By 1862 the imperial troops had been well trained by advisers like 'Chinese' Gordon and joined with European mercenaries in the 'Ever-Victorious Army' which hurled back the Taiping offensive. In 1864 the revolt collapsed, and Hung died by his own hand. His disunited followers simply broke up into bandit gangs.

This does not disguise his achievement

in showing the way in which China was eventually to defeat the West. Where Hung had whipped up mass nationalist enthusiasm, with a bastardized form of Western religion, future leaders would copy Western industry and education and, finally, Western armaments. The lessons of the ill-fated Taiping were well learned by the Chinese revolutionaries of the present century, particularly Sun Yat-sen and the Kuomintang.

The 'Arrow' War

While the Taiping revolt dragged on, Western merchants were still engaged in the humdrum work of increasing their profits. Unfortunately they had still found no answer to the main problem: that the Chinese did not wish to buy anything manufactured in the West. Convinced of the quality of their wares, the merchants put this down to the ill will of the Chinese leaders and the backwardness of their people. Their solution was to push further and further inland and to put pressure on the central government in Peking itself. These were the aims of the 'Arrow' War, named after a British-owned junk which was very properly impounded by Chinese officials after sheltering a local pirate.

This insult to the flag, in 1856, produced swift action. The British and French took Canton in the following year, and Chinese

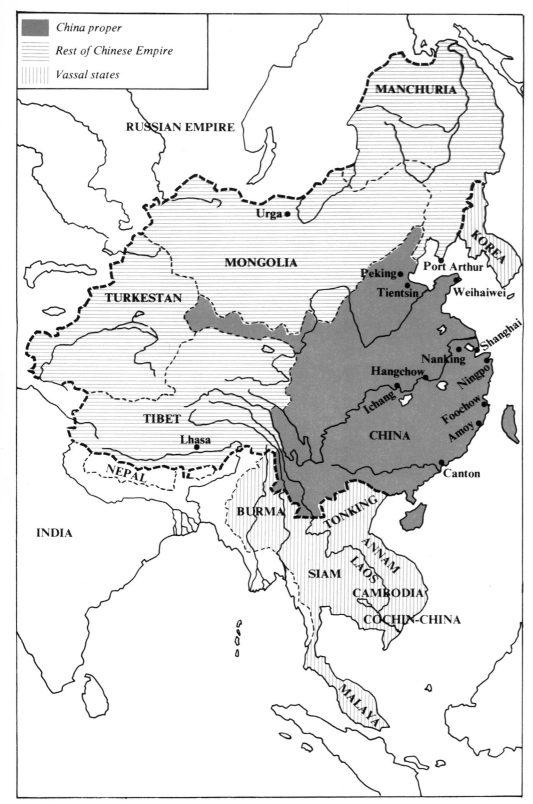

RUSSIAN EMPIRE

MANCHURIA

MONGOLIA

Urga

TURKESTAN

Peking
Tientsin

Port Arthur
Weihaiwei

KOREA

TIBET

Lhasa

Shanghai

Nanking
Hangchow

Ningpo

Ichang

Foochow

CHINA

Amoy

Canton

NEPAL

INDIA

BURMA

TONKING

ANNAM

SIAM

LAOS

CAMBODIA

COCHIN-CHINA

MALAYA

Above, a British merchant trading at Canton: the western presence in China had little impact at first, but gradually, as trading increased, accompanied by missionary and military activity, the authority of the Chinese administration was undermined.

Left, the Far East in the mid-nineteenth century.

Opposite, the British gunboat Nemesis, *one of the first ironplated warships built, attacking Chinese junks during the Opium War.*

resistance collapsed much faster than in the Opium War.

At the Peace of Tientsin in 1858, Britain and France were given sweeping new privileges. Eleven new ports were opened, and free navigation on the Yangtse granted. The commercial heartland of China now lay exposed. Foreign merchants were also given rights of special jurisdiction, which protected them from Chinese civil and even criminal law.

The wretched position of the Manchus soon became even worse. After new brushes, Lord Elgin advanced on Peking and sacked the beautiful Manchu Winter Palace. The subsequent Treaty of Peking gave the Westerners legations in the Chinese capital, which had always been refused in the past. Now they could deal directly with the imperial government, in order to extort whatever privileges they wished. China had surrendered to the West.

The European nations could now trade in China on their own terms. The old Manchu hope that the distasteful outer barbarians could be isolated in a few ports was finally dispelled. Much of coastal China had effectively become a European colony, and her major cities were open to any foreigner who wished to visit them. Western *hong* or trade compounds multiplied, even hundreds of miles inland. The Chinese themselves were treated with contempt, as a subject race which had been conquered in open warfare. Some parts of the European compounds even carried notices reading 'No dogs or Chinamen'.

The Chinese themselves adopted the bad habits of the West and distrusted its good ones. European diseases became rampant outside the borders of the concessions. It probably made little difference to the Chinese peasant whether he was oppressed by a Manchu or a European – both were foreigners. But the humiliated gentry and scholarly classes naturally distrusted a civilization which seemed to be superior in nothing but its weapons. Europeans seemed crude, vulgar and incomprehensible.

Indeed the Western population of the Treaty Ports constantly ran the risk of 'incidents' with the hostile Chinese population. Perhaps the worst was the massacre of the French Catholic missionaries at Tientsin in 1870. In this case the fathers were somewhat tactlessly gaining converts by buying infants who would normally have been exposed as a way of getting rid of unwanted mouths in overloaded families.

When rumours got round that the priests were killing and even eating them, the result was the destruction of all mission property by a hostile mob, which also murdered all the Frenchmen who fell into its hands. The Chinese authorities gave ample satisfaction but nothing could improve the misunderstanding and bitterness between the races. Such incidents were many during the long era of concessions. They looked forward to the nationalist revolutions which produced the independent China of our own century.

The transformation of Japan

As in China, the Western challenge came to Japan at a time when the old order was already being undermined from within. Since the early seventeenth century the shogunate had been in the hands of the Tokugawa family. They had given Japan two and a half centuries of internal peace by maintaining strict control over the great feudal lords, the *daimyo*, and their military retainers, the privileged warrior class called the samurai. But in a period of peace the samurai had been encouraged to become men of learning as well as warriors. This proved dangerous, when samurai scholars began to question the legitimacy of Tokugawa rule and whether it was time for the emperor himself to resume power. The study of European books, which could be imported so long as they did not propagate Christianity, aroused doubt about the wisdom of isolating Japan from the world.

In addition, an important and wealthy merchant class had grown up, town life developed (Yedo, the future Tokyo, had a population of a million in the eighteenth century), the manufacture of Japanese handicrafts was flourishing. Merchant financiers were gaining control of the Japanese economy which was becoming more capitalistic, and Japanese society was changing with it.

The threat from America and Europe hastened the political revolution. With its prestige badly shaken by the country's helplessness, the shogunate faced mounting opposition from the *daimyo* and samurai, especially those from Choshu and Satsuma in western Japan. When, in 1867, a fifteen-year-old boy succeeded to the throne as the Emperor Meiji, the shogun Keiki restored to him power over the state, hoping that he would become the leading figure in the new regime. Opponents of the shogunate were determined to prevent any such compromise from taking place and intended to drive the Tokugawa family from power altogether. A group of samurai, led by Saigo Takamori of Satsuma, proclaimed in January 1868 a provisional government in the name of the emperor. Keiki's forces resisted, but were defeated. The imperial court moved into the shogun's castle at Yedo, which in future was to be known as Tokyo. The Meiji restoration was complete.

Although there was a restoration in form, the real rulers of Japan were a group of young and vigorous samurai bent on a revival of Japanese power by a revolution from above, which they accomplished with skill and determination. They abolished feudalism after convincing the principal *daimyo* that this was in the interests of the state. They created a conscript army, following the French example, to replace the warrior class to which they themselves belonged. With this army they were able to crush a samurai rebellion led by Saigo Takamori himself, who believed that reforms destructive of samarai traditions were damaging to Japan. The samurai reorganized the state's finances according to Western practice and built up a national network of schools and universities aimed at turning out loyal, patriotic and efficient citizens from all classes of society. They westernized their legal system in an attempt to bypass the unequal trade treaties to which they had agreed and which gave the foreigners control over tariffs and exempted them from jurisdiction by Japanese courts.

In addition to these radical measures, the young samurais brought about an industrial revolution. Because Japanese merchants were slow to risk their capital in industrial ventures, the government built railways, introduced postal and telegraph services, took over control of the mines and shipyards, set up model factories and lent money to men who were willing to invest in factories. The samurai reformers did everything possible to speed Japan towards the industrialization which their travels abroad had convinced them was the secret of national greatness and imperial expansion.

The samurai oligarchy were less enthusiastic about the political institutions of the West. Most of them believed that rapid modernization must have priority and that representative government and democratic institutions might get in the way. Only after a number of samurai rebellions did the oligarchy accept the idea of a Japanese constitution. In 1881 a constitution was promised, and in 1889 it was finally proclaimed, modelled on the Prussian one, with the emperor keeping control of foreign policy and the armed forces and being largely independent of parliament in money matters. Parliament was to be elected by only a small fraction of the population. The rights of the subject were only vaguely outlined in the constitution, which was not unlike the one which Nicholas II granted to the Russian people in 1906. Nevertheless, while the tsar continued to exercise power with disastrous results, in Japan the emperor allowed the samurai leaders who had emerged after 1868 to govern in his name with conspicuous success. When political parties were formed in the 1880s, however, Japan's leaders found it increasingly difficult to subdue them.

Within twenty years Japan had acquired the basic apparatus of industrial civiliza-

tion, and with it came the inevitable demands for democracy. Even a small, illegal socialist party had emerged by the early years of the twentieth century. Like the Prussians and the Russians, the rulers of Japan staved off the demand by a very limited constitution and also by a spectacular foreign policy. The extraordinary success of their foreign policy enabled them to preserve the 1889 constitution until 1946, apart from the introduction of universal suffrage in 1925.

Asia's lesser lands

Meanwhile the Westerners themselves were systematically annexing the smaller kingdoms which controlled the approaches to the China Sea. Both France and Britain were intent on seizing as many possessions as possible without actually dismantling China itself. The British had the advantage of a base in their huge Indian Empire and at the same time were driven by fears that any other power might gain land with strategic control over the approaches to the Indian Ocean.

As early as 1819, the colourful adventurer Stamford Raffles occupied Singapore. The British were now entrenched where they could control all traffic to and from the Far East. Next they turned their attention to Burma, a country torn by internal conflicts. Anxious as always for their Indian interests, and bent on securing the approaches to China, they took advantage of frontier incidents to intervene. Rangoon was occupied in 1824 and by 1852 the whole of southern Burma was under British control. Fifteen years later they gained territory further up the Irrawaddy, and by 1885 the whole of northern Burma had been annexed. Across the frontier from them was Yunnan province – in China.

Above, Commodore Matthew Perry (1794–1858) landing at Yokohama, with his officers and men, 8 March 1854: except for a few Dutch traders, Japan had been closed to all westerners since the seventeenth century. Now, after an initial period of uncertainty, Japan adapted well to the influence of the West, borrowing many of its better institutions but managing to retain much of her traditional identity.

Opposite top, an attack on Canton during the 'Arrow' War.

Opposite bottom, the guard at the British Legation at Peking, 1863: though she never officially became a colony, by the 1860s increasing western influence on Chinese government and society meant that effectively China was being colonized.

became the main aim of French policy in southeast Asia in the 1860s.

In 1863 Cambodia became a French protectorate. Much to the disgust of the French government, however, the great explorer François Garnier then returned from an expedition up the Mekong to announce that the river did not in fact go anywhere near the prosperous parts of China. It now seemed that the road to the Chinese market was by way of the Red River, which runs into the Gulf of Tonkin.

After they had recovered from the disaster of the Franco-Prussian War, the French began the search for an inland route into China all over again. By 1885 Tonkin, Annam, and Laos had joined Cambodia and Cochin-China as French dependencies. In 1887 all were reorganized as French Indo-China.

The only southeast Asian state to survive was Siam (or Thailand), which profited from the mutual distrust of the French and British. Wedged between Burma and Indo-China, it became a sort of buffer state or no man's land, where neither of its great Western neighbours could annex land without risking a major conflict.

The South Seas

Europe's stranglehold on the Far East became complete with the occupation of the islands of the South Pacific. Because they lacked the obvious wealth of China and Japan, missionaries were more important in exploring or even annexing them than merchants or soldiers. This is not to say that conflicts with the Polynesians, or between rival groups of missionaries, did not produce incidents which might involve governments at home.

After Captain Cook's exploring voyages, the great British missionary societies, especially the London Missionary Society and the Anglican Church Missionary Society, sent mission after mission to the South Seas. Their impulse was almost wholly religious, although some businessmen hoped that they could sell endless bales of Manchester cotton to the islanders once the missionaries had convinced them that nakedness was sinful. Working from the British settlement in Australia, missionaries soon founded posts in Tahiti, Fiji, the Marquesas and the New Hebrides. American missions became active in Hawaii.

However, Catholic missionaries soon appeared on the scene too. After the voyages of Dumont d'Urville in 1826 and 1827, the French government gave its support to missions in Tahiti, Samoa, the Marquesas and New Caledonia. The Protestant and Catholic missionaries soon quarrelled. In Tahiti, their spectacular squabbles produced a full-scale international incident between the British and French in 1844. Although the French responded well to Palmerston's fury at their activities, they retained the

Apart from constant border troubles with Burmese rulers, the British advance had been speeded up by fears of French activities in South-East Asia. When France joined in the race for China and Chinese markets, she at once began to consolidate her power in Indo-China. French missionaries and traders had always been prominent in Siam and Vietnam and, indeed, they had made every effort to get government assistance from Paris to advance their claims. Whether their interest was in Bibles or cashbooks, they agreed that they would have greater scope with the help of French gunboats.

However, for many years southeast Asia was too far away for French governments with plenty of problems at home to wish to become involved there. Only the empire of Napoleon III, proclaimed in 1852, set enough store by French prestige overseas to consider a forward policy worthwhile. Vietnamese distrust of Christians continually led to incidents involving French missionaries, one of which provided the pretext for an attack on Hanoi. Annam (north Vietnam) was forced to cede what became Cochin-China, the first French colony in southeast Asia.

Cochin-China included the Mekong Delta, which the French believed would provide a waterway into China, thus short-circuiting the traditional trade-routes to the treaty ports of the empire. If they could gain control over the whole course of the Mekong, the profits to be made at the expense of other European powers would be fabulous. This

Society Islands, and Napoleon III was also able to annex New Caledonia in 1853. It became a colony for French convicts, similar to the British penal colony in Australia or the Siberian settlement in tsarist Russia.

The atmosphere of the Pacific islands in the early years of settlement – their beauty, calm and richness – is nowhere better described than in Herman Melville's *Typee* or in Joseph Conrad's much later *Victory*. Both novelists had roamed through the South Seas. Melville had nothing good to say of the missionaries, and indeed the islands were changing by the time he wrote. Like everywhere else, they had business possibilities. For instance, Hawaii, although independent until 1898, was under the control of American businessmen by the 1850s. The impact of the Europeans on the simple islanders was disastrous.

Japan defeats China

Japan won her spurs as a great power by defeating both China and Russia during ten momentous years of war and diplomacy, the bone of contention between the three countries being Korea. The kingdom of Korea was one of the states bordering China which acknowledged Chinese suzerainty by paying regular tribute to Peking. Burma, Siam and Laos were other such states. Korea's main frontier was with China, but it also touched the southeastern tip of the Russian Empire near Vladivostock, and Japan lay only a hundred miles away by sea. Since the sixteenth century Korea, which had been strongly influenced by Chinese civilization, confined her relations with the outside world to China, Meiji Japan was determined to prise Korea open in the same way as she herself and China had been. In 1875 an incident involving Japanese warships off the Korean coast led to a threat of war from Tokyo. The Korean government gave way and signed a commercial treaty opening three of Korea's ports to Japanese traders. China did not intervene, but in the years that followed her foreign minister, Li Hung-chang, tried to re-assert Chinese influence in the Korean capital, Seoul.

A battle for predominance over Korea now began. Within Korea rival political groups looked either to Peking or to Tokyo. China seemed to be in a stronger position and held off growing Russian as well as Japanese penetration. Russia began in 1891 to build the great Trans-Siberian Railway. Japan saw this as the opening move in a Russian programme of imperialist expansion in east Asia and concluded that she would have to act quickly if she were to realize her own plans in the region. The Japanese government had for a long time been under pressure at home to take a more aggressive line. Despite governmental attempts to muffle them, Japan's new political

parties were giving trouble in parliament, and the government leaders realized that a victorious war would unite the nation and serve the national interest by forestalling Russia.

A pretext for war was easily found. Rebellion broke out in Korea in 1894, which, like the Taiping Rebellion in China, sprang from a religious movement. The Tong Hak was a society which aimed to preserve the spiritual traditions of the East against Western influences by reconciling Buddhism, Confucianism and Taoism. It became politically-minded and appealed to the country's oppressed peasantry. When the Korean army failed to crush the rebellion both China and Japan sent in troops, but China refused Japan's idea of joint action to reform Korea. At the end of July 1894, Japan set up a pro-Japanese government in Seoul, sank a ship carrying Chinese reinforcements to Korea and attacked the Chinese forces already there. China was taken by surprise.

Japan was overwhelmingly victorious on land and sea. The Chinese navy was defeated, enabling Japanese commanders

Above, the Battle of the Yellow Sea, 1894, during the Sino-Japanese War.

Top, Japanese troops landing in China in 1894: the rapid westernization of Japan in the second half of the nineteenth century was accompanied by an increasingly aggressive imperialism, culminating in the total defeat of China and Russia within ten years.

Opposite, late nineteenth-century painting illustrating the increasing westernization of Japan.

to pour troops into Korea and into China's neighbouring province of Manchuria. By the spring of 1895 Japanese armies were marching on Peking. Li Hung-chang promptly made peace. The Treaty of Shimonoseki was a landmark in Asian history, when China, which had grudgingly accepted the military superiority of the West, was now forced to realize that the western formula for success had transformed her small island neighbour into a major threat. The contrast between the response of the old order in China and the new order in Japan to the challenge of the West was now tragically revealed.

The powers close in on China

The terms of the Treaty of Shimonoseki called for China to pay a large indemnity to Japan for the cost of the war, grant Japan further trading rights, give up the islands of Formosa and the Pescadores and surrender to Japan the southernmost part of Manchuria, the Liaotung peninsula. This area contained the important naval base of Port Arthur, and its occupation would put Japan within striking distance of Peking.

The provisions of the treaty did not please Russia, who planned to dominate Manchuria herself and immediately launched a diplomatic rescue operation to save China from having to cede the peninsula. France, as Russia's ally, agreed, while Germany was only too pleased to encourage Russia in adventures so far away from the German frontier. Japan had found the war exhausting, despite her victory, and was in no position to resist the pressure from Europe. She gave up her claim to the peninsula.

China now had to pay the price of her rescue operation, which was higher than that extorted by the Japanese. Apart from Britain, the powers did not take Japan too seriously and assumed that her easy victory simply proved how ripe China was for domination. The Chinese who had been reluctant to import foreign capital and skill for the sake of rapid modernization now had no alternative but to seek foreign loans, which inevitably extended the European grip on China. A defensive alliance with Russia in 1896 was bought at the cost of allowing Russia to build a section of the Trans-Siberian Railway across Manchuria. This not only shortened the route for Russia but was a step towards her economic domination of Manchuria.

The other powers now closed in on China. In 1898 Germany seized Kiaochow Bay on the grounds that two German missionaries had been murdered in the area. Russia took the Liaotung Peninsula and Port Arthur, which she had just forced Japan to give back to China. France and Britain also obtained naval bases and forced China to grant long leases to these territories. The powers began to bargain with one another over their 'spheres of influence' in China, so

that they could exploit the country without coming to blows. America, realizing she was being left out of the territorial scramble, tried to persuade the other powers to accept an 'Open Door' to their spheres of influence so that all foreign commercial interests could share. She got a dusty answer.

Although China seemed on the verge of partition, she survived, as the Ottoman Empire survived, because her enemies were too much at odds among themselves. Britain and Japan were determined to prevent Russia from getting the lion's share of China. They succeeded.

The Boxer uprising

At first, events seemed to favour Russia. The aftermath of the scramble of 1898 was a fresh upheaval inside China, which was to bring foreign troops again to Peking. When the turmoil subsided, Russia seemed a step nearer her ambition of becoming the dominant power in Asia.

The upheaval known as the Boxer Rebellion was a popular movement directed against foreigners and, more especially, against Christians. It got its name from a secret organization whose name was translated as The Society of Harmonious Fists, popularly known as Boxers, which had previously attacked the Manchu dynasty and now redirected its attention towards western imperialism and Christians. The ill feeling aroused among peasants in northern China against European commerce and the acquisition of territories there was surreptitiously encouraged by the government.

For a few months in 1898 it had seemed that China might at last have started on the road to radical reform. The Emperor Kuang Hsu, horrified by the disasters to China which had marked his reign, was won over to proposals for modernization. The most influential of the reformers was K'ang Yu-wei, who had managed to reconcile modernization in the western manner with the doctrines of Confucianism. Between June and September 1898 the emperor and his advisers introduced important changes. They hoped to reform the civil service examination system, which was the heart of the Chinese tradition of government, and

make it relevant to the problems of the day and not just based on the study of ancient texts. Peking University was founded. Army reorganization was set in motion. And many sinecures were abolished.

The emperor's 'Hundred Days of Reform' touched too many vested interests. Though she had supposedly retired, Empress Tz'u Hsi continued to exercise a controlling influence over affairs and now organized a palace revolution which ended with the emperor in prison, his advisers in exile or dead, and the reforms mostly countermanded. The triumph of reaction seemed complete.

It was Tz'u Hsi and her supporters who saw the Boxer rebels as a means of driving out the foreigners. In 1900, the Boxers seized Peking and besieged the foreign legations there. The German ambassador and other diplomats were murdered, and the Boxer policy of slaughtering Chinese converts to Christianity went into action.

With the lives of their ambassadors endangered, China's enemies got together an international brigade of Japanese, Russian, British, American, French and German troops. A smaller force had previously been repulsed, but in the summer of 1900 Peking was captured and the legations relieved. Tz'u Hsi and her supporters fled from the capital, and Li Hung-chang was recalled to make peace with the invaders.

By the 'Boxer Protocol' of 1901 the powers forced China to punish officials deemed responsible for the anti-foreign movement, to pay a large indemnity and to agree to the stationing of foreign troops to police the legations and the route between Peking and the sea. China's humiliation was complete.

The foreign intervention to suppress the Boxers finally discredited the Manchu dynasty. At last Tz'u Hsi realized the inevitability of the reforms she had tried for so long to suppress. She and her successors tried to make up for lost time: systems of communication and education were to be modernized, reforms in the civil service and the army were planned more systematically than before; a constitution similar to Japan's was projected. It left the emperor with wide powers, but, whereas the Japanese emperor had god-like prestige, the Manchu dynasty was non-Chinese in origin, had

kept its separate identity and by the beginning of the twentieth century had lost its prestige altogether. The last-minute effort to enact reforms merely emphasized the corruption of the dynasty and had come too late to save China from foreign exploitation. The Manchu dynasty was soon to go down to revolution.

The Boxer affair also strengthened Russia's position in Manchuria, which she occupied as part of the foreign 'police action'. Her 'arrangements' to evacuate her troops after the rebellion had been crushed contained loopholes which she fully exploited. In 1903 Russia evaded her undertaking to withdraw and thereby made it quite clear that she envisaged Manchuria becoming a Russian protectorate. Japan might have been willing to concede Russian control over Manchuria provided Russia had accepted Japanese predominance in Korea. The independence of Korea had been stipulated by the Treaty of Shimonoseki in 1896, and Japan was sufficiently versed in imperialist terminology to assume that other powers would understand this was a prelude to Korean dependence on Japan. Russia showed no such understanding, and her rulers were to pay as heavily as had China's for underestimating Japanese power.

The battle for east Asia

Japan's principal aim was still to establish her control over Korea. Her victory in 1895 had merely brought Russia into the field as her main rival. Both Japan and Russia alienated the Koreans by their clumsy attempts to assert themselves by direct interference in Korean politics. There were rumours in Tokyo and St Petersburg that factions in both governments favoured a deal between the two governments at the expense of Korea.

Ito Hirobumi, the Japanese statesman responsible for the 1889 constitution, worked for an alliance with Russia whereby the two countries would share power in east Asia. He was opposed by Yamagata Aritomo, founder of the new Japanese army, who believed that sooner or later Japan would have to fight Russia for supremacy in east Asia.

Yamagata's view was the more popular, since Japanese resentment over the move by Russia, France and Germany to deprive her of the spoils of war in 1895 had been deep and bitter. Her indignation had been all the greater in 1898 when Russia forced China to lease her the Liaotung peninsula. The desire for revenge against Russia was also influenced by the popular feeling that Japan's historical mission was to lead Asia against the European intruders – a viewpoint which was to inspire Japanese policies especially in the years before 1945. But the principal emotion was Japanese pride in the achievements of its army and navy and willingness to trust them in settling accounts with Russia. The prestige of the armed forces gave them a strong voice in the cabinet, where officers controlled the military ministries.

As the conviction grew that war with Russia was inevitable, Japan began to make preparations. This time she took care that they were diplomatic as well as military preparations. There was one, and only one, obvious ally. Britain was Russia's main rival in Asia and was openly alarmed at Russia's designs on China and Korea. Britain had dominated China's trade in the nineteenth century, but her prospects for the future had been dimmed by the success of her rivals in extracting economic concessions from China in the 1890s. The power Britain feared most was Russia. If Russia gained economic predominance over China and used it to secure a controlling influence over Chinese policy, the balance of power in Asia would shift decisively against Britain. She tried and failed to do a deal with Russia, she tried and failed to mobilize German support against Russia. For Britain too the obvious ally was Japan.

After a last-minute attempt by Ito to secure an alliance with Russia had failed, Britain and Japan came to terms. According to the terms of their alliance of 1902, if Japan should become involved in war with Russia, Britain would try to prevent any of the power from siding with Russia. Japan's fears of a coalition against her as in 1895 were relieved, and she had the satisfaction of being accepted as an equal by the greatest of the imperialist powers. For their part, the British had never shared the scepticism of other states about Japan's real strength. They knew the potentialities of an island nation with a strong navy, and their opinion of the Japanese navy was high. The consequences, however, of underwriting Japanese imperialism in Asia had more far-reaching consequences than Britain could possibly imagine, and forty years later her

猛烈なる砲撃ハ砲臺其他へ々損害を加へ我ハ無事引揚たり

own empire in Asia was to face a mortal blow from her former ally.

Japan's triumph

Throughout 1902 and 1903 Japan continued to negotiate with Russia. Time was on Russia's side. The Trans-Siberian Railway was nearing completion, and Russia would soon be able to bring her full weight to bear in the Far East. This was exactly the situation Japan feared, and it soon became evident that the Russians did not intend to give Japan the free hand in Korea which she demanded.

By the end of 1903 Japan had decided to fight, and her surprise attack on the Russian fleet at Port Arthur in February 1904 was the signal for war. In order to transfer her troops freely from Japan to Korea and Manchuria, the Japanese hoped to be able to keep Russia's fleet in Port Arthur and Vladivostok. Her plan was to inflict an early heavy defeat on Russia, since Russia's resources were vastly greater and Japan could not expect to win a war of attrition. She hoped for a rapid triumph of the sort she had enjoyed against China.

Japan's calculations worked, though only just, and her troops quickly seized control of Korea, invaded Manchuria and besieged the Russian forces in Port Arthur. In August 1904 at the Battle of the Yellow Sea the Japanese admiral, Togo, drove the Russian fleet back into Port Arthur while another Japanese naval victory kept the Vladivostok squadron in port. From that point on Japan kept control of the sea, and Russia lost the chance to threaten Japanese communications. The siege of Port Arthur lasted nearly a year, and both sides suffered heavy losses. Russian attempts to relieve the base failed. After a massive Japanese assault under General Oyama in January 1905, the Russians surrendered Port Arthur.

News of the defeat struck a great blow at tsarist prestige and was an important motivation for the Revolution of 1905. The civil strife within her borders sapped the Russian government's will to fight and two more Japanese victories made Russia abandon the struggle. In March 1905, Japan won a great and costly battle at Mukden. This was followed in May by Admiral Togo's annihilation of the Baltic fleet, which had sailed around the world in a desperate attempt to recapture for Russia the initiative in the war. Japan was finding the war dangerously exhausting and suggested mediation, to which Russia agreed.

The Treaty of Portsmouth gave Japan the right to dominate Korea with control over the Liaotung Peninsula, Port Arthur and the southern part of the railway the Russians had built in Manchuria. She was also given control of half of the island of Sakhalin.

Japan's victories in 1895 and 1905 showed how a nation's power could be dramatically increased even in the early stages of industrialization. Like the Franco-British victory over Russia in the Crimean War, the Japanese victory over China showed that a small nation could defeat a large one provided its economy was more advanced. But Japan and Russia had reached similar stages in their advance towards industrialization – both were well on the way to becoming

Above, an incident during the 1904–05 Russo-Japanese war.

Opposite, Boxer print of foreign prisoners being brought before a military court, 1900.

industrial societies, though in 1914 both were still more agrarian than industrial. The difference between the two countries was that the Japanese political system, after the Meiji restoration, was more likely than the unreformed tsarist system to turn out efficient military and civilian leaders. Victory was, however, as dangerous for Japan as it was for imperial Germany. It concealed the long-term weaknesses of the state and bred a feeling of over-confidence. The Treaty of Portsmouth set Japan on the dangerous road to Pearl Harbor and Hiroshima.

The Russo-Japanese war was an important landmark in world history. An Asian state had defeated one of the great powers of Europe, heralding the end of a world order dominated by Europe. The economic and military power stimulated by industrialization had ceased to be a monopoly of the white-skinned peoples of the world.

Sun Yat-sen

Revolution from above had made Japan a major world power and its more energetic and adaptable leaders had forced the old governing class to accept a modern outlook. Conversely, in China the grudging acceptance of social and political reforms by the governing class opened the way to revolution from below. The aftermath of the Boxer rebellion saw an outpouring of revolutionary propaganda from Chinese outraged by a regime which had allowed China to suffer the humiliation of foreign invasion.

In 1905 the T'ung Meng Hui was formed and served to unite revolutionary societies all over China, attacking the Manchu dynasty for its failure either to learn from the West or to resist its encroachments. The T'ung Meng Hui was primarily made up of students who had been abroad to study, and their leader was Sun Yat-sen.

Sun Yat-sen, the son of a peasant, was born in 1866 near the Portuguese commercial centre of Macao in southern China. He acquired an elementary education on western lines from an Anglican school in Hawaii and continued his schooling in Canton and Hongkong, eventually qualifying as a doctor. During these years he became aware of the need for some sort of revolution against the corrupt rule of the Manchus in China.

The failure of the Manchu government to assert itself against France in 1885 convinced Sun that they should be overthrown. In 1895, after China's defeat by Japan, a revolutionary society led by Sun was foiled in its plans to seize Canton and challenge the regime. This was the first of ten attempts by Sun to rid China of the Manchus before their eventual downfall in 1911.

During his travels in Europe and America Sun achieved unintentional publicity for his cause when in 1896 the Chinese legation in

London involved itself in an international incident by holding him prisoner for ten days. More important was the influence on him of European socialism and of radical thought in America.

By the time he founded the T'ung Meng Hui (Alliance Society) in 1905, Sun had organized enough rebellions – all unsuccessful – to earn him a nationwide reputation and to give the revolutionary movement the rudiments of an ideology. The 'Three Principles of the People' which he planned to realize through revolution were: the unity of the Chinese nation, a democratic and republican form of government and a redistribution of land to benefit the peasants. He foresaw this revolution coming about after a period of military rule, which would uproot the old order, and a subsequent period of local self-government, which would serve to teach the nation the meaning of democratic government. The introduction of democracy on a national level would complete the revolutionary process. This was Sun's attempt to apply an assortment of Western ideas to the Chinese situation.

The spread of revolutionary ideas to the army proved to be crucial to the success of Sun Yat-sen's plans, which as yet seemed obscure to the peasants of China. The revolutionaries were forced however to act before they were ready because the discovery in October 1911 of their headquarters in Hankow led to a disturbance. Troops at the neighbouring town of Wu-chang made a rather desperate bid to start a rising. Hankow was seized, a provisional government was proclaimed and a general call to revolt was issued.

The Manchus were sufficiently alarmed by the uprising to recall Yuan Shih-k'ai, who had been summoned before by Tz'u

Hsi in 1898 at the time of the hundred days of reform. Yuan agreed to take command if the Manchus would offer some compromise political solution. The dynasty eventually agreed to a British style constitutional monarchy and made Yuan prime minister.

Meanwhile, the revolutionaries had established control of southern China as firmly as Yuan controlled the north. Sun returned from exile to become president of the provisional government in January 1912 and soon realized that Yuan was too strong to be ignored. He, therefore, offered to step down and arrange for Yuan to become president of a Chinese republic if Yuan would get rid of the Manchu dynasty. As Yuan was aiming throughout to secure supreme power for himself, he fell in with Sun's proposal. The Manchus found themselves without support, and they agreed to the abdication of their emperor, a boy of six. In February 1912, the last of the great Chinese dynasties came to an end. The revolutionaries had achieved their aim of establishing a republic.

The rest of Sun's revolutionary programme, however, was as far from realization as ever. Yuan was bent on using the revolution to make himself ruler of China, not to make her democratic or socialist. And once the Manchus were gone it soon became clear that Yuan was their real successor.

In 1913 a parliament was elected under the new republican constitution. Sun organized a new party, the Kuomintang, in an attempt to fight the elections and unite the forces of republicanism which were divided as to the future course of the republic. The Kuomintang was successful in the elections but almost immediately clashed with Yuan over the conditions of a foreign loan. The parliamentary struggle turned into a rebellion, which Yuan crushed. The Kuomintang was dissolved, Sun went back into exile and Yuan made himself dictator. He died in 1916 after trying unsuccessfully to make himself emperor. China fell under the control of a number of 'warlords' or military leaders who had taken advantage of the breakdown of the old order to carve out little empires for themselves in the provinces. Thus she entered a period of conflict and turmoil which continued until the triumph of Mao's communist movement in 1949.

Left, the heads of decapitated offenders hanging
for all to see during the 1911 Chinese Revolution.

Opposite, Sun Yat-sen (1867–1925), founder
and leader of the Kuomintang, the Chinese
nationalist party, and briefly president of the new
Chinese republic in 1912: his life was spent trying
first to overthrow the Manchu dynasty and then
to combat the warlords.

Chapter 12

The United States Industrialization and Imperialism

Of the dramatic events of the years 1895–1905 in Asia none was more momentous than the intervention of the United States, which until then had counted for little in world affairs. Her rise to power had been noticed with alarm only by the British with their imperial interests in North America. Europeans were quick to realize the significance of Prussia's victories against Austria and France in the years between 1866 and 1870. Prussia, transformed into the German Empire, would henceforth be the leading power in Europe. The significance of the American Civil War, however, fought between 1861 and 1865, did not seem so important to the Europeans. This was a war which showed, nevertheless, more clearly than any of those yet fought in Europe how wars were to be waged in an age of industrialism. Moreover, the victory of the northern states meant that the United States of America would survive as an entity, whose fast developing industries and expanding population would contribute to making her a leading world nation by the end of the nineteenth century. America's role in Asia at the turn of the century marked her emergence as a world power.

While the Civil War decided the question of America's unity, it left unsettled the question of what sort of state America was to be. The war had been fought because the southern states of the federation felt that they were a minority, unfairly discriminated against by the federal government in Washington and more specifically by the northern states, who favoured the maintenance of unity in the territories of the United States. The fundamental issue between North and South was that of negro slavery, which the South regarded as essential to their economy and way of life. The North saw the eventual disappearance of slavery as an inevitable part of economic and social progress much as critics of serfdom did in Russia in these same years.

In 1860 the new Republican Party elected Abraham Lincoln as president. The party had been formed to advance a programme of high tariffs and economic development on a national scale. The radical wing of the party, to which Lincoln did not belong, was very anti-slavery and anti-southern in sentiment. The South saw the election of Lincoln as a challenge to their future, however, and the secession of ten southern states from the union in 1861 precipitated the Civil War.

The war of southern independence, which lasted for four years, involved battles as great and devastating as those of Napoleon. It was not until the southern armies had been greatly weakened by divisions among themselves that the Confederate general, Robert E. Lee, finally surrendered to General Ulysses Grant at Appomattox on 9 April 1865. The industrialized North had defeated the agrarian South.

Reconstruction

During the course of the struggle, President Lincoln had used his wartime powers to abolish slavery in the Confederate states by the Emancipation Proclamation of 1863, but the victors remained at odds as to what that emancipation was to mean in practice. Lincoln gave his first priority to healing the wounds of the Civil War for the sake of national unity. As long as the South abandoned plans to break up the federation he was prepared to be conciliatory over working out the practical consequences of freeing the slaves. Though he was assassinated in April 1865 in the last days of the war, his successor, Andrew Johnson, had much the same attitude. He was opposed, however, by radical Republicans in the Senate and the House of Representatives, who believed that the North should use its victory to impose efficient government on the South and make its leaders conform to the democratic political principles which America had long proclaimed.

The radicals had their way in the aftermath of victory, when most people in the North felt that the South should pay a heavy penalty for such a bloody and costly war. In the South Reconstruction entailed the establishment of freed slaves as effective citizens, whose votes could be used to elect new legislatures in each of the southern states, where it was hoped that democratic state constitutions would be adopted. In

THE CONSTITUTIONAL AMENDMENT!

GEARY
Is for Negro Suffrage.

STEVENS
Advocates it.

FORNEY
Howls for it.

McCLURE
Speaks for it.

CAMERON
Wants it.

The LEAGUE
Sustains it.

They are rich, and want to make

The Negro the Equal
OF THE POOR WHITE MAN,
and then rule them both.

The BLACK Roll
CANDIDATES FOR CONGRESS
WHO VOTED FOR THIS BILL

THAD. STEVENS
WM. D. KELLEY
CHAS. O'NEILL
LEONARD MYERS
JNO. M. BROOMALL
GEORGE F. MILLER
STEPHEN F. WILSON
ULYSSES MERCUR
GEO. V. LAWRENCE
GLENNI W. SCHOFIELD
J. K. MOORHEAD
THOMAS WILLIAMS

THE RADICAL PLATFORM--"NEGRO SUFFRAGE THE ONLY ISSUE!"

Every man who votes for Geary or for a Radical Candidate for Congress, votes as surely for Negro Suffrage and Negro Equality, as if they were printed on his ballot.

"ONE VOTE LESS."—*Richmond Whig.*

Above, cartoon by Thomas Nash, published in the New York journal, Harper's Weekly, *after an incident during the 1868 presidential election, in which a black was killed because he tried to vote.*

Left, election handbill produced in about 1866 (the constitutional amendment referred to is the fourteenth, which guaranteed negro suffrage): advocated by the radical wing of the Republican Party, negro suffrage was an unpopular cause even in the North and became non-existent in the South after the withdrawal of Federal troops.

Opposite, a family of freed slaves on a South Carolina plantation, 1862: a few blacks were granted their freedom by enlightened owners, but the vast majority had to await the end of the Civil War; then lack of economic strength and the hatred of the whites meant that freedom brought meagre benefits.

particular, Reconstruction entailed the enforcement of the Fourteenth Amendment to the American constitution, which abolished slavery everywhere in the country and made the national government the guardian of every person's right to 'life, liberty and property'.

Radical leaders like Thaddeus Stevens worked for a more democratic and humane system of government in the South. At first these radicals enjoyed a good deal of success, but reform was obtained only by the unscrupulous use of authority which enhanced the bitterness between North and South. This might not have been so important if the reforms could have been made permanent, but popular enthusiasm for reform in the North faded in time; after the withdrawal of the last federal troops from Louisiana and South Carolina in 1877 the southern states had again something like home rule. The radicals had failed.

Negroes in the South were left insecure, third-class citizens by the failure of radical reconstruction. Immediately after the Civil War secret societies like the Ku Klux Klan dedicated themselves to keeping negroes in as subservient a position in society as they had endured under slavery. Klan intimidation often took the form of horrifying cruelties and lynchings. By the end of the century southern legislatures had found more systematic methods of keeping negroes 'in their place' – like the use of poll taxes to deprive them of their right to vote and the segregation of public transportation and schools.

Although the negroes were little better off as freemen than as slaves, they could at least escape to the towns in the North, where racial discrimination was less blatant. A small but important negro middle class emerged, and negro education developed

under the leadership of men like Booker T. Washington, who saw no future in political action and concentrated on educating negroes to improve their economic well-being. The failure to force or persuade the South to emancipate the negroes after the Civil War postponed the settlement of a problem which was to survive into the second half of the twentieth century and prove a source of weakness and embarrassment when America aspired to the leadership of a world whose people were mostly coloured.

Emigration

Although the Civil War left divisions in American society which still persist, America did succeed in dealing with the problem of immigration. Over 30,000,000 immigrants poured into the United States from every European country and some Asian ones during the nineteenth century. National minorities did not prove a danger to America as they had to most European states, and immigrants were quite easily integrated into American society.

Most of Europe industrialized too slowly to support the continent's rapidly rising population, and land hunger drove millions to the spacious American plains and cities. Political, religious and nationalist oppression drove millions of others to the comparative tolerance and freedom of opportunity offered by America. Between the Civil War and 1890 most of the immigrants were German, Irish, British and Scandinavian. Between 1890 and 1914 they came mainly from Italy, Austria-Hungary and Russia. As immigration mounted, many Americans demanded some restrictions,

especially when Chinese and Japanese immigration became prominent on the west coast. But there were few restrictions until after the First World War. Generally speaking, Americans were proud of their tradition as the land of the free to which the victims of less enlightened governments fled; and the booming American economy was hungry for all the cheap skilled labour Europe could provide.

The opportunities for hard-working and enterprising men in American industry largely explains why most immigrants were quite easily assimilated. Immigrants were likely to be above average in enterprise, and in a society which admired those who raised themselves to wealth by their own efforts many immigrants climbed high in the social scale within a generation or so. America's educational system overcame the language problem and indoctrinated the newcomers' children in the rights and duties of American citizens. The Democratic and Republican party machines were hungry for voting fodder, and although organizations like Tammany Hall (the famous Democratic political machine in New York) were notorious for corruption they made the town immigrant feel an active citizen and involved him in political life. Corrupting 'hand-outs' at least alleviated poverty when immigrants were finding their feet in a society which did not believe in welfare services.

Immigration on this vast scale enriched not only industrialization but America's scientific and artistic development as well. For example, Andrew Carnegie, by origin a poor Scottish immigrant boy, built up one of the largest steel producing companies in the world. The German born physicist, Albert Einstein, who emigrated to America in the 1930s, revolutionized the scientific world with his theory of relativity.

Nevertheless, people who wanted to restrict immigration argued that the slum conditions to which immigrants came and in which the unsuccessful ones stayed bred crime and corruption and lowered the standards of city life. The United States tried to maintain an industrial society which left individuals to sort out their own destinies and had little sympathy for failure. The prospects of success were high enough to gratify the expectations of most of her new citizens.

Railroads

Though at the beginning of the nineteenth century America had been a thoroughly agrarian society, between 1830 and 1860 industrialization developed rapidly. Because of the high labour costs American industrialists eagerly adopted labour-saving machinery from the other side of the Atlantic and improved on it. American workers, who were generally better educated than those in Britain and other European countries, eagerly accepted the new machines as easing their tasks. By the time of the Civil War America had become second only to Britain as a manufacturing country.

As in Russia, the size of the country made the transportation of goods a major problem which could best be solved by a network of railways. In Russia industrialization began only when the construction of railways was started while America had become an important industrial power before the big trans-continental lines were laid down. The first of these lines, begun in 1863, was the result of two separate enterprises, one starting from Chicago as the Union Pacific Railway, the other, the Central Pacific, driving east from California. In 1869 the two lines came together in Utah after their

promoters had overcome phenomenal difficulties by brutal determination and often by shady financial operations. Other lines stretching across the American continent followed in the next twenty years.

As in other countries America's great railway network was an immense stimulus to industry, and American industrialists rose to the challenge of providing the coal and steel needed in such huge quantities. As the network developed, the costs of transporting raw materials, agricultural produce and manufactured goods fell. Apart from the economic benefits, the railways, together with the simultaneous development of telegraphic and telephone communications, helped to supply a sense of unity especially valuable in such a sprawling and scattered nation.

The triumph of capitalism

Although the urban population remained smaller than that of the countryside until after the First World War, the most striking feature of American history between the end of the Civil War and 1914 was the staggering growth of industry. By the time she entered the First World War in 1917, the US had outstripped every other industrial nation in terms of manufacturing output, and she could claim the highest per capita income in the world. As the leading industrial state America was to become the most powerful as well as the richest of the great powers.

The big business corporations which emerged during the late nineteenth century dwarfed those of Europe. The United States, even more than Britain, offered unrivalled opportunities for building great industrial empires. Remarkable and ruthless industrialists, like John D. Rockefeller, and Andrew Carnegie, emerged. They saw the

world of business as evolving through an endless struggle in which the fittest survived; and both Carnegie and Rockefeller, who survived as the fittest in their industries of steel and oil, saw it as their duty to use their enormous wealth to benefit the community at large. They became philanthropists on the same giant scale as their industrial enterprises. The Rockefeller Foundation continues to finance projects for the benefit of society, and Carnegie's fortune still promotes educational enterprise in Scotland as well as America.

The great issue in American politics in the ten years after the Civil War was the extent to which Reconstruction could impose on the defeated southern states the necessity of liberty and equality for all its citizens. General Grant, the North's hero in the Civil War, became president in 1868 and backed the radicals in their zeal to reform the South.

After the presidential election of 1876, however, when a congressional electoral commission had to decide the winner, a more conservative conciliatory mood descended on the Republican Party and the country as a whole. The new president, Rutherford B. Hayes, favoured an end to the strife with the South, and this seemed to be in tune with the rest of public opinion.

With the decline of radical influences in the Republican Party, both the main parties became conservative in their approach to the problems of government. The Republicans,

who won every presidential election between 1860 and 1912 except for those in 1884 and 1892, emerged as a middle-class party with a good deal of working class support. The Republicans bore some resemblance to the British Liberals and were similarly in tune with the spirit of industrialism. In the late nineteenth century they became increasingly linked to the interests of big business. Republican presidents in this period saw their role as ensuring efficiency in the rather limited work of central government, allowing private industry to develop to the nation's advantage.

Similarly, the Democrats, who elected only one president in these years (Grover Cleveland) but who frequently had a majority in both houses of congress, had a narrow view of the scope of central government. The experience of radical Republicanism left the South solidly Democratic during the following hundred years, and the Democrats in the South defended the rights of the old landowning class. The Democratic Party was also the party of the farmers, who believed that their interests were being sacrificed to the growing power of big business. Above all, the Democrats were for states' rights and against the power of the federal government in Washington, and they saw the presidency as a means of protecting the states. Their future role as the reforming party of Franklin D. Roosevelt's New Deal was still very distant.

Above, a railway construction crew by their locomotive: the years between the Civil War and the end of the First World War were the heyday of American railways; the transcontinental link was completed in 1869 and the network covered the entire country, increasing from 35,000 miles in 1865 to 254,000 in 1916, when one worker in every twenty-five was a railway employee.

Opposite right, the completion of the first transcontinental rail link, Promontory, Utah, 10 May 1869.

Opposite left, Italian immigrants at Ellis Island, the reception centre in New York Harbour for immigrants from Europe: more than twelve million people entered the USA through Ellis Island between 1892 and 1924, when mass immigration ended and immigrants were inspected in their country of origin.

181

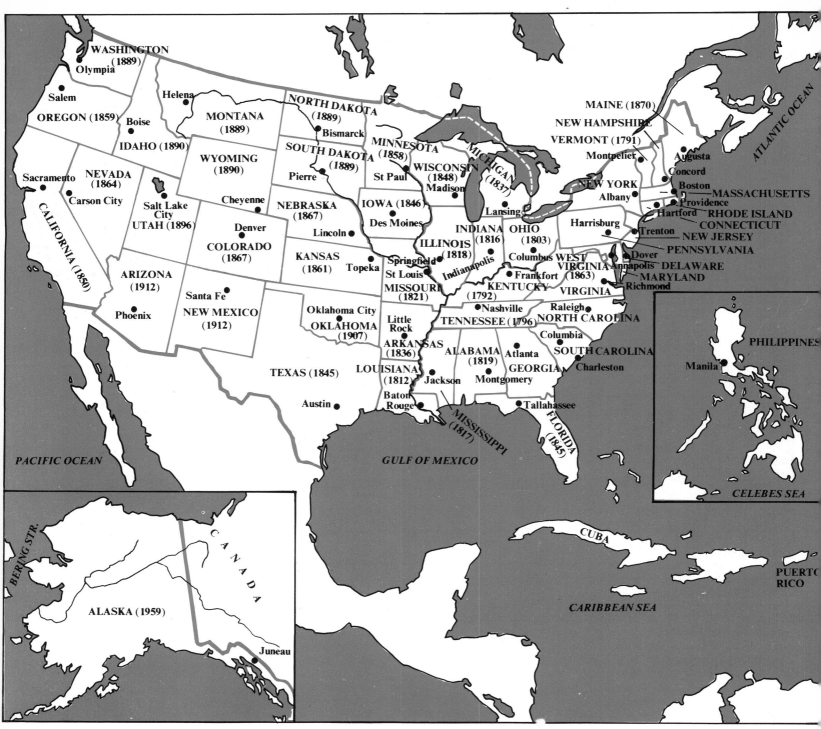

The presidents in these years of conservatism were worthy and efficient men but left no great mark on American society. While Abraham Lincoln's name became known the world over, Hayes, James Garfield, Chester Arthur, Grover Cleveland and William McKinley acquired little fame outside America. Two of them were assassinated: Garfield was succeeded by the sound but unspectacular Chester Arthur, but McKinley, who was shot by an anarchist in 1901, was succeeded by his dynamic vice-president, Theodore Roosevelt. With Roosevelt's accession the United States had for the first time since 1865 a leader of world stature to coincide with her emergence as a world power. Roosevelt's energy, which alarmed many of his fellow Republicans, was to bring an end to the era of conservatism.

Roosevelt came to power at a time when strong minorities were becoming openly discontented with the way the country was run. Both industrial workers and farmers had grievances against the system; and although they failed to change it, their behaviour was turbulent enough to draw attention to the need for reform.

Industrialization in the United States was not accompanied by a rapid growth of trade unionism, and employers were in a stronger position than those in Europe in these years. Millions of immigrants supplied them with an ever-growing labour force accustomed to a lower standard of living and, therefore, initially less demanding. The prevailing philosophy in America favoured rugged individualism which saw trade unions as disrupting the process by which free enterprise created wealth. Middle-class opinion was hostile to organized labour; the farming community had little interest in or sympathy for the problems of factory workers; and the courts were likely to find against them in disputes. The more militant workers, especially those with experience of labour politics in Europe, tended to become despairingly violent when peaceful pressure failed. Incidents like the riot in the Haymarket, Chicago, in 1886, when over a hundred people were killed or wounded, further alienated public opinion and discouraged

the average worker from pressing for the establishment of unions.

The mainstream of the American labour movement abandoned any attempt to play politics in the manner of European workers. The Knights of Labour, founded in 1869, aimed at building a nation-wide labour organization for all kinds of workers. It proved too big, unwieldy and lacking in discipline to outwit employers willing to use a private army of hired detectives to break up strikes. However, smaller unions of skilled workers in particular trades had more success. The most influential leader thrown up by this kind or organization was Samuel Gompers of the Cigarmakers Union. A Londoner by birth, Gompers built up his union into a closely knit and disciplined one with a national fund and welfare benefits. In 1886 a number of these smaller unions joined together to form the American Federation of Labour, with Gompers as president and the dominating personality in the federation until 1924.

Samuel Gompers believed that there was no point in trying to challenge the entrenched Republican and Democratic parties by creating a separate labour party. He was hostile to socialism and worked to secure high benefits for his members within the capitalist system instead of trying to replace the system or even to change it. He tried without success to organize the labour movements of the world in a new non-socialist International. In America, however, Gompers' programme had wide appeal. Despite periodic depressions, prosperity was too obviously increasing for many American workers to be attracted by ideas of revolution or even radical political change. The American labour movement was to develop firmly on the lines laid down by Gompers.

In the period before the First World War, however, the American Federation of Labour represented only a fraction of American workers. Long hours and insecurity for the majority were not countered by effective trade unionism or state welfare provisions. A number of spectacular, violent and unsuccessful strikes towards the end of the century made more of an impression on public opinion than the ultimately more

significant work of Gompers. Although industrialists were able to withstand the demands of frustrated workers, their brutal methods in the 1890s helped to swing influential sections of society to greater sympathy with the workers' problems. This sympathy was one aspect of the Progressivist movement which Theodore Roosevelt came to represent.

The Populist Party

It was a curious fact that in the most flourishing industrial society in the world the farming community seemed a more powerful political force than the industrial workers. Farmers had a more deep-rooted grievance to express. While workers in the towns wanted to reform industrialization in their favour, the farmers opposed the capitalist system as a whole. For example, they opposed the railway owners who disregarded the rights of farmers in areas through which their railways passed. During periods of economic depression the farmers blamed high interest rates and an inadequate supply of credit on the east coast financiers, who wanted to impress foreign investors by establishing the gold standard in the United States. In 1892 the farmers formed the Populist Party.

The Populists denounced the capitalist system as immoral, and, in particular, they demanded a reform of the currency to allow an unlimited amount of silver coinage to augment the gold supply. Both Republican and Democratic party leaders were agreed on the need for the gold standard because an industrial economy had to have a 'sound' currency if it were to attract foreign investors. A depression in the mid-1890s intensified debate on the issue, and the propaganda of the Populists began to have its effect. In 1896 the Democrats split on the currency question and nominated as their presidential candidate for that year William Jennings Bryan, whose splendid and emotional tirade against conventional financial wisdom contained the famous words, 'you shall not crucify mankind upon a cross of gold.'

By persuading the Democrats to adopt their policy, the Populists enjoyed a remarkable triumph. But their triumph was short-lived when Bryan lost the election to the 'sound money' Republican candidate, William McKinley. The immense wealth of America's great banks and corporations was enlisted by the Republicans to counter Populist propaganda and the powerful oratory of Bryan. Moreover, the country was recovering from the depression, and prosperity was returning.

Whatever the merits of the gold standard the importance of which was probably exaggerated, Bryan's defeat was a significant event in American politics. Agrarian America had been defeated by industrial America. The radical Populist movement was backward-looking and romantic and

had some affinity with the very different Russian populist movement in its hostility to industrialism. By the end of the nineteenth century in the United States the future lay with industrialism. The campaign of 1896 was a brilliant rearguard action, but afterwards Populism faded, and the Democratic Party did not revive until 1912.

Progressivism

The farming protest had failed and trade unionism was slow to develop. A socialist movement under Eugene Debs attracted widespread interest but never became a serious contender for political power. The failure of populism and socialism did not mean that public opinion was complacent, however, for at the turn of the century an influential reform movement grew up known as Progressivism.

Progressivism arose from a growing distaste for the way in which the giant corporations pursued their aims without regard for the interests of the community as a whole. For many intellectuals the idea of the 'survival of the fittest' turned sour when they saw some of the triumphant survivors. The older generation of American capitalists were offended by the newer, more ruthless brand of tycoon and resented their success. 'Muckraking' journalists highlighted the seamier side of big business with stories of corruption and all sorts of abuses and helped to convince middle-class opinion that American society was getting out of control.

Not that Progressivism sought any radical change. Its followers aimed to make politics more democratic and to make businessmen responsive to public as well as private interests. They also favoured a limited amount of labour legislation to limit working hours, to compensate workmen for injury – the kinds of provisions which were becoming standard practice in most industrial societies. Some Progressives traced the causes of corruption and the evils of social and political life to immigrants and alcohol, and they started campaigns to restrict immigration and to prohibit the sale of alcohol. The more liberal side of the movement worked for the right of women to vote.

This moderate, mainly middle-class movement did something towards cleaning up the corruption in American political life. One important achievement was the adoption of 'primary' elections in many states in response to the demand that party voters should be directly involved in the nomination of party candidates instead of leaving it to corrupt party 'machines'. In general, the achievements of Progressivism matched its modest aims.

Progressivism gained from the assassin's bullet which ended McKinley's presidential career and put Theodore Roosevelt in the White House. 'T.R.', as he was affectionately referred to, was an energetic, colourful, restless figure with wide-ranging interests

and many enthusiasms. By the time he became president in 1901 he had written several books, worked on a cattle ranch and seen public service as assistant secretary of the navy, governor of New York State and vice-president of the United States. In everything he did he took a positive approach to the job and attacked corruption and inefficiency with gusto. Characteristically, he had found organizing the navy too tame during the war with Spain in 1898 and had instead played a dashing role as colonel of the 'Rough Rider' volunteers in Cuba.

Roosevelt was an appropriate president for an age of Progressivism and imperialism, very different in style from the conservative administrators of previous decades. He believed in using his office to ensure that the big corporations behaved themselves in a more public-spirited way and directed his administration to investigate monopolistic 'trusts' in the major industries. In an unprecedented extension of his executive office, Roosevelt intervened in a major coal mining strike in 1902 to get both sides to accept arbitration. In addition, he instituted federal control over the rates charged by the railways; he put through a pure food act which current scandals had proved necessary. Conservation was another interest of the indefatigable Roosevelt, who tackled the problem of protecting America's forests, rivers and natural resources from exploitation by private concerns.

Roosevelt was in office from 1901 until 1908, having been returned in 1904 with massive popular support. Even as interpreted by Roosevelt, the presidency did not carry enough power to do more than tinker with the problems which both he and the

Above, Colonel Theodore Roosevelt (1858–1919) and his 'Rough Riders' on San Juan Hill, Cuba, during the 1898 Spanish American War.

Opposite top, troops protecting a train during the Pullman strike in 1894: George Pullman (1831–97), in many respects a beneficent employer who had built a model village for his employees, cut wages and sacked workers during the 1893–94 economic depression but refused to lower rents. His employees struck, but, though Pullman cars were boycotted nationally and two-thirds of the railway system came to a halt, the strike was eventually broken.

Opposite centre, a Nebraska farmstead in the late 1880s: agriculture experienced a boom period in the last decades of the nineteenth century, as the rich soil of the Plains states was put under the plough, its products shipped east by the newly-built railroads; many small farmers, unable to cope with the development of agricultural capitalism, turned to the Populist movement to express their grievances.

Opposite bottom, ranchers and cattle, 1902: though the myth still endures, the reality of the wild west – the cowboy roaming the plains, driving his stock hundreds of miles to slaughter – lasted for only about twenty years, homesteaders then putting the Plains under cultivation and ranchers introducing industrialized methods of stockfarming.

Progressives saw as urgent. But he made regulation of the jungle warfare of American capitalism a popular cause to which future presidents would return.

Imperialism in Latin America

Roosevelt's approach to international affairs was as flamboyant as his approach to domestic problems and far more widely appreciated. Like the rest of the world's industrial powers, the United States was seized with imperialist fervour at the turn of the century.

During the nineteenth century she had taken the obvious course of extending her frontiers within the north American continent. The Indian wars between 1862 and 1886 resulted from the intrusion by white settlers on the hunting grounds of Indian tribes like the Sioux and the Cheyenne. After numerous Indian attacks on the settlers' camps had been savagely repulsed, America's Indian population was persuaded or compelled to settle peacefully in areas allocated to them by the federal government. War with Mexico in 1846–8 had forced the Mexicans to recognise US sovereignty over Texas and to cede New Mexico and California, where gold had been recently discovered. Settlers had moved steadily west during the century, and Americans were told by the historian Frederick Jackson Turner in 1893 that this moving frontier was the secret of their dynamic national character. By the end of the century the frontier was 'closed' – the great plains, where the cowboys and the pioneer farmers had left their legends, had become settled regions.

As in Britain and Germany, the achievements of the age of industrialism were so obvious to the eye, and the changes it wrought so rapid, that an exhilarating sense of national pride and confidence characterized the period. The United States now looked for fresh fields to conquer with her immense economic and military power. Alfred Mahan's *Influence of Sea Power upon History*, published in 1890, strongly influenced American – and European – opinion as to the need for naval bases and colonies in the quest for national security and power. As in Britain, the popular press sensationalized international issues and aroused resentment and alarm at European encroachments or interventions in Asia and even Latin America.

Pacific naval bases like Midway and Pearl Harbor had already been acquired before the imperialist movement got under way. It was the war with Spain in 1898 which released imperialist passions in America. Spain was an especially suitable victim, a European intruder in America's global backyard who possessed Cuba and the Philippines. She was also a reactionary colonial power, whose presence was hated by those she ruled. The United States had ample opportunity to experience the mixed emotions of national interest and sincere self-righteousness which were the hallmark of imperialism in the industrial age. In 1895 the US had strongly supported the Cubans in their revolt against Spain, which had dragged on despite brutal repression by the Spanish colonial administration. American opinion was angered by events so close to her shores, and the idea of a liberating war grew popular. They mysterious explosion which destroyed the American battleship *Maine* in Havana excited feelings still further. In April 1898 Congress was practically unanimous in agreeing to war.

The ease with which victory was won was predictable enough given Spanish weakness and distance from her Cuban colony. The defeat of Spain's troops in Cuba and of her navy in the Philippines was very gratifying to American national pride. By August 1898 peace was being negotiated; Spain evacuated Cuba and handed over Puerto Rico and the Philippines to the United States. The annexation of the Philippines, whose population had rebelled against Spain and in the meantime set up their own government, caused much soul-searching and debate and was considered by some to be an act of colonialism. The misgivings were sincere enough, but imperialistic fervour was stronger than the feeling that Philippine self-determination should prevail. The argument of a civilizing mission, so familiar to European ears, eventually proved adequate to convince the Senate to ratify the treaty signed in Paris in 1898. Cuba was evacuated but only after the Cubans had accepted limitations on their freedom to manage their affairs which made the island something like an American protectorate.

This was also the year when the industrial powers began closing in on China. In 1899 the United States secretary of state, John Hay, made his famous 'Open Door' proposal to the other interested nations, hoping to keep China open to US economic penetration.

Dollar Diplomacy

American imperialism had thus been already launched in dramatic style when Roosevelt became president, and he himself had played an important part in both the planning and the fighting of the war against Spain. Roosevelt was a convinced imperialist on both moral and political grounds. He accepted the idea that the era in which he lived was witnessing the carve-up of the world by the most civilized nations and believed it America's duty to join in the work of civilization. If she did not, she would fall behind in the race for power and influence in world affairs.

Although Roosevelt was a whole-hearted imperialist, he was not a greedy one and concentrated on emphasizing America's world image and her areas of influence. His only really spectacular international coup concerned the Panama Canal. When de Lessep's attempt to build a canal linking the Pacific and Atlantic oceans had collapsed in financial scandal, the US proposed to take over the project. In 1901 they at last got rid of the treaty by which they had agreed to share construction of the canal with Britain and internationalize it. Colombia, through whose territory the canal was to pass, put off ratifying an agreement by which America would get perpetual control of the canal area in Panama. Roosevelt, angry at the hitch, helped to engineer a revolution in Panama which declared itself independent of Colombia. The US government made payments to both the Republic of Colombia and the new Republic of Panama and got control of the Canal Zone in return. Even though Roosevelt's action was strongly criticized at home, he had secured effective control of the future Panama Canal, which was opened for traffic in August 1914.

After British, German and Italian intervention in Venezuela on a debt collecting expedition, Roosevelt, to forestall future ventures of this kind, enunciated his corollary of the Monroe Doctrine. The Monroe Doctrine, as proclaimed by President Monroe in 1823, had declared European colonization or intervention in the Americas to be acts unfriendly to the United States. In 1904 Roosevelt argued that if America's neighbours provoked other powers by failing to live up to their international obligations, it would be necessary for the US herself to act as an international policeman in the American continent. In 1907 the United States intervened in Santo Domingo in fulfilment of Roosevelt's doctrine and left again when her mission was completed.

On the world stage Roosevelt mediated in the Russo-Japanese war and in so doing notified the other powers of America's interests in the fate of east Asia. In 1906 Roosevelt agreed to support a conference to settle the dispute between Germany and France over Morocco and sent American representatives to the conference at Algeciras. In 1908 he sent the US fleet around the world to demonstrate her naval power. The voyage boosted American morale and was more significant than perhaps the rest of the world appreciated.

Although Roosevelt was a moderate imperialist by the standards of the time and had little blood on his hands, the decade after 1898 was a landmark in world history, signalizing the arrival of the richest and potentially the strongest state in the world.

The Republican split

When Roosevelt's term of office ended in 1908 he was succeeded by his secretary of state, William Howard Taft, who had been Roosevelt's choice but who lacked his predecessor's skilful political touch. Taft moved away from the Progressivist stance of the previous administration at a time when the tide of public opinion was still flowing strongly that way.

His administration was to become memorable for an event quite removed from politics. In 1909 the Ford Motor Company in Detroit, Michigan, produced the Model T, the first cheap, standardized car to be constructed on an assembly line. This method of production brought the motor car within the reach of the average man's pocket and inaugurated a worldwide expansion of the automobile industry.

When he left office in 1908 Roosevelt had gone on a big-game expedition to Africa and then a triumphal tour of European cities. He returned to the US to find the Republican Party threatened with a split over the 1912 presidential nomination. Encouraged by the enthusiasm with which he was greeted, Roosevelt challenged Taft for the presidential nomination in 1912, but the Republican convention was controlled by the conservatives who nominated Taft. Roosevelt led his supporters out of the convention and organized his own Progressive Party, also known as the 'Bull Moose' party. He stood for re-election on a platform of reform in industrial and political life.

In the three-sided electoral campaign which followed, Roosevelt and Taft faced the Democratic candidate, Woodrow Wilson, who won a great victory over his rivals. As always, American voting habits did not favour third parties.

Wilson was an academic who had specialized in law and history and had worked out theories about the nature of the presidential office and how it could best be used for

reform. While he lacked Roosevelt's boisterous personality, Wilson had great political skill. After entering office in 1913 he immediately called for a series of reforms which he had called the New Freedom in his presidential campaign, such as anti-trust measures, and he reorganized the national banking system by the Federal Reserve Act of 1913. His interventions in Latin America were also in the Roosevelt tradition. Moderate reform and moderate imperialism distinguished America on the eve of the First World War.

Wilson's dilemma

The outbreak of war in Europe in 1914 took Wilson by surprise. He had so far concentrated his attention on domestic politics rather than international affairs, and his knowledge of European problems was sketchy. Almost immediately his friend and confidant Colonel House was sent by Wilson to see if the United States could help to resolve the conflicts among the European powers. House reported more optimistically than the situation warranted, and war was declared by the various angry nations before he had returned to Washington.

There was no question of the United States doing more than declaring her neutrality in a struggle so remote from her shores. Wilson hoped that she would eventually be able to restore peace, as Roosevelt had done between Russia and Japan in 1905.

It was impossible for the United States to remain an aloof and impartial bystander. The Allies needed her great wealth of raw materials, munitions and manufactured goods; and American industry was eager to supply them. They also wanted to prevent these goods being sold to the enemy. Inevitably Wilson was soon involved in trying both to protect domestic interests and seek international accord; and gradually the threat to United States interests grew to such an extent that it submerged the wish to mediate and remain neutral. Only after the United States had altered the course of the war by sending its armed forces to support the Allies was Wilson able to pursue his role of peacemaker.

Above, Sitting Bull (c.1831–90) the Sioux chief, in about 1885: his death at the hands of Indian police led to the Massacre of Wounded Knee.

Top, an Indian camp on a reservation: deprived of their former lands and their buffalo, the staple of their economy, destroyed, the Indians were confined to relatively small reservations providing an inadequate living; full legal rights and citizenship were only granted in 1924.

Opposite, US troops in Santo Domingo: the years around the turn of the century saw US imperialism confidently exercised in the Caribbean and Latin America, as the nation, internal expansion now complete, turned its attention to international events.

Chapter 13

Nations in Turmoil

Bismarck's German Empire was, like the America of Roosevelt and Wilson, characterized by moderate reform and moderate imperialism. German development had in some ways paralleled that of America as she experienced a steady growth of industry in the first half of the nineteenth century and then in the second half expanded at such a remarkable rate as to become one of the wealthiest and most powerful states in the world. Germany, like America, was a federation of states with different traditions, and these and other sources of discontent brought internal divisions which the empire's rulers never succeeded in healing.

In other respects the German Empire was a very different kind of state. Bismarck and his successors faced greater problems than any American president after the Civil War. German unity was achieved by war in the same decade that American unity was being confirmed by war. While the Americans could fight out their own quarrels remote from the interference of other great powers, the Germans were in the heart of Europe, where every change was anxiously watched by fearful neighbours. The historical experience of the German people set them on an entirely different political road from the Americans, although their economic development was similar.

By the nineteenth century the number of German states had been reduced to thirty-nine, Austria and Prussia predominating. Austria had a German dynasty and was the traditional leader among the German states, although it was divided into seventeen provinces and encompassed many nationalities besides Germans – Czechs, Poles, Slovenes, Italians, Croats, Serbs and a large community of Jews settled mostly in Vienna. In the first half of the nineteenth century the idea of drawing the German states together into one great central European empire began to have increasing appeal to the small number of politically educated Germans. Ideas of nationalism were in the air, and the economic advantages of a united Germany without commercial and other barriers became obvious as trade and industry developed.

These ideas were realized when the King of Prussia, under the inspiration of his brilliant and forceful minister, Otto von Bismarck, challenged Austria over Germany in the 1860s. Prussia defeated Austria in 1866, and formed the North German Confederation. After her defeat of France, Prussia was able to go a stage further and draw the southern German states into her orbit. In January 1871, a German Empire was proclaimed, which united all Germans except those living under the Habsburg dynasty in Austria.

Although the new empire was a federation of the various German states, for all practical purposes it was a Prussian empire which Bismarck had created. Until his fall from office in 1890 Bismarck was the real ruler of Prussia and Germany because of the trust placed in him by Emperor William I and because of his immense prestige as the most successful statesman in Europe. The empire's constitution, however, made the emperor the key figure in political life, and in 1888 there came to the throne a man determined to use his power. William II became the emperor of Germany in fact as well as in name by getting rid of Bismarck in 1890. But whether the emperor or his chancellor ruled, the most influential class in Prussia was the *junkers*, the old landowning aristocracy from east of the river Elbe. They were prominent at court, in the army and in the civil service, and they were looked on by all the emperors as the mainstay of their regime. Bismarck was, of course, himself a *junker*, though of a rather eccentric kind. The *junkers* and their king dominated Prussia, and Prussia dominated Germany, with the result that the most dynamic industrial state in Europe was controlled by one of the most reactionary of the old European aristocracies. In this respect Germany was closer to Russia than Britain and totally remote from the United States.

Germany was also very different from Britain and the US in the strategic problems imposed on her by geography. Access to the sea and the power to control it allowed Britain and America feel secure during the upheavals of industrial change. Japan, once she had built a modern fleet, had a similar advantage, but Germany was hemmed in on all sides by other major powers. Although she was stronger than any one of them, a coalition of France, Russia and Austria-Hungary would be very formidable. The only other European power surrounded by enemies was Poland, which had been carved up by her neighbours. Prussia had come close to the same fate more than once and had come to trust in militarism as the only way of guaranteeing her survival. Even after the establishment of the German Empire with its huge resources and proven strength, her rulers felt uneasy about the dangers surrounding them.

They differed about what should be done to make Germany safe. Bismarck suffered nightmares about coalitions, but his remedies were restrained. He tried to impose discipline and unity at home by a combination of comparatively mild repression and moderate reform. Abroad he tried to make sure that Germany was always a member of a powerful coalition and thus unlikely to be a victim of one. His successors abandoned his moderation with calamitous results.

The more thoughtful members of the German aristocracy had long realized that they could play off the new middle-class employers against the new lower-class industrial workers. Bismarck had studied the way in which Napoleon III in France had used universal suffrage to bolster the existing social order. The *junkers* favoured the idea that the masses were conservative when not led astray by agitators and when their conditions were alleviated by a fatherly system of government – the same thinking which had influenced the Russian tsar after the 1905 revolution.

As usual, Bismarck put the idea into practice with more imagination and boldness than other statesmen. The *Reichstag*, the lower house of the imperial parliament, was elected by universal suffrage, an arrangement which had been adopted by the North German Confederation, whose constitution served as a model for the empire's. The confederation had been set up in 1867, the year when Britain had cautiously enfranchised better-paid workers in towns and the tenant farmers in rural districts. Bismarck could afford to be bolder than Disraeli. The composition of the British House of Commons determined who governed Britain, while the more democratically elected *Reichstag* had little real power. Ministers in the government were responsible to the emperor not to the *Reichstag*, which could resist legislation but had little control over the budget or the army. Moreover, the granting of universal suffrage in a country so divided as Germany created numerous political parties which the government could manipulate as it wished. The upper house of the imperial parliament or the *Bundersrat* was designed to represent the states and not their people and was composed of delegates appointed and recalled at pleasure by the state governments which they represented.

The various states making up the federation also had their own assemblies, the Prussian *Landtag* being the most important of these bodies. It was elected by giving equal representation to three classes of electors – roughly the wealthy, the rather less wealthy and the rest. This kind of franchise produced a safe assembly of *junkers* who were ever ready for a coup d'état to end the limited democracy which Germany had. One of them got a standing ovation from his colleagues in 1910 when he declared: 'The King of Prussia and the German Emperor must always be in a position to say to any lieutenant: "Take ten men and shoot the *Reichstag*".'

The middle class in Germany, which had become so prominent with the rise of industrialization, was also unwilling to fight for greater democracy. Its fear of socialism, and the pleasure which so many of its members took in gaining even limited access to the privileges of the old nobility, meant that it was firmly on the side of the emperor and his government. The governmental system in the empire was democratic enough to allow pressure to be brought successfully in exceptional cases, but the government's overriding interest was for industrial growth and the creation of as much wealth as possible. Organized labour had absolutely no chance of putting fetters on capitalism.

Thus Bismarck's semi-democratic system worked by removing the one issue which had traditionally united the mass of German people against the old ruling class – the desire for an elected assembly. Employers and employees could now fight among themselves while the emperor and his *junkers* held sway.

The *Kulturkampf*

Bismarck's main aim was always to hold together the old Prussian state in face of threats from within its borders and from its foreign rivals. In the 1860s his victories over Austria and France had united the nation in nationalist fervour at a time when German liberals were bent on turning Prussia into a genuinely parliamentary state. Because Bismarck knew that further wars would be dangerous, he had to ensure Prussian unity without them – a task made more difficult in the new empire which had extended Prussian power but given it more internal enemies. This expansion had greatly increased the proportion of Catholics in a predominantly Protestant country. While religion had long been one of the forces which united Prussia, Bismarck was now haunted by the divisive effect of the Catholics, who felt as much loyalty to Rome as to Berlin. His fears were confirmed when the Catholic Centre Party emerged as the second strongest in the elections to the *Reichstag*. They were led by a particularly skilful politician, Ludwig Windthorst, whom Bismarck detested.

In 1871 Bismarck undertook to subject the church, both Catholic and Protestant, to the authority of the state and make the latter supreme in both political and religious matters. In 1872 the campaign was extended to expel the Jesuits from the empire. In May 1873 Dr Adalbert Falk, who had been made Prussian minister of public worship (schools and churches were administered by individual states not by the empire), introduced a number of anti-Catholic measures known as the May Laws. The Prussian government was to have the right to veto church appointments, to supervise the education of the clergy, to control the church's discipline over its clergy and generally to restrict the church's freedom in various other ways. In 1875 grants to the Church were cut off in those Sees which resisted the new laws, and by 1877 many bishoprics were vacant, the bishops having been imprisoned or driven into exile, and many parishes were without priests for the same reason.

Bismarck's attack on the Catholics and his speeches against the Centre Party in the *Reichstag* were popular among German liberals. Pope Pius IX's denunciation in 1864 of progress, liberalism and contemporary civilization had been followed in 1870 by the dogma that papal decisions on matters of faith and morals were infallible. The Catholic Church was seen as the enemy

Above, cartoon from an 1875 number of Kladderadatsch *depicting Bismarck's conflict with the Catholic church.*

Opposite, drilling at barracks as depicted in a painting of about 1880: though the Second Reich was a parliamentary semi-democracy, the army, along with the bureaucracy and the landowners, remained a strongly conservative and authoritarian influence.

of reason and progress, and Bismarck's war was described as a *Kulturkampf*, or struggle between rival cultures.

Resistance from Germany's Catholic clergy was strong. Fines and imprisonment were imposed over and over again but without persuading the bishops and priests of the need to conform to Falk's laws. The more they resisted, the more Bismarck and German Protestants and liberals were convinced there was a plot against the empire inspired by the pope and Catholic France. It was at this time that the royalists in France had high hopes of a restoration of monarchy, and Bismarck believed that a monarchy would start a war of revenge against Germany. In 1875 there were signs that Bismarck was preparing for such a war, perhaps even by attacking France first. This 'war in sight' crisis moved other powers to make clear their position to a preventive war against France. Bismarck's exaggerated belief in the Catholic and French danger had brought him failure at home and humiliation abroad.

The campaign against the Catholics proved futile. The Centre Party was not destroyed and the Catholic Church was not intimidated. After five years of *Kulturkampf* Bismarck began to have second thoughts. The death of Pope Pius IX in 1878 and the conciliatory attitude of his successor Leo XIII gave him the chance to come to terms and wind up the affair. Falk resigned in 1879. The May Laws went into disuse or were repealed over the next few years, and by 1883 the *Kulturkampf* had died away.

The socialist threat

One of Bismarck's reasons for deciding that the Catholic threat to the empire's unity was less deadly than he had supposed was that he had sensed another more serious threat from German socialism.

In the 1860s, with Germany's industrial revolution in full swing, two workers' parties had been formed. The German Working Men's Association was founded by Ferdinand Lassalle, who believed in the peaceful achievement of socialism through political democracy. When the working-class votes were in a majority they could usher in socialism. Bismarck was interested in Lassalle's ideas as a means of diverting working-class political energies into peaceful channels, and he had secret talks with him. Lassalle was killed in a duel in 1864, but his followers continued to work for his ideas. A rival Marxist party was formed in 1869. Karl Marx had sent Wilhelm Liebknecht to Germany to organize labour there, after the foundation of the First International socialist movement in 1864. By 1869, with the help of August Bebel, Liebknecht had organized enough support to set up the Social Democratic Working Men's Party. In 1875 they united with Lassalle's group at the Gotha Congress to put forward their programme,

which was a mixture of Marx and Lassalle.

Bismarck was even more alarmed by international socialism than by international Catholicism. He thought in terms of an alliance of conservative powers to act against revolutionary conspiracies. He was determined to get the Reichstag to pass laws persecuting the social democrats. Here he ran into difficulties, as the National Liberals were suspicious of measures which might be a precedent for repressing liberalism as well as socialism. One of the advantages Bismarck could gain from ending the *Kulturkampf* was the support of the Centre Party for his anti-socialist legislation.

Bismarck's campaign was assisted by the occurrence of two attempts on the emperor's life in 1878. Though the would-be assassins were not socialists, Bismarck used the incidents to paint a picture of the empire threatened by revolutionary agitators whose propaganda drove people to violence. The anti-socialist law of 1878 banned public meetings and other open political activities by socialists.

Like the Catholics, the Social Democrats were strengthened by the persecution, which was too mild to achieve its purpose. Bismarck had exaggerated the threat to Germany's unity.

After Bismarck was forced to resign in 1890 the anti-socialist law was dropped. The Social Democratic Party was reorganized in 1891 with a full-blooded revolutionary programme on Marxist lines, which seemed to confirm Bismarck's worst fears and to prove him right. But the revolutionary ardour of the German Social Democrats was of the surface variety. A booming economy convinced German trade union leaders that they could win high benefits for their members within a capitalist system. In elections to the *Reichstag* the Social Democrats went from strength to strength until in 1912 they were the biggest single party. This seemed to suggest that with time they might become so powerfully supported in the country as to force concessions from the regime; but behind the revolutionary slogans and despite provocative action by employers and the government, the Social Democrats gradually became part of the 'establishment'.

The change of climate was summed up in the writings of Eduard Bernstein, an influential German socialist, who put forward his revisionist Marxist theory. Bernstein argued that socialism would not arise from the breakdown of capitalism as Marx had predicted. Capitalism had learned how to adjust itself to major crises. As capitalism led to a wider distribution of wealth, social tensions would die down and society would move towards socialism as the most reasonable and ethical way of living. Bernstein became an arch-villan to orthodox Marxists, and 'revisionist' is still their deadliest term of abuse.

Although Bernstein's views were officially denounced, the Social Democrat Party moved steadily towards his position in

practice. With more tolerance on the part of the government they would have been more easily reconciled to peaceful change. As it was, Bismarck and his successors helped to keep the revolutionary wing of the party alive.

Bismarck's failure to suppress socialism or the Catholic Church showed that he was never at his best in pursuing negative policies. In foreign affairs his greatest triumphs had been the result of bold and aggressive action, notably the wars of the 1860s. His later attempts to ward off a French war of revenge by keeping France isolated were much more clumsy and in the end unsuccessful. Similarly, in Germany itself Bismarck's genius was displayed not in the *Kulturkampf* or the anti-socialist law but in his bold adoption of universal suffrage in 1867 and the welfare legislation of his later years.

Bismarck realized that the best antidote to the socialism he feared was for the state to provide enough welfare services to take the edge off the German workers' appetite for change. The old idea of the ruler being the father of his people and alleviating their sufferings was still as strong as the liberal idea of people providing for themselves by enterprise and initiative. Bismarck could, therefore, depend on support from the *junkers* for state welfare schemes.

He began in 1881 with a bill providing for accident insurance. The National Liberals opposed the legislation as being socialist and were deaf to arguments that welfare measures would divert the workers from wanting power to redistribute wealth themselves. Eventually Bismarck got his measures through: a bill providing for sickness insurance was passed in 1882, and his accident insurance bill went into effect in 1884. In 1889 he introduced an old-age insurance law.

Although Bismarck's welfare legislation was in the old paternalistic spirit, the measures proposed were in tune with the needs of an industrial age. It was a statesmanlike and imaginative programme, valuable in itself and a precursor of the twentieth century welfare state. Other nations copied

it or drew inspiration from it, and the British later followed the German example.

By introducing 'state socialism' after his anti-socialist law, Bismarck failed in his main purpose. The working class was not converted from socialism, and the continued persecution of the Social Democrats convinced them of the enmity of the old ruling class. Even though socialism survived as the favourite creed of the German industrial workers, it was less of an immediate threat to the regime. It would have been even less of a threat if Bismarck had simply stuck to his legislative programme for old age pensions and industrial insurance. His creative statesmanship paid off in the age of democracy and industrialism.

Restrained imperialism

Just as Bismarck had some success in his bid to satisfy German socialist yearnings, he also managed to satisfy nationalist urges by his adoption of imperialistic tactics overseas. Although he preserved the old regime in Germany by a popular and victorious foreign policy, after 1871 he could not afford to risk the empire's destruction by further adventures. He sensed that the moment of easy victories was over because Germany was now the strongest power in Europe – and, as the strongest, the most likely to arouse hostile coalitions. He therefore spent the next twenty years building up coalitions himself and trying without much success to persuade the rest of Europe that Germany had got all she wanted.

A new outlet for German nationalism was found in overseas expansion, as agitation grew for an active colonial policy. Books and pamphlets glorifying imperialism proliferated throughout Germany to satisfy the popular belief that an empire was something no great power should be without. Bismarck was not himself swayed by these arguments and was sceptical of the value of colonies; but the growing membership of colonial societies after 1882 showed that it was a popular cause. By supporting an imperialistic foreign policy Bismarck could perhaps rekindle the spirit of national unity shaken by his campaigns against the Catholics and Social Democrats.

In 1882 he promised protection to a German trader, Lüderitz, if he could acquire territory in southwest Africa not already claimed by another power. This was the first step in a dramatic imperialist campaign which brought Germany a sizeable African and Pacific empire in a few years.

Bismarck embarked on this with less careful preparation than he had devoted in the past to major international ventures. In 1884–85 he got involved in an unnecessary quarrel with Britain over German ambitions in southwest Africa by failing to make his policy clear; but he soon adjusted himself to this new and unfamiliar field of international politics. There was still plenty of room to expand in Africa and the Pacific without offending France, Italy or Russia; and the only power he risked quarrelling with was Britain, the least dangerous opponent for Germany. Between 1885 and

Above, drawing dating from about 1890 of the restaurant at the Berlin Zoological Garden, favourite dining-spot of Berlin's haute bourgeoisie.

Opposite, woodcut dating from 1890 entitled The Blessings of Old Age Pensions and Sickness Insurance: *Bismarck's social welfare legislation, pioneering measures in this field, was extended after his retirement, so that by 1914 German workers were better protected than those in any other country.*

1890 Bismarck established a satisfactory working relationship regarding imperial questions with Lord Salisbury, the British prime minister. He found his new overseas interests useful weapons in blackmailing the British to side with him in European affairs.

The acquisition of a German colonial empire was a popular move, and the spectacular exploits of explorers like Karl Peters excited the imagination and pride of the German public. Imperialism also resulted in increased influence in international relations, as the interests of the other powers shifted outside Europe. The colonies however proved of little economic value, and the Germans began to feel cheated and jealous of the other powers who seemed to have got more than their fair share of the spoils. This attitude was dangerous. Bismarck had been able to keep German nationalism from demanding more than Germany could safely try to get. His successors were less cautious.

Bismarck's successors abandoned his moderate imperialistic policies because the immense increase in German strength brought about by industrialization made moderation seem less necessary. That their neighbours – especially Russia – were eventually acquiring the same amount of power from industrialization also made a quick and drastic solution to Germany's strategic problems seem all the more necessary.

The lead which Germany had built up over countries like Russia, France and Austria-Hungary during the second half of the nineteenth century was remarkable enough strongly to influence her rulers. Her population grew rapidly from about 40,000,000 in 1870 to 66,000,000 in 1913. By the early 1880s there were roughly as many Germans engaged in industry as in agriculture and by 1907 there were nearly twice as many. German production of coal, iron and steel – key industries in the industrial revolution in the nineteenth century – leapt to quantities comparable with the output of Britain though well behind that of America. Alfred Krupp had already built up his steel works at Essen into one of the major establishments of its kind in the world. Germany became a major shipbuilding country more or less from scratch. In the newer electrical and chemical industries, whose power to speed up production and create new materials and goods was so great as to constitute something like a second industrial revolution, Germany was particularly advanced. The automobile industry was pioneered by men like Gottlieb Daimler, who patented his small high-speed internal combustion engine and in 1890 founded the Daimler motor car company. Germany had not merely caught up with the pioneer of industrialism, Britain, but she was in the van of progress towards the science-based industries of the twentieth century.

Prussia had played an important part in initiating Germany's industrial revolution. In the first half of the nineteenth century, the Prussian government created a customs union, the *Zollverein*, to remove the barriers to trade produced by so many German frontiers. In order to improve transportation between her widely scattered provinces, Prussia encouraged the establishment of a network of railways, which were eventually to be nationalized. The value of technical education was realized by Prussia early in the century, and this farsightedness was to pay rich dividends later on. After Prussia's acquisition of Schleswig-Holstein in 1866, the Kiel Canal was built linking the North Sea with the port of Kiel and the Baltic. Prussia's annexation of Alsace-Lorraine after the war with France in 1870–1 brought in important iron-ore deposits.

Once the state had overcome political resistance to economic growth, there was a ready response from private enterprise. Joint-stock companies blossomed in the middle of the century, and later on Germany, like America, became the scene of giant industrial undertakings. The big companies tended to cooperate more and more towards the end of the century, drawing together in associations known as 'cartels' to fix prices, share out the market and avoid over-production. The great German electrical combine AEG was an example of a successful cartel. As in America the banks were important to industrial growth, as they supplied credit to investors, helped to organize cartels, financed overseas projects and became involved in the running of industries by being represented on management boards. Capitalism flourished in the Prussian state, controlled as it was by a pre-industrial monarchy and aristocracy. By 1914 Prussian leadership had contributed much towards making the German empire, together with America and Britain, the three most industrialized and powerful nations in the world.

William II and Germany's world role

In 1890 Bismarck was forced to resign his chancellorship after a quarrel with the young Kaiser, William II. His successors as chancellor – Caprivi, Hohenlohe, Bulow and Bethmann-Hollweg – were men of lesser ability and easily manipulated by William II, who was intelligent and imaginative but impetuous and easily persuaded of the value of dramatic departures in policy. William II was to prove himself too much infected by nationalist fervour to be able to use it in the calculating and cautious manner of Bismarck.

As soon as Bismarck had resigned, William II's government began the blundering course which was to lead them to the disasters of the 1914 war. They refused to renew their alliance with Russia, and they signed the Heligoland treaty with Britain. The alliance with Russia had always been regarded by Bismarck as crucial to German security. He knew that France would always be an enemy as long as Germany controlled Alsace-Lorraine but that Germany could feel confident of defeating France if she were isolated from and unallied with Austria-Hungary or Russia.

To make sure there was no link between Vienna and Paris Bismarck had negotiated an alliance with Austria-Hungary in 1879 which was to last down to the First World War. An alliance between Paris and St Petersburg Bismarck knew could be even more dangerous. Although Russia was suspicious of Germany and frequently at odds with Austria-Hungary, Bismarck had succeeded with great difficulty in forming a Three Emperors' Alliance with Russia and Austria-Hungary between 1881 and 1887. When his two allies quarrelled over the Balkans, he made a separate Reinsurance treaty with Russia. It was this latter treaty which William II refused to renew in 1890.

William's motives were sound. Bismarck's policy was complicated and difficult to operate. It was not easy to remain friendly with two powers who disliked one another so decidedly as did Russia and Austria-Hungary. The only alternative was to ally with Britain. A combination of Germany, Austria-Hungary, Italy (who had joined the other two in 1882) and Britain might be enough to deter both France and Russia. Even though Bismarck had tried and failed to make an alliance with Great Britain, William II and his ministers went on believing they would succeed. They therefore followed their rebuff of Russia by making a major colonial agreement with Britain, allowing big concessions in Africa in return for the island of Heligoland, which the British had controlled since the Napoleonic Wars. The Heligoland Agreement was spectacular enough to convince Russia and France that Britain must have for all practical purposes joined the Triple Alliance. Russia began to move towards the fateful step of an alliance with France. France had emerged from isolation, and Bismarck's policy was in ruins.

William II's Germany never overcame the problem presented by the Franco-Russian Alliance which his policy had done so much to bring about. Although Britain's growing difficulties made her look at times with favour on an alliance with Germany, what she wanted more was an ally to help combat her chief colonial rivals, France and Russia. Germany could not risk a war on two fronts with France and Russia, knowing that British help in such a war could be of little value. Though there was no real basis for an alliance, William II maintained his belief that the British would eventually be forced into an agreement on Germany's terms.

Imperialist emotion was, moreover, continuing to grow in Germany in the 1890s, and William II was infected by it. The new generation in Germany thought in global terms like the British, the Americans and the Russians. Germany was becoming less worried by the prospect of what would happen in Europe and more concerned by the thought of being dwarfed by the great world empires. Thus there developed a feeling that Germany must assert herself on the world stage more boldly than in the Bismarck era. A few colonies were not enough – after 1898 the Kaiser's foreign policy was geared to the acquisition of 'spheres of influence' and an overseas empire.

Hence Germany enthusiastically engaged in the battle for concessions from China. In 1898 Admiral Alfred von Tirpitz set in motion his plans for a great fleet. German financing of the Baghdad railway project from Constantinople to the Persian Gulf was one of many signs of German influence in the Ottoman Empire. In 1905 Germany made clear her interest in the decaying state of Morocco.

Germany's world policy got her into far more difficulties than would have been involved in handling Austro-Russian relations in the Balkans. Tirpitz's naval programme alarmed Britain so much that she decided Germany was a greater threat than either France or Russia. The agreements reached between Britain and France in 1904 and between Russia and Britain in 1907 shifted the balance of power and made Germany's position in Europe more hazardous than ever before. German backing for Austria-Hungary in the Balkans and her growing influence in the Ottoman Empire worsened her relations with Russia. When the consequences of a world policy proved to be growing isolation, the Kaiser was strongly criticized. The Moroccan crisis of 1905–06 showed how isolated Germany was, and her reputation was further damaged by revolt against German rule in South West Africa. The Catholic Centre Party, which since the end of the *Kulturkampf* had supported the government in return for valuable concessions, now opposed the government and joined the left wing parties in refusing funds for the colonial war and demanding a reform of colonial administration.

In 1907 Chancellor von Bulow held a general election which was dominated by the question of Germany's world policy. Nationalist and imperialist societies worked hard on the electorate, and their arguments made a considerable impression. Von Bulow's claim that the government was being prevented from making Germany a world power by meddling from the opposition parties was sympathetically received. The Social Democrats, who had been attacked as 'anti-national', were shattered and lost half their seats in the *Reichstag*.

The appeal to nationalism had succeeded. The electorate was clearly responsive to the idea of Germany as a world power, and the Social Democrat advance had been checked. There was no doubt that nationalist and imperialist sentiment was strong in all sections of society. In the years that followed despite intensified industrial trouble the government maintained its ability to rally the nation with an expansionist foreign policy.

This was a dangerous consolation. Crisis succeeded crisis among the European countries, and Germany's leaders became ever more nervous and frustrated as the hostility

of France, Russia and Britain grew. Since Bismarck's time the influence of the army in politics had greatly increased. The army thought in terms of a future war which would finish Germany's enemies in Europe once and for all. Political leaders dreamed of a Europe after such a war in which the German frontiers would be extended so far as to make her secure against all possible enemies. Once secure in Europe, Germany could take her proper place on the world stage. In 1914 they succumbed to their dreams.

The Habsburg Empire after 1848

Both Germany and Russia ruled over other nationalities, notably the Poles, who were kept in subjection by discriminating tactics.

The presence of active political nationalists like the Poles was disturbing to governments bent on national unity. Bismarck tried to 'Germanize' the Polish provinces of the empire, and the tsars tried to 'Russify' their various non-Russian groups, from whom many of the leading revolutionaries were to come.

Neither Germany nor Russia, however, had to deal with nationalities as various as those comprising the Habsburg realm – Germans, Hungarians, Czechs, Poles, Croats, Italians, Ruthenians, Romanians, Slovaks, Serbs and Slovenes – no one national group outnumbering the others. Though the Habsburg dynasty was German in origin, and Germans were the predominant group in their empire, in terms of numbers the Germans amounted to less

than a quarter of the population. The next largest nationality were the Hungarians, who until 1848 gave most trouble to the Habsburg rulers. In 1848, however, when revolution engulfed most of the European states, the other nationalities showed themselves ambitious for greater freedom or even independence.

Although the Habsburg Empire nearly disintegrated as a result of the uprisings of 1848, it did not finally break up until 1918, towards the end of the First World War. In the seventy intervening years the emperor, Francis Joseph, who had succeeded to the throne in 1848, desperately tried to keep his empire together. He failed because he fought three wars and lost them all. If he and his ministers had been less obsessed with the problems of nationalist minorities, or more successful in solving them, they might have seen more clearly that economic backwardness was the secret of Habsburg weakness.

The empire survived in 1848–9 because the army was strong enough to crush the Czech and Italian rebels and to recapture Vienna and because the Russian army helped to defeat the Hungarians. Francis Joseph tried in the 1850s to follow up the victory over the rebellious nationalities by a system of direct rule from Vienna. German civil servants and German police were set to rule over the non-German nations, and national rights and privileges were swept away. The minister of the interior, Alexander Bach, was charged with the 'Germanization' of the empire, which became known as the Bach system.

It is possible that if the Habsburgs had been able to concentrate on maintaining this centralized absolutism for a generation or so national resistance might have died away. But the Habsburgs could not hope for enough time to make the Bach system work, and like the Prussians they were surrounded by enemies only too anxious to exploit their difficulties. Their only friend was the Russian tsar, who believed that monarchs must stand together against revolution, but they lost Russia's friendship by exploiting her difficulties during the Crimean War.

In 1859 war came with Piedmont and her ally, Napoleon III's France. The stake was Habsburg control of Italy, and defeat would mean that Habsburg control in the Italian peninsula would be confined to Venice. It would also mean that a united Italy could come into being – another probable enemy on the frontier. Austria's defeat, which was largely a result of the disaffection of the Magyars and Slavs, encouraged the Hungarians to resist the Bach system at a time when the Habsburg government was in no position to persist with it.

A state of emergency followed during which Francis Joseph was forced to consider the advisability of establishing a federal state system of rule, allowing each nationality within the empire the autonomy guaranteed by its historic constitutions. The 'October Diploma' which restored the old local diets was issued by Francis in October 1860, but its terms satisfied nobody, and another constitution was announced in February 1861 (the 'February Patent'). This returned to something like centralized government, but with a representative assembly in Vienna.

Although Austria had become a constitutional state, this was bound to be a temporary arrangement because of the Hungarians' hostile attitude. The prospect of a new war was looming up, this time with Prussia. Francis Joseph knew that to enter another war with the Hungarians ready to revolt would be like fighting with one hand tied behind his back. He opened negotiations with the most realistic and statesman-like of the Hungarian nobility, Francis Deák, but before a compromise could be reached war with Prussia broke out in the summer of 1866.

The Compromise of 1867

The first of Francis Joseph's wars, in 1859, had destroyed Habsburg power in Italy and forced him to realize that a compromise with the Hungarians was essential. The second disastrous war for the emperor was fought for the leadership of Germany and was quickly won by the Prussian armies, directed by Helmuth von Moltke. Considering the ease of the Prussian victory, Bismarck's terms were mild – Prussian domination of northern Germany and the transfer of Venice to Italy, which had been Prussia's ally in the war.

After the signing of the peace treaty, Francis Joseph resumed negotiations with the Hungarians, knowing that he was in no position to haggle with Deák over terms. The Compromise worked out between them provided for a unique political system whereby Hungary should have her own constitution but accept the Habsburg emperor as the King of Hungary. Although the Compromise was far less than many Hungarians demanded, it was far more than Francis Joseph would have consented to before the war with Prussia. The essential feature of the Compromise, which was formally accepted in 1867, was that it gave the Habsburg Empire three governments. The central government consisted of the emperor and three common ministers – for foreign affairs, the armed forces and finance. Austria's government was based on the February Patent, with the emperor as a constitutional monarch and a complicated system of representative assemblies in Vienna and in the provinces to be elected by an even more complicated voting procedure. The kingdom of Hungary was also a constitutional monarchy, with a two chamber parliament elected in such a way as to assure Hungarian predominance. County assemblies were to have nominal control over local

matters and were again to be Hungarian dominated. The emperor still had very considerable power in practice, though he would find it hard to have his way in Hungary without parliamentary support.

This 'dual monarchy' of Austria-Hungary survived until the end of the First World War. It made the Hungarians and the Germans the ruling nationalities within the empire at the expense of the Slavs, who in numbers made up nearly half the total population. Count Gyula Andrássy, who helped Deák negotiate the Compromise, is reported to have said to Francis Joseph: 'You look after your Slavs and we will look after ours.'

Although Andrássy's remark sounded sinister, both the Austrian and Hungarian governments at first approached the question of the other nationalities within their territories in a liberal enough fashion. Francis Joseph was above all concerned with the survival of his dynasty and had no special affection for the Germans in the Austrian half of the empire. They made up only a third of the population there, and the emperor was alarmed at the allegiance many of them showed towards the new German Empire to the north. He was inclined to support demands for special rights from the Poles and the Czechs especially, the most advanced of the Habsburg Slavs. From Budapest, Deák and his colleagues gave a measure of autonomy to the Croats, and introduced laws to enable the various nationalities to use their own languages as far as possible in their dealings with officials.

Within a few years the two parts of the empire diverged in their approach to the nationality question. In Austria, Francis Joseph continued to experiment with laws to avoid tension between the Germans and the Slavs. Czechs and Poles were prominent in Count Eduard Taaffe's ministry, which was in office from 1879 to 1893. One of Taaffe's successors as premier was Count Badeni, a Polish landowner. In 1907 universal suffrage was introduced in Austria. Although the Germans and Czechs still

Above, Europe between 1871 and 1914: during this time the boundaries of most states remained unchanged. The Congress of Berlin, 1878, readjusted the boundaries of the Balkan States, creating Bulgaria and confirming Serbian, Romanian and Montenegrin independence as well as making other changes. In 1908 Austria annexed Bosnia, and after the 1912–13 Balkan Wars Albania became independent and Greece and Serbia larger.

Top, Count Badeni (1846–1909), Prime Minister of Austria 1895–97: his recognition of Czech as an official language provoked intense resistance by German speakers and compelled the Emperor to dismiss him.

Top left, the Emperor Francis Joseph I (1830–1916, ruled 1848–1916) in 1890; his benevolent autocracy, perhaps still acceptable in the mid-nineteenth century, had become completely unacceptable fifty years later.

Opposite top, Vienna burning during the 1848 Revolution: still strong enough then to maintain its unity, the Empire went into a slow decline thereafter under the pressure of economic weakness and the increasingly vociferous demands of its subject races for independence.

Opposite bottom, the Emperor Francis Joseph and his court on the steps of Schönbrunn Palace, June 1857. Schloss Schönbrunn, Vienna

remained bitter enemies despite all attempts at compromise, the Habsburg dynasty remained remote from the squabbles and persisted in their efforts to reach a settlement.

In Hungary the moderates who had negotiated the Compromise were soon replaced by Kálmán Tisza's Liberal Party, which won the election of 1875 and stayed in power for the next fifteen years. Tisza, who was a powerful orator and a ruthless and able politician, used his gifts to consolidate the supremacy of the Magyars in their half of the empire. By means of education laws he tried to force the children of other nationalities to learn the Magyar language, and the government took steps to uproot other languages and cultures. Before long Magyar was made the official language of the government – to be used in railways, post offices and schools. This process of Magyarization was resisted by the Slavs and Romanians, but it stimulated demands among still more extreme nationalists for a complete break with Vienna. Francis Joseph countered these demands by backing the popular idea of universal suffrage. This would have swept away the Magyar nobility, who had kept power in their own hands.

The Yugoslav problem

The nationality question took a new and dangerous turn for the Habsburgs when states surrounding the empire began to cast acquisitive eyes on areas of the empire inhabited by their fellow nationals. Italy had never given up hope of bringing those Italians still under Habsburg rule into the kingdom of Italy. Romania, independent since 1878, wanted Transylvania where Romanians were subject to Hungarian rule. Most dangerous of all was Serbia who saw

herself as the Piedmont of the Balkans, and hoped to unite the South Slav people under the Serbian monarchy in much the same way as Piedmont had united Italy. As so many of the South Slavs lived in Austria-Hungary such a programme could only be accomplished at the expense of the Habsburgs. It was determination to stop Serbia fomenting revolution in her South Slav provinces that decided the Dual Monarchy to try to destroy Serbian power in the Balkans. The assassination in June 1914 of the heir to the Habsburg throne by a Serbian student gave her a pretext. After delivering an unacceptable ultimatum to the Serbian government and insisting that the government was behind the assassination at Sarajevo, the Austrians declared war on the Serbs on 28 July and thus precipitated the First World War. Francis Joseph's third war brought an end to the empire, whose various nationalities would found their own small independent states.

Such a drastic solution was probably unnecessary. Although there was serious discontent in Austria-Hungary, as in every other state, only a minority of extremists wanted to break up the empire. What most of the nationalists wanted was more privileges within the empire. Probably no solution satisfactory to all nationalities, Germans, Hungarians, Slavs and Romanians, could have been devised, but the empire could probably have staggered along until growing prosperity did its usual work of reconcilation.

What was fatal to the empire was the prolonged world war which its economy was too undeveloped to stand. Industrialization had been making impressive strides in Austria in the middle of the century, but the depression of the 1870s had shaken confidence, and the interests of the landowners generally got priority over those of the industrialists. There was also the fact that

Hungary was much poorer and much more decidedly an agricultural society. Steady progress had been resumed in the years before 1914. A sizeable working class had established itself (about twenty percent of the population), and there was a flourishing Social Democrat Party favourable to change within the empire. Welfare legislation similar to Germany's had been introduced. Within a generation Austria-Hungary might have become sufficiently industrialized to risk an aggressive foreign policy. But the persistent tensions of dealing with rival national groups seems to have worn down the patience and nerve of the empire's leaders. They gambled on war as they had done in 1859 and 1866.

Vienna

Despite its failure, an air of romance still clings to the Habsburg Empire. Although Francis Joseph was not a romantic figure, his beautiful wife, Elizabeth, who rebelled against the formalities of court life and was eventually murdered by an anarchist, had the makings of a tragic heroine. Their son, Rudolph, died with his mistress, Marie Vetsera, in mysterious circumstances in his hunting-lodge at Mayerling. However the most attractive thing about the empire was the flourishing artistic and intellectual life centred around Vienna, which since the middle of the eighteenth century had been the musical capital of the world. Gustav Mahler, Anton Bruckner, Richard Strauss, Arnold Schoenberg, Alban Berg, Johann Strauss and Franz Lehar are just a few of the composers who worked in Vienna during the latter part of the nineteenth century and the early twentieth. It was in Vienna that Sigmund Freud developed his revolutionary techniques of psychoanalysis during this same period.

There was unfortunately a darker side to Vienna. The worst manifestations of nationalism naturally occurred in an empire so divided. Demagogues whipped up nationalist emotion, more especially anti-semitic emotion. They were studied by one particularly apt pupil in the years before 1914 – Adolf Hitler was a subject of Francis Joseph and the formative years of his political education were spent in Vienna.

Revolution and repression in Spain

In 1808 the French emperor Napoleon I had invaded Spain and placed his brother Joseph on the throne. After the French army had been driven out by British troops commanded by the Duke of Wellington, the Spanish Bourbon dynasty was restored. In 1814 King Ferdinand VII returned to the throne.

Spain for the most part was a poor and backward country, whose peasant population were devoted to the old monarchy and the Catholic church. As Ferdinand VII intended to be an absolute monarch he could rely on the support of the church and the mass of the population. Unfortunately for him, an important minority of the Spanish people were bent on preventing a return to absolute monarchy. They included aristocratic landowners, army officers, manufacturers, municipal clerks, lawyers, journalists; and they had all been influenced by the ideas of the Enlightenment which had spread from France and Britain in the eighteenth century. When Ferdinand made clear his determination to crush the forces of liberalism, which had become prominent in the fight against Napoleon, he was faced with resistance from people whose position in society made them dangerous opponents.

Spain's colonies in South America were in revolt. An army to reconquer them was assembled at Cadiz. A group of young army officers exploited the reluctance of the troops to leave for service in America, and led a revolt against Ferdinand. Their principal leader was Rafael del Riego. In January 1820, Riego, an officer in the army encamped near Cadiz, proclaimed the constitution which a liberal assembly had drawn up in 1812 to be in effect. This constitution reduced the king to a cipher.

Riego's *pronunciamento* was the first of many revolts by politically minded army officers in nineteenth-century Spain.

Gradually Riego's attempt to stir up southern Spain spread to the north where liberals and their local armies began to proclaim the constitution of 1812. When riots broke out in Madrid, Ferdinand gave in and announced himself ready to accept the constitution. Because he was never sincere about the new government, Ferdinand was closely guarded by the rebels until 1823, when French troops invaded Spain as part of an international rescue

operation to restore Ferdinand's power. fearful of the spread of liberalism. The French troops were welcomed by peasants equally nervous of liberalism, and the revolution was crushed. Ferdinand had ignored the advice of his rescuers to concede a limited constitution and spent the last ten years of his reign in chronic bankruptcy, suppressing any further attempts at liberal reform.

Above, an incident in Barcelona during the 1835 uprising: though Isabella's claim to the throne was supported by the liberals, when once she became queen her reign was notably repressive. Museo de Historia de la Ciudad, Barcelona.

Opposite left, the Crown Prince Rudolf (1858–89) on his deathbed at Mayerling.

Opposite right, the Ringstrasse in Vienna, 1891.

The Carlist Wars

Before Ferdinand's death in 1833, he had firmly supported his wife's desire that their only child, Isabella, should succeed to the throne in preference to Don Carlos, Ferdinand's brother. This he agreed to even in the face of Salic Law which disputed the right of women to rule. Don Carlos and his supporters were prepared to fight for the throne. The queen, Maria Cristina turned to the liberals for help as the most fervent opponents of Don Carlos, who was a convinced absolutist. A protracted war was necessary to determine the issue.

In the civil war which raged between 1834 and 1839 the advantage lay with the liberals and the infant Isabella. The Carlists commanded a great deal of support in the poorer parts of the countryside, while the monarchy and the liberals had the resources of the big towns, which were prospering during this period because of the industrial development in Catalonia and other areas. Isabella's cause attracted the support of Great Britain and France, who were very conscious of being constitutional states in a continent dominated by absolute monarchies. Money, supplies and volunteers therefore were organized to ensure the triumph of liberalism in Spain. Britain and France formed an alliance with Spain and Portugal, which was experiencing similar troubles. Fighting in difficult country dragged on until 1839, but there was little doubt as to the outcome.

Carlism continued to find loyal adherents especially in the Basque region, but its inability to prosper even in the chaotic political conditions of nineteenth-century Spain showed how weak it really was. The rest of Isabella's reign down to 1868 was marked by instability and revolutions. In 1834, Maria Cristina had proclaimed a constitution as the price of liberal backing. The liberals were divided over the constitution – the Moderates, who were primarily aristocrats and the wealthy middle class, accepted it, while the Progressives, who represented the less well-to-do sections of the middle class in the towns, wanted a return to the more democratic constitution of 1812. Both groups of liberals looked for support to the army, which held the key to power in Spain. Liberalism in these years entailed the prevention of a return to absolute monarchy, experimentation with different constitutions and the encouragement of economic expansion.

For most of Isabella's reign, therefore, Spain was ruled by politically-minded generals acting in the name of either the Moderates or the Progressives. Between 1840 and 1843 the Progressive general Espartero was in power. He was overthrown in favour of the Moderate general Narváez, whose brand of liberalism was summed up in his alleged deathbed remark: 'I have no enemies, I have shot them all.' In 1854 an army revolt was accompanied by a popular rising from below which alarmed Moderates and Progressives alike. Another general, O'Donnell, emerged to try to unite the less extreme members of both parties, and his ascendancy lasted, on and off, until 1863. During these years foreign capital had enabled Spain to build a railway network and exploit the mineral wealth, which was her principal economic asset. The sale of church and common land helped to increase the number of prosperous peasant farmers. These economic developments, however, only complicated Spain's political life further by increasing the number of people whose lives had been disrupted by change but failing to increase the standard of living of the majority of Spanish people.

Republican interlude

The monarchy continued to play an active part in the petty politics, court intrigues and corruption which characterized Isabella's reign. Isabella herself became unpopular and like her mother found relief from the political tensions thrust upon her since infancy in a colourful love life. This scandalized Spanish society and caused discontent to be centred on the monarchy as much as the politicians and the generals. In 1868 navy and army leaders overthrew the dynasty, resulting in Isabella's exile to Paris. Then the leading revolutionaries, General

198

Francisco Serrano and General Juan Prim y Prats, hunted Europe for a democratically-minded king, which Prim declared was like looking for an atheist in heaven. After innocently sparking off the Franco-Prussian war by offering the throne to a relative of the King of Prussia, they found a suitable candidate in Italy. A son of the Italian king became Amadeo I of Spain.

Amadeo was well suited to the role of being a constitutional monarch in an orderly political system, but the chaos of Spanish politics placed him in an impossible position. To the left of the liberal parties the Democrats and the Republicans had emerged. O'Donnell's attempt to find a compromise between the Moderates and Progressives had produced a party of Liberal Unionists. The revolution which overthrew Isabella had been led by a coalition of Liberal Unionists, Progressives and Democrats whose ablest leader was Prim; but after his assassination the coalition broke up. Amadeo found himself shunned by the more conservative elements in Spanish politics, yet unable to unite the groups which had called him to the throne. After ruling for two years, he gave up the task as hopeless and abdicated in 1873.

Radical elements in the *cortes*, Spain's parliament, were strong enough to proclaim the First Spanish Republic, but this was to last less than two years. Its supporters were mainly interested in trying to make Spain into a federal state. Strong regional feelings, most notably in Catalonia and the Basque area, had always resisted centralization from Madrid. The geography of the country made communications difficult, and the uneven distribution of wealth among the various regions resulted in jealousy and rivalries. There was considerable support for federalism, though no agreement on what form it should take; but when federalism was endorsed by the *cortes*, the provinces set about running their own affairs without waiting for elections. A new Carlist revolt flared up. Chaos and violence forced republican leaders to abandon the idea of federalism and concentrate on restoring order. They were alarmed, too, at the propaganda of the First International, which took the opportunity to sow the seeds of revolutionary socialism in Spain. Spain's fourth president in less than a year, Emilio Castelar, abandoned federalism and assumed dictatorial powers to re-unify the country. Under him and his successor, Serrano, the republic swung steadily to the right.

Opinion in the country swung in favour of restoring the monarchy. Isabella's son, Alfonso, came of age in 1874 and succeeded to the throne at the end of the year.

The leading statesman of the restoration was Cánovas del Castillo, who did much to win acceptance for the idea that political life should be orderly. The constitution of 1876, which survived for nearly fifty years, provided for a limited monarchy in which ministers were responsible to the *cortes*.

Alfonso was not anxious to put the dynasty at risk again, and followed Cánovas' advice to use his powers sparingly and let parliamentary government work. Cánovas led the Liberal-Conservatives, a party formed from Moderates and Liberal Unionists. Práxedes Sagasta founded the Liberal Party out of the old Progressives. Cánovas aimed to make these two parties the governing parties of Spain in the way Conservatives and Liberals governed Britain. Since Spanish electoral conditions were less likely to produce the 'swing of the pendulum' which made British parties confident they would get their turn of office, Cánovas, Sagasta and Alfonso collaborated to give each of the two parties its turn. The feeling that neither would try to influence the king to exclude the other from power and that power would alternate between Liberal-Conservatives and Liberals made revolution and army support unnecessary. Spanish politics entered a period of order and stability. When Alfonso died in 1885, his widow acted as regent for their son until 1902. The succession passed smoothly to Alfonso XIII.

In the years after the restoration Spanish liberalism had some notable achievements in securing more religious freedom than Spain had ever known, trial by jury and universal suffrage. But in a predominantly peasant country this did not bring democracy. It only established the conditions within which local party bosses and priests had to work in their efforts to shape opinion. A growing number of people were demanding more freedom and by the end of the century anarchism and socialism were attracting considerable support from the Spaniards.

Anarchism flourished more in Spain than in any other European country. Ideas of peasant socialism brought to western Europe by the Russian revolutionary Bakunin took firm root among the poverty-stricken peasants of Andalusia in southern Spain. Anarcho-syndicalism spread from France to Barcelona and the other towns of Catalonia, where industrial workers looked to the general strike for salvation. The terrorist wing of the anarchists was active in Spain at this time as in other European states and gave the movement dramatic publicity with its bombs and assassinations. Cánovas was among the victims. Socialism grew more slowly than anarchism. A socialist party was founded in 1879 and was influenced by the rigidly orthodox French socialist, Jules Guesde. A socialist trade union was set up in 1882. Socialism was strong in the industrial areas of northern Spain, which were beginning to rival Catalonia in importance. Spain's first serious strikes occurred there in the 1890s.

Spain's vanishing empire

The successive Spanish governments were unable to divert public opinion by managing any spectacular manoeuvres abroad.

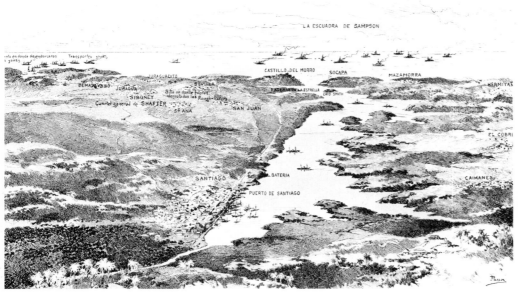

Spanish imperialism was persistent but largely unsuccessful. O'Donnell had won plaudits in the 1860s by a victory against Morocco, although it brought no concrete gain. Spain still hoped that she might regain something from her lost colonial empire in Latin America. She joined in an international debt collecting expedition to Mexico in 1861, but it led to nothing else. She got involved in a minor and inglorious war with Peru in 1864. An unexpected success came in 1861 when Santo Domingo asked to return to Spanish rule, but the inhabitants had regretted their move by 1865, and Spain withdrew in face of a revolution.

The only important colonies remaining to her after the achievement of independence by her Latin American colonies in the first quarter of the nineteenth century were Cuba, Puerto Rico and the Philippines. Although Cuba and Puerto Rico had remained loyal during the wars of independence, the Cubans became increasingly embittered by Spanish rule. A civil war broke out over liberal reforms in 1868, and the fighting continued for ten years. In 1895 a fresh revolutionary outbreak led to ruthless repression followed by offers of partial self-government which came too late. The continued strife was one of the causes of the Spanish American War.

That war which began in 1898 was a great blow to Spain, whose people still harboured delusions about their country's strength. With the loss of Cuba, Puerto Rico and the

Philippines, Spanish prestige was at its lowest ebb. National unity under the Bourbon dynasty became more difficult to visualize as regional discontent grew. Anarchist and socialist influence among the slowly expanding urban population increased. A general strike in Catalonia in 1909 was accompanied by the killing of Catholic clergy. Brutal repression and the execution of the anti-clerical writer, Francisco Ferrer, embittered feelings still further. On the eve of the 1914 war, Spain's weakness, backwardness and disunity were breaking through the orderly façade of constitutional government.

Portugal

Events in Portugal followed a remarkably similar pattern to those in Spain. The aftermath of the Napoleonic wars brought dispute over the kind of constitution which should be adopted. In 1826 the throne passed to an infant girl, Maria, and her uncle, Dom Miguel, played the same sort of role as Isabella's uncle, Don Carlos, in Spain. Maria was actually overthrown in 1828, and Miguel made himself absolute monarch. Like Don Carlos, he was defeated during the 1830s by Maria's supporters, aided by the British and French. Maria was restored and reigned until 1853.

Thereafter, similar developments to those in Spain occur only in a different order. A party system like that of Cánovas developed, the conservative Regenerators agreeing to alternate with the liberal Progressives. After Carlos I came to the throne in 1889, his extravagant and scandalous behaviour lowered the reputation of the monarchy. In the face of rising discontent, Carlos suppressed parliamentary government in 1906 and gave dictatorial powers to João Franco. Then in 1908 Carlos and his eldest son were assassinated, and his second son, Manuel II, reigned for only two years. A republican

movement which had been gathering strength since the 1880s received the support of the army in 1910. When a cruiser in the Tagus River shelled the royal palace at Lisbon, Manuel fled into exile.

A republic was proclaimed which offered no immediate remedy for the chronic insolvency and economic backwardness which had characterized Portugal, like Spain, in the nineteenth century. The idea of syndicalism began to be accepted by the small working class in the towns, and Lisbon experienced a general strike in 1912.

In one respect Portugal's history in this period diverged considerably from that of Spain: while Spain lost most of her overseas empire and made only minor gains in northwest Africa, Portugal greatly expanded her African possessions by developing Angola and Mozambique. She avoided a clash with Britain, comparable with the Spanish-American war when in 1890 she gave way to a British ultimatum designed to prevent her linking the two territories together. In Portugal's case imperialism was not enough to save the monarchy.

Italian Unification – the disappointed hopes

'Italy is made, all is safe', Cavour was reported to have said in 1861. Cavour's skill in exploiting events which his own state of Piedmont was too small to control had been largely responsible for the expulsion of Austria from the Italian peninsula and the creation of a united Italy. He had used Napoleon III's desire to revise the map of Europe in France's favour to secure an alliance with France against Austria. After the war of 1859, Austria controlled only Venetia. When Garibaldi and his thousand Redshirts seized southern Italy – to the surprise of everyone, including Cavour – it was Cavour who made sure that his own monarch, Victor Emmanuel of Piedmont,

was the beneficiary. The kingdom of Italy was proclaimed in 1861, Piedmont dominating the kingdom as surely as Prussia dominated the German Empire, which was established ten years later.

Italy had been united by a combination of spectacular warfare, tortuous diplomacy and nationalist propaganda of the more idealistic kind. The Italian unification was one of the most heroic and glamorous episodes of nineteenth-century history and gave Italy many admirers abroad, especially in Britain. The aftermath of unification disappointed Italian hopes, however, for within a generation Italy was being treated in patronizing fashion by the other European states.

It took only ten years to round off the work of unification. In 1861 only Venetia and Rome, held by Austria and the Pope respectively, remained outside Victor Emmanuel's kingdom. In 1866 Italy got control of Venetia, having allied herself with Prussia in the latter's duel with Austria. In 1870 Italian troops entered Rome and made it the capital of the new Italy. Nevertheless the way in which these gains were made was ominous. In the war of 1866 the Italian army and navy were defeated by the Austrians in contrast with the overwhelming victory of the Prussians. Venetia was won by Prussian not Italian arms, and Rome was occupied in 1870 only because the Pope's protector, Napoleon III, had had to withdraw his troops to meet the Prussian invasion of France. Again, Italy owed her success to Prussian arms.

Italy's role in international politics became more depressing as the years went by. Italians had no sense of greatness abroad to compensate for their even more depressing inability to solve the country's basic social and economic problems. The tragic contrast between the fairly prosperous north and the dismally poor south, and the widening gap between rich and poor, continued to provide distressing evidence of how little unification

had achieved. Italy had been made, but her future was far from safe.

The guerrilla leader, Garibaldi, and the revolutionary thinker and organizer, Giuseppe Mazzini, had wanted to involve the whole Italian people in the work of unification. But the Piedmontese politicians with whom the real power lay were not democrats. They were ultra-cautious liberals who believed it best to let Italy develop at her own pace within the framework of a constitutional monarchy and a national parliament.

Italian politics, therefore, were played between a small electorate and politicians who had very limited ideas of reform. Cavour, whose vision might have brought wider changes, died in 1861, and his colleagues of the more conservative kind dominated the political scene from 1861 to 1876. Quintino Sella was the ablest of them, and his skilful handling of the nation's finances by a scheme of rigorous taxation and the reduction of government expenditure balanced the budget. By 1876 results were beginning to show in the form of completed unification, increased revenue, a reformed army and navy, a virtually newly created merchant marine, railway building and the beginning of industrialization. But the cost to the Italian people was heavy. High taxation was not accompanied by any measures to alleviate the immediate hardships it produced. Voters became impatient of waiting for long-term results.

In 1876 the Right were defeated and replaced by the Leftist groups who brought no radical change into the government of the country. The first prime minister under the new Left regime was Agostino Depretis, who was in power from 1876 to 1887. He was a man of moderation and political skill, who extended the franchise by widening the age and tax qualifications; during his time in office some ineffective welfare legislation was also introduced. Otherwise the political groups known as the Left did little to justify their claims in opposition, and Depretis

Above, Pope Pius IX blessing the French troops of the Papal Guard withdrawn by Napoleon II for service against Prussia: now that the papacy was unprotected, Italian troops entered Rome and the Papal States declared in favour of union with Italy, completing national unification.

Above left, revolutionary troops at the Royal Palace during the 1910 revolution: Manuel II fled to London and a republic was formed under the presidency of Theofilo Braga.

Opposite top right, Maria II of Portugal (1819–53): periodically threatened with overthrow during her reign, Maria nevertheless maintained the good name of the monarchy and kept her country together, unlike Isabella in Spain.

Opposite top left, plan of the harbour of Santiago da Cuba in 1898: in the war that year against the USA Spain lost the last remains of her once great empire and faced national humiliation as a result.

Opposite bottom, the bodies of Catholic clergy killed during the so-called 'Tragic Week' in Barcelona, 1909, a popular uprising directed against conscription for the North African campaigns.

became best known for his success in influencing elections by various corrupt methods and for his skill in organizing coalitions in parliament to support his policies. The latter technique was known as 'transformism', because contending groups were transformed into government coalitions.

Parliamentary government therefore disappointed many Italians as being slow, dull and corrupt. But the politically conscious classes on whom both Right and Left relied for support wanted a middle course between the clericalism and reaction of the old Italy and the radical and socialist ideas which were emerging. A cautious liberalism was probably all Italy could hope for at this time. The political system was self-regulating in that the principal bar to the majority of Italians taking part in politics was the literacy test. As literacy spread with the needs of a developing economy, so more of the nation would participate. The high ideals and hopes which had inspired unification made most Italians expect too much too quickly.

Crispi and Italian imperialism

Between 1887 and 1896 the most important figure in Italian politics was Francesco Crispi. Crispi was more radical than most of his colleagues on the Left, and when he succeeded to the premiership this was expressed in reform of the legal system, the prisons, public health and in a strongly anti-clerical policy, which included the abolition of compulsory religious education. Relations between the Italian government and the pope, who had been confined to the Vatican since the annexation of Rome, became worse.

Crispi's period in office was most notable for his aggressive policy overseas. Ever since unification Italy had been regarded as a great power by most of the other European countries; but in fact Italy lacked the means to maintain her new status. There were few natural resources, and the lack of coal and iron were especially detrimental. The Italian coastline was so vulnerable that friendly relations with Britain, the principal naval power, were an essential aspect of her foreign policy. It soon became clear that Italy's chances of winning control of the Trentino, the Italian-speaking area still held by the Habsburgs, were slight. Since the upheavals of the years between the Crimean War and the unification of Germany, Europe had settled down to a period of stable frontiers. Italy would have to look elsewhere if her appetite for additional territory were gratified.

The obvious course was to expand into North Africa and increase her standing as a Mediterranean power. As a result of the French annexation of Tunis in 1881, on which Italy had fixed her eyes, she began to quarrel with France, and in the following year allied herself with Germany and her old enemy, Austria, to form the Triple Alliance.

Crispi stuck firmly to this alliance and to close relations with Britain, which he tried unsuccessfully to turn into an alliance. Using this combination as a shield against France, he set out to build an empire for Italy in Africa. What was left of North Africa was technically part of the Ottoman Empire, whose further dismemberment Italy's allies were anxious to prevent. Crispi marked out the Red Sea coast as the area for Italian expansion. In 1887 Italian activities led to war with Ethiopia, the most powerful of the African states, in which Italy fared badly. Crispi had agreed to back the contender for the Ethiopian throne, Menelek, and claimed he had agreed to make Ethiopia an Italian protectorate. When Italy tried to realize this claim, Menelek took up the challenge and the Italian army suffered a disastrous defeat at Adowa in 1896. Crispi was forced to recognize Ethiopian independence and to confine Italian ambitions to the coastal colony of Eretrea.

The disaster at Adowa ended Crispi's career, and Italy's basic military weakness thirty-five years after unification was exposed in humiliating fashion. Britain had, of course, suffered humiliating defeats in Africa and Asia, but Britain could afford them. Italy could not, or believed she could not.

Crispi's successors prepared the next colonial conquest more carefully. They aimed to get Tripoli, the Turkish province lying east of Tunisia on the African coast. After years of diplomatic soundings, the Italians finally declared war on Turkey in October 1911 confident that no other European power would intervene. Italy's victory over the Turks and her acquisition of Tripoli encouraged the forces of Italian nationalism, although the victory reflected Turkish weakness rather than Italian strength. For Italy imperialism had proved to be a more difficult way of raising morale at home and prestige abroad than it was for the more industrialized European nations.

Economic backwardness contributed to Italy's inglorious foreign and imperial policy, and conversely the excessive attention which the government paid to foreign affairs diverted their energies from the task of promoting economic progress. At the time of unification the mass of the Italian peasantry lived in a state of continual poverty and insecurity. Industry did not begin to make strides until the 1880s and even then developed in slow and troubled fashion. The railway network which was built after unification, had begun by then to open up a nationwide market. Significantly, an armaments industry was an early achievement.

As in Spain, both anarchism and socialism flourished in an essentially peasant society with small concentrations of industry. Anarchist ideas imported by the Russian revolutionary Bakunin had the same appeal to the peasants of Sicily as they had to those in Andalusia. Syndicalism was popular with Italian workers as with those of France as

Spain. Orthodox socialism was promoted initially by journalists and intellectuals, and a socialist party was founded in 1892 which, though it accepted a Marxist interpretation of Italy's development, was less clear about how it might revolt against the evils of capitalism.

Peasant uprisings in Sicily in the 1890s were savagely suppressed by Crispi, and laws against anarchist and socialist organizations introduced. In 1898 there was street fighting in Milan, and socialist leaders were severely punished for agitation. King Umberto of Italy was assassinated by an anarchist in 1900. In the early years of the twentieth century there were widespread strikes in the northern industrial towns. By 1914, when election returns showed the growing strength of socialism, Italy was again in the grip of strikes and riots.

Giolitti

These years of industrial and agrarian unrest was also the period when Italy was moving towards parliamentary democracy. In 1903 Giovanni Giolitti became prime minister and for more than a decade was to dominate Italian politics. He tried to bring about a mood of reconcilation and consensus in Italian political life. He made concessions to the Catholic Church, which had been bitterly opposed by the Liberals in the past; he introduced laws to improve working conditions and cut food taxes in a bid for socialist support. Socialists were invited to join the government. In 1912 he extended voting rights to something approaching manhood suffrage.

Italy was at last undergoing an industrial revolution, and in the long run this would have brought benefits to a large enough section of the working class to give them some faith in a system which was no longer inclined to use authoritarian methods against industrial unrest. But Giolitti's policy of conciliating all important sections of opinion also entailed the pacification of

strident nationalists, who were demanding the aggressive foreign policy Italy could not afford. They were granted the war with Turkey in 1911–12, but the cost of this resulted in increased taxation at home and further industrial trouble. Without a long period of peace Giolitti's policy for neutrality in the struggle between capital and labour had little chance of success. Parliamentary government had not worked sufficiently well to convince the majority of politically conscious Italians that it was unquestionably the best system. The only way to establish parliamentary government on a firm base was to associate it with prosperity at home. This took time and, with so much industrial strife, nerve. Italy's involvement in the First World War provided momentary relief from the wave of industrial and agricultural strikes, but it was eventually to create the inflammatory situation which heralded the rise of Fascism and the dictatorship of Mussolini.

The new Balkan states

The impact of industrialism on the relatively primitive and undeveloped states in the Balkans was even more disturbing than its effect on the highly organized agrarian nations of China and Japan, Spain and Italy, Russia and Austria-Hungary. After most of the Balkan nations had won their independence from the Ottoman Empire during the nineteenth century, they risked becoming dependent instead on the wealthy and powerful states of Europe. What

affected them most was not industrial development in their own countries, which remained very small, but the unavoidable influence of a foreign industrial civilization on their way of life.

The growing weakness of the Turks and the rise of nationalism among the Balkan Christians brought revolt and liberation: Greece became independent in 1830; Serbia, Montenegro and Romania were recognized as independent in 1878, (although they had effectively thrown off Turkish rule long before then); Bulgaria declared her independence in 1908, although in practice she too had been free for over twenty years. The Muslim Albanians freed themselves in 1912. Turkey had been driven almost entirely out of Europe.

The price of independence was high. The Balkans remained a turbulent area whose rulers saw territorial expansion as a prime duty. In order to militarize their new states, rulers had to get loans from the larger European countries, who frequently attached burdensome conditions to their agreements. Taxation was another source of revenue, but one which made for discontent. To pay their taxes the peasants had to raise enough money by producing for the European market or by borrowing at high rates of interest. The situation which resulted upset the age-old patterns of village life and added the complication of political instability. Success in foreign adventure became urgent

but very much dependent on the backing of an industrialized nation. All the new Balkan states found their independence limited by their need of the industrial world.

The Greek kingdom remained under foreign tutelage throughout the century. Her monarch was chosen according to the wishes of the great powers, who on three occasions prevented her from making war

and saved her from the consequences of defeat by Turkey in 1897. Her finances were subject to international control after this war had reduced her to bankruptcy. The economic backwardness which was responsible for Greek impotence was scarcely tackled by her political leaders, who conducted a dangerous foreign policy appropriate only to powerful and wealthy states.

Serbia, Montenegro, Romania and Bulgaria were rather more independent than Greece because they could play off Russia and Austria against one another. Between 1905 and 1907 Serbia successfully defied the attempt by Austria-Hungary to wage a tariff war against Serbia to induce her to return to Austrian control. The rivalry between the European powers encouraged the Balkan states to expand and thereby risk both their own survival and the peace of the rest of Europe. Thus the imperialistic designs of the powers in the Balkans pushed the small nationalistic states into imperialist projects of their own with disastrous results in 1914.

The Young Turks

In its struggle to survive during the nineteenth century the once-great Ottoman Empire had introduced a remarkable amount of reform based on western European examples, the high point of which

Date	Western and Central Europe	Russia and Asia	United States
1850			
	Great Exhibition in Britain (1851)	Taiping Rebellion	
	Second Empire in France (1852)		
	Bessemer steel (1856)	Crimean War (1853) Arrow War in China (1856) Indian Mutiny (1857)	
			First oil well drilled (1859)
1860	Kingdom of Italy (1861)	Emancipation of Russian serfs (1861)	Outbreak of Civil War (1861)
	British make first all iron warship (1861)		Gatling machine gun (1861)
	First International (1864	Polish rebellion (1863)	Emancipation Proclamation (1863)
	Whitehead's self-propelled torpedo (1864)		
	Siemens-Martin open-hearth steel (1866)		Lincoln assassinated (1865)
	Battle of Sadowa (1866)		Fourteenth Amendment (1866)
	England's Second Reform Act (1867)		Transatlantic cable laid (1866)
	Austro-Hungarian Compromise (1867)		Purchase of Alaska (1867)
	First volume of Marx's *Das Kapital* (1867)		British North America Act (1867)
	Nobel manufactures dynamite (1867)	Meiji restoration in Japan (1868)	
			First transcontinental railroad completed (1869)
1870	Dogma of papal infallibility		
	Establishment of German Empire (1871)		
	Paris Commune (1871)		
			Alabama settlement (1872)
	First Spanish Republic (1873)		
	Gotha congress of German Social Democrats (1875)		
	Constitution of Third French Republic (1875)		
	Restoration of monarchy in Spain (1875)		
		Midhat Pasha's Turkish constitution (1876)	Bell's telephone (1876)
		Russo-Turkish War (1877)	
	Congress of Berlin (1878)		
	Austro-German alliance (1879)		
1880		Assassination of Alexander II (1881)	
	Fabian Society (1883)		
	Gladstone's Franchise Act (1884)		
	Maxim gun (1884)		
	Daimler's petrol engine (1885)	Penjdeh crisis (1885)	Canadian Pacific Railway completed (1885)
	Benz's first motor car (1885)	Indian National Congress (1885)	American Federation of Labor (1886)
			First Pan-American Congress (1889)
	Second International (1889)	Japanese constitution (1889)	Brazil becomes a republic (1889)
1890	Bismarck dismissed		Sherman Anti-Trust Law
		Great famine in Russia (1891)	Populist Party (1892)
	Trial of Dreyfus (1894)	Franco-Russian alliance (1894)	
		Sino-Japanese War (1894)	
			Marconi invented wireless telegraph (1895)
			Venezuela boundary dispute (1895)
	Diesel's heavy oil engine manufactured (1897)		
	French quick-firing artillery (1898)	China leases territory to Powers (1898)	Spanish-American War (1898)
	Tirpitz's first naval law (1898)	China's Hundred Days of Reform (1898)	
		Russian Social Democrat party formed (1898)	
	Bernstein's revision of Marxism (1899)		
1900	First Zeppelin launched Labour Representation Committee	Boxer uprising	
		Commonwealth of Australia (1901)	Theodore Roosevelt president (1901)
		Russian Socialist Revolutionary party formed (1901)	
		Japan allies with Britain (1902)	
	Serbian revolution (1903)		Wright brothers' flight (1903)
			Panama independent (1903)
	Franco-British Entente (1904)	Russo-Japanese War (1904)	
	Separation of Norway from Sweden (1905)	Bloody Sunday and the October Manifesto (1905)	
	Separation of church and state in France (1905)		
	British launch *Dreadnought* (1906)		
		Russo-British Entente over Asia (1907)	
	Annexation of Bosnia-Herzegovina (1908)	Young Turk revolution (1908)	
	Lloyd George's People's Budget (1909)		Ford's Model T car begins mass production (1909)
1910	Portugal a republic		
		Assassination of Stolypin (1911)	
		Chinese revolution (1911)	
	First Balkan War (1912)		Woodrow Wilson elected president (1912)
		Coup in Turkey by Enver Pasha (1913)	Federal Reserve Bank Act (1913)
	Assassination of Francis Ferdinand. Outbreak of First World War (1914)		Opening of Panama Canal (1914)

was the proclamation of a constitution in 1876 by the Turkish statesman, Midhat Pasha. The adequacy of the reforms to enable the empire to cope with its problems was doubtful, but the movement was abruptly ended by Sultan Abdul Hamid. The Ottoman Empire reverted to a further period of stagnation and tyranny.

In 1908 a revolutionary organization, the Young Turks, which had strong support in the sultan's army, made its bid for power. The sultan hastily revived Midhat's constitution to save his throne, but his endorsement of a counter-revolution in 1909 led to his disposition and replacement by a puppet sultan. The reformers were at odds over the future form of the empire. After military disaster at the hands of Italy in 1911 and the Balkan states in 1912, power was seized by the extreme nationalists among the Young Turks. Although their movement was to end in a brutal dictatorship, they initiated many valuable reforms in education and municipal government in the meantime and pointed the way to Turkey's westernization by Kemal Ataturk after the First World War. Like her former Balkan subjects Turkey developed in response to the challenge of the industrialized nations of Europe.

By 1914 this challenge was being faced in every part of the world. It had been taken up vigorously and successfully by America and Germany and later by Japan and Russia. With Britain and France they formed a new aristocracy among the nations. Elsewhere the response was slow and uncertain. In Austria-Hungary, Italy, Spain and Portugal political and social conditions were not conducive to rapid change, and the gap widened between them and the leading powers. Far less enviable was the position of countries like China, Turkey and the Balkan states as they struggled to avoid becoming the victims of a new and potent kind of imperialism. The great industrial states were often reckless and irresponsible in using the wealth and power they had created. In 1914 they turned their strength against one another.

Opposite top, Midhat Pasha proclaims the constitution at Constantinople, 1876, the culmination of a series of administrative reforms over the previous two decades. The constitution failed to survive the succession of the Sultan Abdul Hamid II.

Opposite bottom, delegates from the Young Turks and the Balkan Committee are received personally by the Sultan Abdul Hamid, who restored the constitution in Turkey on 24 July 1908.

Part IV

THE FIRST WORLD WAR: CAUSES AND CONSEQUENCES

Introduction

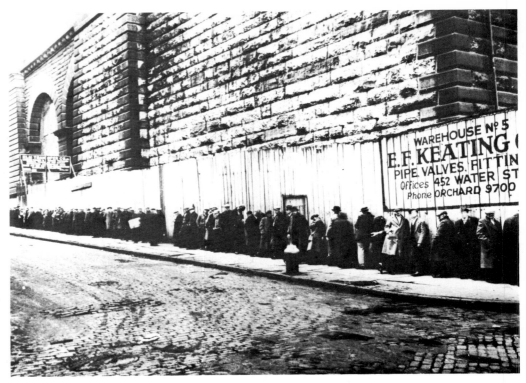

The Great War of 1914–18 still appears as a cataclysmic event, even though well over half a century has elapsed since it ended. The great powers of Europe had avoided war with one another for some forty-three years. In August 1914 they seemed to stumble into it unintentionally. Everyone thought that the battle would be short and that they would be 'home in time for Christmas'. In fact the war was to last for four years and people were driven by events to abandon their optimistic and consoling misapprehensions. Instead they persuaded themselves, with equal fallaciousness, that they were engaged in the last general conflict, a 'war to end wars'. Certainly no government expected, or was adequately prepared for, the extravagant sort of warfare in which it found itself embroiled.

Naturally enough, the causes of this surprising and unwanted war have, ever since, been a matter of controversy among both politicians and historians. Even today, the relative importance of the different policies, conflicting interests, circumstances and personalities which contributed to its outbreak remains in dispute.

The most intractable conflict of all was the Balkan rivalry between Russia and Austria-Hungary. Britain, France, Italy and even Germany had repeatedly shown that over colonial disputes they were all, in the end, prepared to seek a settlement without war. The French desire for revenge against Germany for 1871, and for recovery of Alsace and Lorraine, had never quite died, but it had died down. But the clash between the two ancient dynastic empires of Russia and Austria-Hungary seemed to be beyond compromise. Linked as it was with rival hot-headed nationalist movements in the Balkans on the one hand and through the system of great alliances with the fears and tensions of Europe on the other, here was the flash-point of the explosion.

The Great War (as it was called throughout the 1920s and 1930s) began, then, as a civil war in Europe. Only in 1917 did it become more genuinely a world war. But for various reasons the conflict was, from quite an early stage, worldwide in its repercussions and its future consequences. This came about because of the vast colonial empires of the major European powers,

which collectively dominated world trade, and not least because the war released the momentous new world force of the Bolshevik Revolution in Russia. The new idealism which crept into allied statements of peace-aims, notably through President Woodrow Wilson's 'Fourteen Points', roused the hopes of disunited nationalities. The victory of the western maritime powers of Britain, France, the United States, Belgium and the Commonwealth proclaimed a new world made 'safe for democracy'.

What most wrecked these hopes, highest at the moment of the Paris peace conference of 1919, were the uncontrollable effects of the war on the pre-war world economy. It was not simply that vast wealth and millions of lives had been destroyed or that individual countries, notably Great Britain, had now lost their lucrative overseas investments and become debtor-nations. What mattered most in a material sense was that the pre-war economy, the fabric of international trade and investment, was hopelessly disrupted and dislocated. With the central market of Germany temporarily gone, the Russian market closed, industrial production everywhere distorted by wartime needs. Europe needed more drastic and deliberate reconstruction than was possible in the desperate conditions of the immediate post-war years. Politics, as Maynard Keynes pointed out, seemed destined to frustrate economic recovery at every point. It created a host of new states whose frontiers often made little economic sense, it exaggerated attempts to exact monetary reparations from Germany, it insisted on the repayment of war debts, and it sought too hasty a return to 'normalcy'.

Economics, as it were, had its reprisals on politics. The resulting unemployment

of the inter-war years, the slumps induced by the shrinkage of international trade, the revulsions of inflamed nationalism, especially important in Italy and in Germany, ruined hopes of democracy's survival in the worst-hit countries. Militant, ruthless authoritarian movements arose during the 1920s and were quick to learn from the successful Bolsheviks the potency of a single-party state monopolizing all the resources of modern terror, propaganda and state power. The dictatorships of Mussolini in Italy and of Hitler in Germany were, in a real sense, consequences of the Great War.

Indeed, fascism was perhaps the chief beneficiary of the war, for it could hardly have gained power and flourished so much without the war's aftermath. But another beneficiary was communism, and not only because the collapse in war of both the tsarist regime and the liberal provisional government which succeeded it in 1917 opened the door to Lenin's Bolshevik Party.

Communist agents and propagandists exploited fully the conditions of unrest and distress which prevailed after the war. They saw in them the best guarantee of a world proletarian revolution. It took nearly two decades to prove that the fears their methods aroused did far more to help fascism than to promote communism. Repeatedly, communist agitation was the perfect excuse for fascist coups, and weak parliamentary democracies did not give place to proletarian dictatorship, only to fascist dictatorship.

Economic crisis, then, gave rise to political crisis, and to revolution, during the inter-war years: and political crisis gave rise to international crisis and eventually to a second world war. The new League of Nations was gravely weakened from birth

by the exclusion of Soviet Russia and Germany and by the abstention of the United States, its chief sponsor. We cannot but speculate whether it might have succeeded more but for the mounting challenges of Italy, Japan and Germany. Perhaps it could have achieved fuller international cooperation in social and economic affairs, but still without succeeding in its ultimate purpose of preventing war. But once aggressive military movements were in complete power in Japan, Italy and Germany and these three powers even drew together in common cause under the misleading title of the 'Anti-Comintern Pact', a major war was probably inevitable. The collapse of the League of Nations as a peace-keeping organization and the inertia of its major props in Europe, Britain and France increased the probability.

In these ways, there are certain links of cause and effect between the two world wars. It would be oversimplifying to see them entirely, as Winston Churchill once suggested, as parts of one 'Thirty Years' War' or as one great German challenge to the rest of Europe. The strongest evidence to the contrary is the role in contemporary history of China and Japan. Both during and after the Great War, Japan progressively rose to a position of supremacy in Asia. It was above all, as the author shows, China's chronic division and weakness that made this possible.

The shifting balance of power in the Far East is as much a part of world history, helping to explain the drift of events during the inter-war years, as is the rise of fascist dictatorships in Europe. It has even been suggested, with some reason, that the Second World War should be seen as having begun not in 1939, parochially, with a German attack on Poland but in 1937, when Japan embarked on full-scale war against a disintegrating China. In the same sense, China's communist revolution is probably the most important single event amid the complex aftermath of the Second World War.

Since 1945 the serious study of so-called 'contemporary history' (i.e. twentieth-century history) has become both fashionable and respectable. Much harm was done by the ignorance and the myths about the peace settlement of 1919 and the Allied treatment of Germany in the 1920s, and it is entirely to the good that research and better perspective have now made possible more objective accounts of those years.

There is little doubt that, just as the causes of the First must be looked for in the whole sequence of events from at least 1871 onwards and in the unique situation which they had produced by 1914, so historians will trace the origins of the Second back to the events here chronicled. History never divides sharply into separate phases, and it is wise to recall how small a part conscious human intention plays in determining the outcome of great events. Nobody went to war in 1914 to precipitate a communist revolution in Russia, or to set up a League of Nations, or to provide a home for the Jews in Palestine, yet these were among its most important consequences. The moral to be drawn from this period is, perhaps, that modern warfare is not only an exceptionally extravagant mode of action but also a most unreliable and uncontrollable means of achieving one's aims.

Chapter 14

The Approach to War

For most of its history, the continent of Europe has been more often at war than at peace. Viewed against this background, the four years of war which followed August 1914 were less remarkable than the forty-three years of peace between the great powers of Europe which had preceded them. What was most surprising about the great age of European imperialism in the later nineteenth century was not the national rivalries which it inevitably produced but the success with which these rivalries were contained. For centuries past, wars had been fought in Europe to decide the ownership of a few hundred square miles of territory. During the thirty years after 1871, the great powers of Europe divided between them more than ten million square miles of the earth's surface without once coming to blows among themselves.

Within Europe itself, the most serious and persistent source of tension during the half century before the First World War was the Balkan rivalry between Russia and Austria-Hungary. This rivalry was an inevitable consequence both of the geographic position of these two powers and of the progressive disintegration of the Turkish Empire in the Balkans. What was remarkable was not that this rivalry gave rise to a series of international crises but that these crises were so often settled without recourse to war.

The long period of peace between the great powers of Europe was partly produced by the even distribution of power between them during the later nineteenth century: a balance eventually disturbed by the enormous growth of German strength. But it was a consequence also of the fact that the great powers had learned a self-restraint unthinkable only a century before; Europe, in short, had become more civilized. By 1909 a generation had grown up which, for the first time in European history, thought of warfare as a thing of the past. Even when Europe finally went to war, many believed that they were doing so for the last time, that they were fighting a war to end all wars.

The alliance system

There had been no war between major European powers since 1871. The Franco-Prussian War, concluded in that year, had been one of the turning-points in the history of nineteenth-century Europe. It had ended two centuries of French supremacy on the continent of Europe and, at the same time, had enabled Bismarck to complete the unification of Germany under Prussian leadership. The war changed Bismarck himself from poacher to gamekeeper. For a decade he had used war ruthlessly for the aggrandizement of Prussia. But in 1871 he suddenly discovered a new role as the chief defender of the peace of Europe. The new state of Germany, Bismarck believed, was 'a satiated power' with no further territorial ambitions. France, on the other hand, robbed by Germany of Alsace-Lorraine, would 'regard revenge as its principal mission'.

The main object of Bismarck's diplomacy, therefore, was to preserve the position Germany had won and guard against the danger of a French war of revenge. He relied at first on an informal understanding between the three great continental monarchies – Germany, Russia and Austria-Hungary – to keep the French Republic in its place. That understanding, however, broke down in 1878 because of Austro-Russian rivalry in the Balkans. From 1879 onwards, Bismarck began to replace the informal understanding of the 1870s by a series of formal (and sometimes overlapping) alliances – with Austria from 1879, with Russia from 1881, with Italy from 1882 – all concluded with the same aim of keeping France isolated, and therefore powerless.

Great Britain became increasingly convinced during the later nineteenth century that its 'splendid isolation' from European alliances was a tribute to its strength. France, on the contrary, never regarded its own isolation during the twenty years after the Franco-Prussian War as less than ignominous. The first chance for France to escape from this isolation came soon after Bismarck's fall from power in 1890. With Bismarck safely out of the way, Kaiser William II rashly decided to allow the alliance with Russia to lapse. Hitherto, though Russia had sometimes tried to frighten Bismarck by threatening to ally with France, it had never seriously intended to carry out its threat. The Russian court, in particular, had an almost physical horror of the French Republic which it regarded as an inherently subversive institution. The future Tsar Nicholas II, the last of the Romanov dynasty, declared in 1887: 'May God preserve us from alliance with France. . . . It would mean the invasion of Russia by revolution.'

Russia's diplomatic estrangement from Germany in 1890, however, was accompanied by a growing financial dependence on France. Russia in the late nineteenth century was at one and the same time an underdeveloped country and a great military power, increasingly conscious that its future as a great power depended upon the modernization of the Russian economy. This, in turn, required massive foreign investment, investment which was available only from France. It was, above all, its dependence on French investment which persuaded the Russian government to conclude, by stages, an alliance with France which was finally ratified in 1894.

By 1894, therefore, the four great powers of continental Europe were already grouped in two rival alliances. Germany, Austria-Hungary and Italy were joined together in the Triple Alliance (though Italy was neither a great power nor, by 1902, an effective member of the Triple Alliance). France and Russia were united in the Dual Alliance. The making of these two alliances was later blamed by many as the root cause of the First World War. It was, said Jagow, the German foreign minister, in his final meeting with the British ambassador in August 1914, 'this damned system of alliances' which had dragged Europe into war.

At the beginning of the twentieth century, however, there still seemed no real likelihood of war between the Dual and Triple Alliances. The two major rivalries which divided these alliances – France's desire for revenge against Germany, Austria's rivalry with Russia in the Balkans – had both receded into the background. No French statesman of any consequence still dreamed of a war of revenge against Germany. Austria and Russia both seemed determined to abide by the agreement which they had made in 1897 to put the Balkans 'on ice'. To most European statesmen at the beginning of the twentieth century, the only serious threat of European conflict seemed to lie in the imperial rivalries between Britain and her future allies in the First World War, France and Russia. And within a few years these rivalries, too, were to have been resolved without war.

German *Weltpolitik*

The growth of tension between the two alliances which first became apparent during the first Moroccan crisis of 1905–6 was the result, not of the nature of the alliances themselves, but of the new course of German foreign policy, German *Weltpolitik*. *Weltpolitik* ('world policy') arose in part from Germany's consciousness of its own enormous strength. At the time of the Franco-Prussian War, Germany had been only marginally superior to France in the size of its population and economic production. For the remainder of the nineteenth century, however, Germany's birth rate was the highest in Europe while France's was the lowest, and the German economy expanded at almost twice the rate of the French.

At the end of the century Germany towered, both militarily and economically, over every other state in the continent of Europe. *Weltpolitik* was partly an expression of this strength. In part also, it was simply one expression of the imperialist mood common to other European powers.

Imperialism, in both France and Britain, became a popular movement only in the closing years of the nineteenth century, after the French and British Empires were virtually complete. World policy emerged in Germany at almost exactly the same moment. Its first acts were the seizure of the Chinese port of Kiaochow in 1897, and the decision by the German parliament, the *Reichstag*, a year later to build a new German battle fleet.

Weltpolitik reversed the assumptions on which Bismarck's foreign policy had been based. Germany was no longer 'a satiated power', content with its position in Europe. It aspired, instead, to become a world power, with world ambitions. 'The German Empire', declared the Kaiser optimistically, 'has become a world empire'. By the time that Germany began to demand a place in the sun, however, almost all the available places had been taken. Had the nineteenth-century scramble for Africa been followed, as many European statesmen expected, by a twentieth-century scramble for China, Germany might still have been able to satisfy its imperial ambitions. But it was not to be.

Largely because of the lack of outlets for its imperial ambitions, *Weltpolitik* assumed a peculiarly restless character, undecided on which area of the world to focus its ambitions. Even the purpose of the new German navy was never made quite clear. Bethmann-Hollweg, Germany's chancellor on the outbreak of war, said vaguely that Germany needed the new navy 'for the general purposes of German greatness'. The Kaiser was almost equally vague. He told the King of Italy: 'All the years of my reign my colleagues, the monarchs of Europe, have paid little attention to what I have to say. Soon, with my great navy to endorse my words, they will be more respectful.'

The fact that the ambitions of *Weltpolitik* were so ill-defined only increased the extent to which Britain, France and Russia all came to feel threatened by them. Each power interpreted these ambitions with a different emphasis. Britain came to look on *Weltpolitik* primarily as a threat to British naval supremacy, Russia as a challenge to Russian influence in the Near East, France as a threat to the French position in the Mediterranean.

It was partly because of the lack of overseas outlets for German imperialism that, during the early years of the twentieth century, the ambitions of *Weltpolitik* turned increasingly towards the European continent. Among some sections of German opinion there was growing interest in the idea of a German *Mitteleuropa*, a new order in central Europe embracing not merely Germany and Austria-Hungary but also large areas of the Balkans and eastern Europe and even parts of Belgium. Though this idea became the official policy of the German government only after the outbreak of war in 1914, *Mitteleuropa* was the logical outcome of these vaguer ambitions formulated before the war.

The most curious characteristic of Germany's foreign policy during the decade before the First World War was the degree to which it combined an often arrogant assertion of German strength with a chronic feeling of insecurity. To a considerable degree this insecurity was a product of its ambitions: a fear that Germany's neighbours were jealous of its growing strength and might conspire to deny it the world power status which was its by right. Germany's insecurity showed itself, for example, in a fear that England might attempt the destruction of the new German fleet before it had grown large enough to challenge the supremacy of the Royal Navy. This fear, though greatly exaggerated, was not entirely without foundation. Sir John Fisher, the volatile First Lord of the Admiralty, suggested just such a scheme to Edward VII in 1904. The king was horrified. 'Good God, Fisher,' he replied, 'you must be mad.'

Insecurity was a consequence also of Germany's geographic position in the heart of Europe which forced it, unlike its two main continental rivals, France and Russia, to face the possibility of war on two fronts. Bismarck himself confessed that he suffered throughout his career from 'a nightmare fear of coalitions'. Time and time again in the years before the First World War, German statesmen showed that they could feel secure only in a world in which Germany's neighbours were at odds with one another. Much of the confidence felt by the Kaiser and his ministers at the turn of the twentieth century derived from the deep hostility (which Germany was at pains to encourage) between both England and France and England and Russia. It was the violent German reaction to the relaxation of this hostility with the signing of the Entente Cordiale in 1904 which began the decade of tension in European affairs which was to culminate in the First World War.

Above, the ceremonial start to construction work on the Baghdad Railway, 1903: financed and built by Germany, the railway, which ran from Constantinople to Baghdad and was not completed until 1918, was viewed with anxiety in London and Paris as yet another attempt by Germany to extend her political and economic power.

The Entente Cordiale

The Entente Cordiale has come to seem a much more romantic agreement than it appeared to be to the statesmen who concluded it. President Auriol of France claimed, on its fiftieth anniversary, that 'the convention of 8 April 1904 embodied the agreement of our two peoples on the necessity of safeguarding the spiritual values of which we were the common trustees.' The interpretation given on the same occasion by the British foreign secretary, Sir Anthony Eden, was less romantic but more accurate. He told the House of Commons:

At the time when it was concluded the Entente Cordiale did not represent some great surge of public opinion on either side of the Channel. It was in fact an instrument of political policy at the time, calculated to attempt to remove the differences which had long complicated Anglo-French relations in Egypt and Morocco.

The solution to these differences was a somewhat unscrupulous arrangment, characteristic of the diplomacy of imperialism. England and France signed a public undertaking to respect the integrity of both Egypt and Morocco. Secretly, they simply agreed to take them over: Egypt was to go to Britain, Morocco to France.

In itself, the Entente Cordiale did nothing to make war between the two European alliances more likely than before. Nor did it give any indication that England was any readier than before to take part in a continental war. What made the Entente Cordiale a major turning-point in international relations was, quite simply, the German reaction to it. The sight of Germany's neighbours settling differences which the German Foreign Office had assumed to be permanent immediately revived in German statesmen their nightmare fear of hostile coalitions. Once the agreement was signed, Germany was determined to demonstrate publicly that it was worthless. Its attempt to do so provoked the first Moroccan crisis, the first in the series of European crises which characterized the decade before the outbreak of war in 1914.

The German government calculated that if it were to provoke a crisis with France over Morocco, Russia would be unable (because of its involvement in a war with Japan) and Britain unwilling to offer France effective support. At one stroke, therefore, Germany would demonstrate the ineffectiveness of both the Dual Alliance and the Entente Cordiale. Germany might then be able to draw France into dependence on it and transform the European balance of power dramatically in its favour.

The Moroccan crisis began with the Kaiser's visit to Tangier in the spring of 1905. At Tangier he declared that Germany regarded the sultan as the ruler of a free and independent state: a clear warning that

Germany would not be prepared to tolerate a French protectorate. The significance of his visit was summed up by the Moroccan grand vizier in a particularly picturesque metaphor. 'Whilst in the act of ravishing Morocco,' he declared, 'France has received a tremendous kick in the behind from the Emperor William.'

Supported by Germany, the sultan now demanded an international conference to discuss Moroccan affairs. Simultaneously, Germany began a war of nerves directed against France. Rouvier, the weak and inexperienced French prime minister, soon had visions of a second Franco-Prussian War, followed by a second Paris Commune. By the summer of 1905, his nerve had given way. As a peace-offering to Germany he forced the resignation of his foreign minister, Delcassé, the French architect of the Entente Cordiale. Germany's failure at this time to exploit the spectacular success of its war of nerves was one of the greatest missed opportunities in the entire history of German diplomacy.

For the first time since the Franco-Prussian War, a French prime minister appeared ready and even anxious to cooperate with Germany. Rouvier offered Germany compensation in the Congo for French supremacy in Morocco, as well as cooperation in a variety of other fields. Had Germany accepted these terms, France might well have been drawn into a policy of continuing cooperation with Germany, so shifting the balance of power decisively in Germany's favour.

The German government, however, found itself trapped by its own propaganda. Having publicly demanded an international conference and having posed as the defender

of Moroccan independence, it felt unable to back down and reach an agreement with France. By its inflexibility Germany alienated those Frenchmen most anxious for agreement with it. Even Rouvier gradually recovered his spirits. In November he told one of his advisers: 'If Berlin thinks it can intimidate me, it has made a mistake. Henceforth I shall make no further concessions, come what may.'

The German war of nerves against France strengthened the suspicions aroused in Britain by the building of the new German fleet. At the beginning of the crisis the British government denounced the attitude of Germany as 'most unreasonable' and offered France 'all the support in its power'. Sir John Fisher begged the Foreign Office to go further and 'send a telegram to Paris that the English and French fleets are one'. At the end of 1905 British and French service chiefs began secret talks about cooperation in a war with Germany. By its own policy, therefore, the German government had transformed the character of the Entente Cordiale. What had begun as a settlement of colonial differences had now become a defensive coalition against Germany, regarded by both Britain and France as essential to their own security.

The new significance of the Entente Cordiale was apparent as soon as the international conference on Morocco met at Algeciras in January 1906. Throughout the conference France depended on British support. Grey, the British foreign secretary, dared not refuse that support for fear of damaging the Entente Cordiale. Even when he thought the French unreasonable and believed they should make concessions towards Germany, he still maintained that

Above, 'Are You Sitting Comfortably?' was the caption to this Punch *cartoon of March 1906 mocking German ambitions at the Algeciras Conference which settled the Moroccan crisis.*

Above left, Kaiser William II (1859–1941, ruled 1888–1918) and his escort in the streets of Tangier, 1905: Germany's attempt (unsuccessful as it turned out) to assert herself in Morocco strengthened the Anglo-French resolve to resist and brought alliance with Russia closer.

Opposite, French vessels welcome the British squadron at a naval review at Brest, 1905. The Anglo-French Entente concluded the previous year brought long-standing differences between Britain and France to a conclusion and signalled reviving British interest in European power politics.

'we can't press our advice on them to the point of breaking up the Entente.'

The conference itself ended in a major defeat for German diplomacy. Germany had been convinced that France would find itself almost isolated at Algeciras and that neither Britain nor Russia would offer it effective support. In the event it was Germany which was almost isolated, supported only by Austria-Hungary and Morocco.

The first Moroccan crisis convinced Grey of the wisdom of turning the Entente with France into a Triple Entente with both France and Russia. He wrote during the Algeciras conference: 'An Entente between Russia, France, and ourselves would be absolutely secure. If it were necessary to check Germany it could then be done.' As soon as the conference was over, he began the negotiations, which led eventually to the Anglo-Russian agreement of August 1907 and the creation of the Triple Entente. Even now, Grey remained genuinely anxious to reduce the tension between Britain and Germany. Both he and his Foreign Office advisers, however, were constantly afraid of taking any initiative to improve relations with Germany which might endanger the Triple Entente with France and Russia on which, they believed, British security depended. 'If we sacrifice the other powers to Germany', Grey believed, 'we shall eventually be attacked.'

Tension in the Balkans

One of the unforeseen consequences of the first Moroccan crisis was its effect on Germany's relations with Austria-Hungary. Only a few years earlier, relations between the two countries had been rather distant.

At Algeciras, however, Austria-Hungary suddenly emerged as Germany's only reliable ally. In a Europe in which the other three great powers seemed to be uniting against it Germany now regarded the alliance with Austria as vital for its own security. Unhappily for the peace of Europe, the moment at which Germany found itself reduced to dependence on the Austrian alliance coincided almost exactly with the moment chosen by Austria to resume a forward policy in the Balkans.

The new course in Austrian foreign policy was partly the result of the rise of new men to power. In the autumn of 1906 Aehrenthal became Austrian foreign minister and Conrad chief of staff. Their predecessors had been cautious men, anxious not to disturb the understanding with Russia in the Balkans. Aehrenthal and Conrad were arrogant, aggressive and ambitious, eager to restore the prestige of the Austrian Empire by a dramatic success in the Balkans.

At a deeper level, however, Aehrenthal's foreign policy was a response to the internal tensions of the Austrian Empire. Like Turkey, Austria had to face the enormous problems involved in holding together a multinational empire beset by the growing nationalism of its subject peoples. Many European statesmen believed these problems to be insoluble and concluded that the Austrian, like the Turkish, Empire was doomed to disintegration.

The most restive nationality within the Austrian Empire were the South Slavs. Many were attracted by the prospect of joining with their fellow Slavs in the independent kingdom of Serbia and in the provinces of Bosnia-Herzegovina (still a part of the Turkish Empire though under

Austrian administration) to form a united South Slav state.

Serbia, which openly considered itself the nucleus of this future South Slav state, thus came to be considered by Austrian statesmen as a threat to the continued existence of Austria-Hungary. Austria-Hungary would be secure, Aehrenthal believed, 'only when we decide to grasp the nettle firmly and make a final end to the pan-Slav dream'. And for both Aehrenthal and Conrad the only 'final end to the pan-Slav dream' was the complete destruction of the kingdom of Serbia.

The signal for the revival of tension in the Balkans was the Young Turk revolution at Constantinople in the summer of 1908. The Turks, now fired, like their Balkan subjects, with a new spirit of nationalism, seemed likely to reclaim full sovereignty over the provinces of Bosnia-Herzegovina. Aehrenthal's reply was to announce the annexation of these provinces by the Austrian Empire. By bringing another million Slavs under Austrian rule, he believed that he had struck a first blow against South Slav dreams of a united South Slav state. So too did the Serbs. Serbia mobilized its forces and appealed for Russian support. Russia, as the largest of the Slav nations, considered itself the protector of the Balkan Slavs and demanded that the question of Bosnia-Herzegovina be submitted to an international conference.

Aehrenthal had planned the annexation without giving any warning to Berlin. He had acted, however, in the conviction that, once the crisis had begun, Germany dare not risk the defeat of its only reliable ally by denying it German support. In the event, Germany promised support, not merely over the annexation of Bosnia-Herzegovina but in whatever action Austria thought fit to deal with Serbia. The German chancellor wrote to Aehrenthal a fortnight after the annexation. 'I know you doubt whether the present nasty state of affairs in Serbia can be allowed to go on indefinitely. I trust your judgement and shall regard whatever decision you come to as appropriate to the circumstances.'

After six months of tension it was Germany which brought the crisis to an end. In March 1909 it presented Russia with what amounted to an ultimatum demanding that it recognize the annexation. With its army still unprepared for European war, Russia was forced to give way. Serbia, now deprived of Russian support, had no option but to follow suit. Germany, boasted the kaiser, had stood by its ally like a knight 'in shining armour'.

'Here', wrote the Austrian minister, in the Serbian capital soon after the crisis had ended, 'all think of revenge, which is only to be carried out with the help of the Russians.' Russia was unlikely to desert the Serbs a second time as it had done in 1909.

Having been humiliated once by Germany, it was unwilling to risk humiliation again. As soon as the crisis was over, Russia began a large-scale reconstruction of its armed forces. The settlement of the Bosnian crisis had only postponed a final showdown between Serbia and Austria-Hungary. When that showdown came, it was already clear what Germany's policy would be. It was Germany's willingness, and even eagerness, to underwrite Austrian action against Serbia – already clearly demonstrated in the crisis of 1908–9 – which, in August 1914, was to be the immediate cause of the First World War.

The naval arms-race

During the last five years before the outbreak of war two sources of European tension dominated all the rest: the Balkan rivalry between Austria and Serbia (and Serbia's protector, Russia) and the naval rivalry between Britain and Germany. Naval rivalry, unlike Balkan rivalry, did not cause a European war, but it did much to explain British participation in it.

Until the first Moroccan crisis the new German battle fleet had posed only a symbolic threat to British naval supremacy. The new fleet had succeeded in making Britain suspicious but not really apprehensive. The sheer size of the Royal Navy made it impossible, for the foreseeable future, to

envisage any real rival to it. Or so it seemed until the launching of the new British battleship *Dreadnought* in 1906. By its size and firepower the *Dreadnought* made all other battleships obsolete. With ten twelve-inch guns, each with a range of more than eight miles, it was more than a match for any two of its predecessors. Overnight the Royal Navy, like every other navy in the world, discovered that it was out of date.

The launching of the *Dreadnought* gave a new and more dangerous dimension to naval rivalry between Britain and Germany. The discovery by the British public that British naval supremacy was no longer secure was a traumatic experience. Almost inevitably, rumours spread that Germany was planning a secret acceleration of its naval programme which, within a few years, would give it more dreadnoughts than the Royal Navy. By the final stages of the Bosnian crisis in the spring of 1909 British public opinion had been roused to a state of almost frenzied agitation. Asquith's government, which had originally intended to build only four dreadnoughts during the next year, was assailed by the slogan 'We want eight and we won't wait' and capitulated to it.

Talks between Britain and Germany on methods of slowing down the naval arms race began in August 1909 and continued intermittently for two years. The stumbling block throughout the negotiations was

Germany's insistence that a naval agreement be accompanied by a political agreement. This was to bind each power to observe 'a benevolent neutrality' if the other went to war with other powers. To Britain it seemed increasingly clear that Germany's real aim in the negotiations was to destroy the Triple Entente. The slim prospect of a compromise agreement that still remained after nearly two years' negotiation was destroyed altogether by Germany's action in provoking the Agadir crisis in the summer of 1911.

Early in 1911 the Sultan of Morocco was forced to appeal for French troops in order to protect himself against a rebellion by his subjects. It soon became clear that a French protectorate would not be long delayed. Kiderlen, the German foreign minister, concluded that some dramatic gesture was necessary to make France offer Germany compensation for its absorption of Morocco. In his own words: 'It is necessary to thump the table, but the only object is to make the French negotiate.' Kiderlen's method of thumping the table was to send a gunboat to the Moroccan port of Agadir, allegedly for the protection of German citizens whose lives might be endangered by the Moroccan rising. Unfortunately, as A. J. P. Taylor has observed, the nearest German was at the more northerly port of Mogador. He was therefore ordered to proceed to Agadir at once, in order to put

Above, The Sure Shield of Britain and Her Empire, *painting dating from about 1914.*

Opposite, illustration from the Illustrated London News *of 21 September 1912 of 'the German Navy as it will be in the Near Future': the artist based his forecast on the provision recently made in a new German Navy Law for an increase in the size of the fleet. Command of the sea was essential for the survival of Britain and her empire and it was this German naval challenge above all other issues that alarmed both the government and public opinion in Britain.*

215

himself in danger and so justify the sending of a gunboat. The crisis was ended in November 1911 by a compromise. Germany agreed to recognize a French protectorate in Morocco and received a large slice of the French Congo in exchange.

Public reaction to this agreement was striking evidence of the serious worsening in Franco-German relations since the first Moroccan crisis of 1905. In 1905 most Germans had been indifferent to Morocco and most Frenchmen had been in favour of making concessions to Germany. In 1911, however, public opinion in both France and Germany was indignant at the conclusion of a compromise settlement. In Germany the minister of colonies resigned over the agreement, and attacks on it were ostentatiously applauded by the Crown Prince. To his fury the Kaiser found himself accused of loss of nerve for having let the settlement go through. In France public hostility to the treaty led to the overthrow of the government which had concluded it and to the rise to power, first as prime minister and then as president, of Raymond Poincaré, one of the leading advocates of a tough policy towards Germany.

The Agadir crisis was interpreted in Britain, like the first Moroccan crisis in 1905, as yet another German attempt to destroy the Entente Cordiale by a war of nerves against France. At the height of the crisis British and French chiefs of staff discussed, for the first time, the transfer of British troops to France to meet a German attack. At the same time Lloyd George, the chancellor of the exchequer, hitherto considered the most pro-German member of Asquith's cabinet, delivered the strongest public warning to Germany so far given by a British statesman. The British government, he said, would prefer war to a peace achieved 'by allowing Britain to be treated as if she were of no account in the cabinet of nations'. The British public believed that Germany had intended to make war on France and that Lloyd George's warning had stopped the German army in its tracks. The inevitable result of the passions aroused by the Agadir crisis was an intensification of Anglo-German naval rivalry. In Germany Tirpitz, the architect of the new German battle fleet, was able to use the crisis to push through a new German navy law. Britain replied with an enlarged naval programme of her own and a naval agreement with France.

The Balkan wars

The Agadir crisis led, by a roundabout route, to war in the Balkans. Italy took advantage of the crisis to begin an attack on Libya, now all that remained of the former Turkish empire on the north coast of Africa. In itself the Italian conquest of Libya was only a minor episode in the history of European imperialism. But, by making plain the unexpected extent of Turkey's military

vulnerability, it provided a powerful stimulus to the territorial ambitions of the Balkan states, anxious to divide between them what remained of Turkey's European empire. Bulgaria, Greece and Serbia temporarily set aside their differences, formed the Balkan League and declared war on Turkey in October 1912. The extent of their successes took the whole of Europe by surprise. After an illness lasting 150 years, European Turkey, the 'sick man of Europe', suddenly expired.

The First Balkan War, however, only strengthened the rivalries among the Balkan states themselves. It was followed in 1913 by a Second Balkan War in which the victors of the first fell out among themselves. In this war Serbia and Greece, the protégés of Russia, defeated Bulgaria, the protégé of Austria. Berchtold, who had succeeded Aehrenthal as Austrian foreign minister, declared at the beginning of the war: 'In view of the open hostility of Serbia towards us, a further material and moral strengthening of Serbia at the expense of Bulgaria would be absolutely contrary to our interests.' Yet this was precisely what the Second Balkan War achieved. It thus strengthened still further Austria's determination to put an end to the Serbian menace. Once again, the Kaiser reaffirmed Germany's readiness to support whatever action against Serbia Austria thought necessary. 'You can be certain', he told Berchtold, 'that I stand behind you, ready to draw sword whenever your action makes it necessary.'

The Sarajevo crisis

Bismarck had predicted, long ago, that the immediate cause of the next European war would be 'some damned foolish thing in the Balkans'. His prophecy was fulfilled by the murder of the Archduke Francis Ferdinand

at the Bosnian capital of Sarajevo on 28 June 1914. Francis Ferdinand had chosen as the date for his visit St Vitus' Day, the Serbian national festival. The effect on Serbian opinion has been compared to the likely effect in Ireland of a visit to Dublin on St Patrick's Day by a British monarch at the height of the Irish troubles. The Archduke and his wife only narrowly escaped a bomb attack soon after their arrival in Sarajevo. They were killed early in the afternoon while on their way to visit an officer wounded during the first assassination attempt a few hours earlier. The assassin, Gavrilo Princip, was a nineteen-year-old Bosnian, the first student revolutionary to change the course of European history.

Though Princip was an Austrian subject, the assassination had been planned in Serbia by a Serbian terrorist organization, the 'Union of Death' (better known as the 'Black Hand'), dedicated, as its name implies, to achieving the union of all South Slavs under the Serbian crown. Francis Ferdinand was selected as its victim, not merely because he was the heir to the throne of Austria-Hungary, but also, paradoxically, because he stood for a policy of conciliation towards the South Slavs of the Austrian Empire. He intended, once he became emperor, to offer the South Slavs an autonomy similar to that already enjoyed by the Magyars. Such a scheme was probably impracticable. The 'Black Hand', however, feared that it might succeed. If it did, it would end all hope of a united South Slav state. Francis Ferdinand was killed because, in his assassin's words, 'as future sovereign he would have prevented our union and carried out certain reforms which would have been clearly against our interests.'

Throughout the Sarajevo crisis the Austrian government possessed no proof whatever of Serbian complicity in the assassination. Even the existence of the 'Black Hand' was not discovered until much later. Conrad, nonetheless, insisted that the time had come for the Serbian nest of vipers' to be finally destroyed. Berchtold, after some hesitation, rallied to his view. The final decision of peace or war, however, rested not with the Austrian but with the German government. Even Conrad recognized that war with Serbia was out of the question unless Austria possessed a guarantee of German support.

Germany, however, not merely promised Austria support but urged it to lose no time in launching an attack. 'The Serbs', wrote the Kaiser, 'must be wiped out and quickly too.' Germany believed that Austria's survival as a great power was essential to its own security: and, in the opinion of both the Kaiser and his government, Austria could not remain a great power unless it dealt with Serbia. 'The maintenance of Austria, and in fact of the most powerful Austria possible', said Jagow, the foreign minister, 'is a necessity for us.'

But Germany's belligerence was not solely

Left, 28 June 1914, and the Austrian Archduke Francis Ferdinand (1863–1914), the heir to the Austrian throne, and his wife descend the steps of Sarajevo town hall: a few minutes later they were assassinated, and the almost unstoppable train of events that led six weeks later to the outbreak of war was set in motion.

Below left, Gavrilo Princip, the Archduke's assassin, is hustled into custody.

Opposite, a Montenegrin soldier firing a Turkish blockhouse during the First Balkan War, 1912.

dictated by concern for Austria-Hungary. Each succeeding crisis had strengthened the feeling in Berlin – as in other European capitals – that war between the two alliances was, sooner or later, inevitable. In the summer of 1914, German generals were agreed that now was the time to fight. 'Any delay', argued Moltke, 'means a worsening in our chances.' The alacrity with which the German government adopted the aim of a German *Mitteleuropa* once the war had started suggests, however, that Germany was not simply thinking in terms of a preventive war. Only through war could the frustrated ambitions of *Weltpolitik* hope to find fulfilment. The German writer, Plehn, wrote in 1913: 'It is an almost universal belief throughout the country that we shall only win our freedom to participate in world politics through a major European war.' Germany's ambitions did not cause the Sarajevo crisis, but once the crisis had arisen they inevitably conditioned its response to it.

Both Austria and Germany were careful to throw a smoke screen over their intentions. Early in July the Kaiser sent birthday greetings to the King of Serbia and left for his annual cruise off Scandinavia in his steam yacht. For almost a month after the assassination most European statesmen assumed that the crisis between Austria and Serbia would be settled without war. By mid-July the crisis was no longer headline news. English newspaper readers were more concerned with events in Ireland and French newspaper readers with the trial of a former prime minister's wife, accused of shooting a newspaper editor who had threatened to publish her husband's correspondence with his mistress. As late as 23 July, Lloyd George was confidently forecasting both 'substantial economies' in naval expenditure and a world-wide reaction against the growth of armaments. He told the House of Commons:

I cannot help thinking that civilization which is able to deal with disputes among individuals and small communities at home, and is able to regulate these by means of some sane and well-ordered arbitrament should be able to extend its operations to the larger sphere of disputes between states.

The approach to war

In the evening of 23 July, while Lloyd George was still speaking to the Commons, Austria delivered an ultimatum to Serbia, based on an assumption of Serbian responsibility for the assassination and making demands which were intended to be unacceptable. Serbia's refusal of these demands was intended to provide a pretext for war. To Austria's astonishment – and embarrassment – Serbia accepted, either outright or with reservations, all but one of Austria's demands. 'A great moral victory for Vienna!', wrote the Kaiser, when he learned of the reply, 'but with it every reason for war drops away.'

Though the Kaiser was beginning to have second thoughts, however, the German government continued to press Austria for an immediate declaration of war in order to make mediation impossible. In response to German pressure Austria formally declared war on Serbia on 28 July, a fortnight earlier than it had intended. The Kaiser's view that war was now unnecessary was passed on to Vienna by the German Foreign Office only when it was too late. Bethmann-Hollweg, the German chancellor, had no intention of trying to avert a war. He recognized that an Austrian war with Serbia would mean a European war with France and Russia but was confident of victory.

Bethmann-Hollweg, however, had counted on obtaining British neutrality. Only on 30 July, when he learned that it was not to be secured on the terms offered by Germany, did Bethmann-Hollweg at last make a serious attempt to restrain Austria. He urged Austria to halt its forces at Belgrade and agree to talks with Russia. By now, however, it was too late to hold Austria back. Nor was Germany speaking with a single voice. While Bethmann-Hollweg was counselling moderation, Moltke was telegraphing Conrad: 'Mobilize against Russia at once. Germany will follow suit.'

Even Bethmann-Hollweg's eleventh-hour attempt to hold Austria back was not wholly dictated by a desire to preserve the peace. He was also concerned – perhaps mainly concerned – to fix on Russia the responsibility for transforming a local war with Serbia into a continental war between the great powers of Europe. If Russia were the

first to mobilize its forces for a continental war, Bethmann-Hollweg believed it would be possible for Germany to brand Russia as the aggressor.

Russia went to war against Austria, as Austria went to war against Serbia, because it believed that its status as a great power left it no alternative. Just as Austria believed that it could not remain a great power without war with Serbia, so Russia believed that it could not remain a great power if it abandoned Serbia. On 30 July Russia became, as Bethmann-Hollweg had hoped, the first of the great powers to order general mobilization. This decision, however, reflected less a desire for war than a consciousness of its own military inferiority. Russia was well aware that its mobilization would be much slower, and less efficient, than that of Germany. Unlike Germany, therefore, Russia could not take the risk of allowing its opponents to be the first to mobilize.

Once Russia had decided to mobilize, control of German policy passed from the statesmen to the soldiers. The only plan of campaign which the German high command possessed was that devised by General Schlieffen ten years before. The Schlieffen Plan assumed (wrongly as it turned out) that Germany's only chance of victory in a war on two fronts was to win a quick victory over France by a sweep through Belgium before Russia was ready for war in the east. Once Russia had begun to mobilize, therefore, the Schlieffen Plan made it essential for war to begin without delay.

On 31 July Germany issued an ultimatum to Russia to demobilize within twelve hours. When this was refused, Germany declared

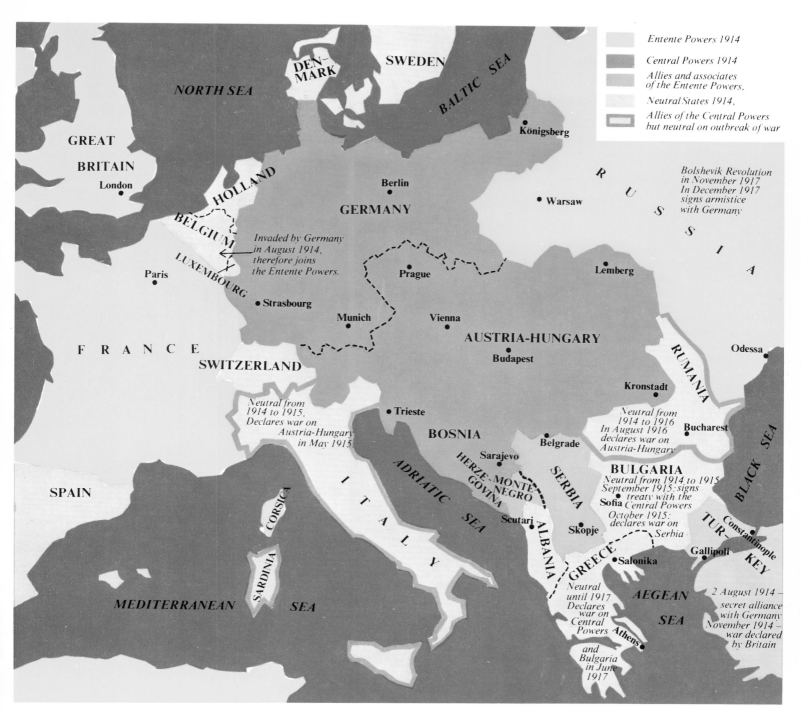

*Bolshevik Revolution
in November 1917
In December 1917
signs armistice
with Germany*

*Invaded by Germany
in August 1914,
therefore joins
the Entente Powers.*

*Neutral from
1914 to 1915.
Declares war on
Austria-Hungary
in May 1915.*

*Neutral from
1914 to 1916
In August 1916
declares war on
Austria-Hungary*

*Neutral from 1914 to 1915
September 1915: signs
treaty with the
Central Powers
October 1915:
declares war on
Serbia*

*Neutral
until 1917
Declares
war on
Central
Powers*

*and
Bulgaria
in June
1917*

*2 August 1914 –
secret alliance
with Germany
November 1914 –
war declared
by Britain*

war on 1 August. Two days later, on 3 August, Germany declared war on France, using the trumped-up pretext of French violations of the German frontier. Britain's last doubts about intervention were removed by the German ultimatum to Belgium, demanding free passage for an invasion of France. Britain replied with an ultimatum of her own, demanding German respect for Belgian neutrality. When Germany failed to reply, Britain entered the war at midnight on 4 August.

After forty-three years of peace the great powers of Europe went joyfully to war. Crowds in all the five main European capitals greeted the declaration of war with delirious enthusiasm. The social and political conflicts of the pre-war years seemed to be forgotten in the enthusiasm of the moment. In Germany the Kaiser told cheering crowds, 'I see no more parties, I see only Germans.' In France all parties buried their differences in the *Union sacrée*. Even in Russia, the wave of strikes which had paralysed Russian industry in the spring and summer of 1914 ceased almost overnight. The Second International, which had sought to replace national rivalries by the international solidarity of the European working class, sank without a trace. Often, it was the young and idealistic who greeted war with the greatest enthusiasm. Peace had come to seem unheroic and they were bored by it, hoping to discover in war a sense of purpose lacking before. All over Europe a generation echoed the English poet, Rupert Brooke: 'Now God be thanked, Who has matched us with His hour.'

Above, Europe on the eve of the First World War.

Opposite top and centre, the last days of peace: citizens of Budapest read the mobilization order and Londoners demonstrate outside the War Office. How many of these, who confidently expected to be home from the front by Christmas, survived the four years' slaughter?

Opposite bottom, the first days of war: newly mobilized troops on their way to the front, a sight repeated in every town throughout Europe.

Chapter 15

The First World War

Almost no-one, in August 1914, had any idea of what war would be like. There had been moments in the decade before the war when at least some generals had had a premonition of what lay in store for them. Moltke had spoken in 1905 of 'a war that, even should we be victorious, will push our people to the limits of exhaustion'. Joffre, the French commander-in-chief, had spoken in 1912 of a war which might be 'of indefinite duration'. These fears seemed to be forgotten in August 1914. No country possessed plans for a war of more than a few months. Most generals on both sides thought such plans unnecessary. 'You will be home', the Kaiser told the German army, 'before the leaves have fallen from the trees.' Only Kitchener, recalled to become secretary of state for war on the day that Britain entered the conflict, foresaw a war which would involve millions of men and take years to decide.

And yet, on the Western Front at least, the war was almost won and lost within the space of one campaign. In both 1870 and 1940 the French were routed by the Germans in six weeks. The same thing very nearly happened in 1914. Though Joffre knew of the Schlieffen plan, he did not take it seriously. While the Germans were struggling through Belgium, the French would pour across the frontier into the heart of Germany. The whole French army in August 1914 shared Joffre's sublime confidence in attack. While the British and Germans tried to make themselves inconspicuous in khaki and field-grey, the French sought to make themselves as conspicuous as possible. Confident that their *élan* would shatter the enemy's nerve, their infantry went to battle in blue overcoats and red pantaloons. 'The French army', said its Field Regulations, 'knows no law but the offensive.' French *élan*, however, was no match for German firepower. The French assault on the German frontier ended in a series of disasters, collectively known as the Battles of the Frontiers. Unable to comprehend what had gone wrong, Joffre blamed the defeats on 'a lack of offensive spirit'.

The Germans, meanwhile, had swept through Belgium and were advancing into northern France. By early September they had reached the Marne, Paris was in a panic and the French government had left for Bordeaux. The very speed of its advance, however, had led the German army to over-reach itself. Corps commanders were often out of touch both with headquarters and with one another. Moltke hardly knew where his armies were for days on end. Instead of enveloping Paris, as Moltke had planned, the German army wheeled to the southeast, leaving its flank exposed to a brilliantly successful counter-attack on the Marne by the Paris garrison.

Some historians have since concluded that the Schlieffen Plan was doomed from the beginning. The French, however, believed that they had been saved only by a miracle: 'the miracle of the Marne'. Perhaps the crucial factor in the German failure was that Moltke had been forced, at a critical stage of the French campaign, to transfer two army corps to the Eastern Front to meet an unexpected Russian attack in East Prussia. The miracle of the Marne was won as much in East Prussia as on the Marne itself.

The Western Front

The 'miracle of the Marne' was followed by a race to the sea, each side trying, unsuccessfully, to turn the other's flank before the sea was reached. Though Germany had failed to win a quick victory, it still retained the initiative in the war. When the race to the sea was over, Germany remained in control of one-tenth of France's territory, eighty percent of its coal and almost the whole of its iron ore. For the next three and a half years Germany was usually content to remain on the defensive behind an impregnable line of

trenches, against which the Allied armies battered in vain. At no time before the spring of 1918 did the front lines established during the race to the sea in 1914 vary in depth by as much as ten miles. 'The Western Front', wrote Robert Graves, 'was known among its embittered inhabitants as the Sausage Machine because it was fed with live men, churned out corpses, and remained firmly screwed in place.'

The reason for this stalemate was technological. The invention of barbed wire and the machine gun had given a temporary, but overwhelming, advantage to the defence. Only a further technological advance could turn the advantage once more in favour of attack. Some historians have argued that by the end of 1916 the invention of the tank already provided just such a technological advance and that only the blindness of both the French and British high commands

prevented them from achieving a breakthrough. Until the closing months of the war, however, tanks were too deficient, both in quality and quantity, to end the stalemate on the Western Front. Even at their greatest victory, the Battle of Amiens, in August 1918, 270 of a total of 415 tanks were destroyed in one day's fighting. Deadlock in the west continued for so long not because generals were more incompetent than in the past but, quite simply, because they lacked the means to break it.

'The German lines in France', wrote Kitchener at the beginning of 1915, 'may be looked on as a fortress that cannot be carried by assault.' With the exception of Kitchener, however, most Allied generals were confident of an early breakthrough. The greatest criticism that can be levelled at the Allied commanders on the Western Front is not that they failed to make this breakthrough but that they refused for so long, against all the evidence, to recognize the enormous strength of the enemy's position.

Joffre's plan to win the war in 1915 was for a gigantic pincer movement against the German lines, Anglo-French forces attacking in Artois and the French alone further south in Champagne. Offensives on these fronts continued intermittently throughout the year, none achieving an advance of more than three miles. At the end of the year Joffre comforted himself with the thought that, even if the Germans had yet to be defeated, they were being worn down by a war of attrition. Pinning his faith in inflated estimates of German losses, he refused, like most other Allied generals (and many later historians), to accept the simple truth that a war of attrition on the Western Front was bound to bear most heavily on the attacker. In fact, French and English losses in 1915 were almost double those of Ger-Germany: probably 1,600,000 killed and wounded as against 850,000 of the enemy.

Enormous though these losses were, they were surpassed by even greater losses in the east. In 1915 Falkenhayn, the new German commander-in-chief, had chosen to remain on the defensive in the west, while launching his main offensive in the east. In five months, between May and September 1915, Russia lost a million men in prisoners alone, at least a million more (perhaps far more) in killed and wounded and more territory than the whole area of France. Judging by size alone, Falkenhayn had won what has been called 'the greatest battle in history'. But it was not, and could not be, a decisive victory. Though the Russians had been forced to retreat three hundred miles,

they were left with a shorter line to defend and still possessed vast reserves of man-power. In the east, as in the west, 1915 ended in deadlock.

Verdun

The plan of campaign devised by the Allies for 1916 simply proposed to repeat the mistakes of 1915 on a larger scale. Joffre convinced himself and many others that, on the Western Front at least, the Allies had been on the verge of a breakthrough in 1915, robbed of a victory only by a lack of heavy guns and ammunition. Next year, with plenty of munitions and the first British conscript armies, things would be different. As soon as sufficient shells were available, Haig told *The Times* correspondent, 'we could walk through the German lines at several places'. To make sure of victory in 1916 it was agreed to launch all-out offensives simultaneously on both the Western and the Eastern Fronts. Italy, which had entered the war on the side of the Allies in 1915, would join in with an attack on Austria from the south.

Falkenhayn's plan for victory was much more subtle. He proposed to win the war

not by defeating the enemy in battle but by bleeding him to death – a new and ingenious addition to the theory of warfare. The power on whom Falkenhayn proposed to perform this experiment was France:

Within our reach behind the French sector of the Western Front there are objectives for the retention of which the French General Staff would be compelled to throw in every man they have. If they do so, the forces of France will bleed to death – as there can be no question of voluntary withdrawal – whether we reach our goal or not.

Falkenhayn selected as his target the great French fortress of Verdun, already half encircled by German lines and one of the few places on the Western Front where the defenders seemed to be at a disadvantage. German communications to the Verdun salient were excellent, and their heavy guns had closed all French routes to the fortress, except for one light railway and one road, which became known as the *voie sacrée*. Throughout the Battle of Verdun supply remained as great a problem as the fighting itself. For months 3,000 lorries passed every day along the *voie sacrée* carrying 20,000 men and 4,000 tons of supplies.

The Battle of Verdun became, as Falkenhayn had intended, the supreme symbol of attrition even in a war of attrition. It lasted ten months, from February to November 1916, longer than any battle had ever lasted before. In no other battle in the history of warfare have so many died on so small an area of ground. As the battle progressed, however, it became increasingly clear that Falkenhayn had made one fatal miscalculation. 'Germany is perfectly free', he had written, 'to accelerate or draw out the offensive, to intensify it or to break it off from time to time as suits its purpose.'

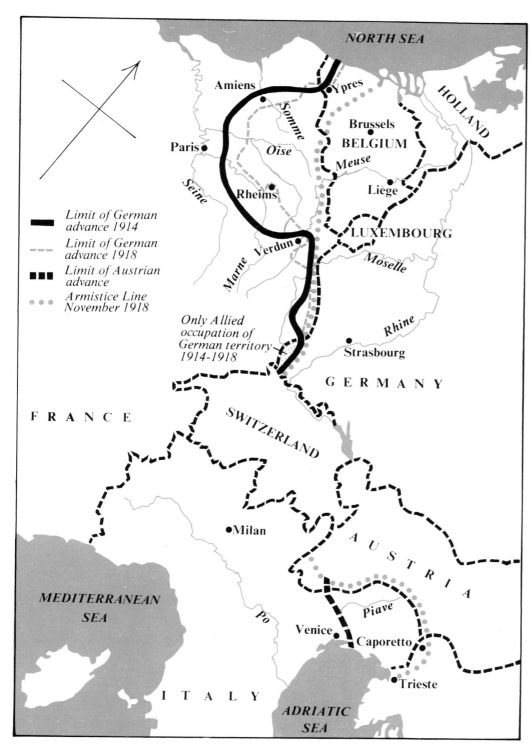

NORTH SEA
Amiens
Ypres
HOLLAND
Brussels
BELGIUM
Paris
Somme
Oise
Meuse
Seine
Rheims
Liège
Limit of German advance 1914
Limit of German advance 1918
Limit of Austrian advance
Armistice Line November 1918
LUXEMBOURG
Verdun
Marne
Moselle
Only Allied occupation of German territory 1914-1918
Rhine
Strasbourg
GERMANY
FRANCE
SWITZERLAND
Milan
AUSTRIA
MEDITERRANEAN SEA
Po
Piave
Venice
Caporetto
Trieste
ITALY
ADRIATIC SEA

Left, the western and Italian fronts during the First World War.

Above and opposite top left and right, First World War recruiting posters from Australia and Great Britain.

Opposite bottom, French survivors from the Battle of Verdun.

After the first week of the battle Falkenhayn's freedom of action had disappeared. Just as French prestige was involved in the defence of Verdun, so German prestige increasingly demanded its capture. The Battle of Verdun ended by bleeding the German army almost as disastrously as it bled the French.

Had Germany been able to press home its attack after the capture of Fort Vaux on 7 June however, it could, in the opinion of the historian Alistair Horne, 'almost certainly have broken through to Verdun'. In June 1916, as in the other great crisis of the war in September 1914, the French were saved by a Russian offensive in the east. Partly in response to desperate appeals from France to relieve the pressure on Verdun, Brusilov, the ablest of the Russian generals, attacked the Austrians on the southeast front with forty divisions. Many German officers had long believed that, by its alliance with Austria, 'Germany was fettered to a corpse'. They were confirmed in this opinion by the spectacular success of the Brusilov offensive. What began as a diversionary attack rapidly turned into a rout of the Austrian army along a three hundred mile front. By the time German troops arrived to try and stem the Austrian retreat in September, Brusilov had taken almost half a million prisoners.

Despite its ultimate failure, the Brusilov offensive had far-reaching consequences on both the Eastern and Western Fronts. In the east it brought nearer the disintegration of the Austrian Empire. In the west it changed the course of the battle for Verdun. At a crucial moment, Falkenhayn was forced to divert to the Eastern Front divisions intended to push home the assault on Verdun. At a time when French reserves were almost exhausted, General Pétain, who had been summoned to the defence of Verdun, was given a vital ten days' breathing space in which to strengthen his defences and bring up fresh troops. When the Germans were able to resume their offensive, on 22 June, their chance of victory had gone.

The Somme offensive

Verdun was a turning point in the history of the Western Front. From now on, the main burden of the fighting passed from France to Britain. The French had been so weakened at Verdun that they were no longer capable of assuming the major role in the planned summer offensive on the Somme. When the battle began on 1 July the French contingent had been reduced by Verdun from forty to fourteen divisions alongside Haig's twenty-five. Yet what successes were achieved on the first day of the offensive were mainly because of the French. The latter moved swiftly in small groups supported by machine guns, using methods learnt from the Germans at Verdun, and overran most of the German front line. The British, weighed down by sixty-six pound packs, advanced at walking pace in even lines, presenting the German machine guns with their best target of the war. As one line was cut down, so others came on, regularly spaced at intervals of a hundred

yards. On 1 July the British lost almost 60,000 men killed and wounded in a single day, more than on any other day in the history of the British army and greater, too, than the losses suffered by any other army on any day of the First World War.

Neither Haig nor any of his staff officers had any idea of the extent of the catastrophe that had befallen them. Haig wrote in his diary on the following day: 'The enemy has undoubtedly been severely shaken. Our correct course, therefore, is to press him hard with the least possible delay.' The Battle of the Somme was to last five months. Only when the winter rains had reduced the battleground to a wilderness of mud was Haig, at last, forced to call a halt. When the battle ended, though the front line had here and there advanced about five miles, some of the objectives set for the first day's offensive had still not been achieved. Like Joffre after the Battle of Champagne a year before, Haig comforted himself with the

delusion, strengthened by inflated estimates of enemy casualties, that the Somme had been successful as a battle of attrition. 'The results of the Somme', he wrote, 'fully justify confidence in our ability to master the enemy's power of resistance.'

'The wars that are won', it has been said, 'never are the wars that were begun.' Wars, once begun, invariably generate war aims for which the combatants would never at the outset have gone to battle. Thus it was after 1914, Russia would not have started a war to capture Constantinople and the Straits, nor Germany for the creation of a Belgian satellite, nor France for the recovery of Alsace-Lorraine. Yet once they had gone to war for other reasons, all these ambitions, and others like them, were swiftly adopted as war aims. And war aims multiplied still further as each side struggled to win over neutrals or retain existing allies by territorial bribes.

Italy's entry into the war in 1915 was preceded by a protracted auction in which each side competed for its favours and Italy played off one against the other. Much the same process preceded the entry of Bulgaria on the side of the Central Powers in 1915 and Romania on the side of the Allies a year later, though – like Italy – neither significantly influenced the outcome of the war.

Despite the stalemate in the war at the end of 1916, despite the growing exhaustion on each side, the extent of the war aims of each alliance condemned attempts to arrange a compromise peace to inevitable failure. Neither side was prepared to accept anything approaching a return to the status quo of July 1914, though both were understandably reluctant to reveal the full extent of their ambitions.

There was one further reason why a compromise peace was impossible. The French writer, de Tocqueville, had long ago predicted that though democracies might be reluctant to involve themselves in war, once embarked on war they would not readily make peace. In an age of mass education, the people of Europe were no longer content to accept the pretexts which for centuries had served as an excuse for war. They needed to believe, instead, that they were involved in a moral crusade to protect civilization itself. Only such a cause could justify the millions of lives whose sacrifice the war demanded. To bolster its belief in the rightness of its cause, each side convinced itself of the wickedness of its opponent. The people of Britain swiftly came to credit Germans with an enormous variety of mythical atrocities: priests hung as clappers in cathedral bells, crucified prisoners of war and children with their hands cut off. With so evil an enemy a compromise peace must be unthinkable. As Lloyd George put it shortly before he succeeded Asquith as prime minister in December 1916: 'The fight must be to a finish – to a knock-out.'

The war at sea

Britain possessed two decisive advantages over Germany at sea. The first was the size of her fleet: the British battle fleet – the 'Grand Fleet' – had thirty-one dreadnoughts against Germany's eighteen. Britain's strategic advantages were equally great. The fact that the British Isles lay between German ports and the seaways of the world meant that the German High Seas fleet could venture into the Atlantic only at the risk of having its retreat cut off – a risk it dare not take. For sixteen years the Germans had been building a fleet with which to challenge British supremacy at sea. When war came they dared not make the challenge. For almost two years the German battle fleet stayed cooped up in the Baltic, with only occasional sorties by detachments into the North Sea.

Yet the Grand Fleet did possess two serious weaknesses which the Germans failed either to detect or exploit. First, the fact that the fleet was based in the north at Scapa Flow and Rosyth made it impossible to offer real protection to the troop carriers taking British forces to the Western Front. Jellicoe, the commander of the Grand Fleet, later admitted that the German fleet 'could have stood a good chance of making the attack [on the troop carriers] and returning to his base before the [British] fleet could intervene'.

The second great weakness of the Grand Fleet was its lack, either at Rosyth or Scapa Flow, of a really secure naval base. Throughout the early stages of the war Jellicoe was constantly preoccupied by the danger of submarine attack. In November 1914 a false sighting of an enemy submarine off Scapa Flow actually succeeded in putting the Grand Fleet to flight. Once the war was over, Jellicoe himself expressed surprise that Germany had not attempted an attack on the Grand Fleet while it lay in harbour: 'It may have seemed impossible to the German mind that we should place our Fleet, on which the Empire depended for its very existence, in a position where it was open to submarine and destroyer attack.'

In past European wars Britain had traditionally used its command of the seas to land its forces at the most vulnerable point of the enemy's coastline. In accordance with this strategy the Admiralty had drawn up plans before 1914 for an amphibious assault on Germany's Baltic coast. Once the war began, however, the overwhelming demands of the Western Front forced Britain to follow a continental rather than a maritime strategy. The only large-scale amphibious operation launched by Britain during the war was the Gallipoli campaign of 1915. Its principal purpose was to force the Straits and reestablish a supply route to Russia, with whom communications had been broken by Turkey's entry into the war on the side of the Central Powers.

From first to last, however, the operation was terribly bungled. An unsuccessful attempt by the Royal Navy, in February 1915, to force the Straits without the use of troops sacrificed the crucial advantage of surprise and allowed the Turks time in which to dig themselves in. Churchill himself later claimed, probably correctly, that: 'Three divisions in February could have occupied the Gallipoli peninsula with little fighting.'

By the time the first Allied landings were made in April, however, seven divisions were insufficient. Thereafter, reinforcements were either too few or failed to arrive in time. 'We have', said Churchill in June, 'always sent two-thirds of what was necessary a month too late.' Though fighting on the peninsula continued for the rest of the year, the operation had finally to be abandoned and Allied troops evacuated in December. The failure at Gallipoli had important consequences. By being interpreted as a failure of design, rather than a failure of execution, it discredited the whole policy of amphibious operations for the remainder of the war. And it seemed to clinch the argument of those who claimed that the only route to victory lay on the Western Front.

In Europe itself, the Royal Navy played a less direct part in the fighting than in previous European wars. Outside Europe, however, it won the war. The fact that Germany lost naval contact with its overseas empire meant that its colonies could be picked off one by one by Britain and its allies. Samoa and New Guinea fell to Australia and New Zealand within little more than a month of the outbreak of war. Early in November 1914 Japan, which entered the war as an ally of Britain, captured the German naval base at Kiaochow.

Above, troops and their horses on the beach at Suvla Bay, August 1915: the failure of the Gallipoli offensive, which might have removed Turkey from the war and would have opened a new supply route to Russia, meant that from now on the generals could pursue trench warfare on the western front undistracted by campaigns elsewhere.

Opposite top, the front line at Ovillers, July 1916, during the Battle of the Somme, in which the Allies gained ten miles and lost 600,000 men.

Opposite bottom, field hospital during the Battle of the Somme.

Togoland fell to the British, German South West Africa to the South Africans and the Cameroun, after an eighteen-month campaign, to English, French and Belgian forces advancing from three sides. Only in German East Africa, the largest and richest of the German colonies, did a commander of genius, General von Lettow-Vorbeck, succeed in continuing a guerrilla resistance until the end of the war.

The 'sideshows' in the German colonies, like other 'sideshows' nearer home, in Mesopotamia or at Salonika, had little influence on the outcome of the war in Europe. Even the fate of the German overseas empire was finally decided, not in the German colonies themselves, but on the Western Front. The true importance of the sideshows outside Europe – their impact on the growth of nationalism in India, China and Japan (and, to a far lesser extent, in Africa) became apparent only after the war was over.

In Europe itself the main function of the Royal Navy was to impose a naval blockade on Germany and its allies. Britain claimed the right to stop and search any ship suspected of making for German ports. Neutral countries bordering on Germany even had quotas imposed upon their imports, for fear that some of these might find their way to Germany. The United States protested that Britain was violating the freedom of the seas; but it protested more vigorously still against Germany's attempt to counter-

blockade Britain by the use of mines and submarines.

In April 1915 the British liner *Lusitania* was torpedoed by a German submarine and sank with the loss of 1,200 lives, of whom more than a hundred were American citizens. The reaction of American public opinion was so violent (and so well exploited by British propaganda) that Germany was deterred for the next two years from continuing unrestricted U-boat warfare.

The war at sea, like the war on land, defied most men's expectations. Instead of ending in the naval Armaggedon which both sides had expected, the war became instead a war of attrition aimed, not at destroying the enemy's fleet, but at destroying its economy and starving its civilian population into submission. The two great battle fleets, the source of so much pre-war rivalry, began to seem almost irrelevant.

In spring 1916, however, the growing success of the British blockade persuaded Admiral von Scheer, the new commander of the German High Seas Fleet, to make Germany's first direct challenge to British naval supremacy. Scheer's plan was to lure a part of the Grand Fleet into battle and then suddenly confront it with the whole of the German High Seas Fleet. On 31 May 1916 a decoy force under Admiral Hipper (followed at a distance by Scheer himself) succeeded in making contact with a British squadron commanded by Admiral Beatty. The battle which followed began very badly

for Britain. As Beatty himself laconically remarked, 'There seems to be something wrong with our bloody ships today.' In little more than half an hour two of his six battle-cruisers had been sunk and his flagship seriously damaged. At this point, however, Beatty himself became a decoy. Turning north, apparently in flight, he succeeded in luring Scheer towards the whole of the Grand Fleet. Suddenly, Scheer found himself heavily outnumbered. The Royal Navy seemed within sight of a decisive victory.

Jellicoe, however, was acutely conscious that he was, in Churchill's words, 'the only man on either side who could lose the war in an afternoon'. He was doubtful whether even a decisive victory would do much to improve Britain's existing naval supremacy. Starting from such premises, Jellicoe was unlikely to take risks. He was deeply concerned, too, by the possibility of serious damage to the Grand Fleet from enemy torpedoes. Ever since the beginning of the war he had been convinced that a pursuit of the German battle fleet would be a hazardous undertaking. In October 1914 he had written in a memorandum to the Admiralty: 'If . . . the enemy battle fleet were to turn away from our advancing fleet, I should assume that the intention was to lead us over mines and submarines and decline to be so drawn.' Twice during the Battle of Jutland the hail of fire from the Grand Fleet forced Scheer to break off the engagement and turn his fleet away. On both occasions a determined pursuit might have led to a decisive British victory. On both occasions Jellicoe refused a pursuit because of the danger of torpedo attack.

When night fell on 31 May, Jellicoe still lay between the German fleet and its home base and hoped for victory on the following day. Scheer, however, had two alternative routes back to base. Tragically, Jellicoe chose to cover the wrong one. Part of the blame for this critical decision lies with Jellicoe himself. Even with the information he possessed, he might have deduced that Scheer was heading for home, under cover of darkness, by the Horn Reef passage off the coast of Denmark.

An even greater share of the blame, however, belongs to the Admiralty. During the night of 31 May a series of signals from the German fleet was intercepted and deciphered in Whitehall. Some of the most important were, inexcusably, never passed on to Jellicoe. 'These errors', claimed Jellicoe later, 'were absolutely fatal, as the information if passed to me would have clearly shown that Scheer was making for the Horn Reef.' When morning came on, the German fleet was safe in Wilhelmshaven and the battle was over.

Both sides claimed the battle of Jutland as a victory: the British on the grounds that they had put the enemy to flight, the Germans on the more convincing grounds that, with a smaller fleet, they had inflicted the greater damage. The Grand Fleet had lost ships totalling 111,980 tons and 6,097 men killed, the Germans 62,233 tons and 2,551 men.

Jutland had shown serious deficiencies both in the construction of British warships and in the training of their crews. In the building of the Grand Fleet armour had been sacrificed to speed and firepower. All three British battlecruisers sunk at Jutland had been lost because their magazines were not protected against flash. Most serious of all was the inability of the Royal Navy to fight at night. German crews were already trained in the use of starshell and the co-ordination of guns and searchlights — techniques which were not adopted by the Royal Navy until ten years after the war had ended. It was the Grand Fleet's ignorance of these techniques which allowed Scheer to make his escape under cover of darkness.

Despite the failings of the Grand Fleet Scheer dared not risk another Jutland. He now concluded that Germany's only hope of surviving the British blockade was to step up her own blockade of Britain. This decision to intensify the German blockade was to lead in 1917 to the resumption of unrestricted U-boat warfare. Scheer was confident that German submarines could bring Britain to her knees before Britain had been able to ruin the German war economy. 'I guarantee', said the chief of the German naval staff, 'that the U-boat war will lead us to victory.' His prediction very nearly proved correct. In April 1917 alone, German U-boats sank 835,000 tons of Allied ship-ping. Britain's reserves of wheat rapidly diminished to a month and a half's supply. 'There is no good discussing plans for next spring', Jellicoe told the war cabinet in June, 'we cannot go on.' Only the convoy system, forced on the Admiralty by Lloyd George against its wishes, saved Britain from almost certain disaster.

Ultimately, however, the decision to resume unrestricted U-boat warfare was to have even more important consequences on land than on sea. By bringing about the intervention of the United States, it made the war, for the first time, truly a world war.

American intervention

At the beginning of 1917 the United States seemed to have done well out of its neu-trality. Its overseas trading surplus had increased from $690 million in 1913 to $3,000 million in 1916. The first three years of the war saw the emergence of no less than 8,000 new American millionaires. The basis of this remarkable prosperity was the dependence of the Allied war economies on massive imports from the United States. While American exports to the Central Powers declined sharply as a result of the British blockade, her exports to France and Britain increased fourfold in two years. To finance their imports from the United States, the Allies were forced to rely on large

American loans. By the end of 1916 the Allied debt stood at almost $2,000 million. As the United States stake in Allies econom-ies increased, so also did its stake in an Allied victory. If the Allies were to lose the war a vast American investment would stand at risk.

Though intervention on the Allied side may have been in the economic interests of the United States there is no convincing evidence that the decision to intervene was taken for economic reasons. There had been no sign, even at the end of 1916, that the United States proposed to abandon her neutrality. Indeed, Woodrow Wilson had been re-elected president in November on a

WAKE UP, AMERICA!

CIVILIZATION CALLS EVERY MAN WOMAN AND CHILD!

MAYOR'S COMMITTEE 50 EAST 42ⁿᵈ ST

Above, American wartime recruiting poster.

Opposite, captured 'U' boats at Harwich on England's east coast: in 1917, German U-boat attacks on Allied and neutral shipping brought Britain to the brink of starvation (before the war she had imported 40 percent of her meat, 80 percent of her wheat), staved off only by the institution, in the face of Admiralty opposition, of the convoy system.

programme that proclaimed, 'He kept us out of war'.

Had the Russian revolution of March 1917 come only two months earlier the United States might never have entered the war at all. If Germany, at the beginning of 1917, had been able to foresee the possibility of a quick victory in the east which would allow it to concentrate all its forces on the Western Front, it might well have decided not to take the risks involved in trying to decide the war at sea. As Tirpitz was later to write: 'Had we been able to foresee in Germany the Russian revolution we should not have needed to regard the submarine campaign of 1917 as our last hope. But in January 1917 there was no visible sign of the revolution.'

Germany's decision to begin unrestricted submarine warfare was announced on 1 February 1917. It was followed in March by the sinking of American merchant vessels, without warning and with heavy loss of life. American intervention, as the German government itself realized, was now inevitable. The German Foreign Office, however, devised a comic opera scheme to cripple the American war effort in Europe by concluding a German alliance with Mexico, which, it was hoped, Japan might later be persuaded to join.

Unhappily for Zimmermann, the German foreign minister, a copy of his telegram outlining the terms of this alliance (and offering Texas, New Mexico and Arizona to Mexico as bait) was intercepted by British Intelligence, passed on to the United States government and published in the American press. Its publication caused a greater uproar even than the sinking of the *Lusitania*.

A second reason for America's decision to enter the war was, quite simply, American idealism. 'Sometimes', said Wilson, 'people call me an idealist. Well, that's the way I know I am an American. America, my fellow citizens, . . . is the only idealistic country in the world.' Time and again Wilson had tried as a neutral, without success, to bring the war in Europe to an end by American mediation. His failure had convinced him that the United States could bring its influence to bear, both on the course of the war and on the peace settlement which would follow it, only by being a belligerent. 'The world', Wilson told Congress, 'must be made safe for democracy.'

It was in this spirit that on 6 April 1917 the United States went to war. For many Americans, the news that Russia had overthrown the tsar and joined the ranks of the democracies for whom the world had to be made safe added a further reason for American intervention. 'The preservation and extension of the liberties so rapidly won in Russia', declared the New York *Nation*, 'are now inextricably bound up with the success of the Allies. A German victory would mean the collapse of free Russia.'

Revolution in Russia

Russian radicals had been predicting revolution in Russia ever since the middle of the nineteenth century. Nor was it only the radicals who made predictions. In 1884, the Russian minister of the interior confided to a foreign diplomat that, if tsarism were ever overthrown, its place would be taken by 'the communism of Mr Marx of London who has just died and whose theories I have studied with much attention and interest'.

Even before 1914, it was already clear that war was the catalyst most likely to lead to revolution. Just as the Crimean War had been followed by the end of serfdom, and the war with Japan by the revolution of 1905, so Russia's involvement in the First World War led to the revolution of March 1917 (known in Russia as the February revolution because the tsarist calendar was thirteen days behind the West's).

By the beginning of 1917 it was clear that both the discontent and dislocation caused by the war were reaching a climax. Russia's casualties already numbered five million (perhaps far more – the government had lost count). On the home front, the cost of living had increased seven-fold since July 1914, and food supplies to the cities were breaking down. During the first two months of 1917 alone there were 1330 strikes, more than in the whole of the previous year. It was one of these strikes in Petrograd, the capital, which developed into the March revolution. The decisive factor in its success was the attitude of the Petrograd garrison. In 1905 the revolution had been broken by the army. In 1917 the army joined the revolution.

On 15 March, the tsar signed an act of abdication and handed over power to a provisional government of liberal politicians. The new government had, however, to contend with a rival authority. First in Petrograd, and then throughout the country, local soviets (councils) were formed, elected by factories and army units and claiming that the provisional government was responsible to them as the true representatives of the Russian people.

Soviet schoolchildren are still brought up on the myth that, in the words of one of their textbooks, 'the Romanovs collapsed under the shattering blows of the people inspired by the Bolshevik party'. In fact, the revolution took the Bolsheviks (the Russian communist party) by surprise. Their leader, Lenin, in exile in Switzerland, had said only a few weeks earlier: 'We, the old, will probably not live to see the decisive battles of the coming revolution.' Even after the March revolution, the Bolshevik following within the soviets lagged far behind that of their two socialist rivals – the Mensheviks and the Social Revolutionaries.

It was through the soviets, none the less – above all, through the Petrograd soviet – that Lenin planned to bring about a Bolshevik Russia. He depicted the rivalry between the soviets and the provisional government as an elemental struggle between the forces of light and darkness, a struggle between the bourgeois order and the revolutionary proletariat. The Bolsheviks must ensure the victory of the soviets in this struggle ('All power to the soviets!') while at the same time winning control of the soviets themselves.

Despite the small size of their following in March 1917, the Bolsheviks possessed one

overwhelming advantage over all their rivals. That advantage was the leadership of Lenin, the greatest political genius in Russian history. Without him, a Bolshevik victory would have been unthinkable.

When Lenin returned from exile in April, he found the Bolsheviks agreed on a policy of 'vigilant control' over the provisional government and contemplating cooperation with the Mensheviks. The first condition of the strategy which Lenin succeeded in imposing on his followers was that, on the contrary, they should adopt a policy of total opposition to the government and refuse all cooperation with other parties. The wisdom of this policy became clear in May when the Mensheviks and Social Revolutionaries joined the provisional government. While their rivals became increasingly compromised by the government's growing unpopularity, the Bolsheviks were able to claim that they alone put forward a truly independent programme.

The Bolshevik programme was based on the three simple slogans – peace, bread and land – which Lenin had formulated on his return from exile. No party could be against bread but, until Lenin's return, the Bolsheviks had been committed to neither peace nor land. Lenin himself had spoken many times in the past in favour of the nationalization of land as well as industry. The proposal that large estates be shared among the peasantry, which Lenin put forward in April 1917, was a policy borrowed by him from the Social Revolutionaries for the sole purpose of winning peasant support. After the March revolution the break-up of large estates was recognized as essential, even by most members of the provisional government. With the single exception of the Bolsheviks, however, all parties were agreed that an immediate redistribution of the land would risk paralysis of the war effort and was therefore impossible. Only the Bolsheviks demanded land for the peasant now.

As long as the war had been conducted by a tsarist government, the majority of Russian socialists had condemned it as an imperialist adventure. Once the tsar had been overthrown, however, the issues no longer seemed as simple. Both Mensheviks and Social Revolutionaries declared their support for 'peace without annexations and without indemnities'. Since there was no prospect of concluding a peace, this policy meant, in practice, reluctant support for a continuation of the war – an attitude shared at first by most Bolsheviks. The slogan 'Down with War!', wrote Joseph Stalin, the editor of *Pravda*, at the end of March, was irrelevant to the present situation. From the moment that Lenin returned to Petrograd, however, he demanded fraternization with the enemy and peace without a moment's delay.

For three months after Lenin's return Bolshevik support grew steadily both in the towns and in the army. Though they remained unable to reach the peasants in the villages, their policies won over large numbers of peasants at the front. Bolshevik party members in the army increased from 20,000 in February to 200,000 in July. During July the growth of support for Bolshevism persuaded a group of Lenin's followers, against Lenin's wishes, to attempt an unsuccessful coup d'état. The failure of the insurrection (which Lenin considered premature) and the publication of forged documents, alleging that Lenin was a German spy, produced a popular reaction against him and reduced the fortunes of the Bolshevik party to their lowest ebb since the March Revolution. Lenin himself had no option but to return to exile – this time in Finland.

The Bolsheviks seize power

It was not long before the Bolsheviks succeeded in re-establishing their position. While the provisional government was restoring order in Petrograd after the Bolshevik rising, General Brusilov was launching a massive new offensive on the Eastern Front in the hope of repeating his successes of the previous year. The collapse of this offensive meant the disintegration

Above, a women's meeting at Petrograd during the first weeks of the February Revolution: the banners call for women's rights. In the first weeks of the Revolution, unity was preserved between the provisional government and the Soviets established in the main towns; only after Lenin's return in April was the authority of the provisional government consistently challenged.

Above left, breadline in Petrograd, 1917: Russia had been prepared for revolution by years of military defeat and food and ammunition shortages and by the gradual collapse of the administration; it was the Bolshevik Party's good fortune to be able to take advantage of this situation.

Opposite, a US gun crew firing on German positions, 1918: though the effects of American entry into the war were not immediately noticeable, by the time of the armistice there were over a million American soldiers in France, a considerable boost to Allied morale as well as to fighting strength.

of most of the Russian army. By October there were no less than two million deserters. 'The soldiers', as Lenin said, 'voted for peace with their feet.' In the countryside the peasants were already dividing noble estates among themselves.

In September, alarmed at the collapse of the government's authority, General Kornilov, the Russian commander-in-chief, attempted to seize power. To defend Petrograd the provisional government was forced to appeal for Bolshevik support and to give arms to the Bolshevik Red Guards. In the event, Kornilov's troops refused even to march on Petrograd, and the insurrection collapsed without a shot being fired. Though unsuccessful, however, the rising destroyed most of the little authority which still remained in the hands of the provisional government. The Bolsheviks claimed to have saved Russia from counter-revolution and became the heroes of the hour. At the end of September they won majorities in the Petrograd and Moscow soviets for the first time.

Once these majorities had been won, Lenin demanded an immediate insurrection. The Bolshevik Central Committee, however, was more cautious and gave its consent only in the last week of October. The armed uprising itself was organized by a Military Revolutionary Committee, led by Leon Trotsky. Though Trotsky's name is now conspicuous by its absence from Russian accounts of the Revolution, it was Trotsky, nonetheless, who was mainly responsible for the immediate success of the Bolshevik seizure of power on 6–7 November 1917 (24–25 October according to the old Russian calendar). As Stalin was to write on the first anniversary of the November Revolution, in an article which must later have embarrassed him:

All the practical organization of the revolution was conducted under the direct leadership of the President of the Petrograd Soviet, Comrade Trotsky. It may be said, with certainty, that the swift passing of the [Petrograd] garrison to the side of the Soviet, and the bold execution of the work of the Military Revolutionary Committee, the party owes principally and above all to Comrade Trotsky.

Within little more than a decade, Stalin had turned himself into the chief architect of the revolution and Trotsky into its

principal opponent. Soviet historians have still to put the record straight.

On 8 November 1917, the day after their seizure of power, the Bolsheviks issued a decree calling for 'a just and democratic peace'. In December they signed an armistice with Germany and began peace negotiations at Brest-Litovsk. Germany demanded, as the price of a peace settlement, the dismemberment of western Russia: the cession to Germany of the Baltic provinces, White Russia, the Ukraine and the Caucasus. Lenin insisted that Russia had no option but to conclude a peace on Germany's terms. 'If you do not know how to adapt yourself', he said, 'if you are not inclined to crawl on your belly through the mud, then you are not a revolutionary but a chatterbox.'

A majority of the Bolshevik Central Committee, however, were unconvinced and wanted to continue the war rather than accept the German terms. Lenin's view prevailed only after he had twice threatened to resign. At last, on 3 March 1918, Russia signed the Peace of Brest-Litovsk. Russia, Lenin argued, had suffered only a temporary reverse which would soon be swept away by the tide of revolution advancing irresistibly across the continent of Europe. In the event, however, the Peace of Brest-Litovsk was to be swept away, not by the tide of revolution, but by the Allied victory on the Western Front.

Victory in the West

The new year in 1917 began with new men, all of them promising a knock-out blow that would bring final victory on the Western Front. In England Lloyd George had replaced Asquith as prime minister at

the end of the previous year. In Germany civilian government gave way to a military dictatorship under the nominal leadership of the new supreme commander, Field Marshall Hindenburg, but with the real power resting in the hands of Hindenburg's deputy, General Ludendorff. In France General Nivelle, the youngest of the French army commanders, succeeded Joffre as commander-in-chief. Nivelle produced a plan for a lightning offensive to end the war in the spring of 1917 which seduced not only the French cabinet but, more surprisingly, Lloyd George, who was usually sceptical of the claims of generals.

Ignoring most of the lessons of the last two years, Nivelle pinned his faith on the 'violence' and 'brutality' of the French onslaught. 'Victory', he promised, would be 'certain, swift, and small in cost': 'One and a half million Frenchmen cannot fail.' The battle began in April and continued for three weeks. When it ended Nivelle had advanced up to four miles in depth along a sixteen-mile front, a result which compared well with the gains achieved in any previous Allied offensive. But it was not the decisive victory he had promised. In May Nivelle was replaced by Pétain, the hero of Verdun.

The failure of the Nivelle offensive to achieve a breakthrough brought to a climax the demoralization of the French army. It was followed by nothing less than a full-scale mutiny: 100,000 French soldiers were court-martialled and 23,000 found guilty. When French deserters revealed the scale of the mutiny to the Germans, their stories seemed so incredible that they were simply not believed. As a result Germany missed perhaps her best opportunity since the beginning of the war for a decisive breakthrough on the Western Front. As Painlevé,

- - - - Frontiers in 1914
━ ━ ━ Front line in October 1917
Russian territory occupied by Germany and Austria in 1918

NORWAY

SWEDEN

BALTIC SEA

• Petrograd

• Tallin

R U S S I A

• Moscow

Danzig •

GERMAN
EMPIRE

Tannenberg

Bug

Warsaw •
Lodz •

Brest-
Litovsk

Vistula

• Kiev

Don

Cracow •

Przemysl

Dnieper

Danube AUSTRIA-

Budapest •
HUNGARY

Jassy •

Odessa •

Belgrade •

RUMANIA
Bucharest •

BLACK   SEA

SERBIA

Nish •

• Sofia

MONTENEGRO

ALBANIA

BULGARIA

Istanbul •

GREECE

• Salonika

↗ Dardanelles

TURKEY

Left, the Eastern front during the First World War.

Opposite right, Lenin addresses a crowd in revolutionary Russia; Trotsky is standing on the right of the platform.

Opposite left, Bolsheviks pose by an armed car captured from forces loyal to the provisional government: in Petrograd the Bolsheviks took power in October without bloodshed, in Moscow after a week's uprising, though it needed years of fighting before the new regime's authority was established throughout the country.

the French minister of war, later admitted: 'There did not remain more than two divisions that could be absolutely relied upon if the Germans had launched a large-scale attack.'

Pétain was faced with an immensely difficult problem. If repression was too severe, the mutiny would become a rebellion. If he were not firm enough, the army might disintegrate. Pétain's success in quelling the mutiny was one of the most remarkable achievements by any Allied general during the war. A number of soldiers were shot *pour encourager les autres* (fifty-five officially, far more unofficially), but leave was doubled and conditions at the front improved. Most important of all, the French army gained the assurance that there would be no new French offensive for the remainder of the year. Pétain's strategy was summed up in the sentence, 'We must wait for the Americans', which meant, in effect, waiting for 1918.

Haig was undismayed by the French mutiny. 'For the last two years', he wrote in his diary at the end of May, 'most of us soldiers have realized that Great Britain must take the necessary steps to win the war by herself.' At the Battle of Passchendaele, fought from July to November 1917, Haig set out to do just that. The French high command condemned the whole offensive

in advance. Even Foch, though temperamentally inclined towards attack, described Haig's plan as a duck's march . . . 'futile, fantastic, and dangerous'.

The offensive coincided with the heaviest rains for thirty years. Even more than the Somme, Passchendaele became, as Lloyd George put it, 'the battle of the mud'. At times more than a dozen men were needed to wade across the battleground with one stretcher case. Haig and his staff officers, Lloyd George wrote bitterly,

never witnessed, not even through a telescope, the attacks [they] had ordained, except on carefully prepared charts where the advancing battalions were represented by the pencil which marched with ease across swamps and marked lines of triumphant progress without the loss of a single point. As for the mud, it never incommoded the movements of the irresistible pencil.

The few gains made in three and a half months' fighting were all to be abandoned without a fight early in 1918 in order to prepare for a new German offensive. Once again, as after the Somme, Haig pinned his faith in exaggerated estimates of German casualties and persuaded himself that he was wearing the Germans down. In fact, British casualties probably outnumbered those of Germany by more than three to two (over 300,000 as against less than 200,000) – and this at a time when Russia's withdrawal from the war made possible to transfer large numbers of German troops from the Eastern to the Western Front.

The last German offensive

As a result of her victory in the east, Germany had by March 1918 twenty divisions more in France than the combined total of the Allies. Ludendorff was well aware, however, that this advantage was only a temporary one. As soon as American forces began to arrive in large numbers in France, the tables would be turned and the Allies could expect to win the war by sheer weight of numbers. Ludendorff drew the conclusion, therefore, that Germany must gamble on a last, all-out offensive, before her numerical advantage was lost.

After the first few days of the German offensive, Pétain was speaking as if the war was almost over. 'The Germans', he told Clemenceau, the French prime minister, 'will beat the English in the open field, after which they will beat us too.' To Haig Pétain 'had the appearance of a commander who was in a funk and had lost his nerve'.

It was Haig's alarm at Pétain's pessimism which led the British to take the initiative, early in April, in the appointment of Foch as the first 'Commander-in-chief of the Allied armies in France'. Even Foch, however, at first seemed less than optimistic. When congratulated by Clemenceau on his appointment, he replied, 'A fine gift! You give me a lost battle and tell me to win it.' By June 1918 the Germans were once more on the Marne and threatening Paris.

By now, though the Allies had little reason to suspect it, their greatest danger was past. Despite the fact that Germany's advance far exceeded anything achieved by the Allies since the opening of the Western Front, German troops had outstripped both their transport and artillery and were incapable of pressing home their attack. During July the tide of battle began to turn, at last, in favour of the Allies.

The real beginning of the German collapse was the British victory at Amiens, on 8 August. Ludendorff wrote later:

August 8th was the blackest day for the German army in the history of the war. This was the worst experience I had to undergo. . . . Our losses had reached such proportions that the Supreme Command was faced with the necessity of having to disband a series of divisions.

The Battle of Amiens already foreshadowed the battles of the Second World War. It showed, too, how far methods of warfare had evolved since the war began. When Britain went to war in August 1914, officers' swords were still being sharpened by the regimental armourer and soldiers at the front were making home-made grenades out of empty tins of jam. At Amiens, in August 1918, British troops advanced behind a shield of tanks, protected by rudimentary air cover directed from the ground by radio.

During the final Allied offensive, Haig's invincible optimism, which had hitherto been something of a liability, became instead a valuable asset. While Foch, even after the Battle of Amiens, did not envisage a decisive breakthrough until April 1919, Haig was convinced that the war could, and must, be won by an all-out offensive in the autumn of 1918 before the enemy had an opportunity to recover. It was the British army, stiffened by strong divisions from Canada and Australia (the latter brilliantly commanded by General Monash), which bore the main brunt of the fighting during the final stages of the war. In the three months between the Battle of Amiens and the armistice of 11 November the British army, under Haig, captured 188,700 prisoners of war and 2,840 guns – almost as many as the other Allies put together. Foch himself was full of praise for Haig's achievement. 'Never at any time in its history', he said, 'has the British army achieved greater results in attack than in this unbroken offensive.'

Germany's defeat was hastened by the collapse of her partners. The Allied forces which had been cooped up in a Balkan bridgehead at Salonika for the past three years at last succeeded in launching a successful offensive and forced Bulgaria to make peace at the end of September. A month later Turkey followed suit, and Austria-Hungary, already in the throes of disintegration, appealed for an armistice.

Germany's collapse was only partly caused by the defeats inflicted on her and on her Allies in the closing months of the war. It was even more because of the conviction that the success of the British blockade and the prospect of large-scale American intervention made Germany's future prospects even bleaker than the present. The longer the war continued, the more the odds would turn against Germany.

In August, at a time when Germany's reserves were almost exhausted, the American army in Europe already numbered one and a half million men and was increasing at the rate of 300,000 a month. When the armistice was signed on 11 November 1918, Germany had still not been invaded, and her front line still lay on French and Belgian soil. Germany capitulated, not because she had been beaten in the field, but because her people and her leaders had lost hope for the future.

Victory, wrote Churchill, had been 'bought so dear as to be almost indistinguishable from defeat'. The war had killed not less than ten million people and maimed as many more. All the great powers of Europe felt, like Britain, that they had lost a generation. The mood of the British people now was very different from the enthusiastic jingoism of August 1914. Once the victory celebrations were over, the overwhelming feeling of the nation was that 'it must never happen again'. The young idealists who had flocked to the colours in 1914, hoping to find at the front a sense of purpose that had been lacking in peace, returned (if they returned at all) overwhelmed instead by the futility of war. The proud, patriotic poetry of Rupert Brooke had given way to the bitter, disillusioned verse of Wilfred Owen and Siegfried Sassoon.

Many men in the years between the wars sought to blame the enormous carnage that Europe had endured, not on the necessities of war, but on the stupidity of generals. And yet, despite the errors of the generals, victory could not have been achieved without the sacrifice of millions of lives. Without

the experience of the terrible battles of the past four years, the German army would not, in November 1918, have lost the will to resist. Despite the enormous technological advances of the next twenty years, no easier way to defeat Germany was discovered during the Second World War. Before Germany could be defeated for a second time in 1945, the massacres of Verdun and the Somme and Passchendaele were to be repeated at Leningrad and Stalingrad and Moscow.

Above, view of an armaments factory: though millions of civilians worked, often in extremely unpleasant conditions, in war-related industries, the very fact that the belligerent nations, except for Belgium, parts of Russia and a small part of France, were never invaded meant that behind the front line the real horror of the war was never fully comprehended and the gulf between soldier and civilian stayed unbridged.

Opposite top right, men of the Inniskillen Fusiliers advancing through the German second line at the Battle of Cambrai, 20 November 1917: tanks were used for the first time at Cambrai, where, instead of the usual yard by yard advance, they advanced five miles at very little cost; the infantry failed to keep up, however, and within ten days the Germans had recovered their position.

Opposite centre right, an early tank in action.

Opposite bottom right, Eddie Rickenbacker, the American ace pilot: considered useful only for front-line reconnaisance duties at the beginning of the war, four years later aircraft had become an important factor in military planning.

Opposite left, Anzacs (Australian and New Zealand Army Corps) at Passchendaele, 1917, described by AJP Taylor as 'the blindest slaughter of a blind war' and the last mass infantry assault of the war.

Chapter 16

Post-war Europe

President Wilson came to Europe in January 1919 expecting to build a new Europe on the ruins of the old, founded on the principles of national self-determination and the rule of law, with a League of Nations to uphold the peace. The rapturous reception given him by the peoples of Europe assured him of their confidence. When he visited London, rose petals were strewn before him. Wilson expected opposition from the Allied governments but was confident that he could overcome it. 'England and France', he had written in the summer of 1917, 'have not the same views with regard to peace that we have by any means. When the war is over, we can force them to our way of thinking.' England and France, however, were to prove less pliable than he supposed.

The basis of the post-war settlement was the Treaty of Versailles, negotiated at the peace conference of Paris, during the first six months of 1919. Unlike most such gatherings in the past, the Paris conference was not a conference between victor and vanquished. It was a conference instead where the victors decided, among themselves, the terms which were to be imposed upon the enemy. The details of the settlement were worked out by a series of more than fifty commissions, which held between them more than 1,600 sessions. Thirty-two states took part in these discussions, among them countries as remote from the fighting as Ecuador and Siam. All the major decisions, however, were taken by three men – Wilson, Lloyd George and Clemenceau, the 'Big Three'.

Two major difficulties stood in the way of the peace without annexations or indemnities which Wilson had come to build. The first was the problem of French security. There is almost no other example in the history of modern Europe of a nation so exhausted by its victory as France appeared to be in November 1918. Britain's security seemed to have been secured by the surrender of the German fleet at the armistice and the conquest of the German colonies during the war, most of which were soon to be shared out between Britain and the dominions.

France, however, seemed to have won something of a pyrrhic victory. Most of the destruction caused by the battles on the

Western Front had been concentrated on French soil, and some of France's principal industries had been ruined. Worse still, with the lowest birth rate of any of the great powers, France had less chance than any other nation of making up its enormous losses in manpower. Even with the recovery of Alsace-Lorraine, France still remained far weaker, both in population and economic resources, than a defeated Germany. Moreover, the alliance with Russia, on which its security against Germany had formerly depended, had been swept away by the Bolshevik revolution.

Despite its victory in the First World War, therefore, the balance of power actually seemed more unfavourable to France at the end of war than at the beginning. Clemenceau at first insisted that the only way to make France secure was to separate the Rhineland from Germany and give France permanent bridgeheads on the right flank of the Rhine. Both Wilson and Lloyd George refused to consider such a scheme. Instead, they made two alternative proposals: first, an Allied occupation of the Rhineland for fifteen years, together with the permanent demilitarization both of the Rhineland itself and of a region fifty kilometres wide on the right bank of the Rhine; secondly, an occupation of the Saar, also for fifteen years (with its coal-mines ceded to France for that period), followed by a plebiscite to decide whether it should go to France or Germany.

France was persuaded to accept these terms only by an Anglo-American promise of immediate armed assistance against any German attack. This promise, however, was not to be honoured. The American Senate later refused to ratify the Versailles treaty, and Britain declared herself thereby released from her own undertaking to France.

The second great obstacle in the way of Wilson's hopes for a peace without victors was the demand for reparations. Public opinion in both France and Britain was in vengeful mood at the moment of victory. The election campaign which returned Lloyd George to power in December 1918 was conducted amid cries of 'Hang the Kaiser' and 'Make Germany Pay', orchestrated by conservative politicians and Lord Northcliffe's newspapers. Sir Eric Geddes, the First Lord of the Admiralty, assured his electors that the government would squeeze Germany 'until you can hear the pips squeak'. Even Lloyd George, though personally anxious to limit the extent of Germany's humiliation, felt compelled to promise that Britain would 'demand the whole cost of the war' in compensation.

Despite the cries for vengeance which surrounded it, the demand for reparations was perfectly justified. It was reasonable to expect that Germany, as the aggressor, should pay a proportion of the appalling losses inflicted by it on the rest of Europe – all the more so since its own economic losses

had been lighter than those of most of its opponents.

Where the Allies were unwise was not in their demand for reparations but in the amount that they demanded and in the way that their demand was phrased. Since they were unable to agree among themselves on the size of reparations, they forced Germany to sign what amounted to a blank cheque. Then, in order to justify this blank cheque, they included in the Versailles treaty the famous war guilt clause, drafted by the young John Foster Dulles (later one of America's least successful secretaries of state):

The Allied and Associated Governments affirm and Germany accepts the responsibility of Germany and her allies for causing all the loss and damage to which the Allied and Associated Governments and their nationals have been subjected as a consequence of the war imposed upon them by the aggression of Germany and her allies.

That Germany should be forced to sign such a declaration was bound to be bitterly resented by the great majority of the German people as a gratuitous insult to the memory of the German dead. Outside Germany itself, the justification for reparations – 'the responsibility of Germany and her allies' for the outbreak of the First World War – is no longer seriously disputed. Most West German schoolchildren are still taught, however, that responsibility for the war was divided, more or less evenly, among all its main participants.

The peace with Germany was, in the words of one of its French critics, 'too mild for its severity'. In certain respects the peace *was* severe. Germany lost its colonies, its air force, most of its fleet, all its army save 100,000 men and over thirteen percent of its territory (though most of its territorial losses, like the surrender of Polish territory or the return of Alsace-Lorraine to France, could be justified by the principle of self-determination). In addition, Germany was faced with a war indemnity, which it was expected to take half a century to pay. And yet the fundamental bases of German strength – the unity achieved by Bismarck in 1871, the great size of its population (even though diminished by ten percent) and the industrial strength which had given it in 1914 the most advanced economy in Europe – remained essentially unchanged. These were the factors which, before 1914, had made Germany incomparably the most powerful state on the continent of Europe. Sooner or later, it was inevitable that they should do so again.

France, Germany's main rival in western Europe, was destined to fall behind Germany economically and demographically even more rapidly after the First World War than it had done before. Already, in 1919, many French critics of Versailles advanced the thesis which was to become widely

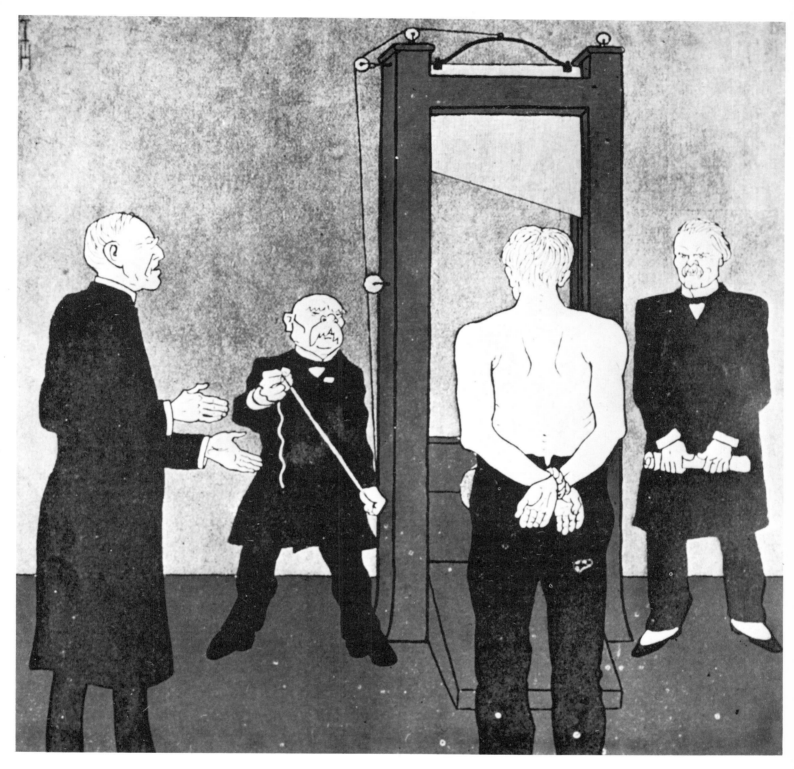

accepted after the Second World War: that European security demanded the sacrifice of the unity achieved in 1871 and the re-creation of a divided Germany.

Having failed to secure the peace without victors which he had come to build, Wilson pinned his faith instead on the League of Nations. Increasingly, as the Paris negotiations dragged on, he came to look on the League as a means whereby injustices in the peace with Germany, which he was powerless to prevent, could be put right as soon as the passions aroused by the war had died down. For that reason, he insisted that the Covenant of the League of Nations should be incorporated in the Versailles settlement itself. One of the articles of the Covenant contained express provision for 'the reconsideration of treaties which have become inapplicable' and the consideration of 'international conditions whose continuance might endanger the peace of the world. The Treaty of Versailles, even if imperfect, contained, in Wilson's view, the eventual remedy for its own imperfections.

Presenting the text of the Versailles treaty to the Senate after his return to the United States in July 1919, Wilson acknowledged that it contained many inadequacies. But he argued that these were redeemed by the

Covenant which conferred on America the moral leadership of all mankind. He ended his speech with a remarkable peroration full of Wilsonian idealism:

The stage is set, the destiny disclosed. It has come about by no plan of our own conceiving, but by the hand of God who led us into this way. We cannot turn back. We can only go forward, with lifted eyes and freshened spirit, to follow the vision. It was this that we dreamed at our birth. America shall in truth show the way. The light streams upon the path ahead, and nowhere else.

The United States, however, refused Wilson's summons 'to follow the vision'. Mainly because of objections to the Covenant of the League, the Senate refused to give the two-thirds majority required to ratify the Treaty of Versailles. That America failed to join the League of Nations was due not merely to Wilson's opponents but also to Wilson himself. The Senate was probably prepared to accept the Covenant with reservations which were no greater than those which most members of the League were in any case to exercise in practice. But Wilson was in no mood to repeat in Washington the kind of compromises which had been forced on him in Paris. All those who opposed him he denounced as 'contemptible quitters'. When officially informed by the French ambassador that the Allies were prepared to accept the reservations on American membership of the League demanded by an influential group of Republican senators, Wilson replied, 'Mr Ambassador, I shall consent to nothing. The Senate must take its medicine.' The Senate, however, refused to take its medicine; and the American people, by electing Warren Harding as their president in 1920, endorsed its decision.

The reshaping of eastern Europe

The second great task of the Paris peacemakers, after the peace with Germany, was the resettlement of eastern Europe. The almost simultaneous defeat of the Russian, German and Austrian empires meant, in effect, that the whole map of eastern Europe, from Finland in the north to the Black Sea in the south, had to be redrawn. The new map of eastern Europe took a year to make and was established by the Allies in three separate treaties: with Austria in September 1919, with Bulgaria in November 1919 and with Hungary in June 1920.

The Baltic states of Finland, Estonia, Latvia and Lithuania, formerly parts of the Russian Empire, all gained their independence. Poland, which in the seventeenth century had been a major European power and in the eighteenth had been divided by its neighbours, was reconstituted as an independent state. The Austrian Empire was divided among half a dozen 'succession

states', of which Austria and Hungary, formerly the two centres of power within the empire, were the smallest.

The guiding principle which underlay the resettlement of eastern Europe was the principle of nationality. Boundaries between states were to coincide as far as possible with boundaries between peoples. This principle was modified in practice by two other considerations. It was doubtless inevitable that Germany's allies in eastern Europe – Austria, Hungary and Bulgaria – should be less fairly treated than their neighbours, but it was difficult to justify either the annexation of German-speaking Austrian South Tyrol by Italy or the inclusion of large Magyar minorities in the territory of Hungary's neighbours. The second factor which limited the application of the principle of

nationality was fear of revolution. All the 'Big Three' were agreed on the need to make Russia's neighbours as large and strong as possible – even at the cost of including in them large alien minorities – in order to strengthen their ability to resist the westwards march of Bolshevism.

No Bolshevik had ever imagined that the revolution in Russia could be other than part of a world revolutionary movement. Early in 1919, Zinoviev, the head of the Communist International, forecast that 'within a year all Europe will be communist'. It is easy now to dismiss such predictions as hopelessly unrealistic. At the time they were taken very seriously indeed. 'Bolshevism', wrote Wilson, 'is moving steadily westward, has overwhelmed Poland, and is poisoning Germany.'

Many other statesmen at the Paris conference feared that the foundations of European society, as they knew it, were crumbling before their eyes. Lloyd George wrote in March: 'The whole of Europe is filled with the spirit of Revolution. The whole existing order in its political, social, and economic aspects is questioned by the masses of the population from one end of Europe to the other.'

Fear of the spread of Bolshevism was strengthened still further when a communist regime, led by Bela Kun, seized power in Hungary for a few months in the spring and summer of 1919. Even though an attempted communist rising in Berlin had been bloodily suppressed at the beginning of 1919, many European statesmen, like Lloyd George, saw a real danger that Germany might yet go the way of Hungary and bring the whole of central and eastern Europe within the Bolshevik orbit.

This fear continued to play upon the minds of the peacemakers throughout the negotiations of 1919. Secret offices were set up in New Scotland Yard and the American State Department to chart the course of Bolshevism as its poison spread through Europe. Ray Stannard Baker, one of Wilson's advisers at Paris, wrote later that the Bolsheviks 'without being represented at Paris at all, were important elements at every turn'. During 1919, western opinion was already coming round to the view expressed by Sir Henry Wilson, the British chief of staff, that 'our real danger is not the Boches but Bolshevism'.

The Civil War in Russia

While Allied statesmen were pondering the Bolshevik menace at the Paris conference,

Russia itself was passing through a period of internal chaos usually, but inadequately, described as the 'Civil War'. The Bolsheviks were challenged by 'White' armies, attacking from three sides: from Siberia, the Gulf of Finland and the Caucasus.

That the Bolsheviks survived these attacks was in part because of Trotsky's brilliant leadership of the Red Army. Their survival owed even more, however, to the failures and divisions of their opponents, some of whom even fell to fighting among themselves. Increasingly, the White armies fell under the control of men of the old, discredited ruling class, hostile not merely to Bolshevism but to the March Revolution. Among the Russian peasant masses, on whom, in the last resort, the outcome of the war depended, the conviction grew that the Bolsheviks were fighting for the people of Russia against White generals whose only programme was reaction and the restoration of their former privileges.

The chaos of the Civil War offered western governments an opportunity which was never to return for reversing the decision of the November Revolution. Two or three Allied divisions landed in the Gulf of Finland in 1919 could probably have forced their way to Moscow (the new capital of Russia) and have overthrown the Bolshevik regime. But in the aftermath of the First World War not even two or three divisions could be found. In none of the Allied countries was public opinion prepared to tolerate intervention on more than a token scale. Those troops which were sent served mainly to discredit the White cause still further. They were too few to affect the outcome of the war but sufficient to allow the Bolsheviks to brand their opponents as the tools of western imperialism.

Above, weighing out an allocation of wood in Petrograd, 1919: the Russian economy had already virtually collapsed in 1917, but the Bolshevik policy of war communism, involving total control over all wealth, labour, commerce and agriculture, brought production of food and industrial goods to a standstill; only when Lenin introduced his New Economic Policy – vital if the Revolution were to be saved – did the situation improve.

Top, Admiral Kolchak (1874–1920), leader of the White Russian government based on Omsk, reviewing troops, September 1919: a few months later his advance collapsed (he himself was captured and executed), and by the end of 1920 foreign invervention had come to an end (with the exception of the Japanese occupation of Vladivostock, maintained until November 1922).

Opposite, cover of the October 1919 issue of The Communist International: *initially the Bolsheviks had hoped and expected that their revolution would be the harbinger of a Europe-wide movement towards communism, but by the early 1920s the opportunity for revolution had passed and the Bolshevik regime was forced to concentrate on the development of socialism in one country.*

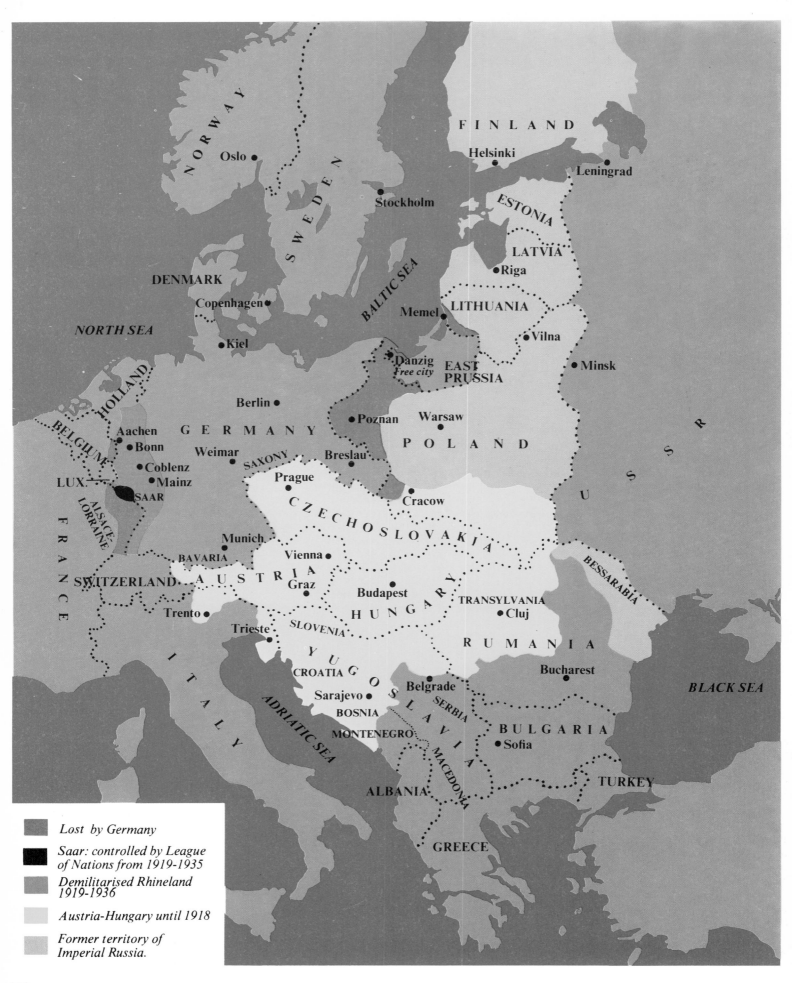

NORWAY

Oslo

SWEDEN

Stockholm

FINLAND

Helsinki

Leningrad

ESTONIA

LATVIA

Riga

DENMARK

Copenhagen

BALTIC SEA

LITHUANIA

Memel

Vilna

Minsk

NORTH SEA

Kiel

Danzig
Free city

EAST
PRUSSIA

U S S R

HOLLAND

Berlin

BELGIUM

Aachen
Bonn

GERMANY

Poznan

Warsaw

POLAND

Weimar

SAXONY

Breslau

LUX.

Coblenz
Mainz

Prague

SAAR

CZECHOSLOVAKIA

Cracow

ALSACE
LORRAINE

Munich

FRANCE

BAVARIA

Vienna

SWITZERLAND

AUSTRIA

Graz

Budapest

TRANSYLVANIA

Cluj

BESSARABIA

Trento

HUNGARY

R U M A N I A

Trieste

SLOVENIA

ITALY

YUGOSLAVIA

CROATIA

Belgrade

Bucharest

ADRIATIC SEA

Sarajevo

SERBIA

BLACK SEA

BOSNIA

BULGARIA

MONTENEGRO

MACEDONIA

Sofia

ALBANIA

TURKEY

GREECE

Lost by Germany

Saar: controlled by League
of Nations from 1919-1935

Demilitarised Rhineland
1919-1936

Austria-Hungary until 1918

Former territory of
Imperial Russia.

Above, Tsarist poster from the time of the Russian Revolution: the dragon symbolizes the Bolsheviks devouring the heart of Russia, indicated by the outline of the buildings of Moscow.

Left, Russian revolutionary poster depicting the combatants in the First World War as capitalist, militaristic money-grabbers.

Opposite, Europe after the Treaty of Versailles, 1919.

By the beginning of 1920 the White forces, though not finally defeated, no longer seemed a serious threat to the Bolshevik regime. In April the Civil War within Russia itself became overshadowed by the beginning of war with Poland. The Poles invaded Russia, nominally in support of Ukrainian nationalists but with the real intention of acquiring the Ukraine for Poland. Within two months the Polish invasion of Russia had given way to a Russian invasion of Poland, followed by the creation of a provisional government of Polish communists.

For a few months in the summer of 1920 many Bolsheviks believed that they were engaged in building a Soviet Poland which would push the borders of Bolshevism to the frontiers of Germany and enable the German communists, with Russian help, to make a successful bid for power. Churchill, among others, was afraid they might succeed. In July 1920 he published an article in the *Evening News* luridly entitled 'The Poison Peril from the East', appealing to the Germans to build, before it was too late, 'a dyke of peaceful, lawful, patient strength and virtue against the flood of red barbarism flowing from the East'. By so doing, he assured them, they would find their way 'as the years pass by back to their own great place in the councils of Christendom'.

In August 1920 the victorious Russian advance was brought to a halt. The Poles, with French assistance, inflicted a decisive defeat on the Red Army at the battle of Warsaw and began a successful counter-offensive which carried them, once again, across the Russian border. In March 1921 the Russians were forced, by the Treaty of

Riga, to leave six million Ukrainians and White Russians in Polish hands. The failure of the Red Army in Poland ended all immediate hope of a European revolution and caused a sharp decline in the Bolsheviks' international prestige. In the year after the treaty of Riga the Italian and Czech communist parties lost more than half their members, the French almost half and the German about a third.

Only in the aftermath of the next European war was Bolshevism able to resume the conquest of eastern Europe. It succeeded after 1945 where it had failed after 1918 less because its ideological appeal had become more persuasive than because its military strength was now immeasurably greater. Between the wars, however, the most serious threat to liberal democracy in Europe came not from Russian communism but from the new menace of fascism, which emerged most rapidly in Italy and more slowly, though in a more vicious form, in Germany. Without the fears aroused by Bolshevism, however, fascism would have been much less serious a menace. Fascism owed its initial impetus in Italy to a panic fear of revolution. The Nazis sought to exploit the same fear in Germany. 'My ambition', said Adolf Hitler after his first, and unsuccessful, bid for power in 1923, 'was to become the destroyer of Marxism. I am going to achieve this task.'

The birth of the Weimar Republic

On 14 August 1919 Germany became a democracy. The first article of the Weimar constitution (named after the city of its birth) proclaimed: 'The German Reich is a Republic. Political authority derives from the people.' Its drafters tried to combine in the new constitution all the best features of the British Bill of Rights, the French Declaration of the Rights of Man and the Citizen and the first Ten Amendments of the American Constitution. In all but one of its articles it was a model of democracy. The solitary exception was article 48, which allowed the president (who in normal circumstances reigned but did not rule) to confer absolute power on the chancellor 'if public order and security are seriously disturbed or endangered'. Three chancellors during the final years of the Weimar Republic assumed absolute power. The last was Adolf Hitler.

The Weimar Republic was aptly described by its first chancellor as a candle burning at both ends. The right, which propagated the myth that the politicians, not the generals, were responsible for the capitulation of 1918, regarded the new republic as both the product and the instrument of Germany's shame. The communists, too, were dedicated to its destruction. From its supporters the Republic received only lukewarm loyalty. From its opponents it encountered passionate opposition. For thirteen years, none the less, the supporters of the Republic outnumbered its opponents. But in July and November 1932, at the last free elections held in a united Germany, the opponents of parliamentary democracy outnumbered its supporters.

During the first four years of its existence the Weimar Republic lived in a state of almost continuous economic and political crisis. The post-war inflation which affected every European state hit Germany worst of all. Reparations provided a convenient excuse for Germany's economic ills. The real cause, however, was the financial irresponsibility of her governments. In Britain during the war, income tax had reached the unheard-of rate of five shillings in the pound. In Germany, on the contrary, not a penny of the war effort was financed out of taxation. The government resorted instead to vast internal loans and the printing of paper money. It pursued the same policy after the war was over.

For the first four years of the Weimar Republic the government spent four times as much as it received in taxes. During these four years the German mark pursued a quickening decline. By 1923 it was worth less – literally – than the paper it was printed on. At its lowest point in November 1923 the mark stood at 4,200,000,000 to the dollar. The rapidity of Germany's financial recovery thereafter was further evidence of the financial irresponsibility of the past four years. That irresponsibility had put at risk not merely the future of the mark but the future of German democracy. By wiping out the savings of the German middle class it destroyed the security of the very class on which, in the long run, the security of the Weimar Republic itself depended.

Financial collapse in Weimar Germany was accompanied by the use of violence for political ends. The leading figures in this wave of violence were the *Freikorps*, groups of out-of-work officers who had earned a spurious respectability by their bloodthirsty suppression of the Bolshevik risings of 1919. In March 1920 5,000 men of the *Freikorps* led by Wolfgang Kapp, a former civil servant, occupied Berlin, declared the government deposed and the Weimar constitution null and void. The *Reichswehr* (the German army) refused to intervene. General von Seeckt refused a government request that he should do so with the curt rejoinder: 'Obviously there can be no question of letting *Reichswehr* fight against *Reichswehr*.' Instead, it was the people of Berlin themselves who paralysed the capital by a general strike and forced Kapp and his comrades to leave Berlin.

All those who had taken part in the Kapp putsch either escaped unpunished or were given an amnesty. Seeckt, who had refused to put the rising down, became head of the *Reichswehr* almost as soon as the rising was over. When workers in the Ruhr called for a purge of the *Reichswehr*, Seeckt branded them as Bolsheviks and sent against them the same *Freikorps* which had just tried to overthrow the government.

For three years after the Kapp putsch, the *Freikorps* took the lead in a well-organized campaign of political terrorism. In 1921 they arranged the assassination of the minister of finance, Mathias Erzberger, the man who had signed the armistice for Germany. 'Erzberger', said one right-wing paper, 'has suffered the fate which the vast majority of patriotic Germans desired for him.' A year later it was the turn of the foreign minister, Walter Rathenau, murdered partly because of his attitude to reparations but chiefly because of his Jewish origins. For several months before his death

STOSSTRUPP-HITLER
MÜNCHEN

Above, French troops occupy the Ruhr, January 1923, in an attempt to collect reparations in kind after the German government had defaulted on its payments. The reparations clauses of the Versailles Treaty, by which Germany was to pay substantial sums, chiefly to France, were ineptly enforced, and overall Germany paid out little.

Above left, members of the Freikorps, early 1920s: large numbers of Germans felt no loyalty to the Weimar Republic, believing it to be the creation of disloyal politicians who had 'stabbed' the army 'in the back' by agreeing to the armistice and the Versailles treaty; they were fertile ground for Hitler's propaganda from the late 1920s onwards.

Left, Hitler's stormtroops during the abortive Munich putsch, November 1923: arrested and tried, Hitler received a remarkably light sentence and spent much of his imprisonment writing Mein Kampf.

Opposite, members of the Berlin Soldiers' Council, November 1918: the Weimar Republic was founded to the accompaniment of uprisings of workers and soldiers throughout Germany, aimed at establishing revolutionary regimes, only put down by the Social Democratic government with the assistance of the army.

nationalists in beer-halls up and down Germany had sung a song which ended with the lines, 'Shoot down Walter Rathenau, The God-damned swine of a Jewish sow'. The most disturbing aspect of these murders was their great popularity with large sections of the German people. Even the courts habitually assumed that right-wing violence (as opposed to left-wing violence) proceeded from praiseworthy motives and were lenient in their treatment of it.

The violence of the postwar years, like the spiral of inflation, reached its peak in 1923. The year began with the French occupation of the Ruhr, an action intended to enforce the payment of reparations which were overdue. For more than eight months, until the German government called a halt, the population of the Ruhr organized a massive campaign of passive, and occasionally violent, resistance. By the end of the summer the Kremlin concluded that Germany was ripe for revolution. On

orders from Moscow there were communist risings, during October, in Hamburg, Saxony and Thuringia. All were quickly suppressed by the *Reichswehr*.

Violence from the left was followed, as usual, by violence from the right. In November there was a nationalist putsch in Bavaria, in imitation of the earlier Kapp putsch in Berlin. As the nationalists marched into the centre of Munich the police opened fire and the putsch collapsed. At the head of the rising were Germany's two most prominent twentieth-century dictators: one, General Ludendorff, nearing the end of his career, the other, Adolf Hitler, at the beginning of his. Ludendorff bore himself splendidly in defeat. Ignoring the gunfire and the confusion around him, he continued to march forward, the police lines opening respectfully to allow him to pass through. Adolf Hitler emerged less creditably from his first bid for power. At the first shot he threw himself to the ground, then sprang up and fled

as is often supposed, the mood of the Italian people as a whole. The general election of November 1919 (unlike the post-war elections in France and Britain) was remarkable for the poor showing not merely of the nationalists and conservatives but of all those groups which had favoured intervention in the war. The newly-founded fascist party, the most extreme of the nationalist groups, failed to win a single seat. Its leader, Benito Mussolini, standing in Milan, gained only two percent of the vote. The fascists were to come to power not by exploiting the nationalism of the Italian people but by playing on their fear of Bolshevism.

Until 1921 Italian socialists and communists were members of a single socialist party, united in its admiration for the Russian revolution. At the 1919 election the socialist party gained a third of the vote and trebled its pre-war representation in parliament. The socialist newspaper, *Avanti!*, declared in triumph, 'Revolutionary Italy is born!' The wave of social unrest which swept through Italy during 1919 and 1920 seemed to prove its point. Many thousands of peasants settled on large estates and seized holdings for themselves. The government seemed powerless to prevent them. Industrial unrest, too, was worse in Italy than anywhere else in Europe. It reached its peak in August 1920 when half a million workers occupied their factories and raised the red flag over them.

Ever since the end of the war the socialist party had been openly demanding 'the violent overthrow of bourgeois society'. In August 1920 its bluff was called. A Lenin would have used the occupation of the factories as the springboard for revolution. The Italian socialists, however, had not the slightest idea of how to put their revolutionary theories into practice. In September the factories were handed back to their owners, in return for a rise in wages and improved conditions.

The end result of all the talk of revolution in post-war Italy was not revolution itself but the rise of fascism. As the anarchist, Enrico Malatesta, prophetically remarked during the occupation of the factories: 'If we do not go on to the end we shall have to pay with blood and tears for the fear we are now causing the bourgeoisie.' With the return of the factories to their owners, all real danger of revolution had passed. 'Italian Bolshevism', wrote Mussolini privately, 'is mortally wounded.' The Italian middle classes, however, were more convinced than ever that Bolshevism was preparing for its final assault. It was by exploiting this fear, and by posing as the saviours of Italy from red revolution, that the fascists were able to raise themselves from obscurity to a position which enabled them to make a bid for power.

In July 1920, on the eve of the occupation of the factories, there were, at most, a hundred fascist groups (*fasci*) in the whole of Italy. Six months later, there were over a

for cover, leaving his followers to fend for themselves. Though many formidable problems still confronted the Weimar Republic at the end of 1923, Adolf Hitler did not seem to be one of them.

Fascism in Italy

Italy, as Bismarck had long ago observed, was gifted with a voracious territorial appetite but inadequate teeth. Its gains at Versailles – the South Tyrol, Trieste, islands in the Aegean and Adriatic – were an exaggerated reward for its minor contribution to the Allied victory. But Italy had wanted more – more, in particular, of the Dalmatian coast.

In September 1919 the nationalist poet, Gabriel D'Annunzio, marched into the

Dalmatian port of Fiume at the head of a thousand of his followers. To the embarrassment of the Italian government, which shared his ambitions but disavowed his methods, D'Annunzio announced the annexation of Fiume to Italy. For the next year, until the Italian government plucked up courage to dislodge him, he ruled a comic opera régime, which developed many of the theatrical absurdities later borrowed, without acknowledgement, by Mussolini. His followers wore black shirts, greeted one another with arms outstretched in the Roman salute and communed with their leader at open-air rallies through a rhythmic and platitudinous series of questions and answers.

But the mood of nationalist hysteria reflected in D'Annunzio's adventure was not, thousand. By now the fascists had the financial backing of many large industrialists and landowners who feared for their factories and estates. They had the support, too, of the same group of out-of-work army officers who made up the *Freikorps* in Germany. And, like the *Freikorps*, the paramilitary fascist *squadre d'azione* had the blessing of the government. Soon after the occupation of the factories, the ministry of war agreed to pay all ex-officers who led the *squadre* four-fifths of their former pay. In many parts of Italy, Mussolini and his followers were able to rely on the support of prefects, police and army commanders, anxious to pay off old scores against the socialists.

Confident of the collusion of the state authorities, the fascists began an intensive series of terrorist raids on left-wing organizations. They became quite open in boasting about their brutality. During one raid near Siena, for example, a fascist leader ordered one of his victims to balance a cup on his head so that he could demonstrate his markmanship. He missed and the man was killed. The incident was reported in the local newspaper under the humorous headline, 'An unfortunate William Tell'.

The Italian middle classes found it impossible to conceive of a threat to the social order other than from the left. Impressed by years of socialist propaganda calling for the violent overthrow of bourgeois society, many were inclined to accept as legitimate the fascist argument that violence could be met only by violence. Even among liberals who deplored the fascists' methods, the illusion persisted that these excesses were no more than a passing phase. One of those who shared this illusion was the liberal minister Giolitti, who compared the fascists with the British irregulars in Ireland. 'The fascists', he told a British diplomat, 'are our Black and Tans.'

At the election of May 1921 Giolitti included the fascists on his own electoral list, thus helping them to gain a foothold in parliament for the first time. As yet few heeded Mussolini's warning that the fascists were destroying Bolshevism not as an end in itself but 'in preparation for the settling of accounts with the liberal state which survives'. When the liberal state finally recognized the nature of the fascist threat to its existence, it proved unequal to the challenge.

There were two crucial turning points in the fascists' bid for power. The first was the government's failure to suppress the paramilitary *squadre d'azione* on which fascist power was based. Without the *squadre* the March on Rome would have been impossible. A government decree issued in December 1921 ordered the prefects throughout Italy to suppress all unofficial armed organizations. Mussolini immediately declared that all fascists were members of the *squadre*, confident that no government would dare dissolve the whole fascist party. His confidence proved to be well-founded, and the

decree remained a dead letter. 'The government', boasted Mussolini, 'can do nothing against us.' Its nerve had failed.

The fascist leader in Ferrara wrote in his diary on the first day of 1922: 'We have not only broken the resistance of our enemies but we also control the organs of the state. The prefect has to submit to orders given by me in the name of the fascists.' During the next nine months the fascists made themselves the masters of northern Italy, forcibly taking over most of its town councils. By October they were ready to make their bid for power. Mussolini told his followers on 24 October: 'Either the government will be given to us or we shall descend on Rome and take it.' Three days later the March on Rome began.

At the eleventh hour the Italian government seemed suddenly to recover its nerve. On the evening of 29 October the cabinet formally requested the king, Victor Emmanuel, to declare a state of martial law and use the army to put down the fascist march. Had the king granted this request, as constitutionally he was bound to do, the March on Rome would have ended in a fiasco from which the fascist movement would have had difficulty in recovering. Instead, Victor Emmanuel invited Mussolini

Above, Benito Mussolini (1883–1945), fascist dictator of Italy: authoritarian, militaristic, imperialist and pompous though his regime was, it never wholeheartedly espoused the racialist doctrines of Nazi Germany (though anti-Semitic campaigns were waged) and in 1943 simply crumbled away, leaving little or no mark on the nation.

Opposite, revolutionary poster issued in Germany 1918–19 depicting a spartacist slaying the forces of militarism, capitalism and the Junkers, *the great Prussian landowners.*

to become prime minister. Hitherto, Mussolini had taken no part in the March on Rome, preferring to remain out of harm's way in Milan. On receiving the king's invitation, however, he donned a bowler hat, boarded a sleeping car and arrived in Rome ahead of his followers. When the fascists entered Rome on 30 October, Mussolini was already prime minister.

Mussolini established his dictatorship only by degrees. For eighteen months he remained head of a coalition government. For more than two years opposition parties and an opposition press continued to exist. As late as the summer of 1924, after the murder by fascists of a socialist deputy, the opposition almost succeeded in bringing Mussolini down. In January 1925, as a result of this experience, Mussolini declared Italy a one-party state.

At the time of the March on Rome no-one, not even Mussolini, had had much idea what fascist government would be like. Like the rest of Italy, Mussolini discovered as he went along. He declared:

We do not believe in dogmatic programmes. . . . We permit ourselves the luxury of being aristocratic and democratic, conservative and progressive, reactionary and revolutionary, legalists and illegalists, according to the circumstances of the moment, the place and the environment.

Though he was vague about his policies Mussolini was clear about the poses which he wanted to adopt. He was, he informed the readers of his *Autobiography*, the man who had preserved Italy from the threat of Bolshevism, cleansed it from the corruption of parliamentary government and had given it a new sense of national pride. Many foreign statesmen were taken in. Winston Churchill called Mussolini 'the saviour of his country'; Sir Austen Chamberlain, the British foreign secretary, felt 'confident that he is a patriot and a sincere man'. Ramsay MacDonald, Britain's first Labour prime minister, wrote him friendly letters even while Mussolini was busy destroying the Italian socialist party. Mussolini made much of his friendship with British statesmen and their wives. In 1925 he ordered no less than one and a half million copies of a postcard showing himself in conversation with Lady Chamberlain and had them distributed all over Italy.

Whatever their attitude to Mussolini himself, almost all European observers during the 1920s utterly mistook the significance of the fascist movement. They regarded fascism not as the beginning of a European movement but as a peculiarly Italian response to a peculiarly Italian situation. Mussolini himself endorsed their judgement. 'Fascism', he declared as late as 1928, 'is not an article for export.' Only the Nazis seemed to understand the European significance of the fascist revolution. 'The March on Rome', wrote Goebbels later, 'was a warning, a storm-signal for liberal democracy. It was the first attempt to destroy the world of the liberal, democratic spirit.'

Chapter 17

Europe and the Outside World

يہ سپاہی ہندوستان کی حفاظت کر رہا ہے۔ وہ اپنے گھر اور گھر والوں کی حفاظت کر رہا ہے۔

اپنے گھر والوں کی مدد کرنے کا سب سے اچھا طریقہ یہ ہے کہ فوج میں بھرتی ہو جاؤ۔

To acute political observers it had long been obvious that Europe's supremacy in world affairs would one day be replaced by global rivalry between the United States and Russia. These two nations, wrote de Tocqueville in 1835, were each of them 'marked out by the will of heaven to sway the destinies of half the globe'. The First World War seemed to have brought the prophecies of both Cobden and de Tocqueville to fulfilment. The United States, now beyond dispute the greatest economic power on earth, emerged from the war apparently intent on claiming what Wilson called 'the moral leadership of all mankind'. Russia shared the same ambition. The November Revolution had made it the centre of a new world faith which, within a single generation, was to rule the destiny of a third of mankind and of whose powers of attraction the statesmen gathered at Versailles seemed to have no doubt.

The age of European supremacy was not to end, however, with the First World War. It was reprieved for twenty years by the simultaneous retreat of the United States and Russia from world affairs. In his inaugural address, in January 1921, President Harding formally renounced the vision of the future which Wilson had laid before the American people. 'We seek no part', he said, 'in directing the destinies of the world.' Most Americans, during the 1920s, came to the conclusion that the United States ought never to have entered 'Wilson's war' at all. As late as 1937, an opinion poll showed that seventy percent of Americans were still of this opinion.

While the United States was unwilling to 'direct the destinies of the world', the Soviet Union (as Russia renamed itself in 1922) was anxious, but unable, to do so. By the time of Lenin's death, in January 1924, the prospect of European revolution, which had earlier seemed so real both to the Bolsheviks themselves and to the peacemakers in Paris, had become remote. In his last article before his death, Lenin consoled himself for the Bolsheviks' disappointments in Europe with the optimistic reflection that 'the East has already entered the revolutionary movement' and that 'Russia, India, China, etc., constitute a huge majority of the world's population.'

The torch of revolution had begun to pass from the peoples of industrial Europe, for whom it had been intended, to the backward peasant masses of Asia. But even in Asia there seemed no immediate prospect of a successful revolution. The communist risings in Chinese cities during the later 1920s were no more successful than the risings in German cities during the early 1920s. Revolution in Asia, like revolution in Europe, could come about only as a result of war.

Though the primacy of Europe continued after the First World War, its basis had been seriously undermined by the European powers themselves. The principle of self-determination proclaimed by the Allies in Europe was one which colonial peoples were bound to apply to the European empires: and which, a generation later, was to provide the ideological basis for decolonization. In both Asia and the Middle East (though not in Africa) it was the First World War which

Above, Indian recruiting poster issued during the First World War: the caption reads 'this soldier is guarding India. He is guarding his home and his household. Thus we are guarding your home and you must join the army.' Like other parts of the Empire, India contributed large numbers of troops to the Allied war effort.

Opposite, Mussolini's blackshirts at Milan railway station: it was from here that Mussolini embarked on his personal march on Rome in October 1922–by train.

245

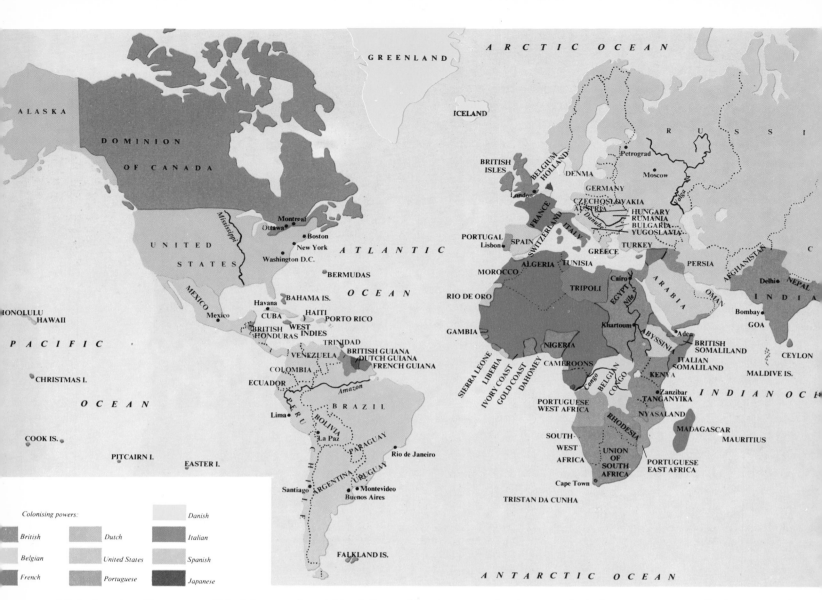

ARCTIC OCEAN

GREENLAND

ALASKA

DOMINION

OF CANADA

UNITED

STATES

MEXICO

ICELAND

BRITISH ISLES

London

BELGIUM
HOLLAND

FRANCE

PORTUGAL

SPAIN

Lisbon

DENMA

GERMANY

CZECHOSLOVAKIA

AUSTRIA

SWITZERLAND

ITALY

Danube

HUNGARY
RUMANIA
BULGARIA
YUGOSLAVIA

GREECE

Petrograd

Moscow

Volga

R U S S I

TURKEY

PERSIA

AFGHANISTAN

Montreal

Ottawa

Boston

New York

Washington D.C.

ATLANTIC

OCEAN

BERMUDAS

MOROCCO

ALGERIA

TUNISIA

Cairo

TRIPOLI

EGYPT

Nile

ARABIA

OMAN

Delhi

NEPAL

Bombay

INDIA

GOA

Havana

HAWAII

HONOLULU

BAHAMA IS.

CUBA

Mexico

HAITI

PORTO RICO

RIO DE ORO

GAMBIA

Khartoum

ABYSSINIA

Aden

BRITISH SOMALILAND

CEYLON

PACIFIC

BRITISH HONDURAS

WEST INDIES

TRINIDAD

VENEZUELA

BRITISH GUIANA
DUTCH GUIANA
FRENCH GUIANA

SIERRA LEONE

LIBERIA

IVORY COAST

GOLD COAST

DAHOMEY

NIGERIA

CAMEROONS

Congo

BELGIAN CONGO

KENYA

Zanzibar

TANGANYIKA

ITALIAN SOMALILAND

MALDIVE IS.

INDIAN OCE

CHRISTMAS I.

COLOMBIA

ECUADOR

Amazon

BRAZIL

OCEAN

Lima

PERU

BOLIVIA

La Paz

PORTUGUESE WEST AFRICA

RHODESIA

NYASALAND

MADAGASCAR

MAURITIUS

COOK IS.

PITCAIRN I.

EASTER I.

PARAGUAY

Rio de Janeiro

SOUTH-WEST AFRICA

UNION OF SOUTH AFRICA

PORTUGUESE EAST AFRICA

Santiago

CHILE

ARGENTINA

URUGUAY

Montevideo

Buenos Aires

Cape Town

TRISTAN DA CUNHA

FALKLAND IS.

ANTARCTIC OCEAN

Colonising powers:

British   Dutch   Danish

Belgian   United States   Italian

French   Portuguese   Spanish

                               Japanese

---

established nationalism as a political force.

In the Middle East the Allies deliberately encouraged the growth of Arab nationalism against the Turkish Empire, only to find the same nationalism turning against themselves as soon as the war was over. In the two largest Asian colonies, India and Indonesia, the war witnessed the emergence of the National Congress and Sarekat Islam – hitherto middle class in membership and moderate in their demands – as mass movements demanding for the first time complete national independence.

The British Commonwealth of Nations

The First World War also transformed the relationship of the British dominions with the mother country. Responsibility for the foreign policy of the empire, Asquith had said in 1911, could never be shared with the dominions. In 1914 the dominions, like the rest of the empire, found themselves at war by a decision not of their own making but of the British government. Though the dominions accepted this decision without question, their governments came to resent

Asquith's failure either to consult them about the conduct of the war or even to keep them adequately informed about British policy. The very scale of the dominions' contribution to the war – 458,000 men from Canada, 332,000 from Australia, 112,000 from New Zealand, 76,000 from South Africa – made it inevitable that their voice should eventually be heard.

One of Lloyd George's earliest acts as prime minister was to announce the formation of an Imperial War Cabinet composed of the prime ministers and other representatives of Britain and the dominions. The new cabinet met in London for several weeks during both 1917 and 1918 to co-ordinate the imperial war effort and prepare for peace negotiations.

At the Imperial Conference of 1926 the dominions were formally conceded in theory the status which had been theirs in fact since 1917, couched in words which has passed into British constitutional history:

They are autonomous communities within the British Empire, equal in status, in no way subordinate one to another in any aspect of their domestic or external affairs, though

united by a common allegiance to the Crown, and freely associated as members of the British Commonwealth of Nations.

There was a deliberate and calculated ambiguity in the definition. Australian loyalists could pride themselves on remaining part of the British Empire; Afrikaaner nationalists, by contract, gained the satisfaction of being recognized as members of an autonomous community.

To many the whole idea of the Commonwealth of Nations was a piece of constitutional metaphysics which defied rational analysis. This was particularly true of the position of King George V, who, having begun his reign as ruler of a united empire, now found himself, rather to his annoyance, the owner of seven technically separate crowns: one for Britain and the colonies and one each for the six dominions (Australia, New Zealand, South Africa, Canada, Newfoundland, and, from 1922, Ireland). He was not amused by comments such as that of the sceptical Canadian historian, Professor Lower, who remarked: 'God in three persons is outnumbered by the British King in seven persons.'

For its supporters the Commonwealth had from the first a sentimental as much as a constitutional significance. Many probably shared the feelings of the future Australian prime minister, Sir Robert Menzies, who wrote later that the Commonwealth meant to him:

King George and Queen Mary coming to their Jubilee in Westminster Hall . . . at Canberra, at Wellington, at Ottawa, at Pretoria, the men of Parliament meeting as those who met at Westminster seven hundred years ago . . . Hammond at Sydney and Bradman at Lords and McCabe at Trent Bridge, with the ghosts of Grace and Trumble looking on.

The First World War was followed by a steady drift of the dominions away from dependence on Britain. Between the wars most Canadian politicians accepted the dictum of Henri Bourassa, the leader of the French Canadians, that 'There is not a single problem of either internal or external policy which we can settle without reference to the policy of the United States.' Sir Robert Borden, the Canadian prime minister, warned Lloyd George at the Paris peace conference that 'if the future policy of the British Empire meant working in co-operation with some European nation as against the United States, that policy could not reckon on the approval or support of Canada.' In 1921 Borden's successor, Arthur Meighen, supported by South Africa, put pressure on Britain to abandon her alliance with Japan because of America's opposition to it.

Australasia followed, more slowly, the same path of growing dependence on the United States. For most of the interwar years Australia and New Zealand were overwhelmingly concerned with domestic problems, almost to the exclusion of foreign policy. Though their inhabitants were, by 1939, more prosperous than any other people in the world, neither as yet even possessed a diplomatic service in non-Commonwealth countries. As early as March 1914, however, Winston Churchill, as First Lord of the Admiralty, had warned Australasia that it could not depend on British naval support in the Pacific if Britain were involved in war in Europe. And without the Royal Navy to defend them, 'the only course of the five millions of white men in the Pacific would be to seek the protection of the United States'.

The rise of Japan during the 1930s and the realization that the Far East had now become, in the words of one New Zealand newspaper, 'Australasia's Near North', slowly convinced the governments of Australasia of the truth of Churchill's warning. At the beginning of 1942, even before the surrender of Singapore, the Australian prime minister, John Curtin, declared: 'Without any inhibitions of any kind, I make it quite clear that Australia looks to America, free of any pangs as to our traditional links of kinship with the United Kingdom.' Though the bluntness of Curtin's statement angered even Churchill (despite his earlier warning), it has remained ever since the underlying premise of Australia's defence policy.

The Irish Free State

The most restless of the dominions between the wars was also the newest and the nearest home. Until the First World War Ireland had been represented at Westminster by her own members of parliament, most of whom had demanded 'Home Rule', a formula which combined internal self-government with continued British sovereignty. The First World War made Irish nationalism, like the nationalism of other subject peoples, more extreme. At Easter 1916 a group of extremists seized the centre of Dublin and proclaimed an Irish republic 'in the name of God and of the dead generations'. After four days of street fighting the new republic surrendered and all but one of its leaders were executed. The single exception was the future president of

Opposite, the colonial empires after the First World War.

247

in the House of Commons, 'which would disgrace the blackest annals of the lowest despotism in Europe.' In the summer of 1921 Lloyd George abandoned hope of subduing Ireland by force, and the rebels agreed to a truce. In January 1922 the *Dáil* approved a treaty by which the Irish Free State was established with dominion status and Ulster was allowed to remain part of the United Kingdom.

In England the treaty helped to bring about the break-up of Lloyd George's coalition and the return to traditional party politics. In Ireland the bitterest phase of 'the troubles' now began. A republican minority, led by de Valéra, denounced the treaty as a surrender and began a civil war against their former colleagues. Some British ministers found it difficult to suppress a feeling of gratification at the sight of Irish nationalists tearing one another to pieces. Birkenhead, the lord chancellor, told the Lords in the summer of 1922: 'I, for one, rejoice, as I have said before in this House, that this task [the suppression of the rebellion], painful, costly, bloody as it must ultimately prove, is being undertaken by those to whom it properly falls.'

The atrocities committed by Irish against Irish after independence exceeded even those of the 'Black and Tans'. Government forces took to disposing of groups of their opponents by tying them to mines which were then exploded. Before the civil war ended in the spring of 1923, the Free State government had executed more than three times as many Irishmen as the British had done in the two years before independence. After independence de Valéra remained for a decade in the political wilderness. But in 1932 he returned to power at the head of a new party, the *Fianna Fáil* ('Soldiers of Destiny') and began gradually to dismantle Ireland's last links with Britain.

Imperial superiority

Few Europeans after the First World War realized that the decline of Europe had begun. The fact that Europe now controlled more of the outside world than ever before seemed more impressive than the faint stirrings of opposition to its rule. The British Empire had gained a million square miles at the expense of Turkey and Germany. It now contained a quarter of the earth's surface and a quarter of mankind. Few British people had any suspicion that the power of their empire was being weakened by the growth of a Commonwealth within it. The South African prime minister, Jan Smuts, the most persuasive advocate of the Commonwealth of Nations, emphatically denied that this was so. The British Empire, he told the Imperial Conference of 1921, 'emerged from the war quite the greatest power in the world, and it is only unwisdom or unsound policy that could rob her of that great position'.

Ireland, Eamon de Valéra, born in the United States of a Spanish father and Irish mother, whose American nationality earned him a reprieve.

In the short term the Easter Rising achieved only the destruction of much of central Dublin. In the longer term, it meant the abandonment of Home Rule. The 450 Irish lives lost during the rising, and the sixteen executions which followed it ('few but corroding', as Churchill described them), shocked most Irishmen outside Ulster into supporting the nationalist demand for complete independence.

By the end of the war most Irish MPs had already left Westminster. After the 1918 elections they established an independent Irish parliament, the *Dáil Eireann*, and an independent Irish government under Eamon de Valéra. The new government hoped at first, by levying its own taxes and administering its own justice, simply to take over peacefully from the discredited British administration. Over much of Ireland it might well have done so. The Irish Republican Army, however, thought otherwise. Against the wishes of the *Dáil*, it began its own guerrilla war against the British.

In 1920 the British brought in their own *Freikorps*, the so-called 'Black and Tans' and 'Auxis', whose atrocities rivalled, and perhaps exceeded, those of the IRA. 'Things are being done in Ireland', said Asquith

Patriotic pride in the British Empire was still a recent phenomenon. The idea that Britain possessed some kind of mission to the 'lesser breeds without the law' had captured a hold on the popular imagination only in the last decade of the nineteenth century. By 1918, however, most British people already regarded this mission as one of their oldest traditions. Their mood was reflected in the tune and words of 'Land of Hope and Glory', by now so popular that it had come to be regarded as a second national anthem. There were few who doubted the immense moral superiority of the British Empire over all other empires past and present. It was, said Lloyd George in 1921, 'the most hopeful experiment in human organization which the world has yet seen'. Hardly anyone was eccentric enough to suppose that within half a century the empire would have almost disappeared.

European rule in Africa

European rule over most of the African continent, though profound in its effects, was comparatively brief – less, in many cases, than a single lifetime. Between the wars, however, most British people thought of Africans as rather child-like people, probably incapable of ever running their own affairs, in general cheerful and easy-going but retaining beneath a thin layer of civilization an aura of primeval savagery.

This, at least, was the image of the peoples of Africa which most school-children in Britain learned from their geography textbooks. One of the most popular of these textbooks was *Children Far Away*, by Ernest Young, a fellow of the Royal Geographical Society, which was first published in 1919 and reprinted twelve times in the next six years. Young's book devotes two of its seven chapters to the children of Africa: one to the negroes, the other to the pygmies. White negro children ('the little blackies') emerge from Young's description as mindless but moderately benevolent. Pygmy children are portrayed as both mindless and malevolent: 'The pygmy children do not love their father or mother, and their fathers and mothers do not love them. They care nothing for their own land or people. All they want is to hunt and to eat. They are cruel to one another.'

White rule in English-speaking Africa took two quite different forms. In West Africa and much of East Africa it was based on the system of 'indirect rule' made famous by the most celebrated of Britain's African proconsuls, Sir Frederick Lugard. Lugard believed in strengthening traditional government by tribal chiefs – if necessary even creating tribal goverments where there had been none before – and placing the chiefs themselves under the paternal care of British district officers. By these means he succeeded in governing the whole of Nigeria, the largest state in Africa (with one-fifth of Africa's population), with a civil service of little more than a few hundred men.

Just as Lugard's Nigeria became the showcase of British imperial administration, so his book, *The Dual Mandate in Tropical Africa*, first published in 1922, became the bible of British imperialism between the wars. In it Lugard argued that Britain possessed a duty both to the peoples of Africa and to civilization itself: to the peoples of Africa, to watch over their political and economic advancement; and to civilized society as a whole, to make sure that Africa's natural resources were available to it. 'The merchant, the miner and the manufacturer', he wrote, 'do not enter the tropics on sufferance or employ their technical skill, their energy, and their capital as interlopers or as "greedy capitalists", but in fulfilment of the mandate of civilization.' The eventual goal of European rule should be to prepare the peoples of Africa to manage their own affairs. But Lugard warned against going at too fast a pace: 'The danger of going too fast with native races is more likely to lead to disappointment, if not to disaster, than the danger of not going fast enough.'

Neither South Africa nor Southern Rhodesia (which, though not independent, gained virtual self-government in 1923) had any thought of preparing their native populations for eventual independence, however remote that independence might be. Their aim, which was shared by many white settlers in other parts of East Africa, was to create new white nations in southern Africa and 'keep the kaffir in his place'. The case for white rule in southern Africa was bluntly put by a government official in Southern Rhodesia: 'We are in this country because we are better men. It is our only excuse for having taken the land. For us to turn round now and ask the natives to help in directing the government of ourselves is ridiculous.' After the First World War many people in both Britain and South Africa (including

Above, members of the 'Black and Tans', British troops sent to Ireland with orders to crush the Irish revolt by no matter what means.

Opposite top, Dublin during the 1916 Easter Rising by the Irish Volunteers: by now the demands for Home Rule made at the beginning of the century were increasingly being replaced by a determination to achieve complete independence from British rule.

Opposite bottom, Eamon de Valera (1882–1975) inspecting troops of the Irish Republican Army, 1921: de Valera's Army refused to accept the settlement negotiations with the British government, by which the Irish Free State became an independent member of the Commonwealth and Northern Ireland remained part of the United Kingdom.

both Churchill and Smuts) expected Southern Rhodesia to seek union with South Africa. To their surprise, a referendum in Southern Rhodesia in 1922 turned down a proposal for union. This decision was a momentous one for the whole of Africa. As a fifth province within the Union of South Africa, Southern Rhodesia might have tipped the balance in favour of the English-speaking population and made less likely both the dominance of the Afrikaner nationalists after World War Two and the era of apartheid which they inaugurated.

On the eve of World War Two there seemed no reason to anticipate either the racial tensions which were soon to show themselves in southern Africa or the pressures for independence which were soon to emerge within Africa as a whole. Though the phrase 'racial conflict' was in common use in southern Africa, it referred at that time not to tensions between black and white but to rivalry between the English and Afrikaner communities. Except in the Arab north, African opposition to European rule still seemed a negligible quantity. There was not a single nationalist movement of any importance struggling to achieve independence in any African colony south of the Sahara Desert.

The future of the African continent was decided far less by events in Africa itself between the wars than by India's struggle for independence. India, as the popular platitude put it, was 'the brightest jewel in the imperial crown'. Its population of 315,000,000 was three-quarters of that of the entire British Empire. It was in India that the decline of the British Empire began.

The Indian subcontinent

At the outbreak of the First World War British rule had seemed as secure in India as it appeared to be in Africa on the eve of the Second. The outburst of patriotism which greeted the declaration of war in Calcutta almost equalled that in London. In 1857 the use of Indian troops outside India had been one of the causes of the Indian Mutiny. Yet in 1914 Indian princes competed for the privilege of being the first to lead their forces to the front. While the princes offered troops, the middle classes offered money, and the Legislative Assembly volunteered to pay part of the cost of the war in Europe.

In retrospect, however, the war was to prove the beginning of the end of the British raj and the beginning of the end, also, of the British Empire. As the war continued the war-weariness which became common in Europe spread to India, but, while soldiers on the Western Front at least believed that they were fighting for national survival, Indians seemed to be giving their lives in Mesopotamia and the Middle East simply for the extension of the British Empire. At the beginning of the war there

had been no shortage of Indian recruits. During its later stages Britain was reduced to using press gangs.

Resentment against Britain was less serious for the future of the raj than the decline of British prestige. British rule in India rested, in the last resort, not on military coercion but on respect for the moral, as well as material, superiority of British civilization. As soon as belief in that superiority disappeared, as it began to do during the First World War, the days of the British raj were numbered.

The British government responded to the unrest caused by the war with a pledge – the Montagu Declaration of 1917 – which was interpreted in India as a promise of dominion status. But by raising hopes which Britain seemed reluctant to fulfil the Montagu Declaration only hastened the growth of opposition to British rule. The reforms introduced immediately after the war by the Government of India Act of 1919, though a substantial departure from the autocracy of the pre-war raj, seemed utterly inadequate as a preparation for self-government. As Adolf Hitler was later to observe, 'Britain has given to the Indians the opportunity of using as a weapon against her the non-fulfilment of her promises regarding a constitution.'

Before the First World War there had been no movement in India capable of organizing a mass demand for independence. The Indian National Congress was still a middle-class debating society which met briefly each December and then lapsed into inactivity for another year. There was nothing in 1914 to suggest that Congress would emerge from the war as a mass movement which would become the focus of resistance to the British raj. The man who brought about this transformation was Mohandas Gandhi, a barrister of the Inner Temple who, more than any other man, set in motion the process which was to lead to the downfall of the British Empire.

Until the war Gandhi had lived almost all his adult life outside India. He had made his name as the champion of the Indian community in South Africa, and it was there that he developed the technique of *satyagraha*, or passive resistance, which he was to use against the raj. Much of Gandhi's political success was a result of the aura of sanctity about his person which won him the devotion of the Hindu masses. After his return to India he abandoned western dress in favour of a loincloth, rigorously and ostentatiously adhered to the rules of poverty and chastity and identified himself with the cause of 'the untouchables', the lowest class in Indian society, whom he renamed the *Harijans*, or the sons of God. Gandhi sought not merely political freedom from British rule but spiritual emancipation from the materialism of western civilization. He claimed for India precisely that moral superiority which the British raj had hitherto assumed for itself.

The war was followed by an influenza epidemic which killed more Indians than the Western Front had killed Europeans. The epidemic added to the unrest caused by the war. The chief centre of unrest was the Punjab where most of the British press gangs had been concentrated. In April 1919 a prohibited meeting at the Punjabi town of Amritsar was dispersed without warning by troops using rifles and machine guns. The official casualty list was 379 dead and more than 1,000 wounded. General Dyer, the officer responsible for the order to open fire, was unrepentant. He followed the massacre by public floggings and forced all Indians using a street where a British woman missionary had been assaulted to crawl along it on all fours.

The Amritsar massacre has been called 'the worst atrocity in the history of the British Empire'. But it was less the massacre itself than the attempts to justify it in Britain which produced a revulsion against British rule. Though Dyer was dismissed by the Indian government, there were many in Britain who vigorously defended his conduct. The House of Lords passed, by a large majority, a motion in Dyer's favour, and the readers of the *Morning Post* subscribed £30,000 in appreciation of his action.

The result of Amritsar was to give Gandhi control of Congress and its endorsement for his view that 'cooperation in any shape or form with this satanic government is sinful.' In the summer of 1920 Gandhi began a campaign of non-cooperation which, he forecast optimistically, would bring the British raj to its knees within a year. But though thousands of students left their schools and colleges, and thousands of middle-class members of Congress began spinning cotton by hand (an activity to which Gandhi attributed spiritual as well as economic significance) instead of buying it from Lancashire, non-cooperation failed. It did so because thousands of Indian civil servants, even though sympathetic to Gandhi's aims, dared not take the enormous risk of resigning from their posts. By the end of 1921 many of Gandhi's followers were already losing heart.

Early in 1922, after twenty-two policemen had been burnt to death by a Hindu mob, Gandhi himself called off his campaign. The people of India, he concluded sadly, did not yet possess a sufficient understanding of the principle of non-violence for non-cooperation to achieve its aims. Soon afterwards, Gandhi was arrested and found guilty of incitement. 'It would be impossible', Gandhi was told by his judge, 'to ignore the fact that, in the eyes of millions of your countrymen, you are a great patriot and a great leader. Even those who differ from you in politics look upon you as a man of high ideals and of noble and even saintly life.' But Gandhi would 'not consider it unreasonable', the judge believed, that he should go to prison for six years: 'And I should like to say . . . that, if the course of events in India should make it possible for the government to reduce the period and release you, no one will be better pleased than I.'

On Gandhi's imprisonment, organized resistance to British rule seemed to have collapsed. By 1924 the Indian government felt, as Gandhi's judge had hoped, that it could safely release Gandhi from prison on the grounds of ill-health.

The British government still had no serious intention of preparing India for self-rule. Lord Birkenhead, the secretary of state for India, admitted in a letter to the viceroy in 1925: 'To me it is frankly inconceivable that India will ever be fit for Dominion self-government.' But Birkenhead thought it as well to anticipate further trouble by making some conciliatory gesture to Indian opinion. In 1927, therefore, the British government established the all-party Simon Commission (which included among its members the young Clement Attlee) to enquire into the Indian constitution.

By omitting to include on it any Indian member, however, Britain made the Simon Commission appear a calculated insult to the Indian people. Even those Indians best disposed towards Britain refused to have anything to do with it. Like the Amritsar massacre, the Simon Commission discredited the moderates and played into the hands of the militants. In December 1928 Congress issued an ultimatum to the British government demanding self-government within a year. When the year expired it declared India an independent state and authorized Gandhi to launch a new campaign of civil disobedience. The new campaign was to include, for the first time, sins of commission as well as omission: a programme of non-violent crime on so vast a scale that Gandhi believed the administration of justice would grind to a halt.

Gandhi began his campaign with a crime brilliantly calculated to show the raj at its most ridiculous and its most unjust. Probably the least defensible of all the methods of taxation used by the raj was its salt monopoly, reminiscent of the hated *gabelle* in pre-revolutionary France. It was an offence not merely to sell but even to possess salt not purchased from the British monopoly, and it was this monopoly which Gandhi decided to challenge. Amid the glare of world-wide publicity he began a three-week walk to the Indian Ocean. Having arrived at the seashore, he was photographed by newsreel cameras solemnly breaking the law by extracting salt from the sea. After a brief period of uncertainty while the raj made up its mind, Gandhi was sent to prison, soon to be joined by 60,000 of his followers. The British government hurriedly called a 'round-table conference' to discuss the future of India, but its discussions were made meaningless by the absence of any Congress representative.

Early in 1931 the British viceroy, Lord Irwin (later, as Lord Halifax, British foreign

secretary at the time of the Munich crisis), released Gandhi from prison and invited him to begin talks with him. Gandhi replied that he would like to meet 'not the viceroy but the man within the viceroy'. He displayed that the same flair for publicity in his meetings with Irwin that he had earlier shown on his walk to the sea. He went on foot each day to the viceroy's palace, surrounded by crowds of his supporters and large numbers of reporters and carrying an aluminium saucepan containing his food for the day. In Britain Winston Churchill fulminated against

the nauseating and humiliating spectacle of this one-time Inner Temple lawyer, now seditious fakir, striding half-naked up the steps of the viceroy's palace, there to negotiate and parley on equal terms with the representative of the King-Emperor.

Above, Mohandas (Mahatma) Gandhi (1869–1948) leading the Salt March, 1930: Gandhi's Congress Party played a central role in the campaign first for Indian self-government, then for complete independence.

Top, Indian demonstration against the Simon Commission: the Commission, headed by Sir John Simon (1873–1954), later to become foreign secretary, proposed indirect elections for the central legislature and increased local democracy, but the India Act passed in 1935 went considerably further in devolving power.

The result of the talks was the 'Gandhi-Irwin truce'. Irwin agreed to the release of all political prisoners, except those convicted of crimes of violence. Gandhi agreed to call off the civil disobedience campaign and attend a second round-table conference in London.

The truce, however, lasted less than a year. In London Gandhi demanded immediate dominion status, and the conference ended in deadlock. Within a few weeks of his return to India at the beginning of 1932, Gandhi was once again in prison. Congress fell, once more, into partial eclipse, as it had done ten years before when he was first imprisoned. Most Indians remained sympathetic towards its aims, but few were yet prepared to continue an indefinite struggle with the raj.

The British government and parliament continued nonetheless to be preoccupied with the future of the Indian subcontinent. A succession of 'fact-finding' commissions went back and forth to India, returning, as Churchill complained, laden with 'bulky and indigestible sheaves'. The final result of these deliberations was the Government of India Act of 1935, ridiculed by Churchill as 'a monstrous monument of sham built by the pygmies'. Under it central government remained safely in the hands of the viceroy but the provinces acquired a high degree of local autonomy and responsible government.

Congress was at first bitterly divided over its attitude to the new constitution, its left wing under Jawaharlal Nehru urging rejection of it. Eventually, however, Congress agreed to contest the first elections held under the new constitution in 1937 and won control of eight of the eleven provinces. The experience of government during the two years before the Second World War was a turning-point in the history of Congress. It marked its transformation from a movement seeking to gain its ends by unconstitutional means into a parliamentary party. Congress politicians and British officials, who had hitherto regarded each other with deep suspicion, now discovered that relations between them were often surprisingly good – a discovery which did much to smooth the course of independence negotiations after the war.

The great mistake made by Congress during the 1930s was in its treatment of the Muslims. During the 1920s Congress leaders had, on the whole, been conscious of the need for the Hindu majority to respect the rights of the Muslim minority. In ten years there had been five Muslim presidents of Congress. 'Hindu-Muslim unity', said Gandhi, 'is our breath of life.' The idea of Pakistan ('the land of the pure') originated, not on the Indian subcontinent itself, but among a group of Muslim undergraduates studying in England at Cambridge University in 1932.

Even in the middle of the 1930s, despite signs of tension between the Hindu and Muslim communities, a separate Muslim state after independence was still the ambition of only a small minority of Indian Muslims. Jinnah, the leader of the Muslim League, declared in 1937: 'There is really no difference between the League and Congress. . . . We shall always be glad to cooperate with Congress in their constructive programme.'

At the 1937 elections the League declared its willingness to form coalitions with Congress in the new provincial governments. Elated with their electoral success, however, Congress leaders refused to allow the Muslim League any share of power in the states which they controlled. No British government between the wars made any mistake of comparable magnitude in its Indian policy. Denied its rightful share in the government of India, the Muslim League was forced back on the idea of Pakistan: an ambition which was to be fulfilled only at the cost of a religious civil war on the Indian subcontinent and the loss of a million lives.

The Middle East

Britain's relations with the people of Egypt were worse than with any other of its subject peoples. The Egyptians became derisively known as 'wogs', a term later more broadly used to indicate the British image of the shifty foreigner. The British themselves, however, had shown a degree of shiftiness in establishing themselves in Egypt which had no parallel in the history of Victorian imperialism.

Britain had sent troops to Egypt in 1882 to put down an anti-European uprising, insisting that these troops would leave as soon as order had been restored. 'An indefinite occupation', declared Gladstone, the British prime minister, 'would be absolutely at variance with all the principles and views of Her Majesty's Government, and the pledges they have given Europe.' Though this pledge was many times repeated, the 'temporary occupation' was to last for seventy years.

Britain broke her word for strategic, rather than for economic, reasons. Even between the wars oil was still only a minor consideration in British policy in the Middle East. On the eve of the Second World War the whole of the Middle East produced no more than five percent of the world's oil. But the Suez canal, which ran through Egyptian territory, was regarded as the most vital link in Britain's imperial communications, the 'lifeline of the Empire'. In British eyes the safety of this lifeline demanded the permanent presence of British troops on Egyptian soil and British control of Egyptian foreign policy.

Despite the length of its military occupation, Britain's protectorate in Egypt lasted officially for only eight years. Its protectorate began soon after the outbreak of

the First World War and came allegedly to an end in 1922 when Britain declared Egypt independent. Both British troops and the British high commissioner remained, however, and Britain claimed continued responsibility for Egypt's defence and foreign policy and for the protection of foreign interests in Egypt. The nationalist Wafd party reasonably declared that independence on these terms would be a farce. The sultan, Ahmed Fuad, was torn between his dislike of the British and his loathing for the politicians of the Wafd, most of whom combined nationalism and corruption in about equal proportions.

After a year's haggling, largely devoted to increasing his own powers, Fuad agreed to independence on terms which raised him from sultan to the status of a rather more than constitutional monarch. Though Britain slightly relaxed its grip on Egypt after the accession of King Farouk in 1936, British troops remained in Egypt for another twenty years.

The greater part of the Middle East in 1914 still belonged to the decaying Turkish Empire. Besides Egypt, only Cyprus and an assortment of sheikdoms under British protection in the Persian Gulf were under European control. The peace settlement which followed the First World War, however, established European rule over almost the whole of the Middle East. Britain's part in bringing about this transformation was more disreputable than any other episode in the history of its twentieth-century diplomacy. Ramsay MacDonald described it thus:

We encouraged a revolt in Turkey by a promise [in 1915] to create an Arab kingdom from the Arab provinces of the [Turkish] Empire including Palestine. At the same time we were encouraging the Jews to help us by promising them that Palestine would be placed at their disposal for settlement and government; and also at the same time, we were making with the French the Sykes-Picot Agreement partitioning the territories which we had instructed our governor-general in Egypt to promise to the Arabs. The story is one of crude duplicity, and we cannot expect to escape the reprobation which is bound to follow as a sequel.

As part of the post-war settlement Britain and France divided between them most of Turkey's former Arab empire. France took Syria and Lebanon, Britain acquired Iraq (formerly known as Mesopotamia), Transjordan and Palestine. Saudi Arabia, which neither country wanted, was given to the Arabs as an independent kingdom.

The horse-trading between Britain and France in the Middle East was made more respectable by the new principle of 'trusteeship'. Both countries acquired their shares of the Turkish Empire not as colonies but as mandates from the League of Nations and recognized a duty to watch over their

'progressive development . . . until such time as they can stand alone'. Most of the Middle East, however, gained its independence only after World War Two. Though the British mandate in Iraq ended formally in 1932, Britain continued, as in Egypt, a form of indirect rule by virtue of so-called 'treaty rights' which gave it military and financial control.

One unexpected by-product of British rule in Iraq was the birth of the Royal Air Force as an independent service. In 1922 Britain succeeded in quelling a tribal revolt in Iraq not, as in the past, by a military expedition but by bombing from the air. For the first time it seemed possible to envisage a European war decided as much in the air as on the ground. As a result, Britain became in 1923 the first country in the world to free its air force from dependence on the other services.

The most serious long-term problem bequeathed by Britain's devious wartime diplomacy in the Middle East arose from its promise to the Jews. The terms of Britain's mandate in Palestine made it responsible for putting this promise into effect by 'the establishment in Palestine of a national home for the Jewish people'. The Arabs, who made up more than ninety percent of the Palestinian population, were at once assured by Britain that the Jewish national home would not become a Jewish national state and that all their 'civil and religious rights' would be respected. A national state, however, was precisely what the Zionist movement (which was responsible for the idea of a 'national home' in Palestine) intended to achieve – a state which, in the words of Dr Weizmann, its leader, would be 'as Jewish as England is English'.

As a first step towards this goal, Zionists insisted on the strict separation of Arab and Jewish communities. Jewish parents refused to send their children to mixed government schools. Arab tenants and farm workers were evicted from all land bought by the Jewish National Fund. David Ben-Gurion, later the first prime minister of the state of Israel, organized a series of strikes against Jewish employers of Arab labour. The Jewish Agency, which coordinated Jewish settlement in Palestine, sought, with some success, to make itself a state within a state. Until the First World War the Arabs had been the only people living in contact with the Jews who had never persecuted them. The birth of Arab anti-semitism between the wars was the work not of Adolf Hitler but of the Zionists.

One of the first British ministers to deal with the Palestinian problem was Winston Churchill, colonial secretary during the final year of Lloyd George's coalition. In a White Paper published in 1922, Churchill correctly defined the crux of the problem (though in an uncharacteristically inelegant phrase) as one of relating Jewish immigration to Palestine's 'absorptive capacity'. During the 1920s Palestine's 'absorptive capacity' never seemed in danger. In most years, there were no more than 5,000 Jewish immigrants. At such a rate of immigration, Arab predominance in Palestine was not in danger, and British administrators could look forward to an eventual lessening of the tension between the two communities.

What no British government during the 1920s could be expected to foresee was the vast influx, in the next decade, of Jewish refugees from Nazi persecution. Though Britain tried in vain to stem the flow in 1939, the Second World War made it unstoppable. It was less the Zionists than Adolf Hitler who made possible the creation, in 1948, of the Jewish state of Israel out of most of pre-war Palestine.

The European empires

The British Empire was larger, both in size and population, than all other European empires put together. The empires of Italy, Belgium, Spain and Portugal were all virtually confined to Africa. That of the

Above, illegal Jewish immigrants to Palestine wading ashore, having dodged the Royal Navy's blockade, late 1930s: throughout that decade the British government restricted the number of Jews entering Palestine, so condemning many to remain in Europe to await eventual death in Hitler's concentration camps.

Above left, Chaim Weizmann (1874–1952), appointed head of the World Zionist Movement in 1920, with King Faisal I of Syria, later of Iraq (1885–1933), 1921: at this time, Jewish immigration into Palestine was small, and Jewish leaders tried to gain the cooperation of Arab leaders, though it was not long before open hostility broke out.

Netherlands consisted only of the Dutch East Indies and Dutch Guiana. Germany had no empire at all. Curiously, it was the oldest and most decrepit empires – those of Spain and Portugal – which were to last the longest. In Asia the last European colony to gain its independence was the tiny Portuguese enclave of Goa, on the Indian subcontinent. In Africa, by the end of the 1960s, Portugal's empire was larger than Great Britain's.

Apart from Britain, only France – with colonies in Africa, Asia, the Middle East, the West Indies and the Pacific – could claim to be a world power. But even France's empire, both in size and population, was less than half Britain's. It was also far more rebellious. In Africa, Asia and the Middle East, France was faced with armed rebellion on a scale not encountered by Britain until after the Second World War. During the 1920s there were serious revolts in both Syria and Morocco. The pacification of Morocco was not complete until the middle of the 1930s and Syria never really accepted French rule. In Indo-China the French administration seemed during 1930 to have caught a nationalist rebellion in its early stages and restored order by hundreds of executions. But by the beginning of the Second World War, there was already a powerful communist underground movement led by Ho Chi Minh which, once the war was over, was to launch a successful struggle for independence.

Though the French Empire was more autocratic than the British, Frenchmen were less troubled than Englishmen by racial differences between themselves and their colonial peoples. The long-term aim of the French colonial administration was to turn its subjects into Frenchmen. A British minister remarked in 1926:

In these matters we are apparently by nature the exact opposite of the French. The French have no doubt that the more French they can make French Africa in language, sentiment, custom, and outlook, the better. We cannot help doubting whether any persons not of our race can really become British in this way.

Increasingly French colonial enthusiasts regarded their colonies – especially in Africa – not as colonies at all but as extensions of France itself. For this reason many Frenchmen regarded their own empire, even though far smaller than the British, as superior to it. As one Gaullist minister was later to remark, referring to the supposed enthusiasm of Algerians for union with France: 'This is something unique! Whoever heard of any Pakistani shouting *"Pakistan anglais"*?'

The imperial mission was a transitory experience. Most people in France and Britain did not take it seriously until the very end of the nineteenth century. By the 1960s, most of them no longer believed in it. The young Disraeli had described most British colonies in the nineteenth century as 'wretched millstones'. Little more than a century later, such a description exactly fitted Britain's only remaining mainland colony, Rhodesia. But the imperial mission left a legacy behind. During the 1950s Dean Acheson described Britain as having 'lost an empire but not yet found a role'. Other peoples who were equally civilized and equally prosperous, like the Swiss and Scandinavians, did not feel that they needed to find a role precisely because they had never had an empire to lose. The imperial mission left in post-imperial Britain and in post-imperial France the conviction that the world still needed the light of their example.

Chapter 18

Prosperity and Depression

The later 1920s were the last period of real optimism in the history of Europe. The years of optimism began in 1925 with the treaty of Locarno, a non-aggression pact between France, Germany and Belgium, guaranteed by Britain and Italy. Locarno, said Sir Austen Chamberlain, would be remembered as 'the real dividing line between the years of war and the years of peace'. To many European statesmen it seemed a landmark in European history, the end of an era of deep hostility between France and Germany which had continued without a break from the Franco-Prussian war of 1870 to the occupation of the Ruhr in 1923. Geneviève Tabouis, the most famous French journalist of her generation, wrote of her reaction to Locarno:

I was literally drunk with joy. It seemed too good to be true that Germany, our enemy of yesterday, had actually signed the pact with its eight clauses of reconciliation! From now on, no more fears for the future! No more war!

The reconciliation between France and Germany was strengthened by the friendship of their foreign ministers, Aristide Briand and Gustav Stresemann. Briand was the greatest exponent of what A. P. Herbert called 'Locarno blarney', the emotional incantations to peace which flowed from the lips of most statesmen of the period. His oratory earned him the title of 'the archangel of peace', and he was regularly depicted by French cartoonists in the act of turning swords into ploughshares. Briand's most famous speech was his welcome to Stresemann on Germany's admission to the League of Nations in September 1926. In retrospect, his speech seems tinged with bathos: 'From this day forth women will be able to fix their eyes on little children without feeling their hearts torn by anxiety!' But it captured completely the mood of the Locarno honeymoon. No speech in European history has aroused so much enthusiasm over so much of Europe.

Soon after welcoming Stresemann to the League of Nations, Briand invited him to a private lunch at Thoiry in the French Alps. The two men announced after lunch that they had 'established the basis for a political

understanding', though the nature of this understanding was never afterwards discovered. 'You can call it the mystery of Thoiry,' Briand told journalists, 'What a good title for a thriller!' But, he added whimsically, 'while we were sitting at luncheon we watched the clouds lift from the top of Mont Blanc, and we both agreed that its snows were no whiter than the bottom of our two hearts.'

The high point of the Locarno honeymoon was the Briand-Kellogg treaty of 1928. In April 1927 Briand proposed to the American government that France and the United States should celebrate the tenth anniversary of the American entry into the

Above, Gustav Stresemann (1878–1929), briefly chancellor of Germany in 1923 and then foreign minister until his death: he brought Germany out of her diplomatic isolation following the First World War.

Opposite, Moorish troops during the 1921 uprising in North Africa, when the Spanish garrisons in Morocco were overwhelmed: it was five years before Spanish control was firmly re-established.

First World War by a pact renouncing war as an instrument of national policy. Kellogg, the American secretary of state, replied six months later by suggesting (with one eye on the next presidential election) that such a pact should be extended to include the whole world. As a first step towards this end, the representatives of fifteen leading powers met in Paris in August 1928 to sign a treaty by which all agreed (though sometimes with reservations) to outlaw war.

The signature of the pact was surrounded by a slightly idiotic ceremonial, devised by Briand and satirized by one French newspaper as 'the celebration of Briand's spiritual wedding with peace'. Almost every state in the world hastened to add its signature to it, including even the Soviet Union which, like the United States, was not a member of the League. Only five states – Argentina, Bolivia, Brazil, Saudi Arabia and the Yemen – refused to sign. The pact was the supreme example of 'Locarno blarney', of the belief that words alone possessed the power to prevent aggression. Its only effect during the 1930s was possibly to make states more reluctant to declare war before they began to wage it.

The League of Nations

Looking back in 1930 on the achievements of the 1920s, most European statesmen still felt optimistic for the future. The League of Nations, though derided at its outset by those who considered themselves political realists, was now an accepted part of international diplomacy. It had, according to *The Times*, 'quietly made good'. The League had had so far to face only one major challenge to its authority: Mussolini's seizure of the Greek island of Corfu in 1923 after the murder in Greece of an Italian general. As a result of mediation through the League, Mussolini had undertaken to

withdraw from Corfu in return for fifty million lire from Greece. Though this settlement clearly favoured the stronger power, it was widely regarded as a victory for so new an organization. Without the League, it was argued, the seizure of Corfu might have developed into a European war. The fact that for the remainder of the 1920s the League had to face no further challenge to its authority from any major power seemed to demonstrate its growing authority.

Introducing a report on the League's first ten years in 1930, its secretary-general summed up the prospects for the future by quoting from a speech by General Smuts:

Looked at in its true light, in the light of the age and of the time-honoured ideas and practice of mankind, we are beholding an amazing thing – we are witnessing one of the great miracles of history. . . . The League may be a difficult scheme to work, but the significant thing is that the Powers have pledged themselves to work it . . . Mankind has, as it were, at one bound and in the short space of ten years, jumped from the old order to the new, across a gulf which may yet prove to be the greatest break or divide in human history.

The return of prosperity

The optimism of the Locarno honeymoon was in part a consequence of economic prosperity. In 1925, the year of the Locarno pact, European production for the first time reached its pre-war level. The return of prosperity was symbolized by Winston Churchill's decision as chancellor of the exchequer to put Britain back on the gold standard in the same year and make sterling once again freely convertible into gold. By 1928 all other European currencies had followed suit. Between 1925 and 1929, the volume of international trade rose by

almost twenty percent and by 1929 Europe's share of world production was once again as large as before the First World War.

The prosperous years of the later 1920s were characterized by conservative statesmen who contrived to make a virtue of their own inertia. Calvin Coolidge had won the 1924 election in the United States by telling the electorate to 'Keep Cool with Coolidge'. Stanley Baldwin, similarly, urged the British people to trust 'honest Stanley' and be content with a policy of 'safety first'. Though there were many gaps in the prosperity of the later 1920s, the Conservative governments of the time paid little attention to them. In Britain, for example, there were never less than a million unemployed. Yet, even after the General Strike of 1926, parliament contrived to spend more time discussing the revision of the Anglican Prayer Book than the problem of unemployment. Happily for the Conservative party, the inactivity of Baldwin's government enabled it to lose the 1929 election, just in time to leave a Labour government to face the depression.

The great flaw in the European prosperity of the Locarno era was that it depended for its continuance on the unstable prosperity of the American economy. This dependence was one of the most important consequences of the First World War. For a century before 1914 investment had flowed across the Atlantic from east to west. Ever since it has flowed emphatically in the opposite direction. The European economy in the 1920s depended for its prosperity on massive American investment. In the five years from 1925 to 1929 alone, this investment amounted to no less than $2,900 million. Germany, with a total debt of $1,000 million, depended on American investment not merely to remain prosperous but even to remain solvent. Yet the continued availability of American investment depended on the continuation of a speculative boom which ran increasingly out of control.

By the summer of 1929 share prices on Wall Street were nearly four times higher than four years before, and five million shares were changing hands every day. Most Americans seemed to imagine that the prosperity of the Locarno era would go on for ever. President Coolidge told Congress in his last message on the State of the Union, in December 1928:

No Congress of the United States ever assembled, on surveying the state of the Union, has met with a more pleasing prospect than that which appears at the present time. In the domestic field there is tranquillity and contentment and the highest record of years of prosperity. In the foreign field there is peace, the goodwill which comes from mutual understanding.

Herbert Hoover, Coolidge's successor as president of the United States, was equally optimistic. In his election campaign he promised Americans not merely 'a full

dinner pail but 'a full garage' too. Not even the economists seemed to have any premonition of what was coming. A fortnight before the biggest crash in the history of the American stock market, Professor Irving Fisher, the doyen of Yale economists confidently predicted, 'I expect to see the stock market a good deal higher than it is today within a few months.'

The Great Depression

On 'Black Thursday', 24 October 1929, the speculative bubble burst. In the next nine days $40,000 million were wiped off the value of American securities. With the collapse of the stock market, lending to Europe ceased and all existing loans were recalled as soon as their term expired. Since most American loans had been short-term, their withdrawal from Europe came with catastrophic suddenness. Yet, while calling in its loans, the United States continued until the summer of 1931 to demand punctilious payment of war debts owing to it. And by raising import duties to an average level of forty percent the United States made it impossible for its foreign debtors to pay their way by increased exports. As one country after another sought to balance its books by cutting imports, the inevitable result was the collapse of world trade.

The prosperity of the world economy depended not merely on American foreign investment but on a high rate of American consumption. In 1928 the United States consumed nearly forty percent of the world's nine chief primary products (food and raw materials). In the long run it was the primary producers who were hardest hit, both by the collapse of world trade and by the contraction of the American market. Even on the eve of the Second World War most primary producers were still unable to

afford much more than a third of what they had been able to buy from abroad before the Great Depression.

Contrary to popular belief, Britain was not one of the countries which suffered most from the depression. Despite its loss of foreign earnings, the slump in the price of its imports of food and raw materials meant that at the worst moments of the depression the net loss to its balance of payments was only £25,000,000 a year. While industrial production in Germany and the United States fell by almost fifty percent in three years, British production in 1932 was still eighty-four percent of the figure for 1929. Though there was heavy unemployment in Britain's export industries, there were also large sections of industry (especially in the southeast) which found themselves almost unaffected by the slump and in which real wages actually rose during the depression.

In the long run, the political consequences of the depression were more serious than

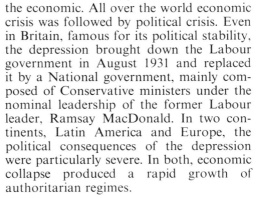

the economic. All over the world economic crisis was followed by political crisis. Even in Britain, famous for its political stability, the depression brought down the Labour government in August 1931 and replaced it by a National government, mainly composed of Conservative ministers under the nominal leadership of the former Labour leader, Ramsay MacDonald. In two continents, Latin America and Europe, the political consequences of the depression were particularly severe. In both, economic collapse produced a rapid growth of authoritarian regimes.

Latin America

For Latin America, as for Europe, the 1920s had been a period of relative stability. In most of the score of independent Latin American states revolution seemed, by 1930, to have become a thing of the past. Foreign investment had poured into Latin America at the rate of more than $5,000 million in a single decade, while Europe and North America provided steadily expanding markets for Latin American foodstuffs and raw materials. Then, in 1930, both the foreign capital and foreign markets,

on which the prosperity of the 1920s depended, were suddenly cut off.

For the first time in its history, Latin America had to face the problem of large-scale unemployment. In Brazil half the civil service was thrown out of work in a matter of months. In Chile 100,000 of the 140,000 miners lost their jobs within two years. The depression years were more violent than any others in Latin America's history since the early years of independence. In the first year of the depression the governments of the three major South American states, Argentina, Brazil and Chile (the 'ABC states') were all overthrown. In Argentina, none of whose governments had been forcibly overthrown for half a century, General José Uriburu, a professed admirer of Mussolini, established a military dictatorship. Two months later a military coup in Brazil handed power to another admirer of Mussolini, Getulio Vargas, who established what he called 'a disciplined democracy'. Chile, which suffered more severely from the depression than any other Latin American country, dissolved for eighteen months into a condition close to anarchy with, at one time, six governments being overthrown in the space of a hundred days. Of all the states of Latin America, only Colombia and Costa Rica managed to preserve relatively stable government throughout the 1930s.

Like Uriburu and Vargas, many of the men who came to power during the depression were attracted by the methods used by Mussolini in Italy. A few, like Calles, the Mexican dictator, claimed to model themselves on Hitler. It would be a mistake, however, to draw too close a parallel between the dictatorships of Europe and Latin America. Everywhere in Latin America dictatorship was tempered by incompetence. No government possessed the means to make itself totalitarian, even if it wished to do so. Political programmes, too, frequently contained a bewildering mixture of ideologies which would have been unthinkable in Europe. Calles, for example, though an admirer of Hitler, chose a moderate Marxist, Lázaro Cárdenas, to succeed him as President of Mexico in 1934. In 1938 a left-wing Popular Front government was established in Chile with the support of the Chilean Nazi party. The most striking characteristic of the regimes of the 1930s was their nationalism and xenophobia. Marxists, fascists and conservatives alike all blamed the outside world for Latin America's ills.

The depression in Europe

The first international consequence of the European depression was to strengthen France. France was not, like Germany, dependent on American investment, nor, like Britain, did she have to export to live. While the mark and the pound fell, the franc remained firm, supported by one third of the world's gold reserves. Dr Luther, the president of the German Reichsbank, was forced to fly cap in hand to Paris in search of credit, and France was able to make her financial goodwill dependent on German political concessions.

Until 1932 many Frenchmen thought they might escape the depression altogether. 'For our part', said *Le Figaro* in October 1931, 'let us rejoice in our timid yet prosperous economy in contrast to the presumptuous and decadent economy of the Anglo-Saxon races.' This euphoria was short-lived. Though the depression reached France last, it lingered longer there than anywhere else in western Europe. When Germany had recovered from the depression, and was planning its second bid for the mastery of Europe, France was still in the midst of an economic crisis. Even on the eve of the Second World War French industrial production was only three-quarters of the pre-depression level.

For more than half a century Marxists had been predicting the collapse of the European economy. Yet when the collapse came they were not the ones to profit from it. Not a single country became communist

as a result of the Great Depression. Instead, the depression changed fascism, communism's most virulent opponent, from an Italian to a European movement. The change in the nature of fascism is aptly reflected in the utterances of its founding father, Benito Mussolini. Having declared in 1928 that 'Fascism is not an article for export', he changed his mind soon after the depression had begun and declared in 1930, 'I never said that fascism is not an article for export.'

Over much of Europe democracy was still a new and fragile institution, unable to withstand the shock of an economic cataclysm. The greatest tragedy of the European depression was that it struck hardest in Germany, the great power where democracy was weakest. Once democracy had been destroyed in Germany, democracy in the rest of Europe stood at risk.

Above, Franklin D. Roosevelt (1882–1945, president from 1933), whose programme of New Deal legislation did much to alleviate the worst effects of the Depression.

Top, election poster issued by the French Communist Party, 1937, attacking bankers for working against the national interest.

Above left, combing a slag heap for coal during the 1930s.

Opposite top right, in Great Britain the effects of the Depression varied enormously from region to region and from class to class. The depressed areas of the north were especially badly hit, and in 1936 the Jarrow miners shown here marched to London to protest at continuing lack of work.

Opposite centre and bottom right, the upper and the lower classes face the camera: throughout the 1930s, and indeed well beyond that decade, Britain remained divided by class and wealth.

Opposite left, Dance Bar in Baden-Baden by the German Expressionist painter Max Beckmann (1884–1950), a typical image of the inter-war period as it is now recalled. Galerie Günther Franke, Munich.

259

Chapter 19

China and Japan

China is the oldest civilized state on earth. It is also the only large country in the world which has never at any time passed under European rule. For two thousand years after its unification in 221 BC the Chinese Empire came into contact with no civilization which could be considered the equal of its own.

China was not merely ignorant of the outside world. It was also uninterested in it. The Middle Kingdom found it inconceivable that the barbarians beyond its borders had anything of value to offer. Only the first Opium War of 1840–2 forced China to open its doors to the West. Its wars with the West led to the establishment of 'treaty ports', semi-colonial enclaves on Chinese territory which became the bases for the determined European exploitation of the Chinese economy. For a hundred years China itself became a semi-colonial nation. Its tax system, its ports and its largest industrial city fell into the hands of foreign powers. The Chinese government became, in the words of Mao Tse-tung, 'the counting house of our foreign masters'. The colonial privileges first established by the West in China in 1842 were finally abandoned only a hundred years later, in 1943, at a time when much of China was in Japanese hands.

For the first fifty years of its exploitation by western capital China still kept itself aloof from western ideas. Except for a half-hearted attempt to modernize its army, the Chinese government sought refuge in 'a return to old ways'. It was, paradoxically, not Europe but Japan which was responsible for bringing China's intellectual isolation from the West to an end. For centuries the Japanese had been contemptuously known in China as the 'dwarf pirates', inferior beings who had copied Chinese civilization. But in 1895 China was heavily defeated in a war with Japan and lost Formosa. Defeat by the 'dwarf pirates' was the greatest humiliation in the entire history of the Chinese Empire. Yet the reason for this humiliation seemed obvious. It lay in Japan's determination to learn from the West. The conclusion drawn by most educated Chinese was that China must end her traditional isolation and do the same.

The emergence of Japan

Japan's response to the challenge of the West was quite different from that of China. In the mid-eighteenth century Japan came swiftly to the conclusion that, if it were to avoid the fate of China, it must learn from the West the secrets of its strength.

The speed of Japan's modernization has no parallel in the history of the modern world. In the 1850s its islands had been defenceless even against a small detachment of American warships. Half a century later, in 1905, it inflicted a crushing defeat on Russia, which for most of the nineteenth century had been considered the greatest military power on earth. Japan's transformation into a modern state began with the accession of the Emperor Mitsuhito in 1867. For centuries the emperor had been a mere figurehead, dominated by a noble clan, the Tokugawa, who had been the real rulers of Japan. But in 1867 the Tokugawa were overthrown by reformers who restored the emperor and used his authority and prestige to gain acceptance for an ambitious programme of reforms.

Mitsuhito gave to his reign the name of Meiji, or 'enlightened rule'. When he died in 1912 Japan possessed a strong army, a modern navy and the basis of an industrialized economy. It had conquered Formosa and Korea and had gained the foothold in Manchuria from which in the 1930s it would begin the conquest of China. Though continuing to insist on his own divinity, Mitsuhito bestowed on Japan an autocratic system of government modelled on Bismarckian Germany, with the additional refinement that the army and navy ministers had always to be drawn from the armed services. This meant, in effect, that Japanese service chiefs had something approaching a power of veto over any cabinet of which they disapproved. The army thus acquired, with disastrous consequences for the future, an influence on government which it possessed in no other country in the world outside Latin America.

The First World War changed the balance of power in the Far East more than in any other part of the world. In Europe Germany's bid for European hegemony had only been interrupted. In the western hemisphere the war had merely confirmed the existing supremacy of the United States. But in the Far East the war established, for the first and only time in its history, the supremacy of Japan.

Before the First World War Japan had been only one of a number of powers competing among themselves for a privileged position in China. On the outbreak of war, however, Japan's competitors were forced to abandon the struggle for influence in China and concentrate instead on the struggle in Europe. Japan took advantage of the war to capture the German base at Kiaochow on the Chinese mainland and

take possession of all the German islands in the north Pacific. Even the United States, hitherto deeply suspicious of Japan's ambitions, formally recognized after its entry into the war that 'Japan has special interests in China.' The Far Eastern problem', wrote the British minister in Peking at the end of the war, 'may now be defined as the problem of Japan's position in China.'

Japanese supremacy in the Far East was guaranteed by an international conference called at Washington in 1921 to discuss the limitation of naval armaments. Japan agreed to limit its navy to three-fifths the size of the navies of Britain and the United States and to give up Kiaochow, though it still retained the Pacific islands which it had won from Germany. In return for these concessions (which still left it with the third largest navy in the world and a strong foothold in China) Japan was able to insist that the West construct no naval bases within striking distance of its islands. Britain was to build no naval base north of Singapore, the United States no base west of Hawaii. Japan thus acquired the naval supremacy of the western Pacific.

This supremacy could have been challenged only by naval cooperation between the world's two greatest naval powers, Britain and the United States. Anthony Eden, as British foreign secretary in the years before the Munich crisis, tried several times to reach agreement on Far Eastern policy with the United States. He declared publicly that he was prepared to 'go from Melbourne to Alaska' to secure American cooperation. But the United States refused to commit itself to more than moral condemnation of Japanese aggression. Just as American isolation made possible Hitler's 'New Order' in Europe, so in the Far East it made possible Japan's 'New Order in East Asia'.

Besides transforming Japan's political position, the First World War also made it a fully industrial state for the first time. No country in the world – not even the United States – derived greater economic advantages from the war. All over Asia Japan was able to capture markets which Europe had once dominated but was now unable to supply because of the demands of the war effort. Part of Lancashire's economic troubles between the wars stemmed from Japan's conquest of much of the Asian cotton textile market during the First World War. Japan was transformed by the war from a debtor to a creditor nation. Until 1914 Japan had always been in deficit on its balance of payments. During the war years alone, it accumulated a trading surplus of 1,400 million yen – a greater sum than the total value of her industrial production in 1913. Its gold reserves in the same period increased almost a hundred times.

The causes of Japan's rise to Asian supremacy during the First World War, however, lie as much in China as in Japan. Throughout history the greatness of one power has invariably been built on the weakness of its neighbours. This principle was as true of twentieth-century Japan as of classical Rome, or the France of Louis XIV, or the Germany of Adolf Hitler. The real basis of Japanese power was less its own strength than the weakness of China. China was twelve times larger than Japan in area (even after the acquisitions of the Meiji era), eight times larger in the size of its population and richer by far in its natural resources. In the long term the modernization of China, begun at the turn of the twentieth century, was bound to make it, once again, the greatest power in Asia. In the short term, however, it destroyed China's internal cohesion. It was the interval of chaos in China which accompanied its emergence as a modern state which allowed Japan to make its bid for the mastery of Asia.

The Chinese warlords

Each of the dynasties which had ruled China for the past two thousand years had claimed to derive its throne from 'the Mandate of Heaven'. Each time a dynasty was overthrown its demise was interpreted by the Chinese people as a sign that heaven had withdrawn its mandate. Thus it was with the fall of the Manchus in 1911. But with their fall the traditional dynastic pattern of Chinese history was broken. They were succeeded not by a new dynasty but by a republic inspired by the alien ideals of western liberal democracy. 'History', said *The Times*, 'has witnessed few such surprising revolutions.' But *The Times* was less than optimistic for the future. It declared:

Some of those who know China best cannot but doubt whether a form of government so utterly alien to Oriental traditions as a Republic can be suddenly substituted for a monarchy in a nation of 400 millions of men whom Kings with semi-divine attributes have ruled since the first dim twilight of history.

The aim of the republican nationalists in the 1911 revolution was to replace the decentralized autocracy of the Manchu Empire with a strong and centralized Chinese state. In the short term, however, they achieved precisely the opposite. The new republic could not unite China because it could not control the army. Of the thirty-six divisions in the Manchu army in 1911, only five were paid and controlled directly by Peking. The other thirty-one were financed by the provinces in which they were stationed. The provincial commanders – 'warlords' as they were romantically called by the Western press – looked on the fall of the Manchus as an opportunity to entrench themselves as feudal rulers

of their respective provinces. Not until Mao Tse-tung proclaimed the Chinese People's Republic in 1949 was any government able to end the rule of the warlords.

The Chinese Republic was officially proclaimed on 1 January 1912. Six weeks later, in order to prevent civil war, its first president, Sun Yat-sen, was forced to hand over power to Yuan Shih-k'ai, the former commander of the Manchu army. Yuan was optimistically referred to by republican politicians as the 'Washington of the Chinese Republic'. His aim, however, was not to defend the Republic but to destroy it. On New Year's Day 1916 he proclaimed himself the founder of a new imperial dynasty. Yuan died six months later while trying, without success, to quell the rebellions which his proclamation had brought about.

The twelve years after Yuan's death were the most chaotic in Chinese history since the peasant rebellions which had brought down the Ming dynasty in the middle of the seventeenth century (at almost the same moment when the Stuart dynasty was being overthrown in England). In 1917 Sun Yat-sen and his republican followers left Peking and set up their own government in Canton. At the Paris peace conference two years later China was in the remarkable position of being jointly represented by separate delegations from the rival regimes in Peking and Canton, each claiming to be the only legitimate Chinese government and each conducting a civil war against the other. Neither government, however, controlled more than a fraction of the Chinese provinces, and both were at the mercy of the local warlords. Sun was forced on several occasions to flee for refuge to one of the foreign enclaves on Chinese soil.

Until the Japanese invasion of 1937 the real rulers of most of China were the warlords. Some made genuine, though sometimes misguided, attempts to modernize their provinces. One of the most famous,

Above, a warlord being received at American headquarters in Tientsin with full military honours: after the fall of the Manchu dynasty, numerous warlords – one estimate suggests that there were some 1300 between 1912 and 1928 – came forward to fill the political vacuum, but none succeeded in establishing a permanent, firmly based regime.

Feng Yu-hsiang, the 'Christian marshal', ordered the mass baptism of his troops with fire hoses and mounted his cavalry for a time on bicycles. Many warlords, however, were simply content to feather their own nests. Conscious that their reigns were likely to be brief, they were anxious to extract as much as possible from the population of their provinces before they could be deposed by a rival. No warlord after Yuan had any hope of founding even a local dynasty. Having amassed their fortunes, many then retired to the security of one of the 'treaty ports'. By 1926 Tientsin contained twenty-five major, and many minor, warlords living in retirement.

The consequences of the First World War in China were less dramatic than in Japan. In the long run, however, they were of even greater importance. The war produced a massive disillusionment among educated Chinese with the alien ideals which had inspired the foundation of the Chinese Republic. China's reaction against the West, like its earlier interest in western ideas, was once again the result of its humiliation by Japan. Japan took advantage of the war to deliver to Yuan Shih-k'ai in 1915 the notorious Twenty-one Demands, which were intended to turn China into a virtual Japanese protectorate. Japan tried to keep these demands secret for fear of their effect on the outside world. Precisely for that reason China made sure that knowledge of them reached Europe and the United States. Though the pressure of world opinion forced Japan to modify its more extreme demands, China was forced to concede to Japan both Kiaochow and the various privileges formerly enjoyed by Germany and to agree to an extension of Japan's existing foothold in Manchuria. The day on which Yuan agreed to these concessions became known in China as National Humiliation Day.

In August 1917 the Peking government yielded to American pressure to enter the war on the Allied side. By so doing, said the United States, China would win a place at the peace conference from which it could challenge Japan's encroachment on its soil. China's delegations set out for Paris at the end of the war confident that the principle of self-determination which the Allies had proclaimed in Europe would also be applied in China. What China did not know was that Britain and France were already committed by secret treaties to supporting Japan. The Treaty of Versailles brushed aside all China's claims and formally recognized the transfer to Japan of the former German base at Kiaochow. The American minister in Peking wrote:

Probably nowhere else in the world had expectations of America's leadership at Paris been raised so high as in China. The Chinese trusted America, they trusted the frequent declarations of principle uttered by President Wilson, whose words had

reached China in its remotest parts. The more intense was their disappointment and disillusionment due to the decisions of the old men controlling the Peace Conference. It sickened and disheartened me to think how the Chinese people would receive this blow which meant the blasting of their hopes and the destruction of their confidence in the equity of nations.

China's treatment by its allies made Chinese nationalism a mass movement for the first time. Its leaders were the Chinese students. On 4 May 1919 demonstrators taking part in a protest rally against the Paris peace conference organized by students from Peking University burned down the house of Ts'ao Ju-lin, who had negotiated the Chinese reply to the Twenty-one Demands and beat up Chang Tsung-hsiang, the former Chinese minister in Tokyo, whose life was saved only by the arrival of troops. The Fourth of May Movement, as it became known, spread to two hundred towns and cities throughout China, involving twenty million people in a series of strikes and demonstrations and a boycott of Japanese goods.

In response to pressure from the movement, the Chinese delegation at the Paris peace conference refused to sign the Versailles treaty (which thus did not receive the signature of any one of the world's three largest independent nations – China, Russia, and the United States). One of the leaders of the movement in Hunan was the young Mao Tse-tung, not yet a Marxist but already an ardent nationalist. His article, *The Great Union of the Popular Masses of the Whole Country*, written in July 1919, was widely read as far afield as Peking. In it Mao declared:

We students are already living in the twentieth century, and yet they [China's rulers] still compel us to observe the old ceremonies and the old methods. The country is about to perish, and yet they put up posters forbidding us to love our country. . . . The great union of the Chinese people must be achieved. Gentlemen! We must all exert ourselves, we must all advance with the utmost strength. Our golden age, our age of brilliance and splendour, lies ahead!

Western observers were taken aback by the student leadership of the Fourth of May Movement. The American philosopher, John Dewey, who came to lecture in Peking in 1919, wrote back to America: 'To think of kids in our country from fourteen on taking the lead in starting a big clean-up reform politics movement and shaming merchants and professional men into joining them! This is sure some country!'

In Europe student protest had begun to emerge as a political force only in the nineteenth century and even then on a small scale. But in China student protest was as old as the Empire itself. During the first century BC some 30,000 students from the

Imperial College had joined in an organized protest against the dismissal of an imperial official. At a number of times of crisis during the next two millenia, students at schools and colleges claimed the right to act as spokesmen for Chinese public opinion. The publications of the Fourth of May Movement make it clear that Chinese students in 1919 saw themselves in this traditional role.

Just as Soviet historians attribute the success of the March Revolution in Russia to the leadership of the Bolshevik party, so the few remaining historians on the Chinese mainland now claim to discern in the Fourth of May Movement the leadership of the Chinese Communist party – a remarkable achievement for a party which was not founded until two years later. The events of 4 May 1919 do, nonetheless, mark a turning-point in China's relations with the West, and the beginning of a new sympathy for Soviet Russia.

Until the First World War, Chinese intellectuals, though not entirely ignorant of Marxism, had been uninterested in it. Even Ch'en Tu-hsin, who in 1921 was to become the first leader of the Chinese communist party, had looked for the salvation of China not to ideas of Marx and Lenin but to 'Mr Democracy' and 'Mr Science', whom he considered the personifications of western civilization. China's betrayal at Versailles, however, left Ch'en, like most other Chinese intellectuals, disillusioned not merely with western governments but with western ideas as well. 'No sun', it was said, 'rises for China in the West.'

Less than a month after the Treaty of Versailles, Bolshevik Russia offered to renounce all the 'unequal treaties' imposed on China by the tsars and return all the territory taken from it. The contrast between Russia's behaviour towards China and that of the Western imperialists could hardly have seemed more striking. Sun Yat-sen, formerly an ardent admirer of the American system of government, now looked for inspiration not to Wilson but to Lenin. 'The only allies and brothers of the Chinese people in the struggle for national freedom', said Sun in a manifesto of July 1919, 'are the Russian workers and peasants of the Red Army.'

To most Chinese intellectuals the Russian revolution seemed to have changed Russia from a European to an Asian nation which had left the ranks of imperialist powers to side with the peoples of Asia in their struggle for freedom from foreign exploitation. 'Russia', said Sun, 'is attempting to separate from the white peoples of Europe. . . . She joins the East and leaves the West.'

Sun Yat-sen and the republicans at Canton (now renamed the Kuomintang or Nationalist party) were ignored by the Western powers, most of which hoped vaguely for the emergence of a warlord sufficiently strong to bring the whole country under his control. Only the Russian communists offered Sun and his followers their sympathy and support. In January 1922 Kuomintang delegates attended in Moscow a 'Congress of Toilers of the Far East'. In the following autumn one of the ablest Russian diplomats, Adolf Joffe, arrived in China to negotiate an alliance with Sun. By the terms of this alliance both men agreed that 'Communism was not suited to Chinese conditions' (Joffe doubtless adding 'not yet' under his breath).

The Kuomintang was promised Russian arms, money and political and military advisers. The political advisers, inspired by the principles of 'democratic centralism', made the Kuomintang an efficient political organization for the first time. The military advisers established the Whampoa military academy which, within a few years, had given the Canton government (previously at the mercy of the local warlords) the most powerful army in China. The first commandant of the new academy was the young and ambitious Nationalist general, Chiang Kai-shek.

The alliance with Russia brought with it the support of the still infant Chinese communist party. For several years, a number of communists held important posts in the Kuomintang administration. Mao Tse-tung ran the propaganda department of the Kuomintang Central Committee. Chou En-lai, later the first prime minister of the Chinese People's Republic, became chief political adviser at the Whampoa military academy. On his deathbed in 1925 Sun wrote a last letter to the Central Committee of the Russian communist party in which he looked forward to the alliance of 'a free and strong China' with the Soviet Union 'in the great fight for the emancipation of the oppressed peoples of the whole world'. In communist China today Sun's portraits are hung alongside those of Marx and Lenin. The places of his birth and burial have become centres of pilgrimage for the communist faithful.

Before his death Sun Yat-sen had dreamed of the day when the armies of the Kuomintang would sweep northwards from Canton and bring the whole of China under nationalist control. In July 1926 the Northern Expedition, commanded by General Chiang Kai-shek, set out from Canton to turn Sun's dreams into reality. Less than two years later, in June 1928, Chiang's forces entered the rival capital of Peking. In the following month he led his generals to the monastery of the Green Cloud, where for three years Sun's body had lain awaiting burial in a glass-topped coffin presented by the Russian government. In Sun's presence Chiang solemnly declared that the unity of China had been restored. That unity, however, was no more than nominal. Though Chiang had won the support of many of the warlords, he had not brought them under his control. The Nationalist government was never able to free itself from dependence on them.

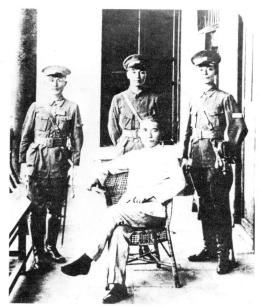

Chiang was no friend of the West, but he had no faith either in the friendship of Soviet Russia. He returned from a visit to Moscow in 1923, privately convinced that 'what the Russians call "Internationalism" and "World Revolution" are nothing but old-fashioned imperialism.' Publicly Chiang proclaimed:

If Russia aids the Chinese revolution, does that mean she wants to oblige China to apply communism? No, she wants us to carry out the national revolution. If the communists join the Kuomintang, does this mean that they want to apply communism? No, they do not want to do that either.

Privately he believed the opposite. The Russians, though suspicious of Chiang's intentions, believed that Chinese communists should cooperate with him until they were strong enough to overthrow him. Chiang, said Stalin, 'should be squeezed like a lemon and then thrown away'.

Chiang, however, sought to use the Northern Expedition not merely to unify China but to destroy Chinese communism. In April 1927 a communist-led rising delivered Shanghai into his hands. Having gained control of Shanghai, Chiang then began the systematic massacre of the communists who had captured it for him. The 'purification movement', as the attempted extermination of the Chinese communist party was euphemistically described, spread quickly to other parts of China controlled by the Kuomintang and sympathetic warlords and continued for a year. The communists, on Stalin's instructions, replied with a series of armed risings – the Nanchang rising in August among units of the Nationalist army, the 'Autumn Harvest Rising' led by Mao Tse-tung in Hunan and the Canton Commune in December. All were disastrous failures.

In the late 1960s the leadership of Communist China consisted largely of

Above, Chiang Kai-shek (1887–1975): by the late 1920s Chiang had ordered the destruction of the communist wing of the Kuomitang, but he never succeeded in eradicating the party entirely. Commander-in-chief of Chinese forces fighting against Japan during the war, he failed to prevent the 1949 revolution and had to withdraw to Taiwan.

Left, Sun Yat-sen (centre) with Chiang Kai-shek (standing, centre): Sun Yat-sen, whose 'three principles' were national unification, democracy and social progress, accepted Soviet support, but the alliance with Russia was broken by Chiang after Sun Yat-sen's death.

men who by various means had survived the disasters of 1927. Mao himself was captured and almost executed but succeeded in escaping from his guards and hiding in a field of long grass. 'Once or twice', Mao said later, 'they came so close I could almost have touched them, but somehow I escaped discovery. At last when it was dusk they abandoned the search.' Chou En-lai had an even more fortunate escape. The officer in charge of his execution squad turned out to be one of Chou's former pupils at Whampoa and set him free.

Japan's bid for Asian mastery

Many Western observers in the 1920s thought of Japan as the 'Britain of the Far East'. Japan seemed rapidly to be establishing itself as Asia's only stable parliamentary democracy. In 1925, only seven years later than in Britain, all Japanese men gained the vote (though, as in France, women had to wait until after the Second World War). When Hirohito became emperor in the following year, he gave his reign the symbolic name of *showa* or 'enlightened peace'. At the time it seemed an appropriate title. The Japanese government, if not the Japanese army, appeared to have abandoned its wartime ambition of turning the Chinese Republic into a Japanese protectorate. 'Japan', said its foreign minister, Shidehara, 'has no intention of interfering in China's internal affairs.'

The most hopeful sign, both for the peace of Asia and the future of Japanese democracy, was the declining influence in the 1920s of the Japanese armed forces. The army suffered a severe blow to its prestige from its intervention in the Russian Civil War. In 1918, encouraged by its Western allies, Japan had sent an expedition to Siberia, which remained until 1922, long after all other foreign troops had been withdrawn from Russia. The contrast between the long drawn-out failure of intervention against the Bolsheviks and the swift and crushing victory of 1905 could hardly fail to impress Japanese opinion.

In 1924 the army, despite the protests of its high command, was forced to cut its strength by four divisions. For the remainder of the 1920s it was refused the funds it needed to supply itself with up-to-date tanks and aircraft. The government was equally firm with the navy. It agreed at the London Naval Conference in 1930 to curtail its naval building programme, despite the resignation of the naval chief of staff. At the end of the 1920s there seemed less reason to suppose that the military would soon capture control of Japanese foreign policy than at any time since the dawn of the Meiji era.

The weaknesses of Japanese democracy derived mainly from its newness. The Japanese parliament still showed little of the decorum which Japanese people held so important to their way of life. Debates often ended in fist fights between the two main parties, the Seiyukai and the Kenseikai. On one occasion the Seiyukai even arranged for a poisonous snake to be thrown among its opponents from the public gallery, but the plan misfired and the snake landed on the Seiyukai's own benches.

Both parties, too, received regular bribes from rival groups within the *Zaibatsu*, the huge industrial and financial combines which dominated the Japanese economy. The inadequacies of Japanese democracy were tolerated as long as economic prosperity continued. But by destroying Japanese prosperity the Great Depression also destroyed the shallow roots of Japanese parliamentary government.

Within a year of the Wall Street crash the world price of silk, which accounted for two-fifths of Japanese exports, had fallen by half. Silk production provided a secondary source of income for almost half the farmers in Japan. Without it many were unable to make ends meet. Unrest in the countryside spread swiftly to the army. Until the Meiji era all Japanese army officers had been samurai, members of the old warrior aristocracy. By the 1920s, however, most officers, like the men they led, were the sons of peasants. The army's chief recruiting grounds in Japan were, significantly, also the areas worst hit by the depression. For most of the Japanese army the only answer to the problems created by the depression was strong government at home and expansion abroad. The depression created a climate of opinion in which the army was able to end its subjection to the politicians and win for its ambitions the support of the majority of the Japanese people.

The Manchurian incident

On 18 September 1931 Japanese troops stationed near the Japanese-owned South Manchurian railway blew up a section of the line. They then accused Chinese troops of responsibility for the explosion and used this as an excuse to begin the occupation of Manchuria. The Japanese government had been warned beforehand of the intentions of its army. On 15 September it had despatched an envoy to the Japanese commander in Manchuria with strict instructions to prevent any clash with Chinese troops. The envoy, however, was waylaid by army officers and persuaded to break his journey in an officers' brothel. By the time he emerged to deliver his letter, the Manchurian incident had already taken place.

Control of Japanese foreign policy now passed abruptly from the politicians to the soldiers. On 30 September 1931 the Japanese government accepted a resolution by the Council of the League of Nations calling for the withdrawal of Japanese troops to the South Manchuria railway zone. But in the face of the nationalist fervour which swept Japan, the government was powerless to carry out its promise. The army simply proceeded with the conquest of Manchuria. Early in 1932 it established in Manchuria the puppet state of Manchukuo, under the nominal rule of the last of the Manchu emperors.

For the next five years the Japanese army followed a policy of creeping imperialism by armed aggression and political intrigue in northern China. Western injunctions to Japan not to interfere in China were, said the minister of war, General Araki Sadao, in 1936, 'like telling a man not to get involved with a woman who was already pregnant by him'. When open war was declared between Japan and China in 1937, the Japanese army had already established indirect control over much of northeast China.

The Manchurian incident was to mark a turning-point in the history of the world between the wars. Eight days before it happened Lord Robert Cecil, the British delegate in Geneva, told the League of Nations: 'There has scarcely been a period in the world's history when war seemed less likely than it does at present.' For a year after war had started in Manchuria, most Western statesmen tried to persuade themselves that nothing had changed. Walter Lippmann, the most famous American journalist of his generation, insisted that 'the Japanese army is, in a word, carrying on not "a war" but "an intervention" ' which in no way contravened the Briand-Kellogg pact. The establishment of Manchukuo, *The Times* assured its readers, 'is undoubtedly intended to provide Manchuria with an efficient government and an honest financial administration.'

In October 1932 the illusion ended. The report of the League's commission of enquiry, though phrased in the most tactful language, condemned Japan. The Japanese delegate at Geneva compared his country to Jesus Christ; Japan, he claimed, was being 'crucified for her opinions'. Early in 1933 Japan left the League in protest. For the first time in its history, a great power had defied the authority of the League of Nations. Others were soon to follow Japan's example.

The Manchurian incident was a characteristic episode in the history of military imperialism. Throughout the period of the expansion of Europe, governments had tended to lose control of their colonial armies. At the dawn of European imperialism, in the sixteenth century, the government of Spain had lost control of its conquistadores in the New World. During the final phase of European imperialism, four centuries later, the government of France was overthrown by the rebellion of its armies in Algeria. Like many of the provincial armies in the later Roman Empire, the Japanese army in Manchuria possessed political as well as imperial ambitions. Not content with carving out an empire of its own, it

set out to destroy parliamentary democracy in Japan itself.

In May 1932, a group of young army and navy officers assassinated the prime minister, Inukai Tsuyoshi, after forcing their way into his official residence. The military high command, while disclaiming responsibility for the assassination, announced that it would no longer tolerate any government headed by a party leader. But the army did not in fact establish a military dictatorship until the Second World War. It failed to do so largely because for several years the army itself was torn between two rival factions: the Kodo-ha, which wanted war with Soviet Russia and something resembling a National-Socialist Japan, and the less radical and less adventurous Tosei-ha, whose ambitions were centred on China.

Their rivalry came to a head in February 1936 with an attempted coup d'état by the Kodo-ha and the victory of the Tosei-ha. Henceforth, the victorious Tosei-ha demanded the power to nominate, as well as to veto, ministerial appointments. From now on major policy decisions were made not by the Japanese cabinet but in meetings between the prime minister, the foreign minister and the service ministers and chiefs of staff.

Japan was never, in the European sense, a fascist state. It acquired neither a Führer nor a monolithic party system. But it shared with Nazi Germany (with whom Japan signed an alliance in 1936) both a violently aggressive nationalism and a conviction that parliamentary democracy was incompatible with national greatness. The argument used by Japan to justify its expansion on the Asia mainland was the same as that used by Germany in Europe: the need for *Lebensraum* or 'living space'. Without expansion, its rulers argued, the Japanese islands would soon find it impossible to support their teeming population. The extraordinary expansion of the Japanese (like the German) economy after the Second World War is a sufficient demonstration of the falsehood of their argument.

The rise of Mao Tse-tung

After the defeat of his Autumn Harvest Rising in 1927, Mao Tse-tung was forced to take to the hills with what remained of his followers. In 1928 he was joined by Chu Teh, who had led the army rising in Nanchang. Together the two men, soon collectively known as Chu-Mao, succeeded in establishing an independent communist soviet in the province of Kiangsi, protected by a Red Army commanded by Chu and with Mao as its political commissar.

In Kiangsi Mao began to evolve a new strategy of revolution. Hitherto, the object of all communist risings both in Europe and China (Mao's included) had been to capture the cities. This was the only strategy which Moscow understood. Once the cities had been taken, said Stalin, control of the countryside would automatically follow. Mao, however, reversed this strategy. He believed first in gaining control of the countryside by organizing the Chinese peasants into rural soviets and then in 'encircling the cities from the countryside'. The enemy, said Mao, would be defeated not by pitched battles or town risings but by guerrilla warfare waged in the countryside. He summed up his strategy of warfare in four famous sentences:

When the enemy advances, we retreat.
When he camps, we harass
When he tires, we attack
When he retreats, we pursue.

Mao spread revolution in the countryside by giving the peasants the land, often lynching landlords and moneylenders in the process. 'Whoever wins the peasants', he believed, 'will win China. Whoever solves the land question will win the peasants.' Mao's faith in the revolutionary potential of the Chinese countryside sprang partly from his experience in organizing peasant movements in his native Hunan. But it sprang also, like much of his thought, from his interpretation of the Chinese past.

Above, Pu Yi, the Japanese controlled puppet Emperor of Manchuria, arriving at his inauguration ceremony, March 1932: the Japanese seizure of Manchuria in 1931 was the first step towards the new Japanese order in Asia.

Above left, a Japanese armoured car in the streets of Shanghai, part of the forces that took over the city in 1932 in response to a Chinese boycott of Japanese goods in protest at the takeover of Manchuria. In 1933 they penetrated further inland, crossing the Great Wall.

Looking back on the two thousand years of the Chinese empire, Mao wrote in 1940:

The gigantic scale of the peasant uprisings and peasant wars in China's history is without parallel in the history of the world. These peasant uprisings and peasant wars alone have formed the real motive force of China's historical evolution.

To an orthodox Marxist, Mao's views could hardly fail to sound like heresy. Though Lenin had looked forward to the participation of the Asian peasant masses in an Asian revolutionary movement, he had never failed to insist that this movement must be led by the industrial working class. 'The city', he had said, 'inevitably leads the village. The village inevitably follows the city.' But Mao for many years paid little more than lip-service to the leadership of the working class, a class which, as he realized, as yet composed only a tiny fragment of China's population.

By the 1950s even Mao himself had concluded that his views of only twenty years before were insufficiently orthodox. Since then his earlier writings have been published in China only in bowdlerized editions which play down his earlier emphasis on the peasant base of the Chinese revolution and contain a number of insertions which stress, instead, the leading role of the proletariat.

By the end of 1930 there were eleven rural soviets in China, most of them modelled on the Chu-Mao soviet in Kiangsi. In 1931 delegates from these areas met in Mao's capital at Juchen and proclaimed the establishment of the Chinese Soviet Republic with Mao as its first chairman. Despite the failure of a second series of town risings in 1930, however, the official leadership of the Chinese communist party (all trained in Moscow and known in China as the 'Returned Students') remained deeply suspicious of Mao's preference for peasant guerrilla warfare. In 1931, the Central Committee, from which Mao had been dropped a few years earlier because of fears for his orthodoxy, moved to Juchen. It spent the next three years trying to reduce Mao's role as Chairman of the Soviet Republic to that of a figurehead.

The Long March

For three years after Mao's flight to the mountains Chiang Kai-shek had been unable, because of the intrigues of his warlord supporters, to send a large-scale expedition against him. At the end of 1930, however, he began the first of five 'annihilation campaigns' against the rural soviets. Even after the Manchurian incident Chiang still insisted that China's first priority, before resistance to the Japanese, must be the destruction of the communism within its borders. By 1934 he had come within an inch of success.

To avoid annihilation, the Kiangsi soviet, and what remained of the rest of the Chinese Soviet Republic were forced to begin a 6,000-mile march to the mountain stronghold of Shensi in northwest China. The Red Army later claimed to have crossed in its journey eighteen mountain ranges and twenty-four rivers, to have occupied at various times more than sixty cities and to have broken through the armies of ten warlords and dozens of Kuomintang regiments.

Of the 130,000 who set out (100,000 soldiers and 30,000 civilians), only 30,000 reached Shensi. But they arrived with their cohesion unbroken and their morale high. 'In the whole of history', wrote Mao, 'has there ever been a march like ours?' He was probably right to reply to his own question in the negative. Napoleon's retreat from Moscow had been a third as long and over less difficult ground, but the army of the greatest general in European history had been broken and demoralized by it.

Besides ensuring the survival of the Chinese communist party, the Long March also won it over to Mao's strategy of peasant revolution. In January 1935, while the March was still in its early stages, the Returned Students were forced to surrender power to Mao, who became the new chairman of the party's central committee. Mao's battle cry, from the moment the Red Army reached Shensi, was to call for a united front against Japan. Many of Chiang's own supporters were by now disillusioned with his policy of waging war on the communists while allowing Japan to strengthen her hold on northern China. In December 1936 he was kidnapped by some of his own troops and forced to agree to an alliance with Mao. This alliance was one of the factors which persuaded the Japanese army to end its previous policy of creeping imperialism and provoke an open war with China in the following year.

In 1937 few people, even in China, expected Mao and the Chinese communists to emerge from the war with Japan poised for

the final conquest of power in China. Already, however, the Kuomintang possessed two crucial weaknesses which in the end were to prove decisive. Under the leadership of Chiang Kai-shek the Kuomintang, which had once considered itself a revolutionary party, had become an ideological vacuum. On the question of land reform, the most serious of all the internal problems facing China, it had no policy at all. In the areas which it recaptured from the communists, it took the land from the peasants and returned it to the landlords. In the long term it could not hope to compete with the communists for the loyalty of China's peasant masses.

The second great weakness of the Kuomintang was its inability to fight a guerrilla war. After 1939, with much of China in Japanese hands, Chiang went on the defensive for the remainder of the war. The communists, however, waged a continuous series of guerrilla campaigns within occupied China with the aim not merely of fighting the Japanese but of spreading the revolution in the countryside. 'The Red

Above, in 1937 war between China and Japan broke out again, and Japanese troops occupied the north of the country and almost all the coastline. Here, Japanese forces march through the streets of Hainan, 1939.

Top, the Long March, the epic journey to the Shensi stronghold, from where the communist revolution was planned, has inspired Mao's followers and provided propagandists with a central theme: this post-1949 painting shows Mao on the March.

Top left, Mao Tse-tung addressing a meeting in the Shensi stronghold.

Opposite top, the Far East in the 1920s and 1930s: the main features of these decades were the remorseless advance of Japanese power and the Chinese communists' abandonment of their bases in southern China, followed by the Long March and the establishment of their stronghold in Shensi.

Opposite bottom, Mao Tse-tung (1893–1976): his strategy of rural revolution, contrary to orthodox Marxist thinking, saved the communist party after it had been destroyed in the cities.

Army', wrote Mao, 'fights not merely for the sake of fighting, but to agitate the masses, to organize them, to arm them, and to help them establish revolutionary political power.' Just as Japanese aggression during the First World War had led China to turn her back on the West, so Japanese aggression on a far larger scale during the Second World War was to create the conditions for a communist victory.

The century from the Opium Wars to the birth of the Chinese People's Republic now seems, in retrospect, an abnormal interlude in the course of China's history. By the middle of the twentieth century China would once again find itself almost as isolated from the West as in the middle of the nineteenth century, as convinced as before that it had nothing of real importance to learn from the West. Once again China thought of itself as the Middle Kingdom, the centre of civilization in a world otherwise almost entirely composed of oppressed peoples, imperialists and revolutionists. But its experience of the outside world during the last century had left China convinced for the first time in its history of a world mission.

Mao's strategy of revolution, first devised during the days of the Kiangsi Soviet, though careful to emphasize the leading role of the proletariat, remained essentially unchanged. That strategy, however, was now applied on a world scale. 'Taking the entire globe', wrote Mao's 'close comrade in arms', Lin Piao, 'if North America and western Europe can be called "the cities of the world", Asia, Africa, and Latin America constitute "the countryside of the world". . . . In a sense, the contemporary world revolution presents a picture of the encirclement of the cities by the countryside.' The strategy of Chinese revolution had become the strategy of world revolution.

Chapter 20

The Decline of Democracy

The sheer frightfulness of Adolf Hitler has made historians reluctant to recognize his extraordinary genius. No other man in the history of modern Europe, perhaps not even Lenin, has seemed so able to bend history to his will. Yet Hitler began his political career in Germany with almost every conceivable disadvantage. He was, to begin with, not a German at all but an Austrian who acquired German citizenship only a year before he became German chancellor. Until the First World War when he became a lance-corporal in the German army, Hitler had lived in the slums of Vienna and Munich, struggling to earn a living as an unsuccessful artist selling poster designs and water colours painted on the back of postcards. After the war he was several times afraid that his new career as a political agitator in Germany would be cut short by deportation to Austria.

Unlike Lenin, Hitler did not have behind him an established political party bound together by a long revolutionary tradition. The Nazi party in Germany was Hitler's own creation. Yet Hitler's vision of the future, though far more malevolent than Lenin's, also came closer to fulfilment. The European revolution of which Lenin had been so confident in 1917 never came, and the party which he had believed would make Russia free became the instrument instead of the most absolute despotism in Russian history. But in 1924, at the lowest ebb of his political career after the failure of the Munich putsch, Hitler was already able in *Mein Kampf* to describe with horrifying accuracy the Europe which he later almost succeeded in creating.

The great Swiss historian, Jacob Burkhardt, writing at the end of the nineteenth century, had foreseen that the greatest danger to the future of the liberal state in twentieth-century Europe would come from 'terrible simplifiers' who would take control of it and 'rule with utter brutality'. This is what Hitler was. 'I have', he said privately in 1932, 'the gift of reducing all problems to their simplest proportions.' This gift, Hitler was convinced, was the key to his success. 'I shall tell you', he told a journalist,

what has carried me to the position I have reached. Our political problems appeared complicated. The German people could make nothing of them. . . . I, on the other hand, simplified these problems and reduced them to the simplest terms. The masses realized this and followed me.

Part of Hitler's political genius was his ability to provide a simple and persuasive explanation for Germany's complex misfortunes. He told his followers in 1925:

To make a struggle intelligible to the broad masses, it must always be carried on against two things, against a person and against a cause. Against whom did England fight? Against the German emperor as a person, and against militarism as a cause. . . . Against whom, therefore, must our movement fight? Against the Jew as a person and against Marxism as a cause.

Hitler portrayed Marxism itself as an essentially Jewish movement, the creation of 'that modern Mordecai, Karl Marx'. By a remarkable intellectual sleight of hand he convinced both himself and his followers that international capitalism, which was responsible for Germany's economic distress, and international communism, which sought to make Germany its captive, were both part of the same 'Judaeo-Bolshevik conspiracy' which was at the root of all Germany's misfortunes.

Despite the undoubted appeal to many of his followers of Hitler's simple diagnosis of Germany's misfortune, it was his even simpler solution to them which was the real secret of his success. This solution, Hitler insisted, was not a question of this or that policy but 'a matter of will-power'. 'No word', writes his biographer, Alan Bullock, 'was more frequently on Hitler's lips than "will".' Will-power alone, Hitler insisted – his own will-power – could make Germany prosperous and strong once more.

The fact that so many Germans believed Hitler was above all because of the extraordinary magnetism of his personality. Nor, as is sometimes implied, was his appeal confined to mass rallies of the simple-minded herded together in the Nuremberg stadium. Hitler excelled in varying his appeal according to his audience. Lloyd George, himself one of the most powerful personalities in the history of British politics, returned in 1936 from a visit to Germany convinced that Hitler was 'a born leader, a magnetic, dynamic personality' (with, incidentally, no desire 'to invade any other land'). A series of eminent visitors left Hitler's country retreat at Berchtesgaden with the same impression.

The collapse of German democracy

Until the Great Depression the mass resentments to which Hitler needed to appeal did not exist. After the fiasco of the Munich putsch in 1923 most people both inside

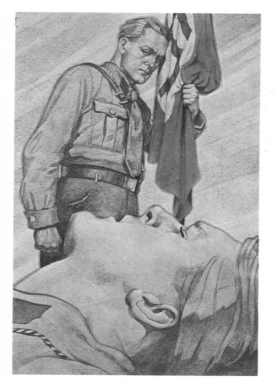

Wir bauen auf!

Unsere Bausteine:

Arbeit
Freiheit
Brot

Also
National-
Sozialisten

Baupläne der anderen.

and outside Germany had written Hitler off. When Lord D'Abernon, the former British ambassador in Berlin, published two volumes of his memoirs in 1929, he mentioned Hitler only in a footnote. After referring briefly to Hitler's imprisonment after the putsch, he concluded: 'He was finally released after six months and bound over for the rest of his sentence, thereafter fading into oblivion.'

The early 1920s had already shown that the Nazis needed an economic crisis to come to power. In May 1924, during the aftermath of the postwar inflation, the Nazis gained thirty-two seats at their first general election, even though Hitler himself was still in prison. But at the next election in the following December, when the economic climate was beginning to improve, they held only fifteen of these seats. In 1928, when the Weimar Republic was at the height of its prosperity, the Nazis lost three more seats. As long as that prosperity continued the Nazis were doomed to remain on the fringe of German politics.

In the short term the depression did more damage to the German economy than to any other economy in Europe. By 1932 industrial production had fallen by almost a half, and six million men – one-third of the German labour force – were unemployed. Parliamentary government in Germany survived the Wall Street crash by only six months.

After the breakdown of the coalition government led by the social democrat, Hermann Müller, in March 1930, effective political power passed from the chancellor to President Hindenburg and the 'palace camarilla' which surrounded him, dominated by Hindenburg's son Oscar and Oscar's friend, General Schleicher. Ever since his

election in 1925 Hindenburg had been the model of a constitutional president, accepting the decisions of his ministers and the votes of the *Reichstag*. After Müller's resignation, however, no chancellor until Adolf Hitler was able to win a stable majority in the *Reichstag*. Hitler's three predecessors as chancellor (Bruning in March 1930, von Papen in April 1932, Schleicher in December 1932) were the nominees of the 'palace camarilla'. All relied not on the consent of the *Reichstag* but on emergency decrees signed by the president.

The depression made the Nazis a major political force for the first time. In 1930, at the first election after the Wall Street crash, Nazi seats in the *Reichstag* shot up from 12 to 107. In July 1932, at the worst moment of the Depression, the Nazis won thirty-seven percent of the vote and 230 seats, more than any other party in the history of the Weimar Republic (though still well short of an absolute majority in the *Reichstag*). By the autumn of 1932, however, it seemed that the party had passed its peak.

At the next election in November 1932 the Nazis lost two million votes. The party was on the verge of bankruptcy. By the end of the year it had run out of funds to finance the 400,000 men of the SA, its private army of stormtroopers. The SA were given collecting boxes and told to beg in the streets. 'This year', wrote Goebbels in his diary at the end of 1932, 'has brought us eternal ill luck. . . . The future looks dark and gloomy.' At the polls the Nazis seemed condemned to a gradual decline as prosperity returned. The only alternative appeared to be a Nazi coup d'état. But this was an alternative which Hitler himself had ruled out ever since the failure of the Munich putsch.

Above, Joseph Goebbels (1897–1945), Nazi propaganda chief from 1929: his enormous skills and unceasing work ensured the Party's success in the early 1930s and in the later part of the war did much to maintain morale.

Above left, Nazi election poster promising work, freedom and bread: the uncomplicated, direct appeal of Nazi propaganda won many converts in the early 1930s, at a time when the other parties seemed helpless and unimaginative, able only to react to events.

Above far left, honouring a fallen comrade: the simplicity and realism of this Nazi painting capture the essence of the movement's propaganda appeal.

Opposite, portrait of Hitler taken for his fiftieth birthday, 20 April 1939.

271

That the Nazis became the masters of Germany in 1933 was less because of their own strength than because of the failures of their opponents. At the elections of November 1932 the German left – the social democrats and communists – had won more votes than the Nazis. But the two parties of the left were hopelessly divided between themselves. The socialists had lost the will to govern. Like the Labour Party in England, they could not reconcile themselves to carrying out an economic policy of deflation which was bound to bear most heavily on their own supporters. The communists believed that a Nazi victory in Germany would signal the death throes of German capitalism. On instructions from Moscow they concentrated not on resisting Hitler but on establishing themselves as the only party of the left. 'Our principal struggle', said the party newspaper on the eve of Hitler's rise to power, 'is against social democracy.'

But the divisions of the left were less crucial than the miscalculations of the right. Baron von Papen, ousted as chancellor by General Schleicher, devised a scheme to use an alliance with Hitler to recover political power. As a preliminary he persuaded a group of Rhineland businessmen to save the Nazis from bankruptcy. Then he helped Hitler to arrange an alliance between the Nazis and the right-wing Nationalist party. At this critical moment the army high command came out in favour of a Hitler government. Hitler himself believed that its support was crucial. 'If the army had not stood on our side', he declared after he became chancellor, 'we should not have been standing here today.'

'You will not think it possible, gentlemen', Hindenburg told two of his generals on 26 January 1933, 'that I should appoint that Austrian lance-corporal chancellor.' He had the best constitutional reasons for changing his mind four days later. If, as then seemed possible, the Nazi-Nationalist alliance won the support of the Catholic Centre party, it would be the first coalition to win a majority in the *Reichstag* since the fall of Müller's government three years before. On 30 January 1933 Adolf Hitler became Chancellor of Germany.

Nazi Germany

The politicians, industrialists and generals who had brought Hitler to power had done so in the belief that they could use him for their own purposes. The coalition government which Hitler headed contained only two other Nazi ministers. Papen, as vice-chancellor, was confident that with nine non-Nazis in a cabinet of twelve real power would remain with him. But they failed to realize that with the two Nazi ministers, Frick and Goering, in control of internal affairs, and the pro-Nazi General Blomberg as minister of defence, Hitler effectively controlled the police and was assured of the army's benevolent neutrality.

Hitler's first act as chancellor was to ensure the failure of the negotiations with the Catholic Centre Party which might have given his government a majority in the *Reichstag*. His colleagues in the cabinet were then persuaded to agree to a new election, which Hitler intended to precede by a campaign of intimidation designed to

give him the absolute majority he could not win in a free election.

The mastermind of this campaign was Hermann Goering, whose gross exterior concealed surprising energy and ruthlessness. In only a few weeks Goering had laid the foundations of the Nazi police state: 40,000 men of the SA and the SS (Hitler's praetorian guard) were drafted into the police force and given unlimited opportunity to indulge the pent-up sadism accumulated during the years in opposition. Goering declared:

Police officers who make use of firearms in the execution of their duties will, without regard to the consequences of such use, benefit by my protection; those who, out of a misplaced regard for the consequences fail in their duty will be punished in accordance with the regulations.

In several parts of Germany local Nazi leaders founded concentration camps on their own initiative as centres of imprisonment and torture for anyone thought to oppose the regime. To assist them in tracking down their victims, Goering transformed the political police of the Weimar Republic into the infinitely more sinister Gestapo – the secret police.

Despite a brilliantly sustained campaign of intimidation, however, the Nazis won only forty-four percent of the vote at the March election. By outlawing all the communist deputies (most of whom were already in concentration camps) Hitler succeeded nonetheless in giving himself a clear overall majority. He then bullied the new *Reichstag*

into passing an 'Enabling Law' which made him the dictator of Germany.

Gleichschaltung

Hitler now began the subordination of every facet of German life to the control of the Nazi party, a process euphemistically described as *Gleichschaltung* or 'coordination'. All other political parties and the trade unions were abolished. The *Reichstag* was reduced to a cipher which met occasionally to be harangued by the Führer. Mass communications and German culture were handed over to Dr Goebbels whose preposterous title was 'minister of propaganda and public enlightenment'.

No legal redress was possible against Nazi tyranny. 'The law and the will of the Führer', said Goering, 'are one.' Hitler himself gave a striking practical demonstration of this principle on the 'Night of the Long Knives' in June 1934, when he ordered the simultaneous assassination of a number of past opponents and disaffected supporters (notably Röhm, the leader of the SA). In a speech to the *Reichstag* Hitler explained that he had acted as 'the supreme justiciar of the German people'.

After Hindenburg's death in August 1934 Hitler also became the head of state. The offices of chancellor and president, he announced, had now been combined in his person. As president (though he still preferred to call himself Führer) Hitler automatically became the new commander-in-chief of the German army, which was now required to pledge its loyalty not to the Fatherland but to Hitler himself.

Only one section of German society remained outside the process of *Gleichschaltung*. This was the Jewish community, which Hitler sought to isolate from the remainder of the German people in preparation for its eventual liquidation. Jews were excluded from the civil service, from the professions, from sport and from the arts. Boycotts were organized of Jewish shops, and blacklists were published of those housewives who dared to defy it.

In 1935 the Nuremberg Race Laws made illegal either marriage or sexual relations between Jews and other Germans. The so-called 'Crystal Night' in November 1938, when hundreds of Jews were murdered and synagogues throughout Germany were burnt to the ground, showed how far anti-semitism had been accepted by the German people as part of their way of life. A climate of opinion was emerging in which the majority of the German people, though not supporting the mass extermination of the Jews, would be prepared to turn a blind eye to it. And it was already clear what the fate of the Jewish people would be when Hitler went to war. He told the *Reichstag* at the beginning of 1939 that if the Jews brought about another world war (and, by definition, all world wars were brought about by Jews) its result would be 'the annihilation of the Jewish race in Europe'.

'I ask of you, German people', Hitler had said in January 1933, 'that after you have given the others fourteen years, you should give us four.' At the Nuremberg rally in November 1936 Hitler gave his own account of the achievements of those four years.

Below, left-wingers rounded up in the early days of the Nazi regime: the government acted quickly to silence all possible opposition.

Centre, Jews forced to scrub the pavements after the Nazi takeover of Austria, March 1938: the Jewish population of central Europe encountered vicious discrimination from the moment the Nazis came to power, though it was not until the early 1940s that the 'final solution', which Hitler had long had in mind, began to be put into operation.

Bottom, the Nuremberg rally, 1933: these massive, skilfully staged propaganda exercises served as a public reinforcement of the power of the Nazi movement.

No peacetime prime minister has ever been able to point to such a triumphant record of success. Unemployment had fallen in four years from six million to less than a million. Industrial production had recovered to the pre-depression level.

Hitler could claim, too, to have made Germany great as well as prosperous. In 1935 the Saar had voted to rejoin Germany and in March 1936 the German army had marched into the demilitarized Rhineland. The German government no longer recognized the restrictions of the Versailles treaty and had begun a massive programme of rearmament. For the first time since the First World War Germany was once again feared and respected as the greatest power on the continent of Europe.

Many Germans were so enthusiastic about Hitler's achievements that they were willing to overlook the methods which he used. But there were many too who were attracted by the violence of those methods. The *Freikorps* era had already shown the popularity of violence among large sections of the German public. After witnessing the organized brutality of Hitler's storm-troopers during the election campaign of 1933, Germans flocked to join them. In a single year membership of the SA rose from 400,000 to three million men. The smaller and even more sinister SS was also never short of recruits. Indeed it was somewhat embarrassed by the profusion of them. Its leader, Heinrich Himmler, declared in 1937:

'We still choose only fifteen out of every hundred candidates who present themselves to us.'

Hitler's supporters before he came to power had been concentrated among the members of the lower middle class: artisans, small shopkeepers, skilled craftsmen, minor civil servants. The depression threatened these men in a way in which it affected no other segment of German society. They felt menaced not merely with a lower standard of living (as did every class in German society) but with the loss of their middle-class status and reduction to the ranks of the working class which they despised.

Before he became chancellor Hitler did not succeed in making any serious inroads into the working-class vote. At both elections in 1932 the combined vote of the two working-class parties, the communists and social democrats, was higher than ever before. Once in power, however, Hitler rapidly established his claim to be the Führer of the whole German people.

During his first years as the ruler of Germany Hitler held a series of plebiscites to demonstrate the strength of his support. At the first of these, held only eighteen months after becoming chancellor, he gained ninety percent of the vote in a poll of ninety-six percent. In March 1936, after the re-occupation of the Rhineland, he won a majority of over ninety-eight percent. Whatever the reliability of these figures, there can be no doubt that the mood of the German

people as a whole was, in the words of Alan Bullock, one of 'overwhelming gratitude and approval'.

Nowhere was Hitler's support more secure than among the youth of Germany. The Nazis had captured control of the German student movement as early as 1931. Once the Nazis came to power, all German children aged six or over were compelled to join the Hitler Youth. At school their teachers brought them up in the Nazi faith. No wonder, then, that Hitler could declare in 1933: 'When an opponent says, "I will not come over to your side", I calmly reply, 'Your child belongs to us already.'

The opposition to Hitler was both weak and powerless. Even the concentration camps, to which the Nazis had no hesitation in despatching their opponents, had a population of only 25,000 at the outbreak of war out of a total German population which numbered eighty million. No government anywhere in the world between the wars commanded the enthusiasm which Adolf Hitler earned from the German people.

Stalin's Russia

'Having become General Secretary', wrote Lenin in his political testament, 'Comrade Stalin has acquired immense power in his hands, and I am not certain that he will always know how to use this power with

sufficient caution.' A few days later he added a final postscript suggesting that Stalin be replaced by someone 'more patient, more loyal, more polite and considerate to other comrades, less capricious and so on'. Lenin had intended that his testament should be read to delegates to the party congress after his death in January 1924. Instead Stalin ensured that it was not published in Russia during his lifetime. It is difficult to think of any other document in modern history whose suppression has had consequences of comparable magnitude.

Two things enabled Stalin to win the struggle for power which followed Lenin's death: his lack of any obvious talent and his control of the party machine. In 1924 Stalin was not even considered a serious candidate for the succession. Had it been otherwise his rivals would hardly have agreed to suppress Lenin's condemnation of him. As yet no one heeded Lenin's warning of the 'immense power' which Stalin had gathered in his hands. The most obvious candidate to succeed Lenin was Leon Trotsky, at once the party's leading intellectual, the organizer of the November Revolution and the hero of the Civil War. By comparison Stalin seemed what Trotsky called him: 'a dull mediocrity'.

To defeat Trotsky Stalin joined forces with his two main rivals, Kamenev and Zinoviev, the chairmen respectively of the Moscow and Leningrad (formerly Petro-

grad) Bolshevik parties. Trotsky lost the battle for power essentially because he was less unscrupulous than Stalin. His control of the Red Army gave him an even more powerful weapon than Stalin's command of the party machine, had he been prepared to use it. But Trotsky, unlike Stalin, had a horror of becoming the Bonaparte of the Russian Revolution. In January 1925 Stalin was able to force Trotsky's resignation from his key position as commissar for war. Having disposed of Trotsky, Stalin now turned on his former allies, Kamenev and Zinoviev, using his power as general secretary to undermine their control of the Moscow and Leningrad party machines. At the 1927 party congress Stalin emerged as the ruler of Russia.

The Bolsheviks in the 1920s found themselves out on a limb. In 1917 they had been sublimely confident that their own

Above, German troops occupying the demilitarized Rhineland, perhaps the biggest, and most successful, gamble of Hitler's career: all too well aware of their own military weakness, the western powers put up no resistance, though Germany would almost certainly have withdrawn had they done so.

Above left, Members of the Hitler Youth at one of the many ceremonial events designed to capture and retain their loyalty to the movement: the movement's appeal was especially attractive to the young, many of whom in the early 1930s felt that they had no future.

Opposite, Hitler amid some of his followers: as the head of the Nazi movement, Hitler acted as its entire focus and attracted devoted loyalty, the propaganda machine building him up as the one man who could save Germany.

revolution in Russia would quickly be followed by the rest of Europe. By the time of Lenin's death this confidence had gone. Europe by now showed little sign of following Russia's example. The most logical course of action, in Marxist terms, seemed either to concentrate all Russia's resources on an all-out attempt to spread the revolution to the rest of Europe (a view favoured by Trotsky) or else to postpone the establishment of socialism in Russia itself. In the autumn of 1924, however, Stalin instead formulated the slogan of 'socialism in one country'. Russia, he argued, must advance to socialism without waiting for the rest of Europe.

Stalin's excursion into the world of ideology took his colleagues by surprise. 'Don't make a fool of yourself', one old Marxist told him, 'Everyone knows that theory is not exactly your line.' But within a few years 'socialism in one country' had become the new test of orthodoxy: all those, like Trotsky, who disagreed were banished from the party. A few years more and Stalin was being hailed, with his evident approval, as the greatest philosopher the world had ever known – not merely the infallible head of the Marxist faith but the first man to solve certain problems in the interpretation of Aristotle and the only man who really understood both Kant and Hegel.

In the chaos left by the Civil War, Russia was at first in no position to build a fully socialist economy. 'We are paupers', Lenin had written in 1921, 'starving, destitute paupers. A comprehensive plan for us equals bureaucratic utopia.' By the New Economic Policy (NEP for short) begun in that year, though big business ('the commanding heights of the economy') was run by the state, almost all the land remained divided into individual peasant plots and a limited degree of private enterprise was allowed in the towns. Only in 1927 did production both on the land and in industry recover to the pre-war level.

The transformation of the Russian economy

The moderate wing of the Bolshevik party, led by Bukharin, was content to continue 'riding towards socialism at the pace of a peasant nag', continuing the gradual industrialization of the Russian economy while, at the same time, seeking slowly to persuade the peasants to merge their private holdings into collective farms. Stalin, however, decided that the doctrine of 'socialism in one country' made necessary a crash programme of rapid industrialization. A socialist Russia, Stalin argued, could survive encirclement by the imperialist powers only by ending her economic backwardness: 'We are fifty or a hundred years behind the advanced countries. We must make good this lag in ten years. Either we do it or they crush us.'

Rapid industrialization was necessary also for the security of the Bolshevik regime within Russia itself. A party which claimed to base itself on the dictatorship of the proletariat was bound to feel insecure so long as it ruled a predominantly peasant Russia. A crash programme of industrialization, however, could only be financed by larger agricultural surpluses from the Russian peasants, both to feed the increased labour force in the towns and to pay for imports of foreign machinery. The obvious way to obtain these surpluses was to encourage the *kulaks* or 'rich peasants' who were the most efficient producers. Since this solution was unacceptable for ideological reasons, the only alternative was compulsory collectivization.

In assessing the progress of the Russian economy after the end of NEP in 1928, the historian is faced with a massive falsification of evidence on a scale that has no parallel in the history of Europe. We know, for example, by the Soviet government's own subsequent admission, that even as late as 1952 grain production was deliberately exaggerated by no less than sixty percent. There is scarcely a single economic statistic published during the period of the first three five-year plans (begun respectively in 1928, 1933 and 1938) on whose accuracy it is possible to rely. Stalin himself lived during these years in a fantasy world largely of his own construction. In 1935, for example, he claimed that 'We have had no

Left, harvest-time political meeting in the Ukraine, 1929: enforced collectivization, in which the kulaks were eliminated, set Soviet agriculture back twenty-five years.

Left, harvest-time political meeting in the Ukraine, 1929: enforced collectivization, in which the kulaks *were eliminated, set Soviet agriculture back twenty-five years.*

Opposite, blast furnaces at the giant Magnitogorosk iron works in the Urals: the vast industrialization in the 1920s and 1930s was achieved by direction of labour and the sacrifice of personal living standards and without foreign investment; by the end of the first Five-Year Plan in 1933 industrial production was four times higher than it had been in 1913.

poor now for two or three years' – and this at a time when, as Professor Nove has observed, the price of bread stood higher in relation to wages than at any other time in Soviet history.

And yet it is clear, despite the fantasy world of Soviet statistics, that by draconian methods and a massive rate of capital investment, Russia became a major industrial state in the space of a single decade – more rapidly than any other state in European history. By 1939 its total industrial production was probably exceeded only by that of Germany and the United States. Russia's industrial achievement compelled even Hitler's reluctant admiration. He admitted privately in 1942:

The arms and equipment of the Russian armies are the best proof of [Russia's] efficiency in handling industrial manpower . . . Stalin, in his own way, is a hell of a fellow. He knows his models, Genghis Khan and the others, very well.

The achievements of collectivized agriculture are far less impressive. In the short term they were nearly disastrous. The peasants' response to the collectivization of their livestock was simply to slaughter as much of it as possible. By 1934, even according to official statistics, the total number of horses, cattle and pigs had dropped by half and the total number of sheep by two thirds. Production on the collective farms did not recover to

the 1928 level until the 1950s. A party congress, held soon after Stalin's death in 1953, was told that after twenty-five years of collectivized agriculture grain production per head of the population and numbers of livestock absolutely were still lower than in Tsarist Russia.

Both the failures of collectivized agriculture and the successes of Soviet industry were purchased at an appalling cost in human suffering. Stalin later told Churchill that of the ten million *kulaks* (a term rather loosely applied by Stalin) who had resisted collectivization, 'the great bulk' had been 'wiped out'. During the first five-year plan Stalin created the world's first man-made famine. To pay for imports of foreign machinery and feed the growing labour force in the towns, he insisted on a vast increase in food expropriations from the countryside at the very time when food production was in decline. In 1931, when the famine was beginning, five million tons of wheat were sold abroad. Though Stalin, characteristically, denied that a famine even existed, more than five million Russians died of starvation. 'We were', Bukharin was to say later, 'conducting a mass annihilation.'

The Great Terror

The barbarism which accompanied collectivization and the first five-year plan inevitably aroused opposition within the

Communist party itself. Those, like Bukharin, who opposed 'mass annihilation' seem to have pinned their hopes on the influence of Sergei Kirov, the party boss in Leningrad. Though a devoted admirer of Stalin, whom he described as 'the greatest man of all times and ages', Kirov was thought to be concerned by the brutality of Stalin's methods. In December 1934 he was murdered, probably on Stalin's orders. His death was the signal for the beginning of the Terror.

It seems increasingly clear that the immediate explanation for the Terror has to be sought less within the needs of Russian industrialization or the interests of the Russian communist party than in the personal paranoia of Joseph Stalin. For this paranoia we have the evidence of, amongst others, one of Stalin's successors, Nikita Krushchev:

Stalin was a very distrustful man, sickly suspicious; we knew this from our work with him. He could look at a man and say, 'Why are your eyes so shifty today?' or 'Why are you turning so much today and avoiding looking me directly in the eyes?' This sickly suspicion created in him a general distrust even toward eminent party workers whom he had known for years. Everywhere and in everything he saw 'enemies', 'double dealers', and 'spies'.

The most that can be said for Stalin is that, like many other despots, he probably convinced himself that his own enemies (real or imagined) were also the enemies of the state.

The Terror reached its peak in the years from 1936 to 1938. Everyone who had ever opposed Stalin on any issue was systematically sought out, accused of usually imaginary crimes and executed. This, however, was only the beginning. Many of the relatives of Stalin's victims were shot or sent to labour camps. Stalin had the penal code altered to permit the execution of children of twelve years and over. All those arrested had, in addition, to provide the names of their accomplices in their imaginary crimes. If they refused, they were tortured until they did so. By its very nature, therefore, the Terror provided itself with an increasing number of victims. 'Today', said the Russian writer, Isaac Babel, 'a man talks freely only with his wife – at night with the blankets drawn over his head.'

The purge began to slacken in the later months of 1938 largely because the administration of the Terror was beginning to collapse under the sheer weight of those it persecuted. By now perhaps one in twenty of the entire Russian population had been arrested. Even the vast network of Soviet labour camps had become hopelessly overstretched. At the height of the Terror probably some nine million people were in captivity, eight million of them in labour camps which could boast an annual death rate of twenty percent. 'We shall have no further need', Stalin told the 1939 party congress, 'of resorting to the method of mass purges.'

The section of Soviet society which suffered most from the Terror was, appropriately enough, the Russian communist party. Less than two percent of the ordinary delegates to the 1935 party congress reappeared at the next congress held four years later. Of those who failed to reappear, well over half had been shot. Of the 139 full members and candidate members of the Central Committee in 1934 only twenty-four were re-elected in 1939: ninety-eight of the remainder are known to have been shot. By a process of natural selection those members of the Soviet leadership who survived the jungle conditions of the Terror, or who rose to power during it, were likely to possess extremely unusual qualities of ruthlessness and servility. Both these qualities are aptly illustrated by the comments on a letter from General Yakir, before his execution on a trumped-up charge in 1937, pleading for the safety of his family. The letter was published by the Soviet government in 1961. It has on it four marginal comments:

Stalin: 'Yakir, trash and traitor.'
Voroshilov: 'An exact description.'
Molotov: 'Entire agreement with Stalin.'
Kaganovich: 'A traitor, a pig.'

By a curious coincidence Voroshilov, Molotov and Kaganovich were the only members of the Politburo at the time of Kirov's murder to escape the purges which followed. All three continued to hold high office after Stalin's death.

After the communist party, the Red Army was the principal target of Stalin's paranoia. Seventy-seven of its eighty-eight most senior commanders were purged. In all, about half the entire officer corps, totalling some 35,000 men, were shot or imprisoned, together with many of their wives and children. The Terror, as Krushchev later recognized, 'also undermined military discipline, because for several years officers of all ranks and even soldiers in the Party and Komsomol cells were taught to "unmask" their superiors as hidden enemies'.

The havoc wrought by the Terror was one of the factors which determined the timing of the German invasion in 1941. German intelligence reports concluded that it would be another three years before the Russian high command recovered from the consequences of the purges. Though a new and efficient command emerged under the pressure of the German invasion, the Terror had to be paid for during the war, as Robert Conquest observes, 'with the lives of hundreds of thousands of Russian soldiers, with hundreds of miles of Russian territory, and a great prolongation of the war itself'.

Opposite, Joseph Stalin (1871–1953), dictator of the USSR from the 1920s: among the achievements of his rule, industrialization, the collectivization of agriculture, the purges of suspected opponents, the extension of Soviet power in central and western Europe and the mobilization of fanatical resistance to the Nazi invasion.

The cult of personality

While Stalin was busy decimating the Russian people he was also, in the words of his protégé, Krushchev, engaged in 'the glorification of his own person by all conceivable means'. Russian writers vied with one another in the extravagance of their praise. One of them, Avdeienko, told the Seventh Congress of Soviets in 1935:

I write books, I am an author; I dream of creating a lasting work. I love a girl in a new way; I am perpetuated in my children . . . All this is thanks to thee, O great teacher Stalin. Our love, our devotion, our strength, our heroism, our life – all are thine. Take them, great Stalin, all is thine, O leader of this great country . . . When the woman I love gives me a child the first word I shall teach it shall be 'Stalin'.

Almost every Soviet achievement in whatever field was invariably attributed at least in part to a personal initiative by Stalin himself. During April 1935, for example, *Pravda* reported that Stalin's ideas were 'invaluable directions for all the work done in the sphere of fruit-growing in this country'; that improvements in mechanized bakeries owed much to 'the genius of our leader and master, comrade Stalin'; and that 'the daily instructions of comrade Stalin were the decisive factors which ensured the victory of Soviet cinematography.'

The 'cult of personality' nowadays provides a convenient explanation in the Soviet Union for those enormities which are publicly admitted. But the abnormalities of Stalin's personality and the glorification of it provide only an immediate explanation. It still remains necessary to explain how a situation could develop in which it was possible for the personal paranoia of one man to hold to ransom a nation of two hundred million people. It is difficult to avoid the conclusion that the ultimate responsibility lies with Lenin.

Lenin had set out in November 1917 to establish the dictatorship of the proletariat, in order to prepare the way for the communist millenium. It had soon become clear, however, that the dictatorship of the proletariat meant in practice the dictatorship of the Bolshevik party. Before he came to power Lenin had insisted that 'what we do not want is the element of compulsion. We do not want to drive people into paradise with a bludgeon.' Once he became the ruler of Russia, however, he was prepared to argue that since the party knew the interests of the proletariat better than the proletariat itself it must, if necessary, use 'revolutionary violence' to defend the proletariat against itself. In 1921 he ordered the suppression of a mutiny of Kronstadt sailors, who had taken seriously his talk of the people's participation in the government of Russia and who felt themselves betrayed by him.

The Bolshevik party under Lenin's leadership was now, in Trotsky's words, persuaded that 'the party is always right'. From a state in which one party was always right it was to be only a short step to a state in which one man was always right.

The retreat from democracy

One of the most basic weaknesses of the Western democracies in the face of Hitler's

Germany was their inability to grasp the extraordinary extent of Hitler's ambitions. Hitler had stated these ambitions quite clearly in *Mein Kampf*. Having first united all the German-speaking peoples, he proposed to revive the *Drang nach Osten*, the eastwards march of the Teutonic knights in the Middle Ages and then to recreate on a larger scale the slave empire they had founded in Eastern Europe: 'We start where they stopped six centuries before.' Germany, said Hitler, needed *Lebensraum* (living space) in the East. Once she had acquired it, the existing populations would either be removed or enslaved. Precisely because this malevolent vision of a new German empire seemed so fantastic, hardly anyone outside Germany took it seriously. And yet it was just such an empire that Hitler set out to build.

While communism claimed to have abandoned nationalism for internationalism, fascism prided itself instead on an exaggerated nationalism. And yet, during the 1930s at least, fascism was the more powerful international force. Fascist movements sprang up almost simultaneously all over Europe, looking for inspiration more to Hitler than to Mussolini. These movements took many different national forms, but everywhere they shared the same militarist nationalism (usually with racialist overtones) and the same militant hostility to both communism and democracy. Everywhere, too, they sought to establish a one-party state in which the party, as in Germany, would control every facet of national life.

Outside Germany and Italy fascism was strongest in the relatively backward countries of eastern Europe and the Iberian peninsula. Except in Spain, which experienced a brief interlude of democratic government from 1930 to 1936, democracy in these countries had already largely disappeared by the time of the Great Depression. The fascist parties of Portugal and eastern Europe (and in Spain after Franco became head of state) therefore aimed not, as Hitler and Mussolini had done, at the destruction of a democratic system of government but at the transformation of authoritarian regimes from within into fascist dictatorships.

Nowhere were they completely successful. Even in Spain, though the Falangists (the Spanish fascists) supported Franco's appointment by the army as head of state in 1936 in opposition to the legal government, they had, as they themselves privately admitted, little influence on his policies. Many European states during the 1930s – among them Spain, Portugal, Poland, Hungary, Romania, Yugoslavia and Greece – acquired fascist overtones or mouthed fascist slogans. None had the means, however, even had they wished to do so, to become fully-fledged fascist states. They lacked the highly developed machinery of oppression and control which enabled Hitler and Stalin to establish the world's first completely totalitarian societies. Even Mussolini, though he devised the celebrated fascist slogan, 'Everything for the state, nothing against the state, nothing outside the state', lacked the means to put that slogan fully into effect. *Gleichschaltung* in Italy was never complete.

Though the victory of fascism was still far from complete at the outbreak of the Second World War, it seemed clear that democracy was in decline. It survived (except in Switzerland) only on the north-western fringes of the European continent: in Britain, France, the Low Countries and Scandinavia. Even here democracy seemed to be losing faith in itself. The idea of progress which had been so popular only a generation earlier had now become desperately unfashionable. The inefficiency of democratic governments in finding effective solutions to the problems posed by the depression contrasted both with the rapid recovery of Nazi Germany and the apparent immunity of Stalin's Russia from the afflictions of capitalist economies.

The 1930s saw something like a *trahison des clercs* among liberal intellectuals. Instead of defending democracy when it was under siege they poured scorn on it. 'Contemporary society', said T. S. Eliot in 1935, 'is worm-eaten with liberalism.' Only Sir Arthur Quiller-Couch, the much mocked editor of the Oxford Book of English Verse, challenged Eliot's contempt for liberal democracy: 'What is the alternative? It is suppression; tyranny; in its final, brutal word-force. Look around Europe today.'

The resistance of the two great Western democracies, France and Britain, to the challenge of Hitler's Germany was far less determined than their opposition to the lesser menace of the kaiser's Germany only a quarter of a century before. But in the years before 1914 they had not been plagued by the economic crisis and intellectual doubts which beset them in the 1930s. There had been a profound change, too, in the mood of public opinion. During the decade before the First World War the peoples of France and Britain had grown steadily more convinced that war with Germany was sooner or later inevitable, and were ready for it. During the 1930s they tried instead to cling to the illusion that the Europe of the Locarno honeymoon had not really disappeared.

Appeasement

The classic example of the capitulation of Western democracy in the 30s is generally considered to be the Munich agreement of 1938, by which Britain and France jointly betrayed Czechoslovakia to Germany in the belief that they could thus appease Adolf Hitler. But the crucial capitulation had come two years earlier with Hitler's occupation of the Rhineland.

As long as the Rhineland remained demilitarized in accordance with the terms of the Versailles treaty, the heart of industrial Germany lay exposed to the menace of a French invasion. The French system of alliances with the smaller states of Eastern Europe (which since the First World War had replaced its earlier alliance with Tsarist Russia) made sense only if France was able to counter German aggression in the East with retaliation through the Rhineland. Hitler, equally, could embark on a policy

FRANÇAIS ALERTE !

E COMMUNISME A DEJA MIS LE FEU
UX DEUX BOUTS DE L'EUROPE

Yo Mich

of expansion in eastern Europe only when he had protected his rear against French attack by the fortification of the Rhineland. The French journalist Alfred Fabre-Luce predicted in January 1936 the remilitarization of the Rhineland which took place two months later – and he accurately predicted its significance:

It would really be a way of asking France what her attitude would be in the event of war in eastern Europe. The lack of any military response on our part would be taken as a sufficient indication. . . . Germany would then prepare her war in the East, confident of being able to resist us on the Rhine which she had fortified.

Hitler's reoccupation of the Rhineland was, as he later admitted, one of the biggest gambles of his career:

If the French had then marched into the Rhineland we would have had to withdraw with our tails between our legs, for the military resources then at our disposal would have been wholly inadequate for even a moderate resistance.

Ten years, even five years before, there is no doubt that the French army would have

called Hitler's bluff. Even in 1936 France lacked not the ability to call Hitler's bluff but the will to do so. Britain, which grudgingly agreed to supply only two divisions if France invaded the Rhineland, heaved a sigh of relief when it failed to do so. Just as the achievements of Nazi Germany during the 1930s were not unfairly described by Hitler as 'the triumph of will', so the failures of Western democracy during the same period were, above all, a failure of will.

After Hitler's invasion of the Rhineland, Germany replaced France as the leading state on the continent of Europe. France herself was by now afflicted with a growing feeling of inferiority towards Germany. As late as 1931 France had seemed almost immune from the worst effects of the depression, while Germany had been forced to come cap in hand to Paris seeking financial help. By 1936 the tables had been turned with a vengeance. While the German economy forged rapidly ahead, France was still in the middle of an economic crisis. Worse still was the problem of France's declining manpower. During the 1930s deaths began to exceed births for the first time. France's population was actually

lower in 1940 than it had been fifty years before. The most striking fact about France's international position, observed Colonel Charles de Gaulle in 1934, was that two Germans were reaching military age for every one Frenchman.

During the middle of the 1930s European affairs seemed increasingly polarized into an international struggle between fascism and communism. In 1935 Stalin reversed his earlier instructions to European communists to concentrate on the destruction

LE PÉRIL JUIF

Above, bare-footed Abyssinian soldiers, 1935: they could do little against Italian airpower, poison gas and superior armaments.

Left, French anti-semitic poster issued during the 1930s: though at its most virulent there, anti-semitism was not confined to Germany, and Jews became a convenient scapegoat for Europe's political and economic ills.

Opposite top, right-wing French election poster of 1936 warning of the perils of communism: despite the fact that there had not been a single successful left-wing revolution anywhere in Europe, until the very late 1930s many people dreaded the Bolshevik menace, ignoring the far more real one posed by Germany.

Opposite bottom, Italian troops leaving Rome for Abyssinia, 1935: the League of Nations condemned Italy's aggression but failed to take any action.

of democratic socialism and advocated instead a new policy of 'Popular Front' alliances between socialists and communists against the menace of fascism. When the Civil War broke out in Spain in 1936 Hitler and Mussolini sent help to Franco, and an International Brigade of left-wing sympathizers partly supplied with Russian arms fought on the side of the republican government. Hitler, however, was in no hurry to ensure Franco's victory. The longer the war continued, he believed, the worse

would be the demoralization of liberal, democratic Europe.

The rest of Europe saw the Civil War in simplified terms as a struggle between fascism and communism. Many European conservatives were by now anxious that by opposing Hitler they might be playing into the hands of Stalin. This attitude was most prevalent in France. Ever since the beginning of the twentieth century the French right-wing parties had been the leading advocates in Europe of a tough,

Above, German troops take part in a victory parade, May 1939: Germany and Italy gave troops and matériel *to Franco, Russia aid (but not troops) to the Republic, while the western democracies stood on the sidelines.*

Above left, Republican militia in the trenches before Irun, September 1936: the Civil War, fought with passion and conviction by both sides, should be viewed as the culmination of long-term internal political and social conflicts and, in the shorter term, of opposition to the Republic of 1931 rather than as the prelude to the Second World War.

Left, after the Munich Agreement, September 1938, the statesmen of Europe pose for the cameras: from left to right, Neville Chamberlain, British prime minister, Edouard Daladier, premier of France, Hitler, Mussolini and Count Ciano, Italian foreign minister; missing was Czechoslovakia, not invited to the conference that dismembered her.

uncompromising policy towards Germany. But in 1936 they suddenly changed their mind. Faced with the prospect of a Popular Front government in France led by the socialist, Léon Blum, they coined the slogan, 'Better Hitler than Blum!'

The policy of appeasement practised by the French and British governments during the 1930s reflected absolutely the wishes of their populations. The Munich agreement of 1938 was the most ignoble surrender in the history of modern British foreign policy. Yet as a direct result of that surrender Neville Chamberlain attained a peak of popularity which few, if any, other peacetime prime ministers have ever equalled. The British people as a whole greeted the betrayal of Czechoslovakia with an almost indecent relief of which they later felt ashamed.

The only British politician who might have rallied the British people from a policy of appeasement was Winston Churchill. But Churchill, after a brilliant early career

in which he had held almost every major cabinet office, had disappeared into the political wilderness. The eccentricity of his views on the Indian subcontinent only served to cast doubt on his constant warnings of Hitler's designs in Europe. His hour was yet to come.

The history of the 1930s suggests perhaps that the First World War, though a war caused by European rivalries and whose battles were overwhelmingly concentrated on the European continent, affected Europe less profoundly than it affected Asia. In Asia it set India on the path to independence, Japan on the road to Asian mastery and turned China's face against the West. In Europe, on the other hand, though the war acted as a catalyst to revolution in the East, in the West it only interrupted Germany's bid for the mastery of Europe. In 1919 Marshal Foch had described the peace settlement of Versailles as 'a twenty years' truce'. In Europe, at least, that was all it proved to be.

Date	Western Europe	Central and Eastern Europe	The outside world
1914	Britain declares war on Germany (4 August) Battle of the Marne (5–12 September) Race for the sea (October–November)	Assassination of Francis Ferdinand (28 June) Austrian ultimatum to Serbia (23 July) Russia mobilizes (30 July) Germany declares war on Russia (1 August) Germany declares war on France and invades Belgium (3 August) Russian defeats in East Prussia (August-September)	New Zealand takes Samoa (August) Britain takes Togoland (August) Australia takes New Guinea (September) Turkey enters the war (October) Japan takes Kiaochow (November) British protectorate in Egypt (December)
1915	Allied offensives in Artois and Champagne (February–October) Italy enters the war (May) Haig British commander-in-chief (December)	Gallipoli campaign (February 1915–January 1916) Large German gains on the eastern front (May-October) Bulgaria enters the war (October)	Japan submits Twenty One Demands to China (January) South African troops take German Southwest Africa
1916	Conscription in Britain (January) Battle of Verdun (February–November) Easter Rising in Dublin Battle of Jutland (31 May) Battle of the Somme (July–November) Lloyd George prime minister (December)	Brusilov offensive (June-September) Romania enters the war (August)	Last German garrison in Cameroun surrenders (February) Sykes-Picot agreement on Middle-East Arab revolt against Turkey Wilson re-elected president of the United States (December)
1917	Imperial War Cabinet meets in London (March) Nivelle offensive (April–May) Mutinies in French army. Passchendaele (July–November)	Germany begins unrestricted submarine warfare (February) Tsar abdicates (15 March) Bolshevik revolution (7 November)	United States enters the war (April) China enters the war (June) Sun Yat-sen sets up rival government in Canton Montague declaration on India (August) Balfour declaration on Palestine (November)
1918	Final German offensive in the West (March–July) Foch 'commander-in-chief of the Allied armies in France' (April) Allied counter-offensive (July–November) Battle of Amiens (8–11 August) Armistice (11 November) Lloyd George coalition re-elected (December)	Treaty of Brest-Litovsk (March) Civil War begins in Russia (1918–20)	Wilson's Fourteen Points (January)
1919	Paris peace conference begins (January) Treaty of Versailles (28 June) Treaty of Saint-Germain with Austria (10 September) Treaty of Neuilly with Bulgaria (19 November)	Communist rising in Berlin (January) Bela Kun in power in Hungary (March–August) Weimar Republic in Germany (August) D'Annunzio occupies Fiume (September 1919–December 1920)	Amritsar massacre in India (April) Fourth of May Movement in China United States Senate rejects the Versailles treaty Government of India Act (December)
1920	Treaty of Trianon with Hungary (4 June) Treaty of Sèvres with Turkey (August) Italian workers occupy their factories (August)	Kapp putsch in Berlin (March) Battle of Warsaw (August)	Non-cooperation begins in India (August)
1921		Treaty of Riga (March) New Economic Policy in Russia	Harding President of the United States End of Anglo-Japanese alliance Foundation of Chinese communist party Washington Naval conference
1922	Irish *Dail* ratifies treaty establishing Irish Free State (January) Bonar Law British prime minister (October) Fascist March on Rome (October)	Stalin secretary-general of Russian communist party	End of British protectorate in Egypt Southern Rhodesia rejects union with South Africa Gandhi imprisoned (1922–24)
1923	Baldwin's first ministry (May)	Occupation of the Ruhr (January) German inflation at its height (November) Hitler leads unsuccessful Munich putsch (November)	Sun Yat-sen signs alliance with Russia (January) Coolidge President of the United States Southern Rhodesia gains virtual self-government

Date	Western Europe	Central and Eastern Europe	The outside world
1924	Ramsay MacDonald Britain's first Labour prime minister (January) Matteoti assassinated in Italy (June) Baldwin's second ministry (November)	Death of Lenin (January)	
1925	Mussolini declares Italy a one-party state (January) Locarno treaties signed in London (December)	Hindenburg President of Germany	Death of Sun Yet-sen Abd-el Krim's rebellion in Morocco (1925–26) Druse rebellion in Syria (1925–27)
1926	General Strike in Britain (May)	Germany enters League of Nations	Chiang Kai-shek begins Northern Expedition Hirohito Emperor of Japan Imperial conference recognizes autonomy of dominions
1927		Stalin wins struggle for power in Russia	Chiang Kai-shek begins attack on Chinese communists Simon commission visits India
1928	Kellogg-Briand pact signed in Paris	First Five Year Plan begins in Russia	Chiang Kai-shek claims re-unification of China
1929	Ramsay MacDonald's second Labour government (June)	Trotsky leaves Russia	Hoover President of United States Chu-Mao soviet in Kiangsi Wall Street crash (October)
1930	London Naval Conference	Effective political power in Germany passes to Hindenburg and palace camarilla (March) Last Allied troops leave Rhineland (June)	Civil disobedience campaign in India Uriburu President of Argentina (September) Vargas President of Brazil (October) Rebellion in Indo-China
1931	National government in Britain led by Ramsay Macdonald (August) Statute of Westminster on British Commonwealth		Gandhi-Irwin truce Manchurian incident (18 September) Mao elected first chairman of Chinese Soviet Republic
1932	Worst year of the Great Depression	Worst year of the Great Depression Nazis emerge as largest party in Germany Russian famine at its height	Worst year of the Great Depression End of British protectorate in Iraq Japanese army establishes puppet state of Manchukuo
1933		Hitler becomes German Chancellor (30 January) Reichstag fire (27 February) Enabling law completes Hitler's dictatorship (23 March)	Franklin D. Roosevelt President of United States Japan leaves League of Nations
1934		Hitler's Night of the Long Knives (30 June) Death of Hindenburg. Hitler head of state (August) Kirov assassinated in Russia (December)	Long March in China (1934–35)
1935	Baldwin's third ministry (June)	Saar returns to Germany (January) Nuremberg race laws (March)	Government of India Act Italy invades Ethiopia
1936	Edward VIII King of England (January). Abdicates and succeeded by George VI (December) Popular Front government in France (1936–38) Spanish Civil War (1936–39)	Hitler reoccupies Rhineland (March) Stalin's Terror at its height (1936)	Italy annexes Ethiopia Anglo-Egyptian treaty Tosei-ha faction in Japanese army defeats Kodo-ha Alliance between Mao and Chiang (December)
1937	Neville Chamberlain prime minister (May)		Congress victory in Indian elections (February) War between China and Japan (1937–45)
1938		German annexation of Austria (March) Munich agreement (September)	
1939	Britain and France declare war on Germany (3 September)	German annexation of Czechoslovakia (March) Germany invades Poland (1 September)	

Part V

THE WORLD SINCE 1939

Introduction

Our age is one of rapid, far-reaching change. Change, by definition, means destruction as well as building up. As some fervently set out to sweep away outmoded institutions and hateful backwardness, others interpret their acts as wanton destruction of all that is good, true and beautiful. In such a situation, who is building and who destroying? Time, perhaps, will tell, but with a cruel partiality, praising whatever survives and portraying what goes under as deserving of its fate.

The confusion such a situation creates makes writing contemporary history in our age particularly difficult. The historian's effort must be to make sense of it all, but his appreciation of the tearing down and building up will not necessarily conform to others' viewpoints – or to the viewpoints of subsequent generations. Yet not to try to make sense of our world would amount to an abdication of the human effort to come to terms with life.

Human experience cannot be reduced to a simple formula. However it is true that a real thread runs through most of the human achievements since 1945. They are aspects of a remarkable growth in the range of human power, exerted usually through corporate organization of expertise rather than by individual men or by the unskilled masses of mankind. The most obvious examples are political and military: how enormously the destructive capacities of the world's armed forces have increased since 1945! How much the jurisdiction of governmental officials has enlarged during the same period, in backward and advanced countries alike. But the power and range of private corporations has also grown and often runs across national boundaries. Similarly, the less closely structured but nonetheless real communities of specialists in innumerable branches of science and technology have also become transnational and in some important respects continue to be self-regulating and capable of influencing even the greatest of the world's governments and corporations. Schools, sects, political parties, advertising agencies, news services and other corporate groupings that seek to affect men's minds have also attained greater scope and range. The globe-girdling television hook-up that reported the first human landing on the moon in 1969 is

only an unusually spectacular example of the interweaving of national information systems that has come to constitute a powerful political force in its own right, even in those lands where there is governmental control of information.

Cumulatively, the effect of such corporate activities is to make all society malleable – capable of being made over, this way or that, according to somebody's more or less rational plan. Zones of behaviour left to themselves – that is, to custom and to age-old traditional routine – have shrunk drastically. More than ever before, man has set out consciously to make and remake himself. The mushroom growth of corporate structures in the 'modernizing' sector of human society is matched by a no less remarkable disruption and breakdown of other types of corporate structures within which human life used to be led. Kindreds, tribes, village communities, as well as occupational, religious, ethnic and other groupings have become far less powerful, that is, far less able to guide men's actions through the vicissitudes of their lives. The great instrumentality breaking up these older structures is the enhanced range of modern communications. Since 1945 radio, television, and newspapers backed up by schools, political parties and ultimately by the whole array of 'modernizing' corporate structures have made most of the world's human beings dissatisfied with their traditional lot in life and hopeful of being able to enjoy other, usually urban, experiences of whose existence and possibility they had scarcely dreamed before.

Aptly named the 'revolution of rising expectations', this change in human attitudes

almost inescapably outruns the practical possibilities of realizing these new desires. To be sure, human life has always known pain and suffering. Traditional styles of life did not abolish suffering; perhaps they made it more tolerable by offering religious solace, but this in itself did not reduce the reality. What is new in our time is the potentiality – glimpsed and not yet attainable – of eliminating physical deprivation and many forms of disease that have haunted and deformed human lives for thousands of years. Yet, paradoxically, this bright vision is balanced by our increased awareness of the dark forces within human personalities that find expression in private, personal violence. On a public, political level, these same forces, allied with the social instincts that urge men to defend their own community – however defined – while fearing and often hating outsiders, open the possibility of mass destruction through war.

The irrational levels of human personality set limits to planning and check the growth of human capacity to control the world around them. Yet awareness of these levels may allow calculation of their effects in particular situations. Statistical regularities in criminal and other kinds of violent behaviour do exist. This may some day allow an ultimate triumph of rationality: planning for and deliberately making use of the irrational levels of the human psyche. Such a tour de force is still far away. In the meanwhile men must observe and take part in a fateful race between the party of construction and the party of destruction. The tricky part is to know which is which: and on this issue men may be expected to disagree in the future as they have in the past. Pending

an outcome, we cannot know for sure in any contested issue who in retrospect will appear right and who wrong. We remain too near, too closely engaged emotionally as well as intellectually in the struggles and debates of our age to see the overall patterns and master movements that will emerge for our descendants in a century or two. Yet each of us must do his best to understand his place in the world, to open new perspectives, batter down old prejudices and diminish narrow parochialisms.

Above, student riots at Kent State University, Ohio, in protest at US military action in Cambodia: the 1960s brought worldwide student protests against virtually every aspect of the established order, though by the late 1970s they could be seen to have had little long-term effect.

Left, Graham Sutherland's tapestry Christ of the Apocalypse *completed in 1962 for the rebuilt Coventry Cathedral.*

Opposite, Las Vegas, temple of American capitalism.

On page 286, at no time in the last four decades has the world been at peace; the Second World War has been followed by a succession of conflicts, more local in scale but no less bloody for those involved. The woman here is a Vietcong suspect being interrogated by a South Vietnamese policeman, but she could be almost anyone almost anywhere.

Chapter 21

The Second World War

Human experience cannot be reduced to a simple formula, but the historian has a duty to try and make sense of even its most recent past. For him not to do so would be to abdicate his professional responsibility. Therefore in offering an account of the last forty years of global history, the writer aims at eschewing bias while maintaining a viewpoint. That viewpoint consists of the belief that the historical process is an amalgam of political, economic and psychological forces, operating in varying conditions, subject to occasional deflection and modification at the touch of outstanding individual personalities and gradually raising the level of the sum total of mankind's consciousness of its own identity.

Unlike the outbreak of the First World War in 1914, which on the whole was unexpected, the hostilities beginning in September 1939 had been dreaded and anticipated for several years. The causes of both these major conflicts lie deep in the history of previous centuries; the causes of the second are rooted in the unfinished business of the first.

Politically they proceeded from the unchecked sovereignty of nation states, which the League of Nations had failed to curb. Economically they were the inevitable concomitant of competing economic systems, entrenched behind tariff barriers. The psychological causes of the war were the frustrations of peace time and were the result of human beings seeking compensatory outlets for their violent and aggressive instincts. All three of these were worldwide in their manifestations, but the occasion which finally triggered off war was entirely European.

That occasion was the German invasion of Poland on 1 September 1939. It, or something like it, had become unavoidable ever since the policies of Communism, Fascism, Nazism and the western democracies began during the 1930s to cut across each other. Directly or indirectly, these powers had all had a kind of dress-rehearsal interest in the Spanish Civil War. By the spring of 1939 this struggle was moving towards victory for General Franco's right-wing regime. The unopposed re-occupation of the demilitarized zone of the Rhineland by German troops in 1936 in defiance of the Treaty of Versailles, the proclamation of the agreement between Italy and Germany resulting in a Rome-Berlin Axis or collaboration pact in the same year, the anti-Comintern Pact (Germany–Italy–Japan) of 1937, which opposed international communism, the futile efforts of France, Britain and the Soviet Union to constitute a counter-alliance – these were stages towards catastrophe.

In March 1938 Hitler invaded Austria and incorporated her into the German Reich. In Czechoslovakia, Nazi Germany was giving more and more support to the Sudeten-Deutsch minority there and threatening military intervention to such a degree that in the late summer partial mobilization by the Great Powers in Europe began. However, on 29 September 1938, by a policy of appeasement towards Hitler, France and Britain bought off war for a few more months: this was the Munich agreement. Its hollowness, as expressed in Neville Chamberlain's fatuous claim that he had obtained 'peace with honour', was demonstrated by its terms. These involved the transfer of the Sudetenland to Germany in exchange for some vague guarantee about the inviolability of the remaining Czechoslovak frontiers – a fatal set-back to all attempts at anti-fascist and anti-Nazi solidarity.

In the ensuing months Czechoslovakia was virtually dismembered; in October 1938 its president, Benes, resigned; in March 1939 German troops occupied Bohemia and Moravia, and Germany annexed Memel from Lithuania. Hitler then proceeded to denounce the German non-aggression pact with Poland, and on 31 March France and Britain pledged their support to Poland in case she were attacked – a belated and ineffective gesture. On 16 April the Soviet Union proposed a defensive alliance with Britain, but it was not until 5 August that a British military mission left for Moscow. Then on 23 August there occurred a dramatic and complete reversal of alliances: suddenly a German-Soviet non-aggression pact was signed. What prompted this was Hitler's desire to guard against being involved in a possible war on two fronts and Stalin's eagerness to secure for the time being a screen behind which his own designs could be furthered.

Next, Germany demanded of Poland the right to build a military highway across the Polish Corridor, which since the First World War had separated west Germany from her eastern provinces, this was accompanied also by a demand for the ceding to Germany of the Free City of Danzig. Strengthened by the guarantee it had recently received from France and Britain, the Polish government refused that demand. This was the actual spark that set off the conflagration. The mixture of ruthless Nazi aggression, Soviet duplicity and Franco-British lethargy had shattered the frail defences of an uneasy armistice in Europe, which had lasted for exactly twenty years.

Before following the course of the Second World War and its extension beyond Europe across the planet, it is necessary to survey the rest of the world scene as it had been shaping during the 1930s and as it appeared in the summer of 1939.

Around the eastern end of the Mediterranean two forces were at work, one being the result of Egyptian national independence gained from Britain in 1936, which retained however certain strategic rights in the Suez canal area in case of war. The other was a legacy of the First World War, namely the problem of Arab-Jewish relations. It had been largely created by the incompatible promises of the British government of that day to the Arabs (Mac-Mahon Pledge 1916) and to the Jews (Balfour Declaration 1917), one guaranteeing rights of national self-determination to the Arab states, the other guaranteeing a national home for the Jews in their midst. This had resulted in the setting up under the League of Nations of a British Mandate for Palestine. By the middle of the 1930s terrorism in this area had become such a problem for the British administration that plans for the partition of Palestine between the two contestants, acceptable to neither Arab nor Jew, were being prepared. These became increasingly urgent under the stimulus of mounting immigration demands from Jewish refugees from Hitler's terror, but when the Second World War broke out no solution to the problem had been found. British arms controlled the strategic points of Cyprus, Malta and Gibraltar.

In North Africa there had been only two independent nations in 1933, Liberia and Ethiopia: the latter was invaded in 1935 and annexed in 1936 by Italy, its Emperor Haile Selassie going into exile. Elsewhere on that vast continent there was as yet, in striking contrast with many parts of Asia, an almost total absence of native nationalist leadership against the dominating European imperialist powers. Yet the policies of these same powers to their African dependencies varied: Belgium and Portugal were patriarchal, France had a policy of assimilation and Britain was paternalistically preparing both East and West Africa for eventual self-government. South Africa was a special case, where a small British and Afrikaans minority completely dominated a huge Bantu, Indian and 'Coloured' majority. This division is particularly notable because, although the then South African prime minister, Smuts, was to bring his country into the Second World War on the side of the Allies, there was a large measure of sympathy within the Afrikaans community for the Nazi cause.

Since 1937 India had been hovering on the verge of independence, but Anglo-Indian understanding was to receive a rude shock. All Congress office holders resigned in protest against the British government's inclusion of India, without consulting her, in the declaration of war on Germany in 1939.

Indian self-government was postponed for another eight years and even when it was achieved there were internal divisions. Meanwhile Indian troops fought on the Allied side, while a dissident anti-British group under Bose looked to the Japanese for support.

In China there had been two struggles going on since the early 1930s: one was between the Chinese and the Japanese invaders of their country (which had been formally in progress since 1937); the other was between Chiang Kai-shek's Chinese Nationalist party and the Communists under the leadership of Mao Tse-Tung. Between 1934 and 1937 the latter, in order to establish and consolidate a firm base for further revolutionary activities, had led his followers on the Long March of 6,000 miles to North East China, converting many of the peasantry to Communism on the way. Although for most of the Second World War the two Chinese leaders faced a common enemy in Japan, they neither trusted each other nor wished for reconciliation – in the end Mao's party was to prevail.

Undoubtedly the most striking phenomenon in the 1930s in the Far East had been the rise of Japanese power from the early days of Japan's violent aggression in Manchuria to the virtual declaration of a 'new order' in East Asia in October 1938. During the summer of 1939 there were Soviet-Japanese hostilities in Outer Mongolia, but with the signing of the Soviet-Nazi Pact Japan, because of her alliance with Germany, had to re-orientate her foreign policy. It was a year before she was ready for the next phase of her expansion. When it came, most of southeast Asia was ripe for shaking. Siam was traditionally pro-Japanese, Burma was restive under British control, Malaya was vulnerable in spite of the British stronghold at Singapore. The Dutch hold on the East Indies could be prised open, and French power in Indo-China was already being seriously challenged by the Vietnamese leader, Ho Chi Minh. The Philippines were on the point of obtaining their independence from the United States.

Of the remaining British Commonwealth countries in the eastern region Ceylon was still a crown colony and together with Australia and New Zealand supported Britain when she declared war in 1939.

Across the Atlantic the United States had been recovering under Roosevelt's New Deal from the post-1929 depression. Externally American policy was defined in terms of various Neutrality Acts and of her 'Good Neighbor' policy to the Latin American countries. Nevertheless, informed circles in the States had begun to sound the alarm against fascist, Nazi and communist movements in Europe and elsewhere, and in December 1938 there had been the joint United States-Latin American Declaration of Lima to the effect that any interference by an outside power in the affairs of the Latin

American continent would be regarded as an act of war.

As for the Latin American countries themselves, most of these had been striving to cope with the aftermath of the economic effects of the Great Depression, mainly by means of dictatorial forms of government. Although some of them displayed pro-Nazi sympathies, most were in due course to declare themselves supporters of the Allied cause. Canada, a young, highly industrialized country and part of the Commonwealth, ranged herself immediately with Britain on the outbreak of war.

Although on 23 September 1939 by the Panama Declaration of Neutrality the United States and the Latin American countries proclaimed their neutrality, this was not to endure. In Europe neutrality quickly became a casualty as Norway, Denmark, Greece, Belgium, the Netherlands, Luxembourg, Iceland and Yugoslavia were swallowed up by the belligerents' activities. Only nine countries retained their neutral status throughout the war years: Afghanistan, Saudi Arabia, Siam, Spain, Portugal, Sweden, Turkey, Switzerland and Eire. Fifty-seven nations went to war, forty-six on the Allied and eleven on the Axis side.

Blitzkrieg

Within the first three weeks of September 1939 German armies raced across Poland; on 17 September troops of the Soviet Union moved in from the East; on 27 September Warsaw itself capitulated to Hitler's might, and the Polish government went into exile. While these events were occurring the French and British military chiefs in the West acted indecisively, although logistically they enjoyed a marked superiority over the German forces opposed to them in that area. The mentality of the French High Command was symbolized by the Maginot

Above, inside the Maginot line, which ran the entire length of France's border with Germany: having constructed these enormous fortifications, the French General staff retired behind them, both mentally and physically, and utterly failed to appreciate the implications of German rearmament, being totally surprised by Hitler's rapid advance. Much of the Maginot line was surrendered without a fight.

Top, Polish cavalry during the September 1939 campaign: valiant though their resistance was, the Polish army could do nothing to withstand the onslaught of Hitler's forces.

line of fortification, behind which it sheltered. Although this was unfinished, it did not conceive of enemy infiltration. It seemed inhibited from advancing and assaulting the western front of Germany, while Nazi fanaticism and military expertise were triumphant in the East.

Yet the relationship between Germany and the Soviet Union was full of mistrust: Hitler had made up his mind to attack the Soviet Union at some stage, while Stalin was bent on securing his own defence by tightening his hold on the Eastern frontier lands of Poland and with German connivance wresting Lithuania, Latvia, Estonia and Finland to his own uses. On the other hand, these two powers could be of economic assistance to each other: food and materials could be brought from Siberia to Germany in return for manufactured goods and munitions from Germany to the Soviet Union.

Meanwhile throughout the autumn and winter months of 1939–40 all the Western Allies seemed capable of doing was to mount and increase the naval blockade of Germany and to await – in the case of Britain with some attempts at civilian defence precautions – the eventual switch of Hitler's *Blitzkrieg* from the Eastern to the Western front. A British expeditionary force had been sent across the channel to support the French armies. This came to be known as the 'phoney war'. At sea there had been a blow and counter-blow: the British battleship, *Royal Oak*, had been sunk when at anchor in Scapa Flow by a daring intrusive raid from a German submarine; the German pocket-battleship, *Admiral Graf Spee*, had been scuttled by her commander on 17 December in Montevideo harbour after being driven in there off the Atlantic by the British navy.

Military action in this first stage of the war was confined to Finland. On 30 November 1939 the Soviet Union attacked that country after failing to secure its unconditional cooperation by mere demand. The Finns, under Field-Marshal Mannerheim, put up an unexpectedly stiff resistance, but in March 1940 the Finnish army collapsed under renewed Soviet military pressure, and the Finnish government was forced to make peace, surrendering their naval base of Hango to the Russians.

Now although Hitler had already prepared for the seizure of power in Norway through the Norwegian Nazi leader, Quisling, he was still determined to finish off the French and British while the Soviet Union was preoccupied with Finland. He had in fact ordered an attack on the West for 17 January 1940, but on 10 January operational plans for this move had fallen into the hands of the Allies, who had also been secretly tipped off about Hitler's programme by the Italians. So, for a few weeks this 'Case Yellow', the code-name for Hitler's plan, was postponed. Instead, he went ahead with the invasion and occupation of Norway and

Denmark. He had strong reasons for doing so for he realized that the Allies were preparing to cut off Germany's imports of high-grade iron-ore via Norwegian territorial waters.

On 9 April 1940 German troops entered Denmark and Norway; the former yielded at once, the latter continued the struggle partly through internal resistance and partly through the Norwegian government which went into exile in London. In spite of a brief excursion of British troops in small numbers to Central Norway, the Germans obtained control of the whole country and Atlantic seaboard and safeguarded their supplies of iron-ore. The only compensation gained by the Allies was a successful British naval action against German warships near Narvik, whereby one-fifth of the

German navy's warship tonnage was destroyed.

In France Prime Minister Daladier was replaced by Paul Reynaud on 20 March 1940, a change which did not fundamentally alter the prevailing French attitude of defeatism. By contrast, in Britain Chamberlain was succeeded by Churchill on 10 May 1940 at the head of a coalition government, and under him the British will to resist stiffened.

Although still not in a position of numerical superiority in the West, the Germans at this stage possessed a clear advantage in morale and leadership. Their offensives in May through the Ardennes and their invasion of Belgium, Luxembourg and the Netherlands, the now fatal advance of British and French troops beyond their prepared positions and the demolition of the

myth of the Maginot line by the German flying columns – all these events meant that by the end of that one month the British forces were reeling back on Dunkirk, where they were to be joined by the defeated remnants of the French and Belgian armies: the Belgian government itself had surrendered on 28 May, and the Dutch government had escaped to England.

Two factors made possible the successful evacuation by 4 June of 222,500 British, 112,000 French and some 1,000 Belgian soldiers from Dunkirk to the shores of Britain. One was Hitler's decision to halt his tanks just south of Dunkirk in order to preserve them for further use elsewhere on the assurance of Goering that the Luftwaffe would suffice with its strafing from the air to prevent the evacuation of the Allied troops. The other was the extraordinary daring and skilful improvization of the British by means of which hundreds of small boats, mostly skippered by amateurs, ferried the soldiers back across the channel from the bombed and blazing beaches of Dunkirk.

Although Gamelin had been succeeded by Weygand as the French commander-in-chief, the latter had been unable to alter the course of France's collapse. On 10 June Mussolini declared war on France and Britain in order not to be left out of gaining some of the spoils of victory. On 22 June the French were forced to sign an armistice, and the old soldier, Marshal Pétain, took over the government of that part of defeated France which the Germans had decided not to occupy – roughly the southwest region with Vichy as the seat of government. General Charles de Gaulle had however escaped with a few followers and rallied what were to be known as the 'Free French' in England, from where he continued to fight in the name of an undefeated France. A bitter dispute then ensued as regards the future of the French navy, the ships of which were impounded by the British navy either in home or in Mediterranean waters in so far as they were outside Vichy-controlled ports, although Vichy still claimed their allegiance.

Meanwhile the Soviet Union, uneasy at her partner's colourful successes in the West, attempted to make a bargain with Hitler for the partition of the Balkan countries. For the time being he had to concede Bessarabia to Stalin, but this was only because he was not yet ready to strike eastwards against the Soviet Union.

Across the Atlantic the dramatic successes of the Nazi *Blitzkrieg* had been forcing a reappraisal of American policy: neutrality was beginning to shade off into non-belligerence – a phrase which described an enormously increased production of munitions and in November 1940 the abandonment of the Neutrality Act. This meant rejecting the embargo on selling arms to belligerents to the extent of imposing 'cash and carry' terms which favoured the Allies.

This then was the position in the early summer of 1940 – a prostrate France, either occupied by Germany or controlled by Vichy, a victorious Germany in control of most of northern Europe, a watchful, predatory Soviet Union, a slowly awakening United States and a defiant Britain. In Churchill's words: 'the battle of France is over. I expect that the battle of Britain is about to begin . . . let us therefore brace ourselves to our duty, and so bear ourselves that, if the British Commonwealth and Empire last for a thousand years, men will still say, "This was their finest hour".'

With the repeated assurances of Goering that the Luftwaffe could gain dominance over the British navy and air force, Hitler decided that the invasion of Britain should take place during the month of August. In spite of this imminent peril, and relying on a huge increase in production of Hurricane and Spitfire fighter planes, the British government sent out reinforcements that summer to its commander in the Middle East, General Wavell, to help him to meet the onset of Italian forces in North Africa.

From 13 August to 17 September 1940 the Battle of Britain was fought, ending with the defeat of Goering's all-out effort to establish supremacy in the air and the calling off of the German invasion. If it is ever justifiable to pinpoint one event in history as being decisively important, then the victory of the Royal Air Force in the Battle of Britain was such an event. Churchill's phrase is the best comment: 'Never in the field of human conflict was so much owed by so many to so few'.

The eastern front

Hitler had been regarding the Soviet Union's propagandist activities in the Balkans with an alarm that only strengthened his determination to attack her early in the spring of 1941. Partly in preparation for this and partly to play on British, Dutch and French weaknesses in Asia, he listened attentively to the voice of Japan, which was about to state its claim to establish a so-called 'Greater Asia Co-prosperity Sphere'.

On 27 September 1940 a Tripartite Pact was signed between Germany, Italy and Japan by which the European partners agreed to underwrite a Japanese 'New Asia' and Japan agreed to underwrite a Nazi-Fascist 'New Europe'.

During the autumn events moved rapidly in southeast Europe: Hitler proclaimed his support for a newly established fascist regime in Romania under the 'Iron Front', anti-Communist General Antonescu, and at the end of October Italy invaded Greece. On 5 November 1940 Roosevelt was elected president of the United States for a third period of office. Thus he was able to lay plans for the granting of large-scale economic aid to Britain, which was to become effective by the Lend-Lease Act of 11 March 1941. Britain was enabled to procure ships and supplies in the form of a loan to be repaid only at some future date.

In April 1941 German troops began the invasion of Greece and Yugoslavia, compelling the Greek and Yugoslav governments to seek asylum in London together with the Free French, Polish, Belgian, Dutch, Norwegian and Czechoslovak governments already established there. Early in February Hitler had despatched one of his ablest generals, Rommel, to Africa with the famous 'Afrika Korps' which proceeded to conduct a massive onslaught against Wavell's forces.

It seemed that the whole world, with the exception of the Soviet Union, was convinced that Hitler was now about to turn eastwards, but Stalin spurned the British offer of a military alliance on 13 June. On 22 June at long last 'Operation Barbarossa', as the invasion of Russia was code-named at German headquarters, began. Hitler had a war on two fronts on his hands.

Turning-points in the struggle

Even at the time it was apparent to some that this action of Hitler must spell his eventual doom, although its manner could not be foretold – least of all the long-term ideological implications of it. With the Battle of the Atlantic causing heavy shipping losses to Britain, the German hold on western Europe from north to south firm, and the United States as yet only committed to economic aid through 'all measures short of war', Hitler's prospects looked bright.

The Nazi occupation of Europe therefore fell into four categories: first, those countries annexed outright and governed direct from Berlin: Austria, Sudetenland, northwest Poland including Danzig and the Polish Corridor, Alsace-Lorraine, Luxembourg and northwest Yugoslavia; second, the 'Eastern Lands': the 'Protectorate of Bohemia and Moravia, 'the Government-General of Poland' and eventually the Baltic states and the temporarily conquered areas of the Soviet Union; third, the 'occupied territories' granted a measure of self-government but under Nazi control: Norway, Denmark, Holland, Belgium, France, Serbia, Greece and (after September 1943) Northern Italy; fourth, Germany's satellite allies: Bulgaria, Hungary, Romania, Croatia, Slovenia and Finland.

Yet in spite of all this, three stubborn facts remained as pointers to the ultimate destruction of the Nazis, namely, an undefeated Britain, a mountingly hostile America and a Japan still neutral to the Soviet Union – a neutrality which, because it was maintained until very near the end of the war, meant that the Soviet Union had not to fear attack from her Asiatic rear while locked in desperate encounter with Hitler's invading armies.

Above, German news photo showing the citizens of Larissa, Greece, welcoming one of their invaders; the reality was rather different – the Greeks were among the dourest resisters, pinning down troops that could more usefully have been deployed elsewhere.

Above left, German reconnaissance group in Yugoslavia, April 1941: the German invasion took just one week, helped by the destruction of Belgrade from the air.

Opposite top, American B-17 Fortresses on a mission supported by a Mustang fighter escort.

Opposite bottom right, Reichsmarshal Herman Goering (1893–1946) visiting a Luftwaffe squadron, autumn 1940: the Luftwaffe's failure to win the Battle of Britain put paid to Hitler's hopes of invading England and helped to ensure his ultimate defeat.

Opposite bottom left, German Dornier 172 aircraft over the London docks in the first daylight bombing raid on London, 7 September 1940: with hindsight, this can be said to have been one of the most crucial days of the war, for the beginning of raids on London meant the end of the attacks on the airfields and radar stations of southern England, which, though still in action, had been severely damaged during the previous weeks, and so enabled the RAF to retain air superiority.

These were making spectacular advances into the Soviet Union on a 1,200-mile front, reaching the suburbs of Moscow and penetrating the Ukraine and the Crimea. But the reserves and resources of Siberia and the Urals remained beyond their reach, a knock-out blow was not achieved during the summer and soon the Russian winter closed in on the German armies.

In August 1941 Churchill and Roosevelt had their first meeting at sea and drew up the Atlantic Charter, a preliminary attempt to sketch the war aims of the Allies. The United States, though still neutral, had been edging nearer to participation by the way in which she was offering protection to convoys in large expanses of the Atlantic and by her steadily increasing deliveries of supplies to Britain.

In the Far East, Japan's governing regime became more and more militaristic as opportunities for further Japanese expansion

began to present themselves with the pre-occupation of the Western Powers in their own hostilities. The American government refused to countenance any accommodation of Japan as long as China remained un-liberated from Japanese pressure. On 17 October 1941, Tojo became head of the Japanese state, and although by then the Americans were expecting Japanese aggres-sion somewhere in the East they were caught entirely by surprise when Japanese aircraft hurled themselves on the American naval base at Pearl Harbor on 7 December 1941. In less than one hour they inflicted greater naval losses than the United States had suffered throughout her First World War participation in 1917–18. This event brought the United States right into the Second World War as a full protagonist.

The war now began to take on its global but bi-partite character. On 1 January 1942, twenty-six of the Allied nations signed the Declaration of the United Nations, but al-ready there were signs both in Asia and Europe of those rifts which were, after 1945, to divide the victors. In China, Chiang Kai-shek, who had not been exerting himself much against the Japanese, was becoming more and more concerned with opposing the spread of Mao's influence and power; yet Roosevelt remained loyal to Chiang's nationalist regime.

In Europe the question was beginning to be raised as to whether the Russians and their Western Allies were prepared to recog-nize the same politicians as the legitimate government of Poland. For the time being they did, in the person of General Sikorski in London, but the problem of Poland's eventual eastern frontier was an unsolved and thorny one because the Russians naturally wished to see this ruled to their advantage and with a Polish regime favour-able to Soviet interests, and such a regime

Above, the Japanese attack on Pearl Harbor, 7 December 1941, which brought the Japanese strategic freedom for several months. The longer-term consequence – American entry into the war – was far graver for the Axis powers.

Opposite top right, Waffen SS troops in Yugoslavia. The Nazi belief in the inferiority of the peoples of eastern Europe deprived the Germans of much-needed support they might have gained from the population of the invaded territories.

Opposite top left, German officers watching the performance in a Paris nightclub.

Opposite centre right, German troops sweep into Russia, summer 1941. The German invaders became bogged down within six months, giving Russia time to recover herself and to draw on her enormous reserves of manpower.

Opposite bottom, Muscovites digging trenches during the German assault on the city.

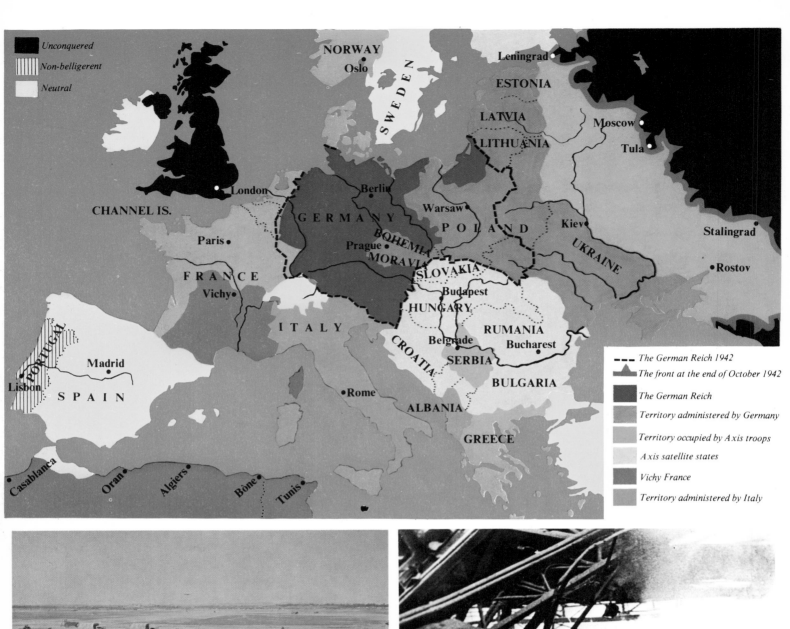

Unconquered

Non-belligerent

Neutral

NORWAY
Oslo

SWEDEN

Leningrad

ESTONIA

LATVIA

LITHUANIA

Moscow

Tula

London

Berlin

Warsaw

Kiev

Stalingrad

CHANNEL IS.

GERMANY

POLAND

Paris

BOHEMIA

Prague

MORAVIA

Rostov

UKRAINE

FRANCE

SLOVAKIA

Vichy

Budapest

HUNGARY

RUMANIA

ITALY

CROATIA

Belgrade

Bucharest

PORTUGAL

Madrid

SERBIA

Lisbon

SPAIN

BULGARIA

Rome

ALBANIA

GREECE

Casablanca

Oran

Algiers

Bone

Tunis

- - - The German Reich 1942

The front at the end of October 1942

The German Reich

Territory administered by Germany

Territory occupied by Axis troops

Axis satellite states

Vichy France

Territory administered by Italy

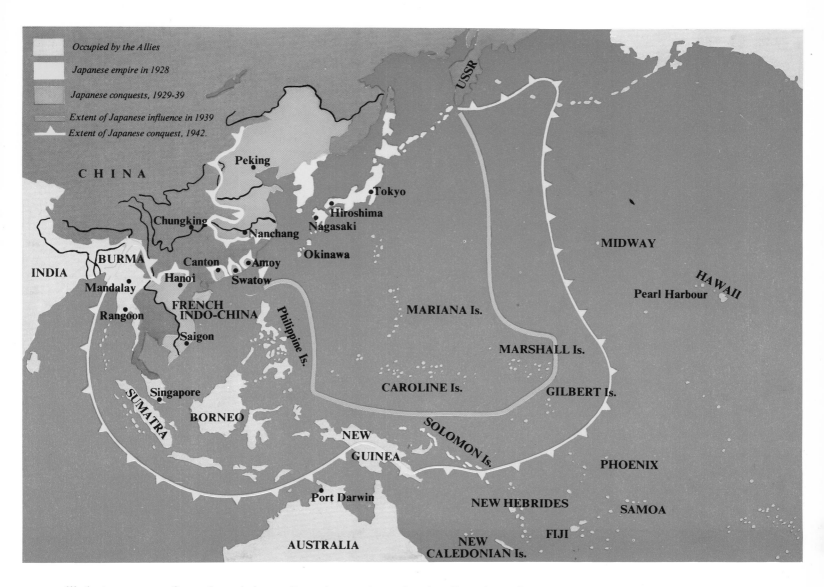

Legend:
- Occupied by the Allies
- Japanese empire in 1928
- Japanese conquests, 1929-39
- Extent of Japanese influence in 1939
- Extent of Japanese conquest, 1942.

USSR

CHINA

Peking

Tokyo

Hiroshima

Nagasaki

Chungking

Nanchang

Okinawa

MIDWAY

BURMA

Canton

Amoy

HAWAII

INDIA

Hanoi

Swatow

Pearl Harbour

Mandalay

FRENCH
INDO-CHINA

MARIANA Is.

Rangoon

Saigon

Philippine Is.

MARSHALL Is.

CAROLINE Is.

GILBERT Is.

Singapore

SUMATRA

BORNEO

SOLOMON Is.

NEW
GUINEA

PHOENIX

Port Darwin

NEW HEBRIDES

SAMOA

FIJI

AUSTRALIA

NEW
CALEDONIAN Is.

was unlikely to emanate from the existing Polish government in exile in England.

The main features of the first six months of 1942 were the rapid expansion of Japanese control in southeast Asia, the start of the anti-British 'Quit India' campaign in India by the Congress leaders there, and the comparative lull in hostilities in the European section except for aerial bombing and the awakening of various anti-Axis resistance movements.

Two events dominated the autumn months. The first was the North African campaign with its climax in General Montgomery's victory at El Alamein on 22 October 1942. This was followed by the landing of an Anglo-American military force on the North African coast in November (Operation Torch). Shortly afterwards Admiral Darlan, who had been looked upon as Pétain's most probable successor as head of Vichy France, was persuaded to bring French Morocco and Algeria over to the Allied side. After his assassination on 24 December 1942, an uneasy co-presidency of the French side was established between General Giraud, commander of French troops in North Africa and the Middle East, and General de Gaulle of the French

Committee of National Liberation. On 11 November 1942, the Germans had already moved into and occupied the previously unoccupied France of the Vichy government.

The second event was Hitler's obsessive and ultimately fatal attempt to capture and hold the city of Stalingrad. His failure to do so, and the surrender on 31 January 1943 of Paulus, the general commanding there, meant that the Nazi initiative on the Eastern front was lost for ever.

Churchill and Roosevelt

When Churchill and Roosevelt met at Casablanca in North Africa in January 1943, their main topic of discussion was how Europe was to be invaded. The former urged the invasion of Italy, while the latter pressed for a direct invasion of northern France. As a compromise it was decided to attack Sicily.

In the early months of 1943 successful preparations were made for the opening up of the Burma road by means of which, as well as by flights over the mountains, supplies could reach Chiang Kai-shek from the

Above, the course of the Second World War in the Far East.

Opposite top, Europe during the Second World War.

Opposite bottom right, fighting during the battle for Stalingrad: 91,000 German soldiers surrendered (70,000 more had already been killed) in what was only one of a series of Russian victories that winter.

Opposite top left, a crashed German Ju-52 troop carrier in the North African desert.

Opposite bottom left, Italian troops in action in the North African desert: Italy became increasingly subordinate to Germany as the war progressed, counting for little in Hitler's calculations.

and Badoglio's government. This resulted in the overthrow of the latter and its replacement by Bonomi, chairman of the National Liberation Committee.

The Allies were now paying increasing attention to the question of how a defeated Germany should be treated, while Stalin pressed more and more vigorously for the opening of a Second Front in the west by Britain and the United States. From 28 November to 3 December 1943, Roosevelt, Churchill and Stalin met for consultation in Teheran. Here the main feature was the split between Churchill and Roosevelt. Roosevelt appeared ready to concede far more, both immediately and by implication for the future, to Stalin's demands for what was virtually the sovietization of the whole of eastern Europe. Moreover, in January 1944 Stalin set up a 'Polish National Council' made up of Polish Communists in Russia as a counterweight to the exiled Polish government in London – the very first seed of what came to be known as the Cold War.

Götterdammerung

General Eisenhower of the United States, Commander of 'Overlord' – the code-name for the invasion of France – settled on 6 June 1944, for D-Day. The landings on the French coast from across the English Channel were successful, but because of a number of factors, chiefly the unexpected and resilient stubbornness of the German resistance, the Allied follow-up into the interior of Europe was delayed for several months. During this time Hitler tried out V1s or flying-bomb weapons on London, but they were countered before they could do extensive damage to morale or material, as was the later V2 version.

On 20 July 1944, the German resistance movement finally failed, though by only the narrowest margin, to assassinate Hitler.

In August 1944 Paris was liberated from German occupation, while in the Balkans there had occurred an extraordinary division of the spoils between the Soviet Union and the Western Allies. This was the so-called 'percentage agreement' or deal between Churchill and Stalin by which ninety percent of Romania went to Russia and ten percent to others, ninety percent of Greece to Britain and ten percent to Russia, fifty percent of Yugoslavia and Hungary each to Russia and fifty percent to others, Bulgaria seventy-five percent to Russia and twenty-five per cent to others. Although things did not in fact work out like this, the arrangement provides a striking if unedifying example of diplomatic horse trading.

In August 1944 there occurred one of the most tragic and sinister events of the war, namely the uprising of the pro-Western Poles in Warsaw against their German oppressors in order to prevent, by anticipation, their being taken over by Stalin's

West. The activities of General Stilwell's American troops and Orde Wingate's 'Chindits' behind the Japanese lines ensured that in the event no Japanese reinforcement landing on the South China coast could succeed.

From January 1943 until July 1944 the Americans conducted an increasingly successful series of counter-offensives in the Pacific by means of which large numbers of Japanese troops, on their over-extended lines of communication, were cut off and left to wither. By spring 1943 the Battle of the Atlantic had at last been won by the Allies, and allied victory in North Africa was completed. In July the invasion of Sicily began, to the accompaniment of

anti-Mussolini movements in Italy. This resulted in the formation of a new Italian goverment under Marshal Badoglio, who immediately began secret talks with the Allies for taking his country out of the war.

Eventually Hitler decided to come to Mussolini's rescue: he despatched twenty-five divisions of German troops to north Italy, captured Rome in September 1943, kept the ignominiously rescued Mussolini under surveillance and delayed the slow and bloody advance of Allied troops up the long Italian peninsula until they eventually recaptured Rome in June 1944. Meanwhile a virtual civil war had developed between the leaders of the Italian resistance movement

Above, German officers in captivity after the liberation of Paris, 25 August 1944: its commander, General von Choltitz, had surrendered, disobeying Hitler's orders to destroy the city.

Above left, the Star-spangled Banner flutters over the citadel at Saint-Malo, surrendered, against his oath, by the German commander after a four-day American assault on 17 August 1944: such was the importance attached to the personal oath of loyalty sworn to Hitler by every officer and the strength of Nazi ideology that most – though not all – commanders resisted to the bitter end.

Left, a Russian soldier hoists the Red Flag over the ruined Reichstag *in Berlin, symbolizing the defeat of Nazism and the start of Soviet hegemony over central and eastern Europe.*

Opposite top, the monastery of Monte Cassino from the air: the Allied forces advancing up Italy towards Rome needed four months to take this heavily fortified stronghold.

Opposite bottom, Allied forces on the Normandy beaches shortly after D-Day: for Nazi Germany, this was the beginning of the end.

puppet 'Polish National Council' from Lublin. While this rising was ruthlessly and systematically crushed, Russian troops stood by without interfering – a cold piece of *Realpolitik* on Stalin's part and evidence of his determination to use any means to attain his national and ideological ends.

During the opening months of 1945 the Allied pincers closed on the crumbling German Reich, the Russians driving from the East, Americans and British from the West. On 30 April Hitler took his own life under the ruins of his Chancellery in Berlin. On 7 May the Germans surrendered unconditionally at General Eisenhower's headquarters in Reims, with a repeat of this act,

on Russian insistence, on the following day in Berlin. It was already evident that the understanding which Roosevelt and Churchill had thought they had reached with Stalin at the Yalta Conference in February 1944 was a hollow one, even though there did emerge from it the San Francisco Conference of April–June 1945 and eventually the United Nations Organization.

In the Far East Japan was reeling under the hammer blows of the victorious American offensive but was not yet invaded herself. The Allies shrank from the possible toll in casualties of such an invasion, especially as now there lay ready to hand the ultimate

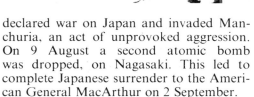

weapon – namely an atomic bomb, successfully tested on 16 July 1945. When Stalin, Churchill and the new American president, Truman, were meeting at Potsdam during that month, the latter two were informed of peace overtures which had been made and were being made through the Soviet Union, still in a state of neutrality with Japan. Nevertheless, on 26 July the Potsdam Declaration continued to demand Japan's unconditional surrender, under threat of 'prompt and utter destruction', which meant the use of an atomic bomb. When the Japanese government failed to respond to this ultimatum, the first atomic bomb was dropped by American aircraft on Hiroshima on 6 August, killing 78,000 people and destroying two-thirds of the city. On 8 August the Soviet Union shamelessly

declared war on Japan and invaded Manchuria, an act of unprovoked aggression. On 9 August a second atomic bomb was dropped, on Nagasaki. This led to complete Japanese surrender to the American General MacArthur on 2 September.

How the war was won

Once war begins, its outcome plainly depends on the skills of those waging it on the seas, on land and in the air, together with the immense resources in manpower, munitions, finance, transport and food essential to the support of both the armed forces and the civilian populations of the protagonists. There are two major considerations to be borne in mind in surveying the respective roles of navy, army and airforce: one is the concept and actuality of waging 'total' war, that is, war not confined to the military; the other is the occurrence of virtually two wars within one, the German and the Japanese, each only occasionally, though significantly, impinging on the other.

Naval affairs were chiefly significant in the long-fought Battle of the Atlantic, where, in the First World War, Britain's very

lifelines were threatened by the German U-boats. That it was won by the Allies was due to the devising of the convoy system, whereby merchant shipping received systematic armed protection when in transit.

It became clear that the day of large battle-fleets was over: carrier-borne aircraft and, as the Americans demonstrated in the Pacific naval operation against the Japanese, the use of a 'task force' supported by a 'fleet train' enabled lengthy operations to be conducted at long distance from the home base. The ever-increasing use made of radar was another distinctive feature of the war at sea, as was also the mounting of 'combined operations' for the invasion of an enemy-held coast line towards the end. Control of the seas still remained vital for whichever of the main contestants hoped to survive and win, but the manner in which that control was exercised was very different from that in previous wars and depended far more than previously on close and active cooperation with the air forces.

With regard to the conduct of armies, the Second World War was far more a war of manoeuvre than the First. This was dramatically demonstrated by the *Blitzkrieg* – the

lightning thrust of armed vehicles penetrating deep into enemy territory without waiting to advance on a uniform front: examples were the German invasion of Poland in 1939 and the German drive to the Channel ports in 1940. Another new feature was the use of airborne troops and the dropping of parachutists behind the enemy's lines, instances being the German drop on Crete (May 1941) and the British drop on Arnhem (September 1944). Further colourful expression of the war of manoeuvre was the North African Campaign with tanks taking the place of traditional cavalry in rapid encircling and outdistancing movements. It was only here that the old romantic elements of warfare still manifested themselves, in the admiration that each side accorded to the other's expertise.

Two other new types of soldiers emerged:

one was the commando unit on the Allied side, men specially selected, trained and toughened for short, violent bouts of intense aggressiveness, the other, also on the Allied side but in Britain alone, the mobilizing of a Home Guard. This consisted of civilians in full-time or part-time employment who drilled and prepared themselves in their free time to defend their homes in case of enemy landings from the sea or the air.

In the early months of the war three things became evident: one, the superb efficiency and high morale of the Germans on the offensive; two, the low morale and defeatism of the French armies hoodwinked by the myth of their own Maginot line and, three, the astonishingly contrived rescue of the bulk of the British expeditionary force from Dunkirk, albeit with the loss of most of its equipment. Later on, when the German

invasion of Russia took place, the Red Army, first in its 'scorched earth' retreat, then in its desperate beleaguering of Stalingrad and finally in its victorious counterattack right into the heart of Central Europe in 1945 vindicated to the full the years of ideological and military preparation. Two other developments may be noted: first, the degree to which women in most countries, but especially on the Allied side, were integrated into the war effort, and, second, the saving of life among the wounded as a result of improvements in medical treatment and the rapidity with which cases could be transported from the front to hospital.

Yet because control of the air proved to be the imperative condition for the successful waging of a naval or a land campaign, it was the contest between rival airforces which provided the truly decisive and dramatic issues. Three examples may be quoted. One was the Battle of Britain, when British fighter aircraft successfully denied the Luftwaffe that superiority over the English Channel and Southern England essential for effective German landings on the island coast. A second example was the Japanese air attack on the American fleet in Pearl Harbor, an event of shattering importance because of its effect on American public opinion and the way in which it dictated subsequent American strategy in the Pacific. A third example was the rather more controversial one of bombing: how much material and moral damage did sustained raids on cities and centres of industrial production actually do? The climax of this argument was expressed in the horrors of Dresden and Coventry, burning in nights of fire-storm, and in the ghastly effects of the atom bomb on Hiroshima and Nagasaki. Did events such as these finally tip the balance between acceptable war and genocide?

In conclusion it should be remembered that all the various naval, military and air encounters need to be surveyed in that confused context of strategic and political motivation which clouded the counsels of the great powers. As examples of 'miscalculations' there may be cited Hitler's underestimate of Russia's military strength and Roosevelt's underestimate of Russia's political ambitions. The tremendous dispute which went on so rancorously between Stalin and the Western Allies about the date for the opening of a Second Front can only be viewed as evidence of the underlying suspicions among the temporarily allied coalition against Hitler. It was because of this that the final German offensive in the west, although militarily a failure, was diplomatically a success in that it inserted still further the wedge of mistrust into the Allied ranks and meant that Berlin, Prague and Vienna were to be liberated not from the west but from the east.

In a very real sense Stalin obtained from Churchill and Roosevelt what he had failed to obtain from Hitler: a seat firmly astride the stricken countries of Central Europe.

Resistance

Any record of the Second World War would be incomplete without reference to war-time resistance movements in Europe and Asia, leading on into full-scale national liberation movements. In the case of the first, three well-defined phases may be detected: one, a period of stunned horror at the experience of defeat and occupation; two, from 22 June 1941, the date when Germany's invasion of the Soviet Union first really mobilized the Communist elements in the resistance movements into active pro-Allied participation and, three, the second half of the war when most of the resistance movements went over to the offensive with large-scale anti-Nazi sabotage and regular liaison with the invading Allied forces. Previously, they had been mainly concerned with social ostracism of the occupying forces, with helping escaping prisoners on their way and with labour strikes.

Of the European resistance movements in the West, in Norway, Denmark, the Netherlands, Belgium, Luxembourg and France, the last was probably the most important. A quite complex and intimate relationship developed between the indigenous resistance fighters and General de Gaulle and the Free French. For instance, in January 1942 the Free French sent one of their resistance heroes into France by parachute to coordinate the various groups into the National Liberation Movement. The organized groups of saboteurs and guerrilla fighters were known collectively as the Maquis: this force liberated Corsica on its own in 1943 and fought a number of costly battles with the Germans

after the opening of the Second Front. It would be fair to say that the leaders of the various resistance movements represented more or less honestly the interests of those elements which were opposed to the Nazi and fascist invaders of their countries – the patriotic motive – and also, though not nearly so cohesively, the interests of those elements which wished to reform the pre-war social system – the ideological motive.

It must also not be forgotten that resistance movements existed in the Axis countries themselves. In Italy this led eventually to collaboration with the forces working for the overthrow of Mussolini. In Germany resistance was ill-organized and ineffective – several attempts at Hitler's assassination misfired: nevertheless, a number of liberal-minded Germans from all sections of the country strove persistently to undermine the Nazi tyranny. They failed to interest the Allies in their clandestine activities and most of them suffered hideous execution at the hands of the Gestapo after the last abortive attempt of von Stauffenberg on Hitler's life on 20 July 1944.

Grim though the story was in western Europe, it was far grimmer and larger in eastern Europe and also rather different. For here, with almost daily massacres of his neighbours going on around him, the ordinary citizen and peasant was drawn more rapidly into active opposition. In the Soviet Union itself this took the form of partisan activities directed by the Soviet government as an ancillary to the campaigns of the Red Army. In Yugoslavia there developed an extraordinarily complex and pitiable situation. At first the Resistance was led by the Serbian Colonal Mihailovitch and his

Above, Soviet citizens executed by the Germans, October 1941: the Soviet partisans could rely on the wholehearted support of the population and operated relatively freely behind the German lines, though the consequences were brutal and immediate if they were caught.

Above top left, a German firing-squad prepares for its victims: Jews, left-wingers, resisters, intellectuals, in fact all who failed to subscribe to Nazi ideology, risked this treatment.

Above left, members of the Corsican Maquis: throughout occupied Europe, resisters did much to make life uncomfortable for the Germans, in addition providing valuable intelligence and assisting escapes; perhaps their most valuable contribution for the future, though, was actually to have resisted.

Opposite top, the City of London in flames during the 1940 Blitz (miraculously, St Paul's Cathedral was not destroyed): though the raids on London and provincial centres did cause short-term disruption, their main long-term effect seems to have been to raise morale in the face of adversity.

Opposite bottom, an oil refinery at Dortmund, Germany, under bombardment by the US 8th Air Force: as in Great Britain, enemy bombing strengthened morale and had little effect on industrial production, output in Germany reaching a peak in 1944.

Cetniks, with the full support of the Allies and the Yugoslav government in exile. But although at first it launched actions against the Germans, Mihailovitch was more concerned with Serbian nationalism and anti-communism than with campaigning against the Nazis. So a second resistance movement developed, especially after the Soviet Union changed sides. This was led by Tito, eventually obtained full Allied support after this had been withdrawn from the Cetniks and was to prove victorious. The unfortunate Mihailovitch was tried and executed by Tito's government.

Whether or not Mihailovitch's policy can be justified, the extent of his resistance movement in the early days of the German invasion of Russia (and at the time there was virtually no other in Yugoslavia) delayed the German offensive by drawing off some of its troops for the Yugoslav front for

as long as four to seven weeks, so that the German armies did not reach the gates of Moscow before winter had got them in its grip. This may well have contributed to one of the turning-points in the Second World War, for German success in Russia then could have prevented or completely altered the nature of the Western counter-measures slowly being prepared during this breathing-space.

With the Albanian resistance movement led by another Communist, the school teacher Enver Hoxha, it could be said that both Yugoslavia and Albania liberated themselves under Communist leadership.

In Poland, occupied by the Nazis for over five years, resistance took the form of sabotage and underground conspiracy. The fate of the Polish Home Army in the summer of 1944 has already been mentioned – a victim of Great Power politics. How could Polish

resistance be communist-inspired when it feared Russian communism as much as German Nazi oppression? The very men and women who had heroically sustained the anti-Nazi underground movement were subsequently liquidated by the Russians as traitors and reactionaries because they were not communists.

In Asia, the great catalyst proved to be the Japanese seizure and occupation of vast areas previously under the imperial control of Britain, France, the Netherlands and the United States. In diverse ways this roused resistance movements against the Japanese in the Philippines, Vietnam, Indonesia, Malaya, Burma and, by indirect implication, in India. Much more than in Europe, these resistance movements not only aimed to eject the invader but to effect a social revolution internally, generally a socialist or communist one.

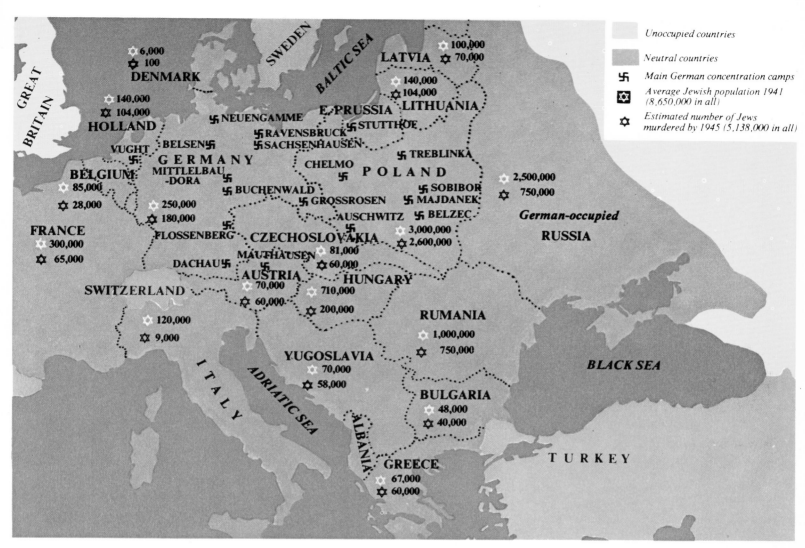

GREAT BRITAIN

SWEDEN

DENMARK ☆ 6,000 ✡ 100

BALTIC SEA

LATVIA ☆ 100,000 ✡ 70,000

HOLLAND ☆ 140,000 ✡ 104,000

E. PRUSSIA
LITHUANIA ☆ 140,000 ✡ 104,000

NEUENGAMME
RAVENSBRUCK STUTTHOF
SACHSENHAUSEN

VUGHT BELSEN
BELGIUM
☆ 85,000 ✡ 28,000

GERMANY
MITTLELBAU-DORA
BUCHENWALD
GROSSROSEN

CHELMO
POLAND

TREBLINKA

SOBIBOR
MAJDANEK
AUSCHWITZ BELZEC

2,500,000 ✡ 750,000

FRANCE ☆ 300,000 ✡ 65,000

FLOSSENBERG

CZECHOSLOVAKIA ✡ 81,000

3,000,000 ✡ 2,600,000

German-occupied
RUSSIA

DACHAU
MAUTHAUSEN ✡ 60,000

AUSTRIA ☆ 70,000 ✡ 60,000

HUNGARY ☆ 710,000 ✡ 200,000

250,000 ✡ 180,000

SWITZERLAND ☆ 120,000 ✡ 9,000

ITALY

YUGOSLAVIA ☆ 70,000 ✡ 58,000

ADRIATIC SEA

ALBANIA

GREECE ☆ 67,000 ✡ 60,000

RUMANIA ☆ 1,000,000 ✡ 750,000

BULGARIA ☆ 48,000 ✡ 40,000

BLACK SEA

TURKEY

The concentration camps

Although the full horror and extent of the concentration camps did not become known until the end of hostilities, nevertheless the naked brutality and inhumanity which their existence symbolized were an essential issue around which the war was fought. The subject, however distressing, belongs to the history of the period and must not be evaded. It is necessary to distinguish clearly between concentration camps and the Warsaw ghetto, which was a particularly ghastly ante-chamber to them, on the one hand and prisoner-of-war camps, still largely governed by Red Cross conventions on the other. Questions which any student of our times is entitled to ask are: when and where were concentration camps set up, by whom and to what purpose and how could such bestiality exist within supposedly civilized societies?

Although concentration camps existed before, during and after the Second World War in the Soviet Union, our focus here will be on those established by the Nazis in Germany and the German-occupied or controlled territories. Their purpose was a double one: to detain all those who in any way could threaten the existence of the Nazi regime and, more ostensibly, to act as centres for forced labour vast numbers of men and women were often transported long distances in appalling conditions to constitute such a labour force. As well as all political deviationists, the inmates consisted of thousands of Jews and the majority of them perished either by deliberate extermination by gas ovens and shooting, or through starvation, overwork and neglect.

The most notorious of the concentration camps were Dachau, Buchenwald, Belsen, Sachsenhausen, Ravensbruck, Maüthausen, Auschwitz, Treblinka and Maidenek. The operations were conducted on a monstrous scale.

The walled ghetto

Although it was not strictly speaking a concentration camp, this is the place to record the story of a specific instance of the policy of genocide, the 'final solution' of the 'Jewish problem', decided on by Hitler in 1941. After the German conquest of Poland, 500,000 Jews were enclosed in one small area of the city of Warsaw. It was sealed off by a high brick wall and life within it was barely sustained at survival level. Then in June 1942 the Nazis decided to liquidate the ghetto, and by October of that year 310,000

Above, Hitler's progress towards the extermination of European Jewry.

Opposite top right, photomontage by John Heartfield (1891–1968), the German Communist propaganda artist, produced in response to the news of the massacre at Lidice: the village of Lidice was wiped from the ground – its men killed, women deported, houses burnt – as part of German reprisals for the assassination in 1942 of Reinhard Heydrich, SS leader in Bohemia.

Opposite centre right, Cetniks manning a mountainside position: Yugoslav resistance was determined and divided, Tito's forces eventually dominating.

Opposite bottom right, Japanese troops parading near Battery Road, Singapore: Singapore, thought by the British to be impregnable, fell on 15 February 1942, only ten weeks after Pearl Harbor.

Opposite left, Adolf Hitler (1889–1945), Chancellor of Germany from 1933: during the war his public appearances became less and less frequent, his health deteriorated, and his grip on reality vanished. Nevertheless he seems to have retained the loyalty of the vast majority of Germans until the very end.

307

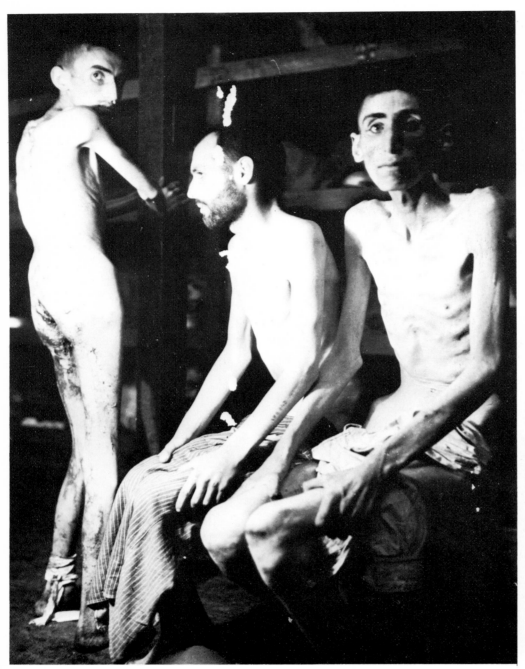

had been deported to extermination camps. News of this reached London via the Polish underground movement: for some weeks it was simply not believed. In April 1943 the 56,000 Jews who were all there were now left of the ghetto rose in heroic resistance against their Nazi tormentors: the ss major-general lost a thousand men in suppressing it and wiping out the ghetto.

This was one episode in the systematic slaughter of six million Jews by Hitler's orders. On 17 December 1942 the Allied governments officially condemned the extermination of the Jews and served notice that those concerned in organizing it would be held criminally responsible. One terrible assumption lay at the root of all these atrocities, namely that those outside the pale of the ruling regime or race were no longer human beings and could therefore be treated and used as mere objects.

Unconditional surrender

The formula of 'unconditional surrender' was hatched by Churchill and Roosevelt at the Casablanca Conference in January 1943. It was applied to Germany in April 1945 and to Japan in August 1945. It expressed a fierce determination to treat the defeated enemy with no other absolute consideration than to make future aggression impossible. Its pathos was twofold: first because its demand was unrealistic because, however unconditional the surrender, certain conditions, such as ensuring food and order, imposed themselves if the vanquished society was to exist at all, and to the establishment of these the victors would have to contribute; second because it veiled the irreconcilability of aims between the Soviet Union and the West, which when the formula was applied could no longer be concealed.

Of the original causes for which the war had been fought none had been realized: politically, in spite of the establishment of UNO, nationalism was as rampant as before, if not more so; economically, individual and collective competition was unrelenting; spiritually, human values had suffered abasement rather than elevation. The most that the historian can record on the credit side – and it is not negligible – is that the Allied victory left the human prospect less gloomy and more open to the chances of avoiding further declines into totalitarianism than if Hitler had triumphed.

The aftermath

As a consequence of hostilities, material damage and trade dislocation were great, but human displacement and penalties

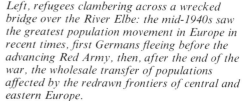

Left, refugees clambering across a wrecked bridge over the River Elbe: the mid-1940s saw the greatest population movement in Europe in recent times, first Germans fleeing before the advancing Red Army, then, after the end of the war, the wholesale transfer of populations affected by the redrawn frontiers of central and eastern Europe.

Below left, German refugees outside Berlin, 1945: the end of the war brought the total collapse of Germany; out of the chaos two radically different states emerged, one providing relative economical and political freedom for its citizens, the other continuing, in the name of another ideology, though on nothing like the same scale, the repression of Nazi Germany.

Opposite top right, the camp orchestra at Auschwitz, humanity amid inhumanity.

Opposite bottom right, a Parisian Jew during the German occupation wearing the yellow star: the Nazi regime was committed, quite simply, to the total extermination of Jewry.

Opposite left, some of the survivors of Buchenwald: the Jewish population of occupied Europe had been about 8.5 million in 1941; some 5.5 million were killed.

were greater still. The major cities of Germany were heaps of rubble, and many urban centres in Europe and Britain bore the marks of heavy bombing. Railways, bridges, factories and private dwellings had been destroyed in the course of war; nor had the countryside escaped, for everywhere land had been 'scorched' by retreating armies. Yet material reconstruction proceeded surprisingly quickly. Far more long-term in their effects were the changed economic relationships between nations, the three chief examples of which were the virtual bankruptcy of the defeated powers in Europe, the impoverishment of Great Britain on such a scale as to transform her into a second-class power, deeply in debt, and the wrecking of much of the Soviet economy which in turn clamoured for disproportionate reparation from the countries she had helped to defeat.

Millions of people were homeless or in exile: refugees from war, enemy occupation and political persecution, prisoners of war in foreign captivity, conscripted workers forcibly driven into Germany to work for the Nazis and now in need of repatriation. Relief and rehabilitation were the crying needs of these postwar months even as the politicians, by the webs they were spinning, laid up further trouble for a peace-hungry, if not peace-loving, mankind. For although men might desire peace very few were prepared to pay its price, and this was the bitter knowledge on the basis of which governments had to shape their policies.

Already during the war much work had been done by the Western Allies in anticipation of postwar needs. This took two forms: one, plans for an emergency relief operation and, two, schemes for securing a social and economic world welfare society.

On 9 November 1943, forty-four Allied and associated nations established the United Nations Relief and Rehabilitation Administration (UNRRA):

Being determined that immediately upon the liberation of any area by the armed forces of the United Nations or as a consequence of retreat of the enemy, the population thereof shall receive aid and relief from their sufferings, food, clothing and shelter, aid in the prevention of pestilence and in the recovery of the health of the people, and that preparation and arrangements shall be made for the return of prisoners and exiles to their homes and for assistance in the resumption of urgently needed agricultural and industrial production and the restoration of essential services.

UNRRA headquarters were in Washington DC, and the organization consisted of a Council representing all the constituent members, a Central Committee and a Director-General and his internationally recruited staff. Relief and rehabilitation were to be distributed and dispersed fairly on the basis of the relative needs of the population in the areas and without discrimination because of race, creed or political belief. By the end of 1945 more than $3,500 million had been contributed to UNRRA funds.

Although UNRRA came in for various criticisms, some well justified on administrative grounds, its personnel laboured heroically and with a fair measure of success. Alongside the official UNRRA teams there worked teams from most of the great voluntary organizations of the world. As a result of this effort many of the war-devastated areas were redeemed and the mass outbreak of infectious epidemics avoided.

Of all UNRRA activities, those concerned with displaced persons were the most poignant and impressive. Many displaced persons were reluctant or unwilling to be repatriated, either because they had lost all ties with their countries of origin or because of changed political conditions there. At the beginning of 1946 some 1,675,000 persons were estimated to be refugees in need of new homes. The International Refugee Organization (IRO) took over this part of UNRRA's work in June 1947.

The need for long-term political and economic measures of reconstruction on a world scale had been realized quite early in the war: the political institutions, together with their social agencies which emerged, will be dealt with later; here may be conveniently summarized the early stages of the economic ones. Two concepts were dominant: one was the need to ensure conditions of full employment as widely as possible, the other was the desirability of establishing a stable international monetary system.

Normal trading relations having been disturbed during the war, and control by

Freedom of Speech   *Freedom of Worship*

Freedom from Want   *Freedom from Fear*

governments over the movements of goods having been greatly increased, the transition from wartime to peacetime economies was bound to prove difficult. For instance there was the wartime machinery employed to control the use of sterling in international transactions, which became the basis of a trading area in the post-war years encouraging freedom of payments and trade within the area. The fact that the United States had entered the war, with all that this implied for her subsequent involvement in world affairs, was another decisive factor. Beginning with the Atlantic Charter both the British and American governments had begun to take initiatives in designing a new economic as well as political order; the 1942 Mutual Aid Agreement between them was a further stage in this development.

By the summer of 1945 some $44 million worth of supplies had been provided to their allies by the Americans. Moreover Article 7 of the Agreement provided that the final settlement of Lend-Lease should include

provision for agreed action by the United States of America and the United Kingdom, open to participation by all other countries of like mind, directed to the expansion by

appropriate international and domestic measures, of production, employment, and the exchange and consumption of goods . . . to the elimination of all forms of discriminatory treatment in international commerce, and to the reduction of tariffs and trade barriers.

This declaration led to the establishment of an International Monetary Fund at a United Nations Monetary and Financial Conference at Bretton Woods in 1944; this became effective in 1947 and had some forty-eight members by 1949. Also discussed at Bretton Woods was a project for establishing another international fund for the provision of longer-term capital, which found realization in the setting up in 1946 of the International Bank for Reconstruction and Development, or World Bank. The third important institution to be founded was the General Agreement on Tariffs and Trade (GATT) in 1947, its constituents being twenty-three countries, which at that time controlled some seventy percent of world trade.

As the history of the international economy in the postwar years is so closely bound up with political developments, discussion of the Marshall Plan for European

Above, Churchill, Roosevelt and Stalin at the Yalta Conference, February 1945: here the three Allied leaders settled the post-war fate of eastern Europe and recognized Russia's de facto *control of the nations they liberated.*

Opposite top right, US wartime poster based on the Four Freedoms enunciated by President Roosevelt.

Opposite top left, Nazi posters proclaiming that 'Bolshevism brings war, unemployment and hunger': much of Nazi propaganda, before they came to power and again at the end of war, was directed at the national fear of communism and the even more traditional fear of the east.

Opposite bottom, Dutch anti-Nazi poster calling on a traditional theme of European iconography.

Date	The European sector	The war in Asia	Other events
1939			
March	Germany occupies Czechoslovakia		End of Spanish Civil War
April	Italian invasion of Albania		
August	German-Russian non-aggression pact; Britain signs pact with Poland		
Sept	Germany attacks Poland: Poland divided between Germany and Russia; Britain and France declare war on Germany		
Sept–Oct	Soviet treaties with Estonia, Latvia, Lithuania		Accession of Pope Pius XII
Dec	Russia expelled from League of Nations		*Graf Spee* scuttled in Montevideo harbour
1940			
April	German fleet attacks Norway; Germany occupies Denmark		
10 May	German troops invade Low Countries		Churchill leads coalition ministry
27 May–4 June	Evacuation of Dunkirk		
22 June	French sign armistice with Germany		
July	Start of the Battle of Britain; German occupation of the Channel Islands		French government moves to Vichy
August	Italy and Britain clash in North Africa		Trotsky assassinated in Mexico
Sept		Japan joins Rome-Berlin axis. French Indo-China invaded	
Oct	Italy invades Greece		
1941			
March	Defeat of Italians at Cape Matapan		
April	Addis Ababa recaptured by British	Russo-Japanese neutrality pact	
May	Germany invades Greece and Yugoslavia; Battle for Crete		
June	Free French and British enter Syria; Turkey makes non-aggression pact with Germany		
22 June	Germany invades Russia		
14 Aug			Atlantic Charter signed by Churchill and Roosevelt
Oct	Attack on Moscow		
Dec		Attack on Pearl Harbor; USA declares war on axis powers; Japanese capture Hong Kong	

Date	The European sector	The war in Asia	Other events
1942			
Jan		Capture of Manila; Dutch East Indies invasion	
Feb		Capture of Singapore, Rangoon	
March		Capture of Mandalay, Philippines; Allied counter offensive in New Guinea	
May		Battle of the Coral Sea	
June	Rommel captures Tobruk		
July	Battle of el Alamein		
Sept	Battle of Stalingrad begins		
Nov	Germany enters unoccupied France		
1943			
Jan	British capture Tripoli; Casablanca conference: 'unconditional surrender' terms agreed		
Feb	Germans surrender at Stalingrad		
May	Axis forces surrender in Tunisia		
July	Allied invasion of Sicily	Australians join American troops in the Pacific	
Sept	Italian government surrenders to Allies; joins Allies		
1944			
Jan	Allied landings at Anzio		
March	Bombardment of Monte Cassino		
June	Allied landings in Normandy	US forces bomb Japan	
July	Bunker bomb plot against Hitler fails		Iceland declares her independence
August	Liberation of Paris		
Sept	Battle of Arnhem		
Oct	Allied landings in Greece		
Nov			Roosevelt elected president for fourth term; Butler Education Act
1945			
Jan	Hungary, Poland, Austria, overrun by Russia		
7 Feb	Yalta Conference		
April	Suicide of Hitler; Mussolini shot	US forces invade Okinawa	Roosevelt dies; Truman President of America
May	Russians enter Berlin; Unconditional surrender of Germany and Italy		
June			Formation of the United Nations; Labour wins British election
July	Start of Potsdam Conference		
August		Russia declares war on Japan and invades Manchuria; Surrender of Japan	

recovery and of the emergency of a number of regional economic groupings will be treated below in the account of ideological alignments and the waging of the Cold War.

Russia and America

At the end of the Second World War there were two great powers left in the world, the United States and the Soviet Union, for China was internally split between Nationalists and Communists and Great Britain was an impoverished victor. Her previous wealth had been stripped off her by vast war-time expenditures and her people were weary.

The Soviet Union had emerged from the conflict militarily victorious but at a terrible cost of human suffering and material damage: the loss both of manpower and resources was such as would require years of reinvestment and hard work for recuperation. Nevertheless the Red Army dominated eastern Europe, and Stalin's might threw long shadows right across Europe to the Channel ports and manifested itself as a no less challenging presence in northern Asia.

When hostilities ceased the United States was the greatest industrial power in the world. She had emerged from isolationism and could no longer seek alibis for her dominance of the global stage. Moreover, at this moment of history she alone possessed the secret of the atom bomb.

The two unsettled issues which straddled the postwar scene were the future of Germany and the fate of Poland. Both had begun to present themselves at the Yalta and Potsdam Conferences, although the former had not yet become as acute as the latter. The victorious Allies were agreed that conquered Germany should be administered by a Four Power Control Commission, American, British, French and Russian, the land being carved up regionally and the city of Berlin under special four-power control.

Reparations were to be exacted from Germany but not in the same totally unrealistic manner as in 1919, in spite of a first but unsuccessful attempt by the Soviet Union to assert a monstrous and disproportionate claim of her own. In general it was also agreed that a policy of denazification should be implemented by means of which all future controlling sectors of German society should be purged of those elements which had supported the Hitler regime. This project proved extremely difficult to execute both for administrative and ideological reasons and was to become one of the most bitter sources of quarrel between the Soviet Union and her Western partners. It was also further agreed that there should be a formal trial of war criminals. In due course this took place at an International War Crimes Court at Nuremberg at which a number of Nazi leaders were brought to trial as war criminals for the atrocities they had committed.

With regard to Poland, the Western Allies had virtually capitulated to the Russian demand for recognition of the former Lublin government as the legitimate government of Poland: the supposed counter-guarantee of 'free elections' to be held in the near future proving worthless in the light of Soviet prevarication and delay. The problem of frontiers was a menacing one, the very simplicity of its proposed solution being both brutal and sinister. The Soviet Union extended her frontiers westwards into former Polish territory, and for this Poland received territorial compensation by herself extending westwards into former German territory to the Oder Neisse line.

Chapter 22

The Headlines of History 1945–1965

In the distant perspective of history what lay behind the headlines often assumes greater significance than what was contained in them. Nevertheless the headlines are essential markers for our story.

The Anglo-American partnership had made an allied victory possible and Anglo-American relations coloured much of the next twenty years of world politics. That is why a glance at the domestic affairs of Britain and the United States during that period is necessary to start with. The first need to be viewed in the light of the decline in influence of a former Great Power; the second must be seen in the light of America's vast international responsibilities, as one of the two giant powers of the postwar world. Both countries are democracies, but each offers its own version of democratic principle and practice.

Great Britain

In July 1945 the Labour Party won a sweeping victory in the general election, which was conducted after the defeat of Germany (8 May 1945) but while the war against Japan was still being fought. In the words of the English historian A. J. P. Taylor: 'The electors cheered Churchill and voted against him.' Why? They believed, it seemed, that a war government was not the right government to tackle the problems of peace and that social reform, which had become a widely held expectation, would more probably be forthcoming from the Left than the Right. With Clement Attlee as prime minister, Herbert Morrison as deputy prime minister, Ernest Bevin at the Foreign Office and Sir Stafford Cripps as president of the Board of Trade until 1947 and then chancellor of the Exchequer, the new government commanded an impressive range of talents.

The team was successful in maintaining full employment and introducing a measure of nationalization in keeping with socialist principles: in 1946 the Bank of England, the coal industry and civil aviation were nationalized; in 1947 the British Transport Commission took over the railways, canals and road haulage, while the electricity and gas industries also came under state control.

In 1951 iron and steel began to be nationalized, but, unlike the others, this branch of the national life was almost entirely denationalized when the Conservatives came to power in 1951. Labour had only just retained its position after the general election of February 1950 with a majority of six; then illness and dissension disturbed its ranks, and, after the dissolution of parliament in September 1951, the Conservatives took office with a majority of seventeen.

Churchill resigns

Although Churchill headed the government, he had aged considerably. He suffered a heart attack in 1953 and finally resigned in 1955 from the premiership. He remained a member of parliament until a few months before his death in 1965, enjoying the veneration of his countrymen whose island he had saved from destruction. At the next general election in the early autumn of 1955 the Conservatives, with Anthony Eden as prime minister were returned to office with a majority of sixty. This was symptomatic of the country's general feeling of recovery and mild satisfaction with things as they were, of continuing friction between the right and left wings of the Labour Party and of the succession of Hugh Gaitskell as its leader.

After the fiasco of Suez and the retirement of Eden in 1957 the succession in the Conservative Party fell to Harold Macmillan, whose government continued from then until the end of 1963. It was a period when, for most of the British, it was true that they 'had never had it so good': there was better housing and more consumer

Above, Princess Elizabeth (now Queen Elizabeth II), Queen Elizabeth (now Queen Elizabeth the Queen Mother), Sir Winston Churchill, King George VI and Princess Margaret greet the VE Day crowds from the balcony of Buckingham Palace, 8 May 1945. The royal family had worked continually throughout the war to maintain popular morale; in two months Churchill, despite his universal popularity, would be swept from power in a socialist landslide, reflection of the widespread belief that the nation was ready for radical reform.

HELP THEM FINISH THEIR JOB!
Give them homes and work!
VOTE LABOUR

goods, increased car ownership and shorter working hours. In the election of October 1959 the Conservative majority was increased to a hundred. Yet beneath the calm, political surface there were serious economic problems, differences of opinion in both major political parties about expenditure on armaments and a growing coherence of viewpoint among the Labour opposition as Gaitskell asserted his leadership. In 1961 the Conservative government opened negotiations for British membership of the European Economic Community – a definite signal that the days of British supremacy as a first-class world power were at an end and that the reality of a united Commonwealth was rapidly disappearing. The rebuff which this initiative received from General de Gaulle, the personal scandal in connection with Mr Profumo, secretary of state for war, and his own ill-health accounted for Macmillan's resignation in October 1963. After an unedifying personal squabble over the leadership, he was succeeded by Sir Alec Douglas-Home, but in October 1964, at the next election, Labour returned to power under Harold Wilson with a tiny majority, Gaitskell having died unexpectedly in 1963.

Actually, the verdict of the polls revealed a three million Liberal vote and an almost equal division between the Conservative and Labour members returned to parliament. However, Labour succeeded in amassing an overwhelming majority at the next election eighteen months later, which implied a mission to do two things: re-align Britain's relations with the outside world in such a way that they corresponded to her actual status as a second-class power and tackle the balance of payments problem.

The end of this particular political sequence, 1945 to 1965, seemed to carry a tang of disillusionment about it. Were the real political decisions any longer being taken in parliament? Was not that august body now incapable of discharging its traditional functions of debate and questioning when the issues involved had become too complex and speculative for the legislative to pass judgment on them? Had the influence of the trade unions increased so enormously as to constitute a political menace? Was the office of prime minister itself assuming dangerously presidential-like powers? These are the kind of questions which an examination of the period brings into focus.

Embedded in wartime promises of social reform, of which Archbishop Temple and William Beveridge were the two most notable proponents, there was the implied assumption that Britain could and should spend more on her welfare services. How far this assumption was to prove well-founded must be judged in the context of her actual rate of economic growth in the postwar years and the relationship of that to her overseas balance of payments problem. Although the country was nothing like so rich relatively as she had been before 1939, the great majority of Britain's inhabitants enjoyed a higher standard of living than ever before at the very time that her share in world trade was steadily declining. Between 1953 and 1963, for example, the volume of British exports increased by less than forty percent while that of the Common Market countries increased by more than 140 percent. Two series of events illustrate this paradoxical tendency.

First, there was the achievement of the welfare state, the main landmarks of which were the Beveridge Report (1942), the creation of the National Health Service (1947) and the National Assistance Act (1948). It must be reckoned to the credit of

both government and governed that all this was achieved during a period when food rationing still continued and the price to be paid involved the public's putting up with the perpetuation in peacetime of many of the wartime austerities and controls. This whole enterprise in welfare democracy was however threatened by three factors. One was the dollar shortage (1949–50), shared with much of Europe and overcome by the imaginative and mass support of Marshall Aid. Another was the practice in business circles of living off expense accounts – particularly in the 1950s – an insidious method of evading taxation and damaging to public morale and efficiency. The third and easily the most important factor was Britain's balance of payments problem – the fact that she was not paying her way in terms of the world money market and was becoming increasingly dependent on foreign loans for the upkeep of her standard of living.

To offset these negative influences, particularly after 1953, attempts were made to invigorate the economy by the government's frequent exhortations to management and labour alike to modernize their methods and increase exports. In 1954 Britain attempted to re-establish her industrial and technological pre-eminence by setting-up the United Kingdom Atomic Energy Authority, which in subsequent years began to pay modest dividends. In 1963 came National Productivity Year, an attempt to infuse new life and energy into the national economic scene, but the notion smacked somewhat of 'whistling in the dark' and did not really catch on.

Another way of improving Britain's prospects was tried, namely, a belated formal move to join the European Community. Both political parties were divided on the issue when Macmillan's Conservative government applied for membership of the Treaty of Rome in July 1962. The chief economic argument was that the European Common Market could offer British manufacturers a larger and better market than the Commonwealth now did. General de Gaulle imposed his veto with a resounding

non in January 1963, on the grounds that the United Kingdom was not really genuine in her desire to join the community and was more likely to be a liability than an asset to it both economically and politically. In this he may not have been entirely incorrect, especially as one of the main arguments of those in Britain who were against 'going into Europe' was that Europe – the Europe of the Six – was not the real Europe, which stretched much further north, and south, but only a fragment of it. Hence Britain developed an alternative trade policy in collaboration with the European Free Trade Association (EFTA).

In the process of economic adjustment between 1945 and 1965 Britain could not help profiting from the general rise in material standards of living common to all the developed countries, but, it may be suggested, to the accompaniment of a degree of domestic demoralization and the derisive criticism of foreign controllers of capital: Britain had become the financial invalid of the international banking scene. In spite of all this Britain's welfare state had come to approximate rather more closely to the 'Great Society' than had the United States, where that slogan originated.

To come closer to an understanding of the political and economic phenomena so far discussed, it is necessary to pay attention to what might be called the spiritual and cultural groundswell of this population of fifty-two million – an average of six hundred of them to the square mile. A clue may be found in such phrases of the 1950s as 'I couldn't care less', 'I'm all right, Jack' and 'You've never had it so good' – themselves manifestations of the delayed shock induced by the huge and often heroic exertions of Britain during the Second World War.

The Festival of Britain in 1951 was an attempt on the part of the British to reassure themselves and their neighbours that they were the same and as good as if not better than their forefathers of 1851. Yet this was at any rate arguable, as was best demonstrated perhaps by the only truly popular movement of this period, the Campaign for Nuclear Disarmament

Above, The Islanders, *a sculpture produced for the 1951 Festival of Britain.*

Above left, a fight between two London dockers waiting for work: the system of competitive casual labour that prevailed in the London docks until the 1960s meant that only a bare minimum wage was guaranteed. It also reflected the widespread failure of British industry to reform its procedures and to attempt to overcome endemic class divisions.

Opposite, poster produced by the Labour Party during the 1945 election reflecting the current belief that the war had been fought not merely to defeat Germany but to create a fairer society at home: Conservative propaganda, by contrast, relied practically entirely on admiration for Churchill.

C. P. Snow, roamed the 'corridors of power' and helped to perpetuate the myth of two opposing cultures, science and the arts.

In the absence of broadly shared moral and political objectives, acceptable to the younger generation, there began the protest of youth. Symptomatic were the 'teddy-boys', the 'beats', the 'mods and rockers'. Also to be taken into account was the erosion of Christian belief, in spite of some attempts, such as the Bishop of Woolwich's book *Honest to God*, to bring fresh air into the stale theological atmosphere.

Yet the process of cultural adjustment to the postwar world was by no means entirely negative. Indeed, in the arts Britain experienced a veritable renaissance. Britten, Fonteyn, Piper, Moore, Murdoch these names suffice to indicate artistic variety and richness. Those in the younger age groups were seeking a new set of coherent values in the fields of politics and ethics – especially those to do with sexual conduct – which they could affirm as being relevant to the conditions of the mid-twentieth century. Perhaps the most hopeful sign of genuine progress was to be found in the sphere of education. The 1944 Education Act had been the climax of a 'silent social revolution' which had been occurring since 1870. Even though not all of its clauses were implemented, it led to a ferment of concern about the upbringing of the nation's children, not least in the desire to get away from selection for secondary education at the age of eleven. Education became news in a way which it had never been before: the Crowther Report on the education of the school child from fifteen to eighteen, the Newsom Report (*Half Our Future*) on the secondary school child of average or less than average ability, the Robbins Report on the expansion of the universities and their proliferation which followed from it, the Public Schools Report, the Plowden Report on primary education, the Albemarle Report on youth and many others all witnessed to a widely-spread feeling that Britain's future in reduced circumstances depended on the overhaul of her educational institutions at all levels to bring them into line with the demands of the atomic age.

By way of summary it may be suggested that after 1945 Britain steadily abandoned traditional forms of morality and religion, pursued material prosperity with inefficient eagerness, questioned her political institutions and placed a hopeful bet on the prospects of her schools and colleges.

The United States

In contrast with postwar Britain, there was in the United States no widespread demand for social reform, but rather for a return to things very much as they had been before the war. However, three mighty factors, which were to be operative throughout the four presidencies of the period

(CND). This effort to express outside official political circles the feeling among many sections of the population that Britain should no longer be a candidate for participation in, or preparation for, a Third World War of nuclear dimensions was a striking one. Although its influence was for a time considerable, it waned during the 1960s as the world seemed to be turning in the direction of several small-scale, contained wars rather than one total one. Another expression of discontent was to be found in literature and drama: J. B. Priestley's *Three Men in New Suits*, about men demobilized from the forces in 1946 and seeking a decent, commonsense way of

life who had turned into the 'angry young men' of the 1950s. What were they angry about? The false flush of health on Britain's body politic, as they saw it, the continuation of class differences and rivalries, the bogus nature of traditional figures of authority in the churches, the universities, the professions and business management.

It was then that much was heard of the 'establishment', a word used to describe the real as distinct from the apparent rulers of Britain – a mixture of the City, Oxford and Cambridge universities, top civil servants, the upper managerial class and a few high-ranking scientists. It was they who, in the words of the novelist and physicist

1945 to 1965, militated against that wish being fulfilled. One was the increasing size and vehemence of black protest, the consequence of black American participation in the armed forces and the experiences of wartime full employment and maximum productivity, with its resultant demand for full black civil rights. The second, to some extent provoked by the first, was a growing demand in the middle and late 1950s for measures to abolish such pockets of white poverty and misery as still existed in parts of the Union. The third was the realization by American citizens of some of the implications, not all of them welcome, of the unavoidable overseas responsibilities of the greatest power in the world.

Owing to the death of Franklin D. Roosevelt in office his vice-president, Harry Truman, automatically succeeded him in the early summer of 1945. Little was known or expected of the new president. He himself at first seemed aghast at the task which had fallen on his shoulders: he was indeed a 'president in the dark'. Yet in the course of his two periods of office, 1945 to 1948 and 1948 to 1952, his performance contradicted its lack of promise both in foreign affairs and in domestic policy. Two issues demonstrated Truman's capacity to interpret accurately the opinion of the mass of his fellow countrymen, who saw much of themselves reflected in his honest-to-goodness, practical common-sense, spiced with folksy humour and occasional outbursts of temper. The first of these was some appreciation of the plight of the negro: the fact that he boldly made the civil rights issue one of his main planks in his 1948 presidential election campaign, which he so unexpectedly won, showed the public that this was not a problem that could just be left; a plan, and when necessary direct federal guidance, were to be called for.

The second incident was his handling of the beginning of the 'Red Scare', which started in 1948 when Alger Hiss, a high-up state department official and president of the Carnegie Endowment for International Peace, was accused by Whittaker Chambers, himself an ex-communist, of having betrayed American secrets to the Russians in the 1930s. This incident, which resulted in Hiss being convicted of perjury but not of treason by the Supreme Court in October 1950, triggered off long smouldering public alarm at what was felt to be the way in which American diplomacy was being outsmarted by Soviet guile in various parts of the world.

Although, a few days after the Hiss verdict, Truman announced that work was to proceed on the hydrogen bomb, this did not suffice to appease the Red-baiters, chief of whom was the Republican senator from Wisconsin, Joseph McCarthy. His main criticism of the Truman administration was that there were communists in high governmental positions. The Tydings Committee, which had been appointed to investigate these charges, reported in July 1950 that there was hardly any foundation in them and that they were a great deal to the discredit of McCarthy for the way in which he had brought them. Yet for a while the country as a whole fell for the attractions of a Red witch-hunt, and quite a number of liberals and moderates suffered from the operation of this scapegoat mechanism. McCarthyism was an ugly scar on the American body politic and undoubtedly exercised considerable influence in the 1951–52 presidential election by making the task of the Democratic candidate, Adlai Stevenson, a virtually impossible one.

The two periods of the Eisenhower presidency (1952–56 and 1956–60) were marked by substantial material progress, massive and often unthinking social conformism and the domination of the 'organization man'. Himself a national hero after his victorious command of the Allied Forces

Above, President Harry S. Truman (1884–1972, president 1945–53) holds aloft a copy of the Chicago Tribune *wrongly announcing his defeat in the 1948 presidential elections: his Republican opponent, Dewey, had widely been expected to win. The crucial decisions made by Truman – to drop atomic bombs on Japan, to commit the USA to the defence of western Europe, to send troops to Korea – set the course of international politics for the next decade and a half.*

Above left, Polish refugees arrive in New York, October 1948: the USA continued to welcome large numbers of immigrants after the Second World War, initially from Europe, later predominantly from the Caribbean, though restrictions ensured that numbers were never as great as they had been at the turn of the century.

Opposite top, CND demonstration against the construction of bases for Polaris submarines in Scotland, February 1961 (the philosopher Bertrand Russell is in the first line of the marchers): the disarmament campaign, the liveliest political movement of the late 1950s and early 1960s, petered out in the late 1960s, disillusion setting in as a result of the failure of the Labour Party, returned to power in 1964, to make any progress towards unilateral disarmament.

Opposite bottom, a scene from John Osborne's play Look Back in Anger, *first produced in 1956: its portrayal of personal relationships and the class society shocked the theatrical world, used to a more comfortable treatment, but the attitudes it embodied seem, twenty years on, as dated as those it attacked.*

from exercising their voting rights by such notorious devices as the 'literacy' tests: they were sent to inferior schools by means of the gerrymandering of school districts, and in most of the South they were excluded from jury service.

This therefore was the situation when there swung into more vigorous action the old-established National Association for the Advancement of Colored People and its Legal Defense and Education Fund: its first triumph was the Supreme Court's decision in May 1954 that 'in the field of education the doctrine of "equal but separate" has no place. Separate educational facilities are inherently unequal.' Eighteen months later segregated seating in buses in Montgomery, Alabama, was abolished as a result of a black bus boycott organized by the Reverend Martin Luther King.

Then at the beginning of the 1957 school year the Little Rock School Board decided to admit seventeen black students to the previously all-white Central High School. In defiance of federal law the governor of Alabama stationed the Arkansas National Guard outside the school, ostensibly 'to prevent racial violence' but actually to prevent blacks entering the school. This was a direct challenge to the federal constitution, and in spite of his own abhorrence of infringing state rights, President Eisenhower felt obliged to intervene to deal with the Little Rock situation, to suppress Governor Faubus' activities and to uphold the Supreme Court's decision. He did so by federalizing the Arkansas National Guard and despatching a thousand paratroopers to Little Rock to enforce law and order for the rest of the school year.

This was the beginning of a creeping malaise, which spread across the United States during the closing months of Eisenhower's presidency. It was compounded of white fears, black aspirations, a general shame at the shortcomings of many American schools, despondency and jealousy at

at the end of the Second World War, 'Ike' was content to be a conscientious, golfing president, who presided over the counsels of his officials, listened to their advice, often took it and emerged ever more clearly as a beloved father-figure of the American people – the very personification at that time of their own desire to be left in peace to enjoy their affluence at home and not to be too much bothered by affairs abroad. As the following summary indicates, neither of these desires was to be realized.

McCarthyism, after a brief and sordid period of triumph in the summer of 1954, was most creditably exposed for the evil thing it was by the Senate resolution in December 1954 to the effect that McCarthy 'had acted contrary to Senatorial ethics and tended to bring the Senate into dishonour and disrepute, to obstruct the constitutional processes of the Senate, and

to impair its dignity – such conduct is hereby condemned'.

Eisenhower's cabinet, a conservative one by his own admission, concentrated on binding up the wounds of the Korean war, on reducing federal expenditure, eliminating corruption and tightening up the national defences. It was his second term of office that was to witness the outbreak of a series of troubles. Revolution in Cuba and the Lebanon, the Soviet launching of Sputnik I, the 'U2' incident and the bungling of the 1959 Paris summit conference need to be taken into review when surveying the American domestic scene. First, there was the school desegregation crisis of Little Rock, Arkansas: this was a definite alarm signal to the entire nation that black patience and white restraint, particularly in the southern states, were almost at an end. Black American citizens were prevented

the achievements of Soviet science. Congress passed the National Defense Education Law for the appropriation of large funds for the financing of a great leap forward in the production of American scientists and political scientists.

Meanwhile the black revolt grew: cafe sit-ins were organized in 1960; the Congress of Racial Equality arranged a series of freedom rides. The Eisenhower era ended in a mood of deep national depression and self-questioning: obviously the political formula of the last eight years had proved inadequate, in spite of all the country's material affluence, to propound solutions to the persistent problems: the plight of blacks in such an affluent society and the international obligations of the United States.

The Kennedy presidency was as brief in duration as it was distinctive in style. At his inauguration in January 1961 John F. Kennedy, the youngest president ever elected and the first Roman Catholic to hold that office, declared his hope that the nations of the world would come together in joint harness, 'explore the stars, conquer the

deserts, eradicate disease, tap the ocean depths and encourage the arts and commerce'. Although thirty-four months later he was dead from an assassin's bullet, his 'new frontier' policy manifested itself vigorously both abroad, where the supreme test came with the Cuban crisis, and at home.

The black revolt continued: in September 1962 the University of Mississippi ('Ole Miss') admitted a black student. In August 1963 a quarter of a million people, black and white, representing all aspects of the civil rights movement, held a huge, peaceful rally in Washington DC. They were listened to sympathetically by Kennedy, who then recommended to Congress the strongest civil rights measure the country had ever seen. That measure became law at the hands of an otherwise reactionary Congress within a year, in spite of and partially because of Kennedy's assassination and by reason of the astute political management of his successor in office, former vice-president Lyndon Johnson.

Otherwise President Kennedy's domestic initiatives were hampered by nominally

Above, seconds after her husband has been shot, Mrs Kennedy drags a secret serviceman on to her car.

Opposite right, John F. Kennedy (1917–63, president 1961–63) addresses an Inaugural Gala on the eve of his inauguration as president, January 1961: Kennedy's administration brought new style and new hope to American politics, though much of the reforming legislation he promised was in fact enacted by his successor, Lyndon Johnson.

Opposite left, American advertisement dating from about 1950: the nation's enormous wealth has enabled it to set the lead in the development of a consumer society.

Democratic Congress with strong conservative prejudices. True, he did achieve the creation of the American Peace Corps for welfare services overseas, and he did see enacted the Trade Expansion Act. Yet, at the time of his assassination in November 1963, it was what he was promising rather than what he had actually achieved that was significant. His youth, intellectual brilliance, attractive family and general lifestyle had brought new energy and hope into American national life when it was badly needed.

Although Lyndon Johnson was personally the complete antithesis of Kennedy, he shared with him the same basic beliefs in progressive policies. As a result of the successful passing of the 1964 Civil Rights Act, integrated civil rights organizations operated in many parts of the United States, chiefly in the south. Their function was to test the degree to which the 'public accommodation' clauses were being implemented, to encourage voter registration and political education in the black communities and to foster urban renewal and slum clearance. Although their plight remained a desperate one in many areas, the blacks and their friends could begin to sing their song, 'We shall overcome', with a fair promise of success.

Yet the shadow of Vietnam spread ever more darkly over the Johnson administration, and there was a strange but understandable correspondence between the fears, doubts and honourable intentions of young Americans drafted to the Far East and the demands of black resistance at home and the small but increasing numbers of white Americans conscientious objectors to military service in Vietnam. It indicated a growing conviction among many Americans that the money being spent in Vietnam would be better spent at home. In the context of that correspondence President Johnson's hopes for the creation of the 'great society' grew paler.

If 'adjustment' is the correct verbal clue to an understanding of the British domestic scene since 1945, then, it may be suggested, 'complacency punctured by concern' is the appropriate phrase for the American one. Their respective accuracies may be tested by setting them in the wider context of the world's ideological alignments.

The beginnings of the Cold War

Ideology is a word used to describe two distinct but related notions, a science of ideas and a set of passionate beliefs. Together they combine to produce various forms of political life: those in which governmental authority is largely internalized may be deemed democratic; those where governmental authority is entirely externalized may be deemed dictatorial and, in the twentieth century, totalitarian. Both have been immensely affected in recent

history by the emergence on a world scale of working classes demanding their rights and by the gigantic leap forward in science and technology.

Where a society has been insufficiently sophisticated and mature to accommodate these forces by self-imposed, free-choice discipline, it has adopted a totalitarian government – fascism and Nazism on the Right, communism on the Left.

The origin of the Cold War is to be found in the Communist Manifesto of 1848, where an implicitly totalitarian challenge was issued to liberal and social democratic policies in the name of dialectical materialism, the dictatorship of the proletariat and a planned economy. That challenge received powerful reinforcement with the triumph of Leninism and Stalinism, the German-Soviet pact at the outbreak of the Second World War was only a tactical deviation from it, and by the time of the Potsdam Conference if not of the Yalta Conference in 1945, it had begun to emerge unmistakably once again. Because of the persistent strength of the power-politics of nation-states, the utopian ends of what is in theory an international communist policy became submerged in the conventional power-struggle of the Great Powers, which by 1945 had been reduced to two, the United States and the Soviet Union. No

wonder that the code name which Churchill used for Potsdam in 1945 was 'Terminal': no wonder that uneasy peace was to slither into cold war.

At the end of hostilities US policy rested on the assumption of harmonious cooperation with the Soviet Union and the strengthening of the United Nations: it continued so to rest for a year and a half, during which time the Soviet Union issued its own unmistakable challenge to the non-communist world. Soviet control was to extend between 1945 and 1948 across a vast area, from the 38th parallel in Korea to the Elbe; only in Yugoslavia did the Titoist regime presume to go its own way, while in Czechoslovakia there was but an interval of reprieve before the Soviet hand was outstretched over Prague in 1948. Soviet pressure was exerted on Turkey, Persia and Greece, and in the case of the last was to result in three years of civil war.

Recognition of the importance of these events was voiced by Churchill in the presence of President Truman at Fulton, Missouri, on 5 March 1946:

A shadow has fallen upon the scenes so lately lighted by the Allied victory. Nobody knows what Soviet Russia and its Communist international organization intends to do in the immediate future, or what are the

Above, the Potsdam Conference, July 1945, at which the Allied powers met to ratify the decisions made at Yalta about their spheres of influence in Europe and to discuss the future of Germany; initial attempts to govern Germany jointly failed, and by 1948 two separate states had already taken on an embryonic existence.

Opposite top, race riot in New York City, July 1964: in the mid- and late 1960s, the focus of racial tension moved from the south, where integration had at least in theory been enforced, to the urban areas of the north, where blacks formed a poorly housed, badly paid minority living in deprived city centres. Only in the 1970s did the tension seem to ease, though the inequalities that gave rise to it remained.

Opposite bottom, freedom marchers in Mississippi fleeing from their tents after highway patrolmen had attacked with tear gas, June 1966.

ALL OUR COLOURS TO THE MAST

began. 'I believe', said the President to Congress,

that it must be the policy of the United States to support free peoples who are resisting attempted subjugation by armed minorities or by outside pressures. . . . I believe that our help should be primarily through economic and financial aid, which is essential to economic stability and orderly political progress.

'Let us not be deceived', said the American financier, Bernard Baruch on 16 April 1947, 'today we are in the midst of a cold war.'

On 5 June 1947 the US secretary of state, General Marshall, made a speech offering substantial economic aid:

Our policy is directed not against any country or doctrine but against hunger, poverty, desperation and chaos. Its purpose shall be a revival of a working economy. . . . Any government that is willing to assist in the task of recovery will find full cooperation . . . on the part of the United States Government. . . . The initiative, I think, must come from Europe.

It did, chiefly from Britain and France, but the Soviet Union had such strong reservations, namely that the plan should be applied separately to each nation state and not to the continent as a whole, that in fact the Marshall Plan was confined to the West. Within a year the Organization of European Economic Cooperation (OEEC) had come into being, to implement the plan to the tune of some $17 billion from American resources.

At the same time as this economic buttressing of Western Europe, George Kennan, head of the State Department's

limits, if any, to their expansive and prose-lytising tendencies. . . . From Stettin, in the Baltic, to Trieste, in the Adriatic, an iron curtain has descended across the continent. Behind that line are all the capitals of the ancient states of central and eastern Europe – Warsaw, Berlin, Prague, Vienna, Buda-pest, Belgrade, Bucharest and Sofia. All these famous cities, and the populations around them, lie in the Soviet sphere, and all are subject in one form or another, not only to Soviet influence, but to a very high and increasing measure of control from Moscow. . . . Whatever the conclusions may be drawn from these facts – and facts they are – this is certainly not the liberated Europe we fought to build up. Nor is it one which contains the essentials of permanent peace.

Germany was the focus of all this con-tention, for here the Soviet had sealed off

their zone from the British, French and American zones – not only politically but economically. This last fact meant that the Anglo-Americans were both supplying re-parations to the Soviet Union from their zones and at the same time pouring their own money into their own zones to enable the West German economy to function. This trend was reversed when in May 1946 reparations from the American zone were withheld; Bizonia was created in January 1947, and shortly after came an American declaration of intent to leave troops in Germany as long as there were occupation troops in Europe at all. When early in 1947 Britain informed the United States that she could no longer afford economic as-sistance to Turkey and Greece, America replied with the Truman doctrine of 12 March 1947. With this the phase of contain-ment of the Soviet Union by the West

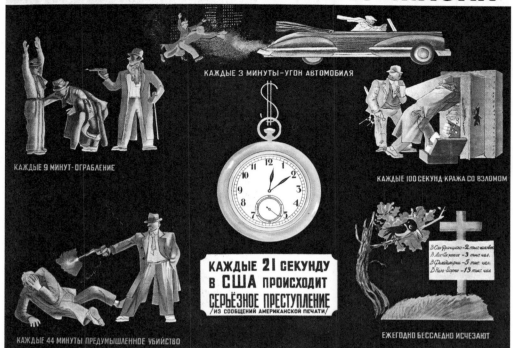

АМЕРИКАНСКИЙ ОБРАЗ ЖИЗНИ

КАЖДЫЕ 3 МИНУТЫ—УГОН АВТОМОБИЛЯ

КАЖДЫЕ 9 МИНУТ—ОГРАБЛЕНИЕ

КАЖДЫЕ 100 СЕКУНД КРАЖА СО ВЗЛОМОМ

КАЖДЫЕ 21 СЕКУНДУ в США ПРОИСХОДИТ СЕРЬЁЗНОЕ ПРЕСТУПЛЕНИЕ /из сообщений американской печати/

КАЖДЫЕ 44 МИНУТЫ ПРЕДУМЫШЛЕННОЕ УБИЙСТВО

ЕЖЕГОДНО БЕССЛЕДНО ИСЧЕЗАЮТ

Above, bystanders weep as Russian tanks roll into Prague during the Communist takeover in 1948: hopes for the restoration of a democratic Czechoslovakia, faint enough at the end of the war, now vanished for twenty years.

Left, Russian poster produced in about 1950 for home consumption: its message, that the American way of life is corrupt, is supported by statistical evidence. Thus, 'every three minutes a car is stolen'; 'in San Francisco 2,000 people disappear every day,' etc.

Left, world communist leaders gathered in Moscow to celebrate Stalin's seventieth birthday, December 1949 (fourth from left at the front is Mao Tse-tung, at this time still closely supported by Russia): Stalin held power unchallenged until his death in 1953, but within three years his successor, Nikita Kruschev, had vehemently denounced his policies.

Opposite right, poster produced to commemorate the Marshall Plan of 1947, under which American aid was offered to Europe (and accepted by the nations of western Europe): the aid, vital to the rapid economic recovery of Europe, also helped to prevent a post-war slump in the USA.

Opposite left, Europe in the years immediately after the Second World War: though a Communist government came to power in Yugoslavia, in 1948 it broke with the USSR and has never been a member of the Soviet block.

Policy Planning Staff, developed a coherent policy of containment based on the conviction that Soviet Russia's plans were potentially aggressive and must be resisted not only by economic and defence measures on the part of the West but by a positive affirmation of Western civilization's political ideals.

Nine communist countries in eastern and central Europe responded to this by setting up a Communist Information Bureau (COMINFORM). This body described the Marshall Plan as 'a European brand of the general world plan of political expansion being realised by the US.' As a result of this counter-charge the Communist parties of western Europe immediately went into active opposition to their various national governments, and from the winter of 1948 onwards the cold war quickly became hotter.

During the spring and early summer of 1948 there were communist uprisings in Malaya against British colonial government and in the Philippines against the new independent Manila government: it was however in Indo-China that the communist offensive was most sustained and effective. Meanwhile, in Europe, a coup against Benes and Masaryk established a communist government in Czechoslovakia in February 1948; in June Yugoslavia was expelled from the Cominform, and between then and the autumn of 1949 Stalin's policy was responsible for the liquidation of communist leaders in eastern Europe suspected of deviation from the orthodox Moscow line.

The crux of the Cold War, however, was the city of Berlin, itself a symbol by reason of its municipal division, marking the rift between the Soviet Union and her former

States, the United Kingdom, France, Benelux, Italy, Iceland, Canada, Denmark, Norway and Portugal, it simply asserted: 'The Parties agree that an armed attack against one or more of them in Europe or North America should be considered an attack against them all.'

The policy of containment had been firmly and successfully initiated by the autumn of 1949, but its future was bound to be affected by two other events of that season: Soviet Russia's explosion of her own first atom bomb and the predominance of the Chinese People's Republic in Peking.

As we have already seen, conflict between Chiang Kai-shek and Mao Tse-tung had existed throughout the Second World War and in July 1946 it developed into a full-scale civil war in China. Chiang Kai-shek failed to make good his bid for victory in Manchuria, Mao's Communist armies triumphed, and by October 1949 the former had been compelled to retreat with the remnants of his troops to the island of Taiwan.

It is against this background that developments in the Far Eastern sector of the Cold War must be viewed. In 1945, to make the surrender of Japan easier, Korea had been divided at the 38th parallel, the northern half under Russian and the southern half under American supervision. By 1948 the now more or less independent Republic of Korea (in the south) and the Democratic People's Republic of Korea (in the north) each claimed sovereignty over both halves: the 38th parallel had become the Iron Curtain of the Far East.

In June 1949 American occupation troops were withdrawn from South Korea: this served as an opportunity for the Soviet Union, operating through its North Korean puppets, to instigate a North Korean invasion of the South, beginning on 25 June 1950. The Americans responded immediately to this challenge by dispatching troops and supplies to South Korea, and shortly afterwards the United Nations recommended military action by the UN 'to repel the armed attack'. In the end some fifteen member states contributed to the UN forces sent to Korea, 'although essentially they depended on the backing of American military power.

In September 1950 American troops landed at Inchon, and US policy was one of fighting a limited war, that is, one unlikely to provoke either the Soviet Union or China to participate in it. However, the American commander, General MacArthur, had more aggressive aims, and as in October 1950 the advance of his troops towards the Yalu river took place it seemed as if the traditional containment policy of the United States might be going to alter into a drive to 'liberate' a communist satellite country north of the 38th parallel.

However, the Soviet Union did not rise to this incitement: instead, Communist China under Mao came to the rescue of the reeling

allies. This was dramatically exposed by the fact that only a narrow corridor running through the Soviet zone connected Berlin's western half under British, American and French occupation by road and rail with the West.

In June 1948 the Western powers announced a currency reform in West Germany, including West Berlin, and at 6 a.m. on 24 June 1948 the Soviet forces closed all road and rail routes from Berlin to the West for reasons, as Moscow declared, of 'technical difficulties'. In fact, it was an attempt to drive out the Western

powers and starve West Berlin into submission. The Allies replied by organizing an air-lift of supplies into the beleaguered city and maintained this successfully until the blockade was lifted by the Russians in May 1949 – a resounding victory for the West.

This incident, combined with a worldwide series of Communist threats, led to closer ties between the United States and her West European allies. On 4 April 1949 the North Atlantic Treaty Organization (NATO) was initiated and came into force on 24 August 1949. Consisting of the United

North Korean armies and effectively halted the American forces – to such good purpose that in December 1950 America and Britain abandoned the aim of uniting North and South Korea and contented themselves with a declaration of their intention simply to stand firm on the 38th parallel.

In terms of world perspective the intervention of China was of the highest significance: it meant that the arena was changing from one dominated by two Great Powers to one dominated by three: America, the Soviet Union and China.

In April 1951 General MacArthur, who still advocated a forward, aggressive policy in Korea, was dismissed by his own president, who re-affirmed a US policy of containment and the conduct of a limited war only. Once again General Marshall defined the nature of the struggle:

There can be, I think, no quick and decisive solution to the global struggle short of resorting to another world war. The cost of such a conflict is beyond calculation. It is therefore our policy to contain Communist aggression in different fashions in different areas without resorting to total war.

Further Chinese and North Korean offensives in the peninsula in April and May 1951 were defeated by American and UN forces

Above, Korean war refugees: though the war ended as it had begun, with the country divided along the 38th parallel, it had brought a new power – the People's Republic of China – to the centre of international affairs and revealed the essentially defensive nature of the USA's role of guardian of the free world.

Left, General Douglas MacArthur (1880–1964) on his return to the USA after being dismissed as commander-in-chief of the UN forces in Korea: he had wanted to take the war into Chinese territory.

Opposite top, a British Dakota takes on passengers after delivering food supplies to blockaded Berlin, July 1948: the success of the airlift ensured the survival of West Berlin.

Opposite bottom, the ceremonial signing of the North Atlantic Treaty, 4 April 1949: the Treaty established NATO and formalized the USA's commitment to the defence of western Europe; it remains the backbone of the western defensive alliance today.

and negotiations for an armistice began. These extended for many more months while battles in the air and on the ground continued, accompanied by threats from the United States of unleashing atomic war on the Chinese mainland. Eventually an armistice was signed on 27 July 1953 at Panmunjom, confirming the partition of Korea.

Their experiences in the Far East, and the fact that although Stalin had died in March 1953 there was as yet no sign of change in the European sector of the Cold War, now led the Americans to embark on a huge rearmament programme and the establishment in Europe of the Supreme Headquarters Allied Powers Europe (SHAPE). This marked a new phase, namely the US policy of negotiation from strength, something sharper and, in the opinion of the American secretary of state, Dean Acheson, more likely to be effective as an international attitude. Aspects of this change were the signing of a peace treaty with Japan in September 1951 (to which the Soviet Union was *not* a party), the joining of NATO by Greece and Turkey, and the emergence of a virtually independent Western Germany – the German Federal Republic – soon to become a full and equal member of the Western alliance.

'Negotiation from strength' assumed extreme and flamboyant expression in the activities of Senator McCarthy, who whipped up an anti-communist witch hunt in the States. But on the election to the American presidency of the Republican candidate, General Eisenhower, in November 1952, and the death in March 1953 of Stalin, the position was once again greatly stabilized: neither communist expansion nor American counter-aggression were sustained for reasons which had to do with the

emergence of China as a third world power, the terror of nuclear weapons and the sensing of some degree of common interest between America and the Soviet Union. Power in the Soviet Union was passing via Malenkov to Kruschev: in June 1953 an uprising in East Germany was suppressed by Soviet troops; in March 1954 the Americans exploded a new nuclear device at Bikini – the hydrogen bomb.

The new American secretary of state, Foster Dulles, somewhat rhetorically practised the art of brinkmanship in international relations between East and West; there was talk of massive retaliation by the United States in case of attack; in September 1954 a further anti-communist bastion was established by the formation of the South East Asia Treaty Organization (SEATO), the United States, Britain, France, Thailand, Pakistan, Australia and New Zealand.

Yet in spite of, or because of, these events, the year 1954 marked a move towards mutual accommodation of a limited kind between Russia and America. There were signs that the Soviet Union might be ready to settle for a divided 'two Germany' agreement, and in April 1954 there had occurred the Geneva Conference, summoned to discuss the future of Korea and Indo-China. Nothing was achieved about the former, but as a result of the defeat of the French at Dien Bien Phu by the Vietminh yet another partition was agreed upon as a temporary modus vivendi, namely the partitioning of Vietnam into South and North. It seemed that a thaw in the cold war might be coming, not because of the end of the dispute but because of the deadlock of partition in Berlin and Germany, in Korea and in Vietnam.

The beginning of the year 1955 provided an epitome of the constant clash between the

major ideologies in the world. In January the offshore islands of Quemoy and Matsu, held by the Nationalist government in Formosa, were threatened with attack by Chinese communists from the mainland. Immediately the American president obtained authorization from Congress to resort to arms should they need to be defended. An apparent easing of tension followed soon after. In April 1955 there was an Afro-Asian conference in Bandung, Indonesia, where the Chinese foreign minister, Chou En-lai, carefully commended the 'peaceful' liberation of Formosa. This was the prelude to a lull of almost three years in the Far Eastern sector of the Cold War.

In Europe the German Federal Republic formally became a member of the Western Alliance on 6 May 1955. In the same month the Soviet Union organized a defence system for the Eastern countries, the Warsaw Pact; it came to terms with Tito's Yugoslavia and agreed to a treaty establishing the neutral state of Austria. At the same time the Soviet Union fired its first intermediate range ballistic missile. Both sides had been putting their respective houses in order before coming to the summit conference in Geneva in July 1955. Although this led nowhere, because of the basic intransigence of the United States and the Soviet Union, especially on the subject of Germany, a little progress towards some degree of coexistence was made in the shape of agreement to a measure of cultural exchange.

The Cold War drama was next played out in a Middle East setting. As part of US strategy there had come into existence in April 1955 the Baghdad Pact between Turkey, Iraq and Britain and a little later Pakistan and Persia – the so-called 'Northern Tier' of anti-communist defence in that region of the world. However, it was the cause of serious trouble, for Nasser of Egypt saw in it an increase in the power of Iraq to rival his own leadership of the Arab world. Unable to obtain arms to support his anti-Israel guerrilla warfare from the West, he acquired these in September 1956 from the Soviet Union via Czechoslovakia. At the same time he was planning the Aswan High Dam with the help of American capital. When in the spring of 1956 it was known that the Egyptian leader had recognized communist China, American and British promises of aid for the Aswan project were withdrawn.

This was the moment for Nasser to play his trump card: on 26 July 1956 he nationalized the Suez Canal. There then developed the Suez crisis, which revealed an Anglo-American split of the most serious kind, and that it coincided with the Hungarian uprising and its suppression by Russian tanks. A nationalistic and an ideological clash had become so confused that for a time Western anti-communist solidarity was ruptured, with the inevitable consequence that none but moral protests could be made against Soviet actions in Budapest.

Nevertheless it was sufficiently in the common interest of both the chief ideological protagonists, the United States and the Soviet Union, to prevent the spread of Middle Eastern hostilities into world war. However, the dispatch of a UN peace-keeping force to the Middle East was made possible largely by the prompt skill with which the then UN Secretary-General, Dag Hammarskjold acted.

In spite or because of these explosive situations, the era of coexistence was dawning. It was heralded in a sinister fashion by the bringing into production in 1957 of two neutralizing weapons of terror, the intermediate range ballistic missile and the intercontinental ballistic missile. Even more significantly, there had already occurred in February 1956 Khrushchev's 'secret speech' to his Party, violently attacking Stalin and all his policies.

This speech had repercussions, first in Poland, where riots against the Stalinist regime broke out in June, to be succeeded in October by the establishment of a revisionist Polish government under Gomulka – the exact opposite of what occurred in Hungary, where Soviet intervention prevented such a liberalization of government.

With the launching of the Sputnik satellite in October 1957 the diplomatic phase of coexistence pursued its course, but to the accompaniment of a tremendously fierce race between America and the Soviet Union to obtain 'missile superiority'. Meanwhile the nations of western Europe had recovered economically from the ravages of war and six of them (France, Germany, Belgium,

failed to resolve the problem; Khrushchev's attempt to initiate a revisionist policy in European internal affairs to the advantage of the Soviet Union and the discomfiture of the West had not made much progress by the end of 1959. Its very stalemate served as a spur both to Khrushchev and to the new American president to attempt another Summit meeting in the hope of breaking deadlock without sacrificing what were conceived of as essential mutual interests.

Undoubtedly the single greatest factor to dominate these and succeeding years was the rift between the communist regimes of Moscow and Peking, the former failing to sustain its claim to be the sole and final arbitrator of Marxist-Leninism. The rift was caused by difference of opinion between Russia and China with regard to communist theory, tactics and strategy. The chief of these stemmed from the fact that Mao's revolution had been achieved by peasant-based guerrilla armies with little help from the Soviet Union. Moreover, in China the nationalist ingredient was as strong if not stronger than it had been in Russia. The Chinese Communist Party disapproved of Russia's coexistence policy; it regarded it as weak and deviating from true Marxist-Leninist principles. Furthermore, China was attempting her 'Great Leap Forward' during the late 1950s, an attempt to modernize and industrialize an age-old civilization and way of life overnight. In July 1960 at the Bucharest Conference of Communist Parties, Moscow was already abusing Peking as heretical and warmongering. The climax of the argument reached in November 1960 with a seeming compromise, which failed however to disguise underlying distrust and differences of policies with regard to world revolution and the pattern of national liberation movements.

Khrushchev had been continuing his version of coexistence with the West, not least by his attempt to wreck the November 1960 UN Congo peace-keeping effort. And by his insistence at the UN Assembly that 'there are no neutral men', when he tried unsuccessfully to have Hammarskjold replaced by a troika, or three-man committee.

The year 1961 could be reckoned as the decisive one in the long drawn-out Cold War, for with the assumption of the presidency by John Kennedy in January the stage was set for three great trials of strength, Cuba, Berlin and the Far East (Laos and Vietnam). In April 1961 there had been the ill-fated and misconceived attempt by the American Central Intelligence Agency to back a landing at the Bay of Pigs of Cubans opposed to the communistic regime of Fidel Castro. This was followed by the building of missile launching sites by the Soviet on Cuban soil and the ultimatum dispatched by Kennedy to Khrushchev on 22 October 1961 which virtually said that he

Italy, the Netherlands and Luxembourg) were entering into closer union, already economic and by intention political. This was signalized by the Treaty of Rome in March 1957, which brought the European Economic Community into formal existence on 1 January 1958. The diplomatic initiative still remained in the hands of Moscow, with the desire to establish a coexistence via a summit meeting on terms which would have meant the withdrawal of American military forces from Europe. However, in the summer of 1958 the Iraqi government was overthrown, and although British and American troops moved into Lebanon and Jordan to preclude any possible Soviet exploitation of the situation Iraq left the Baghdad Pact, which was later renamed the Central Eastern Treaty Organization

(CENTO). At about the same time threatening noises were heard in the Far East against the offshore islands, and these were met by strong pressure from the United States on Peking.

Once again the Berlin issue came alive to highlight the perpetual ideological quarrel. On 10 November 1958, Khrushchev proposed that the Potsdam signatories, the United States, the Soviet Union and Great Britain; should agree that Berlin should be turned into a demilitarized free city – on the territory, however, of the German Democratic Republic. This was in the nature of a Soviet notice to quit to the Western Allies, but its dangerous tone and the stiffening of Western resistance compelled Khrushchev eventually to withdraw it. Further consultations in Moscow, Paris and Washington

must have the sites dismantled or be bombed out of existence. The Soviet Union capitulated: it did so in the knowledge that in case of non-compliance 144 Polaris, 103 Atlas, 105 Thor and Jupiter and 54 Titan missiles were ready to be used against them.

On 3 and 4 June 1961, Kennedy had met Khrushchev in Vienna, where he learned of the latter's determination to bring the Berlin issue to a head. Khrushchev repeated the Soviet demands of 1958, with a threat to sign a separate peace treaty with East Germany, and again suggested demilitarized status for West Berlin. Kennedy responded with a firm declaration of the American intention to protect the independence of West Berlin, and in the face of this and the alarming rate at which refugees were pouring through Berlin from East to West Germany Khrushchev decided to build the Berlin Wall. On 13 August 1961, that flow was brutally and effectively stopped.

In the Far East, events in Laos, which centred upon the emergence of pro-communist and anti-Western forces, resulted after mediation by the UN in a declaration of Laotian neutrality, but the situation in Vietnam developed into an open sore.

Apart from Vietnam, the next three years witnessed a continuing lull in East-West tensions. In August 1963 the nuclear test ban treaty was signed by the United States, Soviet Union and Britain, though not by China and France. Then on 1 June 1963, the so-called 'hot-line' was set up, a direct teleprinter circuit between Moscow and Washington, whereby the respective chiefs could make instantaneous contact in case of world crisis.

Yet armaments on each side remained huge and menacing, and such a balance as has been achieved between the previous two great contestants, America and the Soviet Union, must be regarded as one based on fear and not on trust, with the hope of survival as the only kind of cementing force.

A wave of nationalism

The nationalisms of Asia, Africa and elsewhere mostly developed in and after the Second World War as a consequence partly of the various resistance movements, partly of the disfigurement of the white man's image in the non-white world, partly of the increase in awareness among previously ignorant races of how other people in regions of the world hitherto unknown to them existed.

From a complete list of those which have either attained or reaffirmed in modern terms their independent national identities, a selection will be made to illustrate such points as underlying similarities or basic differences, types of government, relations with the ideological alignments of the Great Powers and the degree of domestic social alienation or solidarity. One touchstone of reality may usefully be John Stuart Mill's 1861 definition of the nation as

a portion of mankind . . . united among themselves by common sympathies which do not exist between them and any others – which make them cooperate with each other more willingly than with other people, desire to be under the same government, and desire that it should be government by

themselves or a portion of themselves exclusively.

The main nationalist movements of Asia were: Mongolian People's Republic (1945); Philippines (1946); India (1947); Pakistan (1947); Ceylon (1948); Burma (1948); Indonesia (1949); Laos (1949); Cambodia (1953–54); Vietnam (1954); Malaysia (1957–63); Singapore (1965); Maldive Islands (1965).

Because the entire Asian scene was deeply affected and continues to be strongly influenced by two events, it is appropriate that both should receive comment at the outset. One was the establishment of the Chinese People's Republic in 1949 under Mao Tse-tung and the emergence of a kind of renovated nationalism. In terms of ideology, domestic reform and potential power in foreign affairs Mao's China has taken its place as a third world power, whose word is listened to with admiration or revulsion not only throughout Asia but on the continents of Europe, Africa and Latin America and – most attentively of all – in the Kremlin. The other event was the manner of Japan's defeat at the end of the Second World War, and the reappearance of that country apparently shorn of its imperialistic and chauvinistic qualities as the small but immensely energetic and modernized industrial power of the Far East.

Asian nationalism was both cause and consequence of the retreat of the Western imperialism of America, Britain, France and the Netherlands. Three instances must suffice to illustrate a general phenomenon. The Dutch East Indies had, ever since the seventeenth century, formed a rich part of the Netherlands' overseas empire. Between 1929 and 1945 one man, the Indonesian Sukarno, had dreamed of and planned for the national independence of his country. When the Japanese occupation took place during the Second World War, the occupying power declared the country to be independent of the Netherlands. When at the end of the war the Dutch tried to re-establish their control, Sukarno led the

Indonesian National Party into action against them. For three and a half years a fierce, violent struggle took place, but when in 1949 Sukarno had to admit military defeat the United Nations, in response to world opinion, organized a conference at The Hague, as a result of which national independence was granted in 1950.

In spite of Sukarno's lofty speeches about the Indonesian Revolution occurring within the context of the revolution of mankind based on 'the awakened conscience of mankind', and in spite of the success with which Indonesia played host at the Bandung Conference of 1955, social reform did not go fast or far enough. As a result the local communist party gained rapidly in power. In a curious bid to stave it off Sukarno turned to Mao's China for help, but then the military stepped in, the generals demanding strong national government without foreign strings. These developments were viewed with alarm and suspicion by the United States, the Soviet Union and

China respectively, none of which could afford to see Indonesia fall exclusively into any one ideological lap. It has therefore remained so far a non-aligned dictatorship, still plagued with the problem of social alienation internally and with its original charismatic leader, Sukarno now having given place to Suharto.

India and Pakistan are two further examples of renovated nationalism. For two hundred years the two together had formed British India. After a long struggle for 'Swaraj' or Home Rule under the Hindu Gandhi and the Muslim Jinnah and, it must be stressed, a longer and more thorough administrative training for independence at the hands of its imperialist masters than any other part of the overseas empires of Europe, the Indian continent had to achieve liberation on the tragic basis of partition in 1947 into two independent nation states, Indian and Pakistan (West and East). That this occurred was a result of irreconcilable religious differences, and also

because of the fact that independence which was almost achieved by 1939, was then deferred because of the war until the Allies had won – a period during which political and economic factions which might have come together went instead in opposite directions.

Enmity between the two countries thus partitioned continued long after 1947 and absorbed much of the energy which both the respective governments could more happily have applied to the solution of immense food and population problems. Prime Minister Nehru, the outstanding leader of independent India, steered his country on a course which sought to avoid communist extremes at home and to cultivate neutrality for India and create a Third World somewhere between the two Cold War power blocs.

What made any kind of rapprochement between India and Pakistan impossible was their dispute about Kashmir. It was claimed by India, but Pakistan objected on the grounds that seventy-five percent of Kashmir's population was Muslim. Military skirmishes took place, and in 1948–9 the United Nations attempted to impose truce and demarcation lines without obtaining any agreed settlement. Then the leadership changed: Ayub Khan took control in Pakistan in 1957, turning his country into a military state with pro-Chinese and anti-Russian tendencies; in 1964 Nehru died and was succeeded by Shastri. Shortly afterwards hostilities broke out again, chiefly as a result of Pakistan's offensives in Kashmir. These continued until a peace was patched up at Tashkent on Soviet initiative in January 1966.

The renovated emergent nationalisms of the Indian subcontinent have neither ministered to their domestic well-being nor to their external security, witness the ceaseless India-China frontier disputes after the Chinese occupation of Tibet.

The history of Vietnam was strangely interwoven with the total history of the

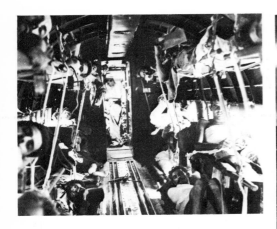

THẾ PHANH THẦY

UỐNG MÁU ĐỒNG BÀO.

world: indeed, the story of the latter could be told in terms of the former, for here a renovated nationalism sought to emerge in a situation permeated with the ideological jealousies of the Great Powers beyond Vietnam herself.

Like Indonesia, Vietnam, or French Indo-China, of which it was then a part, was declared liberated from its former colonial status by the Japanese invaders. Even during the Japanese occupation guerrilla warfare had been started up against the Japanese troops by Ho Chi Minh. In 1945 he set up his own independent Democratic Republic of North Vietnam. As the French refused to recognize this, he organized further resistance (Viet Minh) against the French attempt to reassert their position. Under the brilliant leadership of General Giap the French were continually harassed, and 15,000 French soldiers were trapped by Giap in the fortress of Dien Bieu Phu and finally forced to surrender in May 1954.

Such an event bred alarm among all the leading powers for the future of Indo-China as a whole, and under their auspices the Geneva Conference convened. Here it was decided to make a fourfold division of the region: a communist North Vietnam under Ho Chi Minh, a non-communist South Vietnam and two neutral states to the west, Laos and Cambodia. The plan was that all foreign troops should then vacate Indo-China and that within two years free elections should be held in both parts of Vietnam to elect a government of the people's own choice for the whole area.

However, the very act of partition had serious consequences: essential rice supplies from the Mekong Delta were cut off from North Vietnam; moreover former Viet Minh now found themselves existing in the South, although many were communists and some were Buddhist-nationalists linked, if in nothing else, by their common hatred of the South Vietnam regime in Saigon, which was headed by the Roman Catholic Premier Diem.

In the years 1955–56 sporadic fighting against Diem's regime broke out, the rebels calling themselves Viet Cong (Vietnamese Communists). Diem appealed to the United States for help in suppressing them, and

16,000 American 'military advisers' soon arrived. In spite of this the Viet Cong had by 1961 gained control of more than half the South Vietnam countryside. A group of discontented army officers then turned on Diem and murdered him in 1963. One short-lived South Vietnamese government followed another, each supported more and more by the Americans, for the US government now began to see the Vietnam struggle as a great world issue and applied to it their theory that if what they regarded as the communist threat were not countered here, one after the other the other cards in the pack, Laos, Cambodia, Thailand, Burma, India, Pakistan, would collapse and go communist.

In August 1964 the war began to spread: communist torpedoes menaced US warships in the Bay of Tonking; US planes bombed North Vietnamese naval bases. Thousands more US troops were brought over the America, numbers of communist soldiers came down from the North by the 'Ho Chi Minh Trail' to help the Viet Cong. Soon a full-scale war was in progress around and among a piteously suffering native population. A military impasse seemed to have been reached, and largely

because of war-weariness in America and a fear shared by other powers that the Vietnam issue could at any moment spark off a world war, negotiations for a settlement at last began in Paris in January 1969 at a round table at which were seated representatives of North Vietnam, South Vietnam, the National Liberation front and the US Government.

Africa

African states which achieved independence were: (formerly under British control) South Africa, which became an independent Republic in 1961; Southern Rhodesia which issued its Unilateral Declaration of Independence (UDI) in 1965; South West Africa under UN and South African Trusteeship (special cases). Ghana (1957); Nigeria (1960); Sierra Leone (1960); Uganda (1962); Kenya (1963); Malawi (1964); Zambia (1964); Tanzania (1964); Gambia (1965); Botswana (1968); Lesotho (1966); Mauritius (1968); Swaziland (1968).

(Formerly under French control) Guinea (1958); Senegal (1958); Togo (1958); Cameroun Republic (1960); Central African Republic (1960); Chad (1960); Congo

(1960); Dahomey (1960); Gabon (1960); Ivory Coast (1960); Malagasy Republic (1960); Mali (1960); Mauritania (1960); Niger Republic (1960); Upper Volta (1960).

(Formerly under Belgian control) The Congolese Republic (1960); Rwanda (1961); Burundi (1962).

(Formerly under Italian rule) Libya (1949); Somali Republic (1960).

It is necessary to comment briefly on the special cases of the Independent Republic of South Africa (1961), South West Africa and Southern Rhodesia. In the first country a British-Afrikaans white minority of three and a half million rules over the remaining majority of fourteen millions (made up of Bantu, Coloured and Asiatics). The official policy of the government is one of apartheid or separate development. This has been implemented in two ways, by the creation under the Group Areas Act of segregated black African townships and job reservations, and by the state of Bantustan Transkei for the sole occupation of Bantus, which enjoys a measure of internal autonomy but in reality depends for its existence on the will of the white South African government. There were attempts on the part of the non-whites to organize resistance against this state of affairs, but in spite of the efforts of men like Luthuli and Mandela the African National Congress became a forbidden organization and almost all anti-white leaders are in gaol or exile. Because of the circumstances described above, South Africa was expelled from the United Nations on 6 November 1962 by resolution of the General Assembly.

To the northwest lies the former German colony, surrendered to South African mandate after the First World War. In spite of UN resolutions and a judgement of the International Court of Justice to the effect that the imposition of South African white supremacy policy on this territory is illegal, it in fact continues. The black nationalist party was here led by Hosea Kutako, Paramount Chief of the Hereros.

After the break-up of the attempted Federation of Rhodesia in 1963, the northern part (Nyasaland) went its independent way as Malawi under Hastings Banda, and its eastern part (Northern Rhodesia) as Zambia under Kenneth Kaunda, leaving Southern Rhodesia still as a British colony with a white settler population of 224,000 ruling a black majority of four millions. Because of the mounting determination of successive white governments to perpetuate white supremacy and their refusal to make concessions to the British demand for eventual racial equality, under Ian Smith's premiership a Unilateral Declaration of Independence was made in 1965.

Those main features which characterized the emergence of Kenya as an independent nation-state can be clearly discerned. First, as a result of British colonization, the native population were able to gain some experience of administration and responsibility for a considerable period before independence. Together with this had gone the development by white settlers of the Kenya highlands which had served partly as a model and partly as a spur for the Africans. Secondly, there was the slow evolution from tribal conditions to the rudiments of party political life. Thirdly, there was the personality and leadership of an outstanding African leader in Jomo Kenyatta, who after a long spell in Britain (1934–46) returned to Kenya to head his country's national liberation movement. This was interrupted by imprisonment at the hands of the British between 1953 and 1959, while the movement had also from 1950 onwards acquired a terrorist wing in the shape of Mau Mau – an organization

Above, suspected Mau Mau guerrillas being led away for questioning, November 1952: Mau Mau violence was directed against both black and white (in fact it claimed some 8,000 African victims, 68 European) but failed in the end to prevent relatively peaceful progress towards independence.

Opposite right, a South Vietnamese poster warning of Communist brutalities: most peasants supported the Communists – or were in no position to do otherwise, since much of the south was under Viet Cong control by 1960 – rather than the government in Saigon, its existence only maintained by American aid, first financial, then military.

Opposite left, wounded French and Vietnamese troops being evacuated by air from Dien Bien Phu, May 1954: after their defeat and the division of Vietnam the French withdrew from Indo-China and were gradually replaced by the Americans.

which committed atrocities against white settlers. The combination of all these factors, especially the outstanding qualities of Kenyatta and the readiness, albeit gradual and reluctant, of the white rulers to acquiesce in their own dispossession meant that the transition from colonialism to independence in this East African country was managed with less friction than elsewhere on that continent.

On the opposite western flank of Africa the story is a sadder and more sombre one. The huge country of Nigeria, a former British colony with an almost entirely African population, had been evolving quite differently. With four hundred tribes, chief of which are the Hausa, Yoruba and Ibo, and many most able politicians, Nigeria failed to make her governmental institutions function effectively when white power was withdrawn. After a troubled period of six years a military takeover occurred in January 1966, federal and regional constitutions being suspended. In May 1967 the country was divided into twelve new states, but this action led to the break-away of the Ibo-controlled part of the country in a bid for complete independence as a nation with a name of its own, Biafra. After a bitter civil war waged with appalling sufferings for the civil population the break-away state finally succumbed to Nigeria's greater military strength.

After these two examples of post-British imperialism it is instructive to turn to the former French colony of Senegal. Here as elsewhere in their overseas empire the French had attempted to turn the indigenous population into Frenchmen. Even under the pressure of wartime events and the growth of a strong *presence africaine* in the post-war years, when native leaders pressed with eventual success for independence, the French cultural influence lingered strongly. The President of Senegal, Leopold Senghor, contributed as poet and man of letters to the creation of that rich cultural concept known as 'negritude'. As a consequence of a prolonged period of governmental apprenticeship under the French, Senegalese political life developed with a strong, if violent, force, although it failed to maintain the attempted 1959 Federation of Mali, Senegal, French Sudan, Dahomey and Upper Volta.

The vast, sprawling, former Belgian Congo achieved its independence in 1960 with a shocking legacy from the past. This consisted of a period of extortionate exploitation by the imperialist power, especially in the days of its personal leadership by King Leopold II, and the deliberate policy of the Belgian government not to give higher education to more than a tiny fraction of the black African population. This meant that when the forces pressing for liberation from colonial rule became so menacing as to compel Belgian political withdrawal there was not an adequate supply of native leaders to carry on effective government.

Because of the commercial and industrial interests of two or three Western powers, especially in the mineral deposits of the province of Katanga, and the accompanying Great Power rivalry for control of Congolese internal politics, that country very nearly became the occasion for a world conflict. That it did not do so was due to the skill and energy with which the then secretary-general of the United Nations, first in New York and subsequently with the aid of a UN peacekeeping force in the Congo, succeeded in balancing the rival power bids for a period of more than two years and avoiding Russian and American confrontation on African soil.

Even this short glance at only four of the emergent nationalisms of modern Africa will have sufficed to illustrate the immense importance of certain factors in determining the manner of post-colonial development. These are the presence or absence of white settlers, the pre-independence policies of the colonizing powers with regard to training the natives for independence, and the personalities of the African leaders. There are two further influences, neither of which has yet been explicitly mentioned. One is the economic resources of the particular African region in question, coffee in Kenya, cocoa in Nigeria for example, related to the natural climatic conditions prevailing; the other is education. On these the young independent country's future has depended.

In North Africa, nationalism centred upon three main issues: the Algerian struggle for independence, Nasser and Arab nationalism and the case of Israel.

The independent states of North Africa,

the Middle East and the Mediterranean are as follows: Tunisia (1956); Morocco (1956); Sudan (1956); Syria (1941); Egypt (1953); Algeria (1962); Yemen (1962); South Yemen People's Republic (1967); Israel (1948); Cyprus (1960); Malta (1964).

Acquired by the French in 1830, Algeria had in 1871 become three departments of metropolitan France, and many European immigrants had settled there. Between them and the government in Paris there had developed over the years a tension stemming from the resentment which the settlers felt at the amount of money being spent by the metropolitan government on the education of the native Muslim population of Algeria. After the First World War there were the first stirrings of native nationalism, and then in 1942 during the Second World War there appeared the Manifesto of the Algerian People, making a claim for independent Algerian sovereignty as soon as hostilities were over. The situation was a particularly delicate one, as during the closing months of the world struggle Algiers had become the seat of General de Gaulle's provisional French government. In an attempt to accommodate native demands, it allocated voting rights for the French Chamber in 1944 to all the population over twenty-one years of age, further evidence of the way in which national liberation movements could be influenced by their connection with events on a wider world stage. However, compromise on these lines proved impossible in the face of mounting terrorist activity on the part of the extremist national-

ists: these came to a head in the formation in March 1954 of a Revolutionary Council for Unity and Action. In spite of further attempts at settlement at the Evian Conference of 1962, what now constituted a full-scale civil war was in progress in Algeria.

This had three aspects: the French metropolitan government ineffectually seeking a compromise, the white settlers seeking to preserve their own position of privilege and power in Algeria, and the black African rebels seeking to overthrow both. By the end of 1962 General de Gaulle, with statesmanlike realism, conceded full independence to the *Front de la libération nationale* as the necessary price to be paid for the cessation of a ruinous and cruel war, which had had unsettling repercussions on political life in France herself. In August 1962 the now fully independent state of Algeria was admitted to the Arab League. The case of Algeria illustrated admirably the dual aspect of most national liberation movements, namely that independence of the former colonial power is a stage of development and that some degree of domestic social revolution is an inevitable accompaniment.

The Middle East

The seeds of Arab nationalism are in part religious, the common legacy of Islam, and in part political, resulting from growing,

Above, UN forces on the alert in Leopoldville, January 1963: some mistakes notwithstanding, the four-year UN presence in the Congo kept the Congolese economy going and prevented the secession of Katanga.

Opposite, Federal troops capture the airport at Enugu, the capital of the rebel Biafran state, October 1967: Biafra finally capitulated in January 1970 after three years' fighting, but reconciliation came about relatively quickly.

He proceeded energetically to galvanize his country, particularly concentrating on the building of the Aswan Dam as a vital contribution to Egypt's modernization. The international ramifications of this have already been traced and so all that needs to be noted here is the perpetuation of Arab-Israeli antagonism and the increased prestige of Nasser in other Arab countries. If the stories of the other Arab states over the last twenty years are studied, it will be found that two factors are constant. The first is a positive one, namely the attainment of their nationalist objectives in most cases, in the sense of abolishing foreign control. The second is a negative one, namely the failure of Arab nationalism to implement itself in the form of Pan-Arabism: this is a result of the deep mistrust persisting between Arab rulers.

The emergence of the modern state of Israel needs to be viewed against the background of Zionism, the 1917 Balfour Declaration guaranteeing the creation of a Jewish National Home, and Hitler's persecution of the Jews. When on 14 May 1948 the British Mandate of Palestine ended, partition took place. Immediate war brought victory for the Israelis, but the armistice of 1949 satisfied no one: Israel felt insecure and the Arab countries were still set on her destruction. This position was further exacerbated by Israeli policy during the Suez crisis and a long continuing series of border incidents culminating in the Arab-Israeli war of 1967, when the Arab armies were annihilated and considerable gains in territory were made by Israel.

The Caribbean and Latin America

Countries which achieved independence are: Jamaica (1962); Trinidad and Tobago (1962); Barbados (1966); Guyana (1966); Cuba (1959).

Nationalism in the Caribbean and Latin America has come under three dominant influences: former British imperialism in the West Indies, the economic pressures of US 'good neighbourliness' and the recent development of national liberation movements in Latin America, the origins of which lie in the nineteenth century.

The Caribbean group takes in the many islands with a population composed of white settlers, indigenous inhabitants, many of them of black slave origin, and half-castes and with an economy based mainly on the export of sugar, rum and bananas. With the cooperation of Britain, mother country of the British Commonwealth, its former members tried to establish their full independence in 1958 by forming the Federation of the West Indies. By 1962 this had collapsed, chiefly because of the unreadiness of Jamaica and Trinidad to give material assistance to the smaller islands. Unemployment remained a serious domestic

if ill-organized and sporadic, resistance to European imperialism, chiefly British, French and Italian. As a consequence of irreconcilable and opposed pledges given by the British to Jews and Arabs during the First World War (Balfour Declaration, 1917, and Mac-Mahon Pledge, 1916), the precursors of the contemporary Arab-Israeli conflict, interlaced with Great Power rivalry in the Middle East, particularly with regard to oil interests, helped to fan the flames of varying types of local Arab feeling. This took its most powerful shape in Egypt, where after the Second World War British power had to retreat in

the face of nationalist demands for complete independence, which was attained in 1953. Already in 1945 there had been formed an Arab League in the hope of building up concerted action for all the Middle Eastern Arab States to eliminate the Jews. However, in the 1948 Arab-Jewish war, which followed Britain's abandonment of her Palestine mandate and the failure of UN mediation, both Egypt and Jordan suffered humiliating military reverses. The truce of 1949 merely marked Arab ignominy and Jewish triumph. It was this defeat which paved the way for a military takeover in Egypt first under Neguib and then from 1954 under Nasser.

problem with the consequence that considerable numbers of West Indians emigrated to Britain.

The second and third influences are dramatically illustrated by the history of Cuba, which may be treated as a paradigm of many national liberation movements. From 1933 to 1958, with the exception of the years 1944 to 1952, Cuba existed under the dictatorial government of Fulgenicio Batista – a regime of brutality and terror. During this period US financial interests established a grip on the whole country, controlling its sugar industry, half the railways, most of the electronic and telegraph services and the tourist industry and mining. In spite of the rural poverty, illiteracy and disease which afflicted the population, the land itself was rich and had been industrialized with some success, but only to the benefit of a limited upper-middle class. This provided the opportunity for social revolution, which was seized by the young law student Fidel Castro. At his trial in 1953 after he had been arrested for attacking a barracks he made a long accusatory speech against Batista, outlining a programme of economic and political reform.

When, as a result of a general amnesty, Castro was released from prison two years after beginning to serve his fifteen years' sentence, he organized an expedition from Mexico in November 1956 but suffered complete defeat at the hands of Batista's troops. However, he retreated into the mountains with a faithful band of fellow-revolutionaries and then gradually built up a tiny but determined guerrilla band.

On 1 January 1959, as a result of successful harrying tactics, Castro came to power after the disintegration of the Batista regime; he established what at first seemed a just and not illiberal form of government. However, with the Agrarian Reform Law of May 1959, which provided for the expropriation of many properties, including foreign held ones, moderation vanished, and the Communist Party assumed a well-organized and tight control of affairs. This had international implications, for Castro not unnaturally sought support from the Soviet Union, an action which itself precipitated American counter-action in the shape of the suspension of the Cuban sugar quota. In July 1960 Castro expropriated all American interests, and this was followed by the series of events leading up to the missile site crisis in 1961. Once again an emergent nationalism had become entangled with ideology.

Above, Fidel Castro (b. 1927) (centre), whose Marxist revolution in Cuba survived American attempts to undermine it in the early 1960s but failed to extend to the rest of the Caribbean.

Opposite top, President Ben Bella of Algeria, Nikita Kruschev, President Nasser of Egypt and President Aref of Iraq at the temple of Karnak during a ceremony to divert the waters of the River Nile at Aswan, 1964: the Dam, begun in 1960, became a symbol of Egypt's membership of the modern world and a vital factor in international negotiations.

Opposite bottom, an immigrant ship arriving in Palestine, 1947: only in 1948, after the formation of the state of Israel, was unrestricted Jewish immigration permitted; before then, the British authorities had imposed a limited quota, turning away the survivors of the concentration camps and, before 1939, refugees from Nazi terror.

Chapter 23

The Headlines of History 1965–1978

While this period was dominated by the three giant powers, the United States, the Soviet Union and the People's Republic of China, the European continent began to assume an identity and to some degree an unity of its own. This tendency continued, however, to be sharply contradicted by the tensions between communist East and democratic, pluralist West, the two halves contriving an uneasy relationship of truce over which hovered the military preparedness of both sides to react offensively or defensively. A number of dominant features may be discerned.

The stabilization of the two Germanys: After Herr Willy Brandt became Chancellor of the German Federal Republic in October 1969, he and the Polish Premier signed a treaty in December 1970 which recognized the Oder/Neisse line as Poland's western frontier. After Walter Ulbricht, leader of the German Democratic Republic, retired in May 1971, to be succeeded by Herr Honecker, the way was clear for further accommodation between the two Germanys. In December 1971 agreement was reached regarding East-West German travel and traffic access, and in June 1973 the United Nations Organization admitted both the German Federal Republic and the German Democratic Republic as members. A final touch to stabilization was given by the signing of a Peace Treaty in May 1977 between Poland and East Germany. The cold war in Europe had given place after thirty years to a reluctant peace.

The European Economic Community and Great Britain's entry into it: In July 1966 the EEC became more closely knit through the adoption of a Common Agricultural Policy (CAP). In May 1967 Great Britain, Denmark and Eire registered applications for membership, but General de Gaulle firmly imposed his veto against the first. In July 1968 all EEC internal customs duties ended and a common external tariff was introduced. After the death of General de Gaulle in November 1970, and with the strong advocacy of the Conservative British Prime Minister, Edward Heath, the way was cleared for Great Britain, as well as Denmark and Eire, to enter the EEC in January 1973: British membership was sealed by a Referendum in its favour held

in June 1975, with both Harold Wilson, then leader of a Labour government (until April 1976 when he was succeeded by James Callaghan) and Mrs Margaret Thatcher, newly elected leader of the opposition Conservative party, pledged to full British participation in Europe. Early in the 1970s Great Britain began to feel the economic benefits of her North Sea oil, while a fresh stage in the evolution of European unification began, in 1979 with direct elections to the European Parliament.

The USSR and the West: Growingly pre-occupied with the problem of its relations with the People's Republic of China, the Soviet Union made only one thrust on its Western side, namely the invasion of Czechoslovakia. Some clue as to Russia's internal condition may be obtained from the activities of a dissident minority within its borders, the expulsion of Alexander Solzhenitsyn in 1974 and the fact that, though the eminent Soviet scientist, Andrei Sakharov, received a message of

member-states of the
European Economic Community

nations applying for membership of the
European Economic Community

members of the
European Free Trade Association

encouragement from President Carter of the USA in February 1977, he still remains unapprehended. A visit to the German Federal Republic by Mr Brezhnev on behalf of the Soviet Union in May 1978 confirmed the success of German-Russian detente. A further aid to the improvement of relations between Communist and non-Communist countries was the election of Pope John Paul II – a Pole by nationality – in 1978.

Reform and reaction in Czechoslovakia: In January 1968 the Communist regime in Czechoslovakia began to be modified when Alexander Dubcek came to power as First Secretary of the Communist Party – 'social-ism with a human face' was his slogan. However, removal of the censorship and other measures of relaxation, which were accompanied by clear indications that Czechoslovakia could no longer be regarded as politically reliable by its Russian neigh-bour, resulted in August 1968 in the invasion of the country by a Soviet military force. Ideologically, the clock was set back. In January 1969 Jan Palach, a student of Prague University, burnt himself to death in protest against communist tyranny; in April 1969 Dubcek was forced to resign and a safely pro-Soviet Czechoslovak govern-ment installed. That the battle for liberal-ization had not been entirely lost was shown when in January 1977 Charter 77 was smuggled out of Czechoslovakia, a manifesto from those within proclaiming their anti-totalitarian convictions.

Northern Ireland: The relationships of Northern Ireland to the British parliament at Westminster and to the government of Eire in Dublin were darkened by the fierce and tragic internecine strife in Ulster. This was exacerbated in the autumn and winter of 1968–69 by clashes between Protestants and Catholics, Civil Rights marches and growing terrorist activities mainly, though not exclusively, perpetrated by the Irish Republican Army (IRA). By May 1972 conditions, in spite of the presence of British troops, had deteriorated so greatly

that the province became ungovernable locally, and direct rule from Westminster had to be substituted. Although terrorist activities subsided somewhat after a brief, but unsuccessful, attempt to export them to London, the underlying problems, political, economic and religious, remained no nearer resolution.

Post-Franco Spain: after nearly forty years of dictatorship, Spain became a constitutional monarchy after the death of General Franco in November 1975. Under King Juan Carlos I political life came more to resemble other pluralist democracies of

Above, rioting in the Catholic Bogside area of Derry, Northern Ireland, August 1969: the civil rights movement, which began as a protest at the genuine grievances experienced by the Catholic community, soon degenerated into a sectarian bloodbath indulged in by Catholic and Protestant extremists, the hostility thus created hindering any attempts to reach a long-term solution acceptable to both communities.

Left, satirical placard attacking de Gaulle during a union demonstration in Paris, 1968: the alliance between students and workers was uneasy, many of the former looking for social revolution, the latter concerned to improve pay and conditions.

Opposite top right, Prague during the Russian invasion, 21 August 1968. The Czech government put up no coordinated resistance at this stage, believing Russian success inevitable and hoping to avoid a repetition of the events in Budapest in 1956.

Opposite bottom right, cheering crowds greet the new Spanish monarch, King Juan Carlos, November 1975: Spain's return to democracy has been accomplished more gradually but more peacefully than that of her neighbour Portugal, where extremist elements for some years posed a definite threat to the new state.

Opposite left, demonstration beneath the statue of St Wenceslas, Prague, 1968: the so-called 'Prague spring' – the brief months of liberalization, when even the introduction of a multi-party system and free elections seemed possible – was crushed by Russia in August.

Western Europe, and Spain applied for membership of the European Economic Community.

Finally, no account of the European scene during this period may omit the wave of student unrest which swept across most European universities in 1968 and after, Paris and the London School of Economics becoming notorious. It took the form of protests, some of them violent, and 'sit ins'. They were aimed against university curricula and administration and were partly inspired by left-wing agitation, partly by a sense of genuine grievance at what appeared to many students to be the irrelevance of their prescribed studies to the burning issues of the day, those of war and peace, capitalism versus socialism, social equality and hierarchical privilege.

The Far East

There are two main features, the course of the Vietnam war and the 'Cultural Revolution' and its aftermath in the People's Republic of China. After some four years of savage strife, in January 1969 North

Left, Red Guards assemble in Peking during the Cultural Revolution.

Opposite, survivors of the My Lai massacre, 1967, in which a US army unit killed 300 Vietnamese civilians.

Vietnam received her first diplomatic recognition from Sweden. In January 1973, after months of private and public diplomatic activity, a cease-fire between North and South was arranged. Fighting continued, however, and it was not until 30 April 1975, that President Minh of South Vietnam surrendered unconditionally to the Vietcong. In April 1976 the two halves of the country were re-united and Vietnam was recognized as one state. The most important aspect of the whole Vietnam war was that it demonstrated the inability, short of involvement in total war, of a great power (in this case the USA) to impose its will when met by determined opposition from a society (North Vietnamese) ideologically inspired and in some measure militarily supported from without.

After 1966 Chinese–Russian relations deteriorated, and the Chinese mainland scene was dominated by a mighty struggle within the governing Communist ranks. In August of that year the so-called Red Guards made their first appearance at one of Chairman Mao Tse-tung's huge rallies, and this marked the beginning of what came to be known as the 'Cultural Revolution'. This was an attempt by the ageing Marshall and his colleagues, 'the Rule of Four', to (in the words of its friends) preserve the purity of the original revolution, (in the words of its critics) to fasten a harsh, totalitarian regime on the whole country. In early 1967, after an incident between Russian diplomats at Peking airport and a period of closed schools and considerable social dislocation, Premier Chou en-lai called for discipline, and the Red Guards were ordered to desist from violence. In April 1975 General Chiang Kai-shek died in Taiwan, and on the mainland a Chinese National People's Congress, adopting a new constitution, headed the country in a new direction, towards some degree of domestic ideological relaxation, and of

international contacts, not least with the USA and Europe. On 9 September 1976, Chairman Mao died and was succeeded by Hua Kuo-feng, since when the reaction against the whole Maoist conception of communism as it had developed in Mao's latter years has continued to gain in force.

Other events in the Far East of note in this period are the secession of Singapore from Malaya in August 1965, the short-lived invasion of Laos in February 1971 by South Vietnamese troops supported by American aircraft, the fall of Cambodia in April 1975 to the Khmer Rouge communist forces and its subsequent invasion in 1979 by Vietnam, the establishment in Laos in December 1975 of a People's Democratic Republic. In concluding this summary it

may be noted that the cause of communism triumphed in the Far East, but that this did not lead to confrontation, in spite of armed stalemate within Korea, with the other great power of that hemisphere, namely Japan, which became a world industrial power during these years.

Africa

The dominant theme of events in this gigantic land-mass is the tremendous force of nationalism and its capacity to attract foreign aid, interest and intervention, e.g. the Chinese loan for the Tanzam (Tanzania/Zambia) railway.

Under the leadership of Verwoerd, Vorster and Botha successively, South

Africa continued its policy of white supremacy and apartheid, although its ultimate viability came more and more in question as various national liberation movements around its borders became successful, Angola and Mozambique to mention two.

In spite of sanctions, including an embargo on oil imports, the Smith regime in Rhodesia, in connivance with oil companies and with the tacit acquiescence of Britain, managed to survive for a number of years, declaring itself a Republic in March 1970. However, after an African National Council was set up in Rhodesia in December 1971 and in spite of lack of unity among the black opponents of the Smith regime, guerrilla warfare to destroy it and replace it by the independent state of Zimbabwe began and has not ceased. Under its pressure and that of the departure of many white settlers and constant admonition from the other Black African states, Britain and the USA, Ian Smith agreed in September 1976 to majority (i.e. black) rule within two years. To this end he proposed an internal settlement and took in to partnership two or three moderate Black Rhodesians, notably Bishop Muzarewa, but the Patriotic Front under Nkomo and Mugabe refused to go along with this policy and stepped up the fighting. As 1978 drew to an end, with majority rule now postponed by the Smith government until April 1979, the prospects of a peaceful settlement still eagerly canvassed by Britain and the USA seemed slim indeed.

Among numerous other African struggles, special mention may be made of the trials of Ghana first under President Nkrumah (deposed in 1966) and then an abortive civilian government of democratic style overthrown by the Army; after the deposition of Emperor Haille Selassie in September 1974, the conflict between Ethiopia and Somalia in 1977, and the independence struggle of Namibia (South-West Africa). Set against this pattern of tumultuous, bloody revolt and dislocation there may be posed the emergence of the Organization of African Unity, which held its sixteenth meeting in Khartoum in July 1978 and might possibly be regarded as an early harbinger of eventual black African solidarity.

The Indian Continent

In January 1966 Mrs Indira Gandhi became prime minister of India. In 1967, after a further series of minor border clashes India successfully resisted a sharp thrust by Chinese troops into Sikkim. In March 1971 Sheikh Mujib Rahman declared East Pakistan the free and independent state of Bangladesh, and in spite of bombing attacks from Pakistan, India recognized Bangladesh on 3 December 1971, and on 17 December the war between India and Pakistan ceased. By July 1972

Sheikh Mujib and Mrs Gandhi were co-
operating, and she had also formed an
accord with Mr Bhutto, who in August
1973 became prime minister of Pakistan.

However, in the course of her premiership
the government for which she was responsible began to be attacked for corruption
and intimidation of its opponents. In June
1975 Mrs Gandhi was found guilty of
corrupt practices and disqualified from
holding electoral office for six years. She
was replaced in March 1977 by Mr Desai as
prime minister but, determined to make a
political comeback, she campaigned for
election in a country district in Southern
India and reentered Congress as the leading
member of the Opposition in November
1978. Meanwhile in Bangladesh Sheikh
Mujib and his family had been assassinated
in August 1975, his place as President being
taken by Mr Assad. In Pakistan General
Muhammed Zia al-Hug overthrew Mr
Bhutto in July 1977, since when the latter
has been sentenced to death for treason to
the state.

The Middle East

This ideologically volatile area continued to
be plagued by Arab-Israeli conflict, anxieties all over the world on account of Middle
Eastern oil supplies, and the constant fish-
ing in troubled waters by the Great Powers,
the United States with a leaning to Israel,
the Soviet Union with a leaning to the Arab
world.

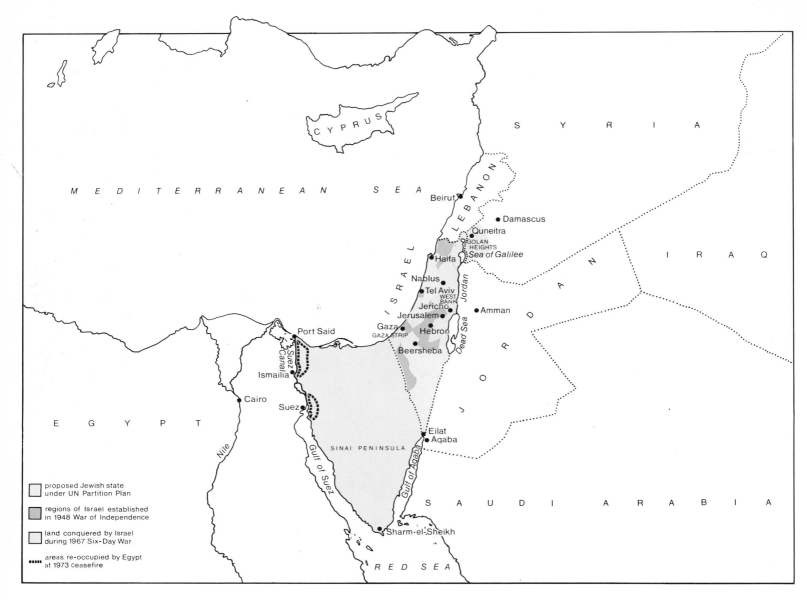

Map legend:
- proposed Jewish state under UN Partition Plan
- regions of Israel established in 1948 War of Independence
- land conquered by Israel during 1967 Six-Day War
- areas re-occupied by Egypt at 1973 ceasefire

Of great significance was the coming into existence of the Palestine Liberation Organization (PLO), pledged to establish an independent Arab State of Palestine on the West bank of the river Jordan. This movement under the leadership of Yassir Arafat sought to promote its cause by methods of terrorism not confined to the Middle East: for example, it attacked an Israeli airplane on the ground at Zurich airport. In February 1969 Mrs Golda Meir became Israeli prime minister.

An additional complication in Middle Eastern affairs was caused by tensions between Syria and the Lebanon, which in the 1970s was to prove a disturbing factor in the internal politics of Lebanon. Meanwhile incidents of varying gravity continued to occur between Israel and Egypt, which were only slightly diminished by a 90-day cease-fire in the Arab-Israeli conflict in the summer of 1970. In September of 1970 Nasser was succeeded by Sadat as ruler of Egypt, and early in 1971 a United Nations mediator in the person of Mr Jarring strove ineffectively to discover a basis for serious peace talks. After King Hussein of Jordan's plan for an autonomous Palestine State

broke down and Israel occupied the whole of the West Bank, further full-scale war developed in October 1973 between Israel and Egypt. Peace talks, held in Geneva, in September 1975 led to the agreed withdrawal of Israeli troops in Sinai and the erection of a new UN buffer zone between them and the Egyptian forces.

Nothing further happened until in December 1977 the new Israeli Premier, Menachem Begin, invited President Sadat to come to Jerusalem for talks, and the latter boldly accepted the invitation. Thus began a new era of life for Israeli-Egyptian rapprochement, eagerly encouraged by President Carter of the USA, who persuaded both men in 1978 to consult together under his aegis at Camp David, his country retreat. As a consequence there emerged the prospect of a real peace settlement

between Israel and Egypt, albeit somewhat dashed by the opposition of some of the other Arab states to any form of agreement which would seem to ratify the permanent status of the state of Israel.

Latin and North America

The main motif in the recent history of this continent of vast potential has been the continuing struggle between varying types of dictatorial government and movements of national liberation with a strong left-wing bias, both striving to be free of undue economic or ideological pressure from the USA. It is perhaps significant that in March 1977 the USA and Cuba resumed official contacts after a lapse of eighteen years. Comparable with the Organization of African Unity, there is an Organization of Latin American Solidarity which seeks to witness to some sense of continental solidarity, but essentially there are twenty-one nation-states (eighteen Spanish-speaking republics, plus Brazil, Haiti and Puerto Rico) with twenty-one histories. Three are mentioned here; Cuba has continued under the rule of General Fidel Castro; Argentina came for a while (1974–76) under the presidency of Senora Peron after the death of her husband and since March 1976 has been ruled by General Videla; and, thirdly, Chile, which between September

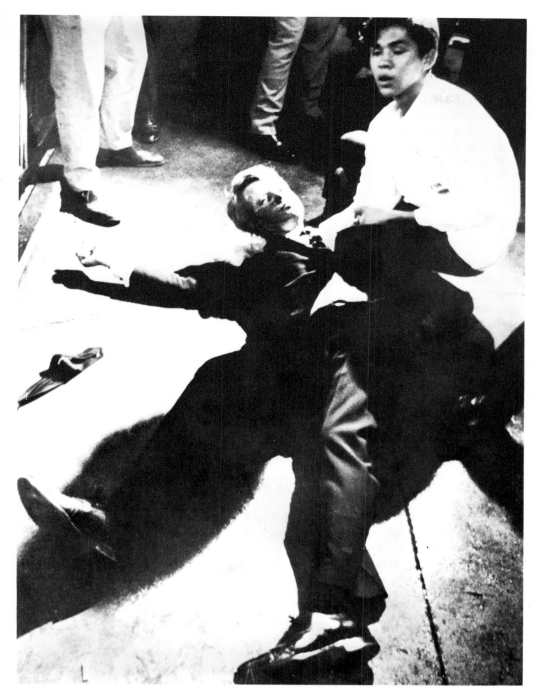

Left, Senator Robert Kennedy lies sprawled on the ground moments after being shot, June 1968: Kennedy, a late but idealistic convert to the cause of America's oppressed minorities, had launched his campaign for the Democratic presidential nomination shortly before.

Left, Senator Robert Kennedy lies sprawled on the ground moments after being shot, June 1968: Kennedy, a late but idealistic convert to the cause of America's oppressed minorities, had launched his campaign for the Democratic presidential nomination shortly before.

Opposite top right, Cuban poster depicting Fidel Castro cutting sugar cane: after twenty years, the Cuban regime no longer arouses the reactions – enthusiastic or hostile – it once did.

Opposite centre right, Senator Robert Kennedy (1925–68) marching in the Reverend Martin Luther King's (1929–68) funeral procession, April 1968: by 1968 Martin Luther King's impassioned, but non-violent, advocacy of black civil rights had contributed to the greater understanding of black ambitions developing at the end of the 1960s.

Opposite bottom right, Salvador Allende; left-wing ruler of Chile whose government was overthrown in September 1973.

Opposite left, President Anwar Sadat of Egypt and Prime Minister Menachem Begin of Israel address a Press conference at the end of Sadat's peace mission in Jerusalem, December 1977: Sadat's visit, a startling breakthrough in the apparent Middle East deadlock, eventually led to the signature of a peace treaty fifteen months later, though division among the Arab nations caused doubts about its effectiveness and permanence.

1970 and September 1973 experienced a brief period of Marxist revolutionary government under Dr Salvador Allende, but, after his reported suicide, reverted to the rule of a junta under General Pinochet.

In Canada the whiffs of French Separatism in Quebec grew stronger after 1967, though this has to some extent been checked by the premiership of Pierre Trudeau since April 1968.

The course of affairs in the USA can best be charted in the form of a chronological summary, keeping a watchful eye on four dominant features, her reversal in Vietnam, her Civil Rights problem with regard to race, the Watergate scandal, and her continuing international influence as still the most powerful of the world's three giants, the United States, the Soviet Union and the People's Republic of China.

In March 1968 it was announced that Robert Kennedy would challenge President Johnson as the Democratic presidential candidate; but in June of that year Kennedy was assassinated. In April 1968 the leader of the American blacks, Dr Martin Luther King, was assassinated, but in the same month a Civil Rights Bill passed through Congress. In August 1968 Mr Richard Nixon obtained the Republican and Mr Hubert Humphrey the Democratic party nominations respectively. During 1969 protests, especially from young Americans, against US involvement in Vietnam mounted steadily, and in December of that year Nixon, now president, announced the gradual withdrawal of American troops.

A beginning of rapprochement between the United States and the People's Republic of China was curiously enough signalled

Date	Europe	America	Asia and the Middle East	Africa	Date	Europe	America	Asia and the Middle East	Africa
1945	War in Europe ends (May 1945) Potsdam talks between Allies (July 1945) Labour government elected in Britain (July 1945); nationalizes Bank of England, civil aviation, coal industry (1946), power and transport (1947) establishes National Health Service (1948) Communism established in: Bulgaria (1946) Poland (1947) Czechoslovakia (1948) Romania (1948) East Germany (1949) Hungary (1949) Marshall Aid instituted (1947) Organization of Europe; Community established (1948) Berlin air lift (1948) Federal Republic of West Germany founded (1949)	Death of F. D. Roosevelt, succeeded by Harry Truman (April 1945) Formation of Organization of American States (1948) Truman re-elected as president (1948)	Atomic bombs dropped on Hiroshima and Nagasaki, bringing war in Far East to an end (August 1945) Civil War in Indo-China (1946) Indian independence: Partition of India (1947) Assassination of Gandhi (1948) Arab-Israeli war: Zionist Jews declare new state of Israel (1948) Communists control North Korea and Northern China (1948) Ceasefire in Kashmir (1949) Laos, Indonesia, Cambodia, Vietnam declared independence (1949) Mao Tse-tung leader of Communist China (1949) Arab-Israeli armistice: Partition of Jerusalem (1949) Korean war starts (1949)	First African nominated for Kenya Legislative Council (1946) South Africa officially adopts apartheid policy (1948)	1960	Uri Gagarin orbits the earth (1961) French veto British entry into Common Market (1963)	John F. Kennedy president (1961) Cuban crisis (1962) Kennedy assassinated: Lyndon Johnson becomes president (1963) Civil Rights Bill passed (1964)	Aswan dam begun (1960) Independence of Algeria (1962)	Nigeria becomes independent (1960) South Africa leaves Commonwealth (1961) Northern Rhodesia becomes Zambia (1964) Ian Smith prime minister of Southern Rhodesia (1964)
					1965	Student riots (1968) Russia invades Czechoslovakia (1968) Willy Brandt becomes Chancellor of West Germany (1969) Solzhenitsyn expelled from Russia (1969)	Martin Luther King assassinated; Robert Kennedy assassinated; race riots (1968) Richard Nixon becomes president (1969) First man lands on moon (21 July 1969)	Cultural Revolution in China (1967) Six-day war between Israel and Arab states (1967)	Rhodesian UDI (Unilateral Declaration of Independence) (1965) Civil war in Nigeria (1967–70)
1950	North Atlantic Treaty Organization established (1950) Conservatives win British election (1951) Accession of Elizabeth II (1952) Death of Stalin (1953)	USA intervenes in Korean War (1950) Un-American Activities Committee set up (1950) Alger Hiss found guilty of perjury (1950) General MacArthur relieved of his command (1951) Dwight D. Eisenhower becomes president (1953)	India becomes an independent republic within the Commonwealth (1950) Iran nationalizes oil (1951) King Farouk of Egypt overthrown (1952) French defeated at Dien Bien Phu, withdraw from Indo-China (1954)	Fanatical anti-white sect, the Mau Mau, terrorizes Kenya (1952)	1970	Death of de Gaulle (1970) Death of Salazar and inauguration of democratic regime in Portugal (1970) Partition of Cyprus between pro-Greek and pro-Turkish governments (1973) Overthrow of right-wing colonels' regime in Greece (1973) Oil crisis (1973)	Nixon re-elected president (1972) Nixon visits China (1973) President Allende of Chile overthrown (1973) General Juan Peron returns to Argentina (1973) Mariner 10 probe reaches Venus (1974)	Bangladesh (formerly East Pakistan) becomes independent (1971) Yom Kippur war between Israel and Arab states followed by Arab restrictions on oil production (1973)	Emperor Haile Selassie of Ethiopia deposed (1974)
1955	Eden resigns over Suez (1956) Soviet troops quell revolt in Hungary (1956) British hydrogen bomb tested (1957) Launching of Sputnik I (1957) Charles de Gaulle president of France (1958) Nikita Krushchev (1958) prime minister of USSR (1958) Cyprus declared independent (1959)	Supreme Court rules against schools segregation (1955) Federal troops sent to Little Rock, Arkansas (1957)	Suez Crisis (1956) Syrian crisis (1957) New constitution for Singapore, CENTO established (1959)	Sir Roy Welensky prime minister of the Federation of Rhodesia (1956) Gold Coast becomes independent state of Ghana, Kwame Nkrumah as prime minister (1957) African National Congress banned in Rhodesia (1959)	1975	Death of General Franco; succession of King Juan Carlos in Spain (1975) Election of a Pole, John-Paul II, as pope, the first non-Italian for four centuries (1978) Conservative election victory in Britain; Margaret Thatcher Europe's first woman prime minister (1979).	Jimmy Carter elected President (1976)	Civil war in Lebanon begins (1975) State of emergency in India (1975) US withdraws from South Vietnam, which falls to North Vietnam (1975) Death of Mao Tse-tung (1976) Mrs Gandhi defeated in elections (1977) Peace talks begin between Israel and Egypt (1977) Shah of Iran in exile (1979) Israel and Egypt sign peace treaty (1979)	Independence of Mozambique (1975) Death of Jomo Kenyatta (1978) First elected government to include non-whites takes office in Zimbabwe (Rhodesia) (1979)

by the visit in April 1971 of American table-tennis players to China.

In May 1972 President Nixon visited Moscow and in November was elected to a second term of office. However, in January 1973 the trial began of seven men accused of bugging Democratic headquarters in the Watergate building in Washington DC. Such damaging evidence then began to come to light concerning the malpractices of the Nixon administration that in October 1973 demands were heard from both the Republican and Democratic parties for the President's impeachment. In July 1974 the Supreme Court ruled that tapes carrying incriminating evidence against the president and his men must be handed over to the judicial enquiry, and on 8 August Nixon resigned his office, being immediately succeeded by the vice-president, Gerald Ford. In January 1975 the three chief defendants in the Watergate case were found guilty and received prison sentences, Nixon had received a pardon from President Ford and retired to his country estate. It would

be no exaggeration to state that Watergate gave a nasty smear to the image of American political life, which Ford and then his successor in November 1976 as Democratic president, Jimmy Carter, sought not unsuccessfully to remove.

Opposite top right, Vietnamese civilians vainly trying to scramble onto a departing transport as the Americans left Saigon, April 1975.

Opposite top left, President Nixon with Premier Chou En-Lai at a Peking banquet, 1972: since the early 1970s events in China have become more and more important to the West, and she must now be ranked with the USA and the USSR as a major world power.

Opposite bottom right, President Jimmy Carter (b. 1924, elected president 1977), walks down Pennsylvania Avenue from the Capitol with his wife and daughter after his inauguration as president. By 1979 Carter's popularity had declined considerably, as much because of changing views among Americans as to the president's role as because of his at times uninspiring performance.

Opposite centre left, cartoon by Herblock from the International Herald Tribune *published on 9 August 1974, the day President Nixon resigned.*

Opposite bottom left, Henry Kissinger (b. 1923), US Secretary of State 1973–77, famous for his 'shuttle diplomacy'.

Chapter 24

Behind the Headlines

There is a paradox about the six topics considered in this section. Each has world-wide ramifications, but not one of them is as yet sufficiently imbued with a sense of shared values that a cooperative programme on a global scale can be implemented. That is why, in spite of their crucial significance, they mostly do not figure in the headlines of contemporary history.

The world economy

While some factors since 1945 continued to make for a still greater degree of economic cooperation than previously, others militated against it. Among the first were the readiness of successive US governments to foster economic collaboration on a large scale, the high level of economic activity and rate of expansion, and a degree of trade liberalization among Western countries. Among the second were the East-West ideological split, which restricted economic relationships between the two blocs and the tendency of small nations to erect trade barriers to defend themselves in the face of overwhelming world competition. Also there was a tendency for many countries to retain economic controls in obedience to the dictates of their own domestic policies. Economic nationalism and economic regionalism thus continued to be notable features of the mid-century. The dollar replaced sterling as the most important currency in the world's monetary system. Steps towards greater European economic unity, although agreed to by the United States as the price of Western European political cohesion, were not welcomed elsewhere. In July 1961 the president of Uruguay remarked:

The formation of a European Common Market and the European Free Trade Area constitute a state of near-war against Latin-American exports. Therefore we must reply to one integration with another; to one increase of acquisitive power by internal enrichment with another; to inter-European cooperation by Latin-American cooperation.

Hence the formation of a Latin America Free Trade Association by the Treaty of Montevideo in 1960 and in 1962 the signing of a General Treaty of Economic Integration by Central American States. Similar initiatives have been attempted in Africa, the Middle East and southeast Asia. The Communist response to the Marshall Plan, namely the Council for Mutual Economic Assistance (COMECON) had already been established in 1949.

Towards the end of the 1960s plans were being made by the International Monetary Fund for the establishment of a new international monetary unit and for the adjustment of exchange rates between national economies. A world concern with inflation, classically described as too much money chasing too few goods, began in 1970, which was exacerbated by a US dollar deficiency. The salient point to grasp however is that during the eighteen months before the end of 1974 the longest period of sustained economic growth ever known in history ceased. It had taken seventy years up to the Second World War for the real output of the industrial world to double. In just one post-war decade (1948–57) it doubled again, and between 1948 and the beginning of 1974 it increased by more than 250 percent. This phenomenon must however be seen in the context of a gross imbalance between the wealth of the rich north and the poor south of the planet. The economies of the Third World still lagged pitifully behind the economic advance of the so-called 'developed' countries. In 1972 a world conference held in Stockholm by the United Nations Organization brought rich and poor countries together to discuss the problems of the environment and to devise patterns for collective economic behaviour. It was realized, as an article in the *Observer* newspaper put it, that 'the car made in Birmingham of Brazilian iron, smelted with Polish coal, may run on Libyan oil, whose exhaust pollutants fall on the waters of the Baltic in which Russians fish.'

World welfare

The population explosion of the mid-twentieth century means that whereas it took sixteen centuries for the world population to double itself between the birth of Jesus Christ and AD 1650, it took only two centuries to double itself between then and 1850. At the present rate of increase it has been estimated that it will double itself again between 1950 and 2000 AD – from about 3,000 million to 6,000 million.

The main cause of this dramatic increase has been death-control, namely the prolongation of human life expectancy without any kind of corresponding decrease in the birth-rate. The effects of this striking mid-twentieth-century phenomenon are apparent in the filling up of open spaces, the crowding of cities, the pollution of nature and the need for a vast increase in the production of goods if even the present pitiable standards of living, viewed from a world perspective, are to be maintained, let alone improved. The salient fact to grasp is that the greatest population increases have been taking place in those countries which, because of their underdevelopment, are least able to deal with them. This imbalance between death- and birth-rate has been and is vividly illustrated by the case of Mexico, whose population looks as it if will double in a mere twenty years. By contrast the reduction in death-rates in industrially developed countries has only caused a moderate acceleration in population growth because it has been gradual and has been accompanied by a decline in births. It is not difficult to perceive how such circumstances as these, accompanied by demands for welfare services for the awakening masses of mankind, have themselves become powerful agents of political unrest.

Recognition of the crucial character of this world problem was given by the appointment in 1945 of a special Population Commission of the United Nations, and some of the measures taken to cope with it will be described when the UN specialized agencies are discussed. Although it is evident that the core of the problem lies in the production and distribution of sufficient food to satisfy the hunger of the mounting numbers of the human species, this itself brings with it a number of other problems. These are the need for long-term capital investment, which competes with the claims for immediate expenditure on education and housing, the differing age-structures in various societies and the differing political systems which the varying societies are innured to tolerate or endure. For a variety of reasons, religious, ideological and technical, birth-control has not yet achieved sufficiently large proportions to make more than a small dent on this problem, although medical science offers in the pill preventing pregnancy hopes of a solution, provided sufficient numbers of people can sufficiently quickly be educated to practise birth-control themselves and to insist that their governments devote the needed priority of their resources to increasing food production as opposed to other forms of expenditure. The only country where this food-population problem has begun to be solved is Japan. There the adoption of an abortion policy on a national scale meant that the birth-rate fell from 34·3 per thousand in 1947 to 19.4 in 1955.

Before probing further into the question of world poverty and affluence and the need for aid on a global basis to deal with the former, it is instructive to ponder the following quotation from a health official in Venezuela, by no means the poorest of the Latin-American countries, which epitomizes the tragic predicament in which mid-twentieth century mankind has found itself:

Our successful campaign to reduce infant mortality has given us more problems. If we do not have adequate food supplies at reasonable prices and an understanding of nutrition, the babies we save may sicken or die of malnutrition before they reach school age; when they reach school-age, there will not be enough schools, unless we can greatly expand our educational facilities; if they lack schools, they may become juvenile delinquents and present us with still other needs for services; if they reach working-age without sufficient training, they will not earn enough to give their own children a good home – even if we manage to get enough housing built; and whether they will find jobs at all will depend on the rate at which we can expand our industry and improve our agriculture and find the capital resources with which to do so. Unless we can move forward on all fronts at the same time, the saving of lives only puts us further behind.

That last sentence provides the clue to understanding why recent world history has to be studied simultaneously in its political, economic and cultural dimensions if it is to make sense.

The dimensions of this topic are best indicated by the following facts: developing countries include about half the world's population, and just over one-sixth lives in the developed countries of Europe, North America, Japan, Australia and New Zealand, the remainder being accounted for by the communist countries of the Soviet Union, Eastern Europe and China; at least half the people of the world are living below what the Western nations would regard as a minimum for subsistence. The criteria which determine whether an economy is developed or underdeveloped are its resources in land, labour and material and the effectiveness with which these have been applied to the welfare of their peoples. The major international developments of the 1950s were the realization that the capital requirements of the underdeveloped countries were far greater than had previously been supposed and that in order for an under-developed country to 'take off' from the flat runway of perpetual poverty and undernourishment a sustained period of capital investment was necessary – capital which could only be supplied from without. Whether such an operation could be successfully conducted without a very large measure of centralized governmental control was also questioned. As the World Bank was by itself inadequate to produce these capital funds, various other forms of

Above, Pakistani women receiving family planning advice: controlling the rate of population growth is one of the greatest problems currently facing the world.

'aid' were attempted, the greatest single handicap being that loans made on ordinary interest terms were themselves so crushing on the frail receiving economy that it could not benefit from them, while others tended to be tied up with a variety of conditional 'strings', strategic, ideological and cultural. The local populations also often failed to respond effectively to new possibilities inherent in the situation.

The main feature of the period between 1950 and 1960 was the increasing prosperity of the developed countries: examples of this are the growth of the British economy by an average 2·6 percent per annum and annual increases in the Western European countries up to 6 or 7 percent, with even higher rates of increase in Japan. The 1960s were declared to be a 'development decade', a sign of conscience-searching among the wealthy nations. Why should the problems of the poor countries concern the rich? The answer to this question lies only marginally in humanitarian terms, in spite of notable voluntary, philanthropic efforts. It lies far more in the political area, namely the fear that, unless something is done to alleviate the economic distress of the majority of the human race living in underdeveloped countries, these will eventually by sheer force of numbers turn and rend the privileged. Self-interest therefore seems to indicate that the rich countries should continue to get richer but that a far larger proportion of their wealth than heretofore should be devoted to the solution of the economic problems of the underdeveloped countries. These have already begun to organize themselves as a united economic pressure group, witness the 1964 UN Conference on Trade and Development (UNCTAD) at Geneva. Here they pressed their objections to certain world trade tendencies such as restrictions and preferences, monetary arrangements and the terms of aid. Yet four years later at the second UNCTAD Conference in New Delhi little had been achieved by way of improvement.

Although between 1959 and 1961 there was a great increase in the flow of aid from developed to underdeveloped countries, since then the various strings with which so much of it is tied up have tended to increase; not the least of these has been the disillusion at the inefficient manner in which so much of the aid supplied has been applied.

For the first time in the history of mankind, the welfare of the species as a whole has been receiving systematic attention. Since 1945 governmental and non-governmental organizations have concerned themselves with the modes and standards of living of ordinary men and women to a degree which is as remarkable as it is pitifully inadequate.

The account which now follows offers a picture of services rendered to the uprooted, hungry and diseased portions of humanity and of the way in which communication between them has thus been improved.

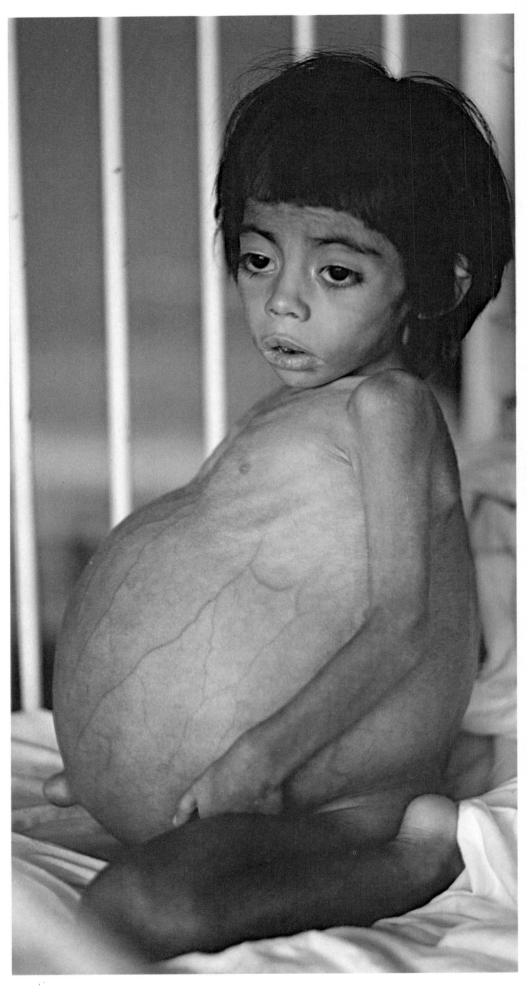

There are the millions of men, women and children who, through war, revolution, political partition of countries and natural disaster, have been forced to quit their homelands, scatter across the planet and eventually put down new roots, often in alien surroundings. Universal recognition of their existence and of their plight was signalized by World Refugee Year, held in 1959–60. The full picture includes those refugees created by the First World War, refugees from totalitarian oppression during the 1930s, and, concerning us here, refugees created by the Second World War and it aftermath – most of these at first European but now mainly Asian and African.

At the beginning of 1946 it was estimated that there were some 1,750,000 people in Europe for whom new, permanent homes would have to be found. The International Refugee Organization (IRO) took up this work where UNRRA left off: IRO's constitution was approved by the UN on 15 December 1946 – a Preparatory Commission gradually took over from UNRRA, and IRO became fully operative on 20 August 1948. Between then and its termination in February 1952 it resettled more than a million displaced persons, had assisted 73,000 to

Above, refugees in Berlin, 1945: wars, internal revolution and natural disasters have made refugees permanent political and humanitarian problems.

Top, starvation in India: vital though the task of feeding the hungry is, it must be accompanied by efforts to release the developing world from its economic dependence on the richer nations.

Opposite, a starving child, victim of the world's inability to organize its food supplies.

return to their own homes and helped in one way or another over 1,600,000 persons.

On 3 December 1949 the UN, recognizing that there would be a long-term problem in connection with those still unsettled and with new refugees, decided to appoint a UN High Commissioner for Refugees. On 1 January 1957 the office of the United Nations High Commissioner for Refugees (UNHCR) came into existence, initially for a period of three years, since when its mandate has frequently been renewed. Its function has been tersely summarized by its present Secretary-General, Prince Sadrunnen Aga Khan: 'We are like doctors, who hasten to help the injured without seeking to know who caused the injury.'

Since 1945 it is reckoned that between forty and fifty million people have become refugees: most of them have been resettled but from ten to fifteen million still remain, who have not yet found an adequate basis for life.

The refugee, then, is a phenomenon of recent world history, asking out of his uprootedness, 'who am I, for what purpose am I living, and what is the sense of my existence?'

The welfare services, to which we now turn, are not answers to those questions but they provide promise of the only condition in which answers can be forthcoming.

The Economic and Social Council of the United Nations (ECOSOC) has twenty-seven members and works with such bodies as the World Health Organization, the Food and Agriculture Organization and UNICEF, to eliminate such causes of war as disease, hunger, illiteracy, poor housing, inadequate clothing and unemployment.

The way in which more than 2,000 international voluntary organizations, formerly rooted in private charitable enterprises, have become integrated with governmental welfare services without losing their own identities, has been a particularly striking feature of recent world history.

Such voluntary organizations, many of which enjoy the status of Non-Governmental Organizations (NGOs) recognized by the Economic and Social Council of the UN, fall into three main categories. The first may be labelled 'religious-spiritual' and consists of the Society of Friends (Quakers), which has made a great contribution to the welfare of humanity out of all proportion to the size of its membership, the Reformed Churches of the Christian Faith, through Christian Aid, and the Roman Catholic Church. The second may be labelled 'cultural-educational' and include such bodies as International Voluntary Service. The third may be labelled 'relief', of which OXFAM (the Oxford Committee for Famine-Relief) is an outstanding example. Through these and hundreds of other voluntary organizations throughout the world private citizens of all shades of colour, class and religion have been steadily doing their best to relieve universal poverty.

Yet mankind in the last quarter of the twentieth century remains confronted with the tragic paradox that the more lives are saved, the more mouths there are to feed. Over a wide area of Asia infant mortality fell by about two-thirds between the late 1940s and the early 1970s, and life expectancy increased by about the same proportion, from a little over thirty years to well over fifty.

Race relations

Relations between peoples of different skin colours have greatly multiplied and altered during the last forty years. Speed of communication, attainment of national independence in large parts of Asia and Africa and ideological propaganda have given the growth of tolerance between people of different races an urgent priority. Although the difference which has so far been most dramatically expressed has been between whites and non-whites, largely as an accompaniment to the retreat of Western imperialism, differences have also clearly arisen between the non-whites themselves, as for example anti-black prejudice by the Chinese in Africa. There has also been anti-black prejudice in the Soviet Union, which is ideologically opposed to such feeling.

By brief reference to the recent history of race relations in South Africa, the United States and Great Britain, some idea can be obtained of the complexity and magnitude of the whole problem. This is not to underestimate its importance elsewhere, as, for instance, in the case of the Maoris in New Zealand, the Red Indians in the United States, the Jews in many parts of the world, and the Creoles, and mixed, coloured populations in South America, especially in Brazil, in the last in particular, apparent absence of racial discrimination often conceals its more subtle presence.

In South Africa race relations are governed according to the official policy of apartheid, or separate development. Although the separation between English and Afrikaaners on the one hand and Bantu, Coloured and Asiatic people on the other goes far back in history, it was only in 1948 that the Nationalist government finally and consistently rationalized the prejudices of its forefathers and presented apartheid as a moral principle. Theoretically apartheid means the creation of separate, self-sufficient, socio-economic units, its justification in the eyes of white South Africans being that this is the only possible alternative to complete integration, which would involve the disappearance of traditional, God-ordained white dominance. Since 1950 a number of laws have been enacted to confirm apartheid policy: of these the most far-reaching

are the Suppression of Communism Act (1950), an act empowering local authorities to arrest without warrant native non-whites in urban areas suspected of being 'idle, dissolute or disorderly' and to send them anywhere to work (1953), an act making it illegal for more than ten non-whites to meet together without permission (1956), the banning of the African National Congress (1958), the abolition of the parliamentary representation of non-whites, the Bantu Investment Corporation Act for the economic development of Bantu areas (1959), and finally the fierce Sabotage Act of 1962 imposing the possible death penalty for almost any act of political defiance.

The major feature of white South African policy has been to start to establish Bantustans, the first being the Transkei; these are to be areas reserved for exclusive occupation by Bantus, and these, it is claimed, will eventually achieve a large measure of self-government and enter into a federal relationship with the white central government. However, as these areas consist of the less good soil, and as above all the education and social welfare of the non-whites as a whole can only make very slow progress because of the relatively small sums of money expended on them, the prospects for the Bantustans are not bright.

Meanwhile a wide gap still yawns between the white minority rulers and the non-white majority ruled, the former absolutely

Above, the aftermath of the massacre at Sharpeville, when South African police fired on a crowd demonstrating against the pass laws, killing dozens and injuring many more: more than any other event, this incident drew the world's attention to the horrors of the South African apartheid policy.

Opposite, Soweto township, Johannesburg, the scene of severe riots during the summer of 1976: despite South Africa's increasing isolation from the international community and her occasional superficial attempts at integration, at the end of the 1970s the apartheid policy seemed as well entrenched as ever.

controlling the politics and economy of South Africa, the latter living in special group areas, particularly in townships on the outskirts of Johannesburg and Cape Town or on the land, domicile in white residential districts being forbidden to them unless they are actually employed in white households. Yet because the national economy is utterly dependent on black labour and is extremely prosperous, the living standard of the average black African is higher in South Africa than elsewhere on the African continent.

Nevertheless, surrounded as it is by an independent Angola and Mozambique and a Rhodesia involved in civil war and hungry for some kind of black nation-status, the prospects of eventual survival for a white-dominated South Africa must be regarded as slim. This is perhaps best evidenced by reference to the World Conference for Action against Apartheid, held in Lagos, Nigeria in August 1977.

The problem of race relations in the United States is governed by more than three centuries of history during which blacks, having been sold out of Africa for profit into the hands of a white governing class in the southern states of America, have endured the terrible and ignominious experience of slavery. After the American civil war of 1861–65, slavery was theoretically abolished, but segregation between black and white and a deadly depression of living standards meant in practice the continued oppression of black by white into most recent times. After some years of ineffective striving on the part of a few dedicated black leaders between the two world wars, followed by the experiences of blacks fighting alongside whites against a common enemy in the Second World War, a much more formidable attempt began on the part of negroes to assert their constitutional rights as American citizens. Quite the most decisive factor has been and continues to be the huge movement of blacks from rural to urban employment in both south and north and in even greater proportions the movement from south to north. With a total US population of some 180 million, of which some 19 million are black and some $1\frac{3}{4}$ million other races, the following figures tell their own story. Between 1940 and 1960 the black population living outside the old southern states increased from under four million to over nine million, most of this increase being concentrated in the central cities of the twelve largest American metropolitan areas.

In 1954 came the Federal Supreme Court decision that segregation of schooling between black and white children was unconstitutional. In 1957 at Little Rock that principle was asserted in the face of strong local white opposition. In 1960 three black members sat in Congress. Blacks attempted to assert their rights to sit in the same places of refreshment as whites by a series of cafe 'sit-ins'. Yet, because of extremist white

opinion, notably the secret society known as the Ku Klux Klan, it still remained desperately hard for blacks to exercise their voting rights in some states. In 1963 occurred the formidable demonstration march of blacks on Washington and their sympathetic reception by President Kennedy, and in 1964 came the enactment of the Civil Rights Act. This was intended to be the crowning act of law-abiding sanction, formal and human justice for American blacks, so long battled for by such men as Luther King and the novelist James Baldwin. Nevertheless, both in the north and south the rise of the blacks was regarded with fear and hatred by many white Americans. The energetic minority of young American university students, however, rallied to the black cause. Civil rights marches by both blacks and whites, the assassination of Luther King in the spring of 1968, and the subsequent appearance of a substantial and sinister white 'backlash' against perfectly legal black pretensions, have had two results. One has been to shift the balance from non-violent to violent agitation among large sections of the negro population; the other has been that the effort of white American liberals to make judicious concessions has become less likely to succeed. As James Baldwin has remarked: 'To be a negro in this country and to be relatively conscious is to be in a rage almost all the time.'

Race relations in Great Britain have only very recently become an acute problem. In 1950 there were 100,000 coloured people in Britain, Caribbean, African, Middle Eastern and Asian. By 1968 the number had swollen to just over one million out of a total population of fifty-two and a half millions. This increase was mainly a result of two causes, the need for labour in the transport and hospital services in Britain and the desire of Commonwealth citizens to improve their conditions of living and employment by exercising their right to seek employment in Britain. As most coloured immigrants have tended to congregate in a few of the densely populated urban and industrial areas of Britain, their presence has given rise to an alarming growth of anti-coloured prejudice among white citizens anxious about their own security. In 1962 there was passed the Commonwealth Immigration Act limiting immigration for work to 7,500 a year. In 1965 a Race Relations Act was passed, making discrimination in public places on grounds of colour illegal. In 1966 a Race Relations Board was established to foster the work of local conciliation committees, and considerable attention was paid to the educational aspects of coloured immigrants' problems through the National Committee for Commonwealth Immigrants. Exact enquiry by public and private bodies showed that discrimination had become undeniable, and in 1968 a new Race Relations Act was passed which set up the Race Relations Board and the Community Relations Commission, appointed by the

Above, anti-racialism rally in north London, late 1970s: the demonstrations held by the National Front, a tiny, fanatically racist party that never gained significant electoral support, provoked widespread counter-demonstrations in favour of racial equality and solidarity, though many people believed the consequent escalation of street violence harmed rather than helped the cause of racial integration.

Above left, immigrants from the West Indies arriving in London in the late 1940s: immigration restrictions, first imposed in the early 1960s, were tightened during the 1970s, allegedly to prevent overcrowding and the consequent demands on the country's social services, though their discriminatory nature – entry for whites remaining far easier than for blacks – suggested that the real reason was electoral popularity.

Opposite, a freedom march at Washington in the mid-1960s: once civil rights legislation had been passed, the struggle for real equality – financial, social, and, above all, in the minds of men – could begin.

Home Secretary to deal with race and community relations in Britain. It is the special function of the former to ensure that the law is upheld by making discrimination unlawful in the provision to the public of goods, facilities and services and in employment and housing.

These three countries alone demonstrate the interpenetration of different races. They epitomize a global predicament, namely the need for men and women of all colours to learn racial tolerance of one another. Methods of doing so obviously vary greatly; in South Africa the method is separate development; in the United States, it is integration with the white community by the reinforcement of civil rights; in Britain, where the problem is still on a manageably small scale, by persuasion and legislation.

Peacekeeping

Four main features dominate the story of peacekeeping since 1945: the birth and evolution of the United Nations Organization, various initiatives at governmental level to halt or at least to limit the manufacture and growth of armaments, the

phenomenon of terrorism and violence in individual and group relationships and the persistant witness of a tiny band of pacifists to their social and spiritual convictions. Although there has been no major war, local armed struggles all over the planet have been plentiful during the last forty years; such peace as precariously exists has seemed to depend on the so-called balance of terror between the powers equipped with nuclear weapons, and the world's armaments industries continue to flourish.

The Charter of the United Nations was drawn up by the representatives of fifty countries at a conference to discuss international organization, held at San Francisco between 25 April and 26 June 1945. The United Nations officially came into existence on 24 October 1945 when the Charter had been ratified by China, France, the Soviet Union, the United Kingdom and the United States and by a majority of the other signatories. Its function, as unequivocally declared in the preamble to the Charter, was to prevent the outbreak of war, to safeguard basic human rights, to ensure justice throughout the world and to foster the social welfare of mankind. Its structure was designed to further this enterprise but, as we

shall see, there was a flaw built into it from the start, which always handicapped and sometimes crippled its effectiveness, namely the constitution and powers of its chief governing organ, the Security Council.

The victorious military coalition which had devised the United Nations indicated its determination to retain control of world affairs by commanding a permanent majority in the Council, a design which later events were to challenge. The main organ, although not so originally designed, is the General Assembly, composed of all member states, numbering at the end of 1978 151. The Security Council is composed of five permanent members and ten non-permanent members elected by the General Assembly for two-year terms.

The Economic and Social Council is responsible for the welfare activities of the United Nations. Special agencies such as the Food and Agricultural Organization and the International Court of Justice are also maintained.

The UN Secretariat consists of a secretary-general, appointed by the General Assembly upon the recommendation of the Security Council, and such staff as may be required. Article 99 of the Charter gives the secretary-general powers to bring to the attention of the Security Council any matter which in his opinion may prove a threat to peace and security.

By 1950 the breakdown of the original grand design for peacekeeping had already become obvious, chiefly as a consequence of Cold War developments, and the UN seemed to be giving place to regional groupings based on ideological and strategic promises. The negative attitude of Stalin to the General Assembly which he simply regarded as the henchman of American imperialism, and his use of the veto in the Security Council seemed to preclude all hope of constructive development.

Yet this proved not to be the case for the following reasons. First, the United States continued to support the UN on a grand scale, contributing forty percent of its budget. Secondly, both Trygve Lie and even more his successor as secretary-general in 1953, Dag Hammarskjold, displayed considerable skill in gradually building up the UN organization and battling to prove its independence. Thirdly, as the Cold War began to alter its character in the mid-1950s, the UN, under Hammarskjold's discreet guidance, began to discover that it could fill a peacemaking role effectively, provided it refrained from attempting to operate where there was head on collision between Russian and American policies, and provided it leaned heavily on the support of the new Asian and African member states, which by then could form a majority in the Assembly.

It is instructive to watch the stages in which this development occurred. Undoubtedly the first and most important occurred in 1950. A Soviet proposal to remove the representative of Nationalist China from his seat on the Security Council had been defeated, which led to the boycott of all the organs of the UN by the Soviet Union. So, when the invasion of South Korea by North Korea took place and was brought to the attention of the Security Council, the Soviet delegate was not present to cast his veto vote prohibiting discussion of the business. The UN therefore went into action, and when in August 1950 the Soviet delegate returned to obstruct further Security Council business the General Assembly at its meeting in October passed the Uniting for Peace Resolution, by means of which any matter involving threats to peace, hitherto the preserve of the Security Council, could in future, if that body failed to agree, be brought before the General Assembly. If the Assembly did not happen to be in session, it could be called together within twenty-four hours at the request of *any* seven members of the Security Council or of a majority of the members of the Assembly. As we shall see, this enabled the UN to mount a number of not unsuccessful 'observer' and policing actions in spite of the original handicap of the veto. Gradually the idea developed that a UN 'presence' in a

trouble area could be a useful, if modest, contribution to the progress of peace.

In 1946 UN observers proceeded to Greece, whose government had complained of the infiltration of communist guerrilla forces: the UN commission could do no more than confirm that this in fact had occurred. In 1947 the partition of India led to the problem of Kashmir, and here the UN succeeded in establishing a ceasefire and left observers behind to keep watch on subsequent developments.

The UN attempted to mediate in the Middle East between Arab and Jew after the war of 1948 without much effect because its commission received little encouragement from either the United States or the Soviet Union. Two outstanding men, Count Folke Bernadotte of Sweden and the African Negro, Ralph Bunche, made high reputations for themselves personally and for the UN, and largely as a result of their efforts the UN truce supervision organization was established in that area.

The Korean War provided occasion for a special kind of UN intervention in 1950, so dependent on American military and financial support as to make the operation, though nominally UN, actually American in direction – 250,000 troops coming from the United States and only 36,000 from other countries.

When in the Suez crisis of 1956 France and Britain used their veto in the Security Council, the 'Uniting for Peace Resolution' enabled the UN to go into action with the despatch of a UN emergency force, twenty-four countries expressing willingness to contribute troops.

In 1958 a UN observer group operated successfully in the Lebanon when insurgents in that country were reported to be receiving help from Egypt and Syria. In 1960 Hammarskjold succeeded in quickly establishing a UN presence in Laos, when that country complained of subversive elements intruding across its frontiers.

In 1960 and 1961 the UN embarked on by far its longest enterprise when attempting to hold the rising in the Congo. Soon after receiving its independence from Belgium, the Congolese government was faced with a mutiny of its own army, and breakaway movements began in the provinces of Katanga and Kasai. To protect their own white nationals against growing domestic strife, the Belgian government sent in paratroopers. The Security Council, in response to an appeal from the Congolese government, agreed to despatch a military force to the Congo with the sole and explicit purpose of preserving order and without taking sides with the various Congolese factions. By August 1960 there were 20,000 UN troops from fourteen different countries in the Congo.

The UN had three undertakings on its hands: to secure the departure of Belgian troops and mercenaries from other countries from the Congo, to prevent Great Power

tried to take over the 900 square kilometres of territory from the Litani river down to the Israeli frontier but are still in dispute with Palestine guerrillas and Israeli armed forces and have been rendered incapable of discharging effectively their peacekeeping function.

Worth noting at this point are two events of historical significance, the admission in October 1971 of the People's Republic of China to the UN and the expulsion from it of the Taiwan government, and the succession in December 1971 of Dr Kurt Waldheim to U-Thant as the fourth secretary-general of the United Nations Organization.

In spite of this rehearsal of some positive achievements of the UN as a peacekeeping agency, it must be admitted that the overall achievement has been pitiably weak. As the political scientist H. G. Nicholas has remarked: 'The UN perfectly embodies in insititutional form the tragic paradox of our age; it has become indispensible before it has become effective.'

UN troops can only enter a country at the declared invitation of a host country and must be withdrawn at its request. Financial resources are lacking to support a sustained campaign, especially when one or more of the stronger member countries refuses to contribute towards it. In any dispute, the number of appropriately neutral countries from which troops can be recruited is limited. And yet the sure fact that both actually and symbolically the blue and white berets of UN forces have been observed in various quarters of the globe and the UN presence experienced as a real factor in international negotiations is of sufficient historical significance not to be ignored.

With regard to the second aspect of peacekeeping, namely governmental actions, the following points may be noted. In January 1967 the United Kingdom, the

intrusion into this African affair, and to safe-guard the economy and welfare of the Congo. This triple task was complicated by the delicate necessity that the UN forces themselves should not become involved in the show or exercise of force on behalf either of the central government or any of its splinter groups or on behalf of Katanga under the energetic leadership of Tshombe.

Inevitably the UN troops did have to fight in self-defence on a number of occasions, and their actions could be and were con-strued by the various interested parties, particularly the British, Soviet and US governments, as departing from the strictly neutral terms of their mandate. Although months of fighting and intrigue were to

occur before the emergence of a degree of settled central control by the Congo govern-ment, and although Hammarskjold's diplo-macy led to bitter disputes at UN head-quarters in Washington and Khruschchevs' attempt to wreck the whole operation, and although the secretary-general himself perished in an aeroplane crash when flying to negotiate with Moise Tshombe, it would be fair to assert that, at the least, without UN intervention the course of events in the Congo would have been more disastrous than it was.

A quite recent example of a UN predica-ment is the entry of UN troops into Lebanon in the aftermath of the Israeli invasion in March 1978. Since then they have steadily

Above, an Israeli camel patrol unit and a UN guard beside the demarcation line in the northern Sinai desert: UN forces can keep the peaces for only as long as the host nation wants them to and can be ordered to withdraw at any moment.

Left, the body of German industrialist Hans Martin Schleyer, kidnapped and then shot by the Baader-Meinhof group, May 1977: by the late 1970s, kidnapping had become a favourite weapon of terrorist groups.

Above left, a member of the Swedish detachment of the UN force sent to the Congo in 1960: neutral nations supply the bulk of the troops used in such operations.

Opposite left, poster issued on behalf of the United Nations Association.

United States and the Soviet Union signed a treaty banning nuclear weapons from outer space. In August 1967 at a Geneva Disarmament Conference the United States and the Soviet Union drafted a treaty on the non-proliferation of nuclear weapons. In July 1968 the same two Great Powers attempted to set limits on the use of offensive and defensive missiles. In November 1969 Strategic Arms Limitation Talks (SALT) began in Helsinki, and these have continued from time to time. In February 1971 a treaty was signed by forty nations banning atomic weapons from the sea-bed. In November 1974 Brezhnev for the Soviet Union and Ford for the United States, signed a ten-year pact to control the

strategic arms race, but the historian can but bleakly record that it still continues.

The use of terrorism and violence grew dramatically in size and frequency from the 1960s. Examples are the activities of the PLO. in the Middle East and elsewhere, the Baader-Meinhof group in Germany, and the protagonists on both sides of the Northern Ireland conflict. As such activites have often taken the form of hijacking aircraft and holding passengers to ransom, national governments have become more and more inclined to seek agreement among themselves about taking measures in common to prevent such actions.

As regards the fourth aspect it can only be reported that the pacifist conscience is

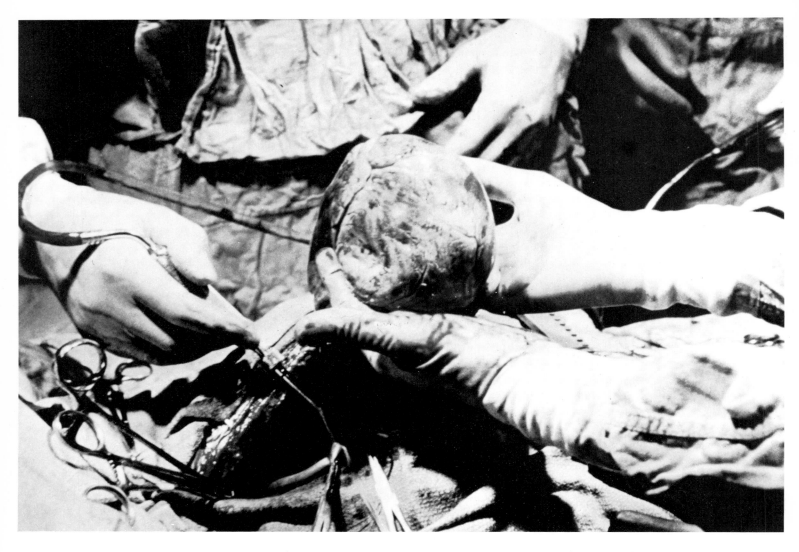

still alive and that in the liberal democracies it commands more serious attention and respect than ever before.

Science and technology

Advances in pure and applied science over the last forty years have been stupendous, so that it is not possible to do more here than suggest a few directions in which to look for evidence of this, both in man's knowledge of himself and the universe in which he is situated.

In 1946 the discovery of carbon-13 further advanced the curing of metabolic diseases, and in the same year it was observed that sunspots emitted radio-waves. In 1949 the drug cortisone made possible the improved treatment of arthritic diseases. In 1956 came the discovery of neutrons and anti-neutrons followed by the declaration of 1957–58 as an International Geophysical Year; in October 1957, the planet earth was circled by the Soviet satellite Sputnik 1. In 1961 Claus and Nagy concluded from their study of the structure of meteorites that the probability of the existence of life in other parts of the universe was high. In the same year Crick and Watson broke the genetic code with their discovery that DNA (deoxyribonucleic acid) has a molecule consisting

of two spirals each made up of a string of atoms: this chemical structure was regarded as possibly holding the key to the very nature of life itself.

In physics the main interest was in work on the neutrino (an atomic particle) while in 1961 there was instituted the European Organization for Nuclear Research (CERN). In the mid-1960s, striking progress was made in molecular biology, while in 1966 Worldwide Communication Satellites began to be planned for 1980. The late 1960s also saw the first attempts in heart surgery and increased efforts in cancer research. The discovery by Sir Martin Ryle of pulsars, announced in 1968, added to astronomical knowledge of the universe.

During 1970 the work of Dr P. G. Edwards at Cambridge made possible the treatment of a woman unable to conceive because of blockage in the Fallopian tube by fertilizing one of her eggs in a test-tube and then replacing it in her body for the production of a normal baby at full term. In 1971 genetic engineering began to look really possible with the prospect of the permanent cure of hereditary diseases; also made public that year was the work of Professor Gabor of London University in three-dimensional photography (holography). In May 1973 'the first babies to

have been conceived outside their mothers' bodies emerged into a world which, for the moment at least, had largely lost faith in the ability of science or technology to provide easy answers for any of the real problems facing mankind' (*The Annual Register of World Events*).

Parallel to these developments in the natural sciences, considerable progress has also been made in the social sciences, although whether on a sufficiently large and rapid scale to enable man to remain in control of his inventiveness still remains an open question. His political skill has not as yet matched his anthropological, sociological and psychological insight.

Social anthropologists by studying primitive societies and sociologists by studying contemporary societies have thrown much new light in recent years on how and why communities of men and women are structured. Yet the World Sociological Congress in 1959 avoided broad generalizations concerning patterns of social life, each scholar preferring to concentrate on the specific situation he was studying. As an instance there may be mentioned Oscar Lewis's five studies of lives lived in Mexican poverty, *Five Families* and *The Children of Sanchez*.

Tremendous progress has also been made in the field of psychology: learning theory

under the influence of Skinner, Tinbergen and Lorenz and the whole question of the nature of intelligence as studied by Burt and Vernon – these have influenced social and educational policies in many, though not all, societies. Yet the two most profound influences springing from the discovery of the unconscious in the early part of the century have been those of depth psychology and parapsychology. What this has meant in aesthetic terms, namely consciousness of the unconscious, receives treatment later. Here it need only be noted that the evidence now collected of unconscious motivation in the individual and the group has provided a new or restored an old dimension to the concept of human personality, namely that the rational conscious 'I' is only partly master in his own house, as in the sphere of the physical sciences he is subject to forces which are discontinuous, improbable and uncertain. It has been demonstrated that, particularly combined with the judicious use of the most recently discovered drugs such as LSD, depth analysis can effect cures of a wide range of hitherto incurable diseases.

Parapsychology, technically a division of psychology that studies personality in men and animals, is the science of psychic phenomena (PSI), which in turn divides into extrasensory perception (ESP) and psychokinesis (PK). ESP is the awareness of a response to something outside of oneself without the use of the sensory channels, e.g. clairvoyance, telepathy, precognition: PK is the phenomenon of an individual producing an effect on his environment without the use of his own motor system. This kind of proposition about the nature of life and personality had belonged to the world of speculation, not to say fantasy or even charlatanism, until the series of experiments undertaken at Duke University in the United States and the soberly factual reports of Professor J. B. Rhine in *The Reach of the Mind* (1948) and *New Worlds of the Mind* (1954) established firmly the existence of the dimension to which ESP and PK belong. Man's voyage into inner as well as outer space had definitely begun by the middle of this century.

Yet it was man's ventures into outer space that undoubtedly captured the human imagination. After experimental flights with dogs and monkeys, Major Yuri Gagarin of the Soviet Union became the first spaceman, being orbited in a 6-ton orbital in April 1961. Although elaborate and eventually sensational, successful space travel preparations were also being made in the United States, it was actually a Russian

who became the first human being to take a walk in space while tethered to his spaceship. In 1968 the American space-craft Apollo 8 circled the moon, and on 21 July 1969 the American Neil Armstrong landed on the moon – 'one small step for a man, one giant leap for mankind'. Subsequent moon explorations were followed by probes in space towards Mars and Venus, and although much valuable scientific information was derived from these investigations no actual evidence of the existence of life in the universe in the human sense is yet to hand. In May 1973 this kind of research was put on permanent footing by the establishment of a Skylab in space by the United States. In July 1975 the American Apollo and the Soviet Soyuz spacecraft docked together safely in space – a triumphant transcendence of ideology by science!

The influences of pure science on industry, commerce and agriculture have been great, notably in the field of communications and especially in the development of electronics. One observable effect has been the emergence of a social and human problem in those areas where the introduction of machines has tended to make human labour redundant, more particularly the increasing tendency for such demand as there is for human labour to be for skilled rather than unskilled hands. Yet another phenomenon has been the spread of mass production and consumption and an increase in the urbanization accompanying industrialization. Whereas in 1950 the number of cities with over a million inhabitants each was eleven, by 1960 it had increased to forty-nine. Yet, to preserve a sense of proportion, it is necessary to note that in that same year, eighty percent of industrial production was still in countries which already in the nineteenth century had accounted for ninety-eight percent. Three other general features may be noted, namely the increase in centralized control of industry, the importance of the role of management, and the effective organization of labour.

Against this general background the main landmarks of the last forty years can now be reviewed. The Second World War itself speeded up technological invention and application: 1942 saw the appearance of the automatic computer and magnetic tape, 1945 the dropping of the first atomic bomb and the manufacture of radar, which had been kept secret during hostilities. In 1946 the first pilotless radio-controlled missile took the air and xerography was invented. In 1947 the first supersonic flight occurred. In 1948 long-playing gramophone records appeared, as also the transistor radio and Piccard's bathyscaphe for the vastly significant exploitation of the world's sea-beds. In 1949 there was a UN conference on the conservation and utilization of resources, a sign of growing anxiety regarding the rate at which these were being devoured by the newly technologized societies. In 1950 it became possible to derive electric power

from atomic energy. Two years later the first hydrogen bomb was exploded, while at the same time there was a rapid development of isotopes for use in medicine: the first contraceptive tablet was successfully manufactured, with all that this presaged for possibilities of population control and alterations in traditional modes of sexual behaviour. In 1955 the Geneva conference on the peaceful uses of atomic energy took place, followed in 1957 by the establishment of EUROATOM (European Atomic Energy Authority) and IAEO (International Atomic Energy Agency). By 1959 submarines and the first passenger ship were being driven by atomic power and the hovercraft made its first appearance. Adventures in space increased almost monthly: there were twenty satellites in orbit round the earth in 1960; in 1961 the Soviet cosmonaut was the first man in space to circle this planet and return safely to earth. By 1962 Telstar was being used for instantaneous world television broadcasting and in the same year the United States had 200 atomic reactors functioning, the British 39 as well as 39 in the Soviet Union. Natural gas began to be extracted from the North Sea on a commercially profitable basis.

However, increasingly in the 1960s and 1970s a world-wide concern arose regarding the menace of nuclear and other forms of pollution to the rivers, oceans and atmosphere. An example of this was the spilling of oil from the Libyan tanker, *Torrey Canyon*, into the sea off Land's End in the far west of England. Hand in hand with this anxiety went a new and lively interest in the conservation of the environment, the protection of the earth's natural heritage, rare animals and soil. In June 1972 the United Nations Organization held a World Conference on Human Environment, and in

Above, the Torrey Canyon, *broken in two off Land's End; her fate highlighted the environmental dangers brought by the development of vast supertankers.*

Opposite, a second New World, as men explore the moon's surface for the first time, July 1969.

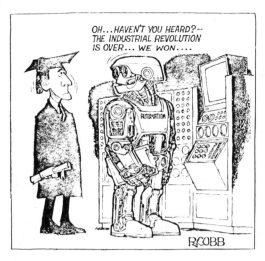

OH...HAVEN'T YOU HEARD?—
THE INDUSTRIAL REVOLUTION
IS OVER...WE WON....

AUTOMATION

R.COBB

April 1975 an important conference was held at the College of Food Technology at Weybridge, England, on Food from Waste. In September 1978 the Intergovernmental Maritime Consultation Organization (IMCO) met to organize preventive measures against pollution of the seas, sparked off by another oil-pollution incident, the *Amoco Cadiz* disaster of that summer.

Finally, the maiden flight of *Concorde*, the Anglo-French aircraft, from Toulouse in March 1969 should be reported as a triumph of technological brilliance combined with doubtful economic viability and a degree of environmental menace.

Education and art

The ways in which the elders of a society bring up their young are indications of the values it holds. Although education is always much more the resultant than the determinant factor in human affairs, it requires distinctive treatment in any general history because, by scrutinizing it, we can get close to the actual processes of social change. The stereotypes adopted in the home by children from their parents, the lessons learnt in school by pupils from their teachers, and the higher forms of knowledge distilled by the university studies of students and professors – these constitute the forces shaping the patterns of relationship between succeeding generations.

Three great educational pressures have been exerting themselves during the last thirty years. One of these is the direct outcome of the growth in population already noted, namely that because there are more people there are a larger number of children to educate. Another is the increase in the sheer size as well as the complexity of the sum total of human knowledge. The third is the huge rise in mass human aspiration to advance from ignorance to understanding of life and the world. These pressures have affected systems of educational administration, the content of curricula and the methods of teaching: their influence can be observed in the war on illiteracy. Other features to

note are the increased availability of education to women and the gradual realization of the need for global perspectives in education as manifested by the activities of the United Nations Educational, Scientific and Cultural Organization (UNESCO) and a host of non-governmental cultural international associations.

As the description 'developed' suggests, education in these countries is supported by a relatively flourishing economy and traditional forms of social and political custom. In them the main feature of recent years has been the extension of free, compulsory education from primary to at least the first three years of secondary education, say to the age of fifteen. This has brought with it the problem of devising universal mass education for a period of ten years' schooling, while at the same time ensuring the training of an elite of highly-skilled technologists, administrators and professionals like doctors and teachers. This in turn has raised the question of the age of selection for different types of secondary education and also the degree of subject specialization to be attempted at any particular age.

The last two issues have been and are being resolved differently in various countries, but, so far as any one general tendency can be detected, it has been towards some kind of comprehensive school for children of all aptitudes to fifteen or sixteen. Although they still play their parts, religion, language and nationalism are less important in these countries than they are in the 'developing' ones. In the 'developed' countries, the educational systems have been less centralized administratively.

A few specific instances of these general tendencies in five 'developed' countries may be mentioned. In England and Wales the 1944 Education Act, making education free and compulsory to the age of fifteen, marked a decisive step forward in what has been called that island's 'silent social revolution'. Yet, curiously enough, in spite of the eglitarian movement, the English public schools, traditional, independent, fee-paying establishments, have more than held their own. As a result of the Nazi regime and defeat in the Second World War, two diametrically opposed types of education developed in Germany, a communist one in the German Democratic Republic and a more or less liberal democratic one in the German Federal Republic. Under Allied occupation a systematic attempt was made to denazify the schools and colleges and to introduce rather more egalitarian practices in both the content and methods of education. In the East this took the form of Marxist-Leninist indoctrination; in the West, after some admirable reforms in a few *Laender*, it has tended to revert to traditional conservative patterns of German socio-political life. In France the general tendency towards a break with traditional, selective education, as exemplified by the classical *lycées* was marked by the introduction in 1959 of the so-called Langevin reforms. In the United States there is now free education almost to the age of eighteen, while it is free and compulsory for all to fifteen; here the great shadow of the race problem has been cast over the scene. In practice the legal enactment of the Civil Rights Bill of 1964 is still being flouted, and desegregation in schools makes but slow and painful progress. In Japan there has been wholesale imitation of European models, administratively through the adoption of the French system and technically through energetic exploitation of the latest inventions in industry and commerce. How far there has been a lasting bond forged between these and traditional Japanese nationalism it is too early to judge. Finally it is worth mentioning the special case of Sweden, where the most scientifically controlled experiment has been made in working out socially just and educationally viable means for educating all the children of a technological society.

Although all 'developing' countries may be distinguished from the developed ones, there are many differences among them, chief of which is the difference between the renovated nation-states of old cultures such as China or India and the new nation-states springing straight from tribalism via imperialism to independence such as Ghana in Africa. None of them has as yet fully achieved the goal of universal compulsory primary education: none of them are free from the crippling handicap of insufficient capital resources and inadequacy of trained manpower. What they mostly have in common is a keen nationalism, severe linguistic problems, some degree of illiteracy, some vestiges of the suppression of women. Largely because of these factors educational systems tend to be more centralized than in the 'developed' countries, not counting the Communist ones. Again it is instructive to take a few instances typical of both kinds of developing countries, those with the background of an old, continuous culture and those without.

The educational problems of the Indian continent are of course dominated by its partition, by the nationalist feeling which has resulted and by the still potent influences of religion and caste and above all by the problem of establishing one national tongue, possibly Hindi, in the transition from English. In Sri Lanka and Malaysia there are in each country two different communities, divided by origin, religion and language. So the majority Sinhalese in Sri Lanka and Malay in Malaysia insist on adequate knowledge of their own languages, while the minorities, Tamil in Sri Lanka and Chinese in Malaysia, insist that public schools be provided with facilities for instruction in their own media.

In most of the African countries the same three difficulties recur: lack of capital for investment in education, hesitation between according priority to primary mass schooling or secondary selective schooling for a badly needed native elite, and the phenomenon of social alienation caused by the coming to power of a Western-educated governing class as, if not more, divorced from the masses of their own people as the previous white imperialist rulers. Adam Curle, in *The Yearbook of Education, 1965*, has defined very clearly the nature of

the relationship between educational aspiration and opportunity on the one hand and openings in employment on the other: his words pertain to many comparable situations in developing countries:

The mass of unemployed primary school-leavers is creating grave political problems in many parts of Africa. Here is one of the most dangerous of social phenomena in a group whose expectations have been raised but not fulfilled. Indeed the danger is even worse, for unemployment on this scale not only means that a certain number are not contributing to (even being a drain on) the economy, but that essential work is either not being done or being badly done. Although many of the young unemployed remain around their homes, they eschew the humble tasks of agriculture – which are nevertheless the mainstay of their countries' economy. And a large minority throng the towns to form the nucleus of an explosively discontented group.

Education in communist countries is necessarily permeated at every level by one ideological assumption – the Marxist-Leninist one: a homogeneous society has produced a homogeneous education system.

Above, Russian students at a lecture: in communist dominated nations education is viewed as a means of reinforcing the nation's ideological basis; in capitalist lands, while offering its students far more opportunities and far greater freedom of self-expression, its basic aim is the same.

Opposite right, laboratories in a South London comprehensive school: though still subject to considerable criticism, the comprehensive system is now in operation almost everywhere in Great Britain.

Opposite left, an ironic comment on the twentieth century industrial revolution.

Yet because of the very nature of the educational process, especially in its most modern forms, this monolithic, rigid, centralized control has begun to be at a disadvantage, at any rate in the more developed communist societies, while the differences as between the Russian and Chinese forms of communist education have become as great as the similarities. Both, however, have been engaged in bringing their enormous population from ignorance and primitivism to modernization in less than half a century – in itself a stupendous achievement – and both have done so by interpreting their people's democracy as being essentially the democracy of collectivity as contrasted with the democracy of the individual. Both in the Soviet Union and China education is employed primarily as a political tool for the construction of a Communist society.

In the Soviet Union 1958 saw a complete set of educational reforms introduced, which were to pave the way for the next stage of advance after the solid achievement of the previous forty years. Two main features should be noted, polytechnic education and the youth movement. The former is linked with the whole scientific bias of Soviet education, which may be defined as

an education aimed at teaching industrial skills with the object of familarizing all children with the most important branches of production in industry and agriculture and of ending of the divorce between manual and clerical work.

The Pioneers and Komsomol movements have in addition successfully mobilized Soviet youth in constructive social and recreative activities out of school hours. Both have been fired with the vision of what Soviet educationalists call the 'New Man', who is a good communist citizen capable of realizing the ideological aims of the state. Children and students receive a highly moral education in terms of the totalitarian philosophy of communism, which in the West would be regarded as intolerant indoctrination.

Education in China must be seen as the essential concomitant of the post-1949 communist educational systems of countries in Asia, Latin America and the Eastern European bloc. It must be soberly recorded that between one quarter and one half of the world's children are being reared on the principles of Marxist-Leninism.

In the light of the above it is paradoxical that, although split ideologically and even split within similar ideologies, the world has

witnessed during the last forty years greater efforts than ever before to educate its children in a consciousness of their global loyalties. UNESCO was founded to foster the mutual understanding of people through the mass media and to encourage popular education and the teaching of science. It has promoted literacy campaigns, East-West understanding, teaching about the United Nations, human rights, exchanges of educationalists and the provision of educational and scientific experts on request to member states.

'Great nations write their autobiographies in three manuscripts, the books of their deeds, the book of their words, and the book of their art. Not one of these books can be understood unless we read the two others, but of the three the only trustworthy one is the last!' If Ruskin was right in making this judgment then the relevance of this part of recent world history is apparent. All art seeks to impose on experience, each epoch carrying its own peculiar stamp; our own twentieth-century one possesses two dominant features which distinguish it from any other. One of these is the new order given to experience through the increased knowledge of the unconscious made possible by depth psychology; the other is the dialogue which has begun between the arts from all over the world, eastern art modifying western and vice versa, primitive art recharging sophisticated art and being in turn transformed by it.

No attempt can be made here to present a descriptive panorama of all the arts for the past forty years: the illustrations in the text must be left to make their own impact. Instead, two outstanding examples from each of the arts are quoted simply as aesthetic signposts for readers to follow or reject.

In painting, Op and Pop art and the work of the Australian painter, Sydney Nolan: in sculpture Epstein's *Lazarus* and Henry Moore's *Reclining Figure*; in architecture Le Corbusier's *Unité d'Habitation*, Marseilles, and the Sydney Opera House; in drama, Dürrenmatt's *The Visit* and the plays of Pinter; in films Satyajfit Ray's *Pather Pathali* and Ingmar Bergman's *The Silence*; in literature Solzhenitsyn's *The First Circle* and Saul Bellow's *Humboldt's Gift*; in music Benjamin Britten's *War Requiem* and Henze's *Der Junge Lord*.

In conclusion it may be appropriate to point out how all artists in their different ways have been increasingly preoccupied with the problem of the very medium through which they seek to communicate their message. Without necessarily subscribing to Marshall McLuhan's message in its entirety, namely that 'the medium is the message', it is significant that in the aesthetic as well as in the scientific field it is the problem of the observer's relationship to and involvement in the observed, the relationship of the medium to the message, that has loomed increasingly large.

Above, Salvador Dali (b. 1904), The Metamorphosis of Narcissus.

Left, the Sydney Opera House, built by Joern Utzon and opened in 1973.

Opposite, the Detroit skyline: stimulating though modern architecure can be, its very size can often swamp the individual.

Personal belief

The word 'belief' is used here in the sense of a faith in 'that which concerns man ultimately'. That is why this recent history of mankind concludes fittingly with a survey of the main types of human belief.

The traditional religions, Christianity, Judaism, Islam, Hinduism, Buddhism, Taoism, Confucianism and Shintoism, these together count some 2,400 million out of a total world population of about 3,000 million as their adherents. How many of these are true believers and how many are nominal it is impossible to calculate, but there is some justification for saying that nowadays most men and women seem to be more motivated by nationalistic, socialistic and secularist impulses than by religious ones in the traditional sense. Christianity (some 900 million – 550 Roman Catholic, 217 Protestant, 137 Eastern Orthodox) is mainly Western in its incidence, Islam (some 440 million) mainly in the Middle East, North Africa and Pakistan, Hinduism (some 150 million) throughout South East Asia and Tibet, Shintoism (some 50 million) in Japan, Judaism (some 12 million) worldwide, Taoism (50 million) and Confucianism (some 400 million) in China.

In face of the common enemy of secularism there have in recent years been two attempts on the part of the traditional religions to unite. One has been limited to the Christian churches, namely the founding of the World Council of Churches in 1948. Even this was a purely Protestant movement, although endeavours have increasingly been made to establish a united front with the Roman Catholic and Eastern churches. Moreover, the example set by Pope John XXIII has introduced a new climate of review of social practice and theological reflection into the lives of Roman Catholic priests and laymen. The other has been the modest but persistent

Above, Wham *by Roy Lichtenstein (b. 1923). Tate Gallery, London.*

Opposite, Madonna and Child *by Henry Moore (b. 1898). St Matthew's Church, Northampton.*

activity of the World Congress of Faiths. It is possible to discern three trends in the traditional religions during the last thirty years: first there has been increased emphasis on the importance of social work, especially in Christianity; secondly, there has been a greater involvement in political issues, for example, whether or not there is today such a thing as a 'just war' in Christian terms, and the role of Buddhist priests in Vietnam; thirdly, attempts have been made to reinterpret sacred doctrine in such a way as to be intellectually acceptable to modern science. Briefly, there has been a swing away from the metaphysics of belief towards ethics, although distinguished exceptions to this may be quoted in the French existentialist Roman Catholic philosopher Gabriel Marcel, the Swiss theologian Karl Barth, the French paleontologist in holy orders Pierre Teilhard de Chardin, and the Japanese scholar of Zen Buddhism Suzuki.

Turning to other forms of belief, it is in the direction of nationalism as an absolute faith, communism as an absolute ideology and science as an absolute authority that we must look. With regard to the first two, it is true that, as Lewis Mumford pointed out in his book *The Condition of Man*, 'when religion ceased to be a political force politics became a substitute religion', or, in Arthur Koestler's language, the Yogi became the Commissar. If by religion is meant that 'which concerns man ultimately', then nationalism has over the last forty years become the religion of most of mankind. It does not answer the deepest question of the why and wherefore of human existence, but it does provide the hope of attainable satisfaction of basic human needs: for most men and women they are the final questions.

Totalitarianism has been the political response to man's demands for the experience of wholeness in an age when the traditional religious faiths have largely proved inadequate to meet them. It has produced the totality of a pseudo-society, the modern police state. Closely allied to these first two 'isms', the nationalist and the totalitarian ones, is a phenomenon known as New Messianism. As Vittorio Lanternari explained in his book, *The Religion of the Oppressed. A Study of Modern Messianic Cults*: 'The Messianic movements of modern times constitute one of the most interesting and astonishing results of the cultural clash between populations in their different stages of developments.' Examples given by him include the encounters between primitive societies and missionary Christianity, nativistic religious movements in Africa, the peyote cult and other prophetic movements in North America, religious movements in Central and South America, and Messianic movements in Melanesia, Polynesia, Asia and Indonesia.

Such Messianic 'cults' involve a belief in society's return to its source, they are expressed in terms of the expectation of the millenium and the cataclysms that are

to precede it, and also embody a belief in the raising of the dead, in the reversal of the existing social order, in the ejection of the white man, in the end of the world and in its regeneration in an age of abundance and happiness.

Belief in the absolute truth of what science claims to have established is probably not as confident as it was fifty years ago, but the method of test and verification has probably come to stay as the essential condition of any investigation of any phenomenon deserving of serious attention. 'The truth is', remarks the hero of Robert Musil's *Man Without Qualities*, 'that science has developed a conception of hard, sober, intellectual strength that makes mankind's old metaphysical and moral actions simply unendurable.'

More than a hundred years ago, in 1856, Hawthorne in his *Journal on Melville* anticipated the crucial position in which modern man finds himself: 'He can neither believe, nor be comfortable in his unbelief, and he is too honest and courageous not to try to be one or the other.'

The historian must at some stage arbitrarily close his narrative even while still being carried forward on its flow. 'History', said Edmund Burke, 'is a teacher of prudence, not of principle'. The history of the last forty years, political, economic and cultural, suggests that the human species would be prudent to transcend its nationalisms, to increase its food supplies and to limit its population, and to identify and respects those values which it holds in common simply by reason of the fact of its humanity.

Above, Unité d'Habitation, *built by Le Corbusier (1887–1965) at Marseilles between 1945 and 1950 as a self-contained vertical street: taken up by planners and architects throughout the developed world, Le Corbusier's ideas led, in debased form, to the wholesale redevelopment of city centres and the erection of tower blocks in the 1950s and 1960s, already by the late 1970s more or less universally reviled.*

Opposite, Pope John Paul II (b. 1920), elected pope 1978), the first non-Italian pope for over 400 years: as a Pole, whose ministry had until his election as pope been entirely conducted under a Communist regime, he is thought by many to be particularly suitable to guide the Catholic church in its increasing dialogue with the non-Christian world.

Further reading

Among the most distinguished texts dealing with modern Europe are Jacques Droz, *Europe between Revolutions 1815–1848* (Fontana/Collins, London, and Harper and Row, New York, 1967); J. A. S. Grenville, *Europe Reshaped 1848–1878* (Fontana/Collins, London, 1976); Elizabeth Wiskemann, *Europe of the Dictators 1919–1945* (Fontana/Collins, London, and Harper and Row, New York, 1966); each contains a useful bibliography.

Excellent on technological change is David S. Landes, *The Unbound Prometheus: Technological Change and Industrial Development in Western Europe from 1750 to the present* (Cambridge University Press, 1969).

On France see the brilliant though somewhat eccentric volumes by Theodore Zeldin, *France 1848–1945*, 2 vols. (Clarendon Press, Oxford and New York, 1973, 1977). On Germany there is a fine book by Gordon A. Craig, *Germany 1866–1945* (Clarendon Press, Oxford, and Oxford University Press, New York, 1978). The best single volume introduction to English history in this period is R. K. Webb, *Modern England from the Eighteenth Century to the Present* (Allen & Unwin, London, and Harper and Row, New York, 1969).

Other good histories of individual European countries include: F. S. L. Lyons, *Ireland since the Famine* (Fontana/Collins, London, 1975); Raymond Carr, *Spain 1808–1939* (Clarendon Press, Oxford and New York, 1966); H. V. Livermore, *A New History of Portugal* (Cambridge University Press, Cambridge, 1966; New York, 1977); René Albrecht-Carrié, *Italy from Napoleon to Mussolini* (Columbia University Press, New York, 1950); J. N. Westwood, *Endurance and Endeavour: Russian History 1812–1971* (Oxford University Press, London, 1973).

Among the more interesting general works on the history of the United States see Marcus Cunliffe, *The Nation Takes Shape: 1789–1837* (University of Chicago Press, Chicago and London, 1960); Roy Nichols, *The Stakes of Power: 1845–1877* (Hill and Wang, New York, 1961); Robert Wiebe, *The Search for Order: 1877–1920* (Hill and Wang, New York, 1968); George E. Mowry, *The Urban Nation: 1920–1960* (Hill and Wang, New York, 1965).

For the world outside Europe and the United States there are several good surveys, including: Kenneth McNaught, *The Pelican History of Canada* (Penguin Books, Harmondsworth, 1969; Penguin, New York, 1970); George Pendle, *History of Latin America* (Penguin Books, Harmondsworth, 1969; Penguin, New York, 1963); John King Fairbank, *East Asia: Tradition and Transformation* (Allen & Unwin, London, 1973; Houghton Mifflin Co., Boston, 1977); O. Edmund Clubb, *20th Century China* (Columbia University Press, New York, 1972); Richard Story, *A History of Modern Japan* (Penguin Books, Harmondsworth, 1965; Penguin, New York, 1960); Percival Spear, *A History of India* (Penguin Books, Harmondsworth, 1965; Penguin, New York, 1966); J. D. Fage, *A History of Africa* (Hutchinson, London, 1978; Alfred Knopf, New York, 1978); Robert Lacour-Gayet, *A Concise History of Australia*, translated by James Grieve (Penguin Books, Harmondsworth, 1976).

On Napoleon see Vincent Cronin, *Napoleon* (Penguin Books, Harmondsworth, 1973), and on what various French historians have said about Napoleon since Waterloo see Pieter Geyl, *Napoleon: For and Against* (Penguin Books, Harmondsworth, 1965).

Other, more specialist, works dealing with topics discussed by this book are William L. Barney, *The Road to Secession* (Praeger, New York, 1972), on the old South; Isaiah Berlin, *Karl Marx: His Life and Environment* (Oxford University Press, London and New York, 1978); Erich Eyck, *Bismarck and the German Empire* (Unwin University Books, London, 1950); Alan Moorehead, *The White Nile* (Penguin Books, Harmondsworth, 1963; Dell Publishing Inc., New York, 1963), a beautifully written account of British expansion in East Africa; G. Kitson Clark, *The Making of Victorian England* (Methuen, London, and Harvard University Press, 1962); Robert Blake, *Disraeli* (Methuen, London, and St. Martin's Press, New York, 1969); *Useful Toil: Autobiographies of Working People from the 1820s to the 1920s,* ed. John Burnett (Penguin Books, Harmondsworth, 1977); Cecil Woodham Smith, *The Great Hunger* (Harper and Row, New York, 1963; New English Library, London, 1977); A. J. P. Taylor, *The First World War: An Illustrated History* (Penguin Books, Harmondsworth, 1966); Edmund Wilson, *To the Finland Station* (Fontana/Collins, and Farrar, Strauss and Giroux, New York, 1974), for the intellectual background to the Russian Revolution, Adam B. Ulam, *Lenin and the Bolsheviks* (Macmillan, New York, 1965; Secker & Warburg, London, 1966); Walter Z. Laqueur, *Weimer: A Cultural History* (Weidenfeld and Nicolson, London, 1974; G. P. Putnam's Sons, New York, 1976); Elizabeth Wiskemann, *Fascism in Italy: Its Development and Influence* (Macmillan, London, 1969; St. Martin's Press, New York, 1970); Hugh Thomas, *The Spanish Civil War* (Penguin Books, Harmondsworth, 1965; Harper and Row, New York, 1977); Isaac Deutscher, *Stalin* (Penguin Books, Harmondsworth, and Oxford University Press, New York, 1970); William E. Leuchtenburg, *Franklin D. Roosevelt and the New Deal* (Harper & Row, London and New York, 1963); A. J. P. Taylor, *The Origins of the Second World War* (Penguin Books, Harmondsworth, 1964); Richard Grunberger, *A Social History of the Third Reich* (Penguin Books, Harmondsworth, 1974); Alan Bullock, *Hitler: A Study in Tyranny* (Penguin Books, Harmondsworth, and Harper and Row, New York, 1962); Stuart Schram, *Mao Tse-Tung* (Penguin Books, Harmondsworth, and Penguin, New York, 1966); Edgar Snow, *Red China Today* (Penguin Books, Harmondsworth, 1970; Random House, New York, 1971); Geoffrey Barraclough, *An Introduction to Contemporary History* (Penguin Books, Harmondsworth, 1967; Penguin, New York, 1968); Robert H. Wiebe, *The Segmented Society: An Introduction to the Meaning of America* (Oxford University Press, London, 1975, and New York, 1976); Peter Mansfield, *The Arabs* (Penguin Books, Harmondsworth, 1978).

A useful pamphlet on some of the problems of considering recent history is James L. Henderson's *The Teaching of World History* (The Historical Association, London, 1979).

Acknowledgements

Colour photographs
Archiv für Kunst und Geschichte, Berlin 191; Art Institute of Chicago, Illinois 154; Berliner Illustrierte Zeitung 270; Bildarchiv Preussischer Kulturbesitz, Berlin 106; Birmingham Museum and Art Gallery 22 top; Bisonte 322, 362 left; Bisonte—U.S. Atomic Energy Comm. 326; Bo Bojesen, London 354, 374; British Museum, London 283 left; Camera Press, London 343; Chicago Historical Society 79, 183 bottom left; Colorific, London 319; Mary Evans Picture Library, London 111, 126 top, 151; Galerie Günther Franke, München 258 left; Photographie Giraudon, Paris 42, 54, 55 top left, 59 top, 63 bottom; Hamlyn Group Picture Library 46, 78 top; Heeresgeschichtliches Museum, Vienna 39; Michael Holford Library, London 371 top; Imperial War Museum, London 298 top left, 310 top right; Institute of Social History, Amsterdam 259 top, 282 top; MacClancy Press, London 86 top, 215, 222 left, 222 top right, 227, 239 left, 242, 267 left, 271 left, 294 top, 302 top left, 302 top right, 303 left, 303 right, 306 left, 306 right, 310 top left, 310 bottom, 311, 314, 323 top; Mansell Collection, London 14, 15, 126 bottom, 163 right; Marshall Cavendish, London 174, 318 left; Marshall Cavendish—National Maritime Museum 166; Mas, Barcelona 198 top; Photo Meyer, Vienna 194 bottom; NASA, Washington 366; National Army Museum, London 127 left; National Portrait Gallery, London 23 top; New York Public Library—Stokes Collection 75 left; Novosti Press Agency, London 47 top; Orbis Publishing—Chicago Historical Society 74; Orbis Publishing—New York Public Library 67; Popperfoto, London 347 top; Scala, Milan 38, 98 left, 99; Taft Museum, Cincinatti, Ohio 183 top left; Time-Life—Ronald Haederle 342; Tokyo Gallery 158, 170, 175; Trades Union Congress, London 138.

Black and white photographs
Aberdeen Central Library 110 top; Archives Photographiques, Paris 8; Associated Press, London 286, 348 bottom right; Barnaby's Picture Library, London 336 top, 348 top right, 367; Bibliothèque Nationale, Paris 63 top right, 105 top; Bildarchiv der Österreichischen Nationalbibliothek, Vienna 35 top, 35 bottom left, 36, 37 right, 195 left, 195 right, 196 left; Bildarchiv Preussischer Kulturbesitz, Berlin 10, 13 left, 13 right, 30 top, 34, 88, 100, 101, 102, 103 top right, 103 centre, 103 bottom, 104, 105 centre, 107 top, 107 centre, 107 bottom, 109, 112 left, 113 bottom, 125, 188, 189, 190, 211, 213 right; Bisonte 331; Bisonte—U.S. Army 321; Bill Brandt 259 left; Brighton Public Library 113 top right; British Museum, London 47 bottom, 280; Bulloz, Paris 58 bottom left; Camera Press, London 288, 332 right, 340–341 top, 340–341 bottom, 341 top right, 341 bottom right, 346, 350 top left, 355 top, 356, 358, 359 left, 359 right, 362–363 top, 368 right, 370; Central Press, London 248 bottom, 332 left; Chicago Historical Society 84 bottom right; Colorific—Alon Reininger 347 bottom, 348 left, 363 top right; Colorific—Rick Smolan 350 bottom right; Comm. for European Communities 328 top; Deutsche Fotothek, Dresden 51 bottom, 115, 192; East African Railways Confederation 125 right; European Picture Service 253 right; Mary Evans Picture Library, London 202, 203; Fox Photos, London 313; Gernsheim Collection, Humanities Research Center, University of Texas at Austin 201 right; Photographie Giraudon, Paris 16 top, 16 bottom, 17 top, 55 top right, 56 bottom, 57 top, 57 bottom, 61, 120, 124; Hamlyn Group Picture Library 11, 12, 21 left, 22 bottom, 32, 33 right, 40, 41 bottom, 44, 60, 63 top left, 92, 95 left, 114 top left, 121, 130 right, 141 bottom, 196 right, 325 top, 372; Heeresgeschichtliches Museum, Vienna 103 top left, 194 top; Lucien Hervé, Paris 375; Lewis W. Hine International Museum of Photography at George Eastman House, New York 183 right; Imperial War Museum, London 43 top, 206, 220 top, 224 top, 225, 232 left, 232 top right, 233, 245; India Office, London 27 top; International Herald Tribune 350 centre left; Kungl. Biblioteket, Stockholm 49 top right, 119 bottom; Library of Congress, Washington 66, 71 bottom right, 72, 73, 75 top right, 76 left, 76 right, 77, 78 bottom, 80 top, 80 bottom, 83, 84 top right, 86 bottom left, 169, 178, 179 left, 179 right, 180 left, 184 top, 184 centre, 184 bottom, 185, 186, 257 bottom, 328 bottom; MacClancy Press, London 84 left, 85 top, 85 bottom, 86 bottom right, 105 bottom, 108, 134, 168 top, 171 top, 171 bottom, 172–173 bottom, 173 top left, 173 top right, 187 bottom, 208, 209, 212, 213 left, 216, 217 bottom, 218 top, 218 centre, 218 bottom, 220 bottom, 221 top left, 221 bottom left, 221 right, 222 bottom right, 224 bottom, 226, 232 centre right, 235, 236, 239 right, 240, 241 top left, 241 top right, 241 bottom, 243, 244, 257 top left, 257 top right, 259 right, 261, 263 right, 265 left, 265 right, 266, 267 bottom right, 268 top, 268 bottom, 271 centre, 271 right, 272–273, 273 top, 273 centre, 274 left, 274–275, 275 right, 282 bottom, 283 right, 284 top left, 284 top right, 284 bottom, 291 top, 291 bottom,

292 top, 292 bottom, 293 left, 294 bottom left, 294 bottom right, 295 left, 295 right, 296 left, 296 top right, 296 centre right, 298 bottom left, 301 top right, 302 bottom left, 302 bottom right, 304 top, 305 top left, 305 bottom left, 306 centre right, 306 bottom right, 308 left, 308 top right, 308 bottom right, 309 top, 309 bottom, 330 top left, 337; The Raymond Mander and Joe Mitchenson Theatre Collection, London 316 bottom; Mansell Collection, London 17 bottom, 19 right, 20, 21 right, 25 left, 25 right, 26, 27 bottom, 28, 70, 71 top right, 93 left, 113 top left, 114 top right, 119 top, 127 top right, 127 bottom, 144 right, 156 bottom, 160 right, 160 left, 161, 162 left, 164 top, 164 bottom, 165, 167, 168 bottom, 176, 177, 204 top, 204 bottom, 214, 217 top, 230 right, 237 top, 256; Marshall Cavendish—Agence France-Presse 330 bottom; Marshall Cavendish—NATO 324 bottom; Marshall Cavendish—United Israel Appeal Photo Archives 336 bottom; Mas, Barcelona 30 bottom, 197, 198 bottom, 200 top left, 200 bottom left; Museum of the City of New York—The Jacob A. Riis Collection 135; National Archives, Washington 232 bottom right, 293 right, 300 bottom, 333; National Army Museum, London 43 bottom; National Library of Ireland, Dublin 142, 143, 249; National Portrait Gallery, London 19 left; Peter Newark's Western Americana, Brentwood 68 left, 68 right, 69 bottom, 71 top left; New York Public Library 71 bottom left; Novosti Press Agency, London 49 top left, 49 bottom, 51 top, 110 bottom, 157 bottom left, 157 bottom right, 159, 162 top right, 163 top left, 229 left, 229 right, 230 left, 237 bottom, 276, 277, 278, 296 bottom, 298 right, 301 bottom, 305 right, 365, 369; Open Road Films, London 129 top; Popperfoto, London 255, 258 top right, 258 centre right, 258 bottom right, 289 top, 316 top, 317 right, 318 right, 320 top, 320 bottom, 323 bottom, 324 top, 325 bottom, 327 top, 327 bottom, 329, 330 top right, 333, 334, 338, 340 left, 344 top, 344 bottom, 345 left, 345 right, 348 centre right, 349, 350 top right, 350 bottom left, 355 bottom, 357, 363 bottom, 364; Pracownia Fotograticzna, Prague 48; Public Library of Cincinatti and Hamilton County 75 bottom right; Radio Times Hulton Picture Library, London 91 top, 91 bottom, 128 top left, 128 top right, 137, 139, 140, 141 top, 144 left, 162 bottom right, 200 right, 201 left, 251 top, 251 bottom, 254, 315 left; Royal Geographical Society, London 130 left; Sawyer Press 368 left; Scala, Milan 37 left, 93 top right, 93 bottom right, 95 right, 96 top, 96 bottom, 97 left, 97 top right, 97 bottom right, 98 right; Smithsonian Institution, Washington 187 top; The Star, Johannesberg—Barnett Collection 128 bottom; State Library of South Australia, Adelaide 114 bottom; Tony Stone Associates, London 371 bottom; Tate Gallery, London 29, 373; Thompson, Coventry 289 bottom; Topix, London 248 top; UNICEF 353; Union Pacific Railroad Museum Collection 180 right; United Nations 335, 360; United Press International, Acme 317 left; U.S. Air Force, Washington 300 top, 304 bottom; U.S. National Archives, Washington 228; U.S. Naval Historical Center, Washington 69 top; U.S. Navy, Washington 297; U.S. Signal Corps, Washington 301 top left; U.S. War Department, General and Special Staff, Washington 84 centre right; University of Washington Library, Seattle 181; Victoria and Albert Museum, London 23 bottom, 24, 44 top, 172 top, 315 right; Roger-Viollet, Paris 33 left, 41 top, 53, 55 bottom, 56 top left, 56 top right, 58 top, 58 bottom right, 59 bottom left, 62 left, 62 right, 64, 65, 94, 112 right, 117, 129 bottom, 132, 145, 146, 147, 148, 149, 150 top, 150 bottom, 152, 153, 156 top, 156 centre, 157 top, 163 bottom left; World Zionist Organisation 253 left. U.S. Research by Research Reports, New York.

Index

Figures in italic type refer to illustrations

Aachen 14
Abd el Kadar 129
Abdul Hamid, Sultan of Turkey 205
Abdul Medjid, Sultan of Turkey 41, 43
Abel, Niels Henrik 17
Abolitionist societies (slavery) 80
Absolutism, Spain 197
Abyssinia *see* Ethiopia
Acheson, Dean 254, 326
Acre 40
Acropolis, Turks attacking *40*
Action française (Maurras) 154
Adams, John Quincy 72, 74, 77
Adams–Onis Treaty 77
Aden 26, 41
Administration, Austria 195; Austria–Hungary 194; British in South Africa 249; French colonies 152; Japan 169; Russia 46, 50, 155
Admiral Graf Spee, sunk 292
Adowa, Battle of 90, 202
Adrianople, Treaty of 40
Advertising 116
Aegean, Egypt's navy dominates 39
Aerenthal, Alois Lexa, Count von 213, 214
Aeroplanes 114; Dakota *324*; Dornier 172, *294*; Heinkel He-45 *284*; Ju-52 troop carrier *302*
Afghanistan 26, 127, 156, 291
Africa 108, 123, 124, 139, 144, 290; education 369; independence for states 332; Italian ambitions 202; nationalism 344; in nineteenth century *123 map*; Portuguese possessions 200 *see also* East, North, South, West Africa
Africa Corps, in Paris 62
African National Congress 333, 357
African National Council, Rhodesia 344
Afrikaaners 128, 290, 333, 357
Afro-Asian Conference, Bandung 326
Agadir Crisis 215, 216
Agrarian Reform Law 1959, Cuba 337
Agricultural labourers, rising of 21
Agriculture 64; British 139; European 12; nineteenth-century 116; Russian 52, 162, 276–7; United States *184*, *257*
Ahmadu Bello (Muslim leader) 130
Ahmed Fuad, Sultan 252
Airborne troops, Second World War 303
Air, control of, Second World War 304
Air force, Japanese *297 see also* Aeroplanes; Luftwaffe; Royal Air Force; Royal Flying Corps
Air-lift, to Berlin 324
Aix-la-Chapelle, Allied congress 30
Alabama 67, 72, 83, 318
Alamo, Battle of 78
Alaska 77, 79, 80; Russian 159
Albania 40, 204, 306
Albemarle Report 316
Albert (Alexandre Martin) 59, 60
Albert, Lake 124
Albert of Saxe-Coburg, Prince *23*
Aldeburgh 18–19
Alexander I, Tsar of Russia *10*, 34, *46*
Alexander II, Tsar of Russia 43, 45, *47*, 50–1, 155–6; death 51, *156*; friendly with Prussia 104; with peasants *51*
Alexander III, Tsar of Russia *152*, 156–9
Alexandra, Empress, Tsarina of Russia *47*, *163*
Alexandria, British fleet 40, 128
Alfonso XII, King of Spain 199
Alfonso XIII, King of Spain 199
Algeciras Conference 212–13, *213*
Algeria 61, 64, 108, 129, 254; independence 334–5; joins Allies 299
Algiers 335
Al Hajj, Umar 130
Ali Pasha, Turkish minister 42
Allende, Salvador 349
Alliances, Bismarck's 210; European 210
Alliance Society (T'ung Meng Hui) 176
Allies, First World War 220–33, 237
Allies. Second World War 290–312
Alma, Battle of 43
Alsace 104
Alsace-Lorraine 152; colonists to Algeria 129; France recovers 234; Germans gain 106–8, 146; iron ore 192
Aluminium 115
Alvensleben, Convention of 102
Amadeo I, King of Spain 199
Amalgamated Society of Engineers 139
America, emigration to 123–4 *see also* United States
American Federation of Labor 183
American Independence, War of 26
American Peace Corps 320
Amiens, Battle of 221, 232
Amiens, Charter of 119, 150
Amoco Cadiz 368
Ampère, André Marie *17*
Amritsar, massacre 250
Anarchism, 119, 199, 202
Anarchists 120, 151
Anarcho-Syndicalism, Spain 199
Ancien régime 53
Ancona 32
Andalusia 31, 199
Andrassy, Count Gyula 195
Andrezième, railway 14
Angkor Wat, palace 125
Anglican Church Missionary Society 170
Angola 200, 344, *344*, 358
Angry young men 316
Annam 131, 170 *see also* Indo-China; Vietnam
Antibiotics, Pasteur 110
Anti-Comintern Pact 209, 290
Anti-communism, United States 326
Anti-Corn Law League 25, *25*
Antietam, Battle of 84
Anti-semitism, Arabs 253; France 147, 148, *283*; Germany 243, 273; Vienna 197
Antonelli, Cardinal 92
Antonescu, General Ion 295
Anzacs, at Passchendaele *232*
Apartheid 250, 333, 357
Apartheid, World Conference for Action against 358
Apollo space craft 367
Appalachians 67, 71
Appeasement 281–4
Appomattox, General Lee surrenders 87
Aquinas, St Thomas 122
Arab–Israeli conflict 345–8, 361
Arab–Israeli war 1967 336
Arab League 335, 336
Arab nationalism 246, 335–6
Arabs 252, 253, 290
Arab states, oppose Egypt–Israel settlement 348
Arafat, Yassir 346
Arago, François Jean Dominique, French scientist and republican, 17, 60
Arakcheyev, General Alexis Andreyevitch 45
Araki Sadao, General 264
Aref, President, of Iraq *336*
Argentina 256, 348
Arkansas, secedes from Union 84
Arkwright, Richard 13, 19
Armenia, Russia gains 40
Arms race, British and German 214–15; United States and Soviet Union 329
Armstrong, Neil 367
Army, Austrian 36, *38*
Army, Belgian, leaving the Congo 361
Army, British 144; Black and Tans 243, 248, *249*; Curragh revolt 143; Dunkirk 292; Egypt occupation 252; gas masks *221*; Indian 26; paratroopers at Arnhem *303*; reorganized 138; Scots in Egypt *128*; Ypres *220*; 1918 campaign 232-3
Army, Chinese 261, 263, *330*
Army, Egyptian 39, 40, 336
Army, Ethiopian *283*
Army, French 90; Dien Bien Phu evacuation *332*; Dreyfus affair 147–8; morale low in Second World War 303; mutiny 230; Napoleon III 104; Pius IX blesses *201*; Prussians fought *105*; republicans promoted 148; Ruhr occupation *241*; silk weavers of Lyons *57*; Verdun weakens 224
Army, German *188*; France occupied 146; Hitler supported 272, 273; Larissa (Greece) welcomes *295*; political influence 194; officers captured *301*; in Russia *296*; Second World War efficiency 303; Spanish victory parade *284*; in Weimar Republic 240
Army, Ghanaian 344
Army, Irish Republican *248*
Army, Italian *282*, *298*
Army, Japanese 174; in China *171*; declining influence 264; in Hainan *267*; imperialist 264; political ambitions 264–5; political power 260; in Shanghai (armoured car) *265*; in Singapore *306*
Army, Moorish *254*
Army, Nigerian 334, *334*
Army, operations in Second World War 303–4
Army, Piedmont, modernized 93
Army, Polish, cavalry *291*
Army, Prussian *103*, 104, *104*, *105*
Army, Russian, Cossacks *221*; deserters 230; humiliation 155; joins revolution 228; and Polish cavalry *48*; Red Army dominates Eastern Europe 312; Red Army in Second World War 304; in Terror 279
Army, Spanish 197, 198, *284*
Army, United Nations *335*, 362, *362–3*
Army, United States, black participation 317; in China *172*; in France 233; in Germany 322; in Santo Domingo *186*; in Second World War *228*; Union (Civil War) *84*, *85*, (Yankee volunteers) *86*
Army, Vietnamese *332*
Arnhem, British paratroopers *303*
Arrow War 166–7, *168*
Arthritis, treatment 364
Arthur, Chester, United States President 182
Artois 221
Artois, Count of 53
Arts, post-1940 316, 370
Ashanti, British in 130
Asia 124; nineteenth-century 164–77; Eastern nineteenth-century *167 map*; Far East 1920–40 *266 map*; during Second World War *299 map*; nationalist movements 330–2
Asquith, Herbert 141, 213, 224, 248
Assad, President of Bangladesh 345
Astor, John Jacob 116
Astronomy, post-1945 364
Aswan High Dam 326, 336
Athens 40, *40*
Atlanta 85, 87
Atlantic, Battle of the 295, 300
Atlantic Charter 311
Atomic bombs 302, 312, 324, 367 *see also* Hydrogen bomb; Nuclear science
Atomic energy 367
Atomic structure, Rutherford 112
Attlee, Clement, British Prime Minister 251, 313
Auriol, Vincent, President of France 212
Auschwitz 308
Austin cars 114
Austin, Texas 71
Australia 26, 27; First World War 246, *222*; greater independence 144; SEATO member 326; Second World War 291; wool exports to Britain 116
Austria, Allied treaty 236; and Balkans 204; denounced at Paris peace talks 94; Emperor 100; Galatia 34; Germany invades 290; in Italy 92; Lombardy and Venetia 31; neutral to Soviet Union 326; Piedmont's war 35; and Prussia 37, 65, 102; succession state 236
Austria–Hungary, calls for armistice 233; and Germany 192, 213; and Russia 208, 223; and Serbia 218
Autocracy, in Russia 155
Automation 367
Autumn Harvest Rising 263
L'Avenir (reform journal) 16
Avogadro, Amedeo 17
Avdienko (Soviet writer) 280
Ayub Khan, Pakistani leader 331

Baader-Meinhof group 363
Babel, Isaac, on the Terror 279
Bach, Alexander 194
Baden 30, 108
Baden-Baden 37, *258*
Badeni, Count *195*
Badoglio, Marshall 300
Baghdad Pact 326; renamed CENTO 328
Baghdad, railway 193, *211*
Bahadur Shah 127
Baiza Bai *127*
Baker, Ray Stannard 237
Bakst, Leon, poster for Diaghilev *153*
Bakunin, Count Mikhail Alexandrovitch *119*, 120, 199
Balaklava, Battle of *43*
Balance of power 90–131
Balbo, Count Cesare 32, 34
Baldwin, James 359
Baldwin, Stanley 256
Balfour, Arthur 140
Balfour Declaration 1917 290, 336
Balkan League, attacks Turkey 216
Balkans, Allies' proposed percentage split 300; Austria–Hungary's policy 213; great power rivalry 208; nineteenth-century *39 map*; Russian ambitions 40; Russians vulnerable 156
Balkan states 203–5
Balkan war *216*
Ballet, Diaghilev 154
Ballistic missiles *see* Missiles
Baltimore 70
Banda, Hastings 333
Bandung, Afro-Asian Conference 326
Bangladesh 344, 345
Banking 15, 74, 192
Bank of England, nationalized 313
Bantu, South Africa 357
Bantustans 333, 357
Barbados, independence 336
Barbarossa, Operation 295
Barbès (French socialist) 57, 60
Barcelona *197*, 199, *200*
Baring (finance and banking house) 15, 116
Barth, Karl 374
Baruch, Bernard 322
Basque region 198, 199
Le Bateau ivre (Rimbaud) 125
Bathyscaphe 367
Batista, Fulgeneio 337
Baton Rouge, revolution 77
Battles *see under name of battle*
Baudin (French deputy) 62
Bavaria 32, 36, 37; constitution 30; nationalist putsch 241; and Prussia 108
Bay of Pigs, Cuba 328
Bazaine, François Achille, General 104

Bazard, Saint-Amand (disciple of Saint-Simon) 16
Beagle, HMS 110
'Beats', Britain 316
Beatty, David, Earl 226
Bebel, August 120
Bechuanaland 129
Beckmann, Max, *Dance Bar in Baden-Baden 258*
Begin, Menachem 347, *348*
Belgian Congo 115, 124, 130, 334, 361
Belgium, African patriarchal approach 290; democracy survives 281; EEC member 327–8; electric motor invented 112; German advance 220, 292; government in London 295; Napoleon III's demands 104; NATO member 324; resistance movement 305; revolution 34; Treaty of Locarno 255
Belgrade, Austrian troops 218
Bell, John 82
Belloc, Hilaire, quoted 90
Bellow, Saul 370
Bell telephone 113
Belsen, concentration camp 307
Ben Bella, Algerian President *336*
Ben-Gurion, David 253
Benedek, General Ludwig von 95
Benedetti, Count Vincent 104
Beneš, Eduard, Czech President 290, 323
Bengal 127
Benz, German car manufacturers 113
Berchtold, Leopold von 216
Berg, Alban 196
Bergman, Ingmar 370
Berlin, airlift *324*; cold war 323–4; Conference 1884 129; decree of Louis Napoleon 68; electric streetcar 112; four-power control 312; general strike 240; Germany surrenders 301; Khrushchev's proposals 328; liberated from East 304; partition 326; population doubled 117; railways 14, 100, Red flag raised *301*; refugees *309*, *355*; restaurant at Zoo *191*; Wall *329*; 1848 riot 36
Berlin Soldiers Council *240*
Bernadotte, Count Folke 361
Bernard, Claude 109
Bernstein, Eduard 120, 190
Berry, Duchess of 57
Berry, Duke of, murder 54
Beryllium 115
Bessarabia, 44, 293
Bessemer, Sir Henry 115
Bethlehem, Holy places 42
Bethmann-Hollweg, Theobald von 192, 211, 218
Beveridge Report 1942 314
Beveridge, William 314
Bevin, Ernest 313
Bhutto (Pakistani leader) 345
Biafra 334, *334*
Biarritz 102
Biddle, Nicholas 74
Bikini atoll 326
Biology 18, 109–10
Biot, Jean Baptiste 17
Birkenhead, Lord 248, 251
Birmingham 19, 21
Birmingham Political Union *21*, *22*
Birth control 352
Bismarck, Count Otto von 37, 92, 101–8, *102*, *107*, *108*, 130, 188, 190, 192; alliance with Italy 97; anti-imperialist 126; and Catholic Church *189*; character 101; foreign policies 191; and France 152; and Pope Pius IX 121; poacher turned gamekeeper 210
'Bizonia', West Germany 322
Black African townships 333, 358
Black and Tans 43, 248, *249*
Black Hand 216
Black movement, United States 318–19
Black progress, United States 320
Black protest, United States 317
Black rule, Rhodesia 344
Black Sea 41, 44, 156
Blackshirts, Mussolini's *244*
Bladensburg 70
Blanc, Louis *16*, 17, 58, 59, 60, *61*
Blanqui, Jerome Adolphe 57, 60
Blériot, Louis 114
Blitzkrieg 291–4, 303
Blitz, on London, 1940 *304*
Blockade of England 20
Blomberg, General 272
Bloody Sunday 159–60, *159*, *160*
'Bloomers' *76*
Blucher, Gebhard Leberecht von 18
Blum, Leon 284
Boers 27; at Mafeking *129*
Boer War 125, 126, 127, 128–9, 143
Bohemia 35, 290
Bokhara 156
Bolivia, rejects Briand treaty 256
Bologna, revolution 32
Bolshevik Revolution *see* Russian Revolution
Bolsheviks 158, 228, 229, *230*
Bolshevism, in Britain and United States 237; in Italy 242, 244; Nazi posters *310*
Bombing, controversy in Second World War 304
Bonaparte family 32, 53 *see also* Napoleon Bonaparte; Napoleon III
Bonaparte, Joseph 197
Bonapartists 53, 56, 57–8
'Bon Marché' 64
Bonomi, Ivanoe 300
Booth, Charles 140
Bordeaux, Duke of 56
Borden, Sir Robert 247
Bose, Subhas Chandra 291
Bosnia-Herzegovina 213–14
Bosporus, Straits of 40
Botha, Louis 344
Botswana, independence 332
Boulanger, General Georges *147*
Boulogne, Louis Napoleon lands 58
Bourassa, Henri 247
Bourbons, restored 53–4; Naples revolt 92; exiled from Spain 104; restored to Spain 197
Bourgeoisie, under Louis Philippe 57
Bourgeois life, Queen Victoria's 23
Bourses de Travail 118
Bowie, Jim 78
Boxer, Chinese *172*
Boxer Protocol 1901 173
Boxer Rebellion 131, 172–4, *174*, 176
Boycott, Captain 142
Bradford 19; ILP founded 140
Brady, Matthew (photographer) *84*
Brandt, Willy 338
Brazil 256, 258, 357
Brazza, Pierre de *124*
Breckinridge, John C. 82
Brest-Litovsk, Russian-German peace 230
Brest, naval review *212*
Bretton Woods, United Nations conference 311
Brezhnev, Leonid 339, 363
Briand, Aristide 120, 151, 255, 256
Briand-Kellogg Pact 1928 255–6, 264
Bridewell prison *22*
Brindley, James 14
Britain, after 1815 18–26; in First World War 220–33; in Second World War 290–312; since 1945 313–16; achievement 28–9; Baghdad pact 326; Battle of 294, 304; class division *258*; democracy survives 281; depression 257; education 368; and EEC 338; Entente Cordiale 211–13; France's ally 131; and Germany 193, 211; Heligoland treaty 192; imports of raw materials 116; industrial power 136; Japanese alliance 174; Locarno treaty 255; NATO member 324; Near East 352–3; nuclear arms ban 362–3; and Pacific Coast 77; Palestine mandate ends 336; paternalism in Africa 290; race relations 359–60; and Rhineland 282; and Rhodesia 344; and Russia in Asia 174; SEATO member 326; Second World War recruiting poster *227*; Suez crisis 361; and United States 68, 313, (Civil War) 84, (Suez Crisis) 326, (War of 1812) 69–70; in Wei-hai-wei 131; West African annexations 123
British Colonies 153, 169, 332
British Commonwealth 246, 314, 359
British East Africa Company 131
British Empire 26–8, *215*; future 139, 143–4; nineteenth-century *126 map*; status of Dominions 246
British Expeditionary Force 292
British legation, Peking *168*
British Somaliland 129 *see also* Somali Republic
British West African Squadron 124
Britten, Benjamin 316, 370
Brooke, Rupert 219, 233
Brooklyn Bridge, breadline at *208*
Brooks, Preston B. 82
Brown, John 82
Bruckner, Anton 196
Brunswick 32
Brusilov, General Alexei 223, 229
Brussels 120, 158
Bryan, William Jennings 184
Buchanan, James 82
Bucharest Conference 1961 328
Buchenwald 307, *308*
Buchner, Georg, banned 32–3
Buckingham Palace *313*
Budapest *218*, *327*
Buddhism 171, 373, 374
Buena Vista, Battle of 79
Buick cars 114
Bukharin, Nikolai Ivanovitch 276, 277
Bulgaria, Allies' treaty 236; Central powers ally 224; independence 204; joins Balkan League 216; peace 233; and Russia 42, 156
Bull Moose party 187
Bullock, Alan, on Hitler 269, 274
Bull Run, Battle of 84
Bulow, Prince Bernhard von 192, 193
Bunch, Ralph 361
Bundersrat, German upper house 189
Bunsen, Christian Karl Josias, Baron *109*
Burke, Edmund 375
Burkhardt, Jacob 269
Burma 26, 127, 131, 169, 291, *302*; communism 332; nationalist movement 330; resistance movement 306; road for supplies 299–300
Burnside, General Ambrose E. 84
Burschenschaft 30–1, 32
Burton, Richard 124
Burt, Sir Cyril 365
Burundi, independence 333
Butler, Andrew P. 82
Byron, George Gordon, Lord 18, *19*, 40

Cables, electric 112–13
Cadiz, insurrection 31, *32*, 197
Cairo, Pasha of 40
Calcutta, Government House *27*
Calhoun, John C. 73, 74
California 77, 78, 81, 180, 186
Callaghan, James, British Prime Minister 338
Calles, Plutarco Elias 259
Calomarde, Francisco de 32
Cambodia 170, 330, 332, 344 *see also* Cochin China; Indo-China
Cambrai, Battle of *232*
Cameroun *88*, 226, 332
Campaign for Nuclear Disarmament (CND) 315–16; demonstration *316*
Campbell, Sir Colin (Lord Clyde), General 127
Campbell-Bannerman, Sir Henry 128, 141
Camp David, Sadat and Begin talks 347
Canada, borders 67; British Empire 26; First World War 246; French separatism 349; independence 27, 144; mining 115; Second World War 291; United States 247, (invasion plans) 69–70
Canals 113; Erie Canal *75*; Germany 192; Panama 80, 147, 150, 186; United States 75 *see also* Kiel Canal; Suez Canal
Canaris (Greek patriot) 39
Cancer research 364
Canning, George 20, 32, 40
Canton 26, 131; in Arrow War *168*; British merchant *167*; and Sun Yat-sen 176, 261; Western trade 164–5
Cape Colony 128
Cape of Good Hope 26, 27, 243
Cape Town *27*; black townships 258
Capitalist system 116, 118
Capital punishment 21
Capitol, Washington *66*
Caprera, Garibaldi at 100
Caprivi, Georg Leo, Graf von 192
Carbonari, Italian secret societies 31–2
Cardenas, Lazaro 259
Caribbean, nationalism 336–7
Carlist wars, Spain 197–8
Carlos I, King of Portugal 200
Carlos, Don 197
Carlyle, Thomas, quoted 22
Carnegie, Andrew 116–17, 180
Carnegie Endowment for International Peace 317
Carnot (physicist) 17
Caroline of Brunswick 20
Carrel, Armand 56
Carson, Sir Edward 143
Cartels, Germany 192
Carter, Jimmy, United States President 339, 347, *351*
Casablanca *129*, 130, 299, 308
Cass, Lewis 81
Castelas, Emilio 199
Castelfidardo, Battle of 98
Castillo, Canovas del 199
Castlereagh, Lord 10, 32
Castro, Fidel 328, *337*, 348, *348*
Catalonia 31, 197, 199, 200
Catherine II, Empress of Russia 45
Catholic Centre Party, Germany 189, 272
Catholic Church *see* Roman Catholic Church
Caucasus 52; and Russia 40
Cavaignac, Louis Eugène, General 61, 62
Cavalry, Russian and Polish *48*
Cavour, Camillo Benso, Count 32, 35, 36, 37, *93*, 200; at conference table 44; death 98, 201; and France 94
Cecil, Lord Robert 264
Censorship, by France 54; by Metternich 32–3
CENTO *see* Central Eastern Treaty Organization
Central Africa 124
Central African Republic 332
Central Asia, Russia conquers 156
Central Eastern Treaty Organization (CENTO) 328
Central Pacific Railway 180
Central Powers, in First World War 220–33
CERN *see* European Organization for Nuclear Research
Cetniks *306*
Ceylon 26, 291, 331 *see also* Sri Lanka
Cézanne, Paul 154
Chad, Lake 124
Chadwick, Edwin 22, 117
Châlons 105
Chamberlain, Sir Austen 244, 255
Chamberlain, Joseph 126, 128, 138, 144, *144*
Chamberlain, Neville 284, *285*
Chamber of Deputies 53, 55, 56, 57, 62
Chamber of Peers 56
Chambers, Whittaker 317
Champagne 221
Champin, J.-J., *Proclamation of Second Republic 59*
Champlain, Lake 70
Champollion, Jean François 18
Chancellorsville 85
Chang Tsung-hsiang 262
Charles X, King of France 40, 54–5, *55*
Charles Albert of Piedmont 34, 35, 36, 96
Charles Felix, of Lombardy 32
Charleston 82, 84
Charter, Atlantic 311
Charter, United Nations 360
Charter 77 (Czechoslovakia) 339
Chartism 24–5, *25*
Chateaubriand, Vicomte de 18, 53
Chatham, Earl of 18
Chattanooga, Battle of 85
Chemistry 17, 109
Ch'en Tu-hsin 262
Cherbourg, steamships 112
Chernyshevsky, Nikolai 51
Chesapeake Bay 70
Chesapeake, US ship 68
Chevalier, Michel 14
Chevreul 17
Cheyenne Indians 186
Chiang Kai-shek *263*, 290; and communist soviets 266–7; death 343; and Mao Tse-tung 267, 297, 324
Chicago 82, 180, 182
Chickamauga, Battle of 85
Chierici, *Gioie di una madre 96*
Child labour *183*
Children, employment 16, 24
Children Far Away (Young) 249
Children of Sanchez (Lewis) 364
Child, starving *354*
Chile 258, 348–9
China 165–8, 171–4, 260–4; British trade 22; communist risings 245, education 369–70; European interest 131; French trade 170; Germany seeks concessions 193; Indian disputes 331; Japanese conflicts 171, 209, 264, 291; and Korea 171, 324–6; Opium War 26; and Palmerston 136; People's Republic 324, 330, 362; racial prejudice 356; road-building *331*; and Russia 143, 159, 172, 328, 343; Sikkim invasion 344; Tanzam railway loan 344; as Third world power 326; and United States 186, 349–51; Vladivostok to Russia 52; Western outlook 164
'Chindits', Wingate's 300
Chinese minority, in Malaysia 369
Chinese National People's Congress 343
Chinese Revolution 1911 *177*
Chou En-lai 264, 326, 343, *350*
Christian IX, King of Denmark 102
Christian churches 256
Christianity 373; Boxers against 172; erosion of in Britain 316
Churchill, Sir Winston 284, *292*, *311*, *313*; on Battle of Britain 293–4; on cold war 321–2; Gold standard for Britain 256; on Indian government act 252; on Irish executions 248; on Mussolini 244; on naval limitations 247; on Palestine problem 253; on Potsdam 321; at Potsdam conference 302; as Prime Minister 292; resigns as Prime Minister 313; and Roosevelt 296, 299; on Russian bolshevism 239; at Teheran 300; at Yalta 301
Chu Teh, joins Mao 265
Cigarmakers Union, United States 183
Cincinnati, Ohio *75*
Civil aviation 313
Civil disobedience 251
Civil rights, Ulster 339, *341*
Civil rights, United States 317, 349; education 368; laws 320, 349, 359; mass rally 319
Civil service 24; Indian 26, 250
Civil War, Cuba 200
Civil War, India 252
Civil War, Russia 237, 275
Civil War, Spain 283
Civil War, United States 28, 82, *84*, 84–7, 178
Civita vecchia 36
Clapperton, Hugh 124
Clark, William *68*
Claus (meteorite study) 364
Clausius, Rudolf 109, 112
Clay, Henry 69, 72, 74, 76, 81
Clemenceau, Georges 148, 151, 232, 234
Cleveland, Grover, President of United States 181–2
Clotilde, Princess of Piedmont 94
CND *see* Campaign for Nuclear Disarmament
Coal industry, in Britain 313
Cobbett, William 20
Cobden, Richard 25
Cochin-China 170 *see also* Cambodia; Indo-China
Coffee plantation, Nairobi *125*
Co-Hong, abolished 165
Cold War 300, 312, 321, 361; and Berlin 323–4; far eastern sector 324, 326
Coleridge, Samuel Taylor 18
Collectivization, Russian 276
Colombia 186, 259
Colonial administration, British and French 254
Colonization, pre-nineteenth-century 123; world empires *246-7 map*
Colored Infantry, 107th *84*
Columbia, District of 81 *see also* Washington, D.C.
Combined operations, Second World War 302
COMECON *see* Council for Mutual Economic Assistance
COMINFORM *see* Communist Information Bureau
Comité d'Afrique Française 129
Commando units, Second World War 303
Commerce *see* Trade
Common Market *see* EEC
Commonwealth *see* British Commonwealth
Commonwealth Immigration Act 1962 359
Commune, Russian, and agriculture 162 *see also* Paris, Commune
Communism, China 209, 263, 265; in Cuba 337; detente 339; education 369–70; Far East 344; First World War gains 208; German risings 241; in Indonesia 330; internationalism adopted 281; international spread 236; Italy and Czechoslovakia discredit 240; Poland fears 306; in Spanish Civil War 283; threat to United States 317; World leaders *323*
Communist Information Bureau (COMINFORM) 323
Communist International 236
Communist League 17
Communist Manifesto (1848) 17, 60, 109, 116, 118, 119, 321
Communist parties, oppose Western governments 323
Communist Party, China 262, 263, 328
Communist Party, France *259*
Communist Party, Germany 240
Communist Party, Russia 279
Communists, in resistance movements, Second World War 305
Community Relations Commission 359
Comprehensive schooling 368
Computers 367
Conakry 124
Concentration camps, Germany 272, 274, 307
Concorde 368
Conditioned reflexes, Pavlov 110
Condition of England question 25
Condition of Man (Mumford) 374
Confederate States 83
Confédération Génerale du Travail 118–19
Confucianism 171, 172, 373
Congo, French 212, 216, 332–3, 334
Congolese Republic 328, 333, 361–2 *see also* Belgian Congo
Congo, River 124, *124*
Congrégation 54
Congress of Paris 1856 *44*
Congress of Racial Equality 319
Connecticut Artillery, 1st *84*
Conquest, Robert 279
Conrad (Austrian chief of staff) 213, 216
Conrad, Joseph, *Nostromo* 98, 171
Conservation 185, 367
Conservative Party 15, 25, 256, 313
Conservatives, and poverty 140
Constant, Benjamin 53, 54
Constantine, Grand Duke 34, 45
Constantinople 38, 42, 193, *204*, 214
Constitutional Democratic Party, Russia 161
Constitution, Austria 195; Britain promises India 250; France 53, 61; Germany, Weimar Republic 240; India 251; Russia after 1905 160; Spain 199; United States, 14th amendment 179
Constitution, US ship *69*
Contraception 367
Convoy system 227, 302
Cook, Captain James 170
Coolidge, Calvin, President of United States 256
Copper 115

Corfu, Mussolini seizes 256
Corn Laws 15, 20, 25–6, 137
Corn Law Repeal Hat *26*
Corridors of power (C.P. Snow) 316
Corruption, Mrs Gandhi convicted 345; United States 185
Corsica, and Maquis *305*
Cortes, Spanish parliaments 31, 199
Cortisone 364
Costa Rica, in depression 259
Cotton-growing 116; and slavery 72
Cotton industry, Robert Owen 16
Cotton mill, United States *183*
Cotton trade 68, 74, 170
Council for Mutual Economic Assistance 352
Council of State, France 62
Courbet, Gustave, portrait of Louis Blanc *16*
Courrier français, le 53
Court, British royal 23
Courts, Russian reformed 50
Cousin, Victor 54
Coventry 304
Coventry Cathedral *289*
Crawford, William H. 72
Creoles, race relations 357
Crete 40, 303
Crick, Francis 364
Crimea, Germans invade 296
Crimean War 43–4, 49–50, 94, 136, 155
Cripps, Sir Stafford 313
Crispi, Francesco 202
Croats, under Hungary 35, 36, 195
Crockett, Davy 78
Crowther Report 316
Cruikshank, George, Andrew Jackson's inauguration *73*; Manchester Heroes *20*; Prince Regent *21*
Cuba 337; Bay of Pigs landing 328; independence 336; poster *348*; revolution 318; T. Roosevelt *185*; Santiago harbour *200*; and Spain 186, 200; and United States 80, 348
Cult of personality 280
Cultural revolution, China 343
Curie, Marie and Pierre *112*
Curle, Adam 369
Currency question, United States Populist Party 184
Currier and Ives *78*
Curtin, John 247
Custine, Marquis de 46
Customs union *see* Zollverein
Custozza, Battle of 36, 99, 102, *103*
Cuvier, Georges 18
Cyprus 252, 335
Czechoslovakia 284; arms to Egypt 326; betrayed by appeasement 281; communist coup 323; communism discredited 240; dismembered 290; government in London 295; and Soviet Union 321, 338, 339
Czechs, in Austria 195

D'Abernon, Lord 271
Dachau, concentration camp 307
Dahomey 130, 333
Dáil, Irish parliament 248
Daily Mail 138
Daimler, Gottlieb 113, *192*
Daladier, Édouard, French Prime Minister *285*, 292
Dalton, John 17
Damascus 40
D'Annunzio, Gabriel 242
Danube, River 40, 44
Danzig, German demands 290
Dardanelles 41, 156
Darlan, Admiral 299
Darlington, railway 14
Darwin, Australia *114*
Darwin, Charles 18, 110, *111*
Darwinism, Social 121
Das Kapital (Marx) 15–16, 119
Daumier, Honoré 57, *58*, *92*
d'Aurelle de Paladines 106
Dawsons Field 347
D-Day invasion of France *296*, 300
Deák, Ferenc 35
Deak, Francis 195
Death control 352
De Beers Mining Corporation 128
Debs, Eugene 185
Décazes, Elie, Duc de 54
Deccan 26
December revolution 49
Decembrists 45–6
De Dion 113, 114
Degas, Edgar 154
De Gaulle, General Charles 282, 293, *293*, *341*; Britain and EEC 314, 315, 338; and French resistance movement 305; and Giraud 299; provisional government at Algiers 335
Degeneration (Nordau) 90
Delacroix, Eugène, *Liberty Guiding the People 8*; *Greece Expiring at Missolonghi 42*
Delaroche, Hippolyte, portrait of François Guizot *57*
Delcassé, Théophile 131, 212
Democracy, in British politics 138; decline in Europe 281
Democratic Party, United States 74, 75, 181, 185, 187, 317
Democratic-Republicans 66, 70
Democrats, Spain 199
Denmark, and EEC 338; Germany invades 292; NATO member 324; resistance movement 305; Schleswig and Holstein 102
Deoxyribonucleic acid (DNA) 364
Depression, Britain after 1815 20; Germany 271; the 'Great' 256–7
Depretis, Agostino 201
Deprez (French engineer) 112
Depth psychology 365
Derby Day, Frith's painting *29*
Déronlède 148
Desai, Mr, Indian Prime Minister 345
Despotism, Alexander I of Russia 46
Detente, Germany and Soviet Union 339
Detroit, model T Ford 187; skyline *370*
De Valera, Eamon *248*
Developed countries, prosperity 354
Development, Third World 354
Devil's Island, Dreyfus condemned 148
Dewey, John 262
Diaghilev, Sergei, 154; ballet poster *153*
Diem, South Vietnam premier 332
Dien Bien Phu, troops evacuated *332*
Diesel, Rudolph 113
Dimitsane 39
Direct rule, of Ulster 340
Disease, treatment 364
Displaced persons, UNRRA'S work 310
Disraeli, Benjamin 25, 118, *137*, 137–8; on British colonies 254; denounces Peel 26; and Suez Canal *127*; and Unions 139
Divine right of kings 37; China 261
DNA *see* Deoxyribonucleic acid
Dockers fighting, London *315*
Dock strike 139
Doll's house, Victorian *24*
Domestic virtues, Victorian 23–4
Doré, Gustave, illustration of London warehouses *11*
Dornier 172; over London docks *294*
Dortmund, oil refinery *304*
Dostoevsky, Feodor 49, 50, 120; *The House of the Dead 49*
Douglas-Home, Sir Alec, British prime minister 314
Douglas, Senator Stephen A 81, 82
Dreadnought, battleship 144, *144*, 215
Dred Scott case 82
Dresden, bombing in Second World War 304
Dreyfus, Captain Alfred 147–8, *148*, 150
Drumont, Édouard 148
Dual Mandate in Tropical Africa (Lugard) 249
Dubcek, Alexander 339
Dublin, Easter Rising 1916 *248*
Duke University 365
Dulles, John Foster 234, 326
Duma 50, 160, 161, *163*
Dumas, Jean Baptiste 109
Dunkirk *292*, 293, 303
Dupré, Jules, view of Normandy *12*
Duralumin 115
Durant, Thomas C 114
Dürrenmatt, Friedrich 370
Dutch East Indies 254, 330 *see also* Indonesia
Dutch Guiana 254
Dyer, General, in India 250

East Africa 90, 130
Eastern church 373 *see also* Greek Orthodox Church; Russian Orthodox Church
Easter 1916 rising 247–8
Eastern lands, German occupied areas 295
Eastern question 38
East Germany *see* German Democratic Republic
East India Company 22, 26
Eatanswill election (satire) *19*
Eaton, John H 74
Economic and Social Council, United Nations 360
Economic development, Russia 52
Economic statistics, Russian falsified 276
Eden, Sir Anthony, British Prime Minister 212, 260, 313
Edinburgh, Congress of 1896 118
Edison, Robert 112
Education 368, 369; Britain 140, 316; France 61, 147; Soviet Union *369*; United States 318
Education Act, 1870 138; 1944 316, 368
Edward VII, King of England 211
Edwards, P. G. 364
EEC 327–8, *338–9 map*, 352; Britain's entry 338; direct elections 338; Spain applies to join 340
EFTA *see* European Free Trade Area
Egypt, Anglo-French relations 212; army 39; and Britain 127, 143, 252; cotton exports 116; independence 41, 252, 290, 335, 336; Lebanese insurgents 361; and Mehemet Ali 40–1; and Nasser 326; and Sadat 346; and Suez Canal *327 see also* United Arab Republic
Egyptology 18
1812, War of *69*, 69–70
1848 crisis 34–7
1848 revolutions 58–60
Einstein, Albert 180
Eire *see* Ireland
Eisenhower, Dwight D., United States President and Allied Commander 300, 301, 317–18, 319
Eisenstein, Sergei, *Potemkin* 160
El Alamein 299
Elbe, River, refugees crossing *309*
Election posters *259*, *271*, *314*
Elections, satire *19*; United States *179*, *183*
Electoral law, France 55
Electoral reform 21, 24; France 58
Electricity 17, 112–13
Electric power 112
Electrolysis 17
Electronics 367
Elements, classification 109
Elgin, Lord, to Peking 167
Eliot, T. S. 281
Elizabeth II, Queen of England, as Princess *313*
Elizabeth, Queen Mother, as Queen Elizabeth *313*
Elizabeth, wife of Francis Joseph 196
Ellis, Havelock 110
Ellis Island, New York *180*
Elysée Palace, Paris 62
Emancipation Proclamation 1863 178
Emigrants, from Ireland *142*
Emigration, and imperialism 123
Employment, Britain 313 *see also* Unemployment; Labour; Working class
Ems telegram 104
Energy sources 112–13
Enfantin, Barthélemy Prosper (disciple of Saint-Simon) 16
Engels, Friedrich 17, 50, 60, 118
Engineers, British 14; United States 139
English Channel, crossed by air 114
English literature, Romantic 18
Enlightened Toryism 20
Enlightenment, Spain 197
Entente Cordiale 211–13
Enugu airport *334*
Environment, Stockholm conference 352; United Nations conference 367
Epidaurus 39
Epstein, Jacob 370
Erie Canal *75*
Erie, railways *75*
Erfurt, Congress 37
Eritrea, Italian 131
Erzberger, Mathias 240
Espartero, Baldomero 198
Essen 192
'Establishment', British 316
Esterhazy 148
Estonia 236, 292
Ethiopia 90, 125, 290, 344
Etienne, Eugène 129
Eugénie, Empress *62*, 63, 95, 104
EURATOM *see* European Atomic Energy Authority
Europe, after Congress of Vienna *31 map*; at end of nineteenth century *195 map*; at start of First World War *219 map*; after Versailles *238 map*; during Second World War *298 map*; after Second World War *322 map*
European Atomic Energy Authority (EURATOM) 367
European Community *see* EEC
European Economic Community *see* EEC
European Free Trade Association (EFTA) 315, 352
European Organization for Nuclear Research (CERN) 364
Europe, emigrants to United States 179; German control 295; map redrawn after First World War 236
Evian Conference 1962, on Algeria 335
Evolution 18
Executions *156*, *305*
Exhibitions 28 *see also* Great Exhibition
Exiled governments, in London 295
Exiles, Russian 50
Expansion *see* Imperialism
Exploration, Asia and Africa 124
Extrasensory perception 365

Fabian Society 140
Fabre-Luce, Alfred 282
Fabvier, Colonel 40
Factories, Italian fascists occupy 242–3
Factory Act 24, 140
Factory, arms *233*
Factory workers 116; Russia *157*
Faidherbe, General Louis Léon Cesar 106, 130
Faidherbe steamer 131
Faisal I, King of Syria and Iraq *253*
Falangists 281
Falk, Dr Adalbert 189, 190
Falkenhayn, Erich von 221, 222
Falloux law 61
Famine, Ireland 1845–9 142; Russia 157; Soviet Union 277
FAO *see* Food and Agriculture Organization
Faraday, Michael 17
Farmers, for Populist party 84
Farming *see* Agriculture
Farny, Henry F, *Song of the Talking Wire 183*
Farouk, King of Egypt 252
Farragut, David G. 85
Fascism, Europe 281; Europe after Depression 259; Italy 240, 242–4; nationalism exaggerated 281; origins 203; post-war elections 242; Romania 295; Second World War gains 208; Spanish Civil War 283
Fashoda 131, 152
Faubourg Saint-Antoine, Paris *33*
Faubus, Governor of Alabama 318
Favre, Jules 106, *107*
Federal Government, power 70–1
Federalists 67, 69, 70
Federal Reserve Act 1913, United States 187
Fédération Nationale des Syndicats 118
Federation of Just Men, Paris 17
Federation of Rhodesia 333
Federation of the West Indies 336
Feng Yu-hsiang 262
Fenian brotherhood 262
Ferdinand I, Emperor of Austria 36
Ferdinand I, King of Naples 31–2, 36
Ferdinand II, King of Naples 92
Ferdinand VII, King of Spain 31, 32, 197
Ferrer, Francisco 200
Ferry, Jules 126, 129, 131, 152
Festival of Britain 315; *The Islanders 315*
Feudalism, in Japan 169; in Two Sicilies 96
Fianna Fáil, Irish party 248
Figaro, Le, on Depression 259
Fiji, missionaries 170
Fillmore, Millard 81, 82
Finance, Europe after depression 259; Germany in Weimar Republic 240; houses 15,116; international 256; Italy 201; after Second World War 310–11; United States 70, 75
Finland 229, 236, 292
First International 119–20, 190, 199
First World War 120, 208–33; Eastern front *231 map*; recruiting posters *222*, *227*; troops mobilizing *218*; United States 187 Western and Italian Fronts 223 *map*
Fisher, Irving 257
Fisher, John, Lord 144, 211, 212
Fiume, D'Annunzio annexes 242
Five Families (Lewis) 364
Florence 36; Italian capital 99
Florida 67, 68, 77, 83
Flying bombs 300
Foch, Ferdinand, Marshal, 232, 233, 284
Fonteyn, Margot 316
Foochow 131
Food and Agriculture Organization (FAO) 356, 360
Food rationing 315
Food riots, Europe 34
Food technology 368
Ford cars 114
Ford, Gerald, United States President 351, 363
Ford Motor Company 187
Ford's theatre 87
Foreign policy, Germany 192–4; United States 68, 186–7
Formosa 172, 260 *see also* Taiwan
Fort Corcoran *84*
Fort Leavenworth 79
Fort McHenry 70
Fort Sumter 84
Fort Vaux 223
Forty-ninth parallel 79
Fourier, François Marie Charles 17, 59
'Fourteen points', 208
Fourth of May Movement, China 262
Foy, General 54
France 53–65, 144–54; Allies invade 300; anarcho-syndicalists 199; Austrian war 94, 194; Bourbons 30; and Britain 131, 144; Chinese trading rights 165; colonies 169, 254, 290, 332–3; constitutional changes 145; democracy survives 281; and depression 259; at Dien Bien Phu 326; education 368; EEC member 327–8; and Egypt 128; 1848 rebellion 34, *59*; Entente Cordiale 211–13; in First World War 220–33, *223 map*; foreign policy 64; and Germany 211, 216; a great power 44; in Indo-China 125; and Italy 293; in Kwang-chow 131; labour movements 118–19; Locarno treaty 255; Louisiana 67; Morocco 215; NATO member 324; in North Africa 129–30; popular front 284; post-war exhaustion 234; and Prussia 102–6; resistance movement 305; and Rhineland 282; and Rome 36; and Russia 156–7; SEATO member 326; Second Empire falls 144–6; Second World War collapse 293, (D-Day) *296*, 300; Spanish rebels 32; Suez crisis 361; Vatican recognizes Third Republic 121; in Vietnam 332 *see also* Vichy France
Franchise Act 1884 138
Francis I 10
Francis II, King of Naples 97
Francis Ferdinand, Archduke 216, *217*
Francis Joseph, Austrian Emperor 36, *95*, 194–5, *194*, *195*
Franco, Francisco 281, 283, 290 340
Franco, Joao 200
Franco-Prussian War 104–6, *105*, 145, 199, 210
Frankfurt, Diet of 32, 101; German assembly 36; Peace of 102, 106, *107*, 108; Prussia takes 102
Fraser, J. B., *Government House, Calcutta 27*
Fredericksburg 84
Frederick William I 100
Frederick William II *10*
Frederick William IV 36, 37
Freedom march, Washington *358*
Free French 293, 295
Freemasonry, in Russia 45
Freeport 82
Free Soil Party, United States 81
Free trade 13–14, 22; Britain 24, 25–6; British Empire restrictions 144; Germany 33; Treaty 1860 64 *see also* European Free Trade Association
Freikorps 240, *241*
Frémont, John C. 82
French Empire 151–2
French literature, romantic 18
French, Sir John 128
Frere, Sir Bartle 128
Freud, Sigmund 110, 196
Frick, Wilhelm 272
Friendly societies 16; France 118
Frith, William, *Derby Day 29*
Fugitive slave law 81
Führer, Hitler's title 273
Fur trade, British 79

Gabon, independence 333
Gabor, Professor 364
Gaeta 97
Gadsden Purchase 80
Gagarin, Yuri *365*
Gaitskell, Hugh 313
Galtaia, Poland 34
Galérie des Glaces, Versailles 108
Galicia, insurrection 31
Gallieni, Joseph Simon 125
Gallipoli campaign 225
Galvani, Luigi 17
Gambetta, Léon 105, 106, 145, 146
Gambia 123, 129, 332
Gamelin, Gustave 293
Gandhi, Mrs Indira 344–5, *345*
Gandhi, Mohandas (Mahatma) 250, 251, *251*, 252, 330
Ganges, British 26; Indian Mutiny 127
Gapon, Father 159–60
Garfield, James, United States President 182
Garibaldi, Giuseppe 92, 96–100, *97*, 200, 201; organizes guerrillas 94; in Naples *98*; 'Red shirt' *98*; in Rome 36
Garnier, François 125, 131, 170
Garnier-Pagès, Etienne Joseph Louis 56
Garrison, William Lloyd 80
Gas, North Sea 367
Gastein, Convention of 102
GATT *see* General Agreement on Tariffs and Trade
Gauguin, Paul 154
Gauss, Johann Karl Friedrich 17
Gay-Lussac, Joseph Louis 17
Gazette de France 53
Geddes, Sir Eric 234
General Agreement on Tariffs and Trade (GATT) 311
General Treaty of Economic Integration 352
Genetics 364
Geneva, Arab-Israeli peace talks 347; conference 1954 326, 332; conference 1955 on atomic energy 367; nuclear weapons treaty 1967 363; UNCTAD conference 1964 354
Genghis Khan 277
Genocide, German extermination of Jews 307–8
George III, King of England 18, 20, 22
George IV, King of England 20, 21, *21*, 22
George V, King of England 246

George VI, King of England *313*
George, Kara 38
Georgia 83, 85
Gerard, Etienne Maurice, Comte, Marshall *56*
German Democratic Republic 326, 329, 338
German East Africa 130, 226 *see also* Tanganyika; Tanzania
German Empire 108, 188–94, 211
German Federal Republic 322, 326, 328; Baader-Meinhoff group 363; economy 322; EEC membership 327–8; joins Western alliance 326
German literature, romantic 18
German South West Africa 130, 226 *see also* Namibia; South West Africa
Germany 32–3; and Africa 130; Brest-Litovsk peace 230; and Britain 28, 144; in Cameroun *88*; in China 131 (ambassador murdered) 173; colonial agreement with Britain 153; colonies taken piecemeal by Allies 225; debts, interwar 256; 1848 revolution 36; Empire formed 146; and Entente Cordiale 212–13; fascism 240; firing squad *305*; First World War 220–33, 234; and France 152, 216; under Hitler 269–74; imperialism after Bismarck 126; industrialization 144; insurance system 141; Italy 300; Kiaochow Bay 172; labour movement 118; nineteenth-century *102 map*; Pacific islands lost 260; partition 326, 338; resistance movement Second World War 305; revolutionary poster *242*; Russian treaty lapses 156; Second World War 290–312; and Soviet Union 210, 279, 290, 296; unification 90, 100–8; Waffen SS *303*; war guilt 234; war plans 218; Weimar Republic 240; *Weltpolitik* 210–11 *see also* German Democratic Republic; German Federal Republic; Prussia
Gestapo 272
Gettysburg, Battle of 85
Ghana 123, 332, 344, 369
Ghent, Treaty of 70
Giap, General 332
Gillray, James, cartoon *164*
Gioberti, Abbé Vincenzo 32, 92
Giolitti, Giovanni 202–3, 243
Giraud, General Henri 299
Gladstone, William Ewart 118, 137, *137*; on Egypt 252; and Ireland 142; and unions 139
Gleichschaltung, Nazi 'coordination' 273
'Glorious revolution', England, 1688 18
'Glorious revolution', Spain, 1868 104
Goa, independence 254
Goebbels, Dr Joseph 271, 273, *275*
Goering, Reichsmarshal Herman 272, 293, *294*
Goethe, Johann Wolfgang von 18
Gogol, Nikolai 18, 48
Goito, Battle of 35
Golan Heights *346*
Gold Coast 129, 130 *see also* Ghana
Goldie, Sir George 130
Gold miners *128*
Gold mines, South Africa 128
Gold standard 184, 256
Gold, United States 186
Gompers, Samuel 183
Gomulka, Wladyslaw 327
Goodyear, introduce vulcanization 115
Gordon, Charles George, General 128
Gotha Congress 190
Gotha Programme 1875 118
Göttingen University 17
Government of India Act 1917 250; 1935 252
Goya, Francisco da *Disasters of War 30*
Gramont, Duke of 104
Grand National Consolidated Trade Union (Owen) 17, 24
Grant, General Ulysses S. 85, 86; President of United States 181
Graves, Robert 220
Great Exhibition 1851 *14*, 28, *28*
Great Lakes 75, 80
Great Leap Forward, China 328
Great Plains 81
Great Salt Lake 80
Great Trek 128
The Great Union of the Popular Masses of the Whole Country (Mao Tse-tung) 262
Great Wall of China *268*
Great War 1914–18 *see* First World War
Greece, archaeology 18; and Balkan League 216; Britain withdraws aid 322; fascist influence 281; foreign dominance 204; Germans invade *295*; independence 18, 38–40, 204; and Italy 256, 295; NATO member 324; Palmerston's ultimatum 137; Soviet Union pressure 321
Greece Expiring at Missolonghi (Delacroix) *42*
Greek National Assembly 39
Greek Orthodox Church 38, 42, 44
Green Cloud, Chinese monastery 263
Grey, Lord 21, 212–13
Guadalupe Hidalgo, Treaty of 80
Guerchoury, Gregory *156*
Guerrière, British frigate 69
Guerrilla warfare, China 265; Rhodesia 344
Guesde, Jules 118, 120, 150, 199
Guiana *see* Dutch Guiana; Guyana
Guinea, French 130, 332
Guizot, François 53, 54, *57*, 57–9
Gutzlaf, Charles 125
Guyana, independence 336

Habsburg empire 194–5
Habsburgs, in Austria-Hungary 35; in Austria 188; and Germany 100; Pope's supporters 92; Sadowa 102
Haggard, Rider 125–6
Haidouks, Serbian war bands 38
Haig, General Douglas 222, 231, 232
Haile Selassie 290, 344
Hainan, Japanese army *267*
Hakka, immigrants in China 166
Haldane, R. B. 144
Half Our Future (Newson) 316
Hall, Charles 115
Hamburg 100
Hamilton, Alexander 66
Ham, Louis Napoleon imprisoned 58, 61
Hammarskjold, Dag 327, 328, 361, 362
Hango 292
Hankow 176
Hanoi 131, 170
Hanover 14, 37, 102
Hardie, James Keir *91*, 120, 140
Harding, Warren, United States President 236, 245
Hargreaves, James 13
Harmsworth, Alfred 138
Harper's Ferry, John Brown's raid 82
Harrison, William Henry 76
Harwich, German U-boats *226*
Hausa tribe, Nigeria 334
Haussmann, Baron Georges Eugène 63
Havana, United States ship 186
Hawaii 170, 176, 260
Hawthorne, Nathaniel 375
Haydon, Benjamin Robert, painting of Birmingham Political Union *22*
Hayes, Rutherford B. United States President 181, 182
Hay, John 131, 186
Heartfield, John *306*
Heart surgery 364
Heath, Edward, British Prime Minister 338
Hegel, Georg Wilhelm Friedrich 50
Heine, Heinrich, banned 32–3
Heinkel He-45 *284*
Heligoland, 192, 193
Helsinki, SALT talks 363
Henry, Colonel, Dreyfus affair 148
Henry, Prince, heir to Charles X 57
Henze, Hans Werner 370
Herbert, A. P. 255
Heredity, Medel's law 110
Herzen, Alexander 48, 50, 155
Hesse-Cassel 32, 37
Hesse, to Prussia 102
Hetaire, Greek secret society 38
Hill, J. W., *View on the Erie Canal 75*
Himalaya, P & O liner *114*
Himalayas 26
Himmler, Heinrich 274
Hindenburg, Oscar 271
Hindenburg, Paul 230, 271, 273
Hinduism 373
Hindus, majority in India 252
Hipper, Franz von, Admiral 226
Hirohito, Emperor of Japan 264
Hiroshima, bombed 302, 304
Hiss, Alger 317
Hitler, Adolf 196, 208, 269–74, *270*, *274*, *285*, *303*, *306*; ambition underestimated 280; assassination attempts 305; in Bavarian putsch 241; Britain and France appease 281; Chancellor 272; imitated in Europe 281; Jews flee to Palestine 253; Marxism attacked 240; Mexican admirers 259; personality and magnetism 269; on Stalin 277; suicide 301
Hitler Youth 274, *274–5*
Hobson, John A. 90
Ho Chi Minh 254, 291, 332
Hohenlohe, Chlodwig, Furst zu 11, 192
Hohenzollerns 100, 104, 108
Holography 364
Holstein, to Prussia 102
Holy Alliance 10, 18, 32, 77; Alexander I's idea 45; end of 40
Holy Places 41–2, 64
Home Guard, in Second World War 303
Home Rule, Ireland 142–3, 247–8
Home, Sir Alec Douglas *see* Douglas-Home, Sir Alec
Honan, village corps *268*
Honecker, German Democratic Republic leader 338
Honest to God (John Robinson) 316
Hong Kong 26, 165, 176
Hong (trade compounds) 168
Hoover, Herbert, United States President 256–7
Hopes (bankers) 15
Horn, Cape, route to California 80
Hospital, field, Battle of the Somme *224*
'Hot-line' 329
House, Colonel Edward Mandell 187
House of Commons 15, 18–19, *23*, 189
House of Lords 18, 140, 141–2, 250
House of the Dead, The (Dostoevsky) 49
Houston, Sam 78
Hoxha, Enver 306
Hua Kuo-feng 344
Hudson Bay Company 79
Hudson Valley 75
Hugo, Victor 18, 62, *63*
Humphrey, Hubert 349
Hunan 165; and Mao Tse-tung 262
Hundred Days, Napoleon's 58
Hung Hsiu-ch'nan 166
Hungarians, and Austria 194, 195
Hungary, Allies treaty 236; and Croats 36; 1848 revolution 35, 36; fascist influence 281; independence 36; a kingdom 195; 1956 rising 326, *327*; succession state 236
Hunt, Henry 20
Huskisson, William 14, 20
Hussein, King of Jordan 346–7
Hyde Park 28
Hydrogen bomb 317, *326*, 367 *see also* Atomic bombs; Nuclear Science
Hyndman, H. M. 140

IAEA *see* International Atomic Energy Agency
Ibo tribe, Nigeria 334
Ibrahim, son of Mehemet Ali 40, 41
Iceland, NATO member 324
Ideologies, world 320–1
Ideology, relaxed in China 343–4
The Idiot (Dostoevsky) 49
IGY *see* International Geophysical Year
Illinois, election campaign 82
Il Risorgimento, Cavour, editor 93
ILP *see* Independent Labour Party
IMF *see* International Monetary Fund
Immaculate conception 121
Immigrants, Britain, numbers limited 359; China (Hakka) 166
Immigration, Jews into Palestine 253; United States 71–2, 179
Imperial Conference 1921 248; 1926 246
Imperialism 11, 90, 123–31; Arab nationalism resists 336; British, after First World War 249; Germany 193; Italy 202; Prussia, Bismarck's policy 191; Russia 156–7; United States 186
Imperial War Cabinet 246
Impressionists 154
Inchon 324
Independence, Missouri 78
Independent Labour Party (ILP) 140
India 250–2, 344; anti-British campaign 299; British Empire 26; British trade 22; communist threat 332; education 369; First World War poster *245*; independence demanded 246; influence on Africa 250; Kashmir dispute 361; leaders *127*; nationalist movement 330–1; Second World War, brought in by Britain 290; Simon Commission *251*; starvation *355*
Indian Civil Service 26, 127
Indian Mutiny 127, 143
Indian National Congress 250
Indian Ocean, British control 127
Indo-China 151, 152; communist rising 323; and France 125, 131, 170; Geneva conference 326; rebellions 254 *see also* Annam; Cambodia; Cochin-China; Laos; North Vietnam; South Vietnam; Vietnam
Indonesia 246, 306, 330, *330 see also* Dutch East Indies
Indonesian National Party 330
Indus, River, British possessions 26
Industrial expansion, United States 75
Industrialization, Austria-Hungary 196; British assessed 144; China, 'Great Leap Forward' 328; France 145; Italy 201; Japan 169, 260; late nineteenth-century 134; Russia 157; Soviet Union 276; United States 180
Industrial revolution 10, 13, 18, 202–3
Industry, nineteenth-century 115; Asia, nineteenth-century 164; British competition 139; depression 257; Europe, nineteenth-century 109; France 149, (working conditions) 60; Germany 100, 192; inventions used 115; Italy 202; Russia 48; transport 114; United States 181, 312; world development 367
Ineffabilis Deus, Pius IX bull 121
Infallibility, papal 121
Infant mortality 353, 356
Influence of Sea Power upon History (Mahan) 186
Influenza, epidemic in India 250
Inkerman, Battle of 43
Inniskillen Fusiliers *232*
Insurance, Bismarck's 190, *190* *see also* National Insurance
Intellectuals, 1848 the year of 109
Intelligence, psychology of 365
Intelligentsia, Russian 48–9, 155
Intergovernmental Maritime Consultation Organization 368
Internal combustion engine 113
International *see* First International; Second International
International Atomic Energy Agency (IAEA) 367
International Bank for Reconstruction and Development 311
International Brigades 283
International Exhibition, Paris 28
International Geophysical Year (IGY) 364
Internationalism and communism 281
International Monetary Fund (IMF) 311, 352
International Refugee Organization 310, 355–6
International socialism 140
International Voluntary Service 356
International War Crimes Tribunal 312
International Working Men's Association 64, 119; membership card *114*
Inukai Tsyoshi 265
Invalides, Les 58
Iowa 81
IRA *see* Irish Republican Army
Iran *see* Persia
Iraq 252, 253, 326, 328
Ireland 247–8; and Britain 142–3; discontent 139; dominion status 246; emigrants *142*; famine 25; independence moves 21; neutral in Second World War 291; peasant eviction *143*
Irish Church, disestablished 142
Irish Free State 143, 248
Irish Republican Army (IRA) 248, 339–40
Iron and steel, nationalization 313; works at Nadezhdinsky *157*
Iron curtain 322, 324
Iron works, Magnitogorsk *276*
Irrawaddy, River 169
Irun, Spain *284*
Irwin, Lord, on India 251–2
Isabella II, Queen of Spain 197, 198, *198*
Islam 373; in Turkey 38
Isle of Wight, royal retreat 23
Ismael Pasha 127
Isolationism, China 260
Isotopes, medical use 367
Israel 345–8; camel patrol unit *363*; Egypt's guerrilla war 326; independence 335; Jordan Left Bank settlement *347*; Lebanon invaded 362; and neighbouring states *346 map*; new state 336
Italians, under Austria 30
Italiens, Boulevard des, Paris *63*
Italy 200–3; in Africa 131; Allied advance slowed 300; communism discredited 240; seizes Corfu 256; EEC member 327–8; 1848 revolution 34; emigrants in New York *180*; Ethiopia defeats 90; Ethiopia annexed 290; fascism 240, 242–4; Federation under Pope 94; First World War 222, *223 map*, 224; Greece invaded 295; as Gulliver *92*; Habsburg lands coveted 196; a Kingdom 98–9; Libya attacked 216; Louis Napoleon 61; NATO member 324; Northern Kingdom 94; resistance movement Second World War 305; revolutionary ideas 31; Risorgimento *94 map*; South Tyrol annexed 236; Southern after unification 98; unification 90, 92–100; Victor Emmanuel II King 98
Ito Hirobuni 174
Ives *see* Currier and Ives
Ivory Coast 130; independence 333

Jackson, Andrew, General, United States President 70, 72–4, *73*, 77, 78
Jackson, Stonewall 84, 85
Jagow, Gottlieb von 210, 216
Jamaica, independence 336–7
Jameson Raid 128
James River 84
Janina, Pasha of 39
Janissaries 39
Japan 174–6, 260–1, 264–5; 'Australasia's Near North' 247; birth control 352; British alliance 225, 247; British trade 22, 26; and China 260, 262, 264, 267–8; and communists 344; constitution 173; education 369; First World War rise 209; German pact 295; and Indo-China 332; and Indonesia 330; industrial power 330; industrial revolution 134; and Korea 171; and Manchuria 125; nationalism 90–1; Pearl Harbor attacked 297; rise in twentieth century 291; and Russia 52, 159; in South East Asia 300; Soviet Union neutral 295; surrenders after Second World War 302; United States peace treaty 326; westernization 168–9, 170
Jarring, Gunner 346
Jarrow march *258*
Jaurès, Jean *120*, *150*
Java, British frigate *69*
Jefferson, Thomas, United States President 66–8, 77
Jellachich, Count (Croat-governor) 36
Jellicoe, John, Admiral 225
Jerusalem, Holy Places 42
Jesuits 54, 189
Jewish National Fund 253
Jew, Parisian, Second World War *308*
Jews, and Arabs 290; Balfour Declaration 336; in concentration camps 307; extermination in Europe *307 map*; Germany isolates 273; Hitler's mission against 269; illegal immigrants to Palestine *253*; immigrant ship in Palestine *336*; and Palestine 253; race relations 357; scrubbing pavements *273*; in Vienna 188 *see also* Anti-semitism; Israel
Jihad (Holy War) 128, 130
Jingoists 126; French 131
Jinnah, Mohammed Ali 252, 330
Joffe, Adolf 263
Joffre, Joseph Jacques Cesaire, Marshal 220, 221, 224
Johannesburg 128, *356*, 358
John XXIII, Pope 373
John-Paul II, Pope 339, *374*
Johnson, Andrew, United States President 87, 178
Johnson, Lyndon B., United States President 319, 320
Jordan 336, 346–7, *347*
Joseph, King of Spain 197
Joule, James 17
Journal on Melville (Hawthorne) 375
Ju-52, German troop carrier, crashed *302*
Juan Carlos I, King of Spain 340, *340–1*
Juchen 266
Judaism 373
July Monarchy 56–7
Junkers 100, 108, 188, 189
Jutland, Battle of 226

Kadets (Russian party) 161
Kaganovitch (Stalin supporter) 279
Kaiser Wilhelm Canal *see* Kiel Canal
Kamenev, Leo, Stalin joins 275
Kampala 131
K'ang Yu-wei 172
Kansas 82
Kansas-Nebraska Act 82
Kapital, Das (Marx) *see Das Kapital*
Kapp, Wolfgang 240
Karakozov 51
Karnak, temple of *336*
Kasai, Congo 361–2
Kashmir 331, 361
Katanga 334, 361–2
Katemu tribe, King of *130*
Kaunda, Kenneth 333
Kautsky, Karl 120
Keats, John 18
Keiki, Japanese shogun 168
Kellogg, Frank Billings 256
Kelvin, Lord 109, 112–13
Kemal Ataturk 205
Kennan, George 322–3
Kennedy, John F, United States President *318*; and promise 319–20, *319*, 328, 359
Kennedy, Senator Robert *348*, 349, *349*
Kenseikai, Japanese Party 264
Kent, Duke of (Queen Victoria's father) 22
Kent State University *289*
Kentucky 71; slavery 72
Kenya 129, 131, 332, 333
Kenyatta, Jomo 333–4
Keynes, John Maynard 116, 134, 208
Khartoum 40, 124, 128, 344
Khiva 156
Khmer palace 125
Khmer Rouge, takes Cambodia 344
Khokand 156
Khrushchev, Nikita 326, 328, *328*, *336*, 362; on Stalin 279, 280, 327
Kiangsi 265, 266
Kiaochow 131, 211, 225, 260, 262
Kiderlen-Wachter, Alfred von 215
Kiel Canal *113*, 192
Kiev 46, 162
King, Martin Luther 318, *348*, 349, 359
Kipling, Rudyard 90, 125
Kirchhoff, Gustav Robert 109
Kirov, Sergei 279
Kir Singh *127*
Kitchener, Herbert, General 128, 131, *220*, 221
Kitty Hawk *114*

Klir, Joseph, *The Lost Bet 183*
Knights of Labor 183
Know-nothing Party 82
Kodo-ha, Japanese army faction 265
Koestler, Arthur 374
Kolchak, Alexander Vasilievitch *237*
Kollar, Jan 35
Komsomol 370
Konieh, Battle of 41
Korea 324, 326; and Japan 171, 174, 260; and Russia 143; stalemate 344 *see also* North Korea; South Korea
Korean War 318, 324–6, *325*, 361
Kornilov, General 230
Kossuth, Louis 35, 36, *37*
Kotzebue, Auguste von 30–1, *30*
Koutaieh, Treaty of 41
Kronstadt 153; sailors' revolt 280
Krudener, Julie de 45
Kruger, Paul *128*
Krupp, Alfred 13, 100, 117, 192
Krupp's works *101*
Kuang Hsu, Emperor of China 172
Ku Klux Klan 179, 359
Kulturkampf 121, 189–90
Kun, Bela 237
Kuomintang, Chinese party 176, 263, 267; at Canton 262; learned from Hung 166
Kutako, Hosea 333
Kwang-Chow 131

Labor unions *see* Trade unions
Labour, agricultural 16; industrial 16; organization of 367; supply, nineteenth century 117 *see also* Employment; Unemployment; Working class
Labour movement, Britain 20; France 119; United States 183
Labour Party, Britain 118, 139–40; election poster *314*; in government 256; internal dissension 313; wins 1945 election 313
Labour unions *see* Trade unions
Lacordaire, Jean Baptiste Henri 16
Ladysmith, relief of 128
La Farina, Giuseppe 93
Lafayette, Marquis de 53, 54, *56*
Lafitte, Jacques *56*
Lagos, World Conference for Action against Apartheid 358
Laibach, Congress of 32, 40
Lakhsmi Bai *127*
Lamarck, Jean Baptiste Antoine Pierre Monet de 18
La Marmora, Alfonso Ferrero, Marquis de 93, 94, 99, 102
Lamartine, Alphonse de 18, 58, 59, 60, 61
Lamennais, Félicité Robert de 16
Lancashire, and textile markets 260
Land Act (Ireland) 1870 142; 1881 142
'Land and Liberty' 51, 155–6, 157
Land enclosures, England 16
Lander Bros 124
Landes, fir tree plantations 64
Land League of Ireland 142
Land nationalization, Russia 229
Land of Hope Glory 249
Landowners, United States 181
Land policy, Russian 276
Land redistribution, Italy 98–9
Landtag, Prussian assembly 189
Lange, Dorothea, photographer, 'Migrant Mother' *257*
Langevin reforms, French education 368
Lanternari, Vittorio 374
Lanterne, La (Rochefort) 65
Laos 131, 170, 332, 344; nationalist movement 330; neutral 329; South Vietnam invades 344; United Nations presence 361
Laplace, Pierre Simon, Marquis de 17
Lassalle, Ferdinand 190
Las Vegas *288*
Lateran Treaty 1929 100
Latin America 348–9; depression 258–9; Free Trade Association 352; nationalism 336–7; trade with Britain 68; and United States 76, 187, 291 *see also* South America
Latin Quarter, Paris 61
Latvia 236, 292
L'Avenir (reform journal) 16
Lawrence, United States town 82
Law, Russian, codification 46; South Africa, racial discrimination 357
League of Nations 208–9, 234, 256; failure 290; Germany admitted 255; Japan leaves 264; Manchurian intercession 264; Woodrow Wilson 235
Learning theory 364–5
Lebanon 252, 318, 346, 361, 362
Lebensraum, Hitler's need 280–1
Leboeuf (French war minister) 104
Lecompton Constitution (Kansas) 82
Lecomte, L. L., painting of fighting in the rue de Roman *55*
Le Corbusier 370; *Unité d'Habitation 375*
Ledru-Rollin, Alexandre Auguste 61
Lee, Robert E. 84, 85, 87
Legien, Karl 118
Lehar, Franz 196
Le Havre 196
Le Mans, Battle of 106
Lena, goldfields massacre 163
Lend-lease 295, 311
Leningrad *see* St Petersburg; Petrograd
Leningrad Bolshevik Party 275
Leninism 321 *see also* Marxism-Leninism
Lenin, Vladimir Ilyich (Ulyanov) 116, 118, 120, 125, 158, 161, *230*; China's inspiration 262; and cult of personality 280; death 245; Finland exile 229; and Hitler 269; leadership 229; and Marxism in Russia 157–8; and revolution 228; on Stalin 274–5
Leo XIII, Pope 121, 149, 190
Leopard, British ship 68
Leopold I, King of Belgium 34
Leopold II, King of Belgium 124, 130, 334
Leopold, Grand Duke of Tuscany 95
Leopold of Saxe-Coburg *see* Leopold I, King of Belgium
Leopoldsville *335*
Leopold von Hohenzollern 104
Lermentov, Mikhail 18, 48, *49*
Lesotho, independence 332
Lesseps, Ferdinand de 127, 147, 186
Lettow-Vorbeck, General Paul von 226
le Verrier, Urbain Jean Joseph 17
Lewis, Meriwether *68*; diary *69*
Lewis, Oscar 364
Liaotang peninsula, Manchuria 172, 174
Liberal Catholic Movement 16
Liberal-Conservatives, Spain 199
Liberalism 30; attacked by intellectuals 281; France 54; Germany against 100; Gladstone 137; Leo XIII 121; Louis Napoleon 64; Piedmont 94; Russia 45
Liberal movement, Russia 51
Liberal parties, nineteenth-century 118; Britain 26, 137, 141, 314; Hungary 196
Liberals, Belgium 34; Italy 243; and poverty 140; Spain 197–8
Liberal Unionists, Spain 199
Liberation of Labour 158
The Liberator (Garrison) 80
Liberia, independent 290
Libraries, public 117
Libya 124, 216, 333
Lichtenstein, Roy, *Wham 273*
Liebig, Justus von 12, *13*, 17
Liebknecht, Karl *120*
Liebknecht, Wilhelm 190
Lie, Trygve 361
Life, expectancy, Asia 356, (increases) 117; extra-terrestrial 367; nature of 364
Light Brigade, Battle of Balaklava *43*, 155
Li Hung-chang 171, 172, 173
Lima, United States–Latin American Declaration 291
Lincoln, Abraham, United States President 82, *83*, 84, *85*, 178; criticized over Civil War 85; President 82–3; re-elected 86; shot 87
Linnaeus, Carl 110
Lin Piao 268
Lin Tse-hsu 165
Lippmann, Walter 264
Lisbon, Royal Palace 200, *201*; strike 200
Lissa, Battle of 99, 102
Lister, Joseph 110
Litani, River 362
Lithuania 236, 290, 292
Little Rock 318, 358
Liverpool, Lord 20
Liverpool, steamships 112
Livestock, Russian 277
Livingstone, David 124, 125
Livingston, Robert 68
Lloyd George, David 141, 218; on British Empire 249; convoy system 227; on European revolution 237; 'fight to a finish' 224; Germany warned 216; on Hitler 269; and Ireland 248; and Palestine 253; at Paris conference 234; on Passchendaele 232
Local government, Britain 22
Locarno Pact 255, *256*
Loigny, Battle of 106
Loire, River 106
Lombardy 32, 34; to Piedmont 95
Lombardy-Venetia 31, 92, 94
London, anti-racialism rally *359*; in Blitz *304*; Chinese legation hold Sun Yat-sen 176; Conference of 1841 41; demonstration at War Office *218*; dockers fighting *315*; docks, air raid *294*; dock strike 139; economic centre 134; an eviction *141*; First International 119; Greek and Yugoslav governments in exile 295; Naval conference 1930 264; poverty 140; Russian Marxist groups meet 158; school-children *140*; school laboratories *368*; Suffragettes *141*; Treaty of 1827 40; Treaty of 1840 41; warehouses *11*; West Indian immigrants *359*
children *140*; school laboratories *368*; Suffragettes *141*; Treaty of 1827 40; Treaty of 1840 41; warehouses *11*; West Indian immigrants *359*
Londonderry, rioting *341*
London Missionary Society 170
London School of Economics 341
London Working Man's Association 24
Long March, China 266–7, *267*
Look Back in Anger (Osborne) 316
Loom, at Great Exhibition *14*
Lorenz, Konrad 365
Louis II, of Bavaria 36, 108
Louis XVIII, King of France 10, 53–4, *53*, *54*
Louis Bonaparte 58
Louisiana Purchase 67–8, 77
Louisiana, secedes 83; slavery 72
Louis Napoleon *see* Napoleon III
Louis Philippe, King of France 13, 15, 32, 37, 55, 56, *56*, 57, *58*
L'Ouverture, Toussaint 67
Louvre 55, 56
Lower, Professor 246
LSD (drug) 365
Luanda, Angola *344*
Lublin, Polish National Council 301
Lucknow 127, *127*
Luddite risings 16
Ludd, Ned *17*
Ludendorff, Erich von, General 230, 241
Ludevitz (German African trader) 191
Luftwaffe 293, *294*
Lugard, Frederick, Lord 90, 125, 130, 131, 249
L'Univers 64
Lusitania sunk 226, 228
Luther, Dr 259
Luthuli 333
Luxembourg, EEC member 327–8; Germany invades 292; and Napoleon III 104; NATO member 324; resistance movement 305
Lyautey, Colonel Louis 130, 152
Lyons, silk industry 56–7; silk weavers' rising 16, (and army) *57*

Macadam, roads 14
Macao 164–5, 176
MacArthur, General Douglas 302, 324, *325*
McCarthy, Senator Joseph 317, 318, 326
Macartney, George, Earl, in China *164*
McClellan, George B. 84, 85
MacDonald, Ramsay British Prime Minister 140, 244, 252, 258
Macedonian, ship 69
Machine guns 220
McKinley, William, United States President 182, 184
McLuhan, Marshall 370
Mac-Mahon, Marie Edme Patrice Maurice de, General 43, 95, 104, 105, 106, 146
Mac-Mahon Pledge 1916 290, 336
Macmillan, Harold, British Prime Minister 313
Macpherson, James (Ossian) 18
Madagascar 151 *see also* Malagasy Republic
Madison, James, United States President 66, 68, 70
Mafeking, Boers at *129*
Magenta, Battle of 95
Maginot Line 291–2, *291*, 293
Magnitogorsk, iron works *276*
Magyar culture 196
Mahan, Alfred Thayer 126, 186
Mahdi 128
Mahler, Gustav 196
Mahmud, Sultan of Turkey 40, 41
Mahratta chiefs, British fight 26
Maidenek, concentration camp 307
Main, River 102
Maine 72
Maine, US ship 186
Malagasy Republic, independence 333 *see also* Madagascar
Malakoff, fort 43, *44*
Malatesta, Enrico 242
Malawi, independence 332, 333
Malaya 291, 306, 323, 344
Malay majority, in Malaysia 369
Malaysia 330, 369
Maldive Islands 330
Malenkov, Georgi 326
Mali, independence 333
Mallarmé, Stéphane 154
Malta, independence 335
Malthus, Thomas 22, 110
Mameluke mercenaries 40
Management 367
Manchester 19, 21, *25*, 118
Manchukuo, Japanese puppet state 264
Manchuria, and Japan 172, 175, 260, 262, 264; Mao Tse-tung and Chiang Kai-shek 324; and Russia 125, 143, 159, 172
Manchus 131, 166, 167, 176; Boxers attack 172; fall in 1911 261
Mandates, League of Nations 252
Mandela 333
Manhattan, New York *71*
Manifest destiny, United States 78
Manin, Daniele 35, 36
Mannerheim, Field Marshal 292
Mann, Tom 139
Manoeuvres, in Second World War 303
Manuel II, King of Portugal 200
Man Without Qualities (Musil) 375
Mao Tse-tung 261, 262, 265–8, *266*, 290, *323*; Autumn Harvest Rising 263; chairman of Republic 266; and Chiang Kai-shek 297, 324; death 344; execution escape 264; funeral *344*; reaction against policies 344; Rule of Four, and cultural revolution 343; in Shensi *267*
Maoris 27; in New Zealand 357
Maquis 305, *305*
Marcel, Gabriel 374
Marchand, Jean Baptiste 131
Marconi, Guglielmo, Marchese 113
Margaret, Princess *313*
Maria II, Queen of Portugal *200*
Maria Cristina, wife of Ferdinand VII 197
Marmont, Auguste Frederick de, General 55
Marne, River 220, *302*
Marquesas Islands 170
Marsala, Garibaldi lands 97
Marseillaise 59, 153
Marseilles, Le Corbusier 370; *Unité d'habitation 375*
Marshall, General George C., European economic aid 322; policy of containment 325 *see also* Marshall Plan
Marshall, John 70, 73
Marshall Plan 311–12, 315, 322, *322*; attacks on 323, 352
Mars, space probe 367
Martignac, Jean Baptiste, Viscomte de 54
Martov (Menshevik leader) 158
Marxism 90; British socialists reject 140; in Chile 349; in China 262; in France 150; in Germany 190; Hitler's mission against 269; Plekhanov 158
Marxism-Leninism 328, 368
Marx, Karl 15–16, 17, 49, 50, 60, 61, 64, 109, 116, 117, 118, 119, 228; *Rhine Gazette* 37
Maryland, Lee advances 84
Masaryk, Jan 323
Massacre, French catholic missionaries in China 168; Lena Goldfields 163; My Lai *342*; Sharpeville *357*
Matchmakers' Union, members *139*
Matisse, Henri 154
Matsu, attacked by China 326
Mau Mau terrorists *333*, 333–4
Maupas (prefect of police) 62
Maupassant, Guy de 154
Mauritania, independence 333
Mauritius 26; independence 332
Maurras, Charles 154
Mauthausen concentration camp 307
Mavrokordatos, Alexander 39, 40
Maxim brothers 90
Maxim gun 90
Maximilian of Bavaria 36
Maxwell, James 109
Maybach, German car manufacturer 113
Mayerling 176
May Laws, Prussian anti-church 189
Maysville veto 73
Mazzini, Giuseppe 32, *33*, 36, 92, 93, 201
Meade, General George 85
Mecca, seized by Ali 40
Medicine 18, 110; Second World War 304; technical advances 367
Medina, seized by Ali 40
Mediterranean, British convoy *302*
Mehemet Ali 39, 40–1, *41*
Meighen Arthur 247
Meiji, Japanese Emperor 168
Mein Kampf (Hitler) 269, 280
Meir, Mrs Golda 346
Mekong delta 170, 332
Mekong River 125, 131
Melbourne, Lord 23
Melville, Herman 171
Memel, Germany annexes 290
Memoirs (Saint-Simon) 16
Mendeleev, Dmitri Ivanovich 109
Mendel, Gregor 110
Menelek II of Ethiopia 90, 202
Menschikoff 42
Mensheviks 158, 228, 229
Menzel, Adolph von *106*
Menzies, Sir Robert 247
Mercier, General *148*
Merlino, Dr 120
Mesopotamia, archaeology 18; campaign First World War 226 *see also* Iraq
Messianism, new 374
Messina, Garibaldi takes 97
Mesta 12
Metropolitan Police 21
Metternich, Klemens von 10, 30, *35*; on Eastern troubles 40; fear of revolutions 32; Italian revolution 32; influence on Lombardy-Venetia 92; outlaws Burschenschaft 31; students and liberals against 35
Metz 104–6, *104*
Mexico, California question 79; Castro's invasion base 337; depression 259; German alliance 228; independent 78; population 352; Spanish expedition to 200; United States, naval engagement *80*; United States war 186
Mexico City *79*
Michelin 115, 117
Middle East 252–3; cold war 326–7 *see also* Near East
Middle Kingdom, China's concept 268
Midhat Pasha *204*, 205
Midway, United States naval base 186
Miguel, Dom, Portuguese leader 200
Mihailovitch, Colonel 305–6
Milan, Blackshirts at railway station *244*; 1848 fighting 34; Louis Napoleon's decree 68; Mazzini's rebels 93; street fighting 1898 *202*
Militarism, Germany trusts in 188
Milner, Sir Arthur 128
Millerand, Alexandre 119, *120*, 150
Millionaires, in United States 116
Mill, James 13
Mill, John Stuart 329–30
Miners, strike march *151*
Mines, nationalization 118
Minh, President South Vietnam 343
Mining 115
Minoulis, Greek patriot 39
Mirs, Russian councils 50, 160
Missiles 326–7, 328–9, 367
Missionaries 124, 125; to China 125; European 122; French massacred in Tientsin 168; South Pacific 170
Mississippi 77, 85; freedom marchers *320*; secedes from Union 83; slavery 72
Mississippi, River 67, 76, *78*, 80
Mississippi, University of 318
Mississippi, Valley 85, 86–7
Missolonghi 18, 40
Missouri 72, 81
Mitsuhito, Emperor of Japan 260
Mitteleuropa 211, 217
Mobile 77
Modena 31, 32, 36, 92
Modena, Duke of 35
Moderates, Spain 198
'Mods and Rockers', Britain 316
Mogador 215
Moldavia 40, 42, 43, 44
Molecular biology 364
Molotov, Vyacheslav 279
Moltke, Helmuth, Count von 101, 102, *103*, 104, *107*
Moltke, Helmuth von (nephew of preceding) 195, 217, 218, 220
Monarchy, British 20, 23; France 145, 146
Monash, General 232
Monet, Claude 154
Monge, Gaspard 17
Mongolia, nationalism 330
Mongolia, Outer 291
Monroe doctrine 77–8, 186
Monroe, James, United States President 66, 67–8, 70, 71
Montagu Declaration 1917 250
Montalembert, Count of 16
Mont Cenis, tunnel 64
Monte Cassino *300*
Montenegro, independence 204
Montevideo 292, 352
Montgomery, Alabama 83, 318
Montgomery, General Bernard 299
Moon *366*, 367
Moore, Henry 316, 370; *Madonna and Child 372*
Morale, Britain after 1945 315
Morality, changing in Britain 316
Moravia, Germany occupies 290
Morea, Guerilla fighting 39
Morgan (finance house) 116, 117
Mormon settlers 80
Morny, Charles Auguste 62
Morocco, Anglo-French relations 212; crisis of 1905–6 210, 212; French 129–30, 151, (joins Allies) 279; German interest 193, 216; independence 335; Moorish troops *254*; revolts against France 254; Spanish victory 200; United States as mediator 187
Morocco, Sultan of 215
Morrison, Herbert 313
Morse (telegraph) 17
Moscow *49*, 52; Bolshevik Party 275; Bolsheviks control Soviets 230; Chinese communists trained 266; Communist leaders *323*; Germans reach suburbs 296; 'hotline' 329; industry 157; Nixon and Khrushchev *328*; Nixon visits 351; railways 48, 114
Motor vehicles 113, 192
Mozambique 200, 344, 358
Mugabe, Robert 344
Muhammed Zia al-Hug 345
Mujib Rahman, Sheikh 344–5
Mukden, Battle of 175

Müller, Hermann 271
Mumford, Lewis 374
Munich, agreement 1938 281, 284; Hitler's home 269; putsch *241*, 269
Municipal Corporations Act 1835 22
Murdoch, Iris 316
Music, Vienna 196
Musil, Robert 375
Muslim League 252
Muslims, education in Algeria 335; Indian Congress 252; prophet 'Mahdi' 128
Mussolini, Benito 203, 208, *243*, *285*, *303*; Corfu seized 256; election bid 242; fascism 259; and fascists 243; and Hitler 281; and Latin America 258, 259; movements against 300
Mutiny, British army, at Curragh 143; French army 230; Indian 127, 143
Mutual Aid Agreement 1942 311
Muzarewa, Bishop Abel 344
My Lai, massacre survivors *342*

Nachtigal, Gustave 124, *125*
Nadezhdinsky, iron and steel works *157*
Nagasaki 302, 304
Nagy (meteorite study) 364
Nairobi, coffee plantation *125*
Namibia, independence 344 *see also* German South West Africa; South West Africa
Namier, Sir Lewis 109
Nana Sahib *127*
Nanchang rising 263
Nanking, British advance 165, *165*, 166
Nantes, Duchess of Berry arrested 57
Naples, Bourbons reactionary 96; 1848 rising *93*; Garibaldi's entry *98*; industry and free trade 99; Mazzini's followers 92; revolt 31–2; royal family *96*; Sicily seeks independence 34; taken for Piedmont 98; voting *99*
Napoleon III (Louis Napoleon) 34, 61–3, *62*, 90, *95*, 145; Cavour's ally 94; and Crimean War 44; Holy Places 42; Orsini's bomb 64; and Pope 149; and Prussia 102–6; suffrage ideas 188
Napoleon Bonaparte (Napoleon I) 18, 58, *58*, 68, *146*
Narvaez, Ramon Maria 198
Narvik, naval battle 292
Nash, Thomas, election cartoon *179*
Nassau, to Prussia 102
Nasser, General 326, *336*
Natal 27, 128
National Assembly, French 61, 145
National Assistance Act 314
National Association for the Advancement of Colored People 318
National Debt, United States 75
National Defense Education Law 319
National Health Service 314
National Humiliation Day, China 262
National Insurance, Britain 118
National Insurance Act 1911 141
Nationalism 11, 30, 90; Africa 344; Afrikaaner 250; Arab 335–6; Asia, Africa etc 329–37; Austria-Hungary 197; Balkan States 203–4; China 262, 328; Egypt 252; and fascism 281; Germany 192–3; Ireland 142, 247; Italy 242; Japan 265; Latin America 259; after Second World War 308; United States 70
Nationalist Party, Germany 272; Ireland 142
National Liberation Front, Vietnam 332
National Liberation Movement, France 305
National Productivity Year, 1963 315
National Republicans, United States 74
National Workshops, France 60
Nationalists, Italy 93
Nationalities, in Austria-Hungary 194; in Germany 188
Nationalization, Britain 118, 313
NATO *see* North Atlantic Treaty Organization
Naval actions, First World War 225–7
Naval operations, Second World War 302
Navarino, Battle of 40, *41*
Navies, nineteenth-century 126
Navigation Acts, repealed 27
Navy, British 69–70, 144, *212*, 214, 225; convoy in Mediterranean *302*; impounds French navy 293
Navy, French *212*, 293
Navy, German 144, 211, *214*, 214–15, 225
Navy, Italian, destroyed 99
Navy, Japanese 174, 260
Navy, Russian, *Potemkin* mutiny 160
Navy, Turkish, fired by Greeks 39
Navy, United States 69–70, 186
Nazareth, Holy Places 42
Nazi party 240; and Bolshevism *310*; and depression 271; election poster *271*; fascist revolution 244; German prosperity 271; Hitler creates 269; and left-wingers *273*; Nuremberg rally *209*
Near East, after First World War 252–3 *see also* Middle East
Nebraska 81, 82; farm *184*
Nechaev (Bakunin's friend) 120
'Negritude', Senegalese concept 334
Negro conditions, United States 317
Neguib, military takeover 336
Nehru, Jawaharlal 252, 331
Nemesis, British gunboat *166*
Nemours, Duke of 34
Neptune, planet 17
Netherlands, anti-nazi poster *310*; attacks Belgium 34; Cape of Good Hope ceded 27; colonies 253–4; democracy survives 281; and Dutch East Indies 291; EEC member 327–8; Germany invades 292; government in London 295; NATO member 324; resistance movement 305 *see also* Boers; Cape Colony; Dutch East Indies; Dutch Guiana
Neutrality, in Second World War 291
Neutrino 364
Neutrons and anti-neutrons 364
New Caledonia, missionaries 170
New Delhi, UNCTAD conference 354
New Economic Policy (Russia) 276
Newfoundland, dominion 246
New Freedom, United States 187
New Guinea, taken by Allies 225
New Hebrides, missionaries 170
New imperialism *see* Imperialism
New Lanark 16, 24
New Mexico 79, 81, 186
New Moral View of Society (Owen) 16
New Orleans 67, 68, 70, *71*, 85
Newsom Report 316
Newton, Sir Isaac 17
New Worlds of the Mind (Rhine) 365
New York *67*; breadline at Brooklyn Bridge *208*; Italian immigrants *180*; Manhattan *71*; Polish refugees *317*; school *180*
New York Tribune, sends Stanley to Africa 124
New Zealand 26, 27; First World War 246; Maoris 357; SEATO member 326; Second World War 291
Ney, Michel, Marshall 53
Nezib, Battle of 41
Nice, to France 94, 95, 96
Nicholas I, Tsar of Russia 45, 46, *47*, 49; and Austria 36; and Turkey 42
Nicholas II, Tsar of Russia 159–63, *163*; abdicates 228; and France 210
Nicholas, H. G. 362
Niel, Marshal 104
Nietzsche, Friedrich 90
Nigeria 123, 129, 130, 249, 332, 334
Niger Republic 130, 333
Niger, River 124
Nightingale, Florence 155
'Night of the long knives', Germany 273
Nihilism, Russia 52
Nile, River 124, 131, 143, 152
Nivelle, General 230
Nixon, Richard, United States President *328*, 349, *350*, 351
Nkomo, Joshua 344
Nkrumah, President of Ghana 344
Nobility *see* Junkers
Nolan, Sydney 370
Non-governmental organizations 356
Non-intercourse Act, United States 68
Nordau, Max 90
Normandy *12*
North Africa, Allied victory 300; campaign 299; explorations 124; before First World War 290; French 130–1, 151; Italian troops *298*; nationalism
North Atlantic Treaty Organization *324*; Greece and Turkey join 326; Treaty signed *324*
North Carolina 84
Northcliffe, Lord 234
Northern Ireland *see* Ulster
North German Confederation 102, 104
North Korea 324 *see also* Korea
North Sea gas 367
North Sea oil 338
North Vietnam 332, 343
Northwest Frontier 26
Northwest Ordinance 1757 72
Norway 292, 295, 305, 324
Nostromo (Conrad) 98
Novara, Battle of 32, 93
November Revolution 275
Novgorod, revolt 48
Nuclear science 329, 362–3, 364
Nuremberg, International War Crimes Tribunal 312; race laws 273; Nazi rally *209*, *272–3*
Nyasa, Lake 124

Obrenovich, Milos 38
O'Connell, Daniel 21
O'Connor, Feargus 25
Occupied territories, by Germany 295
Odessa 38
O'Donnell, General Leopold 198, 199, 200
OEEC *see* Organization of European Economic Co-operation
Oersted, Hans Christian 17
Offenbach, Jacques 64
Ohio, River 67, 72; at Cincinnati *75*
Ohm, Georg Simon 17
Oil industry, United States 181
Oil pollution 367, 368
Oil supplies 344, 345
Old Age Pension Act 1908 141
Ollivier, Émile *65*, 104
Olmutz 37, 101
Omdurman, Battle of 128
O'Neale, Peggy 74
Ontario, wheat production 114
On the Eve (Turgenev) 120
Op art 370
'Open door', United States trade proposal 186
Operation Barbarossa 295
Operation Overlord 300
Operation Torch, North Africa 299
Opium, trade with China 165
Opium War 1840–2 26, 165, *166*
Orange Free State 27, 128
Orders in Council, maritime trade 68–9
Oregon 77; trail 78; Treaty 79
Organization of African Unity 344, 348
Organization of European Economic Co-operation 322
Organization of Latin American Solidarity 348
Origin of Species (Darwin) 110, 121, 125
Orléanist party 55
Orleans, Duke of 55
Orleans, regained 106
Orsini affair 64, *94*
Osborne, John, *Look Back in Anger 316*
Ossian 18
Ottoman Empire *see* Turkey
Otto of Bavaria, (Otto I of Greece) 40
Overlord, Operation 300
Ovillers, First World War 224
Owen, Robert 16–17, 24
Owen, Wilfred 233
OXFAM *see* Oxford Committee for Famine Relief
Oxford Committee for Famine Relief 356
Oyama, Prince Iwao, General 175
Ozanam, Frederick 16

Pacific 78, 260
Pacifism, Western countries 363–4
Painlevé, Paul 231
Painters, French 154
Pakenham, Edward 70
Pakistan 345; Baghdad Pact 326; East becomes Bangladesh 344; Indian war 344; nationalism 330–1; origins 252; SEATO member 326; United States fears communism 332; women and family planning *353*
Palach, Jan 339
Palacky, Frantisek 35, 36
Palaeontology 18
Palatinate 37
Palermo, revolt 99
Palestine, British mandate 252, 290; guerrillas 362; illegal immigrants *253*; immigrant ship *336*; independence 346; and Jews 252, 253; terrorists *346*
Palestine Liberation Organization 346, 363
Palestro, Battle of 95
Palikares, Greek freedom fighters 38
Palmerston, Lord 41, 43–4, 136–7
Panama, Canal 113; route to California 80; scandal 147, 150; United States coup 186
Panama Declaration of Neutrality 290
Panhard 113
Pankhurst, Mrs Emmeline 142
Panmunjon, Korean armistice 325
Papal army 98; legate 95
Papal States 31, 32, 34
Papen, Baron von 272
Parapsychology 365
Paris, Archbishop killed *60*, 61; Bismarck ambassador 101; Boulevard des Italiens *63*; Commune 90, 106, 146; Congress of 1856 *44*; cultural centre 154; Diaghilev 154; 1830 revolt *33*, 55; 1848 revolt 34, 119; Federation of Just Men 17; Germans in nightclub *296*; International Exhibition 28; liberated from Germany 300; Louis XVIII returns *54*; Louvre attacked *56*; Marne offensive 220; military government 62; Moulin Rouge *154*; Napoleon's funeral *58*; Napoleon's statue *146*; Peace of (Crimean War) 44; Peace Conference 234, 262; railway 14; rebuilding 63; revolts against National Assembly 146; rue de Rivoli 63; Russian revolutionaries 153; Second International *120*; Second Republic proclaimed *59*; siege of 105–6, *145*; slums *117*; social life 63–4; strike meeting *150*; student protests *341*; Treaty of 1856 49, 64; Vietnam peace talks 332
Park, Mungo 124
Parliament, Austria 195; Britain 18, 256, 314; (and Chartism) 25, (not democratic) 19, (House of Lords curbed) 141–2, (reform) 21, 137–8, (working-class interests) 139–40; China 176; France 53, 56; Germany 189, 271; Ireland 248; Italy 201–3; Japan 169, 264; Spain 199
Parma 31, 32, 36, 92, 95
Parma, Duke of 35
Parnell, Charles Stewart 142
Parsons' steam turbine 112
Parti Ouvrier Français 120
Passchendaele, Battle of 231–2, *232*
Passive resistance 250
Pasteur, Louis 110, 117
Patras, Archbishop of 39
Paul I, of Russia 45
Paulus, General 299
Pavlov, Ivan *110*
Payments, balance of 314–15
Peacekeeping 360–4
Pearl Harbor 186, *297*, 304
Pearl, River, opium destroyed 165
Peasants, China 166, (rising) 246; Ireland *143*; Russia 52, 162, (and Alexander II) *51*, (and Bolsheviks) 229, (and Lenin) 158, (union) 160
Pedro I, Dom, of Brazil 96
Peel, Sir Robert 15, 19, 20, 25–6, 137; Corn Laws 142; reforms 136; tariffs 14
Peking, Boxers 131, 173; British legation *168*; Chiang Kai-shek 263; communists welcomed *330*; international relief force 173; Lord Elgin 167; Nixon and Chou En-lai *350*; Red Guard *343*; Treaty of 167; University 173, 262; workers *330*
Pennsylvania 85, 115
Pensions, old age 141
People's charter 1837 24
People's will, Russian society 156
Pepe, General Guglielmo 31–2
Péreire brothers (bankers) 14
Périer, Casimir *56*
Peron, Isabella 348
Perry, Commodore Matthew 90, 91, *169*
Persia 156, 321, 326
Peru, Spain at war 200
Pescadores, to Japan 172
Peschiera, Battle of 35
Pestel, Colonel Paul 45, 46
Pétain, Henri-Philippe, Marshal 224, 230 231, 293, *293*, 299
Peterloo massacre 20, *20*
Peters, Karl 192
Petrachevists 49
Petrograd, breadline *229*; and Kornilov's troops 230; strikes 228; women's meeting *229*; wood rationing *237 see also* St Petersburg
Peugeot 113
Peyote cult 374
Phanar, business sector of Constantinople 38
Phanariots 38
Philippines, communists 323; independence 291; nationalism 330; resistance movement 306; and Spain 186, 200; and United States 131
Phillips, Thomas, portrait of Lord Byron *19*
'Phoney war' 292
Photography, three-dimensional 364
Physical sciences 109
Physics 17
Picasso, Pablo 154
Piccard, Auguste 367
Pickett, General George E. 85
Picquart, Colonel Georges 148
Piedmont 31, 44, 92; alliance ends 35; Austria's war 194; and Crimean War 43; and Custozza 36; 1848 revolt 34; in Italy 32; liberal constitution 37
Pierce, Franlin 81
Pinochet, General 349
Pinter, Harold 370
Pioneers, Soviet Union youth 370
Piper, John 316
Pitt, William, the younger 18
Pius IX, Pope 34, 92, 120–2, *121*, *201*; and Germany 189–90; holds Rome 99; against unified Italy 98; withdraws support from Piedmont 35
Pius X, Pope 121–2, 149
Platte, River 78
Plattsburg Bay, Battle of 70
Plebiscites, France and Italy 95
Plehn (German writer) 217
Plekhanov, George 157–8
PLO *see* Palestine Liberation Organization
Plombières, Napoleon III and Cavour 94
Plowden Report 316
Pocket boroughs 19
Poincaré, Raymond 216
Poland 33–4; and Bismarck 102; 1830 revolt *48*; fascism 281; frontier problems 312, 338; Germany invades 290; Germany occupies 291; legitimate government 297–8; Pope's nationality 339; refugees in New York *317*; resistance movement 300, 306; revolt 1860s 51, (against Russia) 48; riots against Stalin 327; Russian war 239; after Second World War 312
Poles 194, 195
Police, Britain 21; Goering prepares police state 272
Polignac, Prince 54, 55
Polish corridor, Germany demands 290
Polish government, in London 295
Political parties, Germany 273; Japan 169; United States 180
Political stability, Britain 138
Polk, James K. 78, 79
Pollution 367; of the sea 368
Polytechnics, Soviet Union 370
Pondoland, British 129
Poor Law Amendment Act 1834 22
Pop art 370
Popular front 283
Population 10; Britain 19, 315, (immigrants) 359; control 367; Europe 117; France 282; Germany 192; Malthus' theory 22; Russia 155; United States black and white 358; world 352, (three world division) 353; world religions 373
Populism, Russia 155, 156; United States 71–2, 184, 185
Porcelain, demand for 164
Po, River 95
Port Arthur, and Japan 143, 172, 175; and Russia 131, 172
Portsmouth, *Dreadnought* launched *144*; Treaty of 175, 176
Portugal 200; fascists 281; NATO member 324; neutral in Second World War 291; Palmerston 136; patriarchal in Africa 290
Portuguese Empire 254
Posnan, to Prussia 34
The Possessed (Dostoevsky) 50, 120
Potato blight, Ireland 142
Potato famine, Ireland 21
Potemkin, mutiny 160
Potomac, army of 84
Potsdam conference 302, *321*
Poverty, Britain 140
Prague, demonstration *340*; Diet of 35; liberated from East 304; Peace of 102; Soviet Union invasion *323*, *340–1*; Windischgraetz bombards 36
Pravda, Stalin editor 229
Prayer book, Parliament discusses 256
Presidential elections, France 61; United States 72
Priestley, J. B. 316
Prim y Prats, General Juan 104, 199
Princip, Gavrilo 216, *217*
Prison, Bridewell *22*
Prisoner-of-war camps 307
Prisoners, political *161*
Profumo scandal 314
Progressive Party 187
Progressives, Portugal 200; Spain 198; United States 185–6
Proletariat, origin 116
Prophetic religion 374
Protestants, and science 121; and Ulster 143, 339
Proudhon, Pierre Joseph 59, 119
Prussia 65, 100; Austrian war 195; 1848 revolt 36; takes Frankfurt 102; German leadership 37; and Italy 201; gains Posnan 34; Zollverein 14, 33, *100 see also* Franco-Prussian war; Germany
Prussian Diet 101
Psychic phenomena 365
Psychoanalysis (Freud) 196
Psychokinesis 365
Psychology 110, 364–5
Public Health, British 24, 117, 140
Public Schools Report 316
Puerto Rico 186, 200
Pullman strike, railways *184*
Pulsars 364
Punch, Mr 25
Punjab 26, 250
Pushkin, Alexander 48
Puttkamer, Johanna von 101
Pu Yi *265*

Quadrilateral, fortress 95
Quakers 356
Quebec 27; separatism 349
Quemoy 326
Quiller-Couch, Sir Arthur 281

Race relations 320, 356 *see also* Civil rights
Race Relations Act, and Board 359
Radar 367
Radetsky, Field Marshall Joseph *36*, *39*
Radiation hazards 367
Radicalism, Britain 20
Radio 113
Radium 112
Raffles, Stamford 169
Railways, Baghdad 193, *211*; Belgium 14; Britain 14, 114, (nationalization) 118; Erie Railroad *75*; Europe 114; France 14, 58; Germany *13*, 14, 100, 192; Italy 14; locomotives *14*; Russia 48, 114, 157, (strike) *161*; Stephenson 14; United States 75, 81–2, 114, 180, *181*, (Pullman strike) *184*
Rangoon, British 169

Rashid, Grand Vizer Pasha 41
Raspail, Francois Vincent 56
Rasputin, Gregori *162*, 163
Rathenau, Walter 240–1
Rattazzi, Urbano 99
Ravensbruck, concentration camp 307
Ray, Satajit 370
The Reach of the Mind (Rhine) 365
Rearmament, Germany 274
Rebellions, China 261; French colonies 254; Korea 171; Samurai 169
Red Army, Chinese, in Long March 267; Russian, under Trotsky 237, 275
Red Cross, International 95
Red Guards 343, *343*
Red Indians 76–7; Britain arms 69; on reservation *187*; Tippecanoe battle 76; United States 186, 357
Redistribution Act 1885 138
Red, River 131, 170
'Red scare', United States 317
'Red shirts' 92, *98*
Reform, Britain 15, 16–17, 20–1, 24, 137–8; China 173; Piedmont 93; Turkey 41, 204–5; Russia 50; United States 179, 185, 187
Refugees 355–6; at Berlin *309*, *355*; East to West Berlin 329; on River Elbe *309*; Indonesia *330*; Korea *325*; Polish in New York *317*; Second World War 309; United States, Civil War *86*
Regenerators, Portuguese political party 200
Reichstag 189, 271; Hitler dictator 273; North German confederation 102; and Social Democrats 190; William I at *103*
Reief, Piet 128
Reims *see* Rheims
Relief and rehabilitation, UNRRA 310
Religion 316, 373–4
Religion of the Oppressed (Lanternari) 374
Remilitarization *see* Rhineland
Renoir, Pierre Auguste 154
Reparations, Allies demand 234, 240
Republican Party, United States 82, 181, 182
Republicans, France 56, 57, 60, 61, 65, 146; Spain 199
Republic, France *see* Second Republic; Third Republic
Resistance movements, Germany 300; Italy 300; and nationalism 329; Poland 300–1; Second World War 305–6
Revisionism 120; Germany 190; Khrushchev 328
Revolution 10; China 176, 209, 265, (Mao Tse-tung's strategy) 268; in the East 245; France, 1830 55, (1848) 58–60; Italy 32; Latin America 258–9; 'of rising expectations' 288; Russia, 1905 159–60; Turkey 205 *see also* Russian Revolution
Reynaud, Paul 292
Rheims (Reims) 54, 301
Rhine Gazette (Marx) 37
Rhine, J. B. 365
Rhineland 282, 290; Allied occupation 234; businessmen save Nazis 272; 1848 revolution 36; Hitler takes over 274, 281–2; Napoleon III asks for 104; to Prussia 30
Rhodes, Cecil 128, *130*
Rhodesia 129, 254, 344, *345*, 358 *see also* Southern Rhodesia
Rholfe, Gerhard 124
Ribeiros, Anita, Garibaldi's wife 96
Ricardo, David 13
Ricasoli, Baron Bettino 95
Richelieu, Armand Emanuel 53
Richmond Grays *85*
Richmond, Virginia 84, 86, *86*, 87
Richthofen, Baron von 125
Rickenbacker, Eddie *232*
Riego, Rafael del 31, 32, 197
Riga, Treaty of 239–40
Rimbaud, Arthur 90, 125, 154
Rio Grande 79, 80, 96
Risorgimento 32
River transport, United States 75
Rivoli, rue de, Paris *63*
Road-building, China *331*
Robbins Report 316
Roberts, Lord, in South Africa 128
Rochefort, Victor Henri 65
Rockefeller, John D. 180, 181
Rocket, Stephenson's *14*
Rocky Mountains 67, 78, 80
Roentgen, Wilhelm 112
Röhm, Ernst 273
Romagna 32, 95
Roman Catholic Church 373; Belgian rebellion 34; and Bismarck *189*; charitable body 356; clergy attacked 56, (killed at Barcelona) *200*; emancipation 21; France, and education 147; France, under Third Republic 149; Germany 189; Giolitti's concessions 202; Ireland 142; under Louis XVIII 54; and Louis Napoleon 64; missionaries killed at Tientsin 168; missions to South Pacific 170–1; and socialism 118; in Ulster 339–40; United States, President Kennedy 319
Romania 44; ally of Britain, France and Russia 224; fascism 281; Hitler and fascists 295; independence 204; and Magyar culture 196; minorities in Hungary 35; *Potemkin* crew interned 160; and Transylvania 196 *see also* Bessarabia; Moldavia; Walachia
Romanticism 18
Rome, Berlin axis 290; fascist march on 243; Garibaldi 96, 99, 100; and Italy 99, 201; and Mazzinians 36; unification with Italy 100; Treaty of 315, 327, *328*
Rommel, General Erwin 295
Roosevelt, Franklin D., United States President *259*, *311*; at Casablanca 299; death 317; meets Churchill 296; at Teheran 300; third presidential term 295; at Yalta 301
Roosevelt, Theodore, United States President 182, 184, 185, *185*, 187
Rossi, Count 36
Ross, Robert 70
Rosyth, British fleet base 225
Rote Fahne 272
Rothschild, Baron Lionel de 14, 127
Rothschilds (bankers) 11, 15
Rotten boroughs 19
Rough Riders, Roosevelt and *185*
Rouvier, Maurice 212
Rowntree, Seebohm 140
Royal Air Force 253, 294
Royal Flying Corps 114
Royal Niger Company 130, *130*
Royal Oak sunk 292
Rubber, Congo production 115
Rudolph, son of Francis Joseph *196*
Ruhr 114, *241* *see also* Rhineland
Ruskin, John 370
Russia 45–52; sells Alaska to United States 159; Asian advances 143; and Austria 194, 208, 218; and Balkans 204; and Bismarck 102; and Black Sea 40; and British 144; and China 172; Civil War 237–40; First World War, eastern front, *231 map*; and France 152–3; German alliance 193, 210; German threat 211; industrialization 136; Japan beats 91, 143, (antagonism) 174; Japanese war *158*, 175–6, 187; and Manchuria 125, 174; mining 115; Pacific Coast 77; Palmerston 136; and Poland 34, 239; and Port Arthur 239; socialism 120; Triple Entente 213; Turkish treaty 41; United States 245; village in 1890s *162*; Warsaw Duchy 33 *see also* Soviet Union
Russian literature 48–9; romantic 18
Russian Orthodox Church 46, 51
Russian Revolution 125, 208, 228, *239*; Asianizing effect 262; prelude to 155–63
Rutherford, Ernest 112
Rwanda, independence 333
Ryleiev (Russian agitator) 45
Ryle, Sir Martin 364

Saar 234, 274
Sachsenhausen, concentration camp 307
Sadat, Anwar, President of Egypt 346, 347, *348*
Sadowa, Battle of 65, 102, *103*
Sadrunnen Aga Khan, Prince 356
Sagasta, Praxedes 199
Saigon 332
Saigo Takamori 168, 169
Saint-Armand 62
Sainte-Claire Deville, Henri Étienne 115
Saint-Etienne, railway 14
Saint-Germain, railway 14
St Helena 26
Saint-Hilaire 18
St Malo *301*
St Petersburg 52; Alexander II assassinated *156*; Bismarck ambassador 101; 'Bloody Sunday' *159*; Decembrists revolt 45–6; 1835 rising *47*; industry 157; Lenin in revolutionary movement 158; political prisoners *161*; railway 48; Rasputin 163 *see also* Petrograd
Saint-Quentin, Battle of 106
Saint-Simon, Duke of *16*, 59
St Thomas Aquinas 122
St Vincent de Paul, society of 16, 64
Sakhalin, half to Japan 175
Sakharov, Andrei 338–9
Salisbury, Lord 126, 128, 140, 192
Salonika, Allied campaign 226, 233
SALT *see* Strategic Arms Limitation Talks
Salt march, Gandhi *251*
Salt monopoly, Gandhi challenge 251
Samarkand 52
Samoa 170, 225
Samori, Muslim Prince 130
Samurai 168, 169
San Antonio 78
Sand, Karl Ludwig, illustration of murder of Kotzebue *30*
San Francisco 77, 301, *360*
Sanitation improvements 117
San Jacinto 78
Santa Anna, Mexican leader 78
Santa Fé trail 78
Santiago da Cuba, harbour *200*
Santo Domingo 67, 68; and Spain 200; and United States *186*, 186–7
Santos-Dumont, Alberto 114
Sarajevo, Archduke Ferdinand assassination 216
Saratoga Springs *76*
Saratoga, US ship *80*
Sardinia *see* Piedmont
Sarekat Islam 246
Sassoon, Siegfried 233
Satellites, artificial 364; German allies 295
Saturday Review 126
Satyagraha (passive resistance) 250
Saudi Arabia 252, 256, 291
Savannah 87
Savoy, House of *see* Piedmont
Savoy, to France 94, 95
Saxe-Coburg, Albert of *23*
Saxe-Coburg family 22
Saxony 32, 37; Bakunin in jail 120
Say, Jean Baptiste 13
Scandinavia 217, 281
Scapa Flow 225, 292
Schamyh, Imam 52
Scheer, Reinhard, Admiral 226
Schiller, Johann Christoff Friedrich von 18
Schleicher, General Kurt von 271, 272
Schleswig-Holstein 102
Schleyer, Hans Martin *363*
Schlieffen Plan 218
Schoenberg, Arnold 196
Schoolchildren *140*, 180
School laboratories, London *368*
Schwarzenberg, Adam, Count von 37
Science 112–13
Science and technology, post 1945 364; Chinese 164
Scientific applications 112–13
Scientific revolution 17–18
Scientists, United States number increased 319
Scotland 23, 114
Scott, Sir Walter 18
Scott, Winfield 79
Sea-beds, exploration 367
Seas, control vital in Second World War 302–3
'The Seasons' secret society 57
SEATO *see* South East Asia Treaty Organization
Sebastopol *43*
Secession from United States 83
Second Bank of the United States 70, 74
Second Front, Second World War 300, 304
Second International, Paris *120*
Second Republic, France 59–63
Second Reform Act 133
Second World War 290–312; aftermath 308–12; aims not realized 308; assessment 302–4; effect on technology 367; Egypt's importance 252; Russian campaign and the Terror 279
Secret societies, France 54, 56, 57; Greece 38; Italy 32; Russia 51; United States 179
Security Council, United Nations 360–1
Sedan, Battle of 90, 100, *105*
Seeckt, General Heinz von 240
Segregation 179, 358
Seiyukai, Japanese party 264
Self-determination 245, 249
Self-government, countries under Nazis 295
Sella, Quintino 201
Senate, United States 23, 236, 318
Senegal 130, 332, 334
Senghor, Leopold 334
Senior, Nassau, economist 22
Seoul, Korean government 171
Serbia 213, 216; Austria–Hungary 196, 218; Balkan League 216; independence 40, 196, 204; rebellion 38; Russian help 214
Serfdom 45, 48, 50, *51*, 155
Serrano, General Francisco 199
Seward, William H. 82
Sexual conduct 316
Shaftesbury, Lord 24
Shanghai 26, 165, 166, *265*
SHAPE *see* Supreme Headquarters Allied Powers Europe
Sharpeville massacre *357*
Shastri, Lal Bahadour 331
Shaw, Bernard 140
Shelley, Percy Bysshe 18
Shensi, 267, *267*
Sherman, General William T. 86
Shidehara, on Japan in China 264
Shiloh, Battle of 85
Shimonoseki, Treaty of 172
Shintoism 373
Shipbuilding, Germany 192
Shipping, British losses 295
Ships, atomic powered 367
Shogunate, Japan 168
Siam, British trade 26, 131, 291
Siberia, Bakunin in prison 120; colonization 159, 162; Decembrists exiled 46; Dostoevsky exiled 46; Germans fail to reach 296; Japanese expedition 264; Poles exiled 48; railway 114
Sicily, anarchism 202; feudalism persists 96; Garibaldi sails to 97; independence demanded 34; Naples recovers 36; rural life *96*; Second World War 299 *see also* Two Sicilies
Sick man of Europe (Turkey) 40
Siemens-Martin process 115
Siemens, Werner 112
Sierra Leone 123, 130, 332
Sikhs, British war against 26
Sikkim, Chinese invasion 344
Sikorski, General 297
Silk industry 56–7, 264
Silk weavers, rising at Lyons 16, *57*
Simbirsk, Lenin's birthplace 158
Simon Commission 251
Sinai desert 347, *363*
Singapore 26; British naval base 260; Japanese troops *306*; nationalism 330; Raffles occupies 169; secedes from Malaya 344
Sinhalese majority, Sri Lanka 369
Sino-Japanese war *171*
Sinope, Battle of 43
Sioux indians *77*, 186, *187*
Skinner, B. F. 365
Skylab 367
Slave market, United States *74*
Slave risings 67, *80*
Slavery 358; British Empire abolishes 22; South Africa abolishes 27; United States *72*, 80–1, (Lincoln proclaims emancipation) 84, (ended) 178, (Southern states) 72–3
Slaves 39, *178*
Slave trade 22, 124, 125, 128
Slavs, and Austria–Hungary 196, 213
Slidell, John 79
Slumps 116, 126
Slums 117, *117*, 140
Small Holdings Act 1907 141
Smith, Adam, *Wealth of Nations* 13
Smith, Ian 333, 344
Smuts, General Jan 248, 256, 290
Smyrna 39
Snow, C. P. 316
Social anthropology 364
Social Democratic Federation 120, 140
Social Democratic Party, Germany 118, 190, 193; Russia 158, 161
Socialism 16; Britain 140; and communism 283; France 149–51; Germany 190; international 120; Italy 202; Russia 120; Russia 'one country' policy 276; Spain 199
Socialist parties, origins 18; Italy 242, 244; Spain 199
Socialist revolutionaries, Russia 159, 161, 228
Socialists 60, 90; France 59, reconciled to republicans 65; 10,000 executed 61; Tsarist war condemned 229
Social legislation, Britain 144
Social life, Britain 19; Two Sicilies 96
Social reform 314; France 147
Social sciences 364–5
Society for the Rights of Man 57
Society of Friends 356
Society of Harmonious Fists (Boxers) 172
Society Islands, France holds 171
Sociology, Weber 112
Soldiers of Destiny 248
Solferino, Battle of *94*, 95
Sologne, swamps 61
Solzhenitsyn, Alexander 338, *338*, 370
Somaliland, Italian 131
Somali Republic 333, 344
Somme, Battle of *224*
Sorel, Georges 119
Soult, General Nicolas-Jean de Dieu 57
South Africa 333; apartheid 344; British Empire 26; First World War 246; independence 332; mining 115; natives dominated 290; race relations 357; white nation 249
South America 87, 197
Southampton, steamships 112
South Carolina 73, 74, 80, 83, *178*
South East Asia 125, 291, 299
South East Asia Treaty Organization (SEATO) 326
Southern Rhodesia 249, 332 *see also* Rhodesia
Southern states, United States 70–1, 72–3, 80, 179
South Korea 324 *see also* Korea
South Pacific Islands 176
South Vietnam 332, *332*, 343, 344
South West Africa 130, 191, 193, 332, 333 *see also* German South West Africa; Namibia
South Yemen People's Republic 335 *see also* Yemen
Soviets 161, 163, 228; China 266
Soviet Union 274–80, 338–9; anti-American poster *323*; anti-religious poster *280*; Berlin blockade 324; Bessarabia gained 293; Chiang Kai-shek 263; and China 262, 328; Churchill on sphere of influence 322; and cold war 321; concentration camps 307; and Cuba 328, 337; invades Czechoslovakia 338; Eastern Europe defence 326; education 370; and Germany 290, 295, 296; Japan neutral 295; and Kashmir 331; and Nationalist China 361; and nuclear weapons 362–3; and Poland 291, 297–9; racial prejudice 356; Red Army in Second World War 304; space exploration 365–7; Second World War 312; and Stalin 280; and Sun Yat-sen 263
Soweto township *356*
Soyuz spacecraft 367
Space exploration 365–7
Spain 31–2, 197–200; bombed town *284*; Bourbons exiled 104; Civil War 283, 290, (Republican militia) 284, (victory parade) *284*; constitutional monarchy 340; applies to join EEC 341; fascism 281; neutral in Second World War 291; Palmerston's influence 136; loses Philippines to United States 131
Spanish–American War 90, 186, 200
Spanish Empire 254; Florida 77; Louisiana 67; United States takes remnants 123; vanishing 199–200
Speenhamland system 20
Speke, John Hanning 124
Speranski, Michael 45, 46
Sphinx *128*
Sputnik I 318, 327, 364
Squadre d'azione 243
Sri Lanka 369 *see also* Ceylon
Stalingrad, Battle of *298*, 299
Stalinism 321
Stalin, Joseph 229, 274–80, *278*, *311*, *323*; takes Baltic states 292; Budapest statue wrecked *327*; on Chiang Kai-shek 263; death 326; Eastern European purges 323; Germans surrender to 301; paranoia and the Terror 279; as philosopher 276; and popular front 283; at Potsdam 302; at Teheran 300; and Trotsky 230; and United Nations 361; at Yalta 301
Stanford, Leland 114
Stanley, Sir Henry Morton 124, *126*
Starvation *354*, *355*
Stauffenberg, Colonel Klaus von 305
Steam power 112
Steel industry 115, 181, 192
Steel production 115; Ruhr 114
Steinheil (telegraph) 17
Stephens, Joseph, Chartist 25
Stephenson, George 14
Stevenson, Adlai 317
Stilwell, General Joseph W. 300
Stockholm, environment conference 353
Stock market, nineteenth-century 116
Stockton, railway 14
Stoke-on-Trent *115*
Stolypin, Peter *162*
Stowe, Harriet Beecher 81
Strasbourg 58, 106, 108
Strategic Arms Limitation Talks (SALT) 363
Stratford de Redcliffe, Lord 43
Strauss, Johann 196
Strauss, Richard 196
Stresemann, Gustav *255*
Strikes 118; Berlin 240; Britain 141; Catalonia 200; China 262; France 151, 154, (Paris meeting) *150*, (miners march) 151; general 120, (Britain) 256; Italy 202; Lisbon 200; London docks 139; Russia 159, 161, (develop into revolution) 228, (after Bloody Sunday) 160, (railway) *161*; Spain 199; United States 183, (coal mining) 185
Student movement, German 274
Students, black cause 359; China's Fourth of May movement 262; Kent State University *289*; protests, Europe 1968 341, (Paris) *341*; Germany 30–1; Russian 48, *369*; Vienna University *35*
Submarines, atomic powered 367; Britain fears 225; First World War 227; German U-boats *226*; Germans attack Scapa Flow 292
'Succession states' 236
Sudan 40, 124
Sudan Republic, independence 335
Sudetenland, to Germany 290
Suez Canal 64, 113, 139, 252; British control 127; British rights 290; and Disraeli *127*; Egyptian ships *327*; Nasser nationalizes 326
Suez Crisis 313, 361
Suffrage, Austria 195; Italy 202; Spain 199
Suffragettes *141*, 142
Sugar industry 67, 337
Sukarno, Achmad 330
Sumner, Senator Charles 81, 82
Sun Yat-sen 166, *176*, 261, *263*

Supersonic flight 367
Supreme Court, United States 70, 73, 82, 317, 351
Supreme Headquarters Allied Powers Europe (SHAPE) 326
Surgery *110*
Sutherland, Graham, Coventry Cathedral tapestry *289*
Suvla Bay, British landing *225*
Suzuki, Zen Buddhist 374
Swaziland, independence 332
Sweden 254, 291, 343, 369
Switzerland 61, 254, 281, 291
Sydney Opera House 370, *371*
Sykes-Picot Agreement 252
Syndicalism 118–19, 141, 200, 202
Syndicats 150, 151
Syria, to Egypt 41; to France 252, (revolts) 254; independence 335; and Lebanon 346, 361; Mehemet Ali's claim 40–1

Taaffe, Eduard, Count 195
Tabouis, Geneviève 255
Taff Vale Case 1901 140
Taft, William Howard 187
Tahiti, missionaries 170
Taiping revolt 166
Taiwan 324, 326, 362 *see also* Formosa
Talleyrand, Charles Maurice 10, 53, 55
Tallmadge, James 72
Tamil minority in Sri Lanka 369
Tammany Hall 180
Tanganyika, Lake 124
Tangier, William II at 212, *213*
Tanks 220, 221; First World War *232*; German crossing Marne *302*; Soviet Union in Prague *323*
Tanzam railway 344
Tanzania 332, 344 *see also* German East Africa
Tanzimat, Turkish reform 41, 42
Taoism 171, 373
Tao Kuang, Emperor 165
Tariffs, GATT 311; United States 73, 74, 80
Tashkent 52
Taurida Palace 161
Taurus, Ibrahim overruns 40
Taxation, Balkan States 204; British 141; French 60; Italy 98–9
Tax avoidance, Britain 315
Taylor, A. J. P. 215; on Churchill 313
Taylor, General Zachary 79, 81
Tea, demand for Chinese 164
'Teddy-boys' 316
Teheran conference 300
Teilhard de Chardin, Pierre 374
Telegram, Zimmermann 228
Telegraph 14, 17, *114*, *183*
Telford, Thomas 14
Telstar 367
Temple, Archbishop William 314
Tennessee 71, 72
Terrorism 363; Algeria 335; Arabs blowing up planes *347*; Kenyan Mau Mau 333–4; Palestinian *346*; Ulster 339
Terror, Soviet Union 277–9
Test Acts 21
Tewfik Pasha 128
Texas, Austin *71*; and Mexico 78; and New Mexico 81; and Spain 77; United States 78, 186, (secedes from Union) 83
Textile industry 116
Thailand *326*, *332 see also* Siam
Thatcher, Margaret, British Prime Minister 338
Thessaly, excluded from Greece 40
Thiers, Adolphe 55, 57, 62, 64, 106, 145, 146
Third Party, France 65
Third Republic, France 145, 153–4
Third World 361
Third World War, Britain to opt out 316
Thoiry, French–German understanding 255
'Thousand', Garibaldi's *97*
Three Men in New Suits (Priestley) 316
Tibet 127, 331
Tientsin 167, 168, *261*, 262
Tillett, Ben 139
Tin 115
Tinbergen (psychologist) 365
Tinghai, British navy take 165
Tippecanoe 76
Tirpitz, Alfred P. Friedrich von, Admiral 131, 144, 228; fleet prepared 193; navy law 216
Tisza, Kalman 196
Titanium 115
Tito, Josip Broz, Marshal 306, 321
Tobacco trade, United States 74
Tocqueville, Alexis de 34, 58, 224; on Russia 46, 245
Togo 130, 226, 332
Togo, Count Heihachiro, Admiral 175
Tojo, Hideki 297
Tokugawa family 168, 260
Tokyo 168; Perry's arrival 90
Tolpuddle martyrs 24
Tommaseo, Niccolo 35
Tong Hak 171
Tonkin, Gulf of 131, 170
Tonking, United States navy 332
Torch, Operation 299
Tories 19, 20
Torrey Canyon 367
Tosei-ha, Japanese army faction 265
Totalitarianism 320–1, 374
Total war 302
Toulon, Russian fleet visits 153
Toulouse-Lautrec, Henri de 154; *Moulin Rouge 154*
Toussaint l'Ouverture 67
Towns, migration to 16
Trade, Britain with Turkey 41; Britain and colonies 27; Britain and Europe 315; Britain and Far East 26; China and West 164–5; First World War 208; Gatt 311; international 256; Japan 168; Latin America and Britain 68; Russia and Turkey 40; Second World War 310–11; United States 68, 87; United States and Europe 68–9; United States in First World War 227; world 352; world after United States slump 257 *see also* Commerce; Free trade
Trade Expansion Act, United States 320
Trades Union Congress 118, 139, 140; German 118
Trade Unions 20, 118; Britain 139, 314; Europe 120; France 118–19, 150–1; Germany 118, 273; industrial action 141; Matchmakers Union members *139*; membership card *138*; Owen's 17; Russia 119; Spain 199; United States 182–3 *see also* Strikes
Tramway, electric *113*
Transistors 367
Transjordan 252 *see also* Jordan
Transkei, Bantustan 333, 357
Transport 113–14; British nationalized 313; Piedmont 93; revolution 14; United States 75 *see also* Railways
Trans-Siberian Railway 114, *157*, 159, 171, 172, 175
Transvaal 27, 128, *128*
Transylvania, and Romania 196
Travel, two Germanies 338
Trebizond 39
Treblinka, concentration camp 307
Trek, Great 27
Trenches, *206*, 221
Trinidad and Tobago 336–7
Triple Alliance, against Turkey 40
Triple Entente 213
Tripoli 67, 124, 202
Trist, Nicholas P. 79–80
Troppau, Congress 32
Trotsky, Leon 161, 230, *230*, 237, 275
Trubetskoi, Prince Paul 45
Trudeau, Pierre, Canadian Prime Minister 349
Truman, Harry, United States President 302, *317*, 321, 322, *360*
Ts-ao Ju-lin 262
Tshombe 362
Tuaregs, Lyautey defeats 130
TUC *see* Trades Union Congress
Tuileries 55, 69
T'ung Meng Hui 176
Tunis 151, 152
Tunisia 129, 335
Turgenev, Ivan 48, 120
Turin 93, 94
Turkestan, overrun by Russia 52
Turkey 38–44, 203–5, 213–14; Acropolis attacked *40*; African possessions 216; Arab nationalism 246; Baghdad Pact 326; Balkan wars 216; Britain withdraws aid 322; anti-British 156; Central powers 225; Italy gains Tripoli 202; Italian war 203; NATO member 326; peace 233; railways 193; Russian intentions 36; Second World War neutrality 291; Soviet Union pressure 321
Turner, Nat, slave revolt *80*
Tuscany 31, 36, 92, 95, *95*
Two cultures 316
Two Sicilies 31, 92
Tydings Committee 317
Tyler, John 76, 78
Typee (Melville) 171
Tyrol, South, annexed by Italy 236
Tz'u Hsi, Empress *173*

Ubangui, River 131
Uganda 125, 129, 332
Uitlanders 128
Ujiji, Stanley and Livingstone 124
UKAEA *see* United Kingdom Atomic Energy Authority
Ukraine, Germans penetrate 296; industrial regions 157; and Poland 240; political meeting *277*; Russo-Polish war 239
Ulbricht, Walter 338
Ulster 248, 339–40
Ulster Volunteers 143
Ultramontanism 121
Ultra Royalists, French party 53–4
Ulyanov, Alexander, Lenin's brother 158
Ulyanov, Vladimir Ilyich *see* Lenin
Umberto I, King of Italy 202, *203*
Uncle Tom's Cabin (Stowe) 81
Unconditional surrender 308
UNCTAD *see* United Nations Conference on Trade and Development
Underdeveloped countries 353, 354–6
Unemployment, Africa 369; Britain 256; Germany reduced by Hitler 274; Latin America 258
UNESCO 368, 370
UNICEF 356
Unkiar-Skelessi, Secret treaty 41
Union Coloniale 129
Union of Death (Black Hand) 216
Union of Railway Servants 140
Union of South Africa 128 *see also* South Africa
Union Pacific Railway 180
Union sacrée 219
Unions *see* Trade unions
United Arab Republic 335 *see also* Egypt; Syria
United Kingdom *see* Britain
United Kingdom Atomic Energy Authority (UKAEA) 315
United Nations 301, 360–2, 370; Association (poster) *362*; Congo mission 328, 334; conservation conference 367; declaration signed 297; Economic and Social Council 356; Educational, Scientific and Cultural Organization 368, 370; environment conference 367; two Germanies join 338; Kashmir dispute 331; in Leopoldsville *335*; Middle East peacekeeping force 327; Palestine failure 336; on refugees 356; Relief and Rehabilitation Association 310; in Sinai Desert *363*; expels South Africa 333; South Korean action 324; Swedish detachment *363*, trade and development conference 354
United Nations Conference on Trade and Development (UNCTAD) 354
United Nations Relief and Rehabilitation Administration (UNRRA) 310, 355
United States 11, 66–68, 178–87, 316–20, 349–51; *map 182*; Allies buy arms 293; Aswan High Dam financed 326; Briand–Kellogg treaty 256; and Britain 28, 313, (blockades) 226, (convoys) 296; Canada and Australia dependence 247; China, trading rights 165; China into First World War 262; Civil War *87 map*; communications 114; Cuba 248; depression 291; Diem appeals 332; education 368; First World War *182 map*; 227, 228, 233, (poster) *222*; growth industrialization 144; Japanese offensive 301; and Korea 324, 361; lend-lease 295; mining 115; NATO member 324; nuclear arms ban 362–3; Pearl Harbor 297; race relations 358–60; and Russia 245; SEATO member 326; after Second World War 312; space exploration 365–7; Suez Crisis 326; westward expansion 71–2; and world history 90
United States, ship 69
Universities, German 31; Mississippi 319; Peking 173; Russia 50; student unrest 341 *see also* Students
UNRRA *see* United Nations Relief and Rehabilitation Administration
Untouchables, Gandhi joins 250
Upper Volta, independence 333
Urals 296
Uriburu, José 257
Uruguay 96, 352
Urville, Dumont d' 170
Utah 81; railways 180
U Thant 362
Utopian schemes 16–17
Uvarov, Count 46

Vaal, River 27
Van Buren, Martin 74, 76, 81
Vancouver Island 79
Van Gogh 154
Vargas, Getulio 258
Vatican 100, 149
Vauxhall cars 114
Vendée, Prince Henry lands 57
Venetia 99, 200, 201
Venezuela 186, 352
Venice 34–5, 36
Venus, space probes 367
Vera Cruz 79
Verdun, Battle of *222*, 224
Vereeniging, Peace of 128
Vernon (on intelligence) 365
Verona, Congress of 32
Versailles, Second Reich proclaimed 108; William I Emperor *107*
Versailles Treaty 234, *235*, 281; China not signing 262; League of Nations Covenant 235; United States 236
Verwoerd, Hendrik 344
Vetsera, Marie 196
Vichy France 293, 299
Vicksburg, Grant takes 85
Victor Emanuel II, King of Piedmont and Italy 32, 36, *93*, 94, *95*, 200–1
Victor Emanuel III, King of Italy 243–4
Victoria, Queen of England 22–3, *23*; Empress of India 27–8
Victoria, Lake 124
Victoria of Leiningen 22
Victory (Conrad) 171
Videla, General (Argentinian ruler) 348
Vienna, Congress of 10; cultural life 196; 1848 revolution 34, *35*, *194*; Hitler's home 269; liberated from East 304; Peace of 99; Ringstrasse *196*; Schönbrunn Palace *194*; siege 36; student revolution *35*, 36
Vietcong 332; suspect *286*
Vietminh 326, 332
Vietnam 170, 329, 331–2; Buddhist priests 374; ceasefire 343; divided 326; evacuation *332*; nationalism 330; resistance in Second World War 306; and United States 320, 349; war 341–3 *see also* Annam, Indo-China; North Vietnam; South Vietnam
Vigny, Alfred de 18
Vilagos, Hungarians surrender 36
Villafranca, Peace of 95
Ville, Hôtel de 56, *59*
Villèle, Count of 53, 54, *55*
Violence, race relations 359
Virginia, Civil War 66, 84, *84*
Virginia Regiment, 1st *85*
Virgin Mary, guides Charles X 54–5
Vladimir, Grand Duke *160*
Vladivostock 52, 114, 175
Volga, River, *157*
Volta, Alessandro 17
Volturno, Battle of 97
Volunteers, International Voluntary Service 356
Voroshilov, Stalin supporter 279
Vorster, South African leader 344
Vries, Hugo de 110

Wafel, Egyptian party 252
Waffen SS *296*, *303*
Walachia 39, 40, 42, 43, 44
Waldeck-Rousseau, Pierre Marie René 120, 148, 150
Waldheim, Kurt 362
Wall street crash 256–7
War 114, 209, 220, 224, 316; declarations 1914 219; Goya etching *30 see also under name of war*
War criminals, trials 312
War damage, reconstruction 309
War Hawks, United States 69
Warlords, Chinese *261*, 261–4
Warsaw, Battle of 239; Duchy of 33–4; Germany takes 291; ghetto 307–8; rebellion 34; rising 300–1; subjugated 48
Warsaw Pact 326
Washington, Booker T. 179
Washington, D.C. *84*; British take 70; the Capitol *66*; conference on arms 260; black march 359; civil rights rally 319; freedom march *358*; 'hotline' 329; Lincoln shot 87; UNRRA headquarters 310; Watergate scandal 351
Washington, George, President of United States 66
Watergate scandal 349, 351
Waterloo, Battle of 18
Watson, James Dewey 364
Watt, James 13
Wavell, Archibald Percival, Viscount 294, 295
Webb, Beatrice and Sydney 140
Weber, Max 112
Webster-Ashburton Treaty 1842 79
Wei-hai-wei 131
Weimar Republic 240
Weitling (German revolutionary) 17
Weizmann, Dr Chaim *253*
Welfare aid 354–6
Welfare state, Britain 140, 314–15; Germany 190
Wellington, Duke of 20, 21, 25, 197
Weltpolitik 210–11, 217
West Africa 115, 123, 125, 130
Western Front 220
West Germany *see* German Federal Republic
West Indies, emigration to Britain 337; immigrants in London *359*; sugar trade 67
Weygand, General Maxime 293
Whampoa 263, 264
Wheat production, Ontario 114
Whigs, Britain 19, 21; United States 80–1
White Army, in Civil War 237
'White man's burden' 90, 125
WHO *see* World Health Organization
Wilberforce, William 22
Wilderness, Virginia 86
Wilhelmshaven, German fleet 226
William I, Emperor of Germany 100, *103*, *106*, *107*, 108, 188; Napoleon III surrenders *105*
William II, Emperor of Germany 188, 192, *213*; and Austria 216; and Russia 156; Scandinavian cruise 217; and Serbia 217
William IV, King of England 21, 22
William of Orange, King of Belgium 34
Wilmot, David 81
Wilmot Proviso 81
Wilson, Harold, British Prime Minister 314, 338
Wilson, Sir Henry 237
Wilson, Woodrow, United States President 187, 208, 237; and China 262; peacemaking 1919 234; re-elected 227–8; world role renounced 245
Windischgraetz, Prince 36
Windthorst, Ludwig 189
Wine industry 116
Wingate, General Orde, 'Chindits' 300
Winn, Godfrey 284
Winter Palace, Peking 167
Winter Palace, St Petersburg 160
Witte, Count Sergei 52, 114, 157; industrialization 159; Nicholas II dislikes 163; recalled 160
Witwatersrand, gold 128
Wohler, Friedrich 115
Wool, Australia exports to Britain 116
Woollen goods, Scotland 114
Woolwich, Bishop of 316
Women, factory workers 24; Pakistani *353*; Russian universities ban 50; Second World War 304; suffrage 142, 185
Workers, Russia 157; march 159–60
Workhouses, Britain 22
Working class 118; alliance with middle class 24; China 266; France 60, 64, (revolutionaries) 64, 149; movement (Britain) 24–5; as proletariat 116; Roman Catholic Church and 121; United States 183–4 *see also* Labour
Working Men's Association, Germany 190
Workingmen's Compensation Act 1907 141
'Workshop of the world', Britain 136
World Bank 311, 353
World Congress of Faiths 373
World Council of Churches 373
World Health Organization (WHO) 365
World Refugee Year 1959–60 355
World Sociological Congress 1959 364
World War I *see* First World War
World War II *see* Second World War
World War III *see* Third World War
Wright brothers 114
Wurtemburg 30, 108

X-rays *112*

Yakir, General 279
Yalta conference 301, *311*, 321
Yalu, River, MacArthur's advance 324
Yamagata Aritomo 174
Yangtze, River, British advance 165, 167
Yearbook of Education 369
Yedo, change of name to Tokyo 168
Yellow Sea, Battle of *171*, 175
Yemen *256*, 335
Yokohama, Perry landing *169*
York, poverty 140
York, River 84
Yoruba tribe, Nigeria 334
Young, Ernest 249
Young Ireland party 21
Young Italy (Mazzini) 32, 96
Young Russia 51
Young Turks 205; revolution 214
Youth 316, 370
Ypres, British troops *220*
Ypsilanti, Alexander 39
Yuan Shi-k'ai 176, 261, 262
Yugoslavia, Cetniks *306*; expelled from COMINFORM 323; fascist influence 281; German reconnaissance group *295*; German SS troops *296*; Germany 295; resistance movement 305–6; Soviet Union 326; Titoist regime 321
Yunnan province 125

Zaibatsu, Japanese firms 264
Zambesi, River 124
Zambia, independence 332, 333, 344
Zanzibar, slave trade 124
Zasulich, Vera 155–6
Zemstvos 50, 52, 159
Zen Buddhism 374
Zimbabwe 344 *see also* Rhodesia; Southern Rhodesia
Zimmerman, Arthur 228
Zinc 115
Zinoviev, Grigori 236, 275
Zionism 253, 336
Zola, Émile 154; Dreyfus affair 148
Zollverein, German customs union 4, 33, *34*, 37, 100, 192
Zululand 129
Zulus, Afrikaaners and 128
Zulu War 128
Zurich, Israeli plane attacked by PLO 346